THE WORLD'S BEST

BEST

Edited by Marian Cooper

Agora Books
824 E. Baltimore St.
Baltimore, MD 21202

ISBN# 0-945332-08-4

THE WORLD'S BEST

Publisher: William R. Bonner

Editor: Marian V. Cooper

Editorial Director: Vivian Lewis

Copy Editor: Kathleen Peddicord

Production Manager: Wilma Vinck

Production Staff: Denise Plowman

Proofreaders: Anne Bonner and Bruce Totaro

Assistant to the Publisher: Jane Lears

Researchers: Gary Almes, Anya Breitenbach, Ellen Chang, Lee Diemer, Loren Fox, Lora Holmberg, Anastasia Hudgins, Josh Kendall, Greg Koren, Beth McNeill, Mike Meresman, Eve Oishi, Janet Schamehorn, Natalie Shelpuk, Nell Wieferich

Writers: Shari Alexander, Gary Almes, Alice Bingner, Anya Breitenbach, David Brinn, Sidney L. Bullene, Roseanne Burke, Marilyn Cantrell, Will Cantrell, Dianne Carter, Douglas Casey, William Chamberlayne, Ellen Chang, Robert J. Cowdy, Gloria L. Charnes, Robert Czeschin, James Davidson, Peter Dickinson, Matthew du Aime, William Dudley, Trish Durbin, Susan Ellis, Gerry Fisher, Loren Fox, Joan Galles, Bill Goodwin, Annamarie Gregory, Thomas Hasler, Humphrey Hawksley, Jack Helbig, Lora Holmberg, Anastasia Hudgins, Sherry Kent, Kenneth Kimpton, Greg Koren, Alison Landes, Jane Lears, Judith V. Lelchook, Vivian Lewis, Beth McNeill, Patrick J. McQuillan, Mike Meresman, Anne-Marie Meuser, Mark Mobley, Francine Modderno, Gene Murphy, Kathleen Murphy, Marilyn Naito, Eve Oishi, Tom and Joanne O'Toole, Kathleen Peddicord, Elizabeth W. Philip, Ladislaw Reday, Bob Reid, Frank Rizzuto, Penny Rogers, Anthony F. Rossi, Lucy Rostelli, Janet Schamehorn, Michael Sedge, Natalie Shelpuk, Sheila Signer, Cathy Smith, Bruce Totaro, Becky Tozer, Warren Trabant, Patti Watts, Natalie Webb, Julia Wilkinson

Cover Design: Jack French
Cover Photography: John Burwell

INTRODUCTION

Who that is besy to mesure and compare
The hevyn and erth and all the worlde large
Descrybynge the clymatis and folke of every place
He is a fole and hath a grevous charge...

—*Alexander Barclay,*
The Ship of Folys, *1509*

When we took on the task of writing *The World's Best,* it seemed simple enough. Just find the world's finest hotels and best restaurants, most amazing sights, highest mountains, biggest lakes, best skiing, finest beaches, ad infinitum. We rolled up our sleeves and got down to work.

Then we realized what a daunting task we had undertaken. The world is huge. What should we cover? Should we write about Europe and not the United States? Hawaii and not Tahiti? Africa and not India? We had to limit our choices. We chose what we thought were the world's most interesting and accessible countries. Some had to be weeded out, not because they don't have beautiful or fascinating sights but because we didn't have the time or space to cover the entire world.

Then we grappled with another question. What exactly does *best* mean? Is it the most expensive, luxurious hotel in town? The cozy little bed and breakfast no one else knows about? The gourmet French restaurant hailed by critics? Or the little Italian place where huge plates of spaghetti are served for a few dollars and the owners visit each table? Some people consider the best night life a frenetic disco frequented by Mick Jagger. Others would rather go to a romantic piano bar with a good choice of wines.

Because each person's idea of best is different, we gave the word a broad definition. We included restaurants with world-famous chefs as well as little-known places serving inexpensive but delicious meals. Luxurious hotels that cater to every whim are mentioned, as are cheap but cozy *pensions*.

Of course, some of the world's bests aren't subject to argument (that's *our* view anyway): the world's best art museum, sunset, surfing, scuba diving, opera house, ski resort, canyon, champagne, couturier, castle, nightclub, island, garden, and safari.

Prices are given, wherever possible, in the currency of the country we are writing about. While this is not as convenient as giving the price in dollars, it is more accurate, because international exchange rates fluctuate wildly. At the back of the book is a table of exchange rates current at the time we went to press.

Unfortunately, hotels, restaurants, nightclubs, and shops go in and out of business rapidly. Many of our old favorites have disappeared. So be sure to verify addresses before making your travel plans. Check prices, too. In some countries inflation is rampant. Even in countries without inflation, hotel and restaurant prices tend to rise every season. In some cases, just listing a place in a travel guide is enough to send prices soaring.

If we have missed any of your favorites, let us know, and we will test them for inclusion in next year's edition of *The World's Best*. This is the third edition of the book; each year we have added readers' suggestions—hotels, restaurants, shops, sights, airlines. With your input, we hope to make this the world's best book.

Bon voyage!

—*Marian Cooper*
Editor

AKNOWLEDGMENTS

Without the help of scores of knowledgeable, creative, and hard-working souls, this book would have been impossible. A special thanks to Editorial Director Vivian Lewis, who poured over each chapter making sure it was up to snuff and adding her own bits of wisdom and wit. And heartfelt thanks to Kathleen Peddicord, our patient copy editor, who scoured each page carefully under a tight deadline. Wilma Vinck, our production manager, is a saint, miraculously converting messy typed pages into attractively laid-out book pages. Her right-hand woman, Denise Plowman, also deserves thanks for the many tedious hours spent making corrections and picking up stray pieces. Jane Lears is a diplomatic soul who kept tempers cool in hot situations and helped to keep us on schedule. And, of course, thanks are due Publisher Bill Bonner, without whom there would be no *World's Best*.

Each chapter had a guardian angel or two. Vivian Lewis and Trish Durbin contributed a wealth of knowledge about Britain. Kathleen Murphy dredged her memory for interesting tidbits on Ireland, New Zealand, and Australia. Warran Trabant and Vivian Lewis shared their secrets in the chapter on France. Lucy Rostelli and Michael Sedge contributed to the file on Italy. Francine Modderno added romance to our chapter on Greece. And Eve Oishi helped with the chapters on East Germany and Japan. Jane Lears gave us insights into Hong Kong, Macao, and Switzerland. Loren Fox brought out the mysteries of Egypt and Israel. Manisha Bhatt described her favorite places in her homeland, India. My Africa-buff sister, Barbara Cooper, kept us out of the dark on the subject of the Dark Continent. And my friend Lisa Bevis lent spice to the chapter on Spain.

Lora Holmberg dug up bests in the Caribbean; Gary Almes patiently researched Brazil; and Janet Schamehorn found many bests in Mexico.

Jack Helbig and Sherry Kent wrote about Chicago with insight and a sense of humor. Many thanks. Natalie Shelpuk unearthed odd and interesting sights in the United States. Anastasia Hudgins shared her love of Tennessee with us.

Josh Kendall and slews of hard-working interns checked the facts throughout the book, making sure they were up-to-date.

Finally, a big thanks to the many patient people at the various national tourist offices, who spent hours on the telephone with us verifying information and suggesting bests. Without them, all this would not have been possible.

As you might suspect, I could go on for pages. But I won't. Thanks again.

—*Marian V. Cooper*
Editor

TABLE OF CONTENTS

Section I

Quality of
Life Index

THE QUALITY OF LIFE INDEX

"The government are very keen on amassing statistics. They collect them, add them, raise them to the nth power, take the cube root, and prepare wonderful diagrams. But you must never forget that every one of these figures comes in the first instance from the village watchman, who just puts down what he damn well pleases."

—*Sir Josiah Stamp*
Director of Inland Revenue
Department of England, 1896-1918

The number of American expatriates grows each year. Some are sent by their employers to live abroad. Others move to foreign countries to pursue trade and investment opportunities. Still others are looking for pleasant retirement havens or simply a change of lifestyle.

Whatever the reason for the move, the choice of where to put down your new roots is an important one. Of all the countries in the world, where would you like to live? Where can an American pension go a long way? Where can you take some dollars offshore out of sight of the taxman? What countries are safe places to raise a family? What countries should be scratched off the list of possibilities altogether?

Most people don't have the time to pour over hundreds of statistics and obscure facts and then make an informed choice. So we've done the work for you. Naming the world's best places to live is the aim of our survey of the world's quality of life. Our Quality of Life Index is the most comprehensive ranking of international destinations that you will find. And we think it is also the best. It rates the overall quality of life in 164 countries and territories and represents hours of research and the painstaking compilation of thousands of statistics—all rounded out by the subjective opinions of our well-traveled staff.

The basic elements

How each country ranks in the final analysis depends upon its individual scores in eight basic categories: health care, economic health, political stability, freedom, infrastructure, recreation and environment, cost of living, and culture.

Health. In this category, we evaluate the most current statistics on life expectancy, infant mortality, and the number of physicians per capita. If life expectancy statistics are high, we conclude that health care, nutrition, and sanitation are good. A low infant mortality rate, such as 6 per 1,000 live births, suggests good health education and maternal health and adequate availability of medical care. A small number of people per physician indicates that the people do not want for medical care.

Economic health. This category includes the average annual inflation rate from 1980 to 1985, the gross national product (GNP) per capita, any growth in the GNP, and the country's ability to pay foreign debts for goods and services. Countries with a low inflation rate, a high GNP per capita, and a low external debt rank highest in this category.

Political stability. This category, new this year, evaluates the level of turmoil and the safety of investments in each country. Countries with low turmoil levels and high investment safety levels rank highest.

Freedom. Countries in this category are ranked according to their inhabitants' civil liberties and political rights. Countries that allow their citizens the most rights receive the highest rankings.

Infrastructure. In this category, we evaluate the quantity and availability of communication and transportation systems. The more developed and far-reaching the system, the higher the ranking.

Recreation and environment. Unlike other categories, this one is subjective. Each country is evaluated according to its geographical attributes and shortcomings. First we look at the environment as a whole. Does the country have lakes, mountains, wildlife preserves, beaches, and jungles? Then we consider the range of activities the country's environment allows—skiing, swimming, mountain climbing, bushwacking, sailing, horseback riding. Countries that offer a wide variety of outdoor activities rank highest.

Cost of living. Here we consider the cost of maintaining a household in each country and the highest income tax that you would be expected to pay.

Culture. This category comprises two subcategories: statistical and subjective. The statistical category includes literacy rates and the number of libraries, museums, cinemas, and daily newspapers per capita. The subjective category is an analysis of the various cultural activities available in each country, including variety and number of restaurants, clubs, festivals, cafés, opera houses, and dance halls. It is based on our personal experiences.

The final judgment

This report must be taken with a grain of salt. Statistics are merely figures. They do not always represent the *real* quality of life in a particular country. After all, what makes up a good life for you may not make up a good life for someone else. When reading our report, remember that it is merely a guide to the best—and worst—countries to live in based on American standards.

This Quality of Life Index isn't magic. It has several inherent problems. Statistics, the base and bane of this report, are only symbols. Numbers cannot actually assess how happy you would be if you moved to Andorra, Portugal, Canada, or Mexico. Furthermore, the same statistics do not always measure the same things. Statistically, the USSR has the most libraries per capita in the world. But what is the government counting? A schoolroom with 10 books and 10,000 political pamphlets may be the Soviets' equivalent of the New York Public Library. It's impossible to say.

The availability of statistics is another problem. Not every country compiles censuses; nor does every country report its findings to the United Nations. Communist countries and poor African countries are extremely difficult to rank. Sometimes the latest statistics, if any exist, date back more than 10 years, thus widening the margin of error.

Our subjective categories provide a more balanced picture. But our Western values, coupled with our individual tastes, do color the final analysis. Someone who likes the quiet intellectual life might enjoy living in Scandinavia rather than southern Europe. Someone who enjoys night life would hate living in New Zealand or the Isle of Man. We can present only an approximate picture of what life is like around the globe. The ultimate choice is up to you.

And the winner is...

The **United States** takes first place, with a total score of 88.88. Although it is not outstanding in all categories, its consistently good scores in most categories averaged out to put it on top.

Here is a breakdown of the United States' category rankings. In health, it ranks 15th. In the culture category, it ranks first. In the economy category, the United States ranks 20th. In the cost of living category, it comes in a mediocre 49th. In political stability, the United States ties for third place with several other countries. It ranks first in the infrastructure category. In recreation/environment, the United States also fares well, tying with Australia, France, Italy, and New Zealand for first place. And in freedom, the United States ties with 21 other countries for first place.

The loser

Afghanistan is at the bottom of the list, with a total score of 7.60. Afghanistan has never been a rich, cultured country, but the Soviet Occupation has increased the nation's poverty. Thousands of Afghans have died as a result of the struggle between the Russians and the guerrillas. And thousands more are refugees stuck in small camps just across the border in Pakistan.

Health care in parts of Afghanistan is practically nonexistant. And more diseases are rampant here than in most countries, including rabies and malaria. Winters are bitter, and the landscape is treacherous. Afghanistan awaits modern technology and development. Culture, as we know it, doesn't exist.

Where freedom rings

In addition to the United States, other countries that are relatively free include: West Germany, France, Trinidad and Tobago, Bermuda, Spain, Portugal, Cyprus, the Channel Islands, Venezuela, and Argentina. These countries allow their citizens a large degree of freedom; however, they are hampered by a few problems, such as press and electoral restrictions, spot searches and seizures, and trial delays and unfairness. (Not every country listed has all these problems.)

The countries of the world with the most freedoms include: the United States, Switzerland, Canada, New Zealand, Sweden, Italy, Australia, Iceland, the Netherlands, Norway, Luxembourg, Denmark, Austria, United Kingdom, Japan, Belgium, San Marino, Isle of Man, Ireland, Barbados, Costa Rica, and Belize.

On the other hand, the following countries offer their citizens few civil liberties and little political freedom (although they are not the worst in terms of freedom): Czechoslovakia, East Germany, Saudi Arabia, Syria, the Congo, Guinea-Bissau, South Yemen, Burundi, Malawi, Mali, Ghana, the Central African Republic, Burkina Faso, Niger, Mauritania, and Mozambique.

The least-free countries of the world include: Bulgaria, USSR, Albania, Romania, North Korea, Laos, Vietnam, Benin, Kampuchea, Equatorial Guinea, Zaire, Iraq, Somalia, Chad, Afghanistan, and Ethiopia.

The 10 most cultured nations

If you're a culture vulture, you'll be in highbrow heaven in any of the top 10 countries in this category. Theater, music, cinema, night life, museums—you name it, and it can be found in abundance in: the United States, France, Italy, the United Kingdom, Monaco, Canada, Sweden, Switzerland, the Netherlands, and Austria.

The 10 least cultured nations

Finding some cerebral exercise in the following countries is somewhat like trying to uproot a tree with your bare hands—all strain, no gain. The culture scenes in these countries, if not non-existent, are pretty sparse: Somalia, Niger, Chad, Mali, Benin, Afghanistan, Ethiopia, Togo, Guinea, and Sudan.

The terrible 10

Most of the world's 10 worst countries, according to our Quality of Life Index, are poor pitiful African nations, wracked by poverty and illness. Afghanistan and Iraq are the only exceptions. If you're looking for the good life, cross these countries off your list: Afghanistan, Mozambique, Chad, Sudan, Mauritania, Angola, Burkina Faso, Ethiopia, Niger, and Iraq.

The greatest of the great outdoors

Australia, France, Italy, New Zealand, and the United States tie for first place in the recreation department. You'll find just about any outdoor activity you're looking for in these nations. Each country has terrific beaches. All have slopes to ski and mountains to climb. And Australia has animals that exist nowhere else on earth. Each country certainly offers something for everyone. In this category, rather than relying on often-unreliable statistics, we called for detailed reports from our far-flung network of inveterate travelers.

The world's best health care

Health care in Scandinavia ranks first. Sweden wins overall, with an infant mortality rate of 6 per 1,000 live births, 430 people per doctor, and an average life expectancy of 76.1 years. But Iceland and Finland don't lag far behind. Both also have low infant mortality rates (six in both countries). And the average life expectancy in Iceland, 79.94, is even higher than that in Sweden. Finland has a doctor for every 496 people; Iceland has a doctor for every 501 people. Two other countries with more than enough health care to go around are the United States, with a doctor for every 452 people, and the USSR, with a doctor for every 281 people.

Statistics on health can be misleading, however. Just because you move to a country where people are genetically predisposed to longevity does not mean *you* will live longer. And while it is obvious that medical problems are greater in countries where there too few doctors, it's not certain that medical problems are fewer in countries where there are too many doctors. At some point (which we would hate to have to define) the increase in the number of physicians ceases to add to the sum of local health. Our statistical method ranks countries by the number of doctors per capita, regardless of the fact that a surplus of doctors can mean unwarranted— and potentially hazardous—health-care practices, such as unnecessary prescriptions, surgery-just-in-case-he-sues, and Cesareans instead of natural delivery of babies.

The countries of the world with the best medical care include: Sweden, Iceland, Finland, Norway, Japan, Spain, Belgium, France, the Netherlands, and West Germany.

Our sources

When creating our Quality of Life Index, we used the following sources: embassies and other government agencies; *Freedom in the World 1986-1987*, Freedom House, Inc., New York; *Kaleidoscope/Current World Data*, ABC Cleo Publishers, Santa Barbara, 1987; *Individual Taxes, A Worldwide Summary*, Price Waterhouse, New York, 1987; *Political Risk Services Letter*, Frost & Sullivan, London, 1987; *The State of the World's Children 1987*, Oxford Press for the World Bank; *The Stateman's Yearbook 1987-1988*, ABC Cleo Publishers, Santa Barbara; UNESCO's *Statistical Index*, St. Martin's Press, New York; the U.S. State Department; *The World Almanac and Book of Facts 1987*, Pharos Books, a division of the Scripps Howard Company, New York; *World Development Report 1987*, Oxford Press for the World Bank.

The scorecard

United States	88.88	Portugal	61.18
Canada	84.92	Bahamas	59.70
Australia	82.24	Channel Islands	57.23
Switzerland	82.11	Venezuela	57.20
New Zealand	80.78	Hungary	56.18
Sweden	79.39	Argentina	55.94
Italy	78.90	Costa Rica	54.30
West Germany (FRG)	78.39	Israel	53.75
Netherlands	76.63	Cyprus	53.63
France	76.08	Malta	53.61
Austria	76.07	Cayman Islands	52.39
Norway	76.05	Trinidad and Tobago	51.24
Japan	76.00	Yugoslavia	49.97
Denmark	75.78	Czechoslovakia	49.90
United Kingdom	75.44	Taiwan	49.59
Belgium	72.54	East Germany (GDR)	48.52
Luxembourg	72.31	Montserrat	48.41
Finland	71.20	Singapore	48.28
Iceland	70.82	Belize	48.01
Isle of Man	70.14	Macau	47.93
San Marino	69.34	Brazil	46.87
Spain	69.02	Jamaica	45.83
Bermuda	68.72	Uruguay	45.09
Liechtenstein	68.28	USSR	44.78
Monaco	66.90	Ecuador	44.63
Andorra	66.52	Dominican Republic	44.12
Ireland	66.13	Nauru	43.96
Hong Kong	63.27	Brunei	43.87
Barbados	62.24	Mexico	43.52

Poland	42.50	Maldive Islands	23.87
Bulgaria	42.35	El Salvador	22.82
People's Republic of China	42.20	Libya	22.80
Grenada	41.35	Gambia	22.45
Fiji	40.81	Madagascar	22.37
Western Samoa	40.73	Côte d'Ivoire	
Thailand	40.24	(Ivory Coast)	22.23
Colombia	39.84	Vietnam	21.78
French Guiana	39.31	Algeria	21.42
Kuwait	38.86	Laos	21.14
Panama	38.71	Guinea	21.08
Cuba	38.15	Bangladesh	21.02
Malaysia	37.82	Yemen PDR	
Paraguay	37.71	(South Yemen)	20.90
United Arab Emirates	37.18	Malawi	20.83
Guatemala	36.71	Haiti	20.46
India	36.44	Congo	20.14
Albania	36.41	Pakistan	20.06
Turkey	36.38	Burundi	19.81
Romania	36.17	Rwanda	19.75
South Korea	36.16	Togo	19.53
Chile	35.62	Nicaragua	18.96
Indonesia	35.39	Ghana	18.92
Sri Lanka	35.36	Cameroon	18.85
Mauritius	35.35	Guinea-Bissau	18.43
Peru	34.70	Yemen Arab Republic	
Bolivia	34.36	(North Yemen)	18.13
Botswana	34.08	Zaire	18.05
South Africa	34.04	Kampuchea (Cambodia)	17.96
Philippines	33.97	Liberia	17.89
Qatar	33.84	Tanzania	17.70
Saudi Arabia	33.76	Benin	17.53
Bahrain	33.40	Equatorial Guinea	17.44
Honduras	32.32	Iran	16.23
North Korea	31.71	Djibouti	16.21
Egypt	31.54	Somalia	15.81
Seychelles	30.20	Nigeria	15.72
Nepal	29.71	Uganda	15.37
Cape Verde	29.32	Mali	14.88
Papua New Guinea	29.31	Central African Republic	13.91
Suriname	28.93	Iraq	12.64
Swaziland	28.91	Niger	11.69
Tunisia	28.58	Ethiopia	11.63
Kenya	28.53	Burkina Faso	11.15
Guyana	28.47	Angola	11.02
Morocco	27.73	Mauritania	10.85
Lebanon	26.71	Sudan	10.75
Syria	26.70	Chad	8.73
Oman	26.59	Mozambique	8.72
Lesotho	25.46	Afghanistan	7.60
Jordan	25.35		
Senegal	24.32		
Zimbabwe	24.09		
Gabon	24.09		
Sierra Leone	23.99		
Zambia	23.99		

Section II

Destinations

THE BEST OF EUROPE

So rich and varied is Europe in culture, history, and beauty that a library of books could be written on its bests. Writing about the most wonderful places in Europe is like trying to name the greatest work of art in the Louvre or the best treasure in the Vatican. The task is so vast that trying to make choices is nearly impossible. After a good deal of thought and research, we came up with some of our favorites on the continent from which most Americans and much of our culture hail.

Chapter 1

THE BEST OF BRITAIN

Britain is the favorite destination of American travelers. Language isn't a barrier, yet the culture and lifestyle are different. Britain's history is linked with that of America. And the land itself is a place of wonders—mighty castles, charming villages with thatched cottages, ancient cathedrals, prehistoric stone circles, misty lakes, dramatic shorelines.

Britain is a land of perfectionism. Shirts must be made with precision. Suits are of good English wool. Tea must be made just so. And politeness is practically law.

Although hundreds of places demand a visit, the number-one sight is London. Here, many of the world's most famous playwrights and artists blossomed; history's most bloody and fascinating tales unfolded; and the outcome of World War II was sealed.

London, the most memorable city

"What has made London the most poignantly memorable city of the world is its continuing ability to recognize the human condition," writer Richard Condon once said. "From Battersea to Woolwich, across the 32 boroughs of the city, humans reign in perpetual celebration of one of the most complex multilayered communities on the planet....Quirky, steeped in the past but actively and civilly pursuing the present, London—and Londoners—continue to honor all that is human. And 1,250 years after its founding, visitors are still drawn to the city's idiosyncrasies—all those facets that endure and enrich life."

The top sights in London

The most famous sight in London, **Big Ben,** is usually misidentified. Many people believe, incorrectly, that Big Ben is the clock in the Parliament tower; it is actually the 13 1/2-ton bell.

The home of **Parliament,** beneath Big Ben, is surprisingly young, built a mere 100 years ago on the site of the old Royal Palace of Westminster. This huge complex of Victorian buildings covers eight acres and includes 1,100 rooms. The guided tour is definitely worth your time.

Westminster Hall, built from 1394-1402, is part of the original palace. The entrance is in Victoria Tower, and today you don't have to be a traitor to get in. Admission is free.

English kings and queens begin and end their careers at Westminster Abbey, where royal coronations and burials have been held since the time of William the Conqueror. **Poets' Corner** in the south transept contains the tombs of Geoffrey Chaucer, Charles Dickens, Robert Browning, and Thomas Hardy.

The **Tate Gallery** has a collection of works by British painters, including Turner, Blake, Hogarth, and Constable. It also contains works by French Impressionists Manet, Monet, Cézanne, and Degas, as well as sculptures by Rodin, Picasso, and Henry Moore. The gallery is on Millbank Street, near the Pimlico underground station.

Whitehall, where fiery King Henry VIII once had his palace, is now an efficient, modern-day government center. The stretch of land is between the Thames River and St. James' Park. **Number 10 Downing St.,** where the Prime Minister lives, is in Whitehall. The War Rooms at 70 Whitehall were Churchill's subterranean headquarters during World War II. You must have reservations to visit; call *(44-1)233-8904*.

The **Banqueting House** in Whitehall, where Charles I was beheaded, is used today for less violent government receptions. Designed by Inigo Jones and completed in 1622, it is decorated with nine allegorical ceiling paintings by Rubens. A bust of Charles I on the staircase marks the position of the window the king walked through to the scaffolding where he was beheaded.

Surrounded by four regal lions, the mighty **Nelson Column** rises from the heart of Trafalgar Square, a monument to Admiral Nelson. (Nelson died in battle with the French off Cape Trafalgar. Here, he spurred his men on to victory with the inspiring words, "England expects every man to do his duty.")

Concerts are held Sundays at noon in the temple-like **St.-Martin-in-the-Fields** (1721-1726), also on the square. Nearby is the **National Gallery,** with works by Vermeer, Turner, Botticelli, Michelangelo, Holbein, El Greco, and Delacroix. Take a look at the gallery's controversial new annex.

Europe's largest medieval fortress

The **Tower of London,** the largest medieval fortress in Europe, has witnessed foul deeds and splendid spectacles. Inside the fortress, on Tower Green, innumerable heads rolled, including those of Anne Boleyn, Lady Jane Grey, Sir Walter Raleigh, and the Earl of Essex, who was Queen Elizabeth I's rejected lover. In the Bloody Tower, as it is known, Richard III supposedly murdered 13-year-old King Edward V and the king's little brother.

The **Crown Jewels** are kept in the Tower of London. The Cullinan diamond here is the largest ever found. It was sent to London from the Transvaal in a brown paper package via third-class mail.

The worst place to tell secrets

St. Paul's, an ornate cathedral built in 1633 by Inigo Jones, has a **Whispering Gallery** where you can hear a word whispered on the other side of the dome as loudly as if the person speaking were right next to you. Of course, it's no secret that Prince Charles and Lady Diana were married here.

The best changing of the guard

The best changing of the guard in London isn't at Buckingham Palace, as you might expect. It is in the middle of **Whitehall,** where the red-suited Horse Guards are stationed. The changing of the guard here is as picturesque as at Buckingham Palace, and a good deal less crowded. (Tourists visit Buckingham Palace by the millions.)

The best repartee

The best entertainment in London is a session of the **House of Commons,** where insults are exchanged with wild abandon. Florence Horsbrugh, once minister of education, suffered the following insult: "I do not know what the Right Honorable Lady, the Minister of Education, is grinning at. This is the face that sank a thousand scholarships." And Winston Churchill, when accused of being drunk by a female political foe, replied, "And you, Madam, are ugly. But tomorrow I shall be sober!"

You can observe these verbal battles from the gallery. Apply for a free visitor's pass in the Admission Order Office at St. Stephen's Hall after 4:15 p.m. (after 11:30 a.m. on Fridays).

London's strangest sight

Cleopatra's Needle is the most surprising monument in London. This Egyptian obelisk dates back to 1500 B.C. Set in the shadow of Waterloo Bridge on the edge of the Thames embankment, it bears the carvings of two of Egypt's greatest rulers: pharaohs Thothmes III and Ramses II. Offered to England in the 19th century by the ruler of Egypt, the obelisk actually had nothing to do with Cleopatra—it was transported down the Nile into the Mediterranean aboard a boat called *Cleopatra.*

When the Needle reached the Bay of Biscay on Oct. 14, 1877, it fell overboard during a storm. Six men volunteered to recover the monument and drowned in the process. (Their names are inscribed on the south face of the base.) Several days later, the monument was rescued by a freighter that lugged it to London.

London's liveliest corner

Piccadilly Circus is as crazy and colorful as its name. Crowded with people and filled with brightly colored billboards, the square is centered around a small statue of Eros and known as a pickup spot and a place for heroin addicts to get their fixes. But don't worry about the criminal elements—Piccadilly is crowded with ordinary citizens and tourists and perfectly safe. And you'll be so busy battling the crowds and construction barricades that you won't even notice any odd goings-on.

Piccadilly is also where you'll find the **Royal Academy of Fine Arts,** the **Ritz,** and **St. James' Church,** which has concerts during the summer.

The artiest neighborhoods

Covent Garden, where Professor Higgins met Eliza Doolittle in *My Fair Lady,* is being renovated. This arts and theater district has become the place for yuppies. You'll find the London Transport Museum, the Theatre Museum, the Theatre Royal and Royal Opera House, and a crafts market here. The area is used as an impromptu stage for clowns, mimes, musicians, and other entertainers, who perform and then pass the hat.

Bloomsbury was once the home of the literary and intellectual "Bloomsbury Group," which included Virginia Woolf, John Maynard Keynes, and E.M. Forster. This charming area offers the British Museum, the Courtland Institute Galleries, and Pollock's Toy Museum.

Chelsea, the literary enclave where Thomas Carlyle, Oscar Wilde, and Bertrand Russell once lived, today is home to blue-haired punkers. Along the main drag, King's Road, you'll see roller skaters and high-fashion strollers.

Seedy **Soho** is home to London's red-light district, but it's also lined with little restaurants and shops. **Berwick Street** has a great produce market. **Leicester Square** was the home of painters Hogarth and Reynolds. **Hampstead** is a writers' and artists' quarter on a hill overlooking the city. Here you can rummage in antique stores and bookshops, then enjoy afternoon tea in area cafes. Visit **Keats' home** on Wentworth Place and **Freud's** home at 20 Maresfield Gardens.

The best place to rant and rave

Amateur orators spout forth at **Speakers Corner** in Hyde Park on Sundays. If you feel the urge to speak from a soap box, this is the place. If you'd rather just listen, be prepared. You never know what you might hear—anarchists, religious zealots, racists, communists, or vegetarians!

Hyde Park is worth a visit even if you aren't interested in all the ranting and raving. On a pretty day you can go boating in the park or just take a long stroll.

London's best flea market

Petticoat Lane Flea Market, held Sundays on Middlesex Street, is chock full of bargains. The lively outdoor market has antiques as well as inexpensive new goods (especially clothing and appliances), bric-a-brac, and used items. The real bargains are found before 8 a.m. Take the underground to Liverpool Street, then walk up Bishop's Gate to Middlesex Street. (You won't find Petticoat Lane on the map; it's a nickname for Middlesex Street.)

The most entertaining flea market

One of the largest and most entertaining flea markets in Europe is held Sundays on **Portobello Road.** To get there, take the underground to Notting Hill Gate, then walk down Pembrook Road to Portobello Road. On Saturdays the road is lined with street performers and part-time vendors selling everything from punk-rock buttons to antiques. Fine hats and shoes that once bedecked Britain's elite can be found here at pauper prices. If you aren't interested in buying, just watch the people. Be careful, though—this West Indian neighborhood can be seedy.

Antique hunting at its best

Camden Passage is the place for antiques—it has more than 100 shops. Decorative and Victorian antiques are especially good quality in this corner of London. Take the underground to the Angel Islington, then walk up Islington High Street. An early-morning flea market is held here on Wednesdays and Saturdays.

Serious antique hunters flock to **New Caledonian Market** (Bermondsey) at the London Bridge underground station. This huge market has quality silver, china, jewelry, memorabilia, and objets d'art. It is open Fridays from 5 a.m. to 1 p.m. Get there early.

The best stuffed shirts

The stuffed shirts of the world know the best shirt shopping is along **Jermyn Street** in London. Here, traditional shirts are made of Sea Island cotton or two-fold poplin. The collars are perfectly shaped and stitched, as are the cuffs. The buttons are mother-of-pearl. The cut is generous, and the shirt tails are long.

Hildich & Key, *87 Jermyn St.,* produces the finest and most expensive shirts in London. Made of soft cotton, they have hand-sewn buttonholes, removable collar stays, and double cuffs. A bright striped shirt here is £79. Less expensive shirts made of poplin are £49.

Turnbull & Asser, *71 and 72 Jermyn St.,* has shirts with collars roomy enough for T&A's generous ties. The cut of the shirts here makes them extra comfortable. A Turnbull & Asser shirt is £55.

London's best tailor

Stovel & Mason, *Old Burlington St.; tel. (44-1)734-4855,* is a London tailor who offers Saville Row quality at more moderate prices. A hand-tailored suit here is £700. (Always have suspenders or brace buttons attached to the inside of your pants, and insist on 13-inch-deep pockets and jacket cuffs that unbutton.)

The best dress maker

Zara, one of the most talented young designers in London, will make you an original dress for about £350. You can contact this blue-blooded aristocrat and jet-setter at *(44-1)736-2872.*

London's finest shoemakers

The three best shoemakers in London are **Lobbs,** *9 St. James Place, London SW1* (the waiting list is six months long); **Wildsmith,** *Prince's Arcade, Piccadilly,* which makes the best, old-fashioned shoes in London; and **Tricker's,** *67 Jermyn St.*

The best brollies

Swaine & Adney in Piccadilly makes umbrellas by hand. The best brolly (a favorite in the House of Lords) is a Brigg umbrella.

The best ways to explore London

If you can afford it, the ritziest way to explore London is by taxi. Government-accredited tour guide-cabbies will lead you on detailed tours of London for a mere $150 a day. Stanley Roth, one of these 60 knowledgeable guides, includes historical, literary, and just plain funny anecdotes in his personalized tours. To reach Mr. Roth (or guides like him), contact the **London Visitor and Convention Bureau,** *tel. (44-1)730-3488,* which keeps a list of "blue badge guides," as they are called. Booking agents that can set you up with guides include: **The Driver Guides Association,** *tel. (44-1)839-2498;* **Take-A-Guide,** *(800)223-6450, (212)628-4823,* or *(44-1)221-5475;* and **British Tours,** *tel. (44-1)629-5267.*

Walking is the best way to see the city if you don't have money to blow on a private guide. And on foot, you can see London in greater detail and mingle with the British. You can take yourself through the city using a guidebook and a map, or you can take one of London's walking tours. One of the best is offered by **Citisights of London,** *12 Alpha Place, London SW3; tel. (44-1)600-3699,* which offers history and archeology walks of Roman, Saxon, and medieval London. The two-hour tours are led by professional archeologists.

London Walks, *139 Conway Road, London N14 7BH; tel. (44-1)882-2763,* follows the footsteps of Jack the Ripper, Shakespeare, Dickens, Virginia Woolf, and other notables.

If your feet get tired, take a double-decker bus or London's famous subway, known as the tube or the underground. The underground is the world's oldest and most extensive rapid transit system, with more than 250 stations and 750 miles of track.

Fares are set according to the length of your ride. On buses, you can pay the conductor, but you must buy an underground ticket before you get on the train. And make sure you don't throw your ticket away—you'll need it to leave the station. Fares are steep. It can cost as much as $2 to go completely across town. Passes save you money in the long run.

A **London Explorer** ticket gives you unlimited travel on the London bus and tube systems. It also allows you one round-trip journey by underground or airbus between London's Heathrow Airport and central London, as well as discounts on tours and admissions. It is available from travel agents and at any subway station or London Regional Transport Travel Information Center. The cost is £3.50 for one day; £9 for three days; £11.50 for four days; or £16 for seven days.

London Travelcards also allow unlimited travel on London buses and the subway. One-day cards are available for £2 for five travel zones, £1.70 for four zones. They can be purchased from underground and bus stations.

Tour buses depart Victoria Station and Piccadilly Circus daily at 9:30 and 11:30 a.m. and 2:30 p.m. The rates are about $5.60 for adults, $1.20 for children.

London double-decker bus tours also are available, *tel. (44-1)222-1234.* The open-topped buses depart Piccadilly Circus, Victoria Station, and Marble Arch daily from 9 a.m. to 4 p.m. The tours last about 2 hours and 20 minutes and cost about £2.95 for adults, £1.50 for children under 16. A free map is included. Reservations aren't necessary.

The best places to take tea

The most elegant place to enjoy a pot of hot tea with scones, Devonshire cream, and strawberry preserves is the **Dorchester Hotel** on Park Lane.

The coziest place for tea is **Brown's,** a Victorian hotel on Dover Street. Rudyard Kipling once stayed here. Men must wear a tie to take tea at Brown's after 4 p.m. (And they should take a moment to glance into the men's room before they leave; the scale is an extremely rare antique.)

Another good place to take tea is the department store **Fortnum and Mason,** *181 Piccadilly, London W1.* If the fashionable Fountain Room is too crowded, go upstairs to the more discreet St. James Restaurant—few people know about it.

A quiet, modest place to have tea, especially if you are shopping, is **Liberty's** on Regent Street. Of the two restaurants here, the one upstairs is the prettiest.

The funniest tea party

The best tea ceremony in Britain is at the **Regents Park Zoo**—and it is taken by chimpanzees, not people. Each summer afternoon, smartly dressed chimps, the girls in pinafores with pink sashes, the boys in Eton shorts and Peter Pan collars, eat cakes and drink tea with milk. The monkeys grab for the prettiest iced cookies and get into wild fights, during which they pour tea (mercifully not hot) on each others' heads and play games with the cream cakes. They break all the rules of good table manners as taught by nanny or Mum—and children visiting the zoo just love it. Apparently the chimps so throw themselves into the game that the zoo has to use different teams on alternate days.

The Regents Park Zoo is also the other place where you can see pandas (besides Washington, D.C. and China).

The best restaurant in London

The **Grill Room** at the **Connaught Hotel,** *Carlos Place, London W1; tel. (44-1)499-7070,* is the best restaurant in London. This elegant establishment serves traditional French and English food to cabinet ministers and art dealers. As an hors d'oeuvre, try the mouth-watering *croustade d'oeufs de caille Maintenon* (quails' egg yolks in a pastry boat). Also try the seafood stew with shrimp and lobster in a wine sauce. Order coffee following your meal—it comes with sugar-glazed grapes and strawberries dipped in chocolate.

The best service in London

The **Terrace Restaurant** at the **Dorchester Hotel,** *Park Lane, London W1; tel. (44-1)629-8888,* has one staff member for every two guests. This marble-columned, elegantly lit institution has exquisite cuisine served in a series of leisurely courses.

The best roast beef in London

At **Simpson's in the Strand,** *100 Strand; tel. (44-1)836-9112,* a maitre d'hotel dressed in tails ushers diners into the paneled dining room. Six 30-pound four-rib loins are roasted simultaneously. Roast beef and saddles of mutton are wheeled directly to guests' tables and carved there. The cattle are chosen by Simpson's agents at auctions in Scotland. The Duke of Wellington and Margaret Thatcher are said to prefer Simpson's.

The best Indian food

Bombay Brasserie, *140 Gloucester Road,* next to **Bailey's Hotel,** *Courtfield Close; tel. (44-1)370-4040,* is the best of the upscale Indian restaurants in London. Especially good are the Goan fish curry, the aromatic chicken dishes, and the bean curries.

London's best night life

One of the trendiest of London's now-trendy wine bars is the **Ebury Wine Bar,** *Ebury Street, Belgravia.* (In case you haven't heard, wine bars are bars that serve good wine by the glass.)

If you'd rather something rowdier, **Brahms and Liszt,** *19 Russell St.,* is the best place for a rip-roaring good time. (*Liszt* is Cockney slang for *pissed,* meaning drunk.)

London's best pub

London's heart is in its pubs. They are located on nearly every street corner and are an integral part of British life. Each has its own inimitable character.

Choosing London's best pub is a big task—everyone has his own favorite. We chose the **Anchor Tavern,** *1 Bankside, Southwark; tel. (44-1)407-1577,* on the south side of the Thames, as our favorite. This cozy riverside pub was frequented by writer Samuel Johnson, as well as by smugglers, rivermen, and wardens from the nearby Clink Prison. (The slang word for prison comes from the Clink.)

The ancient pub originally was built near the site of Shakespeare's Globe Theater; it was rebuilt about 170 years ago. The low-beamed rooms are many and varied.

Legend has it that a special brew known as Russian Imperial Stout was prepared at the pub for the empress of Russia. Besides beer, try the roast forerib of beef or the steak and mushroom pudding. The Anchor is open from noon to 2 p.m. and from 7 p.m. to 10 p.m. It is closed Sunday evenings.

The oldest pub in the world

The **George and Vulture** is the oldest pub in the world. The original, called the George, was built in the 12th century. Sir Richard Wittington, the "thrice-round mayor of London," visited here in the 1500s, as did Chaucer (and Chaucer's father). Daniel Defoe, Jonathan Swift, and Charles Dickens were also customers.

The Pickwick Club meets at the George and Vulture quarterly, and members quote from the many Dickens' passages about the place. The fictional Mr. Pickwick, when asked where he spent his leisure time, replied that he was "at present suspended at the George and Vulture." A framed check written by Dickens to the proprietor hangs on the wall.

The most historic pubs

Ye Olde Cheshire Cheese. This pub was opened in 1538 and rebuilt in 1667 after the Great Fire of London. The Cheese was a favorite of Goldsmith and Johnson and was mentioned by Dickens in *A Tale of Two Cities*. It is one of London's few remaining 17th-century chophouses.

The Cheese has sawdust on the floors (changed twice daily), and the tables are boxed in, with a bench for three diners on each side. An open fire cheers the original bar in winter, which, until recently, was reserved for men only. Try the savory baked cheese and Guinness on toast, the steak and kidney pie, and the Yorkshire pudding.

The Prospect of Whitby. One of the oldest riverfront pubs, the Prospect was popular with painters Whistler and Turner. While drinking here, Hanging Judge Jeffreys watched his sentences being carried out at nearby Execution Dock.

The Trafalgar. This pub is on the Thames at the place where time begins, Greenwich Mean Time. The Greenwich observatory and a maritime museum are located here. The food is good, but expensive. The view is superb and free. Take a ferry from Tower Bridge to Greenwich.

The four best hotels in London

The **Connaught Hotel,** *16 Carlos Place, London W1Y 6AL; tel. (44-1)499-7070,* is the best in town. It has old-fashioned elegance and perfect service. The exterior of the Connaught is elegant, with a gracefully curving facade. Flowers brighten the porch. The interior is cozy, with wood paneling, Oriental rugs, and upholstered chairs.

A magnificent staircase with dark wood banisters leads to bedrooms on the upper floors. The spacious rooms have cheery wallpaper, brass beds, and antique desks. And the bathrooms are luxurious, with grand tubs, fine soaps, thick towels, and a cord to ring for the maid. Breakfast is brought to your room on a cloth-covered table and served on china. The orange juice is fresh. Write to request a room on the Carlos Place side. Book dinner reservations six weeks in advance.

Claridge's, *Brook Street, London W1A 2JQ; tel. (44-1)629-8860,* in the heart of Mayfair, is a close second. It has a Hungarian Quartet that has been playing in the lobby for most of this century. Liveried attendants greet you at the door, and dress-maids are available to help you choose what to wear from your extensive wardrobe. Rooms have fireplaces, bells to ring for the maid or valet, and royally sized bathtubs. The hotel recently underwent a facelift and now has new carpeting, paint, and air conditioning. And a health club is under construction.

Hyde Park, *Knightsbridge, London SW1Y 7LA; tel. (44-1)235-5000,* is the third best hotel in London. It is an enormous hotel that aspires to modern efficiency but doesn't quite succeed.

But it does have a magnificent entrance hall, with marble floors and walls, an enormous mirror, and chandeliers. And the bedrooms are comfortable, with large beds and French doors that open onto balconies.

Last, but not least, is **Brown's**, *19-22 Dover St., London W1A 4SW; tel. (44-1)493-6020.* The building dates back to 1660; it opened for business as Brown's in 1837. Teddy Roosevelt was married at Brown's, Kipling wrote here, and Queen Victoria visited Queen Wilhelmina here. From 1924-1935, it was the official court of the king of Greece. Oak paneling, 19th-century prints, antiques, and stained glass add atmosphere to the 12 connecting buildings that make up Brown's.

Best hotels for the money

11 Cadogan Gardens, *London SW3; tel. (44-1)730-3426,* is so popular that you must book a room months in advance. Bookings from travel agents are not accepted. This Victorian hotel is filled with mahogany and silver. A butler serves breakfast and tea. Double rooms are £94 to £124 (about $145) a night. The hotel is near the intersection of Sloane Square and Draycott Place.

The **Ebury Court**, *26 Ebury St., London SW1; tel. (44-1)730-8147,* is quaint, with white woodwork and chintz curtains. It has a steady British and American clientele. Double rooms are £67.50 (about $102) a night, including breakfast.

The **Cranley Place Hotel**, *1 Cranley Place, South Kensington, London SW7; tel. (44-1)589-7944* or *(44-1)589-7704,* is in a Regency-style house near Harrods. Bedrooms are decorated Laura Ashley-style and furnished with antiques. Breakfast can be taken in the dining room or in your hotel room. Double rooms with private baths are £65-£90 (about $95) a night.

The **Wilbraham**, *1 Wilbraham Place, Sloane St., London SW1; tel. (44-1)730-8296,* feels more like a country inn than a London hotel. It is in a converted Victorian house in Belgravia, near Sloane Square Station. Double rooms with baths are £53 (about $75).

The most punked-out places

Blue-haired, mohawked punks are on the endangered species list, even in London. But you can still find them—they congregate near Oxford Street on King's Road.

If you're adventurous, visit the **Bat Cave** at **Fouberts**, *18 Fouberts Place; tel. (44-1)734-3630,* on Wednesday nights. Slam-dancing is the thing to do in this black-walled place. At 2 a.m. the DJ plays "Batman," and the dancers go crazy.

The world's best theater

London is the world's theater capital. Most of the major theaters are in the West End, a short walk from Trafalgar Square, in Covent Garden, or in Leicester Square. Notable exceptions are the National Theater complex on the South Bank, next to the Royal Festival Hall, and the splendid Barbican Center for the Arts, permanent home of the Royal Shakespeare Company. Numerous fringe theater groups perform all over London.

You can get half-price tickets to major shows at the **Leicester Square Ticket Booth** (right in Leicester Square). Tickets are available for same-day West End shows only, and you'll rarely find tickets for recent hits. Nevertheless, the selection usually is pretty good. What's available is posted on the boards next to the booth. The line is usually long, and the tickets go fast, so keep an eye on the boards for changes as you wait.

On matinee days (Tuesdays, Wednesdays, Thursdays, and Saturdays), two queues form at the Leicester Square Ticket Booth—one for matinees, one for evening tickets. So be sure you're in the right line.

You also can get discounted tickets by going to the theater lobby right before the performance—although you may find yourself running from theater to theater. Last-minute tickets are sometimes also available for sold-out shows, although not at discounted prices.

The best side trips from London

Most Americans who visit Britain see little more than London. Yet it's outside London that you see the real England. The easiest way to get to the sights outside London is by rail or bus (or coach, as the British say). London has eight main train stations, each dealing with a different region—so make sure you are leaving from the right station. Each has an information office.

Buses are the least expensive way to take side trips. London has two main bus services: **National Express** and the **Green Line.** The main station for National Express is **Victoria Coach Station** (NOT Victoria Train Station, which is nearby), *Buckingham Palace Road, London SW1; tel. (44-1)730-0202.* The main station for the Green Line is **Eccleston Bridge,** just down the street, *tel. (44-1)668-7261.* If you are in a hurry, take a National Express bus. The Green Line makes more stops and is slower. However, the Green Line does have some express buses (called Rapid Buses).

Cambridge—the prettiest

Cambridge is the prettiest of England's two rival university towns. A serene place, Cambridge was originally a Roman crossing over the River Cam. At the time of the Domesday Book (1086), Cambridge was a small trading village. Scholars gathered here in 1209 after being ousted from Oxford by irate townspeople. They opened a series of colleges that eventually became the university. The lovely old city (in Britain, any town with a cathedral is called a city) did not always see eye to eye with the university—riots were staged in 1381. The phrase "town and gown" indicates some of the old animosity.

The most impressive Gothic structure

The magnificent architecture of Cambridge and the beautiful surrounding countryside are good reasons to spend several days here. **King's College Chapel** is one of the most impressive Gothic structures in England. "Evensong" on Sunday, sung by a boys' choir at the chapel, is not to be missed.

The best place to buy sheepskin

Cambridge has one more claim to fame. It is the best place we've found to buy sheepskin. **Roy Pett,** *6 Benet St., Cambridge; tel. (44-223)315-855,* has single sheepskins for £40; doubles for £80; four sewn together for £160; and large petal rugs for £300. The friendly proprietor, Roy Pett himself, also offers suede moccasins with wool linings for £10; suede moccasins with sheepskin linings for £15; sheepskin moccasins for £20; and sheepskin booties for £25. Woolens are another good buy at Roy Pett—good wool sweaters are £30.

Oxford—the oldest university

Oxford University, with its 34 colleges and thousands of students, draws visitors from around the world. The college's 100 acres include lawns, gardens, water walks, and a private deer park where the famous Magdalen Deer can be spotted. **New College,** built in the late 14th century, is one of the most inviting colleges on campus, with its medieval cloisters and peaceful gardens. A section of the old city walls can be found here.

While the university was founded in the 12th century, the town itself dates back to A.D. 912. The hero of many Dorothy Sayers mystery stories, Lord Peter Whimsey, studied at Oxford.

The oldest museum in Britain

The oldest public museum in Britain, the **Ashmolean,** is in Oxford. It has a great collection, including works by French Impressionists and Renaissance artists Raphael and Michelangelo. It also contains historical curios, such as the lantern Guy Fawkes carried when he tried to blow up Parliament in 1605.

The best inn

The **Bear Inn,** *Park Street, Woodstock; tel. (44-Woodstock)811511,* is the best place to stay in Oxford. This establishment is seven centuries old and has oak beams and low ceilings. Rooms on the upper stories have sloping floors, and the steps are uneven.

The Bear Inn is an important part of Oxford tradition—students meet here to sing university songs and to hold parties. The famous collection of neckties hanging on one wall here includes more than 4,200 donated by customers since 1951. Each bears the owner's signature. The collection includes ties from members of rowing clubs, cricket teams, student societies, the police, and the military. The ties are divided according to nationality.

England's most charming village

The village of **Shanklin,** on the Isle of Wight off the southern coast of England, is incredibly charming—just what you imagine an English village should be. Thatched-roof cottages, many of them restaurants, pubs, and gift shops, line the streets. St. Blasius, the old parish church, dates in part from the 14th century. Climb down into the Shanklin Chine, a narrow ravine with a waterfall. The Isle of Wight is accessible from Portsmouth or Southampton on the mainland by helicopter or ferry.

The largest inhabited castle in the world

Windsor Castle, still used by royalty after 850 years (construction of the castle was begun by William the Conqueror in the 11th century), is the largest inhabited castle in the world. Many of Britain's kings and queens are buried in **St. George's Chapel** here.

Located on the River Thames, Windsor is a picturesque Victorian town. Across the river from Windsor is **Eton College,** the most exclusive boys' school in Britain. Founded in 1440, it has educated many of the nation's leaders.

Canterbury: Chaucer's favorite

St. Augustine established Christianity in Canterbury in A.D. 597, and in 1197 the martyr Thomas à Becket was murdered in the cathedral. Canterbury has been a settlement since the Iron Age. Visit **Canterbury Cathedral,** the mother church for the Anglican faith and a center for pilgrimages (like the one Chaucer wrote about). The structure was begun in 1070 and completed in 1503.

The world's most famous cliffs

The white cliffs of **Dover** are world-famous for their brilliant white color and their sheer drop into the sea. The best view of the cliffs is from the ferry that crosses the English Channel on its way to France.

England's most romantic bed and breakfast

Hope End, *Ledbury, Hereford and Worcester, HR8 1JQ; tel. (44-531)3613,* is one of the most inviting bed and breakfasts in England. Located in the coach house and stables of the house where Elizabeth Barrett Browning lived for 23 years (her house was demolished in 1873), it is cozy and serves delicious meals. You can ramble the "gentle land" where Browning's "steps in jocund childhood played." Forty acres of wooded valley and park surround the inn.

To get to Hope End, take a train from Paddington Station in London. Get off in Ledbury and take a taxi to the inn. The inn has only seven rooms, so make reservations. Hope's End is closed from Nov. 30 through February.

The most picturesque region: the southwest peninsula

The southwest peninsula—Devon and Cornwall—is for people who like to breathe tangy sea breezes, explore fishing villages, walk harbor walls, swim in the sea, and wallow in England's maritime history. The southern coast faces the English Channel, which affords a mild climate with gentle waves softly lapping the secluded bays and ancient smugglers' coves. The northern coast of the peninsula faces the full force of the Atlantic.

All along the peninsula you'll pass little villages that appear to tumble down the hillsides. Inland are the granite moors. Dartmoor, Exmoor, and Bodmin are designated National Trust areas, protected from development.

Cornwall—the least changed region

Cornwall is one of the last genuinely unchanged counties of England. The motorway doesn't go here, but the A30's meandering route from London is pretty. Cornwall is nearly 300 miles from London (the train journey takes about five hours).

This region, the one-time hideout of smugglers and pirates, is also the location of Tintagel, the legendary home of King Arthur. The tiny village of Camelford is supposedly the original Camelot. You can partake in a medieval banquet in the Great Hall at Tintagel, surrounded by the colors and banners of the Knights of the Round Table.

The best outdoor theater

Penzance, a colorful old South Cornish town of pirates and smugglers, is nearly 300 miles from London. In the summer, open-air opera, including the apt Gilbert and Sullivan work the *Pirates of Penzance,* is performed at the **Minack Theater** at Portcurno.

The Minack Theater is carved out of a cliff. The audience watches the performance in the open air looking out over the Atlantic. Take along a warm sweater and a blanket.

The prettiest Cornish town

St. Mawes, on the southern coast of Cornwall, is one of the prettiest towns in Britain. Located at the mouth of Percuil Creek, it is known for its fine sailing and its castle, which was built by King Henry VIII from 1540-1543. The castle is shaped like a clover leaf for good luck.

Cornwall's best hotels

The best seaside hotel in Cornwall is the **Falmouth Hotel,** *Falmouth, Cornwall; tel. (44-326)314-714.* Overlooking Pendennis Point and Pendennis Castle, it was opened in 1865 and has accommodated Edward VII and stage stars Anna Neagle and Herbert Wilcox.

Allhays Country House, *Talland Bay near Looe, Cornwall PL 132 JB; tel. (44-503)72434,* is one of the best bed and breakfasts in the region. Rooms are £13.50 to £20 through May, £15 to £21.50 in high season.

Truro Farm, *Truro, Cornwall, tel. (44-872)72532,* is a rambling stone house constructed in a jumble of periods from the 16th through the 18th centuries. Rooms have lovely antiques ranging from Georgian to Victorian.

A footpath leads to the village of Malpas, from which you can take boat trips down river to Falmouth. This house is a particularly good bargain—rates are £10 to £15, half price for children younger than 10.

The best moor: Dartmoor

In the heart of Devon is the 365-square-mile **Dartmoor National Park,** which embodies the county's mystery and beauty. Dartmoor is the setting of The *Hound of the Baskervilles,* as well as the location of the notorious Dartmoor Prison. Its desolate moors are relieved by cozy villages and rolling hills.

Wild ponies canter through Dartmoor's fields of wild flowers. Thatched cottages dot the landscape, and towns here—Widecombe-in-the-Moor, Ashburton, Okehampton, and Chagford—are all within walking distance of the moors. Try to be in the area during a village fair or stock show. You will think time has stood still.

If you want to explore the wilds of Dartmoor National Park, pick up an ordinance map of the park, don your waterproof boots, and set out.

After hiking all day, stop in at **Barton's** in Chagford. It serves an authentic Devonshire tea, complete with scones, strawberry preserves, and thick Devonshire cream.

The best stone rows

Dartmoor has the best example of stone **rowsyard**—high rocks set in a line. The rocks are sometimes covered with circular designs. Look carefully—they are often hidden by heather. The rows lead to round barrows or cairns (burial mounds).

The best Bronze Age village

Grimspound in Manaton is one of the best examples of a fortified Bronze Age village on the moor. It is also the largest, with 24 hut circles in a 150-yard enclosure. The protecting wall was originally 10 feet high and had 3 entrances. The hut circles had cooking holes, stone platforms, and flat center stones that supported the roof poles.

The most luxurious hotel in Devon

The most luxurious place to stay in Dartmoor National Park is **Gidleigh Park,** *Chagford, Devon; tel. (44-6473)2367.* This peaceful country manor has blazing fires, chintz-covered furniture, and oak-paneled walls. The hotel has 12 rooms, an exceptional restaurant, and is surrounded by 30 acres.

Gidleigh Park is rather expensive—£108 to £195 a night for two. But it's worth the price. Reserve in the United States through **David B. Mitchell & Company, Inc.,** *(212)696-1323.*

The coziest bed and breakfasts by the moor

Burrator House, *Sheepstor, near Yelverton, Devon PL20 6PF; tel. (44-822)853353,* is a Georgian house on 20 acres. It is on the B3212 Road and has a trout pool, a miniature waterfall, a swimming pool, and a Victorian snooker table (snooker is a form of pool). Double rooms are £26 to £35 per person; a family room with its own bath is £40.

Wray Barton Manor, *Moretonhampstead, Devon TQ13 8SE; tel. (44-647)40246,* is a 17th-century stone house that can be reached by the B3212 (which crosses Dartmoor). Rooms are £13 to £15 without bath, or £16 with bath; children under five stay for free. Dinners are £8.

The best of the Cotswolds

The "Heart of England" lies just an hour and a half (by train) west and slightly north of London. Here, a softly rolling ribbon of hills enfolds rustic villages of another, more romantic age. This region, known as the **Cotswolds,** was the prosperous hub of the wool trade in the 13th through 16th centuries, and you can still glimpse an occasional flock of sheep. Towns and villages nestling in these hills are made up of houses built of the local stone, with steep slate roofs.

The most charming village

Tetbury is the most charming village in the Cotswolds, an old market town with hilly streets that weave and curve around the Old Market House, built in 1655. Early in the morning, bottles of milk with cream on top sit outside the doors of the quaint town houses.

Tetbury has a beautiful church, **St. Mary the Virgin,** some antique shops—and little else. The town is surrounded by royalty—the Prince and Princess of Wales, Princess Anne, and Prince and Princess Michael of Kent all have homes within a few miles.

Shakespeare's favorite

Stratford-upon-Avon, Shakespeare's home town, sits at the northeast tip of the Cotswolds. Despite its commercialized, touristy flavor, Stratford is pretty, with authentic Tudor buildings on practically every street.

You're cheating yourself if you don't make it to one of the Royal Shakespeare Company's productions. Also worth a stop is the Dirty Duck Pub, where actors hang out between shows. It is across from the theater, right up from McDonalds.

The best of Cheltenham

Cheltenham, the tourist base of the Cotswolds, is a melange of old and new. Georgian terraced houses with flower-draped, wrought-iron balconies stand beside gray cube-like office buildings and utilitarian storefront strips.

The nicest strip is the **Promenade,** a tree-lined avenue with ornate Georgian buildings. Visit the Cheltenham Racecourse, one of England's finest steeplechase courses.

The best castle in the Cotswolds

Six miles up A46 from Cheltenham is **Sudeley Castle** in Winchcombe. Catherine Parr, the sixth wife of Henry VIII and the only one to survive him, lived and is buried here. (Henry's fourth wife, Anne of Cleves, also survived him, but their marriage was annulled.)

The best places to stay

Two hotels that make ideal bases for touring the Cotswolds are the Close at Tetbury and the Hotel de la Bere, just outside Cheltenham. The Close was once the home of a 16th-century wool merchant. The Hotel de la Bere is a sprawling, grandiose 16th-century building. For reservations, contact **Ray Morrow Associates,** *360 Main St., Ridgefield, CT 06877; (800)243-9420* or *(203)438-3793.*

The best ways to get there

One of the best things about the Cotswolds is the region's proximity to London. The capital is less than two hours away by the M4 or M40 motorways.

England's best bath

England's most magnificent spa is, appropriately, **Bath.** According to legend, the mineral springs at Bath were first discovered by King Bladud (the father of King Lear), who had been banished into the countryside because of his leprosy. He became a swineherd, and his pigs led him to the springs, which cured him of the disease.

Visit the Roman Baths and the Pump Room, where you can drink the bubbling hot mineral water from the fountain. The Great Bath is exposed to the sky. Next door is a museum displaying Roman and prehistoric relics. Stroll along the Royal Crescent, a sweep of 30 Georgian houses joined by one facade and fronted with Ionic columns.

England's best-preserved town

Chester, on the west coast in Cheshire County, is one of the few English towns still encircled by a medieval wall. The thick wall doubles as an attractive promenade lined with shops. Within the walls are Tudor half-timbered houses.

Founded in A.D. 60, Chester was the headquarters of the Roman XX Legion, and many Roman relics remain.

Residents of this friendly town invite overseas visitors to spend an afternoon in their homes for tea and conversation. The program is called **Chester at Home**. For information, call Mr. and Mrs. Read, *tel. (44-51)339-6615*. Locals also give free tours.

The most inspiring region: Yorkshire

Yorkshire has inspired a number of English writers, including James Herriot and the Bronte family. Herbert Read, the poet and art critic, was a more recent Yorkshire literary light.

James Herriot Country, as Yorkshire County is known, is a patchwork of undulating pastures dotted with sheep and lined with ancient stone walls, desolate moors, rugged coastlines, and medieval towns.

The best of the Brontes

The Brontes lived in **Haworth,** a romantic town perched precariously on a hillside, commanding superb views from its cobblestoned streets. You can visit the parsonage that was their home from 11 a.m. to 5:30 p.m. April through September. It closes at 4:30 p.m. October through March.

The most colorful place to dine or stay in Haworth is the **Black Bull House,** *tel. (44-535)42249,* where Branwell Bronte obtained his supplies of opium.

The best hang gliding

At **Thirsk**, a charming market town in Yorkshire, a natural ridge provides a superb hang-gliding site. Visitors are welcome to take glider rides, enjoying bird's-eye views of the area. For more informatin, contact the **Yorkshire Gliding Club,** *Sulton Bank, Thirsk, Yorkshire, Y072Ey;tel. (44-845)597-237.*

The best guidebook

The guidebook with the most insight into this region is James Herriot's *Yorkshire.* The animal lover and writer loves the region and knows it inside out.

The coziest place to stay

The **Black Swan Hotel,** *Market Place, Helmsley, North Yorkshire; tel. (44-439)70466,* is an old coaching inn on the edge of North York Moors National Park. It serves full English breakfasts, traditional teas, and traditional Sunday lunches. Try the venison, the Barnsley chops, and the puddings. Rooms are £37 to £44 per person.

The most historic city: York

In A.D. 867, the Danish Vikings vanquished York, and many of the street names, such as Micklegate, Bootham, and Walmgate, date from this period. After the Vikings, the Normans took possession. The city's architecture bears witness to their influence. During the fifth or sixth century, King Arthur captured York, and in the seventh century the Saxons moved in. They built a small wooden church, the original **York Minster** (a minster is a church that was once a monastery). Until the 14th century, York was strategically and economically more important than London and was the nation's capital.

In the early 1970s, it was discovered that the foundations of the York Minster were on the move. Draining and underpinning were urgently required. During the work, which began in 1976, evidence of a massive Roman military fortress and a Roman drainage system were discovered. The drains were in such good condition that they could be used for the necessary drainage without repair! Quite impressive for something built in A.D. 71.

During the excavations, one of the workmen on the site insisted that he saw the ghosts of an entire battalion of Roman soldiers marching before him. The British workman was visibly shaken. "One of the strangest things," he said, "was that they were only visible from the knees up. You couldn't see their legs." Further excavations revealed an ancient Roman road at just about the level the soldiers' feet would have been.

Work continues in the south transept of the church, repairing damage caused by a fire started by a bolt of lightning on July 31, 1984. Some say it was divine retribution after disparaging remarks were made by the Bishop of Durham from the minster pulpit about the Trinity. The Queen and Prince Charles have donated ancient oak trees from their estates to help rebuild the roof sections of the transept.

The best city walk

A footpath along the top of the walls that surround York provides a pleasant three-mile saunter on a warm summer evening. You can circle the entire city on the walls, coming down the stone steps at intervals to see the sights. Modern traffic runs between these steps and their ancient gatehouses. The York Minster is visible from the walls at all times. It is a delightful contrast to the black-and-white Tudor buildings that surround it.

The best sightseeing tip

Don't take a car into York. Sights are within easy walking distance of each other, public transportation is available, and parking is a nightmare not to be contemplated.

The Brits' favorite holiday place

If it came to a choice between London and the Lake District, any Briton would choose the **Lake District**. An area of outstanding natural beauty, it covers the northwestern corner of England, just south of the Scottish border. It is easily accessible via the M6 Motorway, approximately a five-hour drive from London.

The Lake District is rich in literary connections. Wordsworth was born here and was visited here often by Shelley and Coleridge. Robert Southey lived in Keswick for more than 40 years. And John Ruskin's name pops up everywhere, from Ruskin House Pottery in Ambleside to the cross commemorating him in the churchyard at Coniston. This is also the country of Beatrix Potter, the much-loved author of delightful children's stories. Charles Lamb vacationed in Keswick.

The best way to see the Lake District

The best way to see the Lake District is slowly. You'll absorb more of the atmosphere by sitting beside one lake for a few hours than by racing around the largest lakes and main towns and villages. The tiny roads that weave between and over the hills will defeat anyone in a hurry. Also keep in mind that wandering sheep have the right of way here, and you'll often have to leave your car to open and close sheep gates that cross the road.

Head first for Brockhole, a country house halfway between Windermere and Ambleside on the main road. The house is an information center and has a pleasant tearoom.

The two most spectacular lakes

Ullswater, which is surrounded by hills and highlands rising from the water's edge, is the most spectacular of the lakes. Wordsworth immortalized the daffodils he saw here and described Ullswater as "perhaps...the happiest combination of beauty and grandeur, which any of the Lakes affords."

The best place to stay on the banks of Ullswater is the **Sharrow Bay Hotel,** *Penrith, Cumbria CA10 2LZ, England; tel. (44-P)08536-301.* Proprietor Francis Coulson goes to great lengths to please his guests. A roaring fire warms the lounge, and rooms are equipped with backgammon and scrabble boards. The views are tremendous.

Mr. Coulson despises cuisine *minceur* and believes in cream with everything, so the food is sinfully delicious. Try the cream of watercress soup and, for dessert, the kiwi fruit pavlova and cream profiteroles with chocolate sauce.

The most beautiful stone circle

Just two miles east of Keswick is **Castlerigg Stone Circle,** the most beautifully situated stone circle in England. And unlike the famous Stonehenge, it is not inundated with tourists.

You can work out a number of astronomical details from this circle, which is 100 feet in diameter with 38 stones in its outer ring (almost all standing in their original positins) and 10 more within.

From Castlerigg you can see the north Lakeland hills. Three miles away is a hill called Threlkeld Knott, over which the sun rises during an equinox.

Wordsworth's favorite

Tiny **Grasmere** village is more famous for its delightful position, nestled as it is beneath Helm Crag and Nab Scar northwest of Lake Windermere, than for its amenities. Wordsworth called it "the loveliest spot that man hath ever found." He made his first home nearby at Dove Cottage. Open to the public, Dove Cottage is tiny and charming, with a museum next door. Historian Philip Crowl says, "The management of this site is a model of graciousness combined with efficiency. Few stately homes, for all their large staffs and high entrance fees, do as well." Even the garden is a delight.

Britain's most regal beach resort

The seaside town of **Brighton** became popular with aristocrats in the mid-18th century. (It later lost standing and became a big favorite of P.G. Wodehouse's Jeeves, the butler, who liked to fish here.) Brighton was originally a tiny fishing village that is mentioned in the Domesday Book.

The best walks in Brighton are along Old Steine, which is the center of activity; out to the Palace Pier, a Victorian structure that juts nearly a third of a mile into the English Channel; and along the Marine Parade, an attractive promenade with 19th-century terraces.

The biggest attraction in town is the restored **Royal Pavilion,** a pseudo-Oriental structure built by the Prince Regent, George, Prince of Wales (later King George IV) from 1787 to 1822. The pavilion graphically demonstrates the excesses and extravagances of the Regency period.

If you tire of the sun—or rain—the most inviting places for tea are the lounge of the Metropole or the veranda of the Grand Hotel (rebuilt after the Irish Republican Army bombed it in 1984 in an attempt on the life of Margaret Thatcher).

Wheeler's Sheridan and English's are Brighton's most elegant restaurants.

The world's best gardens

English gardens are known worldwide for their colorful, wild abandon. Gardening is something the British do well. The rainy weather and mild winters, particularly in the south, provide a congenial environment for trees and plants.

The immense gardens carefully tended on England's estates were once enjoyed only by the wealthy. Now they are open to all garden-lovers. Apart from financial considerations, most owners today believe that it's right to share their historic homes and gardens with the rest of us.

The most beautiful garden

Of all the beautiful gardens in England, the most beautiful is **Sissinghurst Castle**

Garden, two miles northeast of Cranbrook. Created by writer Vita Sackville-West (who wrote a gardening column for the *Daily Telegraph* for many years) and her husband, diplomat Sir Harold Nicolson, Sissinghurst is a series of walled gardens located between the surviving parts of an Elizabethan mansion.

The prettiest is the white garden, planted with only white flowers. Also lovely are the rose garden, with old-fashioned English roses (old-fashioned roses predate hybrids, which are what most gardens grow today), the herb garden, the yew walk, the moat walk, and the orchard. The gardens are open from April to Oct. 15 Tuesday through Friday, 1 p.m. to 6:30 p.m.

The best guides to English gardens

Historic Houses, Castles, and Gardens is an indispensable catalog of more than 1,400 historic properties and gardens in England that are open to the public. Included is a brief history of each, its hours, entry fees, what you'll see, and how to get to the property. Order from **ABC Historic Publications,** *World Timetable Centre, Church Street, Dunstable, Bedfordshire.*

National Gardens Scheme lists private gardens open to the public alphabetically by county. The Scheme is a charitable trust begun in 1927 as a memorial to Queen Alexandra. It now comprises more than 1,600 gardens. Proceeds are administered by the Queen's Nursing Institute. You can order the list from the **National Gardens Scheme Charitable Trust,** *57 Lower Belgrave St., London SW1 W0LR.*

England's best palaces

Castle Howard, in the rugged north, is the most beautiful of England's castles. This 18th-century home 15 miles north of York was the film site for Evelyn Waugh's *Brideshead Revisited,* the renowned British television series.

Actually a palace, Castle Howard was designed in 1699 for Charles Howard, third Earl of Carlisle, and is aglow with paintings by Rubens, Gainsborough, and Reynolds. Some of the furniture is by Sheraton and Chippendale, and the costume galleries have displays dating from the 18th century. The grounds are extensive, with lakes, fountains, and a beautiful Temple of the Four Winds. A replica of an 18th-century rose garden has old-fashioned roses that are no longer available commercially.

Blenheim Palace, in Oxfordshire, is a close second. Near the old town of Woodstock, it was the home of the 11th Duke of Marlborough and the birthplace of Sir Winston Churchill. The gardens and park were designed by Queen Anne's gardener, Henry Wise, and later added to by Capability Brown, an 18th-century landscape gardener who created Blenheim Lake. If you weren't told it was landscaped, you'd think it was all natural. Blenheim is open mid-March through October.

The best English cathedral

Salisbury Cathedral, the only English cathedral built of a single type of stone, can be seen for miles. Set in a grassy plain, the 13th-century structure has the tallest spire in England, rising 404 feet. The best way to see this immense cathedral is to take the 90-minute guided tour, which gives you a look at parts of the cathedral not generally open to the public. The tour is held at 11 a.m. and 2:30 p.m. year-round and at 6:30 p.m. during the summer.

The cloisters and Chapter House that adjoin the cathedral are also worth seeing. The walls of the **Chapter House** are decorated with bas reliefs of the Old Testament. Enjoy the open lawns of the Cathedral Close. Novelist Henry Fielding once lived in one of the houses on the close.

The best of Wales

Wales, that poetic land to the west of England, is renowned for its mighty castles. Dozens can be visited. They perch on rocky cliffs, cling to the mountains, hide in the moors, and rise up from the sea.

Many of the finest Welsh castles were constructed by King Edward I in the 13th century. The best known and grandest Welsh castle is **Caernarfon** in the north, birthplace of Edward II, the first Prince of Wales. Enclosed by 13th-century town walls, it is a masterpiece of medieval architecture. Prince Charles was dubbed Prince of Wales here by his mother when he turned 18. Nearby is the Roman fort **Segontium,** founded in A.D. 78.

The two best hotels in the town of Caernarfon are the Royal, a historic coach house, and Black Boy Inn, which dates back to the 14th century.

Cardiff Castle, in the Welsh capital, is the second-best castle in Wales. Built in the 11th century on the site of an old Roman camp, it was reconstructed in 1865 and given an ornate Victorian exterior. Inside, it is romantic and extravagant, especially the Arab Room and the Chaucer Room. The roof garden is colorful.

Parts of the original Roman fort on which the castle was built still exist. And you still can see the Norman keep in the northwest corner.

Last but not least is **Harlech,** an enormous castle that watches over a tiny village. Built by Edward I in 1283, the castle was the last to yield to the Yorkists in 1468 during the War of the Roses. It is set high on a cliff and protected by a massive double doorway. Because it isn't as well preserved as Caernarfon, it is spared the crowds of tourists. One of the best views of Snowdonia Mountain is from the top of the castle wall. Nearby is the most gorgeous beach on the Welsh coast.

The best fortification in Wales

Offa's Dyke, the eighth-century earthwork created by King Offa to keep out the marauding Welsh, marks the English/Welsh border. The 1,200-year-old earthwork can best be seen from the cliffs near Llanymynech in Shropshire, six miles from Oswestry. (Llanymynech's other claim to fame is the Lion Hotel, which is half in England and half in Wales.)

If you have time, one of the best ways to see Wales is to follow the 176-mile **Offa's Dyke Path** from Prestatyn, on the northern Welsh Coast, to Sedbury Cliff, Chepstow. It leads from sea to sea through the Black Mountains, the Clun Forest, and the Vale of Clwyd. The prettiest part of the path is over the bare central uplands of Clun Forest, where the remains of the Dyke are best preserved.

Another highlight is the beautiful ruin, **Tintern Abbey,** the site of Wordsworth's poem by the same name. Nearby, the devil supposedly tempted the monks. The gabled ends of the 13th-century abbey church rise out of a green meadow. The slate roof of the church was destroyed after Henry VIII dissolved the monasteries in 1537. For more information contact **Offa's Dyke Association,** *Old Primary School, Knighton, Powys.*

The best browsing in Britain

Hay-on-Wye is a charming little border town with typically narrow streets and a surprising number of bookstores. One man's passion for things literary has resulted in a proliferation of bookstores here. His book collection overflowed from his own huge bookstore, with shelves from cellar to attic, into the town's movie theater and dozens of smaller bookstores throughout the town. It is a monument to British eccentricity and well worth a browse.

The two best Welsh national parks

Pembrokeshire Coast National Park is 150 breathtaking miles of immense rocky cliffs that drop into the sea, remote bays, inviting inlets, caves, coves, strangely shaped rock formations, and tranquil islands. Many of the rocks along this coastline are made of lava from volcanoes that erupted 600 million years ago. A marked footpath follows the coastline, passing more than 50 Iron Age fortresses, a number of Celtic churches, and Norman castles at Pembroke, Carew, Havenfordwest, Cardigan, Manorbier, and Tenby.

Visit the seaside towns nearby. Llandudno and Aberystwyth are lively, elegant resorts. Tenby and Aberaeron are quieter places with harbors and whitewashed houses. Baby yourself at the Rock Park Spa in the 19th-century spa town of Llandrindod Wells.

For more information, contact the **Pembrokeshire Coast National Park Development Office,** *County Offices, Haverfordwest, Dyfed SA61 1QZ; tel. (44-437)4391.*

The highest peak in England or Wales

Mt. Snowdon, in Snowdonia National Park, is the highest peak in England or Wales, at 3,560 feet. It is also the steepest and most barren mountain. A narrow-gauge railway climbs to the top. Snowdonia offers 1,000 square miles of rugged mountains and moors, lakes, and rolling green hills. The park can be visited via the Snowdon Sherpa bus service, which runs Monday through Thursday every half-hour from July 15 to Sept. 1. You can catch the bus in Caernarfon. Service is less frequent off-season.

Hiking here is spectacular, but it can be dangerous. Follow an Ordnance Survey map. Be sure to wear sturdy boots and bring a sweater and rain gear. For information on hiking trails and accommodations, contact the **Snowdonia Park Information Office,** *Yr Hen Ysgol, Maentwrog, Blaenau Ffestiniog, Gwynedd LL41 4HW; tel. (44-76685)274.*

The best walled town in Wales

Tenby, a 14th-century walled town, has two sandy beaches (the best is North Beach) and a lovely harbor. The town's narrow streets lead to Castle Hill, a spit of land edged by cliffs that drop to the beach. St. Catherine's Island, which has an abandoned fort, can be seen from Castle Hill.

The nicest place to stay is the **Imperial Hotel,** which uses the town wall as one of its walls. For information, stop at the Croft, above North Beach.

The best Welsh beach resort

Aberystwyth is a popular beach resort with a lively seafront promenade, pastel-colored Victorian houses, black-and-white Welsh houses, and the ruins of a castle. It is also home to the oldest university in Wales (a neo-Gothic building opened in 1877) and the center of the revival of Welsh culture. You can hear traditional Welsh music at the **Cooper's Arms,**

Northgate Street. Stop in at the National Library of Wales, which houses most of the surviving Welsh medieval manuscripts.

The best island in Wales

Holyhead, off the coast of Aberystwyth, is the prettiest island in Wales, complete with palm trees, pastel-colored houses overlooking tranquil bays full of fishing boats and yachts, and a spate of fine restaurants.

The best of Scotland

Scotland's capital, **Edinburgh,** lost its rank as Scotland's largest city to archrival Glasgow in the 19th century. But the result has been to make Edinburgh the more attractive tourist destination (except for Victoriana buffs, who prefer Glasgow).

Edinburgh's **Royal Mile,** which runs along the spine of a hill from Holyrood to Edinburgh Castle, is the most beautiful section of the city. Parts of the stretch date back to the Middle Ages. Few cities in the British Isles have so well preserved a medieval quarter. The Royal Mile has survived because of the 18th-century New Town in the plains below. New Town was built to house the surplus population and to avoid demolition of the old sections.

Follow the Royal Mile beginning at the castle end. It's downhill in this direction. The castle is mostly a shrine to British militarism, complete with red-kneed and kilted Scottish guards at the entrance (the regiment changes daily) and a military museum with historic mementos of these regiments and the parade grounds where they march.

The Palace, or Lodging, in the castle is where Mary Queen of Scots gave birth to James I of England (also known as James VI of Scotland). The Lodging was heavily restored in the last century.

The oldest building in Edinburgh, built in 1076, is the miniscule whitewashed church inside the castle walls called the **Chapel of St. Margaret.** Margaret, queen of Scotland, was canonized for her holy life. (Her immediate predecessor as queen was Lady Macbeth, so she had a hard job of it.) Margaret helped Anglicize the Scots, starting with her husband, King Malcolm III.

The main street running below the castle features historic houses associated with the city's luminaries: John Knox, Robert Burns, Walter Scott, Robert Louis Stevenson. It also provides a fascinating glimpse of historic Scottish life: old shops and breweries, an old printing press, the Presbyterian Cathedral, a school, a sugar refinery, and a bakery.

One of the most interesting sites along the route is the tollbooth, which was the prison setting for Sir Walter Scott's *The Heart of Midlothian.* Another is Golfers' Land, the property purchased by a 17th-century golf champion with his winnings. John Patersone, a shoemaker, began his golfing career as a caddie and later became the partner of James II.

At the bottom of the main road, just one mile from the castle, is **Holyrood,** a converted abbey that was home to Scottish kings. Its style was heavily influenced by the French style Charles II learned about in exile. Charles II also commissioned a series of paintings of his ancestors that graces the Picture Gallery. Dutch artist Jakob de Witt knew how to please his royal patron. He made all 111 forebearers of Charles II look terribly like Charles II.

Holyrood is closely associated with Mary Queen of Scots, who lived and held court here from 1561 to 1567. She married Henry, Lord Darnley in 1565 in the Chapel Royal. You can see the room where she received John Knox (who fulminated against "a monstrous regiment of women") and the room where her secretary, David Riccio, was dragged from her presence and murdered (probably by one of her husbands).

The Royal Mile is one of the best places to buy classic Scottish tweeds and knitwear as well as crafts. Shop around, because prices vary considerably. You can get non-classic knits and tweeds from two fashionable shops: **Canongate Jerseys,** *166 Canongate,* on the Royal Mile, and **Crafts,** *158 Canongate.*

The finest hotel in Edinburgh is the **Caledonian,** *Princes Street, Edinburgh EH1 2AB; tel. (44-31)225-2433.* This grand hotel has magnificent views of the castle. Recently refurbished, the Caledonian, with 212 rooms, 3 dining rooms, and 3 bars, is a favorite among celebrities.

The **Tourist Accommodation Service,** *Waverley Market, 3 Princes St., Edinburgh EH2 2OP, tel. (44-31)557-2727,* can help you find a room. Book early to get the best choice.

The world's best tenement

The best tenement in the world is **Gladstone's Land in Edinburgh,** although until 1934 it was just another grossly overcrowded slum dwelling. Restoration of the house, now a museum on Landmarket along the Royal Mile, has helped tourists understand what the Gladstones set out to erect in 1617 when they put up a tenement. At that time, the tenement was simply a plot of ground on the main street, on which the Gladstones erected a six-story walk-up building with shops on the ground floor.

Britain's best festival: Edinburgh

Millions of visitors visit Edinburgh each summer for the **Edinburgh International Festival,** which draws prominent musicians and theater groups from around the world. In 1987, participating groups came from nine countries (Poland, West Germany, Sweden, China, South Africa, Spain, Japan, France, and the United States).

Tickets range from $5 to $25. **Edwards and Edwards,** *1 Times Square Plaza, New York, NY 10036; (212)944-0290,* sells tickets in the United States.

While known as one of the world's leading musical and theater festivals, the Edinburgh International Festival has a little-known side show. Edinburgh also provides a stage for some of the best avant-garde productions in the English language. The **Fringe,** as part of the festival is called, last year boasted more than 1,000 events and 9,000 performances, including theater, comedy, musicals, cabaret, revues, opera, mime, dance, children's shows, folk, jazz, rock/blues, poetry, and multimedia.

Scotland's best art collections

A medieval city surrounding a 13th-century cathedral, **Glasgow** houses three art collections:

The **Burrell Collection** is housed in a beautiful building with glass walls through which you can see the landscape of Pollok Park. The collection includes Oriental ceramics, French tapestries, and medieval stained glass.

The **Kelvingrove** contains masterpieces by Lippi, Rubens, and Constable. Its pride, however, is its collection of Impressionist paintings. Works by Monet, Pissarro, Matisse, Dégas, and Van Gogh grace the walls.

The **Hunterian Museum** has paintings by Rembrandt, Stubbs, Chardin, and Whistler.

When you tire of art, take tea at the **Willow Tea Room.** Or dine at **Poachers,** *235 Byres Road,* a restaurant in an old farmhouse, or the **Ubiquitous Chip,** *12 Ashton Lane,* off Byres Road.

The **Central,** *Gordon Street, tel. (44-41)221-9680,* is the most comfortable and old-fashioned hotel in Glasgow. A double ranges from £33 to £56. For more information on accommodations in the city, contact the **Greater Glasgow Tourist Board,** *Georges Square, Glasgow, G1 2ER; tel. (44-41)227-4880.*

The best Scottish castle

Stirling Castle in Fife, where Mary Queen of Scots was crowned in 1543, offers views of the Grampian Mountains from its cannonades. For centuries it was Scotland's only defense against English invaders. Once the palace of Stuart kings, Stirling is embellished with Bacchanalian figurines. King Robert Bruce (known simply as The Bruce) and Sir William Wallace held the castle against the English for years. In 1305, however, Wallace was betrayed to the English and hanged, drawn, and quartered in London.

For atmosphere, no hotel in Stirling beats the **Golden Lion,** *8 King St.* It has hosted Robert Burns, members of the royal family, and movie stars.

The world's best golf course

The **Old Course** in St. Andrews, Scotland is the most venerable (and the oldest) golf course in the world. It dates back to the 15th century and has been the site of 24 British Opens. It is a difficult course, with sandy greens and an ever-changing wind, but golfers love to face its constant challenges.

The Old Course, like most Scottish greens, is a links course, which means it is made up of tough seaside dunes covered with only a little grass. You may want to get a few tips on playing links courses before you go.

Contact the **Links Management Committee of St. Andrews,** *Golf Place, St. Andrews, Fife, KY16 9JA Scotland; tel. (44-334)75757,* eight weeks before your visit to apply to play on the Old Course. (You may play in July or August, it is just very difficult to get a tee-time.) If you can't get permission to play on the Old Course, try one of its younger counterparts in St. Andrews: New Course, Eden, or the Jubilee.

The most dramatic region: the Highlands

The desolate beauty of the **Highlands** should not blind you to its violent past. Over the centuries, the Gaelic Highlanders have suffered terrible defeats to the English, fought bloody battles among themselves, and been driven from their homes by wealthy landowners. During the Highland Clearances in the 18th century, crofters were driven from their homes by landowners who wanted to raise sheep. Those who refused to go had their houses and goods burned.

Peaceful today, the Highlands are known for their secluded glens, craggy peaks, and sparkling lochs. The country is virtually unspoiled. Route A82 leads from Glasgow into the Highlands, curving along the west bank of Loch Lomond. When the famed lake turns into a stream, you are in the Highlands. The country is wild, steep, and unfenced.

The bloodiest place in the Highlands

One of the most ruggedly beautiful places in the Highlands is **Glencoe,** the misty valley that was the scene of a brutal massacre on Feb. 13, 1692. Here, the Macdonald clan, which had fought for James II, was butchered by the Campbell clan, soldiers of William of Orange.

The Macdonalds were stabbed to death in their beds at dawn. Their homes were burned and their cattle stolen. Nothing remains of the human inhabitants of the Glen of Weeping, as it's known today. The only residents are golden eagles and red deer.

The most beautiful Highland drives

The **Road to the Isles,** A830, follows the spectacular Atlantic coast. One of the most beautiful passes en route is **Glenfinnan,** where in 1745 Bonnie Prince Charlie, the 25-year-old son of the exiled Stuart Pretender, launched his campaign to reclaim the British crown. The statue of a Jacobite Highlander tops Glenfinnan Monument on the shore where the prince raised the Stuart standard.

The tiny town of **Arisaig** is also steeped in history. Bonnie Prince Charlie landed here to begin his uprising. He hid in a cave in the region. The rocky coast is a short walk away. While here, stay in **Arisaig House,** *Beasdale, Arisaig PH39 4NR; tel. (44-6875)622,* an outstanding hotel with a walled rose garden. Prices are moderate.

On the route to Mallaig from Arisaig is an unpaved track leading to a remote and beautiful hamlet called **Bracora.** The road follows Loch Morar, Scotland's deepest lake, which is 1,017 feet.

Inverary: the prettiest Highland town

Make **Inverary,** on the peaceful shores of Loch Fyne, one of your stops in the Highlands. Meaning "at the mouth of the Aray River," Inverary has been inhabited by the Campbells of Argyll for 500 years. Its white-walled buildings are reflected in the water. Services are still held in Gaelic at the town's church. The **Episcopal Church of All Saints,** *the Avenue,* has the world's second-heaviest ring of 10 bells, which chime every day.

Nearby **Inverary Castle,** home to the Duke and Duchess of Argyll, is open to the public. The Armory Hall, which is 95 feet high, has an impressive display of antique weapons. The family portraits were done by painters such as Reynolds and Raeburn. A tour of the castle takes about an hour and is a good introduction to Highland history. For information call *(44-499)2203.*

Britain's highest mountain

Ben Nevis, at 4,406 feet, is the highest peak in Great Britain. Near Inverness in the Highlands, it guards Glen Nevis. The view from the summit (where the ruins of an observatory remain) seems endless. A precipice on the northeast side drops more than 1,450 feet. Combine a trip to Inverness and Ben Nevis with a look at nearby Loch Ness, home of the most famous monster in the world.

The best place to stay near Inverness is **Culloden House Hotel,** *tel. (44-463)790461,* an 18th-century palace near Culloden Moor where the final Scottish uprising was defeated in 1746. This hotel has spacious rooms, ornate trim, and beautiful antiques.

The best Highland hotel

Inverlochy Castle, *Fort William, Inverness Shire, PH33 6SN, Scotland; tel. (44-397)2177,* is the very best hotel in the Highlands, near Glencoe and Ben Nevis. Reservations can be made in the United States through **David B. Mitchell & Company,** *200 Madison Ave., New York, NY 10016; (212)696-1323.* Rooms are expensive.

The Hebrides: the best escape from civilization

If you are "a mere lover of naked nature," you'll be drawn to the Scottish islands as Dr. Samuel Johnson was in 1775. The **Hebrides** are the best place in Britain to escape civilization.

The most spectacular isle—Skye

The most spectacular island in the Hebrides is the Misty Isle, as **Skye** is known. Sir Walter Scott described the Misty Isle in *The Lord of the Isles*: "The vapour which enveloped the mountain ridges obliged us by assuming a thousand shapes, varying its veils in all sorts of forms, but sometimes clearing off altogether."

Wild still and distant from population centers, Skye is so far north that in June the sun never really sets. From 11 p.m. to 1 a.m., a period of duskiness falls, but that's as close as it gets to darkness.

Canadians, Americans, Australians, and New Zealanders of Scottish descent often look to the isle of Skye with nostalgia. Shiploads of Skyemen were shipped, often unwillingly, to these new lands during the Highland Clearances. Traces of their habitations can be seen all over Skye—foundations of walls, weeds growing over rubble, the outlines of houses, the stones of a hearth.

A trip through Skye's jagged, cloud-enshrouded Cullins and down primitive roads to Glen Brittle leads to excellent hiking country. The Cullins are beautiful seen from across Portree Bay or from Tarskavaig, across the waters of Loch Slapin. The grandest view is from the summit of Bidean Druim nan Ramh or Sgurr a'Mhadaidh.

The easiest defeat

According to British history books, John Paul Jones was turned away from the isle of Skye by a funeral he mistook for an army. The American Navy captain appeared on the coast of Skye in 1779 in the *Bon Homme Richard* (named for Benjamin Franklin's *Poor Richard's Almanack*). He had been harrying the shipping lanes in British waters. The appearance of his gun boat caused a flurry at Dunvegan Castle, because General MacLeod was away on military service in America. But when Jones saw the funeral party bearing the body of Donald MacLeod, he thought it was the MacLeod army in full battle array. He turned and fled. (You might take this with a grain of salt. American history books would probably report the incident differently.)

The favorite holiday isle

The favorite holiday isle among the British is **Arran.** Fluffy Arran sheep graze on green hillsides crossed by miles of hiking trails, especially on Goatfell, the "mountain of the winds." **Brodick Castle,** once the home of the dukes of Hamilton, can be seen in Lochranza. Now a ruin, it was once the hunting lodge of Robert the Bruce, king of the Scots.

Upon arrival in Brodick, check in at Mrs. Henderson's guesthouse in time for her to serve up a true Scottish breakfast—an amazing spread of juice, oatmeal, farm-fresh eggs, bacon, broiled tomatoes, pancakes, oatcakes, toast, and coffee or tea.

The most important sight on Arran is **Holy Island,** containing the cave of St. Molaise and runic inscriptions. It lies off Lamlash Bay.

The Queen of the Hebrides

From Kennecraig, on Kintyre, a day tour crosses to the **Isle of Islay,** known as the Queen of the Hebrides. The island's fertile soil is carpeted with bright emerald fields dotted with sleek cows and ubiquitous sheep. Good roads wind over the moors past salmon-filled lochs and farmhouses snuggled amid tidy flower and vegetable gardens. Wild cliffs tower above secluded sandy bays.

Near Port Charlotte are the graves of U.S. troops who lost their lives when the *Tuscania* and *Otranto* were torpedoed in 1918.

The best island-hopping

For a thrilling three-island hop, take the tour from Oban to **Mull, Staffa,** and **Iona.** Bus rides on Mull are exciting enough, with single-track roads, but the trip to Staffa takes you through six-foot troughs. Huge foaming waves dash against dark columnar rocks on the island's coast. **Fingal's Cave,** a rocky formation beaten by waves, inspired Mendelssohn to compose the *Hebrides Overture* after his visit here in 1829. On calmer days, it is possible to disembark and explore the vast cavern.

The most sacred island

The sacred island of **Iona,** burial place of Scottish kings, is renowned as the location where Christianity was introduced to Scotland by St. Columba in A.D. 563. Abbey ruins, a reconstructed cathedral, and rugged ninth century crosses stand silently on the buffeted shore.

The best Scottish standing stones

The islands of **Harris** and **Lewis** are famous for their Harris tweeds, but most travelers have never heard of the islands' well-preserved standing stones. Yet the prehistoric **Standing Stones of Callanish** on Lewis Island are more complete than Stonehenge in southern England and just as impressive.

The best way to explore the isles

The Scottish Tourist Board sells a **Highlands and Islands Travelpass** that offers unlimited travel for 8 to 12 days. Ferries run by Caledonian MacBrayne Ltd. offer hopscotch fares that cover a sequence of trips priced lower than cumulative single fares.

Scotland's best-known battle sites

The **Scottish Lowlands** were the site of Scotland's two best-known battles: **Stirling Bridge,** where William Wallace drove back the English forces in 1297; and **Bannockburn,** where Robert the Bruce was victorious against the English in 1314.

The most Nordic region

The **Orkney Islands,** north of mainland Scotland, belonged to the Norse from the 9th to 16th centuries. Eventually, they became part of Scotland. The shops here sell Nordic sweaters rather than kilts. Lush and fertile, the islands, populated by birds of all species, are popular among bird-watchers. The pace of life is slow, and in the summer the days are long.

The world's best Scotch whiskeys

The *New York Times Magazine* recommends The Macallan and Glenfarclas-Glenlivet as the best single-malt Scotch whiskeys for their "sherry-like aroma" and "intense flavor," respectively. Among blends, the *New York Times Magazine* prefers sipping Usquaebach (Gaelic whiskey) for its "peat-like aroma and hot finish." Chivas Royal Salute is hailed for its "round, elegant flavor."

Chapter 2

THE
BEST
OF
IRELAND

Of all the people in the world, the Irish are the happiest, according to the Happiness Index developed by two London-based market research firms. The good-natured Irish are a joy to spend time with. So make sure you visit the people of Ireland as well as the Irish countryside. Don't miss the most pleasant occupation in Ireland: sitting in a pub, sipping a Guiness or a Harp, and chatting.

The best way to tour Ireland's emerald countryside, charming villages, and ancient ruins is to circle around its coast, traveling from Dublin, Wicklow, Wexford, Waterford, Cork, Killarney, and Limerick. Venture inland to Kilkenny. Then go beyond the pale to the region the English never conquered: the Burren, Galway, Mayo, and Sligo.

The best way to explore Dublin

The most pleasant way to visit Dublin is to follow the lines of an old song: "Have coffee in Dublin at 11 and walk in Stephen's Green, and you'll be in heaven." Actually, have tea. Coffee in Ireland is usually instant and weak, but the tea is always good. Go to **Bewley's,** either on Grafton or Westmoreland street, for a nice hot cup. Later, spend time shopping along bustling Grafton, Anne, and Duke streets. Look for lace curtains, tailored tweed suits, and Irish knit sweaters.

The most efficient way to explore Dublin, if you are in a hurry, is via the **Dublin Trail.** Well posted, it leads past the city's major sights. A map of the trail is available at the **Dublin Tourist Office,** *14 O'Connell St.*

Another way to explore Dublin is to follow in the footsteps of **James Joyce.** The house where Joyce was born, *41 Brighton Square W.,* in the agreeable suburb of Rathgar, is marked with a plaque. **Mulligan's,** *Poolbeg Street,* a pub Joyce frequented in his student days, has a special aura, especially in the back parlor, where Joyce often sat and wrote. Joyce once lived at **Martello Tower and Museum,** at Sandycove, as did his characters in *Ulysses.*

Also look for the homes of other famous Dubliners: Shelley lived at 1 Grafton St.; Sheridan at 79 Grafton St.; George Bernard Shaw was born at 33 Synge St.

Dublin's greatest treasure

The jewel in Dublin's crown is *The Book of Kells*. More than 1,000 years old, it is the most intricate illuminated manuscript in the Western world.

The manuscript is kept at **Trinity College.** Enter the college through its arched front entrance, then look back at Merrion Square among the tall red-brick houses dominating the skyline, the pristine remains of Georgian Dublin. From there, head for the campus. In the fourth quadrangle on the right is the library. Among the celebrated ghosts that reportedly still haunt Trinity College are those of William Congreve, Oliver Goldsmith, Jonathan Swift, and Oscar Wilde.

Ireland's best stout

The **Guinness Brewery** at St. James' Gate on the banks of the Liffey in Dublin produces Ireland's rich and frothy national drink, the brown stout found on tap in every pub. Tours, conducted from 10 a.m. to 3 p.m. Monday through Friday, end in the tasting room. (You get one free sample.) This English-owned concern is the largest brewery in Europe.

Dublin's best sights

Dublin Castle, restored after a bombing, has handsome state apartments that are open to the public. Castle has been built upon castle on this site. The earliest construction was Celtic. The Vikings later improved upon this, then, in the 13th century, King John of England built a fortress on the site. The British ruled Ireland from this stronghold for 400 years.

The **Records Tower** is the only part of the castle that dates back to the original 13th-century fortress. The **Bedford Tower,** which houses the Heraldic Museum, built in the 15th century, was once used as the state prison. If you are of Irish ancestry, you can trace your family tree in the Genealogical Office.

The **General Post Office,** *O'Connell Street,* was the scene of the 1916 Easter uprising, the major step along Ireland's road to independence. You can read the declaration of Irish independence on the walls. After they proclaimed the free Republic here, the Irish Volunteers were bombed by a British gunboat docked in the River Liffey. Those who surrendered were hanged.

The **Kilmainham Jail Historical Museum,** open only on Sunday afternoons, is another monument to the centuries of struggle against the British. It held political prisoners from 1796 to 1924.

The **National Museum,** *Kildare Street*, has a collection of Irish antiquities from the Stone Age through the War for Independence. It is open daily; admission is free.

The **National Gallery,** *Leinster Lawn,* has a fine collection of old masters, including works by Rembrandt, and also houses the National Portrait Gallery. It is open daily; admission is free.

The creepiest experience

Centuries-old bodies lie perfectly preserved in the dry crypt of **St. Michan's Church,** *Church Street*. The 17th-century church was built on the site of a 10th-century Viking church. Perhaps because of its dryness, the crypt has remarkable preservation qualities. You can actually touch an eight-foot-tall Crusader. It is said to be good luck to shake the hand of one of the corpses here. The crypt is open on weekdays and Saturday mornings.

Dublin's best park

Phoenix Park in Dublin is the largest public park in Western Europe and the largest enclosed city park in the world. The official residence of the Irish president is here, as well as the residence of the American ambassador. The 1,760-acre park includes a racetrack, a soccer field, sports grounds, flower gardens, a herd of fallow deer, a lake, and a monument to Wellington.

The best escape from Dublin

If, by some amazing chance, the weather is hot while you are in Dublin, visit the famous seaside resort called **Bray.** It is about 15 miles south of Dublin City, adjacent to the town of Dunnleaghraigh (pronounced Dunleary) in County Dublin.

Dublin's warmest night life

The best night spots in Dublin are the pubs, with their evenings of Guinness, ballads, and poetry. They roar for a brief three hours—from 8 p.m. to 11 p.m.—in winter; in summer, they stay open until 11:30 p.m., just about the time the sun sets.

The oldest pub in Dublin is **Brazen Head,** which was first licensed in 1666. The low ceilings give this pub an old and cozy air. You'll find it in a courtyard off Usher Quay.

The **Abbey Tavern,** *Abbey Street, Howth; tel. (353-1)322-006,* has good seafood to accompany the entertainment. Reserve ahead, it's popular.

Slattery's Pub, *Capel Street,* features traditional Irish music nightly and Sundays from 12:30 p.m. to 2 p.m.

At the **Culturalann na hEireann,** *32 Belgrave Square,* in Monkstown, you'll hear some of Ireland's finest fiddlers, accordionists, and pipers.

On Wednesdays, you can hear jazz at the **Baggot Inn,** *Baggot Street.* Dance at the Zhivago Club, *Baggot Street,* or **Annabel's,** *Leeson Street.* (Beware, though. Part of Leeson Street is Dublin's red-light district.)

Dublin's finest hotel

The **Shelbourne Hotel,** which graces St. Stephen's Green, is the grand Victorian hotel where the Irish Constitution was drafted. Inside the hotel's turreted red-brick facade are ultramodern rooms with seaweed salt baths (an unusual luxury that is supposed to be good for your health). William Thackeray stayed here.

Don't miss the sumptuous afternoon tea at the Shelbourne, which is served in a restored art-nouveau tearoom. A harpist plays while you enjoy sandwiches, scones, cakes, cookies, and India or China tea.

Double rooms are 105 punts, including tax. To book a room, contact **Trusthouse Forte Hotels, Inc.,** *5700 Broadmoor, Shawnee Mission, Kansas 66202; (800)225-5843.*

Ireland's greenest county

County Wicklow, which is known as the Garden of Ireland, is the greenest of Ireland's counties. The best place to stay while you explore the county is **Wexford,** a small Viking-founded seaside town with narrow streets. Henry II repented at the nearby abbey for the assassination of Thomas à Becket. Oliver Cromwell massacred the townspeople in 1649 in an anti-Catholic rage. The town features a statue of John Barry, father of the U.S. Navy, who was born nearby. John F. Kennedy laid a wreath here. (You can visit the John F. Kennedy Park near the Kennedy family homestead at Dunganstown.)

The **Crown Bar,** an establishment on Monck Street in Wexford, has been in the Kelly family for 100 years. It is a cozy place for a drink or a light meal. Stay at **Killiane Castle,** *off Rosslare Harbour Road, Drinagh,* and enjoy its 230 acres. Rooms in this guesthouse are inexpensive, about 21 punts a night. Wexford is 83 miles from Dublin through the Wicklow Mountains.

Enniskerry, one of Ireland's prettiest villages, is also part of County Wicklow. Located in a wooded hollow and surrounded by hills, the village is famous for Powerscourt, one of Ireland's great estates. The ruins of a Georgian mansion are surrounded by 14,000 acres of grounds, including the 400-foot Powerscourt Waterfall.

Wicklow's other highlight is **Glendalough,** a deep valley in the Wicklow Mountains. In the sixth century, St. Kevin took refuge in this peaceful glen between two lakes. However, his refuge didn't remain secret. His disciples followed him and founded a monastery and a famous center of learning here. View the remains of a medieval round tower, as well as buildings from the 9th to 13th centuries. You can follow nature trails through the valley.

Waterford: the world's best crystal

Waterford, a fine old harbor city and an important shipping port, is best known for producing some of the finest hand-cut crystal in the world. The Waterford Crystal Plant, which you can tour, is about two miles from the city center on the right-hand side of N25, the main road between Waterford and Cork. Craftsmen make about 90,000 pieces of crystal a week; 70% goes to the United States.

Shops selling the products include **Kelly's Ltd.,** *75 The Quay;* **Shaw's,** *53 Barronstrand St.;* and **Joseph Know,** *4 Barronstrand St.* Often you can get better buys in the United States, because of high shipping costs. But these shops are good places to look for rare patterns that are unavailable at home.

Cork: the best Irish market

County Cork's capital, **Cork,** houses the fascinating **English Market,** a vast, covered arcade on Prince's Street that was built in 1788. Here you'll get a bit of local color and hear the unmistakable Cork accent.

When you tire of shopping, sip afternoon tea and eat homemade pastry at the popular **Leprechaun.** The famous **President's Restaurant,** *Longueville House, Mallow; tel. (353-22)4-7156,* on a 500-acre estate, is also nearby. Home-grown produce is served at this superb restaurant. Reservations are required. (Avoid this trip in August, when a mass exodus takes place from Cork City to Mallow.)

The best-named newspaper

Cork boasts the world's best-named newspaper: the *Cork Examiner.* We assume its wine reviews are extensive.

The blarniest sight

Outside Cork City is **Blarney Castle,** where kissing the **Blarney Stone** is said to give the gift of eloquence. Doing so is practically an acrobatic feat. You must lie on your back over a sheer drop and stretch to kiss the stone.

According to one legend, the Blarney Stone was first kissed by a man with a lisp after he had rescued a witch from death. As a reward for saving her life, the witch told him to kiss the stone. He did so, and his lisp disappeared. Another legend says that the lord of Blarney Castle, McCarthy, flabbergasted Queen Elizabeth with his eloquent excuses for having attacked England. She finally dropped the charges against him, calling his excuses "blarney."

The yacht crowd's favorite

Kinsale is an international yachting center overflowing with gourmet restaurants. The *Lusitania* was torpedoed off its coast by a German submarine in 1915. This was also the site of the 1602 Battle of Kinsale, during which the northern chieftains were defeated by the English, establishing English domination of Ireland. The heavy, woolen Kinsale cloak is a popular purchase.

The best base for exploring

The town of **Ennis** in County Clare is the best base for exploring the west of Ireland, from which so many Americans stem. The old market town (population 20,000) has escaped relatively unscathed from the tourist flow, even though Shannon Airport is close by.

The main street in Ennis contains antique shops selling genuine (if pricey) antiques and good crafts shops. But the town's gem is its monastery—the most evocative in Ireland. This roofless, weed-covered ruin's tottering Gothic walls exactly fit Shakespeare's phrase, "baro, ruined choirs."

Bunratty House, built in the 15th century, is worth a visit. (Skip the fake feast in its cellar.) The house gives you an idea of how Irish nobility lived. The folk park behind the elegant house shows how lesser Irishmen survived.

The **Old Ground,** *O'Connell Street; tel. (353-65)28127,* is the most charming place to stay in Ennis. Rooms are well-equipped with comforts such as direct-dial telephones and modern plumbing. Double rooms are 57 punts to 70 punts, including a full Irish breakfast.

The restaurant at the Old Ground is splendid and serves Irish specialties, including Dublin Bay prawns (shrimp), mutton chops with kidneys, and apple pie.

Ireland's most spectacular cliffs

The **Cliffs of Moher,** a few miles north of Ennis, are the most spectacular in Ireland and, perhaps, Europe. The 700-foot black cliff faces weather the constant onslaught of the Atlantic waves.

The most beautiful drives

County Kerry is known for the spectacular **Ring of Kerry,** a 110-mile drive that hugs the coast of the Inveragh Peninsula. Highlights of the drive include **Rossbeigh Beach,** near Glenbeigh on the north coast, which offers the best view of Drung Hill; **Glencar,** near Caragh Lake, a good place to hike; cells carved from solid rock by monks escaping the Vikings at **Skellig Rocks; Ballaghisheen Pass,** which takes you through scenic mountains; and the peaceful beaches that line the southern half of the ring. You can make the drive in a day.

Wild and Gaelic **Dingle Peninsula** is another beautiful drive in County Kerry. Begin the drive in the town of Dingle, on the ocean. Surrounded by hills, this fishing town is protected by an ancient wall. From Dingle, take the road to **Ventry,** which has an inviting beach. Outside Ventry are beehive huts built by monks of early Irish monasteries. **Slea Head,** at the tip of the peninsula, has a lovely view of the seven Blasket Islands. And the beach at Slea Head has water warm enough for swimming, thanks to the Gulf Stream.

Northeast of Slea Head is **Gallerus Oratory,** an unmortared stone building from the ninth century. After 1,000 years it is still watertight. From the **Conair Pass** you can see the lakes and Brandon, Tralee, and Dingle bays. **Sybil Head** has high green-sodded cliffs topped by thatched cottages and washed by the Atlantic below.

While in Kerry stay at the **Ballyseede Castle Hotel,** *tel. (353-66)25799.* Acres of greenery surround this 15th-century castle. Double rooms are 45 punts to 85 punts. Reservations are required.

Where to rent a car

You can rent a car at **Shannon Airport** for as little as $23 per day, including value-added tax (for a two-door Corsa). You receive a discount if you rent for more than 15 days. The fee does not include insurance, which you can waive by making a deposit of approximately $628 with the rental company (a credit card will do). The deposit is reimbursed after you return the car. The fee includes a radio, a roof rack if you ask for one, and unlimited mileage (but not gas). By renting a car you become a member of the Irish Automobile Association. You must be older than 26 to rent a car in Ireland.

Ireland's loveliest lakes

Killarney town offers a dream-like setting of lush green hills and deep blue lakes. Spend time enjoying the town, but concentrate your stay on the surrounding Lower, Middle, and Upper lakes. At their banks, ferns and mosses grow in the shade of oak, birch, holly, and ash trees. Much of this lake district lies within the 11,000-acre Bourne Vincent Memorial Park.

You can do your sightseeing in a horse-drawn jaunting car. Visit Muckross House, a 19th-century manor in the park now used as a folk museum. Pony trek or hike through the mountains and around the lakes.

The kitschiest castle

Bunratty Castle, near Limerick, is one of the kitschiest sights in Ireland. While it does house Lord Gort's superb collection of medieval furniture, tapestries, paintings, and glass, most visitors come for the castle's corny medieval banquet. Guests eat without silverware as they did in the old days, and mead (fermented honey) is served by colleens in low-cut medieval gowns. You sing *Danny Boy* and all the other cliché St. Patrick's Day songs. For reservations, contact **Shannon Castle Tours,** *Shannon Airport, County Clare; tel. (353-61)6-1788.*

The Aran Islands—time's greatest foe

The **Aran Islands** are fascinating, if barely habitable. Gaelic language and traditions survive on these three islands 35 miles from the mainland. The islanders maintain their traditional dress—women wear red skirts and moccasins called pampooties, the men vests and peaked caps. They grow potatoes in a mixture of sand and seaweed and fish in wicker-framed, hide-covered *curraughs,* or boats.

Dun Aengus, an Iron Age fortress built on a cliff on the island of **Inishmore,** has 18-foot-thick walls. The prettiest islands are the two smallest, **Inishmaan,** which is known for its traditional music and dancing, and **Inisheer.** In good weather, boat service is available regularly to most of the islands. The closest point on the mainland is Doolin, where you can catch a boat to Inisheer. Steamers run daily from Galway to Kilronan on Inishmore.

The best horseback riding

The **Connemara Trail,** which winds its way along the coast of Ireland's County Galway, passes through rugged mountains and along deserted beaches. Beginning near the sea in Barna, the trail goes from village to village and mountain to mountain, leading you eventually to the Atlantic Ocean on the beaches near Clifden.

One of the best trail-riding packages is led by William Leahy. A six-day/six-night trail holiday costs 540 punts in the spring and fall, 580 punts in July and August. For information contact Anne Marie Meuser at **Horses and Ireland,** *P.O. Box 10 Clinton Corners, NY 12514; (914)266-3172;* or William Leahy, **Aille Cross Equitation Centre,** *Aille Cross, Loughrea, County Galway, Ireland; tel. (353-91)41216.*

Yeats' favorite land

The dramatic countryside of **Sligo** is where the poet William Butler Yeats spent his childhood summers. He asked to be buried in Drumcliffe Churchyard, five miles north of Sligo proper. At the summit of the nearby Glen of Knocknarea is said to be the grave of the legendary Queen Maeve from the *Queen of the Immortal Faeries.* It is also the site and source of Yeats' best-known poem, *The Lake of Innisfree.* Sixty years ago, Sligo was the center of the Irish literary revival.

The area around Sligo claims one of the largest concentrations of prehistoric graves and monuments in Western Europe. Most are neither fenced off nor mentioned in tourist brochures. You must find them by word-of-mouth.

Donegal: the best tweed

"You'll wear out two suit linings," the Irish brag, "before you'll wear out a Donegal tweed." The county of **Donegal** in northwest Ireland sells some of the best tweed in the world. The town of **Magee** is a good place to begin your search. Magee is easily explored—it has only one main street.

Also try the peninsula just west of Magee. Take the road to Glencolumbkille and stop in **Mt. Charles** (pronounced Charless) at the Tweed Shop. Owen Gillespie and his sister Mary, proprietors of the shop, are both knowledgeable about tweed and tailoring. Their parents owned the shop before them. Spend some time here looking through the selection of herring-bone, houndstooth, and Harris tweeds. If you buy any tweed during your visit, be sure it is labeled "Genuine Donegal Hand-Woven Tweed. Pure New Wool."

The price of tweed is standard throughout Ireland—10 punts to 12 punts per 60-inch-wide yard. A man's suit takes about 4 yards; a jacket 2 1/2.

Ireland's most beautiful ruin

In the northern midlands of Ireland, south of Athlone in County Cavan, is the haunting ruin of **Clonmacnoise,** a flourishing monastic settlement more than 1,000 years ago. Still here are ruins of an abbey founded in A.D. 541 by St. Kieran, the Seven Churches of Clon-macnoise, a castle, a bishop's palace, and two round towers where townspeople watched for invading Vikings in search of Celtic gold. Celtic crosses from the time when Ireland was the Island of Saints and Scholars also stand here still.

Ireland's best accommodations: castles

Stay in Ireland's castle hotels. Scores of these delightful, historic places dot the country-side.

The finest in all Ireland is **Ashford Castle,** *Cong, County Mayo; tel. (353-92)46003.* President Reagan, among other dignitaries, has stayed here. Situated on the shores of the Lough Corrib, it looks like a huge movie set.

A castle was built on this site as early as 1228. In the 16th century, the troops of Queen Elizabeth battled in the area and stormed through the castle, which later became an English fortress. In the 18th century, a French chateau was incorporated into the old complex. Nearby are several ancient abbeys, churches, and points of archeological interest. Note the 20-foot fireplace and the fine woodwork.

The castle became a hotel in 1939. Double rooms range from 120 punts to 160 punts, not including breakfast.

Castle Matrix, *Rathkeale, near Limerick; tel. (353-69)64284,* has seen more than 500 years of history. In 1487, James Fitz-Thomas, ninth earl of Desmond, was murdered in the tower. In 1580, Queen Elizabeth sent Sir Walter Raleigh to subdue the outlaw Desmonds. After Raleigh occupied the castle, the English writer Edmund Spenser lived here. In 1641, during the Irish rebellion, the castle was seized by the Irish, but Cromwell's forces soon took it back. In 1709, it was inhabited by German Protestant refugees. In 1756, John Wesley established a Methodist community here.

The castle fell to ruin over the years but was restored in 1970 by Col. Sean O'Driscoll, an Irish-American architect who converted it to a hotel. Suites have fireplaces and are furnished with Elizabethan and Jacobean antiques. The restaurant serves medieval banquets. During the summer, courses in arts and crafts are held here, but the cold castle is closed during the winter. Rooms are 32.50 punts.

Chapter 3

THE
ISLE
OF
MAN

The politically independent **Isle of Man,** located halfway between Ireland and England and only 20 miles south of Scotland, is one of Europe's hidden bests. It is one of the best banking havens in the world (see our chapter on the world's best banks). Europe's best ice cream is created here. Manx kippers are world-famous, and Man has been noted by the World Health Organization for its high-quality lamb and beef. The fishing here is terrific. And some of Britain's prettiest walking trails flank the isle's shores.

The Isle of Man, covering a mere 343 square miles, is probably the least-known country in Europe. Still a member of the British Commonwealth, the Isle of Man has been ruled by Ireland, Wales, Norway, Scotland, and England. Though it is part of the British Isles, it is not part of the United Kingdom. The island has its own representative assembly and courts.

The world's oldest legislature

The **Tynwald,** as the Manx legislature is called, is more than a thousand years old and has the longest continuous history of any legislature in the world. Tynwald derives from the Norse word *tingvollr,* meaning assembly field.

The **Royal Chapel of St. John the Baptist,** in the town of St. John's, is on the field where the open-air Tynwald ceremony of the Norsemen began 1,000 years ago. Each year on July 5 (or the Monday after, if it falls on a weekend), the Tynwald assembles at the chapel to sign new laws. Any Manx citizen may present a petition on this occasion.

The strangest sight

The Isle of Man's strangest monument in stone is a modern tower in **Corrin's Folly** over-looking Peel Bay. It was built by a man who wanted to be on his feet when Judgement Day arrived. He left instructions to have his glass-lidded coffin stood on its end in front of the tower window. The rest of the family was buried below.

Man's best fishing

Sports fishermen adore the Isle of Man because of its variety of fishing: surf-casting, river fishing, and deep-sea fishing.

Sea fishermen can cast their lines for skate, mackerel, and tope from spring to late summer; pollack (the local name is calig), conger, dogfish, plaice (a flat fish that is a bottom eater), coalfish, bass, and mullet from June to October; and whiting, brill, monkfish, and flounder in the fall.

The best place for surf-casting is **Point of Ayre,** where you can fish at any tide. The best time, however, is low tide.

Sea-angling boat services are available from Douglas. Contact Rodney Kennish or Bobby Pope, **I.C.C. Travel,** *53 Strand St.; tel. (44-624)23441.*

Freshwater fishing in the Isle of Man is for salmon, sea trout, brown trout, and rainbow trout, primarily in the rivers that flow through the Manx national glens. The main run of salmon and sea trout starts in late summer.

For information on fishing and licenses, contact the offices of the **Isle of Man Board of Agriculture and Fisheries,** *Government Offices, Douglas; tel. (44-624)26262.*

Man's best walking trails

The best walking path is the **Millennium Way,** established in 1979 to commemorate the millennium of the Tynwald. It follows the Regia Via, or Royal Way, one of the earliest recorded highways. In medieval times it was used by the king and his attendants traveling to Tynwald from Ramsey. Clearly marked, the Millenium Way is approximately 21 miles long and can be walked by the experienced hiker in a full day.

The Way begins approximately one mile from Ramsey Town Square on the main road to Kirk Michael at the foot of Sky Hill. The Millennium Way ends in Castletown at Castle Rushen, the site of the fortification built by the Norsemen to guard the south of the island.

The world's largest water wheel

Laxey has the largest water wheel in the world, with a diameter of 72 feet, 6 inches, a circumference of 217 feet, and a top speed of two revolutions per minute. Built in 1854, it was christened the Lady Isabella after the wife of the lieutenant governor. Originally, it was used to pump water out of the lead mines.

Exclusive cats

Man is the only place in the world where you can find the tailless Manx cat. Stop in at the **Manx Cattery**, *Nobles Park, Douglas,* to have your name put on the waiting list for the genuine item. (If you don't actually want a cat, you can just look.)

The world's best ice cream

Manx ice cream is the best in the world. This prize-winning concoction is the creamiest and richest we've ever tasted. Visit the **Manx Ice Factory**, *Peel Road, Douglas.*

The isle's best restaurant

The best restaurant on the Isle of Man is **Boncompte's,** *King Edward Road, Onchan; tel. (44-624)5626.* The Continental cuisine is excellent, and the atmosphere is sophisticated. (Onchan is on a hill next to Douglas.)

Hotels with the most charm

Man's most charming hotel is the **Springfield Club Hotel,** *Castletown Road, Douglas; tel. (44-624)20400.* Near Ronaldsway Airport, this old mansion is beautiful and comfortable. It is, as advertised, a haven from the rigors of the business world (though something less of one now that the family that originally owned the place has sold out). The breakfasts at Springfield Club are hearty. The best room is No. 2, an enormous boudoir with huge closets.

For more information on hotels, contact the **Isle of Man Tourist Board,** *Victoria Street, Douglas, Isle of Man; tel. (44-624)74323.*

Chapter 4

THE BEST OF FRANCE

France is the most civilized country in the world. The average Frenchman thinks he is a wine expert, a gourmet, well-versed in art, history, and literature, dressed in the latest fashion, possessing of impeccable manners, and the world's best lover. The best cuisine, wine, and cheeses in the world come from France. High fashion begins in Paris. And the world's artists and writers are drawn to the land of the Gauls.

The best city in the world: Paris

Paris is not only the heart of France, it is also one of the world's most fascinating cities. Four-star restaurants, cozy cafés, wide boulevards, colorful outdoor markets, fascinating museums, theaters, parks, squares, monuments, and churches are found in every section of this capital city. The best way to visit Paris is to stroll. You will pass 17th-century houses, butcher shops with whole pigs hanging in the windows, ancient churches, high-fashion boutiques, street performers, art galleries, Africans selling wooden carvings, and Gypsy beggars. You will smell roasting coffee, expensive perfume, Gauloise cigarettes, crepes, roasting chestnuts, fresh bread, diesel fuel, and the damp breeze coming from the Seine.

When you get tired, stop in a café for a comforting cup of coffee and a chance to watch the people go by. You can sit for hours. Or buy a pastry at one of the hundreds of patisseries in Paris. Your heart will soar as you bite into a flaky, creamy, or fruit-filled delight.

Paris' most famous sight

The **Eiffel Tower** is the most famous Paris landmark. The view from the top is remarkable—if you don't mind waiting in an endless line to get there. Built for the Universal Exposition of 1889, it faced demolition in 1909 but was saved when the French army discovered it could serve as a radio tower.

Since its creation, the Eiffel Tower has been the site of 400 suicide leaps. If you want to prove that you climbed the Eiffel Tower's 1,710 steps (you can cheat and take the elevator), mail a letter from the mailbox at the top. Letters mailed here are canceled with a special Eiffel Tower postmark. New lights make the Eiffel Tower dazzle at night.

The city's most beautiful church

Notre Dame Cathedral is gorgeous, especially at sunset, when the splendid stained-glass rose windows glow. Druids once worshipped on this ground, and the Romans had a temple here before the Christians built Notre Dame in 1163. One of the finest examples of Gothic architecture, the cathedral was used for the coronations of Napoleon. (Napoleon scandalized the world by seizing the crown from Pope Pius VII and crowning himself.)

Beneath the church are the foundations of third-century Roman structures. Take a look at the side portals of the cathedral. According to legend, they were carved by the devil after he bought the soul of the ironsmith Biscornet. (The devil was unable to decorate the central portal, because that is the one the Host was carried through in procession.)

The world's best museum

The **Louvre** is the greatest museum in the world. Begun in the 12th century as a palace it has been a museum since the 18th century. It is now under extensive reconstruction. A controversial glass pyramid (three stories high) will cover a new underground entrance in the main court that faces the Jardin des Tuileries. Parking arrangements, shops, cafés, and restaurants are being added underground.

In 1190, the Louvre was one of Philippe Auguste's fortresses. Charles V made it an official residence, and Catherine de Medici had the long gallery built. It was extended under Henry IV and Louis XIII, and the quadrangle was completed under Louis XIV. Today, the museum is divided into six extensive sections: paintings and drawings, Greek and Roman antiquities, Egyptian antiquities, Oriental antiquities, *objets d'art*, and sculpture.

The *Venus de Milo* and the *Mona Lisa* are just 2 of the 208,500 works of art in the Louvre. The number of masterpieces is overwhelming. So are the crowds, especially on weekends and during the summer. The best way to avoid the masses is to steer clear of the European paintings. Instead, see the collection of ancient art, located in the Cour Carreé. Gigantic statues loom above you, the air is cool, and sounds echo off the walls like long-lost voices of Greek and Egyptian gods.

Paris' biggest attraction

Although it is less famous than the Eiffel Tower, the **Centre Beaubourg,** *rue St. Martin, 4th,* is the biggest attraction in Paris. More than 25,000 visitors are drawn to this arts center each day—twice as many as visit the Eiffel Tower and almost equal to the number who frequent Disneyland. The multicolored modern structure built of steel tubes, concrete, and glass houses the Musée National d'Art Moderne, which displays works by Picasso, Braque, Chagall, Leger, Brancusi, and Calder.

Officially called the Centre National d'Art et de Culture Georges Pompidou, but unofficially known as the Pompidou or the Beaubourg, this arts center also has a 40,000-volume (reference) library, a theater, a restaurant, and temporary exhibits. The library averages 11,000 visitors a day and up to 19,000 a day on weekends. Only 2,000 people are admitted at a time. Outside, street performers breathe fire, perform pantomime, and play guitars.

The world's most beautiful cemetery

Père Lachaise Cemetery, on the northeastern edge of Paris, is the most beautiful cemetery in the world. Located in a wooded park, it is so enormous that the walkways have names, and maps are given out at the entrance. The tombstones are monumental and elaborate. Balzac, Sarah Bernhardt, Chopin, Colette, Corot, Delacroix, Abélard and Héloise, Molière, La Fontaine, Edith Piaf, and Oscar Wilde are among the greats buried here. The most visited grave is that of rock star Jim Morrison.

Four favorite sights in Paris

Sacré-Coeur, a glowing white Byzantine-style church on a hill in Montmartre, can be seen from almost anywhere in Paris. On summer evenings, a cool breeze wafts across the hill. The church was begun in 1876 to celebrate the end of the Franco-Prussian War. It was completed in 1910. Its interior is decorated with mosaics and stained glass. Nearby is a hokey but entertaining pseudo-artist's quarter.

Ste. Chapelle, located in the Palais de Justice on the boulevard du Palais, was built by St. Louis to contain the Crown of Thorns, which he purchased from the Venetians in 1238. (The Crown of Thorns was moved to Notre Dame during the French Revolution. The Gothic chapel has 15 brilliantly colored stained-glass windows and a graceful 247-foot spire. The windows are the oldest in Paris and among the most vivid.

The **Conciergerie,** around Ste. Chapelle, is where Marie Antoinette spent her last days before facing the guillotine. It is also where 1,200 less famous prisoners were held. This fascinating place has dark, dank dungeons. The Concierge was built by Philip the Fair in the 14th century and contains three Gothic halls in addition to the prisons.

St.-Germain-des-Prés is the oldest church in Paris began in A.D. 558 "in the fields" outside the walls of Paris. The steeple and tower date from 1014, when the monastery was rebuilt after attacks by the Vikings. Enlarged in the 12th century, it was once self-sufficient, housing its own bakers, butchers, law courts, and defense force. All that exist of this today, aside from the church, are street names referring to parts of the ancient abbey. The abbey precincts now form a quarter of small hotels, antique shops, bookstores, publishing houses, and l'Ecole des Beaux-Arts.

Paris' seven most charming museums

Musée des Arts de la Mode, *111 rue de Rivoli, 1st,* is the most entertaining museum in Paris. The city that has set fashion for 300 years is an appropriate setting for this institution, which displays the clothing of 19th-century chambermaids as well as 20th-century celebrities.

Musée Carnavalet, *23 rue de Sevigné, 3rd,* is the most Parisian of Paris' museums. Located in a Renaissance mansion in the Marais district, Carnavelet covers the turbulent history of the city and its people from the 16th to the 19th centuries.

Musée Marmottan, *2 rue Louis Boilly, 16th,* has the most significant collection of Monet paintings in Europe. Most of the works were painted at Monet's Normandy home in Giverny. This small, private museum near the Bois de Boulogne is hidden away in what appears a mundane residence. Inside, it boasts 65 paintings by Monet, the Wildenstein collection of medieval illuminated manuscripts, and Renaissance and Empire works. It is open on Tuesdays, when other museums are closed.

Musée d'Orsay, located in the renovated Orsay train station, is the newest in Paris. This museum of the 19th century houses many Impressionist paintings once displayed at the Jeu de Paume. The enormous vaulted glass ceiling gives a 19th-century industrial atmosphere. The exhibits include 1,500 sculptures, 2,300 paintings, 1,100 *objets d'art,* and 13,000 photographs, works by Dégas, Manet, and Rousseau.

Picasso Museum, *5 rue de Thorigny,* in the Marais, is the best place to study Picasso. It contains an intelligent selection of the artist's life's work and provides a complete, carefully documented and illustrated biography. The collection charts Picasso's artistic development through the rooms of a magnificent 17th-century mansion, the Hôtel Salé.

Musée Rodin, *77 rue de Varenne, 7th,* is where the best of Rodin's work is kept. This one-man museum is housed in an imposing 18th-century residence, the Hôtel Biron where Rodin worked and lived toward the end of his life. He presented his art as payment for rent.

Musée de Thermes (Roman baths) and the **Hôtel de Cluny,** *6 place Paul-Painlevé , 5th,* is the most beautiful museum in Paris. A combination of second-century Gallo-Roman remains and an 18th-century mansion, it is set back from the busy corner of the St. Michel and St. Germain boulevards on the Left Bank.

The Cluny, a Gothic house, once the Paris residence of the wealthy abbots of Cluny, houses one of the world's best collections of medieval art, including the exquisite unicorn tapestries. The lion represents chivalric nobility; the unicorn represents bourgeois nobility; and the lady may represent the Le Viste family from Lyons. The Roman baths were used in the third century as a vast public bathhouse.

The three most colorful quarters

The greatest pleasures in Paris are its neighborhoods, which most tourists scarcely notice as they rush from sight to sight. Take time to wander through the streets of Paris. Absorb the smells, sounds, sights. Our favorites for wandering are the Marais, the Latin Quarter, and Montmartre.

The Marais

Marais is vaguely bounded by the rue Beaubourg to the west, the boulevard Beaumarchais to the east, the Seine to the south, and the rues Rèaumur and Bretagne to the north. Within its confines are scores of fine old townhouses, many built with paved forecourts and walled gardens. You'll also find several museums, the National Archives, a half-dozen churches, the Jewish Quarter with its little bakeries, delis, and shops, and the place des Vosges. Tour the Marais is during the week, when it is possible to enter most of the buildings. Begin your walk at the St. Paul metro station.

The Marais (which means marshland) was shunned until the 13th century, when the Knights Templars (a military-religious order) built its headquarters on the rue St. Antoine, a raised highway since Roman times. In the mid-14th century, Charles V built a palace in the area today bounded by the rues St. Antoine, St. Paul, and Petite-Muse (some say it was originally Pute-y-Muse, or whore's muse).

Place des Vosges was given its current shape in 1605, when Henri IV developed a royal square on the site of the former palace. Uniform houses were built, red-brick buildings trimmed with white stone and slate roofs.

After the court moved to Versailles, the quarter began to lose its chic inhabitants, and its popularity. By the end of the French Revolution, it was virtually abandoned. The Marais remained in a declining state until 1962, when the government named the area a historic district. Since then, the Marais gradually has been restored to grandeur.

Don't miss the **Victor Hugo House,** *place des Vosges;* the **Palais Soubise,** *60 rue des Francs-Bourgeois,* which contains the National Archives; the Historical Museum of France; and the **Hôtel de Rohan,** which contains a Gobelins tapestry and the fresco *Horses of Apollo* by Robert le Lorrain on a wall of its former stable.

Montmartre

Renoir was among the many 19th-century artists who lived in **Montmartre** and loved it. When traveling in Italy in 1881 he wrote, "I feel a little lost when away from Montmartre. I am longing for my familiar surroundings and think that even the ugliest girl is preferable to the most beautiful Italian." Renoir painted *La Balançoire* sitting in a large garden, actually an abandoned park, behind the house on rue Cortot.

Traces of the artists who loved the quarter can be found throughout Montmartre. A restaurant called Mère Catherine's, looking out on the place du Tertre, is little changed since it appeared in a painting by Utrillo. The Bonne Franquette on the corner of the rues St. Rustique and des Saules once had a tea garden where Van Gogh painted *La Ginguette*. If you walk down rue des Saules—something few tourists do—you'll pass a tiny vineyard and come to a bar-cabaret called Le Lapin Agile. Here artists and writers such as Picasso and Vlaminck kicked up their heels.

The wrought-iron gate at 11 ave. Junot marks the home of Utrillo's mother, the beautiful Suzanne Valadon. A painter herself and a model for Renoir, she appears among a group of voluptuous nudes in the painting *Les Grandes Baigneuses*.

The Moulin de Galette, a windmill in Montmartre, has been painted almost as often as the Moulin Rouge. Renoir's painting of the *moulin* is well-loved. Corot painted the mill also, and Van Gogh painted it twice. The windmill survives in an altered state—it has been restored as an architectural feature above the roofs of a new development of apartments along avenue Junot and rue Lepic.

Picasso created cubism in his studio above the *bateau-lavoir* (laundry) that once existed next to place Emile Goudeau. This tiny space, with a bench and a fountain, is on the downward slope toward the rue des Abbesses.

The most pleasant spot in Montmartre is the vineyard at the corner of the rues St. Vincent and des Saules, near the Montmartre Museum. The vines still produce a wine called *picolo*. Every autumn, usually the first Sunday in October, when all the grapes are in, a *fête des vendanges* (harvest festival) is held at the vineyard. The more than 300 liters of wine produced are sold, and the proceeds are given to the old age home on the *butte* (hill).

The Quartier Latin

The **Latin Quarter,** surrounding the boulevards St. Germain and St. Michel, is a bustling student quarter with twisting little streets, buskers and street vendors, restaurants, bookstores, and throngs of people.

The Roman conquerors of ancient Gaul settled here, on the Left Bank of the Seine, 50 years before the birth of Christ. They constructed thermal baths, an arena, and a theater. What is now the rue St. Jacques was the Roman road to the south.

The **University of Paris** gave the area its ambience after the departure of the Romans. One of the oldest universities in the Western world, it was established at the beginning of the 12th century. (Its rivals were Bologna, Salerno, Oxford, Cambridge, and Leipzig.) The university was started by Pierre Abèlard, who left the cloisters of Notre Dame to give lessons away from the bishop's influence. He took with him the best students and, at the foot of the Montagne Ste. Geneviève, began new courses taught by liberal masters. Rich benefactors founded colleges to house the students and classrooms. Everyone spoke only Latin, hence the area was named the Latin Quarter.

In 1792, following the revolution, the University of Paris was discontinued. It wasn't until 1806 that the Emperor Napoleon re-established the university. It exists today pretty much as it was set up then, which is one reason its students riot and strike.

The oddest corner of Paris

A place of pilgrimage is hidden in the 7th arrondissement at 140 rue du Bac, next to the department store Bon Marché. Most of the inhabitants of Paris, including those who live in the neighborhood, do not know where the high, wooden door leads. But one-and-a-half-million pilgrims visit a simple chapel at the back of the court every year. It commemorates Catherine Laboure, a 24-year-old novice of the order of the Sisters of St. Vincent-de-Paul.

In November 1830, Catherine swore she had a vision and was told to cast a medal in the image of the vision. She was told that those who carried the medal in faith would be blessed.

The demand for the Miraculous Medal is so great that a slot machine has been installed in the chapel. When three five-franc pieces are put in the slot, the machine discharges a medal.

An odd twist to the story behind the medal: When the body of Sister Laboure was exhumed in 1933, it was miraculously intact. Her eyes were still blue. Her limbs were supple, as if she were sleeping. Dressed in the famous white habit of the Sisters of Charity, the body of the saint can be seen today in the rue du Bac chapel.

The world's finest feathers: haute couture

Paris is not only the city of fashion, but it is the city of haute couture as well. Everyone is fashion-conscious here, from eight-year-old school girls to white-haired grandmothers. To make a splash, you must have an outfit specially made and individually tailored.

Many of the world's finest *couturiers* are found in Paris. (A *couturier,* as opposed to a mere dress designer, is one who presents collections of individually made clothes twice a year.) The world's celebrities come to them looking for flair and unique style.

The top couturiers in Paris include:

Chanel, *31 rue Chambon, 1st; tel. (33-1)4261-54-55* and *42 ave. Montaigne, 8th; tel. (33-1)4273-74-12;*

Christian Dior, *30 ave. Montaigne, 8th; tel. (33-1)4723-54-44;*

Givenchy, *rue Francois I, 8th; tel. (33-1)4723-81-36;*

Madame Grès, *1 rue de la Paix, 2nd; tel. (33-1)4260-51-87;*

Jean Patou, *7 rue San Florentin, 8th; tel. (33-1)4260-36-10;*

Yves St. Laurent, *51 ave. Marceau, 16th; tel. (33-1)4723-72-71;*

Jean-Louis Scherrer, *51 ave. Montaigne, 8th; tel. (33-1)4723-61-94;*

Philippe Venet, *62 rue Francois, 8th; tel. (33-1)4225-33-63.*

The best cure for homesickness

If you feel lonely in Paris and want to hear people speaking English, pop into **Shakespeare and Company,** an English-language bookstore across the river from Notre Dame Cathedral. Writers frequent the bookstore. Poetry readings are held on Monday nights.

The best flea market

For nearly 100 years, **Le Marché aux Puces** (Flea Market) has been operating from Saturday to Monday in the village of St. Ouen, just outside Paris' 18th arrondissement. The largest flea market in Europe, it is a maze of little booths selling everything imaginable, from fine and expensive antiques to cheap, second-hand clothing. To get there, take the metro to Piorte de Champerret, take bus Number 85, Gare de Luxembourg-St. Denis, or the metro to Porte de Clignan court.

The best time to browse (if you can manage to wake up that early) is between 5 a.m. and 7:30 a.m. The buyers at this hour are professionals looking for really good buys. They move fast, checking every item with an experienced eye, then buy without hesitation. Large amounts of cash are exchanged, and the goods are shipped to warehouses.

From 7:30 a.m. until 7 p.m., *le marché* is open officially for the 200,000 visitors it receives each week.

Le Marché aux Puces began in 1890, when sanitation laws first required that used clothing and bedding likely to contain vermin not be sold in the city. The rag pickers moved out to a muddy meadow appropriately called The Plain of the Ill-Seated. They were licensed to sell only to dealers and required to clean all materials before offering them for sale.

Over the years, the market became fashionable and began drawing large crowds.

Today, seven markets make up a huge complex. There is less junk, and more antiques (both good and fake).

Le Jules Valles, a covered market, is the best place to look for collectors' items—toys, postcards, medals, dolls, and old newspapers and magazines. **Le Marché Malik** stocks old clothes. The newest markets, **Le Marché Serpette** and **Le Marché Cambo,** specialize in art deco and period furniture, respectively.

Be careful with your money when you're shopping at Le Marché aux Puces, which is full of plickpockets.

The last of the open markets

For the true flavor of Paris, visit one of the city's 12 covered markets. If you enjoy food, you will appreciate the displays of seasonal fresh fruits and vegetables, meats and cheeses, the stacked mushrooms and melons, and the fall and winter displays of furred and feathered game—hare, deer, boar, wild duck, pigeon, partridge, pheasant, and quail.

The covered markets of Paris include:

Beauvau St. Antoine, *between rues d'Aligre and de Cotte, 12th;*
La Chapelle, *rue de l'Olive, 18th (open until midnight on Fridays and Saturdays);*
Enfants Rouge, *39 rue de Bretagne, 3rd;*
St. Didier, *corner of rues Mesnil and St. Didier, 16th;*
St. Quentin, *85 bis blvd. Magenta,10th;*
Ternes, *rues Lebon, Faraday, and Torricelli, 17th.*

The freshest food

The open-air street markets sell Paris' freshest produce and meats and have the largest selection of cheeses. The supermarkets in Paris just don't compare in price or quality.

The best way to lunch in Paris is to stop at one of the open-air markets, buy a fresh baguette, a chunk of cheese or paté, a few pieces of fruit, and a bottle of wine. Take your bundle to the little Parc du Vert Galant on the Ile de la Cité and have a picnic. Sit on the tip of the island and watch the river flow by on either side.

There are 55 open-air street markets. Each sets up and is ready for business by 7:30 a.m., folding and disappearing at 1:30 p.m. two or three times a week (never on Mondays).

Our favorite open-air market is on **rue de Seine,** near St. Germain-des-Prés. Small but well-rounded, its booths have fresh fruits and vegetables piled high in colorful pyramids.

Other open-air markets operating in Paris include:

Boulevard de Charonne, *between rue de Charonne and rue Alexandre-Dumas, 11th;* Wednesdays and Saturdays;

Carmes, *place Maubert, 5th;* Tuesdays, Thursdays, and Saturdays;

Père Lachaise, *blvd. de Menilmontant, between rue des Panoyaux and rue Tlemcen, 11th;* Fridays and Sundays;

Port-Royal, *along the wall of l'Hôpital Val-de-Grâce, blvd. Port-Royal, 5th;* Tuesday, Thursdays, and Saturdays;

Raspail, *along the center island of blvd. Raspail between rue du Cherche-Midi and rue de Rennes, 6th;* Tuesdays and Fridays;

Woodrow Wilson, *ave. Woodrow Wilson, between the Alma and Iéna metro stops.*

The world's best pastry shops

The best pastries in the world are made in France, where layers of cake, as light as feathers, are molded together with airy, sweet buttercream and topped with curls of fine chocolate. Pastries in France are too beautiful (and too fattening) to eat, but too delicious not to.

Within France, the most tempting *pâtisseries,* or pastry shops, are in Paris, where they adorn every corner. There are 2,300 of them!

One of the best known and most honored *pâtisseries* is **Dalloyau,** which specializes in *marrons glacés* (candied chestnuts), *mogador* (layers of chocolate cake, chocolate mousse, and raspberry confiture), and sherbet cakes. Dalloyau shops can be found at *99 rue Faubourg St. Honoré, 2 place Edmund Rostand, 69 rue de la Convention,* and *16 rue Linois.*

The king of pastry is **Gaston Lenôtre,** who runs Lenôtre shops throughout Paris. His 350 pastry chefs and cooks use at lest 12 tons of butter and 300,000 fresh eggs each month. Lenôtre also has the best chocolates in Paris. His shops are at *44 rue du Bac, 5 rue du Havre, 44 rue d'Auteuil,* and *49 ave. Victor Hugo.*

Ice cream at its best

The most delicious ice cream in Paris is sold at **Berthillon,** *31 rue St. Louis-en-l'Ile.* The list of rich, homemade flavors is long; so are the lines.

The loveliest gardens in Paris

The **Jardin du Luxembourg,** in the heart of the Left Bank, is an oasis for all ages. Children romp in the park's elaborate playground, watch Punch-and-Judy shows in the outdoor theater, and sail their boats in the fountains. Adults stroll through the formal gardens and read in the sun. During the summer, palm trees line the pebble paths. In winter, they are stored in the Château de Medicis, which also houses the French Senate.

The most elaborate fountain is the **Medicis Fountain,** at the end of a long pool. Scores of statues decorate the lawns. The best are those in the Delacroix group by Dalou. Find yourself a bench and relax. But, unless you are younger than six, don't touch the grass.

The formal **Tuileries Gardens,** which lead from the Louvre to the Orangerie, are also magnificent. Colorful flowers are planted in careful formations. A pleasant day can be spent rambling through the park, from one museum to the next, stopping for a picnic in between.

The best woodland escape

Every large city needs its escape valve—even Paris. The **Bois de Boulogne** is where Parisians let off steam. You can lie on the grass in this immense wooded park (a no-no almost everywhere else in Paris). And you can hike for hours around its 2,500 acres. The Bois de Boulogne offers horseback riding, biking, rowing, and a zoo. Don't stay here after dark, however, unless you want to experience Paris' seamy side. When the sun sets, streetwalkers and transvestites work the area.

The creepiest tour of Paris

The creepiest but perhaps most fascinating tour of Paris takes you beneath its streets. Eighty-two feet underground is a series of endlessly branching tunnels—156 miles of them in all. They are corridors left over from when the limestone used in building the city was quarried. In 1785, these tunnels were turned into ossuaries for bones removed from grave-yards. The bones of most of the victims of The Terror were transferred here.

The southern part of the city around Montparnasse and the northern part of the city beneath Montmartre are honeycombed with the old tunnels. It's possible to go from one end of Paris to the other by way of these passages, called *les catacombes* by Parisians.

The section of the catacombs directly under the Place Denfert-Rochereau is open to the public. The entrance is on the southwest side of the square. Escorted tours of the catacombs (which are not for the faint-hearted) are arranged on the first and third Saturdays of each month at 2 p.m. and every Saturday during the summer. (Bring a flashlight.)

The best toilets

Wandering in a strange city often raises unpleasant problems. Where do you go when nature calls? In Paris, this can be a puzzling question. The malodorous *pissoirs* (public urinals) along the street are frequented primarily by smelly old bums. They aren't recommended. Many cafés still have old-fashioned Turkish toilets, which consist of holes with footprints on either side. Also unpleasant. The problem is being ameliorated, however.

More than 400 *sanisettes* recently have been installed throughout the city. Each consists of a block of white cement ridged on the exterior to discourage the posting of bills and graffiti. The interior is heated, expertly ventilated, and wired for muzak. Wash basins, perfumed toilet paper, and hooks for hanging clothing or handbags are provided. All this for a mere one-franc piece. Caution: Don't linger more than 20 minutes. After 20 minutes, the assumption is that you need help, and a siren sounds automatically.

The best cafés in Paris

Cafés are an institution in Paris. Parisians use them as living rooms (apartments in Paris are usually tiny). All that is required is the purchase of one cup of coffee. During the summer, tables are set outdoors. Customers soak in the sun while they watch passers-by. In the winter, cafés smell like good coffee and Gauloise cigarettes.

In the 19th century, cafés were gathering spots for artists. Modigliani, the flamboyant Italian painter, frequented the **Café de la Rotonde** on the boulevard Montparnasse, just around the corner from his atelier on the rue de la Grande Chaumière. He and writer Beatrice Hastings often lingered in the café smoking hashish and drinking absinthe (a potent alcohol now illegal in France). He eventually killed himself on the steps here. The Café de la Rotonde still thrives, cheerful despite its history. You can see its red awnings from a distance.

Le Dôme in Montparnasse is decorated with old photos of bygone customers: Picasso, Bonnard, Dufy, Gauguin, and Modigliani.

Paris cafés continue to draw celebrities. Many famous faces can be seen at **La Coupole** on the boulevard Montparnasse. This café was a favorite of Gauguin and his Javanese mistress.

Three of the most famous cafés in Paris are across the street from St. Germain-des-Prés Church on the boulevard St. Germain: **Café de Flore, Les Deux Magots,** and **Brasserie Lipp.** All three of these cafés have attracted artists, writers, and celebrities for decades. Their notoriety, however, has made them crowded and expensive. Lipp, which is also a restaurant, has art-deco decor and attracts the artistic elite (wine dealer Steven Spurrier is a regular). Les Deux Magots is filled with tourists, but it is a good place to people-watch. The lively Flore was Picasso's favorite.

The hottest night life

You'll find plenty to do in Paris, regardless of the size of your purse. You can stroll for free through the Latin Quarter or Beaubourg, where lively circles of spectators watch street performers. A beer in one of the little cafés won't cost much, and you can sit for hours watching the crowd. Or you can go all out and have dinner in a fine restaurant and then dance until the wee hours of the morning in a *boîte de nuit*.

The coolest clubs

Castel's, *15 rue Princesse, 6th; tel. (33-1)4326-90-22,* is where the jet-set hobnobs. Guests are screened at the door, and only the most prestigious or fashionable are permitted to enter. You might need a bit of help to get into this private club, but it's not impossible, especially if you are staying at a first-class hotel and ask the concierge to make the reservation for you. Some of the most famous people in the world can be spotted in this club, which is made up of a series of little rooms on different levels.

Les Bains-Douches, *7 rue du Bourg l'Abbe', 3rd; tel. (33-1)4887-01-80,* is a super-chic club that attracts the trendiest. Located in an old public bathhouse, it has a small pool. Celebrities can be seen here from time to time.

The jazziest joints

You can hear excellent jazz at **Le Petit Journal,** *71 blvd. St. Michel, 5th; tel. (33-1)4326-28-59.* It has been around for years and features musicians such as Stephane Grappelli, Memphis Slim, and Claude Bolling. Most credit cards are accepted.

New Morning, *7-9 rue des Petites Ecuries, 10th; tel. (33-1)4523-51-41,* is another hot jazz club. Live jazz groups from all over Europe and America perform here.

Le Slow Club, *130 rue de Rivoli,* has good New Orleans-style jazz. It is an old-timer in Paris. Standards from the 1930s and 1940s are played by musicians such as Claude Luter and the Haricot Rouges.

The coziest cave

Paris has a concept missing in most other cities—the *cave* (pronounced *kahv*). These cozy little wine-cellars often have good music and they always have good wine. They are ultra-Parisian. The **Caveau de la Huchette,** *5 rue de la Huchette,* is one of the best. It has jazz bands and a warm atmosphere.

The best cabarets

Parisian cabarets can be good fun. In many you have the choice of a dinner show or drinks and the show. The best of the cabarets is **Crazy Horse,** *12 ave. George V, 8th; tel. (33-1)4723-32-32.* The late show is more fun. It's the best of its genre—a sophisticated and professional performance that never fails to please. A minimum of two drinks is required, a matter of about FFr600.

Cultural bests

Classical music and ballet can be found at numerous theaters. The best performances are at the **Paris Opéra** and the **Opéra-Comique.** but you also can hear good music in the famous concert halls, including Salle Gaveau, Salle Pleyel, Théâtre des Champs-Elysées, and Palais de Chaillot. Up-to-date information is available in *Pariscope*, which you'll find at any newsstand.

The cheapest fun

Churches in the Latin Quarter and Marais offer free concerts. Listen for music wafting out of St. Severin or St. Julien le Pauvre around 8 p.m. The Centre Pompidou also puts on free programs: one night a ballet company, another evening a short play. Street entertainers attract crowds on the plaza outside the building. St. Merry offers concerts Saturday nights and Sunday afternoons. Contribute when the plate is passed around.

The seediest night life

Tawdry Pigalle, on the edge of Montmartre, is beginning to show signs of a renaissance. It was here that Paris acquired its reputation as "Gay Paree" at the turn of the century, when artistic and literary cafés dominated the scene. (The Chat Noir was made famous by Toulouse Lautrec's posters.)

Today, Pigalle is better known for drug traffic, prostitution, and tattoo parlors. But new faces are appearing on stage, new customers in the audience. Below are a few places that have shown enough improvement to warrant a recommendation.

La Cloche, *3 rue Mansart, 9th; tel. (33-1)4874-44-88,* is open every day except Sundays until 2 a.m. It has the atmosphere of rustic Normandy. The audiences from nearby theaters come here for *un pot-au-feu* and *grilled andouillette* (sausage made of chitterling). The entry fee is about FFr150.

La Nouvelle Eve, *25 rue Fontaine, 9th; tel. (33-1)4526-68-18,* is open Friday nights starting at 11 p.m. The entry fee is about FFr96. This is the meeting place once a week for Paris' answer to preppies—the BCBG (*les bon chic, bon genre*).

If you'd rather wallow in the seedy side of Pigalle, the area has quite a few strip joints.

French Lovers, *62 rue Pigalle, 9th; tel. (33-1)4285-32-69,* has live sex shows, pure and simple. It is open every day from 2 p.m. until midnight, except Sundays. The entry fee is FFr252.

The best restaurant in Paris

La Tour d'Argent, *15 Quai de la Tournelle; tel. (33-1)4354-23-31,* has pleased the palate of many a dignitary. Henry III learned to eat with a fork here.

Notre Dame is the backdrop of La Tour, which opened 400 years ago. A 120,000-bottle wine cellar graces this time-honored institution, where 150 employees serve 95 people.

Until the beginning of this century, the place was modest, with sawdust on its wooden floors. Frederic Delair brought it to fame in 1890, when he began numbering the *canard pressé,* the famous duck specialty of the house. Each duck was engraved with a social security number. Since then, about 600,000 ducks have been served. The duck is still delicious, the best dish on the menu. But anything à la carte is good. If the *maître d' hôtel* feels you are ordering something you aren't familiar with, he will explain the dish very carefully and recommend gently that you try something else.

Dinner for two is FFr470 to FFr590.

First-class restaurants

Carré des Feuillants, *14 rue de Castiglione, Paris 1; tel. (33-1)4286-82-82,* serves the cuisine of southwest France with a generous dash of creativity. Chef Alain Dutournier's delicacies include ravioli stuffed with foie gras and truffles.

Ramponneau, *21 ave. Marceau, 16th; tel. (33-1)4720-59-51,* has 1920s charm. The tables are well apart, the tree-shaded terrace is delightful, the wines are excellent, and the service is perfect. The place is always full, but not with tourists.

Robouchon (formerly Jamin), *32 rue Longchamps, 16th; (33-1)4727-12-27,* is a superb restaurant, whose reputation is due to the finesse of chef Joel Robouchon. Enjoy the truffles, foie gras, and seafood.

Best meals for the money

Ambassade d'Auvergne, *22 rue du Grenier St. Lazare, 3rd; tel. (33-1)4272-31-22,* serves the most delicious Auvergnat food in town. Don't miss the *aligot* (mashed potatoes with mountain cheese).

Chez l'Ami Louis, *32 rue du Vertbois, 3rd; tel. (33-1)4887-77-48,* has fine fare—if you can put up with the disgusting atmosphere. The chef is (literally) a dirty old man and can be quite insulting.

Chez Georges, *273 blvd. Péreire, 17th; tel. (33-1)4574-31-00,* is a good place for traditional French meat dishes: *gigot* with *glageolets, pot au feu, navarin, boeuf mode, blanquette de veau,* and *petit salé.* Closed in August.

Chez Pierrot, *18 rue Etienne Marcel, 2nd; tel. (33-1)4508-17-64,* is a traditional restaurant with good food. In 1971, when they tore down Les Halles, a small restaurant disappeared. One of the waiters, Pierrot, retained the old phone number and opened this new place nearby. It captures the flavor of the old food halls and the streets that once surrounded them.

Dominique, *19 rue Bréa, 6th; tel. (33-1)4327-08-80,* is one of the few really great Russian restaurants left in Paris. You can sit at the counter, eat blinis with caviar or smoked salmon with cream, and wash it all down with ice-cold vodka.

La Fontaine de Mars, *129 rue St. Dominique, 7th; tel. (33-1)4705-46-44,* is an authentic and typical neighborhood restaurant. M. and Mme. Launay welcome you with real French food and a touch of Gascony. They serve good bourgeois dishes: *cassoulet de canard, fricassés,* and *saucisson de Toulouse.*

Le Foux, *2 rue Clement, 6th; tel. (33-1)4325-77-66,* received a *Pomme d'Or* (Golden Apple) award from William Chamberlayne, the noted travel writer. The food is Lyonnaise/Niçoise, and the ambience is warm and pleasant. On Saturdays stop here for a typical bistro lunch. Le Foux is located in the center of the book publishing district, St. Germain-des-Prés. Occasionally, the French president drops in.

The best hotels in Paris

The **Ritz**, *15 place Vendôme, 75001; tel. (33-1)4260-38-30,* is the ritziest place in town. Elegant and catering always to the comforts of its clients, the Ritz attracts celebrities such as Bill Blass. Hemingway once said, "When in Paris, the only reason not to stay at the Ritz is if you can't afford it." Indeed, you may not be able to afford it. The deluxe rooms are terribly expensive. They feature Persian and Chinese carpets, large brass beds, down pillows, and fireplaces. The cost of all this is FFr2,550 to FFr7,050 a night. The Imperial Suite is an imperial $5,000 a day! This is where Fiat's owner (Gianni Agnelli) and *New York Times* publisher Punch Sulzberger stay in Paris.

Plaza-Athenée, *25 ave. Montaigne, 8th; tel. (33-1)4723-78-33,* is a close second. Although it isn't as opulent as the Ritz, it is more appealing. Redecorated in 1984, it has an ambience of the 1930s that is more attractive (and less expensive) than the other super-deluxe establishments in Paris. It attracts the likes of Audrey Hepburn. The couches are in silk, and surfaces are marble. You can stroll in the lovely courtyard. Rooms are FFr2,100 a night.

Hôtel de Crillon, *10 place de la Concorde, 8th; tel. (33-1)4265-24-24,* is less famous than the Ritz and the Plaza-Athenée, but more private and peaceful. This grand 18th-century palace across the street from the American embassy was built for Louis XV. Tapestries, columns, and marble baths give it a feeling of luxury. While rooms on the place de la Concorde side have the best views, they are also the noisiest. Rooms begin at FFr1,460 a night.

Hôtel George V, *31 ave. George V, 8th; tel. (33-1)4723-54-00,* is an elegant art deco hotel. It has a lovely courtyard, and rooms have their own balconies with good views. The hotel has a great bar with a bartender who knows how to mix a good martini. Rooms begin at FFr2,200 a night.

Best hotels for the price

Hôtel Angleterre, *44 rue Jacob, 6th; tel. (33-1)4260-34-72,* is an inexpensive hotel near St. Germain-des-Prés. The hotel garden is pretty, and the salon has a grand piano. Rooms are FFr420 to FFr590 a night. Reserve in advance. Credit cards are not accepted.

Hôtel des Deux Iles, *59 rue St. Louis-en-l'Ile, 4th; tel. (33-1)4326-13-35,* is in a 17th-century building on the other island from the one on which Notre Dame is located. The entrance hall is filled with greenery and flowers, and the popular bar has a fireplace. Rooms are small and start at FFr550 a night. Reserve at least a month in advance. Credit cards are not accepted.

Esmeralda, *4 rue St. Julien le Pauvre, 5th; tel. (33-1)4354-19-20,* is popular with the theater crowd. Rooms are cozy with views of Notre Dame and the little park of St. Julien-le-Pauvre. Guests can use the sauna. Three of the smallest rooms go for a mere FFr60 a night, but most rooms are about FFr300. Reserve at least two weeks in advance. Credit cards are not accepted.

L'Hôtel, *13 rue des Beaux Arts; tel. (33-1)4325-2722,* is filled with fresh flowers and antiques. The walls are covered with fabric, and the baths are marble. A winding staircase, marble columns, and stone floors make the entrance rather grand. Oscar Wilde died in one of the rooms. Double rooms are FFr1,400 to FFr1,700. Reserve several months in advance.

Latitudes St. Germain, *7-9 rue St. Benoit, 6th; tel. (33-1)4261-53-53,* is a new hotel on the Left Bank just a few steps from the Café Flore and St. Germain-des-Prés. Although it is only a three-star hotel, the rooms are large and well-equipped. Rooms are FFr700 to FFr1,000.

The **Royal Alma,** *35 rue Jean-Goujon, 8th,* near the place d'Alma and across the street from the Seine, is pleasant. This small, modern hotel has bedrooms with private bathrooms. Prices are reasonable, about FFr1,250, considering the a quiet, elegant neighborhood. Free parking.

The world's best subway

The Paris subway, as *le métro,* will take you anywhere you want to go in Paris quickly, efficiently, and cheaply. Every metro station has a map explaining the system, which is easy to understand. Trains are labeled with their destinations.

A single metro ticket will take you anywhere in the city with as many transfers as you wish. You must use a second ticket on buses if you go beyond two sections of the city, and you must use an additional ticket each time you transfer from one bus to another.

A single ticket (good for the metro or buses) costs FFr4.50 when purchased separately and FFr2.75 when purchased in a *carnet* of 10 (*carnets* are available at metro stations and *tabac* stores).

The most economical and convenient way to travel, however, is to purchase a *carte orange*—a daily or weekly pass to all buses, the metro, and the RER (Réseau Express Régional, or Regional Express System), when used inside the city limits. A second-class one-day *carte orange* can be bought for FFr19. You'll pay FFr43 for a second-class one-week pass.

RER trains go north, south, east, and west to suburbs outside Paris. You can catch them at metro stations in Paris.

The world's most beautiful château

The one side trip from Paris that you must make time for is to **Versailles,** the most magnificent of all French châteaux. Louis XIV created this enormous and elaborate palace and its formal gardens, which cover 250 acres. A river was diverted to feed the gardens' 600 fountains. The king moved the court here to get away from the depressing throngs of Paris. During his reign, Versailles housed 6,000 people.

Be sure to see the Hall of Mirrors, the royal apartments, and the chapel. Le Grand Trianon and le Petit Trianon were smaller retreats for the royal family. Le Hameau was Marie-Antoinette's little farm, where she played at being a shepherdess when she tired of the rigors of palace life.

Versailles' greatest rival

Another château is **Vaux-le-Vicomte,** an hour south of Paris. At the entrance are two enormous stone gods. Beyond the iron gate are pavilions, gardens, terraces, cascades, statuary, and a forest. Across a moat and at the top of two grand staircases is the château itself, which has 5 floors and 80 rooms, 27 open to the public.

Nicholas Fouquet, superintendent of France's treasury and protegé of Cardinal Mazarin, dreamed up the château. He bought 12,000 acres and commissioned three artists to design the building, which was completed in 1661. Le Vau is responsible for the architecture, Le Brun for the paintings, and Le Notre for the gardens.

To celebrate the completion of the château, Fouquet made the mistake of inviting Louis

XIV to a feast there. Three weeks after the visit, the king had Fouquet arrested for embezzlement and imprisoned for life.

The most beautiful cathedral in France

Chartres has the most beautiful cathedral in France—and one of the finest in the world. It once drew thousands of pilgrims, who came to worship at the shrine of the Virgin. Located about 50 miles southwest of Paris, it is known for its stained-glass windows, which date from the 12th and 13th centuries. The present cathedral is the sixth built on the site. The Gothic structure was rebuilt after a fire in 1194.

The best French champagne

Champagne may be made legally only in the province of that name, northeast of Paris. Inferior bubbly cannot be called champagne in Europe (by law). Within Champagne Province, the best champagnes are found in the cathedral town of **Rheims.**

It's great fun to explore the quaint villages and rolling countryside of Rheims, sampling champagne en route. The champagne cellars are often in subterranean caves up to 13 miles long. Two of the best are **Epernay,** about 13 miles south of Rheims on N51, and **Montagne de Rheims,** near the city.

The finest church in the world

The great Gothic cathedral at **Amiens,** north of Paris, was designated the finest religious edifice in the world by UNESCO. Built in 1220, this cathedral is 470 feet long. The nave is 141 feet high, the spire 360 feet high. Four-sided reliefs on the lower-half of the west front portray the virtues and vices and illustrate fables. The 16th-century choir stalls are richly carved, and the rose window glows softly. For more information, contact the **Comité Régionale de Tourisme de Picardie,** *9 rue Allart, BP0342, 80000 Amiens; tel. (33-22)92-64-64* or *(33-22)92-21-20.*

Lyons: the gastronomic capital

Although Parisians may disagree, Lyonnais are sure their city is the gastronomic capital of the world.

Sampling the fare

The best restaurant in the city of great dining is **Vettard,** *7 place Bellecour; tel.(33-7)842-07-59.* It is a favorite of former French prime minister Raymond Barre and other French VIPs. The house specialty is *quenelle de brochet financière* (a pike dumpling), which is incredibly light and airy. Also delicious is the sea bass in olive oil and sherry wine vinegar. The wine list includes the best regional wines at very reasonable prices. The belle epoque decor is pleasant, and the service is friendly. Vettard is closed Sundays and in August.

World-famous chef **Paul Bocuse's restaurant,** too, is excellent. It is located five miles outside Lyons, *69660 Collonges-au-Mont-d'Or; tel. (33-7)822-01-40.* Try the superb Bresse chicken and the Elysées soup, served in a flaky pastry cover. Closed in August.

Henry, *27 rue de la Martinière, 69001; tel. (33-7)828-26-08,* has a solid reputation. It serves traditional food with inventive touches. Try the warm *salade de homard aux pousses d'épinards et au beurre de truffles* (lobster salad with spinach and truffles) and the *gâteau de* *ris de veau á la crème de graine de moutard* (sweetbread in a creamy mustard sauce). The service here is remarkably friendly. The restaurant is closed for lunch on Saturdays; all day Mondays; and from July 15 through Aug. 15.

Léon de Lyons, *1 rue Pleney, 69001; tel. (33-7)828-11-33,* serves the best Lyonnais specialties. If you are adventurous, try the *Lyonnaiseries en salade* (calf's foot, lamb's trotters, cervelas sausage, brawn, blood pudding, and lentil salad). Chef Lancombe's own inventions are also delicious. Try his *pigeonneau cuit en croûte de sel* (squab cooked in salt). The restaurant is closed Sundays and Mondays for lunch and Dec. 22 through Jan. 4. Visa and MasterCard are accepted.

L'Industrie, *95 cours du Docteur-Long, 69003; tel. (33-7)853-27-05,* is a tiny seven-table restaurant. Owner André Perez visits with customers to discuss the cuisine and to explain recipes. The chef is a stickler for high-quality ingredients. L'Industrie is closed on weekends and in mid-August. Make reservations well in advance.

The best chocolate

Before you leave Lyons, purchase some of the world's best chocolates at **Maurice Bernachon,** *42 cours Franklin-Roosevelt, 69006.* Some are sprinkled with gold leaf.

The most heroic past

During World War II, Lyons was the center of the French Resistance. (It was also site of the recent trial of Nazi Klaus Barbie.) Resistance groups hid operational headquarters and clandestine printing presses in the city's complex of covered passages, or *traboules.* Because of this, Lyons has pride and a spirit of independence.

The silkiest city

The city's third claim to fame (aside from being the second-largest business center in France) is its silk industry. Developed in the 17th century, the silk industry in Lyons continued to expand until recent years. The city produces beautiful materials, many involving processes that are mastered nowhere else.

Before you leave the city, explore its silk shops. A good place to buy silk ties, scarves, and shirts is **La Maison des Canuts,** *10 rue d'Ivry, 69004.* **Minouche Picot,** *11 Quai André Lassagne, 69001,* has women's silk clothing. The greatest choice, however, is available at the **Centre Commercial de la Part-Dieu,** *rue de Bonnel, 69003,* an enormous 220-store shopping center.

Lyons' finest hotel

La Cour des Loges, *6 rue du Boeuf, 69005 Lyons; tel. (33-78)42-75-75,* is a Renaissance palace in the old part of Lyons that was recently renovated and turned into a modern hotel. It is decorated in an interesting blend of medieval, Renaissance, and modern. The interior courtyard, circular stairways, beamed ceilings, and terraced gardens add charm.

The fastest way to Lyons

These days, getting from Paris to Lyons is a cinch. A railroad line has been built between the two cities enabling operation of very fast trains called **Trains à Grande Vitesse,** or TGV. They run every hour from Paris' Gare de Lyons (where else?). If you want to combine the train journey with a meal other than breakfast, choose the first-class option, because the food in second class will make you think you are not in France.

Peak experiences: the Alps

The Alps are the most beautiful mountains in the world. Like the Rockies, they are snow-capped and dramatically jagged. But unlike their American counterparts, their valleys and slopes are bedecked with picturesque villages. From the peaks you can look miles down into valleys where tiny church spires are surrounded by gingerbread houses. Stone shepherds' huts offer shelter in the trees. And luxurious hotels pamper tired hikers and skiers.

While the Alps are famous for their tremendous ski slopes, you don't have to be a skier to enjoy them. The Alps are gorgeous year-round. Wildflowers cover the mountains in the spring and summer, and during the fall the leaves turn bright yellow. Hikers, campers, fishermen, and hunters ramble the Alpine peaks long after the ski slopes have closed for the summer.

The mightiest Alp

The mightiest Alp is **Mt. Blanc,** Europe's highest peak, which rises 15,772 feet into the sky. A good place to stay while you enjoy the snow-topped mountain is **Chamonix,** a convenient train ride from Paris. From this posh and expensive ski resort radiate many hiking trails and cable car rides.

The best ride is from the *téléphérique* to the Aiguille du Midi, which costs about $20 round trip. You'll hover thousands of feet above rocky drops and seas of ice. Try to take the ride in the morning, when the view is clearest. Wear warm clothes, because it's chilly at the top! If you'd rather hike through the mountains, you can follow the miles of sign-posted trails. For more information, contact the **Compagnie des Guides,** *Maison de la Montagne, 190 place de l'Eglise, 74400 Chamonix; tel. (33-50)53-00-88.*

The most popular ski resort

Chamonix, *place d'Eglise, 74400 Chamonix, France; tel. (33-50)53-00-24,* is the most popular ski resort in the French Alps. The deep-powder snow and the variety of runs in the 13,000-foot mountain range attract experts from all over the world. The 12.4-mile glacier run down the Vallé Blanche is one of the most exciting in the world.

If you find skiing too tame, Chamonix also offers one of the newest thrills: para-pente, which involves parachuting off steep vertical cliffs high in the mountains. You also can hang-glide in the mountains for about $60 a ride.

The most inviting lakes

Of course, the Alps have more to offer than Mt. Blanc. Lakes Geneva (Lac Leman), Annecy, and Bourget are bordered by charming resorts and invite sailing, water skiing, and fishing.

Lake Annecy is especially attractive. It hasn't yet been discovered by hordes of tourists, and its water is still pure. The town of Annecy, on the lake, is dominated by a 12th-century castle and lined with canals. The 16th-century Palais de l'Isle is surrounded by a picturesque old quarter. And the town's monastery is known for its relics of St. Francis de Sales.

When visiting Lake Annecy, stay in Talloires, a village on the lake. The **Hotel de l'Abbaye,** *74290 Talloires, Haute-Savoie; tel. (33-50)60-77-33,* is located in a converted 11th-century Benedictine Abbey. L'Abbaye has dominated the village for 1,000 years and has a breathtaking view of the lake. About FFr1,025 a night. Closed from Dec. 14 to Jan. 16.

The prettiest ski resort

Les Contamines-Monjoies, *74190 Haute-Savoie; tel. (33-50)47-01-58,* is one of the prettiest ski towns in the Alps—and one of the least known. This small ski area set in a high wooded valley is not far from Chamonix. It has 62 miles of slopes beginning at about 8,000 feet and served by 25 lifts. Facilities also include 15 miles of cross-country ski trails. Lift passes are FFr402 per week. Bus service to Chamonix and other nearby resorts is available for an additional FFr114.

The best place to stay is **Le Gai Soleil,** *tel. (33-50)47-02-94,* just outside town in a small farmhouse. The building itself dates back to 1823. Prices for two range from FFr2,280 to 2,790 per week.

The most spectacular drive

The most spectacular drive through the Alps, the **Route des Grandes Alpes** (D902), can be made only during the summer (from the end of June to the end of September). By October it is covered with snow. Begin at Bourg St. Maurice in the Savoie region and head through the Val d'Isère. You will be on the highest mountain highway in Europe. The highest point is the Iseran Pass, 9,084 feet high. Savor the view of the Tarentaise mountain range and the glacier-covered peaks of Albaron and Charbonel. You also will pass the deepest gorges in France.

Brittany: the most beautiful coastline

Brittany (Bretagne), in the west, has 600 miles of the most ruggedly beautiful coastline in France. Along it are sheltered coves, fishing villages, wide deserted beaches, dramatic cliffs, smart resorts, and lush farmland. The stone-built villages are rich in history.

The Quiberon Peninsula's rocks, caves, and reefs make its coast the most dramatic in the province. Walk the Côte Sauvage (Wild Coast) from one end to the other, stopping at the strange rock formations: Grottes du Taureau (Bull's Cave), la Fenêtre (Window), and La Vieille (Old Woman). East and south of the coast are wide beaches and fishing ports.

Brittany's greatest sight

St. Malo, a fortified island-city in Brittany that dates back to the 12th century, was bombed during World War II but has been restored. Visit the castle (the best view of St. Malo is from its ramparts) and the Quic-en-Groigne waxworks museum.

The best hotel in St. Malo is the **Central,** *Grande-Rue 6; tel. (33-99)40-87-70,* in the heart of the old town.

The oldest culture

Natives of Brittany consider their region a separate country. Its original inhabitants, who left prehistoric megaliths, were overrun by the Gauls, the Celts, and finally the Romans. Brittany didn't become French until 1532. The Breton language and folklore are more like those of Celtic Wales than France.

Carnac is dotted with strange prehistoric megaliths—standing stones that are believed to have been erected by the Druids, but which actually are even older. Especially eerie are the Alignements de Menec two miles outside Carnac on D196. More than 1,000 gigantic rocks are set in perfectly straight, miles-long rows.

The **Gulf of Morbihan** is dotted with islands with prehistoric megaliths that stand against the sky. **Locmariaquer,** an island village, has some of the most important megaliths in Brittany. Another islet contains the Tumulus of Gavrinis, thought to be the tomb of a Celtic king.

The best seafood

Brittany has the most delicious seafood in France—sole, crabs, shrimp, oysters, and smoked salmon. Try a bottle of muscadet, the dry white wine of Brittany, or the potent hard cider.

One of the best places in the region for seafood is **Lorand-Barre,** *Damour, Ponts-Neufs; tel. (33-96)32-78-71.* This rustic Breton restaurant eight miles from St. Brieuc has fabulous grilled lobster and dessert crepes.

Normandy—the Riviera's greatest rival

Normandy's world-famous resorts—Deauville, Trouville, and Cabourg—are the Riviera's colder rivals. These elegant towns along the Cherbourg Peninsula are warmed by the Gulf Stream in summer. And they are far less crowded than their southern counterparts.

Deauville has great shopping (including branches of the leading Paris jewelers and designers), elegant hotels and restaurants, and a casino. A boardwalk runs the length of the beach.

A peaceful contrast is **Honfleur,** a small fishing harbor. At sunset, fishermen bring in the day's catch. A pleasant and comfortable place to stay is **Lechat,** *15 place St. Cathérine; tel. (33-31)89-23-85,* in the heart of the old district.

The most beautiful beach town

The most beautiful beach in France is **Etretat,** in Normandy. Two magnificent white cliffs loom above the wide, rocky beach. While the beach is gorgeous, it is not particularly comfortable. But because of this, it is seldom crowded.

The Hotel Dormy House has a breathtaking view from the top of the cliff.

Incomparable Mt. St. Michel

Mt. St. Michel is an eighth-century abbey that sits atop cliffs rising from a flat island, said to have been built at the command of the Archangel Michael, who appeared on the spot. Guides will show you an indentation in the rock that is supposedly the archangel's footprint. The abbey contains the silver shrine of the archangel, who is supposed to have fought the devil hand to hand on a nearby hill. View the Escalier de Dentelle (Lacework Stairway), the Gothic buildings, and the cloister.

Mére Poulard, *Grand' Rue, tel. (33-33)60-14-01,* has an outdoor terrace where you can dine during the tourist season and a stone fireplace where you can huddle in winter. Try the dessert omelette. A double room with a bathroom is FFr650.

Where saints are made

Rouen, the Norman town where Joan of Arc was burned at the stake, is a medieval treasure. The Maid, as Joan was known, was executed in 1431 at the place du Vieux-Marché.

Of the town's 100 churches, the most beautiful is the cathedral, built in the 11th and 12th centuries. Residents live in 15th-century houses lining narrow old streets. Note the Norman architecture—wide oak beams and sharp roofs.

D-day

Hundreds of American World War II veterans visit the sight of the D-day landing each year. The drama of the Normandy landings can be imagined at Arromanches, Utah, and Omaha beaches. The American Military Cemetery is about 1.5 miles beyond Omaha Beach (Colleville-sur-Mer).

Bayeux was the first town liberated after D-day. The 11th-century cathedral is worth visiting to see the Bayeux tapestry. This shows in elaborate detail the events of the Battle of Hastings in England, during which William the Conqueror won his name. (The tapestry is misnamed; it is actually an embroidery.)

Disneyland come true—the Loire

The **Loire Valley,** southwest of Paris, puts Disneyland to shame. Known as Château Country, the region is filled with turreted castles, where royalty once amused itself. The valley's mild climate, rolling green hills, and lush pastureland attracted French nobility centuries ago. Their early châteaux were fortresses designed to ward off invaders. In later years, they became ornate palaces. Today these châteaux are enjoyed by visitors from around the world. Don't expect to see the 120 castles, 20 abbeys, and 100 churches all at once.

The most beautiful Loire château

Chenonceaux is considered the most beautiful château in the Loire Valley. Straddling the Cher River, it was embellished by eight women over a period of 450 years and has been dubbed "The Castle Women Built." It is approached by a promenade of tall trees. The interior is furnished with tapestries, statues, and portraits.

The château was built between 1513 and 1521 under the supervision of Catherine Briconnet, a wealthy 21-year-old heiress. After Catherine's death, Chenonceaux became the property of Henri II, who presented the castle to his mistress, Diane de Poitiers. She planted fine gardens and had a five-arch bridge built to the far bank of the Cher, where she liked to go hunting.

When King Henri died, his wife, Catherine de Medici, forced her rival out of Chenonceaux. The queen then added her own touches, including a 197-foot gallery filled with fine paintings. Catherine had elaborate, erotic parties at Chenonceaux. One party she gave for the Duke of Anjou included regattas, fireworks, and satyrs chasing wood nymphs in the background. The most beautiful noblewomen in France waited on guests—topless!

The largest Loire château

Chambord is the largest of the Loire châteaux. Designed by Leonardo da Vinci for King Francois I as a pleasure palace, it is set in a 13,600-acre game reserve and surrounded by a 20-mile wall, the longest in France. The 440-room hunting lodge is laced with spires, pinnacles, gables, turrets, towers, and 365 chimneys. The palace has 74 stairways, including a double staircase constructed of twin spirals. One person can ascend while another is descending without meeting.

The most violent château

The **Château d'Amboise** has a violent history. In 1560, 1,000 Huguenots involved in a plot to abduct Francis I and his queen, Mary Stuart (later Mary Queen of Scots), were hanged in the castle courtyard.

Charles VII, who was born here, imported Italian architects, sculptors, decorators, and gardeners to embellish the château. He died from injuries received when he bumped his head on one of the castle's low stone doorways. Leonardo da Vinci spent his last years at Amboise and was buried in the adjoining Gothic chapel.

The most regal castle

Blois was the residence of kings for four centuries. Louis XII, Francois I, Louis XIII, and Henri III lived here and left their respective marks on the architecture. The powerful Duc de Guise, who had plotted to overthrow the king, was assassinated here in Henri III's bedroom in 1588. Catherine de Medici's study has 237 secret panels. The Louis XII wing is now a museum with 16th-century frescoes, furniture, paintings, and sculpture.

Where to sleep like a king

While you are in the Loire Valley, you can live like a king. The region is filled with lovely château-hotels that are beautiful but not expensive.

The **Domaine de Beauvois,** *37230 Luynes; tel. (33 47)55-50-11,* dates from the 15th century. Rooms have beamed ceilings and antique furnishings. The dining area is in the tower. Modern amenities include a heated pool, tennis courts, boating facilities, and an elevator. You can fish and hunt in the region. Rooms start at FFr740.

Château de Pray, *tel. (33-47)57-23-67,* is a lovely old château with moderate prices located two miles northeast of Amboise. Dine on the terrace in the summer. **Château de Chissay,** *Chissay-en-Touraine; tel. (33-1654)32-32-01,* has hosted Charles VII, Louis XI, and General de Gaulle. The 15th-century château-hotel has a restaurant, a tearoom, and an art gallery. Minimum three-day stays are requested. It is located in the heart of the Loire castle region on RN76. Rooms are FFr420 to 1,365 a night.

The best of the Bordeaux wine region

The region around **Bordeaux** is known for its great red wines—Margaux, Mouton-Rothschild, and Haut-Brion. Bordeaux itself is a riverport with fine 18th-century architecture. But a half-hour drive from the city brings you to the heart of wine country. Nearly 100 châteaux in the Médoc region offer wine. They vary from small mansions to splendid castles. All are surrounded by acres of vines.

The best wine stores in Bordeaux are **Badie,** *place Tourny;* **La Vinothèque,** *cours du XXX Juillet;* and **Vignes et Vins de France,** *4 rue des Bahutiers.* The Maison du Vin offers maps of the wine regions and lists châteaux that receive visitors.

The prettiest wine town

St. Emilion is one of the most picturesque villages in France. The medieval town is perched on a plateau looking over the valley of the Dordogne. In the 12th century, pilgrims stopped here on their way to the shrine of St. James of Compostela in Spain. While you are in St. Emilion, visit the seventh-century hermitage, which was hollowed out of rock.

Nearby is the entrance to a chapel with a strange underground shrine. It, too, was carved out of rock 900 years ago. A subterranean passage leads to catacombs containing skeletons in ancient tombs. (You must have a guide to visit the shrine.)

At the **Syndicat d'Initiative,** *place des Crénaux,* you can get a list of wine châteaux nearby. The Château Ausone produces the St. Emilion's vintage.

The best way to explore

From the center of Bordeaux City, follow the signs for Soulac. About two miles beyond the turnoff for the Paris Autoroute, the road branches to the right toward Pauillac. Head to the right, and you will be on D2e—the vineyard road.

Near Cantenac is the entrance to the **Château Prieuré-Lechine,** *tel. (33-56)88-36-28.* This 16th-century wine cellar is the oldest in the Médoc. Wines can be bought and tasted with the permission of the cellar master.

Nearly a mile beyond Cantenac is the well-known **Château Margaux,** *tel. (33-56)88-70-28.* The Empire-style château has swans swimming in the garden ponds. A guide will take you through by prior appointment.

Château Beychevelle, *tel. (33-56)59-23-00,* near St. Julien, is the main attraction along the wine route. Tour the cellars and the gardens.

The Pauillac wine district includes two major vineyards: Lafite-Rothschild and Mouton-Rothschild. Make an appointment to see the cellars, the most impressive in the Médoc. The **Mouton Château,** *tel. (33-56)59-22-22,* is closed in August and weekends.

The wine produced at **Lafite-Rothschild,** *tel. (33-56)59-01-74,* was preferred by two royal mistresses, Madame de Pompadour and Madame du Barry.

The most exotic of the Médoc châteaux is the 19th-century **Château Cos d'Estournal,** *tel. (33-56)44-11-37,* which has pagoda towers and massive carved-wood doors.

A trip to bountiful Burgundy

Bourgogne (Burgundy) is the most bountiful region in France. The food is sumptuous, the wine rich, and the forests filled with game. The landscape is dotted with tiny Romanesque churches, old abbeys, canals, and sleepy towns. The area is known for its medieval churches.

Bourgogne is for those who prefer to pamper themselves while slowly savoring the atmosphere, the wine, and the food. Follow the wine route through the region, sampling the vintages. Treat yourself to Burgundy's legendary casseroles, *coq au vin,* or *boeuf bourguignon,* accompanied by a bottle of local red.

Beaune is the wine capital of the region. Typical of Burgundy, Beaune has narrow cobblestoned streets and old houses with little gardens. It also has tour buses, tourists, and expensive gift shops.

Known for its fine wines, Beaune is also the center for excursions northward to vineyards and châteaux. Ancient cellars in town include Cave du Bourgogne, Maison Patriarche Pére et Fils (a working cellar), and Maison Calvet. Nearby are the wineries around Aloxe-Corton or Nuits St. Georges. The famous Pommard vineyards are just south of the town.

To explore the greatest wine country, drive from Beaune north to Dijon on the Ouche.

Beaune's best sight

Before leaving Beaune to explore the surrounding countryside, visit the **Hospice.** Founded in 1443 by Nicholas Rolin, chancellor of Bourgogne, it used to be a working hospital. It is divided into two sections, the **Hôtel-Dieu** and the **Hospice de la Charité**. The Hôtel-Dieu is the greater attraction, with its Burgundian-Flemish architecture and its art collection. Outside, it is somber, with a stone facade and a steep, multicolored tiled roof. Inside, it is a museum. You must pay for a tour—individual visits are not allowed.

The **Grand' Salle,** or Paupers' Room, in the hospice displays original 15th-century furnishings, including 28 red-canopied beds used by patients 400 years ago. The masterpiece of the museum is *The Last Judgement,* by Roger van der Weyden, in a side annex.

The hospice also owns vineyards all over Bourgogne. Each year on the third weekend in November, the hospice sells the wine at auction and uses the money for charity. Prominent wine growers from around the world attend. (If you plan to be in Beaune that weekend, make sure you have a reservation.)

Burgundy's best restaurant

L'Espérance, *St. Père, 89450 Vezelay; tel. (33-86)33-20-45,* is a classic, three-star restaurant in an 18th-century stone house. Chef Meneau creates a delicious *fricassée de champignons des bois* from wild mushrooms. For dessert have warm raspberries poured over vanilla ice cream. *Parfait.* Closed from Jan. 4 to Feb. 12.

The world's best lodge

The best lodge in the world to join is the **Chevaliers du Tastevin,** which inducts new members twice a year in the Clos de Vougeot, the manor house in the midst of the Burgundy vineyards, whose output alone can bear that prestigious label.

The ceremonies begin with the entrance of the halberdiers (uniformed men carrying medieval weapons), who are followed by the counsels of the order in their scarlet and gold robes. Each new member, or postulant-knight, is welcomed by a witty poem recited by the grandmaster in French. He is then dubbed a knight by being struck three times on the shoulder with a grapewood stick "in the name of Noah the father of the vine, Bacchus the God of wine, St. Vincent the patron of vintners."

The ceremony is followed by a dinner of six courses, each accompanied by a selected vintage—for example meat pies with 1985 Aligoté from the Hautes-Côtes de Nuits; turbot with 1983 Puligny-Montrachet; wine-cooked eggs with 1982 Savigny-lès-Beaune; mustard chicken with 1981 Beaune Grèves; local cheeses with 1980 Latricières-Chambertin; pear ice cream and petits fours with coffee and Marc or Prunelle from Burgundy. You may smoke only at the end of the meal.

The three best hotels

Along the wine route is the **Château d'Igé,** *tel. (33-85)33-33-99,* a hotel in a remodeled 12th-century château near Cluny. Fortified towers, ancient exposed stonework, and a spiral stairway of hewn stone give the hotel a medieval atmosphere. Constructed by the counts of Macon in the 12th century, the castle has six hotel rooms and serves gourmet French cuisine. Expensive.

Another charming old hotel is the **Hostellerie de la Poste,** *13 place Vauban, 89200 Avallon; tel. (33-86)34-06-12,* located off Route Nationale 6 halfway between Chablis and Dijon in Avallon. Napoleon stopped at this inn. Established in 1707, it has one of the best restaurants in France, located in old converted stables and on a cobblestoned terrace. Most of the 30 rooms have baths. The hotel is closed from December to March 11.

The **Hôtel de la Poste,** *1 blvd. Clemenceau; tel. (33-80)22-08-11,* on the site of the former ramparts, is the most popular in **Beaune.** A charming old place with a garden courtyard, it also has the best restaurant in town (try the crayfish in cream sauce or the roast quail). It is closed from late November to March.

Alsace—the most German

Alsatians describe themselves as *entre deux portes,* or between two gates—France and Germany. This French *département* that stretches between the Vosges Mountains and the Rhine River has been passed between France and Germany five times, and, as a result, its culture is an interesting blend of French and German. Try the local dishes: onion pie, *choucrôute* (sauerkraut), and *charcuterie,* accompanied by a glass of the wine or beer of the region. *Kugelhupf,* a yeast-based cake, is the traditional dessert.

Strasbourg: the prettiest old town

Strasbourg, the ancient capital of the province, has a centuries-old center enclosed by the branches of the Ill River and guarded by the Strasbourg Cathedral. Built on Roman foundations, the pink Gothic cathedral was begun in 1176 and completed in the 15th century.

Ancient half-timbered buildings line the cathedral square and surrounding streets. One of the most striking is the **Maison Kammerzell,** a restaurant in a 15th-century house with elaborately carved wood trim. Wander along the rue du Bain aux Plantes to La Petite France. Four massive square towers, remnants of 14th-century ramparts, stand over the covered bridges that cross the Ill.

Alsace at its best

Farther down the river in **Colmar,** where Charlemagne once had his summer villa, are houses with carved-wood gables, balustrades, towers, and balconies. Visit the Customs House and the Musée d'Unterlinden, located in a 13th-century convent and cloister.

Small farming villages dot the Rhine plain as it reaches west to the Vosges. Betschdorf, just north of the Haguenau Forest, is where potters make the region's distinctive blue and gray stoneware.

The best white wines

Regional wines of Alsace, unlike those of the rest of France, are labeled by grape varieties rather than by the name of the village or château. Because they don't understand this German labeling system, the French mistrust Alsatian wines. As a result, vintage Guebwiller Gewurtztraminer is the best wine bargain in France, available for FFr20 a bottle.

Along the Alsatian **Route du Vin** (Wine Road), stretching 90 miles from Marlenheim to Thann, are centuries-old towns surrounded by vineyards. **Eguisheim** is a 16th-century town with half-timbered houses with low doorways. Three medieval towers guarded the town until the 15th century. Stop at the Caveau d'Eguisheim (dated 1603) for lunch.

Riquewihr is a pretty Alsatian town that clings to a vine-covered hill, within a circle of 16th-century walls. Cars may not enter its cobblestoned streets.

Best views in the Vosges

A last line of defense over the centuries, the **Vosges Mountains** are dotted with the ruins of fortresses and with convents and churches. Château de Fleckenstein is carved into a rocky hill high above the German border.

Also in the Vosges, in the Saverne Forest, is the **Rocher de Dabo.** Atop this narrow pinnacle is a small chapel dedicated to Alsace's 11th-century pope, Leon IX. From here the view is terrific.

Dordogne—the least spoiled

This *département* in the heart of France is rural, traditional, and relatively unspoiled. But tourists are beginning to discover the area. The **Dordogne** is known for its prehistoric cave drawings and gourmet cuisine. Deep green valleys and river gorges break up the landscape. In the Dronne Valley, châteaux top nearly every hill.

The best country cuisine

The **Perigord,** a historic province contained within the Dordogne, is famous for its cuisine. This is a place to linger over long meals. The area's foie gras, *confit d'oie,* and truffles are famous. But the game and fish are equally delicious. Try the crayfish and the morels. Wash your meal down with a full-bodied Bergerac.

The world's finest porcelain

Limoges, the largest city in the region, is famous for its fine porcelain. Cross its Roman bridges, stroll the little streets in the old section, and visit the ancient cathedral of St. Etienne. Notice the old half-timbered houses by the river. They have open spaces between the roof and the top floor, held up by wide beams. In the old days, residents dried their wash and kept their food provisions in this airy space below the roof.

Tour the porcelain factories or enamel workshops. You can get lists of factories and workshops from the **Welcome Information Office,** *blvd. de Fleurus,* and from the **Regional Tourist Committee,** *8 cours Bugeaud.*

The most disturbing sight

Northwest of Limoges are the charred remains of **Oradour-sur-Glane,** where 650 men, women, and children were murdered by the Nazis during World War II in reprisal for having sheltered Resistance fighters in their village.

The prettiest town in Dordogne

One of the most charming villages in France is **Brantôme.** Bordered on two sides by the Dronne River, it has an 18th-century Benedictine abbey (now the town hall) and a good museum, the Desmoulin. Stroll along the canals past the old houses, then visit the Monks' Garden.

The superb **Restaurant Chabrol,** *rue Gambetta; tel. (33-5)305-70-15,* makes a trip to Brantôme worthwhile. Try the *magret et saumon fume's maison* (smoked duck and salmon), or the *pigeonneau Rossini* (squab with foie gras). Dinner is FFr100 to FFr350 per person.

The most spectacular town in France

Dordogne boasts medieval castles and walled cities dating back to Richard the Lion-Hearted. The most spectacular of the towns is **Rocamadour,** built into the face of a steep cliff. Narrow, cobblestoned streets climb the cliff to its summit, where the Basilica of St. Sauveur is perched along with several shrines. Pilgrims on their knees have climbed the Great Staircase to the shrine since the Middle Ages. See the black Madonna in Notre Dame chapel.

The **Château de Roumegouse,** located between Rocamadour and Gramat off N140; *tel. (33-65)33-63-81,* is a hotel with views of Rocamadour and a wooded park. It is expensive— rooms start at FFr250 a night.

Medieval musts

East of Le Bugue is the **Château Beynac-et-Cazenac,** a well-preserved fortress atop a cliff. The castle was destroyed and rebuilt twice: in 1189 by Sir Mercadier in the name of Richard the Lion-Hearted and in 1214 by Simon de Montfort during the crusade against Albigensian heretics. From the ramparts of the castle another great fortress, the Château de Castelnaud, can be seen. The restored castle was once a headquarters for Simon de Montfort.

The village of St. Cirq-La Popie, set in a gorgeous valley, sits beneath the ruins of a 1,000-year-old castle. The town's name commemorates St. Cirq, a saint who lived here in the third century, and Sieur La Popie, lord of the castle. St. Cirq is known for its woodcraft, although the art has largely disappeared.

More than 80 walled cities still stand from Perigord to the Pyrenées, including Monpazier, Domme, Lalinde, Villereal, Beaumont, and Ste. Foy-la Grande.

Europe's favorite summer playground

The French Riviera, known as the **Côte d'Azur,** is Europe's favorite summer playground. It is hot, crowded, expensive, and oh-so-trendy. Avoid St. Tropez in July and August, when it is jam-packed. Visit in September and October, after the summer season and before winter. Prices drop, the weather is mild and sunny, and the beaches are yours.

The coast is 72 miles long, with 25 miles of long beaches of pebble or sand, from Marseille to Menton. From Nice to the Italian border, beaches are of gravel or rock. Between Cannes and St. Raphaël, the rocks of Corniche are breathtakingly beautiful. But the best beaches are along the coast from St. Raphaël to Hyères: Cabasson, Le Lavandou, St. Clair, Cavaliere, Tahiti, Pampelone, Salins.

The most famous Riviera town is **St. Tropez.** Its three best-known beaches are Le Plage de Pampelonne, which is spectacular, Le Plage de Tahiti, where the very rich sunbathe, and Le Plage des Slins, where the clothes get skimpy.

The nicest town

Nice is a lovely town with old houses and wide views. Although its beach is rocky, you still can take a pleasant walk along the sea—on the Promenade des Anglais. The casino is elegant. Visit the Terra Amata paleontological museum near the old harbor, located on the spot where the remains of a mammoth-hunters' camp 400,000 years old were discovered.

The **Chantecler,** *37 promenade des Anglais, 06000 Nice; tel. (33-93)88-39-51,* in the Hôtel Negresco, serves the excellent inventions of chef Jacques Maximin. The **Hôtel Negresco** is more an institution than a hotel. It has been revived with splendid authentic antiques and decorated in the styles of the 16th and 18th centuries.

The best casino

In Cannes, the glamorous **Palm Beach Casino** is a big attraction—except when the

French police have closed it. The beaches are sandy, and luxury yachts line the marina. The Promenade of the Croisette is lined with jet-set hotels. And the splendid new Palace of Festivals houses a theater, a casino, a nightclub, boutiques, and a convention center. It is the site of the famous film festival.

St. Yves, *49 blvd. d'Alsace; tel. (33-93)38-65-29,* in Cannes is a charming old hotel in a villa surrounded by palm trees.

The best drive

The drive along the **Grande Corniche,** the high road along the crests of the mountains, is spectacular. At times you will see the high snow-covered peaks of the Alps. At other places you will see the sea. On the way down, visit Roquebrune, where a château was hewn from the rock.

The Corniche is where the Grand Prix de Monte Carlo car races are held and where the spectacular chase in James Bond's *Casino Royal* took place.

The most romantic town

Antibes, the center of the perfume market, has lovely beaches, a quaint old port, and a colorful fruit and flower market.

Hôtel du Cap-Eden Roc, *boulevard Kennedy, 06604 Antibes; tel. (33-93)613-901,* was once a favorite of Scott and Zelda Fitzgerald. It's romantic, glamorous, and has great views.

For a magnificent dinner, take a boat from Antibes to La Napoule and dine at **L'Oasis,** *rue Jean-Honoré-Carle; tel. (93)49-95-52.* Chef Louis Outhier creates unforgettable desserts.

The most royal resort

Monaco, a separate though tiny nation on the Riviera, attracts the world's royalty. The little kingdom set above the sea looks like the setting for a fairy tale. But it's far from innocent, with its casinos, decadent hotels, and beaches where the world's best bodies sun topless.

Monaco's capital, Monte Carlo, has some of the most glamorous hotels, restaurants, and casinos in Europe. The magnificent **Hôtel de Paris,** *place du Casino; tel. (33-93)50-80-80,* attracts jet-setters, gamblers, yachties, and the Grand Prix crowd. It has lovely views of the Mediterranean, a private beach, and a nice pool.

The hotel's greatest feature, however, is its restaurant, **Louis XV.** One of Europe's finest new chefs, 31-year-old Alain Ducasse, is the mastermind behind the marvelous meals served here. (Try the cream of shrimp soup, the crayfish salad, and the strawberries.) The restaurant's wine cellar contains nearly 280,000 bottles. Gold and ivory frescoes decorate the walls.

The hottest nightclub on the Riviera is **No Rock,** *11 rue du Portier, 9800 Monte Carlo; tel. (33-93)25-09-25.* Princess Stéphanie and Prince Albert can be spotted here. The atmosphere is cozy yet exciting, with a piano bar, romantic nooks, and a disco. Drinks are bought by the bottle.

Provence, the sweetest region

The Mediterranean region of **Provence** is a sweet land, literally and figuratively. Its air is scented by the lavender, basil, rosemary, thyme, and sage that grow in its rocky fields. And old traditions and a simple way of life survive here. This is the land of Marcel Pagnol, the beloved French writer, who wrote about his boyhood adventures in these rocky hills, olive groves and stone houses.

Provence looks like an impressionistic painting. Villages climb the white rocks; the pines are a dark green, the soil red, and the olive groves green; and lavender grows in the fields.

Framed by the sea, the Alps, the Rhone and the Durance rivers, and the Italian border, Provence stretches from the medieval town of Aigues-Mortes in the west, beyond Marseille to Cassis in the east. It includes the lower Rhone Valley; the flat, windy marshes of the Camargue; and the foothills of the Alps.

The most typical town

Arles, the most characteristically Provençal town, is also the most Roman town. It has an ancient Roman arena and theater. Around the place du Forum are buildings that date back to the Roman era. Be sure to see the Roman sarcophagi and mosaics at the Museum of Pagan Art in the former Church of St. Anne.

Of the medieval monuments, **St. Trophime** is the most famous, carved details from the Old and New Testaments.

If you happen to be in Arles on a Saturday, visit the outdoor market on boulevard des Lices. Regional produce, lavender, crafts, and homemade sausages are sold.

Le Vaccarès, a restaurant once frequented by Vincent Van Gogh, is the most agreeable place to lunch. It looks over the place du Forum.

Jules César, *boulevard des Lices,* is a beautifully run hotel with a fine restaurant, Lou Marquest. The charming **Hôtel d'Arlatan,** *26 rue du Sauvage; tel. (33-90)93-56-66,* is located in the 15th-century ancestral home of the counts of Arlatan. The courtyard is tranquil with its palm trees and shade. Double rooms are about FFr566.

The Vatican's only rival

Avignon, the seat of the papacy from 1309 to 1403, is famed for its **Papal Palace.** For a time, Avignon was a center of Christianity and medieval civilization. Later is was the home of a schismatic pope, put in power by the ambitious kings of France.

The Papal Palace is a massive, handsome building. Tours in English are offered twice daily. Examine the Gobelin tapestries in the banquet hall, the kitchen tower, the frescoed tower of St. John, the papal bedroom, and the stag room, lined with hunting scenes.

Avignon's place de l'Horloge, between the rue de la Republique and the place du Palais is lively, filled with restaurants, cafés, and street musicians. The Auberge de France is the best restaurant. The Petit Palais, on the square, is filled with 14th- and 15th-century paintings and sculpture, including an early Botticelli.

For the best view of the city, climb to the Rocher des Dômes, just above the Papal Palace. You'll see clearly the **Pont d'Avignon** of the French folk song (it's real name is the Pont St. Benezet). The ruined bridge goes only partway across the river.

Our favorite hotel is **Hôtel d'Europe,** *12 place Crillon, 8400 Avignon; tel. (33-90)82-66-92.* Located in a 16th-century aristocrat's house, it hosted Napoleon in 1799. Rooms are furnished with antiques, and the atmosphere is peaceful. The restaurant serves classic cuisine, as well as the best croissants in France. You can eat outside beside a fountain in the courtyard. Rooms start at FFr350 to FFr870 for a double.

The oldest houses in France

The road to the golden-hued city of Gordes leads through flat vineyards and steep hills to the **Village des Bories.** This collection of prehistoric stone buildings, or *bories,* dates back to 3000 B.C. The huts were used by shepherds until the 18th century. They have been restored to look as they did 4,000 years ago and are filled with old cooking implements and tools.

The wildest region

The **Camargue,** a marshy area where wild horses and bulls live, is the wildest region in France. Horseback riding is a big attraction in the Camargue, which has many horse ranches.

Hotels in Camargue are often built in the style of the traditional low white farmhouse, or *mas.* Two of these hostelries are **Mas de la Fouque,** *tel. (33-90)47-81-02,* and **Mas du Clarousset,** *tel. (33-90)47-81-66.* Mas de la Fouque is a little more than two miles from Stes. Maries de la Mer on the road to Aigues-Mortes. This beautiful *mas* has a shallow lake that attracts flamingos. Rooms start at FFr710 per night. It is open from April 10 to Nov. 2. Mas du Clarousset, also in Stes. Maries de la Mer, has fireplaces, terra-cotta tiles, and flowers everywhere. Rooms start at FFr930 a night.

Stes. Maries-de-la-Mer, the informal capital of the Camargue, is a 20-minute drive from Arles. It is host to Gypsy pilgrims every year. They come by the thousands from all over Europe May 24 and 25 to visit the town's 12th-century church. In a corner of the crypt is the statue of St. Sara, patron saint of the Gypsies, cloaked in purple velvet.

The best-preserved fortified town

Aigues-Mortes, surrounded by marshes, is one of the few perfect surviving examples of a fortified medieval town. The walled city dates back to the 13th century, when Louis IX, later known as St. Louis, sailed off for the Seventh Crusade to the Holy Land.

The best Roman ruins in France

North of this ancient town is **Nîmes,** which has the most splendid Roman arena in the country. Well preserved, it is used for bullfights. Nîmes' Roman temple, known as the Maison Carée, is also perfectly preserved.

The most fragrant town

The sweetest-smelling town in Provence is **Grasse,** 10 miles from Cannes. It is the perfume capital of the world. Violet, lavender, jasmine, lily, rose, jonquil, and mimosa grow here. Once the favorite resort of Queen Victoria, Grasse is a picturesque old village with winding cobblestoned streets and weathered houses.

Each year the perfumeries in Grasse process more than 700 tons of roses, 600 tons of orange blossoms, and 800 tons of jasmine. La Parfumerie Fragonard (named after the painter and engraver born here in 1732) and La Parfumerie **Gallimard** are open daily. English-speaking guides explain how the perfume is made. Villa Fragonard houses paintings by Fragonard.

The most Spanish region: Roussillon

West of the Riviera, stretching the length of the Golfe du Lion, from the Pyrénées to the Rhône Delta, is the **Roussillon** region. Medieval walled cities, the peaks of the Pyrénées, Mediterranean resorts, and quaint villages mark this varied region. Also known as French Catalonia, Roussillon has a Spanish air. It belonged to Spain until 1659, and the people are

Catalan, as are the people of Barcelona. The red and yellow Catalan flag flies over the region's capital, **Perpignan.** Some Catalans would like to see the region become autonomous.

The least-spoiled coast

Traditional fishing villages still can be found along the western end of the Mediterranean coast. **Collioure** is the most charming fishing port. Matisse painted here. **Sète,** the birthplace of Paul Valéry and Georges Brassens, also retains its original appeal.

The largest walled city

Carcassonne, Europe's largest medieval walled city, is west of Narbonne. A mighty circle of towers and battlements surrounds the hilltop town. Parts of the walls were built by the Romans. In the fifth century, the Visigoths enlarged the fortress. Charlemagne laid siege to the city for five years in the ninth century. And in the 13th century it fell to crusaders; Simon de Montfort took it over. St. Louis strengthened the fortress. It was rebuilt in the 19th century by Violet-le-Duc to conform to Victorian ideas of how a walled city should look.

The best place to stay in Carcassonne is the **Hôtel de la Cité,** *place d'Eglise; tel. (33-68)25-03-34,* located in a former Episcopal palace built into the old walls near the Basilica of St. Nazaire. Some rooms have canopy beds, and the dining hall is beautiful. Open from April through October, and for FFr700 a night.

The most exotic region: Basque Country

The southwest of France and the northwest of Spain combine to form an exotic region known as **Basque Country.** The Basques have a common language, culture, and history that is neither French nor Spanish.

The Spanish Basques, in particular, have agitated for autonomy. A separatist movement exists in France as well, but it is milder. The Basque language is related to no other, and is not Indo European. Some people think the cavemen spoke Basque.

The mountainous region is known for its cuisine. The most prized dish is seasonal—the wild dove that migrates from northern Europe to Spain in October.

The most typical town

St. Jean-Pied-de-Port, near the Spanish border, is the most typically Basque town in the region. It was fortified in the time of Louis XIV, and its narrow cobblestoned streets are guarded by a tall citadel. Sheep graze in the moat. The typical Basque houses are stone, sturdy, half-timbered, and white-washed with red or green trim and chalet-like stucco.

The church's clock tower tolls the hour twice, following local custom. A stone bridge crosses the Nive River to the tower. The *fronton,* or ball court, is always filled with *pelote* players. And flat, round tombstones from pre-Christian times can be seen in the graveyards. *Pelote,* or jai alai, is the Basque ball game, played with a hard ball and a racquet. It is very fast.

High fashion and fine surfing

Biarritz, a seaside resort on the Bay of Biscay, has one of the longest beaches in France and offers the best surfing on the French coast. Stroll along the promenade from the Hôtel du Palais to the Côte des Basques. Visit the Rocher de la Vierge for a good view of the ocean.

The lower promenade, along the boulevard du Prince de Galles, leads past the foaming breakers that give the coast its name—Côte d'Argent, the Silver Coast. The lighthouse on the summit of Cap St. Martin has a splendid view.

Biarritz was made famous by the Empress Eugénie (the wife of Napoleon III), who attracted fashionable clientele to the resort. Queen Victoria and Edward VII, among others, slept in Eugénie's villa, now the Hôtel du Palais.

Chapter 5

THE
BEST
OF
ITALY

The Italians live alongside the world's greatest artworks the way Americans live next door to tacky neon signs and billboards. Where else but Italy would an insignificant-looking neighborhood church contain paintings by Botticelli? What city but Rome would go about its business amidst the ruins of the once-great buildings built by their ancestors who ruled the then-known world? What people except Italians can be so surrounded by culture yet so unpretentious?

Rome: the world's most celebrated city

Rome has been the world's most celebrated city for more than two millennia. Before Christ was born, Romans watched gladiators fight lions in the Coliseum. For 1,500 years, Rome has been the center of Christianity. Five centuries ago, Michelangelo painted the Sistine Chapel here. Today, Rome is one of the biggest tourist attractions in the world.

The five most important sights

The **Coliseum** is the greatest architectural remnant of ancient Rome. Shaped like an oval bowl, it was built by Titus and used for month-long spectacles, including battles between animals and gladiators. Christians were fed to the lions here, according to legend. The structure is well-preserved. Today it is inhabited by hundreds of cats, whose eyes glow from dark archways.

The **Roman Forum** was the chief public square and a center of government in ancient Rome. Only a few ruins remain. With a little imagination, you can look at the columns of the **Temple of the Vestal Virgins** and see a full-fledged Roman temple. Vestal Virgins once lived in this elaborate structure and kept the fire in the center of the temple lit around the clock. If they lost their virginity, these maidens were buried alive.

The Forum also has the remains of the **Curia,** where the Roman senators met, and the **Temple of Julius Caesar. The Arch of Titus,** decorated with a seven-branched candelabrum, marks the defeat of the Jews and the destruction of their temple in Jerusalem. The white stone pillars and arches are surrounded by a green lawn and tall trees with inviting benches beneath them. The main entrance to the forum is on via dei Fori Imperiali.

The **Pantheon,** *Piazza della Rotonda,* a heavy circular structure fronted by a porch with 16 Corinthian columns and topped with a cupola, is the architectural and civic symbol of the city. Marcus Agrippa commissioned it in 27 B.C. as a temple to the gods. The first Christian emperors tried to close the pagan structure, but failed. Later, the popes recognized its popularity and made it into a church in A.D. 606. The Pantheon also has been used as a fish market and a fortress. Raphael and the first two kings of Italy chose to be buried here.

The **Piazza di Spagna** (Spanish Steps) is a square dominated by a pair of curved steps filled with vendors, tourists, artists, street musicians, and Romans on their lunch hours. The ornate, flower-bedecked steps lead from a street filled with high-fashion boutiques to a peaceful residential neighborhood of grand houses. Stendhal, Liszt, Balzac, Wagner, Joyce, Keats, and Shelley all lived on this square. Young people from around the world linger on the steps looking for romance, drugs, and the "real" Rome. Watch out for pickpockets!

To ensure your return to Rome, throw a coin in the 18th-century **Trevi Fountain,** at the base of the steps off the via del Corso on Piazza di Trevi. Money from the Trevi is collected by the city and used to improve tourist attractions. On the average, more than 500,000 lire is collected from the fountain each week (more in summer months).

The world's second-smallest country

Vatican City, the world's second-smallest country, occupies one square mile within the city of Rome. It is the headquarters of the Roman Catholic Church and has its own post office and postage stamps, printing press and newspaper, currency, railway, and radio station. It is governed by the pope and protected by Swiss Guards, whose colorful blue and gold uniforms were designed by Michelangelo.

The Vatican museums have the most impressive art collections in the world. The **Sistine Chapel** is one of the great marvels of the Renaissance. The frescoed ceiling was painted by Michelangelo and has recently been restored. Some art critics view the cleaning as a desecration; others applaud. Judge for yourself. A pedestrian walkway leads through the many museums to the Sistine Chapel, which covers an area of more than 40,000 square yards. En route, keep an eye out for the four rooms painted by Raphael and his assistants in the 16th century, as well as the little Chapel of Nicholas V, with frescoes by Fra Angelico.

St. Peter's Basilica in the Vatican reveals both the grandeur of the Papacy and the impact of Catholicism. When 300,000 people gather to hear the pope's blessing, you understand his power. The Basilica was built by Constantine in A.D. 350 on the site where St. Peter was martyred and then buried. Parts of the original building still exist, underground in the crypt. A cupola designed by Michelangelo crowns the church. Be sure to dress modestly when you visit St. Peter's—shorts are forbidden, and women may not wear dresses with hems above the knee or without sleeves. Many travelers are barred from St. Peter's because of improper clothing.

If you would like a papal audience or to attend a special ceremony in St. Peter's, apply in writing to **Prefettura della Casa Pontifica,** *00120 Citta del Vaticano.* When the pope is in Rome, public audiences are held on Wednesdays at 11 a.m.

On the edge of the Vatican is an ancient fortress, **Castel Sant' Angelo,** built in A.D. 135 as a mausoleum for the Emperor Hadrian. The sixth-century chapel on top of the mausoleum was built to commemorate an angel who appeared to announce the end of the plague. Corner towers and bastions were added in the 15th and 16th centuries. Pope Clement VII lived in the castle in 1527. The fortress is connected to the Vatican by a long passage.

Rome's most venerated treasure

Santo Bambino, a two-foot figure carved centuries ago from an olive tree from Gethsemane and then baptized in the Jordan River, is venerated by the Italians for its supposed healing powers. Housed in the chapel of the Santissimo Bambino in the sixth-century **Church of Santa Maria d'Aracoeli,** on the highest point of the Capitoline Hill, the Bambino is brought out four times a year to make sickbed calls. During such excursions, the figure is accompanied by Franciscan monks and an armed escort and sealed behind a bulletproof glass casing. It is said that during a speech given by Mussolini, a Santo Bambino procession passed, and the dictator was left speaking to the backs of a kneeling crowd.

Rome's best markets

Sunday morning, visit the **Porta Portese** flea market. This mile-long sprawl of booths, tables, and ground-cloth displays has everything from glassware and Etruscan relics to Arab carpets. You'll see every manner of Roman here: Gypsy, beggar, well-dressed shopper, street musician, magician, pickpocket. In one section, Arabs sell carpets and blankets. In another, Africans sell wooden sculptures and medicinal cures. Russian Jews have their own section, where they sell linen, caviar, Havana cigars, samovars, and balalaikas.

Campo dei Fiori, a flower market in the middle of the medieval quarter, is a welcome change after days of wandering among ancient monuments and works of art. Every morning, the area is filled with sweet smelling flower stalls. This is Rome's oldest open market

Rome's best park

In the northern section of Rome is the city's most remarkable park—**Villa Borghese.** The gardens around the former estate of Cardinal Scipione Borghese were designed in the 17th century. Rome's zoo is here, as well as two museums housed in the cardinal's palace. The main entrance is at Piazzale Flaminio, just outside the Porta del Popolo. You also can get here by walking up the Spanish Steps and following via Trinita dei Monti to the left until you can see all seven hills of Rome.

The most macabre sight

The mass of skulls in the church of **Santa Maria della Concezione dei Capuccini,** *via Veneto 27,* is the most macabre sight in Rome. Monks at this church maintain a crypt that contains more than 4,000 skulls and bones of past Capuchin monks. Two of the five chapels contain floors of earth brought from Palestine. On Nov. 2 (All Soul's Day), the crypt is brightly lit, making it even more gruesome.

Rome's oldest road

The **Appian Way** (via Appia Antica), a 2,300-year-old road paved by the Romans, still exists in places in and around Rome. In 71 B.C., the gladiator Spartacus and the slaves who rebelled against Rome were strung up side-by-side along this 132-mile route between Rome and Capua. The 6,000 rebels were left to rot.

The **Baths of Caracalla** (Terme di Caracalla) are near the beginning of the Appian Way. Built in the third century, its walls remain on viale delle Terme di Caracalla, near the Piazzale Numa Pompilio.

The **Catacombs of St. Calixtus,** *via Appia Antica 110,* are the most famous sight along the route. These burial tunnels were used by the early Christians as hiding places. St. Cecilia,

St. Eusebius, and many martyred popes are buried here. Also along the road is the Domine Quo Vadis chapel, about half a mile beyond Porta San Sebastiano. It was built in the ninth century on the site where St. Peter, fleeing Nero, had a vision of Christ telling him not to abandon the Christians. Peter then returned to Rome to face his martyrdom.

Rome's six best secrets

San Pietro in Vincoli (St. Peter in Chains), *Piazza di San Pietro in Vincoli,* houses Michelangelo's statue of Moses. The church was built in the fifth century to hold the chains that bound St. Peter.

The **Prehistoric and Ethnographic Museum of Rome,** *1 viale Lincoln,* located on the grounds of the Esposizione Universale di Roma (known as the E.U.R.), has some of the finest remains of ancient civilization in existence today. Highlights of the museum include the collection from the Italian school in Crete; statues of priests and warriors from Sardinia; objects found in cemeteries of Etruria; and tombs dating back to 10 B.C. Closed on Mondays.

Carcere Mamertino, *via San Pietro, Cacere, off via dei Fori Imperiali,* today a chapel consecrated to St. Peter, was once a fearsome prison where St. Peter was imprisoned by Nero. The saint baptized his fellow prisoners using water from a spring that appeared miraculously. The dungeons below may be the oldest structures in Rome.

The villa and gardens of Mussolini (the fascist dictator of Italy from 1922 to 1943), called the **Villa Torlonia,** *via Nomentana,* are now a public park, open from dawn to dusk every day. Many of the buildings on the estate date back to the 17th century. The most outstanding are the twin obelisks carved of red granite. The estate includes a 400-seat theater, two simulated ancient Roman temples, a Moorish hothouse, and a Swiss-style châlet.

Also visit the **Casina delle Civette,** once the playhouse of Giovanni Torlonia Jr., a notorious playboy who brought his many girlfriends into the house via secret passages. The house is decorated with owls. The Italian word for owl, *civette,* also means coquette.

The **Keats-Shelley Memorial House,** *Piazza di Spagna 26,* is overlooked by most visitors to the Spanish Steps. It is identified only by a small brass plaque. Keats died here in 1821, when he was 25. Shelley spent much time here visiting his fellow poet. Fragments of Shelley's bones and some of his letters to Keats are on display. Keats' drawing of the Grecian urn that inspired his most famous poem, "Ode On A Grecian Urn," can be seen.

The oldest café in Rome

Antico Caffè Greco, *via Condotti 86,* is one of the oldest cafés in the world. Founded on July 24, 1760, it has been frequented by artists, celebrities, and politicians, including composer Hector Berlioz, Mark Twain (in fact, a statue of Twain decorates the café), Hans Christian Andersen, James Fenimore Cooper, Sir Walter Scott, Henry James, Lord Alfred Tennyson, Richard Wagner, Benjamin Franklin, Henrik Ibsen, Goethe, Schopenhauer, Orson Welles, Frederico Fellini, Stalin, and Adolph Hitler. The café was declared a national monument by the Italian government in 1953. Homemade ice cream is served, as well as the best cappuccino in Rome.

Rome's most beautiful bridge

Tiber Island, in the middle of the Tiber River, is connected to the rest of Rome by the **Fabricio Bridge,** known to Romans as the Bridge of Four Heads. A pillar in the middle of the bridge is carved with four faces representing the four builders of the bridge, beheaded for not finishing the bridge by the date promised. Tiber Island has been occupied since 292 B.C., when a temple was built in honor of Aesculapius, the Greek god of health.

The most remarkable fountain

The **Fountain of Rivers,** completed in 1651 by Gian Lorenzo Bernini, is the most beautiful fountain in Rome. Located in the heart of Rome's picturesque Piazza Navona, it is a mass of rockwork and grottoes.

Bernini and Borromini competed for the honor of designing the facade of the Church of Sant' Agnese in Agone on the west side of Piazza Navona. The project was awarded to Borromini. When Bernini was later asked to design the piazza's main fountain, he got even. He designed four colossal figures for the fountain's four corners (representing the Danube, Ganges, Nile, and Plate rivers) and placed them so that none would look upon the facade of Sant' Agnese in Agone. The Nile blocks the view of the church with its hand.

Bests beneath Rome

Santissimi Giovanni e Paolo is a little medieval church built over ancient Roman homes on Celio hill, near the Coliseum. A door in the nave leads to a stairway that descends to the old, brick buildings. Patches of mosaic line the cool walls. Saints John and Paul hid from the Romans here. To get to Santissima Giovanni e Paolo, follow Salita di S. Gregorio from Piazza di Porta Capena until the name of the road changes to Clivo di Sauro.

St. Peter's Basilica is also built above a vault of ancient history—in fact, the basilica stands directly over the tomb of St. Peter himself. You can explore the Roman burial ground here. The Pre-Christian tombs are well-preserved, and on one wall is an elaborate tomb with the inscription, "Peter is within." You can visit the necropolis only with special permission, which can be obtained from the **Reverend Fabbrica de San Pietro,** *Ufficio Scavi, 00120 Citta del Vaticano.* Send him your name and your address and telephone number in Rome.

The best Roman shopping

Luxury shops fill the Piazza di Spagna and line the adjoining streets (via del Babuino, via Vittoria, via della Croce, via Condotti, via Borgognona, via Frattina, and via della Vite). Less expensive shops can be found along via del Corso.

Leather goods, gloves, shoes, purses, wallets, belts, and luggage displayed in windows along via Condotti draw credit cards from the pockets of passers-by like magnets. The jewelry displays at Bulgari must be the most sensational in the world.

Few outsiders know about Rome's department stores. Romans of all social levels shop at the **Coin,** *Piarrale Appio, 15,* for high fashion at low prices. Coin has its own designers and stylish collections.

Men, especially, can find good, quality clothing in Rome. **Gioffer,** *via Frattina 118,* is devoted entirely to ties made of quality materials and sold at low prices. **JCA,** *via Cola di Rienzo 183,* is a boutique filled with cotton shirts at good prices. And **Enzo Ceci,** *via della Vite 51,* specializes in Italian brands of men's clothing and offers classic suits, sport shirts, and sweaters with original designs.

Women can buy inexpensive hand-finished linen suits at **Belsiana 19,** *via Mario dei Fiore,* as well as dresses, blouses, and belts by local designers. And hand-painted fabrics are made into skirts and blouses at **Convertite 81,** *via delle Convertite 22.* Silk, cotton, and wool sweaters are sold at **Vittoria 3A,** *via Vittoria 3.* Again, the prices are good.

Leather is a good buy in Rome. **Boris-Pelletterie,** *Corso Rinascimento 43-45, Piazza Navona,* has purses, wallets, briefcases, and men's bags.

You can have a suitcase or a purse handmade to order in Rome—in three weeks!—at **Di Ceglie,** *via S. Claudio 67.*

The world's most beautiful crèches

During the Christmas season, Rome is decorated with crèches rather than lights and Santas. The three most beautiful are on the Spanish Steps, in the Piazza Navona, and in St. Peter's Square.

The oldest Roman crèche, in the **Church of S. Maria Maggiore,** contains figures crafted by Arnolfo di Cambio, the most celebrated architect of the late 13th and early 14th centuries.

However, the crèche most beloved by Romans is at **S. Maria d'Aracoeli,** at the top of 122 stairs on the Capitoline Hill. It features the Santo Bambino. Every afternoon from Christmas Day to Epiphany (Jan. 6), children recite poems and prayers in front of the crèche.

Cosma e Damiano, *via dei Fori Imperiali,* houses an 18th-century Neapolitan masterpiece—the only crèche on display year-round.

The best Midnight Mass

The most beautiful Christmas Midnight Mass in the world is at **St. Peter's Basilica.** The pope conducts the Mass with the assistance of dozens of cardinals. The Choir of the Sistine Chapel sings, and the Vatican ushers, known as San Pietrini, turn on hundreds of lights. You can write in advance for tickets to Midnight Mass. Contact the **Prefettura della Casa Pontifica,** *Città del Vaticano, 00120.*

Rome's best hotel

The **Hassler,** *Piazza Trinità dei Monti 6, 00187 Rome, Italy; tel. (39-6)679-2651,* which crowns the Spanish Steps, has the best view and the best service. The rooms on the fifth floor have little balconies with tables and chairs and views of the Spanish Steps. If you prefer quiet (the steps can be noisy), the most peaceful rooms are in the back, overlooking the courtyard.

The Hassler has been in existence since 1855. The hotel feels like a grand old house or a private club. Its lobby is divided into cozy sitting areas. New rooms are painted cheery pastels; old rooms are decorated with mirrors, dark-wood furniture, and leather-covered paneling. Some of the bathrooms are painted with murals of ancient Roman baths. They all have scales, hair dryers, and heated towel racks.

The Hassler's guestbook contains the signatures of Liza Minelli, Charlie Chaplin, Somerset Maugham, and presidents Eisenhower, Truman, and Kennedy. Doubles are 400,000 lire to 480,000 lire per night. To make reservations in the United States, contact the **Leading Hotels of the World,** *(800)223-6800* or *(212)838-3110.*

Top contenders for second-best hotel

Le Grand Hotel, *via Vittorio Emanuele, Orlando 3, 00185 Rome; tel. (39-6)4709,* truly is a grand hotel. Romans prefer this hotel built above ancient Roman baths. Double rooms are 260,000 lire to 390,000 lire.

Hotel Locarno, *via della Penna 22; tel. (39-6)361-0841,* is popular with Italian artists, writers, and actors, but it has not been discovered by tourists. Intimate and inexpensive, it is near the Piazza del Popolo. Built in the 1920s, the Locarno has art-nouveau touches. Although it was recently renovated, it doesn't have modern (and intrusive) amenities, such as televisions. Double rooms are 135,000 lire.

Hotel Lord Byron, *via G. de Notaris 5; tel. (39-6)360-9541,* in the Parioli neighborhood, is one of the most elegant and discreet hotels in Rome. Set in a garden on a hill at the end of a one-way street near the Borghese Gardens, it is luxurious. Rooms have fine linen, refrigerators filled with champagne, and sumptuous marble bathtubs. The hotel restaurant, Le Jardin, is also outstanding. Double rooms are 380,000 lire a night, including breakfast.

Hotel Raphael, *Largo Febo 2; tel. (39-6)650-881,* just off the Piazza Navona, hosts Prime Minister Bettino Craxi when he is in Rome. Double rooms are 218,000 lire, including breakfast.

Best hotel bargains

Albergo del Sole al Pantheon, *Piazza della Rotonda 63; tel. (39-6)678-0441 or (39-6)679-34-90,* once hosted 16th-century poet Ludovico Ariosto. The hotel has a Renaissance facade, and its lobby is decorated with a fountain. Some rooms look out at the Pantheon and have private baths. Double rooms start at 53,800 lire. Breakfast is extra.

Hotel Columbus, *via della Conciliazione 33; tel. (39-6)656-5435,* is in a 15th-century cardinal's palace near St. Peter's. Plain on the outside, it is sumptuous inside, with sculptured, vaulted halls and rooms, coffered ceilings, carved stone fireplaces, antiques, and paintings. Double rooms start at 60,525 lire.

Scalinata di Spagna, *Piazza Trinita dei Monti 17; tel. (39-6)679-30-06 or (39-6)679-95-82,* is a cozy place near the Spanish Steps. One of the smallest hotels in Rome, it has 14 rooms on 2 floors—so make reservations in advance. The hotel has a long terrace with a vista of Rome. Rooms are simply furnished and have good views. Doubles are about 80,000 lire, including breakfast.

Gourmet bests

Alberto Ciarla, *Piazza San Cosimato 40; tel. (39-6)581-8668,* in the heart of the Trastevere (a colorful working-class neighborhood), is the place for seafood. Try the seafood spaghetti or the seasoned pasta with vegetables. The Tunia wine from Goriza is refreshing. Dinners are about 20,000 lire per person.

Andrea, *via Sardegna 28; tel. (39-6)49-37-07,* is the best place to go for Italian regional cooking. Instead of ordering from the menu, which is designed for tourists, ask the advice of the owner, Aldo, who will suggest unusual, mouth-watering dishes, such as the spaghetti with white truffles. Dinners are about 46,000 lire per person.

A tiny restaurant called **Cicilardone,** *via Merulana 77; tel. (39-6)73-38-06,* is the best bargain in town. Enormous dinners are served for about 26,660 lire. The pasta with broccoli and the vermicelli with cheese and pepper are especially delicious.

Il Drappo, *Vicolo del Malpasso 9; tel. (39-6)65-73-65,* serves creative variations of traditional Sardinian dishes. Near the via Giula, Il Drappo is sophisticated. Try the octopus with wine or the roast breast of veal. For dessert, order the *sedaba,* a cheese fritter topped with honey. Dinners are about 40,000 lire per person.

Ristorante da Sabatino, *Piazza S. Ignazio 169; tel. (39-6)79-7821,* is the homiest restaurant we've come across. This attractive restaurant near the 17th-century Church of San Ignazio has tables in the square. No menu is offered. Instead, a pleasantly round and cheerful *padrona* dishes out a great pot of pasta and oversees the waiters. The shrimp scampi, the specialty of the house, is fresh and delicious. A large plate of crisp, fresh green salad is served. The grand finale is a large bottle of Sambuca served with a glass containing coffee beans. You modify the sweetness of the liquor by crushing a coffee bean between your teeth and sipping the Sambuca through the cracked bean.

Tre Scalini Rossana e Matteo, *via Santi Quattro 30; tel. (39-6)73-26-95,* is an inconspicuous but well-frequented restaurant on a deserted street near the Coliseum. Politicians, bankers, and diplomats are drawn here by the good food and the privacy. Every day a single prix-fixe meal is served for about 35,000 lire. Reservations are required.

Night life at its most Roman

In general, Rome's night life is outdoors, centered around three piazzas. **Piazza di Santa Maria** in Trastevere (Rome's Greenwich Village) is filled with street musicians at all hours of the night. **Piazza Navona,** the most beautiful, stretches between three fountains that are surrounded by vendors. The most fashionable crowd, dressed in leather miniskirts and traveling on shiny motorbikes, appears at the cafés in **Piazza del Pantheon.**

The jet set, however, goes indoors and first-class. And the place they go is **Bella Blu,** *via Luciani 60, 00197; tel. (39-6)360-8840.* Blue-tinted mirrors decorate this small, fashionable nightclub. You can spot actors and Roman nobility on the dance floor.

The most elegant bar in Rome is the outdoor bar of the **Hassler Hotel,** *Piazza Trinità dei Monti 6; tel. (39-6)78-2651.* This enchanted locus, pushed against the verdant bluff of the Villa Medici garden, is a perfect place for starting or finishing an evening in Rome. The elegant red marble bar is tended by an amiable and knowledgeable Roman.

Florence—the most beautiful city

Florence is the most beautiful city in this country of lovely places. Ringed by hills, its streets are lined with red-tiled houses. Graceful domes rise from curving, narrow, cobblestoned streets. The ochre-colored walls of the ancient buildings are decorated with weathered gargoyles and faded coats of arms.

Within Florence are some of the greatest artworks in the world. For three centuries, from Giotto to Michelangelo, Florence was the center of the art world. Paintings and frescoes by the great Renaissance masters decorate even the most mundane churches.

The best way to see Florence is on foot. Don't drive through Florence—the convoluted streets are a navigational nightmare. Parking is even worse—spaces are hard to find, and tickets are a way of life. Besides, most everything is within walking distance.

The world's finest Renaissance art

The immense **Uffizi Museum** has the world's greatest collection of Renaissance art, including paintings by Giotto, Raphael, Titian, and Botticelli. The museum also has a room of modern art. Be sure to see the newly restored *Doni Tondo* by Michelangelo and Botticelli's *Birth of Venus.* The room containing Botticelli's *Primavera, Birth of Venus, Madonna della Melagrana,* and *Pallas and the Centaur* is the most impressive.

The largest dome in Christendom

Il Duomo, one of the world's largest cathedrals, is topped with the largest dome in Christendom. Its marble walls are striped with alternating colors. For this reason, it has been called the Cathedral in Pajamas. Built in 1296 by Brunelleschi, its vast walls are decorated with frescoes illustrating Dante's *Divine Comedy* and works by Ucello. Climb up into the dome for a terrific view of Florence (it is open every day except Sundays between 8:30 a.m. and 12:30 p.m. and 2:30 p.m. and 4:30 p.m.).

Many of the treasures of Il Duomo are stored at **Museo dell'Opera del Duomo,** *Piazza del Duomo 9,* a house behind the church. It contains a pietà by Michelangelo that was never finished and Donatello's *Santa Maria Maddalena,* a nude statue covered only by her hair.

The Gates of Paradise

The **Baptistery,** an octagonal building in Piazza del Duomo dedicated to St. John the Baptist, is famous for its three sets of gilded bronze doors. Michelangelo called the east doors facing the cathedral the "Gates of Paradise." Begun in 1425 by Ghilberti, they weren't completed until 1452, when the artist was 74. They are made up of 10 panels that illustrate the Old Testament. On the Feast of St. John (June 24), the relics of the saint are displayed in the Baptistery, and candles are lit in his honor.

The six most important sights

Pitti Palace, a huge structure built by Renaissance banker Luca Pitti is now divided into five museums, including the Palatine Picture Gallery, where works by Titian, Raphael, and Rubens are displayed. The Silver Museum houses Lorenzo de Medici's vases. The Pitti's Monumental Apartments were once the living quarters for the Royal House of Savoy.

Santa Croce, a striped-marble church, has frescoes by Giotto. The most elegant church in Florence, it contains tombs and monuments to Michelangelo, Galileo, Machiavelli, and Dante. Go through the sacristy into the Leather School started by the monks about 30 years ago.

Accademia is where the original of Michelangelo's magnificent *David* stands. The lines to this museum are incredibly long, however. The worst times to visit are Sundays and Tuesdays; the best times are 8 a.m. and noon, when the lines are shortest.

Bargello, the national museum, was once a fortress that served as a prison. In centuries past, men were strung out of the tower for their misdeeds. Today, the building contains the best of Florentine sculpture. Several early Michelangelos are housed here, including his first unfinished *David* and his statue of Bacchus. Upstairs are Giambologna's bronze animals created for a Medici garden grotto. This museum doesn't draw the crowds it merits.

The **Basilica of San Lorenzo** and the **Palazzo Medici** were built by the Medici family north of the Duomo. Brunelleschi began work on the church in 1419, incorporating the coat of arms of the Medicis in the design. Donatello's sculpture fills the church, and Filippo Lippi designed the altarpiece. The Medici Chapel, adjacent to the basilica, can be reached only from outside. Actually a mausoleum, the chapel has two sections: the Princes' Chapel, which contains the tombs of six Medici grand dukes, and the New Sacristy (Sagrestia Nuova), built by Michelangelo.

Santa Maria Novella is a grand church with splendid frescoes by Ghirlandaio and Filippino Lippi. They are best seen on a sunny day; the chapels are dark. The wealthy merchants of Florence had special chapels built in their honors in this church. Alberti designed the top half of the facade of the church and one of the chapels. And the choir contains Ghirlandaio's most important frescoes, which his student, Michelangelo, helped to create. The cloister of the church is colored with Uccello's frescoes.

Florence's best bridge

Ponte Vecchio, a bridge dating back to Roman times, is lined with goldsmith shops and street musicians. Butchers and tanners originally plied their trade on this bridge, but they were ousted by the Medici family in favor of the more seemly goldsmiths. During World War II, the commander in charge of the German army's retreat refused to blow up the bridge. Instead, he destroyed the buildings at its base so the rubble would block the span.

The prettiest Florentine church

San Miniato al Monte, one of the oldest churches in Florence, has an inlaid marble facade with 13th-century mosaics. Inside, the pavement is patterned with astrological signs, lions, and doves. The church contains superb Della Robbia terra-cottas. You can hear a Gregorian chant at San Miniato al Monte daily starting at 4:45 p.m.

The most interesting shopping

The **Oltrarno,** or artisan quarter on the left bank of the Arno, is a maze of streets spreading out from the Pitti Palace and around the Church of Santo Spirito. Stop in at the workshops, where picture frames are gilded, furniture is restored, and metals are forged.

Vias Tornabuoni and della Vigna Nuova are fashionable shopping areas, where the big names in Italian fashion can be visited.

The best hotels in Florence

Villa Medici, *via il Prato 42; tel. (39-55)26-13-31,* is an elegant hotel in the former Sonnino de Renzis Palace. Among other world-famous guests who have stayed at the hotel are the Shah of Iran, Jack Lemmon, and Hubert Humphrey. The rooms are light, airy, and nicely decorated. The fifth-floor apartment has a terrace that looks out over the skyline of Florence.

Elegance greets you as you enter the lobby at the Medici: Oriental carpets warm the marble-tiled floor; the fireplace is copper-hooded; and through an enormous picture window an elaborate garden can be seen. At the center of the garden is an ancient fountain shaped like the Medici family crest. Double rooms are 335,000 lire, plus 18% tax.

Hotel Regency, *Piazza Massimo d'Azeglio 3, Florence 50125; tel. (39-55)24-52-47,* is certainly the most peaceful hotel in Florence. It is also elegant. Located in a restored old townhouse on a quiet tree-lined square, it is only a 10-minute walk from the center of town. The rooms are splendid, and a quiet walled garden is situated behind the hotel. Rooms are from 350,000 lire to 380,000 lire.

The most charming small hotel in Florence is the **Tornabuoni Beacci,** *via Tornabuoni 3, 50123 Florence, Italy; tel. (39-55)212-645* or *(800)366-1510,* run by Signora Orlandi-Beacci. This old-fashioned hotel has high ceilings, fine furniture, fresh flowers, and lovely rooms. Located in a 14th-century palace on via Tornabuoni, the Beacci occupies the three top floors of the building. Its windows look out over the mauve and coral rooftops of the city. Rooms are 98,000 lire per person, double occupancy.

Scenes from E.M. Forster's romantic *Room With a View* were filmed at **Pensione Quisisana e Pontevecchio,** *Lungarno Archibulsieri 4; tel. (39-55)216-692* or *(39-55)215-046.* A double room with bath is 118,500 lire, including breakfast.

The best dining

The most surprising Tuscan specialty is steak, which is terrific in Florence. To order it, ask for *bistecca alla Fiorentina.*

Our favorite restaurant in Florence is the **Enoteca Pinchiorri,** *via Ghibellina 87; tel. (39-55)24-27-57.* Located in the 15th-century Ciofi-Iacometti Palace, it has a pleasant courtyard for dining and serves nouvelle cuisine. The sweet-and-sour fish and sweetbread salad are good. The 60,000-bottle wine cellar is more than comprehensive. Reservations are required. Dinner for two is about 186,620 lire. Lunch is less expensive, 93,310 lire for two.

The best Tuscan cuisine is served at an inexpensive restaurant called **Trattoria La Beppa,** *via Erta Canina 6/R; tel. (39-55)29-63-90.* It's a friendly, family-style place, where everyone sits at long tables. An elaborate antipasto is served, followed by local specialties, such as rabbit, duck, or quail.

Da Noi, *via Fiesolana 46; tel. (39-55)242-917,* is a homey restaurant that requires reservations. Dishes are traditional, yet imaginative. Try the *crespelle* (crepes) stuffed with spinach and ricotta cheese. Save room for one of the marvelous desserts.

The best night life

The two best nightclubs in Florence are **Manila,** *Plazza Matteucci, Campi Bisenzio; tel. (39-55)894-121,* and **Tenax,** *via Pratense 47; tel. (39-55)373-050.* Manila is avant-garde and decorated with elaborate graffiti. The crowd is ultra-sophisticated. Tenax is in an enormous old warehouse on two floors. The clientele here is also very fashionable.

The best ice cream in Florence

Vivoli's, *via Isola delle Stinche 7,* behind the Santa Croce Square, is a great ice cream bar. The lines are long, but the choice of flavors is great and the ice cream out-of-this-world.

The most magical city: Venice

Venice, a city made up of 118 islets and held together by a maze of 150 narrow canals and 400 lacy bridges, has a magical air. The interlocking waterways are plied by graceful wooden gondolas. Domed churches look over the shadowed pedestrian streets, where throngs of people (but no cars) roam.

Venetians took refuge in their watery home after centuries of invasions by the likes of Attila the Hun, the Goths, and the Vandals. In A.D. 687, they elected a president, called a doge. He was the first in a line of 117 doges, each reigning for life, that ended in 1797.

The five most important sights

The heart of Venice is the **Piazza San Marco,** which is dominated by the beautiful basilica on one side and the Doge's Palace on the other. This huge square, with its five must sees, attracts flocks of pigeons as well as tourists.

Once the doge's private chapel, the **Basilica of San Marco** is now open to the public. Built in the ninth century to house the body of St. Mark, the basilica houses the saint's tomb, paintings by Titian, and the Pala d'Oro, a huge panel behind the altar bedecked with rubies, emeralds, sapphires, pearls, topazes, amethysts, and cloisonné figures, all set in gold. The basilica also has Byzantine treasures. These artifacts and the saint's body were the booty of the fourth crusade, taken from Constantinople by Doge Enrico Dandolo.

The **Palazzo Ducale** (Doge's Palace) is an ornate structure on the water. Its columns are carved with figures symbolizing the trades. On one side are the Quattro Mori, four Moorish warriors embracing each other. Inside are the doges' apartments, the senate chamber, and the Room of the Council of Ten, which is covered with beautiful paintings. The sinister box outside is intended to receive denunciations of traitors or criminals.

The **Bridge of Sighs** passes between the Doge's Palace and the prisons where Casanova was once held. The covered bridge is so named because condemned prisoners sighed as they were led across it to their deaths. They were allowed one last look at Venice from the bridge before their executions.

The **Grand Canal** has been called the finest street in the world. It is lined with 200 marble-covered palaces built between the 12th and 18th centuries. Wagner died in the Palazzo Vendramin-Calergi, now the Municipal Casino. Lord Byron lived in the Palazzo Mocenigo. Gold leaf was used to coat the balls protruding on the facade of the Ca' D'Oro on the right bank. Its pointed arches were influenced by Islam. A good way to see these palazzi is to take a boat ride along the two-mile length of the canal. Take vaporetto (water bus) Number 1 or 4.

The **Galleria dell'Accademia** (Gallery of Fine Arts) houses paintings by Giorgione, Bellini, Tiepolo, Titian, and Canaletto. Admission is free except Sundays.

The Lido—the most fashionable Adriatic resort

Venice is protected from the rage of the Adriatic Sea by a beautiful sand spit called the **Lido.** A fashionable resort, the Lido draws visitors from around the world to its sandy beaches, elegant hotels, and swank casino. To get there, take vaporetto lines 1 and 2 from Venice across the Lagoon.

Before you go to the Lido, read *Death in Venice,* by Thomas Mann. And (if you can afford it) stay at the legendary **Grand Hotel des Bains,** *Lungomare Marconi 17; tel. (39-41)76-59-21,* where Mann's character, Hans Aschenbach, spent his last days. Rooms are expensive, from 336,250 lire to 672,500 lire a night for a double.

The romantic islands of the Lagoon

The **Lagoon** is filled with romantic little islands that can be reached by vaporetto. (Boat 12 leaves from the Fondamenta Nuove, near Campo dei Gesuiti, for Murano, Burano, and Torcello.) Burano and Torcello have especially inviting beaches, fishing villages, and small art museums. Murano is famous for its glass-making.

Burano Island, actually four tiny islets connected by bridges, is a half-hour waterbus ride from the mainland. Everything here is miniature—the canals and bridges are tiny, and the colorfully painted houses look as if they were built for dwarfs. Burano has its own leaning tower, the bell tower of the **Church of San Martino,** *Piazza Baldassare Galuppi.*

However, the island is best-known for its lace-making. Wherever you go on Burano you will see old ladies knitting lace and selling it from outdoor tables. You can buy handmade lace doilies, lace tablecloths, lace mats, hankies, baby bibs, and collars. Prices start at about $2.

Murano Island has dozens of workshops where you can watch glass being blown. The **Museo Vetrario,** *Fondamenta Giustinian,* along the main canal, has an immense collection of glass from the Roman times to the present. It is closed Wednesdays.

San Francesco del Deserto is a tiny, cypress-covered island inhabited by Franciscan monks. According to legend, St. Francis of Assisi was shipwrecked here in 1220. His wooden staff, which he stuck in the ground, turned into a tree, part of which still can be seen. Gardens and lawns surround the cloister and church. Peacocks and bantams wander the grounds freely.

A surprisingly pleasant island is Venice's cemetery, **San Michele**, which is filled with shade trees, flower gardens, and leaf-covered paths. Ornate tombs and mausoleums are surrounded by gardens and terraces. The ferry boat to San Michele is free on Sundays. The entrance is through the cloister of the island's 15th-century church.

The island of **San Lazzaro** has been the site of an Armenian monastery for 200 years. A priest dressed in a black cassock and sporting a heavy beard will give you a two-hour tour of the cloister, which contains an Egyptian mummy, Armenian paintings, ivories from the Orient, and the room where Lord Byron lived in 1816, when he decided to learn Armenian. One of the rooms contains a collection of rare illuminated manuscripts.

Gondolas—romance supreme

Thomas Mann wrote, "Is there anyone but must repress a secret thrill, on arriving in Venice for the first time—or returning thither after a long absence—and stepping into a Venetian gondola? That singular conveyance, come down unchanged from ballad times, black as nothing else on earth except a coffin—what pictures it calls up of lawless, silent adventures in the plashing night...And has anyone remarked that the seat in such a bark, the arm-chair...is the softest, most luxurious, most relaxing seat in the world?"

Long gondola rides, unfortunately, must be reserved for the wealthy or the frivolous. The authorized rate starts at 40,000 lire per 50 minutes—but most gondoliers charge 90,000 lire. Gondolas are rented at Piazzale Roma, the San Marco ferry stop, Campo San Moise, and other points along the canals.

At several points along the Grand Canal where you can't cross via a bridge, you can take a short but cheap gondola ride for about 200 lire. Rides can be taken from south of Campo S. Toma and from Campo del Traghetto to Dorsoduro.

The greatest opera house

Gran Teatro La Fenice, *Campo San Fantin, 30124 Venice, Italy; tel. (39-41)71061,* is one of the greatest opera houses in the world. The 18th-century decor is graceful, with chandeliers, plush armchairs, box seats, mirrored corridors, parquet floors, and a grand staircase with marble columns. The acoustics are flawless.

You cannot make reservations for an opera by telephone; you must visit the box office in person between 9:30 a.m. and 12:30 p.m. or one hour before an evening performance.

The most fantastic hotel in Europe

Venice has the most fantastic hotel in Europe, the luxurious **Hotel Cipriani,** on Giudecca Island. A polished motorboat fetches guests at the Piazza San Marco. Rooms have private, flower-bedecked terraces that gaze out over the water. Marble bathrooms have sliding, hidden doors that open into the bedroom. Excellent seafood is prepared in the dining room. The Cipriani has Venice's only tennis courts and its largest swimming pool. Mitterand and Kissinger are among the dignitaries who have stayed here. Double rooms are 490,000 lire to 690,000 lire per night. To make reservations in the United States, contact **Leading Hotels of the World,** *747 Third Ave., New York, NY 10017; (800)223-6800.*

Venice's homiest hotels

Casa Frollo, *Guidecca 50, Venice 30123; tel. (39-41)522-2723,* is a peaceful establishment in a terraced 17th-century palace. It has a view of Piazza San Marco and the Doge's Palace. Rooms are furnished with Renaissance furniture, and good paintings hang on the walls. The courtyard is cool and colorful. Not all rooms have private baths. Rooms at the front have views of the canal. The hotel is closed from December through February. Doubles start at 69,000 lire.

Pensione Accademia, *Fondamenta Maravegie, Dorsoduro 1058, Venice 30123; tel. (39-41)523-7846 or (39-41)710-188,* located in a 17th-century villa faces a side canal near the Grand Canal at the Accademia bridge. Rooms are elegant, and breakfast and afternoon tea are served at little pink-clothed tables on the patio. Not all rooms have private bathrooms. Double rooms start at 100,000 lire.

Hotel Torino, *via 22 Marzo, Venice 30124; tel. (39-41)705-222,* located in a 14th-century palace between San Marco and Santa Maria del Giglio, is noted for its tiny wrought-iron balconies and flowers. Double rooms start at 120,000 lire.

La Fenice des Artistes, *Campiello de la Fenice 1936, Venice 30124; tel. (39-41)523-2333,* is a quiet hotel behind the Fenice Opera House. The courtyard, where breakfast and drinks are served, backs up onto a canal. Rooms are comfortable. Try to get one at the back. Double rooms start at 127,000 lire.

Hotel Flora, *Calle Bergamaschi 2283/a, Venice 30124; tel. (39-41)705-844,* attracts English travelers. Although it's centrally located, it is quiet and has a gorgeous garden with ivy-clad walls, fountains, flowers, and tables for breakfast and drinks. Some of the rooms are spacious and decorated with painted furniture; others are plainer. Doubles are 168,000 lire.

The best Venetian restaurants

Antica Bessetta, *Santa Croce Salizzada 1395, Zusto, Venice; tel. (39-41)523-7229,* near San Giacomo dell'Orio, is the best place to go for authentic Venetian cuisine. The restaurant is hidden in the back streets of Venice and is very difficult to find.

Corte Sconta, *Calle del Pestrin 3886, Venice; tel. (39-41)27-024,* is the coziest bistro in Venice. Located in the old part of town, behind the Riva degli Schiavoni, it is tiny but very popular. You must make a reservation (preferably two days in advance) or you won't get a table.

Harry's Bar, *Calle Vallaresso 1323, 30124 Venice; tel. (39-41)523-6797,* has two Michelin stars and was one of Hemingway's favorites. Only a few minutes from the piazzetta on the Piazza San Marco, it has been owned and run by the Cipriani family for 50 years.

Europe's largest maze

The largest and most complicated maze in Europe is in Stra, 18 miles south of Venice. Here, the odds are a zillion to one that you will get lost. **Il Labirinto,** as it is known in Italy, is part of the stately gardens of the Villa Pisani. This life-size puzzle is one-third the size of a football field and has four miles of paths lined with tall, thick hedges. Napoleon got himself lost in Il Labirinto in 1807 and had to be rescued. If you too get lost, the caretaker, who has been here for 47 years, will rescue you. He can reach the tower at the center of the maze in three minutes. (You may not photograph the maze from any angle.)

Mantua: Venice without the crowds

Mantua has the charm of Venice without the crowds. The River Mincio wraps around the ducal city like a cloak and threads its way through the city via little canals. Graceful bridges cross the winding waterways. Once the seat of one of the most brilliant courts of Europe, today it is one of the best-preserved medieval cities in Italy.

Mantua feels medieval; it has no modern industry and no high-rise buildings. The **Ducal Palace,** built in the Middle Ages, is actually three interconnected buildings. The palace has 500 rooms, 7 gardens, and 8 courtyards. Frescoes by Pisanello depicting episodes from chivalric tales hang in the Hall of Dukes. Painted in 1440, they were rediscovered in 1969 under two coats of plaster. In the Camera degli Sposi (bridal chamber), built in 1474, hang Andrea Mantegna's frescoes of the Gonzaga family.

A guide is mandatory when you visit the Ducal Palace, but you can explore at your own pace. Take a good guidebook with you. *Mantova Guida Pratica ed Artistica con Pianta della Citta,* by Loretta Santini, is a good one. It is available in English at Mantua bookstores.

After the Ducal Palace, the two most important sights in Mantua are the **Church of Sant' Andrea** and the **Palazzo Te.** The Church of Sant' Andrea has a coffered ceiling and grandiose arches more reminiscent of the Pantheon than a Christian church. This is a good place to get a feeling for the time when the Pagan and Christian worlds met.

The Palazzo Te was a pleasure palace for Federico, the favorite son of Mantua's great lady, Isabella d'Este. Here Federico entertained his mistress for 10 years. The ballroom is decorated with a painting of Federico's favorite horses. Halls are painted with scenes from the Battle of the Titans, the story of David, and the myth of Psyche. Paintings of classical fables cover the scalloped ceiling of Federico's bedroom.

When you tire of sightseeing, enjoy Mantua's delicious egg pasta at **Il Cigno,** *Piazza d'Arco 1; tel. (39-376)327-101,* opposite the Palazzo d'Arco.

Two comfortable hotels in Mantua are the **San Lorenzo,** *Piazza Concordia 14; tel. (39-376) 327-153,* and **Hotel Rechigi,** *via Calvi 30; tel. (39-376)320-718.*

Naples: the most Italian city

Tourists shy away from **Naples,** because of its reputation for crime—although the crime situation here is actually no worse than in New York and other major cities. Because of its rather undeserved bad reputation, Naples is a truly Italian city—free of crowds of gaping foreigners.

A huge, hilly town in the shadows of Mt. Vesuvius, Naples is cooled by the breezes of the Gulf of Naples. The city's waterfront is lined with men and booths selling drinks.

Neapolitans have a lugubrious interest in the macabre. In the **Cappella Sansevero,** for example, is the 16th-century corpse of a family servant mysteriously preserved by the alchemy of the duke of Sansevero. Thousands of capilleries can be seen through the skin of the body. The chapel, which is hidden on a small side street off Piazza San Domenico Maggiore, also holds an uncanny effigy of the body of Christ covered in diaphanous veils carved by the sculptor Sammartino.

The most important sight

The cathedral in Naples is dedicated to San Gennaro. It was built in the 13th century on the site of a previous basilica dedicated to Santa Stefania. The original basilica was built on the foundations of a Roman temple dedicated to Apollo.

Within the cathedral are an ancient round baptistery, which has a deep baptismal pool and mosaics from the fifth century; the Byzantine basilica of Santa Restituta, attached to the north wall of the duomo; and the 17th-century chapel, which holds San Gennaro's head and blood. The blood has liquified from its crystalized state the first Sunday in May and Sept. 19 nearly every year since the Middle Ages. Great crowds gather to see this miracle. If the blood does not liquefy, it is believed that a disaster will happen. (Great importance is placed on San Gennaro in Naples. When Mt. Vesuvius acts up, for instance, the saint's image is taken to the mountain as a pacifier.)

The world's best antiquities

Il **Museo Archeologico Nazionale** in Naples houses one of the most important collections of Greek and Roman antiquities in the world, including many of the treasures excavated from Pompeii and Herculaneum. Among these treasures are the *Young Satyr,* a graceful figure carrying a wine casket, and the famous statues of Apollo and Diana, which once stood at Pompeii's Temple of Apollo. You can't miss the *Farnese Bull,* the largest surviving sculpture from antiquity, carved out of a single block of marble.

Naples' best Renaissance museum

Outside Naples is the **Capodimonte Museum and Picture Gallery,** which houses one of Italy's best collections of paintings from the 14th to 16th centuries. Located in an 18th-century palace in the hills northeast of the city and surrounded by a park, it contains works by Bellini, Botticelli, Correggio, and Titian. Capodimonte is also a famous porcelain.

The best people watching

In the evening, join the Neapolitans in their nightly stroll along the **Lungomare,** a broad promenade along Santa Lucia Port (subject of the famous folk song *Santa Lucia*).

Also in this area is the **Castel dell'Ovo,** *via Partenope,* which sticks out like an island in the bay, and the **Castel Nuovo,** *Piazza Municipio.* Both host evening concerts and exhibitions.

Night life at its hottest

Naples' night life can be found in and around vias Caracciolo and Partenope, commonly referred to as the **Margellina quarter.** Within walking distance is the **San Carlo Theater,** *via San Carlo,* renowned for classical music and dance. Information on the performances here can be obtained at the box office, which is open from 10 a.m. to 1 p.m. and 4:30 p.m. to 6:30 p.m. every day except Mondays.

Naples' nightclubs and discos usually begin to swing at about 10 p.m., when most people have eaten and are ready for some activity. **Il Gabbiano,** *via Partenope 26; tel. (39-81)411-666,* attracts beautiful internationals.

Best ways to thwart thieves

Pickpockets are common in Naples, and they make their livings off tourists. Don't drape your purse over your shoulder. Thieves on motorbikes grab bags as they zoom past, often dragging the person along with the bag. Thieves generally work in pairs. They pull up to people carrying shoulder bags or camera bags. One thug hops off the bike, grabs the loot, hops back on, and the pair speeds away.

Avoid carrying a wallet in your back pocket. Leave all jewelry—including watches—in your hotel. It's best to carry limited amounts of cash and your passport and credit cards in the inside pocket of a jacket or a front pocket of your pants.

When driving, never put anything in the back window of the car. Traffic in Naples is dense, and thieves often break rear windows of cars stuck in traffic jams. And don't leave things in parked cars—not even in the trunks. Most rental cars in Italy have Milan tags, and thieves look for them around hotels, restaurants, and museums.

The most delicious fare

Avellinese da Peppino, *via Silvio Spaventa 31-35; tel. (39-81)28-38-97,* is a friendly place with cheap but good seafood. Try the *pesce frigole,* a mixture of crayfish, octopus, squid, mussels, and clams. Italian singers serenade you as you dine.

La Cantinella, *via Cuma 42; tel. (39-81)40-48-84* or *(39-81)40-53-75,* is a favorite among Neapolitans. The clams and mussels cooked with garlic, parsley, and tomato and served with linguine are exquisite. Dinner for two is about 80,700 lire. The restaurant is closed Sundays.

La Fazenda, *Calata Marechiaro 58; tel. (39-81)769-7420,* serves the best Neapolitan dishes, including home-raised chickens. This rustic restaurant has spectacular views of the bay and is decorated with a profusion of flowers. It is closed Sundays and for two weeks in August. Dinner for two is about 80,700 lire.

Il Gallo Nero, *via Tasso 466; tel. (39-81)64-30-12,* is in an antique-filled 19th-century villa. Dine on the terrace, where you'll have a splendid view of Mergellina. The fresh fish is terrific. Dinner for two is about 80,000 lire.

Sleeping beautifully

The most luxurious hotels in Naples are the Excelsior and the Vesuvio. The **Excelsior,** *via Partenope 48; tel. (39-81)41-71-11,* has terraced seaside rooms with views of the Castel dell'Ovo and the bay. Its restaurant is good. The rather sparsely furnished and old-fashioned double rooms start at 134,000 lire.

The **Vesuvio,** *via Partenope 45; tel. (39-81)41-70-44,* faces the port of Santa Lucia and has a variety of rooms ranging in style from antique to modern. It has air conditioning and a garage. Double rooms start at 134,000 lire.

The strangest sight: the door to the Underworld

Near Naples is one of the strangest sights in Italy—the cave said to have been the door to the Underworld of ancient mythology. Very few people visit the infamous **Grotta della Sibilla,** as it is known.

In the *Aeneid,* the Roman poet Virgil described the cave: "A deep, deep cave there was, its mouth enormously gaping/Shingly, protected by the dark lake and the forest gloom:/Above it, no winged creatures could ever wing their way/With fuming up from its black throat to the vault of heaven:/Wherefore the Greeks called it Avernus, the Birdless Place."

Alessandro, the elderly guide who has given tours and told the tale of the cave for the past 50 years, begins his tour at the entrance of **Lago di Avernus.**

According to the guide, Lago di Avernus was once a volcanic flat whose bubbling mud and sulphur fumes rose into the sky. Because the fumes were poisonous, birds flying over would die and fall into the inferno (*avernus* means *no birds* in Latin). This description matches Virgil's. When Mt. Vesuvius erupted, the volcanic action stopped here, and the crater filled with water. The eruption cut off the tunnel leading to the Underworld.

The guided tour takes about an hour. While no set admission is charged, most visitors tip Signor Alessandro at least 1,000 lira. Open Fridays, Saturdays, and Sundays from 9 a.m. to 5 p.m. and on weekdays from 11 a.m. to 3 p.m.

To get to the cave from the via Domitiana in Naples, turn left after the Olivetti factory toward Archo Felice. At the intersection, turn right onto via Miliscola, which goes along the waterfront toward Baia. Go about one mile, past a newsstand, the Lido di Napoli, and the Sibilla restaurant. A sign points right toward a bumpy road that takes you to a brick wall on your left marked with a white painted sign indicating Grotta della Sibilla.

Volcanic bests

Mt. Vesuvius, 15 miles southeast of Naples, can be seen from the city on a clear day. If you'd like to get closer to Mt. Vesuvius, you can actually hike up to the crater. But remember, it was Vesuvius that did away with Pompeii. It last erupted in 1944, and it averages one eruption every 35 years. You can take a chair lift up to the top, or you can drive part way and then walk. Take the Ercolano exit from the Autostrada, then drive 15 kilometers up a zigzagging path across a sort of moonscape. The oval crater, when you finally get there, is 2,000 feet wide and 525 feet deep. Wisps of smoke rise from the top. If you yell your name, Vesuvius will echo it back.

Pompeii and Herculaneum: the world's best ruins

Pompeii and **Herculaneum,** once bedroom suburbs of Roman Naples, were destroyed when Mt. Vesuvius erupted in A.D. 79. Today, the ruins are preserved in volcanic ash illustrations of everyday life nearly 2,000 years ago. Explore the shops, baths, and houses of ordinary Roman families.

While Pompeii is packed with tourists, Herculaneum is not. What's more, Herculaneum is closer to Naples, and it is better preserved than Pompeii. Known as Ercolano in Italian, Herculaneum once had 5,000 inhabitants. Much of the town remains unexcavated beneath the modern town of Resina. However, among the ruins that have been excavated you'll see cakes in ovens, eggs in cupboards, chicken bones on kitchen tables, fishnets and hooks on a line, and graffiti on bathroom walls. One of the houses has a small cross, the oldest evidence of Christianity in the Roman Empire. The baths are the most interesting sights. You can see cold, warm, and hot water baths, a gym, and a swimming pool. The skeletons of bath attendants have been preserved intact in the men's cloakroom.

The best-preserved Greek temples

The best-preserved Greek Doric temples stand by the sea in **Paestum,** ancient Poseidonia, not far from Naples. The ancient structures are surrounded by a field of flowers and wild grasses. The three major temples are along the ancient via Sacra. The basilica, which is dedicated to Hera, is the oldest, dating back to the sixth century B.C. Next to the basilica is the Temple of Neptune (450 B.C.), one of the most beautiful Doric temples in the world. It is 6 columns across and 14 columns long. See the frescoes of a diver and a dinner party, the earliest surviving Greek paintings, in the museum across the street from the ruins.

The best of the Amalfi Coast

The **Amalfi Coast,** a mountainous peninsula between the Gulf of Naples and the Gulf of Salerno, is a land of legends. Pirates once used the secluded inlets as hideouts. Spectacular views can be enjoyed from the dizzying summits of the mountains. Serpentine roads wind through cliffside villages. Olive groves and grape vines dot the plains.

In July or August, the Amalfi Coast becomes a madhouse, and it is nearly impossible to drive. The spring and fall are idyllic—warm and uncrowded.

The best coastal views

One of the most breathtaking views on the coast is from the old **Capuchin Monastery,** perched on a cliff above Amalfi. An elevator takes you up to the 12th-century building, which today is an inexpensive hotel (rooms are about 47,000 lire a night), *via Annunziatella 46; tel. (39-89)87-10-08.* Theodore Roosevelt and Henry Wadsworth Longfellow have stayed here.

You still can visit a chapel and cloisters within the hotel. The foundations of the convent, which is perched on a sheer cliff, date back to A.D. 1000. Bus service connects the hotel with the beach. If you ask, the staff will pack you a picnic lunch.

Another spectacular view is from the little town of **Ravello,** above Amalfi. A bus will take you to this summit via narrow, twisting roads. **Villa Rufolo,** *84010 Ravello (Salerno); tel. (39-89)85-71-33,* is a lovely 11th-century building now used as an inexpensive hotel (about 40,000 lire a night). It has gorgeous gardens filled with hydrangeas and a Moorish cloister overgrown with flowers. During the summer, concerts are staged here. The villa was once the residence of Pope Adrian IV, the only English pope, who reigned from 1154-1159. Lord Byron, Greta Garbo, and composer Richard Wagner have stayed in here.

The cathedral in Ravello has sculptures of strange-looking animals and contains a reliquary with the skull of Santa Barbara. The blood of the town's patron saint, San Pantaleone, is preserved in a cracked vessel that never leaks (or so it is said).

Hotel Caruso Belvedere, *84010 Ravello (Salerno); tel. (39-89)857-111,* set 900 feet above the Mediterranean coast, has sweeping views of the sea through its arched terrace. This well-known hotel is in the 11th-century d'Afflito Palace. Wines from surrounding vineyards are served in the restaurant. Most rooms have private bathrooms and private balconies. Double rooms start at 40,000 lire.

Hotel Palumbo, *via S. Giovanni del Toro 28, 84010 Ravello (Salerno); tel. (39-89)857-244,* perched 1,200 feet above the coast, also has tremendous views. The 12th-century building was once the Palazzo Confalone. It is a pretty building, with arch and pillar vaulting, stone staircases, tile-inlaid floors, and good paintings. The hotel restaurant serves its own Ravello wines. Three-day stays are requested. Rooms are about 60,475 lire a night.

Capri: Italy's most beautiful island

Capri (pronounced KAH-pree) is a beautiful but crowded island that can be reached by hydrofoil from Naples, Sorrento, or Pozzuoli. After the boat ride, relax and have a pleasant lunch on the terrace of the Hotel Belvedere Tre Re, on the harbor. Take a funicular from the harbor up to the town of Capri. The best view is from the top of Mt. Solaro, where an old monastery stands. To get there, take a bus to Anacapri, then a chair lift to the summit.

The Blue Grotto sea caves are lovely, but touristy. Visit the pagan shrine of the Matromania Cave. Roman Emperor Tiberius built 12 villas on the island to honor the 12 Roman deities. You can best sense his might around Villa Jovis, his headquarters for a decade.

Hotels on the island book up fast, so reservations are a must. One of the most romantic is **Scalanitella,** *via Tragara 8; tel. (39-81)837-0633,* in the town of Capri. A staff member meets visitors upon arrival and leads them along the narrow streets to the little hotel. Cut into a steep and rocky hill, Scalanitella has a Moorish air. Its glistening marble lobby, winding corridors, classical paintings and busts, carved doors, floor-to-ceiling windows, outdoor garden, and little luxuries create a delightful atmosphere. Its pool is one of the best in Capri. Open from Easter to October. Rates range from 289,000 lire to 383,000 lire, including breakfast. Credit cards are not accepted.

The **Quisiana and Grand Hotel,** *tel. (39-81)837-0788,* attracts the jet set with large suites, wide arcades, and an ocean view. **Hotel Luna,** *tel. (39-81)837-0433,* combines old-fashioned style with modern conveniences. Rates are reasonable.

Good food is served at **La Sceriffa,** *via Acquaviva 29; tel. (39-81)837-7953.* **La Pigna,** *via Lo Palazzo 30; tel. (39-81)837-0280,* is another good bet.

The best of the Italian Riviera

The **Italian Riviera,** which stretches from the French border to Tuscany, is less expensive than the French Riviera and just as pretty. It lies within the prosperous northern region of **Liguria,** which has its own lingo and culture. The heart of Liguria is Genoa, a thriving seaport and a good place to stay if you find coastal resorts too pricey. North of Genoa is the Riviera di Levante (Coast of the Rising Sun). Below and to the east is the Riviera di Ponente (Coast of the Setting Sun).

During July and August rooms are almost impossible to come by. The best time to visit is spring or fall, when the weather is warm and hotel rooms are available.

The oldest resort on the Riviera

San Remo, the oldest resort on the Riviera, is overcrowded and overbuilt. But it has a casino and a yacht basin, and the hotels are affordable despite their Edwardian elegance (inexpensive ones are located along the via Matteotti). The **tourist office,** *Palazzo Riviera,* is helpful if you can't find a room.

San Remo has the most memorable restaurant on the Riviera: **Ristorante da Gianino,** *Corso Trento Trieste 23; tel. (39-184)70843.* This high-ceilinged, white-walled restaurant is trimmed in wood and filled with flowers in copper pots. Bamboo furniture gives it a summery charm. Try the *bianchetti,* a specialty of Northern Italy made of inch-long fish flavored lightly with chili and sautéed in olive oil or encased in a golden pancake. A meal for two is about 134,500 lire.

Where the crème de la crème rises

Italy's crème de la crème surfaces in **Portofino** during the summer. Very private and romantic, Portofino is one of the most photographed places in the world. Its remarkably deep natural harbor attracts yachtsmen from all over the world. Everyone who is anyone, from Lauren Bacall and Humphrey Bogart to Aristotle Onassis and Ernest Hemingway, has stayed here. Hike out to the lighthouse following the footpath marked *"al faro"* for a spectacular view of the coastline. For more information on Portofino, contact the **tourist office,** *via Roma; tel. (39-185)690-24.*

Hotel Splendido, *via Salita Baratta 13; tel. (39-185)69551,* is Portofino's most luxurious hotel. Perched in a spectacular setting above the yacht harbor, the hotel was once a private house. It has an old-fashioned charm despite its modern swimming pool on the terrace. For reservations in the United States, contact **David B. Mitchell,** *(212)696-1323* or *(800)372-1323.*

The Riviera's most charming town

From the docks at the coastal town of Camogli, you can take a boat to **San Fruttoso,** the most charming town on the coast. This tiny fishing village on the Portofino Peninsula is accessible only by sea. It is surrounded by pines, olive trees, and oaks that lead down to the sea. Walk through the cloisters and corridors of the Benedictine Abbey of San Fruttoso di Capo di Monte, which consists of a 13th-century palace, an 11th-century church, and a Romanesque cloister.

Camogli has one of the best hotels along the coast, **Cenobio dei Dogi,** *via Cuneo 34, 16032 Camogli; tel. (39-185)770-041,* set in a manor house on the beach. Once the seat of the bishops of Genoa, this manor has lovely grounds, a beach, a swimming pool, tennis courts, facilities for the handicapped, and central heat. Double rooms are about 60,525 lire a night.

Cinque Terre: the least crowded

At the southern end of the coast is one of the least crowded, most picturesque areas. The mountains, woods, vineyards, and hilltop villages of the Cinque Terre cover 15 miles of coastline. The area's five villages—Monterosso, Vernazza, Corniglia, Manarola, and Riomaggiore—are perched on the rocky coast north of La Spezia. Taste of the rare local wine, Sciacchetra.

Monterosso is the largest and most crowded town. But it has a beautiful beach at the southern end of the cove. You can rent boats here for about 6,725 lire an hour. Climb the hill to the Convento dei Cappuccini, which houses Van Dyck's *Crucifixion.* After the strenuous climb, relax at Gigante, Monterosso's best restaurant.

Hiking trails lead from Monterosso to Cinque Terre's quainter towns. A 1 1/2-hour hike along a goat path leads through vineyards and olive groves to **Vernazza.** Another hiking trail leads to **Corniglia,** which has a long, pebbly beach.

If you're up to another hour's walk, follow the trail along the jagged coast to **Manarola,** the most beautiful of the Cinque Terre towns. Here, yellow houses balance on cliffs, and artists and writers seek their muses.

The Alps at their cheapest

The **Dolomites** (Italian Alps) are just as beautiful as their French and Austrian counterparts, but visiting them is far less expensive. The skiing is almost as good as it is to the north, and the hiking can be even better.

Valle d'Aosta is just over the border from France. You can take a cable car to the Italian side from Chamonix, France for 33,625 lire. The panoramic view from the cable car is beautiful—and a bit scary if you fear heights at all.

Alto Badia, 50 miles south of the Brenner Pass through the Dolomites into Austria, is made up of little Tyrolean villages. This region has the beautiful scenery of Austria, but has lower prices, summer skiing, and good Italian restaurants. The best-known and largest among the hamlets is Corvara. Less-crowded are Colfosco, La Villa, Pedraces, and San Cassiano.

The best bargain skiing in the Dolomites

Cortina d'Ampezzo, in the eastern Dolomites, is Italy's most popular ski resort. Although it is crowded, it has some of the best ski facilities in Italy. The area is huge—you can ski for days without doubling back to redo the same runs. When you tire of skiing, you can ice skate in the remnants of the Olympic Stadium, shop in the town's many boutiques, or dine in one of its many restaurants.

Accommodations here are more expensive than in Mt. Livata or Pescasseroli, nearby. The **Cristallo Hotel,** *via R. Menardi 42, Cortina d'Ampezzo 32043, Italy; tel. (39-436)4281,* has spacious, well-appointed rooms and a good restaurant. It is open from mid-December through March and during late summer. Rooms are 150,640 lire to 251,515 lire, including three meals a day. To make reservations in the United States, contact **Ciga Hotels,** *tel. (212)935-9540.*

In **Courmayeur** and **Cervinia** you can ski in the summer as well as the winter. These towns are well-known—and pricey for Italy. The Val d'Ayas is undiscovered and has lower lift prices (and more challenging runs).

Colfosco, a small, quiet ski village with numerous runs, attracts ardent downhill skiers. The area is best-suited to beginning and intermediate skiers—it offers little cross-country skiing and no deep-powder skiing. Its major advantage over the larger, more crowded ski resorts is that it is part of the **Alta Badia,** a five-village ski association. With a Colfosco lift ticket (which costs about 134,500 lire a week), you have access to 75 miles of trails and 53 lifts. For an additional 6,725 lire you can buy the Super Dolomite lift pass, which gives you access to 10 major ski areas that include 650 miles of trails and 430 lifts (not all of them easily accessible). For more information, contact **Azienda Autonoma di Soggiono e Tourismo Corvara-Colfosco,** *39003 Corvara, Badia; tel. (39-471)836-176.*

Hotel Colfosco Hof, *39003 Colfosco, Corvara, Badia; tel. (39-471)836-188,* at the first curve of the Grodner Pass, is the most pleasant hotel in the area. It has good hearty food, a pool, a sauna, and a squash court. Rooms range from 147,950 lire to 209,820 lire, double occupancy, including breakfast and dinner.

For more information on skiing in the Dolomites, contact the **Ufficio Informazioni Turistiche,** *Piazza Chanoux 8, 11100 Aosta.*

The best hiking

Hiking is also terrific in the Dolomites, which are crisscrossed by trails. Bring hiking boots, a windbreaker, a sweater, socks, and gloves. The best time is August and September, when the snow has melted completely. Don't hike in April and May unless you are an expert. The melting snow causes avalanches.

Pedraces, near the Austrian border, is one of the best places for hiking. For one of the most scenic routes, take a chair lift to the foot of the Croce Mountains, then follow Trail 7.

The **National Park of Abruzzi,** near Pescasseroli, is another beautiful place to hike. The trails, which are named for animals, wander through a forest of pine trees blanketed with snow.

The **Grand Hotel del Parco,** *67032 Pescasseroli, Italy; tel. (39-863)91-356,* is the most comfortable hotel in town. Rooms are about 84,735 lire.

The best base for exploring

Aosta is the best base for exploring the Italian peaks. Near mountain trails and several old castles, it has Roman ruins dating from the time of the Emperor Augustus, including a Roman theater, two Roman gates, the Porta Praetoria, and the Arco di Augusto.

The cloister of the medieval **Church of St. Ursus** dates back to A.D. 1000. St. Ursus, who converted the first Christians in the valley, is buried in a crypt below the altar. Modern history can be contemplated at the **Istituto Storico della Resistenza della Valle d'Aosta,** *Xavier de Maistre 22,* which documents the Italian resistance during World War II.

Make hotel reservations early if you plan to be in Aosta in July or August or during the Christmas or Easter seasons. A good place to stay is **Mancuso,** *via Voison 32.* This family-run hotel is clean and has inviting rooms. The hotel restaurant is good and inexpensive.

Italy's most beautiful national park

The **Gran Paradiso National Park** in the Valle d'Aosta is 363 square miles of protected area set aside for wildlife. The park has breathtaking scenery, ibex, wildflowers, and hiking trails. **Cogne** is the best base for exploring the park. You can get there from Aosta by bus. From Cogne, walk to Valnontey, then take Trail 2, which climbs to Rifugio V. Sella. The view from the refuge is mind-boggling. Stop to eat or spend the night, then set out on the six-hour trek to Eau Rousse in Valsavaranche. Again, the views are incredible. Here, stay at the Hotel Col Lauson, a clean little establishment with terrific meals.

Sleeping like royalty in the Italian Alps

A number of old castles have been made into hotels in the mountains of Italy. **Castello Vorst,** *Foresta 39022, Lagundo (Merano),* is one of the most ancient castle hotels in Europe. It incorporates a Roman fortress tower and the feudal castle of Prince Meinhard I of Tyrol, built in 1226. Although the castle has been renovated, its medieval character has been preserved. Rooms are furnished with antiques. A glassed-in sun deck on the tower, an indoor pool, and elevators are modern additions. The dungeon has been made into a cozy bar. Rooms are about 33,625 lire per person.

Schloss Rundegg, *via Scena 2, 39012 Merano; tel. (39-473)34-364,* is an old castle nestled in the mountains of southern Tyrol. Parts, including the square towers, date back to the 12th century. The main structure dates to 1580. Public rooms have grand staircases, vaulted ceilings, and arches. Private rooms are furnished with antiques. A pool, sauna, solarium, and massage center are open to guests. Rooms start at 60,000 lire.

The best of the Italian lake district

Italy's Lake Country has steeply rolling hills and a Mediterranean touch. Olive groves and palm trees surround the warm waters.

The largest and clearest lake

Lake Garda is the largest, clearest, and most visited of the Italian lakes. It is surrounded with Mediterranean scenery—rugged, tawny hills dotted with olive and lemon groves and long, shuttered farmhouses. Desenzano, one of the lake's major and most crowded towns, lies on the Venice-Milan train line. From there, it's easy to get to the other lake towns by bus or boat.

Torbole, at the far end of Lake Garda, is the windsurfing capital of Europe because of the steady breezes that blow across the lake.

Europe's deepest lake

Lake Como is Europe's deepest lake. Sadly, it is too polluted for swimming near the main towns of Como and Bellagio. Como is worldly, wealthy, and refined. Its duomo is one of the most famous churches in Italy. Built between 1457 and 1485, it has a lovely rose window and houses Bernardino Luini's (1475-1533) *Adoration of the Magi.*

The artists' favorite

Bellagio, the lake district's art center, invites artists to spend a month or more there developing works in progress. Located at the point where Lake Como intersects with Lake Lecco, it has narrow streets and ancient buildings. The beach is next to the Villa Serbelloni in the center of town.

The most entertaining restaurant

The most entertaining restaurant in the lake district is on an island in the middle of Lake Como. To get there, drive to Menaggio and then to the Isola Comacina. The restaurant is called, imaginatively, **Locanda dell'Isola Comacina.** Park your car at the edge of the lake, and a boatman will ferry you out to the island.

When you arrive, introduce yourself to the owner, Benvenuto Puricelli. He will show you to your table and start the food coming your way. You do not choose from a menu. The waiters simply bring you the evening's dishes—including warm bread straight from the oven and a vast selection of fresh vegetables, meat, and fish.

As a finale, Benvenuto turns out the lights and puts a torch to an alcoholic concoction. Then, as the liquor burns, he ladles the brew into the air in fiery garlands while reciting the history of the island. (According to legend, a curse was laid on the island in the 12th century.)

Although the restaurant is still obscure, it is acquiring an international reputation. It is one of Bruce Springsteen's favorites.

Europe's finest resort hotel

Villa d'Este, in Cernobbio on Lake Como, is one of Europe's finest resort hotels. Located in a 15th-century villa begun by Cardinal Gallio, it was later used as a palace by an empress of Russia, a princess of Wales, and other members of royalty. In 1873 it became a hotel. It is beautifully furnished and offers concerts, dances, tennis, golf, riding, swimming, watersports, and boating. Open from April to October, the Villa d'Este is very expensive.

The gem of the lakes

Floating in the middle of peaceful **Lago d'Orta** is emerald-green **San Giulio Island,** the little-known gem of the lakes. According to legend, St. Julius (San Giulio) ventured to the forested island in the latter half of the fourth century to rid it of an infestation of snakes and dragons. The island, which is 330 yards long and 175 yards across, hides an age-old settlement and an assembly of Romanesque art treasures. Only one family and the 22 nuns who maintain the island's towering convent live here year-round.

On Wednesday mornings, while mist is still rising off the lake, nuns cross the lake in small fishing boats, as their predecessors did, to attend the weekly open-air market in Orta.

Each year in July, when the population of San Giulio Island reaches 300, townfolk gather in the main square to sing popular island songs. This ancient tradition is believed to date back to the time of St. Julius, when early Christians gathered in front of the island's basilica to sing hymns.

On Sundays in September, San Giulio sponsors concerts that combine classical and regional folk music. But the island's most colorful festival is Jan. 31, St. Julius Day. From midnight until late into the following evening, there are fireworks, music, and dancing.

On San Giulio, among the elegant villas, terraces, clusters of rich green trees, and fragrant flower gardens of the summer, are some of the finest examples of Romanesque art in all Italy. The Romanesque basilica has undergone several renovations. Its history can be traced to the 11th century, but islanders will tell you that it goes back nearly 700 years earlier, to the time of St. Julius.

Inside the basilica is a remarkable collection of frescoes from the 15th century, most by local painters. The masterpiece of the basilica is the 12th-century Pulpit of the Comacine Masters. Gorgeously ornamented with the symbols of the four evangelists and splendid animals, the polychromed wooden bas-reliefs are supported by marble columns. The bells of the basilica ring on Sunday mornings and can be heard for miles around.

The island's only restaurant is the **Ristorante San Giulio,** where succulent regional specialties, such as *minestrone alla Milanese* and *costoletta* (a veal dish), are served, along with a fine selection of sparkling white and red wines.

The island has no hotels. Stay at one of the hotels in nearby Orta.

Umbria: the best of the heartland

Undulating **Umbria** is Italy's heartland, stretching between Rome and Florence. This hilly, forested countryside is dotted with Renaissance architectural gems, ancient farmhouses, vineyards, olive groves, and orchards. Umbria's medieval cities perch on hilltops and hang from mountain sides. St. Francis was born in Umbria, and he left his mark throughout the region.

Umbria's strangest sight

The small town of **Bomarzo** is known for the fascinating but creepy garden at the Villa of Orsini. In the late 15th century, Prince Vicino Orsini created these landscaped gardens, which are dotted with bizarre sculptures. Known as Il Sacro Bosco (the Sacred Wood) or the Parco dei Mostri (Park of Monsters), it is filled with statues of half-human, half-animal monsters.

The most beautiful Umbrian town

Orvieto, perched on an enormous rock, is the most beautiful town in the region. It is known for its **duomo,** built in 1229, which has a golden, mosaic-decorated front that glitters when it reflects the sun. Pope Nicholas IV commissioned the duomo to commemorate a miracle. According to Church lore, drops of blood appeared on the Host consecrated by a Bohemian priest who had doubted the Doctrine of Transubstantiation (the belief that during the sacrament of communion the bread actually becomes the body of Christ and the wine His blood). The blood-stained chalice cloth is kept in the cathedral and carried through town during the feast of Corpus Christi and again on Easter Sunday. The duomo has opaque alabaster windows, a rose window designed by Andrea Orcagna, and frescoes begun by Fra' Angelico.

The best place to stay in Orvieto is three miles outside town in La Badia. The **Hotel La Badia,** *La Badia, Orvieto Scalo 05019; tel. (39-763)90-359,* a former abbey that dates back to the 1100s, has comfortable rooms with private baths and a first-class restaurant that features produce from the abbey's own farm. This beautiful complex has a swimming pool and tennis courts, as well as a church of Romanesque-Lombard style and a 12-sided tower. The buildings contain frescoes from the 12th to 14th centuries. In the 15th century, the abbey was a retreat for cardinals. It has been in the hands of the family of Count Giuseppe Fiumi for the past century. Double rooms start at 134,500 lire.

Perugia: a historical treasure house

Perugia is a town of historic treasures. The most fascinating sight is the **via Bagliona Sotteranea,** an underground street filled with the ruins of 15th-century houses. You enter through the Porta Marzia, a second-century Etruscan doorway. Visit the 13th-century **Fontana Maggiore** and stroll along the palace-lined **Corso Vanucci.** The town's **Collegio del Cambio** was frescoed by Perugino and his helpers, one of whom may have been Raphael, in the early 16th century. Upstairs is the **National Gallery.**

Perugia's best hotel is **La Rosetta,** *Piazza d'Italia 19; tel. (39-75)20841.* Located at the top of the Corso Vannucci, near the main sights, it is friendly and efficient, and the food is delicious. Rooms at the back are quieter.

Umbria's most inviting hotel

Torgiano, a walled town complete with towers, boasts the splendid **Baglioni Palace,** which houses a wine museum founded by the local producers of Chardonnay.

The other reason to stop in Torgiano is the **Hotel Le Tre Vaselle,** *via Garibaldi 8, 06089 Perugia; tel. (39-75)982-447.* Housed in a 300-year-old villa, it has 16th-century wooden doors, thick walls, and hand-hewn ceiling beams and arches. It is a peaceful place on a side street, with spacious bedrooms and views of the countryside. Rooms are decorated with textiles and flowers, and Umbrian specialties are served in the dining room. Try artichoke risotto sage-and-onion bread tarts baked in a wood oven and the traditional Umbrian wafer made in 16th-century molds and flavored with anise. The hotel is often used for conferences of oenologists (wine experts), because it is owned by the Lungarotti Wine Company. Double rooms start at 215,000 lire. To make reservations in the United States, contact **Relais & Châteaux,** *(212)696-1323* or *(800)372-1323.*

In the footsteps of St. Francis

Traces of peace-loving St. Francis are evident throughout **Assisi,** an ethereal mountainside town with medieval houses. Just outside Assisi is the **Basilica Santa Maria,** which includes the fourth-century Chapel of Porziuncola, used by St. Francis and his followers.

St. Francis is buried in the **Basilica of San Francesco**—his remains are kept in the structure's 19th-century crypt. Giotto painted 28 scenes from the life of the saint here. Black-robed pilgrims flock to the basilica from the countryside year-round.

The corpse of St. Clare is exposed and can be viewed in its crystal casket in the crypt of the **Basilica of Santa Chiara,** across town.

Outside Assisi, visit the **Convent of St. Damian,** where St. Francis received his Holy Orders. See the crucifix that supposedly spoke to him and the rooms where St. Clare lived, worked, and fought off marauders. Go on to the Eremo delle Carceri, a minute church hollowed out of a rock by St. Francis and his followers in a nearby wood.

Hotel Fontebella, *via Fontebella 25, Assisi 06081; tel. (39-75)812-883,* is located in a 17th-century palazzo in the center of town. Each room has a balcony with a view of the city. Guests can play cards and drink cocktails in the comfortable sitting room. The hotel restaurant, Il Frantoio, is expensive. Double rooms are 180,000 lire.

The best of Tuscany

Tuscany has historic towns, fashionable beach resorts, and a leading spa favored by the Italian *bene* (elite). The region that gave us Michelangelo and Leonardo da Vinci continues its artistic traditions, creating marble sculpture and fine gold and leather crafts. Yet it is seldom crowded with tourists.

The oldest Tuscan town

Drive up into the hills above Florence to visit **Fiesole,** one of the 12 great towns of ancient Etruria. Long before there was a Florence, this little town sat above the Arno Valley. In 283 B.C., Etruscan Fiesole was conquered by the Romans, who left behind an amphitheater built in 80 B.C. Classical plays are presented in the restored ruins.

An ochre-colored path leads from the Piazza Mino to the San Francesco Monastery in Fiesole. From the path you can enjoy one of the best views of Florence. The Cloister of the Gothic monastery is filled with Chinese art from the era of Marco Polo.

The town's duomo, built in A.D. 1000, has gray Corinthian columns and Romanesque arches. Paintings by Fra' Angelico and Fra' Filippo Lippi are displayed at the Museo Bandini.

The best place to dine in Fiesole is the **Hotel Aurora,** *Piazza Mino.* It has a charming garden and great views, as well as inexpensive Tuscan fare.

Villa San Michele, *via Doccia, Fiesole 50014 Florence; tel. (39-55)59-451,* is a deluxe hotel in a former Franciscan monastery. Monks' cells have been converted into lavishly decorated bedrooms and suites. Michelangelo is supposed to have designed the building.

The best wine-making estate

Not far from Florence, just off Superstrada 67, is the wine-making **Artimino Estate,** with its 740 acres of vineyards, olive groves, and gardens. In the late 16th century, the villa was commissioned by the Grand Duke Ferdinand I to house his court. It became known as La Ferdinanda.

An excellent restaurant, **Biagio Pignatta,** is located on the estate's grounds. It offers Tuscan dishes and the eight wines grown on the estate according to age-old traditions. Wood-burning ovens braise the meats to perfection. The *scaloppina ai carciofi* (veal and artichokes), *bistecca alla Fiorentina* (charcoal-broiled beefsteak), and *faraona alla brace* (broiled guinea hen) are superb.

Hotel Paggeria Medicea, adjacent to the villa, has 37 rooms with wood beams and enormous fireplaces, as well as 20th-century conveniences, such as telephones, televisions, and refrigerated bars. The hotel is in a 17th-century building formerly called Il Corridoio (the Hallway), because it once separated the court residence from the servants' quarters.

The prettiest Tuscan town

Lucca, a small city enclosed within vast ramparts, is the prettiest town in Tuscany. The 12th-century town is beautifully preserved and maintained. Delightfully cool and shaded green walkways follow the massive 16th-century brick and turf walls that surround the town. The curious towers here are typical of Tuscan towns. In the Middle Ages most patrician houses were dominated by very high and slender towers often crowned with ilex trees (the tower of the Palazzo Guinigi, for example). After exploring Lucca's historic churches, wander through the narrow streets, which are filled with boutiques.

Lucca's grand **Romanesque cathedral** is filled with artistic treasures. Jacopo della Quercia designed the tomb of Ilaria del Carretto, wife of the Lord of Lucca in the early 15th century. A strangely lifelike statue of Ilaria reclines on top of the tomb. Other treasures include Tintoretto's *Last Supper* and Ghirlandaio's *Madonna and Saints.* A life-sized statue of Christ that drifted ashore at the nearby town of Luni is kept in a round chapel in the north nave. Every Sept. 13, the statue is carried through town in memory of the day it miraculously appeared. The facade of the cathedral is carved with religious allegories and fantastic animals. Nicola Pisano's *Deposition and Nativity* are above the door on the right.

Inside the **Church of San Michel** is a painting of saints Sebastian, Roch, Jerome, and Helen by Fra' Filippo Lippi.

The **Church of San Frediano** houses the mummy of Santa Zita. On April 26, the townspeople place the body in the middle of the church and stroke and kiss its withered limbs.

The best restaurant in town is the **Buca di Sant'Antonio,** *via della Cervia 1-5, Lucca 55100; tel. (39-583)55881.* Kid roasted on a spit is a specialty. Try the local wine, Rosso delle Colline Lucchesi.

Lucca has a shortage of hotels. Of the nine small hotels here, the most comfortable and convenient is the **Albergo Universo,** *Piazza Puccini, Lucca 55100; tel. (39-583)43678.*

The best-preserved Tuscan town

San Gimignano, with its noble towers, is one of the best-preserved medieval towns in Italy. Unfortunately, tourists flock to this 14th-century gem, crowding the streets. It's difficult to imagine where they all stay—only three hotels are located within the town walls. During the fall, the town is filled with hunters. (Hunting is good in the surrounding hills.)

Fourteen of the 72 towers that once protected this town still stand. At one time all 72 spires crowded around the main square that surrounds the 13th-century *cisterna* (well). The small square is curiously paved with bricks laid on their narrow sides in a herringbone pattern.

The best (and at one time only) hotel is **La Cisterna,** *53037 San Gimignano (Siena); tel. (39-577)940-328,* on the main square. It is an elegant, comfortable, well-run place with an excellent restaurant, La Terrazza. Sit on the terrace to watch the lights blink on in farmhouses and peaceful villages as night falls over the valley.

Tuscany's crown jewel: Siena

The jewel in Tuscany's crown is **Siena,** a beautifully preserved town with wide-open spaces and ancient palaces. It is known for its university, its musical academy, and the annual Palio (a centuries-old horse race). Siena's cathedral, a striped marble structure, reaches high into the sky.

The 14th-century walls that surround Siena were used during World War II to prevent retreating German troops from passing through the city. When the ancient portals were shut, 20th-century tanks couldn't get through!

Siena's most beautiful square is the **Piazza del Campo,** which is bordered by the city's magnificent palaces and the 13th-century Palazzo Pubblico (city hall), which houses the Town Museum. Built of brick, the city hall is a fine specimen of pointed Gothic architecture. The slim, elegant, 334-foot tower (Torre del Mangia) soars high over the city. Its shadow moves across the brick paving as the day progresses. The Sienese Museum is a good introduction to Siena.

In the evening, join the Sienese in their stroll along the *passeggiata,* or promenade, along the curving Banchi di Sopra. The *passeggiata* leads through the banking district. Notice the Monte dei Paschiu di Siena, a bank housed in the 14th-century Palazzo Salimbeni. The bank was founded in 1472 and is still in business. Nearby is Palazzo Tolomei, the oldest private palace in Siena, now home to the Cassa di Risparmio di Firenze, another bank.

The most beautiful Sienese artworks are on display at the **Pinacoteca,** which contains Byzantine paintings and works by Simone Martini.

The best time to visit

The most exciting time to visit Siena is during the **Palio,** which is held July 2 and Aug. 16 each year. This bareback three-lap horse race around the shell-shaped Piazza del Campo is one of the most genuine and fascinating of all Italian spectacles. It lasts all of 90 seconds but generates feuds that continue for decades.

The Palio is a competition between 10 of Siena's 17 *contrade,* or districts. During the days preceding the race, the people of Siena revert to the venality of the Middle Ages. Bribery, meddling, and skulduggery are not only permitted, but also encouraged. *Contrade* captains are expected to indulge in intrigue as part of their efforts to outdo their rivals. Millions of lire are spent bribing the jockeys.

The Palio has its roots in the Middle Ages, when Siena was an independent republic. At that time, the 17 contrade were separate military societies, each defended by its own military forces. Life in Siena in the Middle Ages was not easy. Homes were small, cold, badly ventilated, and had little light. The streets were narrow, murky, and bristled with potential ambush. The walls that surrounded the city and those of the high buildings along the streets were blackened by smoke. The danger of epidemic was great, as was the possibility of dying by the sword or dagger. Considering all this, it is no wonder the people looked for escape. The Compagnie Popolari were organized to help provide distraction. These companies, each from a different section of the city, were intended to keep the people happy and free from worries (and thoughts of revolt, no doubt) by initiating games. One of the games the Compagnie Popolari initiated was the Palio.

The best hotels and restaurants

Park Hotel, *via di Marciano 16; tel. (39-577)44-803,* is the best place to stay in Siena. Located in a 15th-century villa, it has modern amenities, such as air conditioning, a heated swimming pool, and central heating. Terraces, gardens, and vineyards surround the villa. Situated on Marciano Hill, it has good views. Rooms are about 60,000 lire a night.

The best Tuscan castle hotel

The restored Tuscan castle of **Montegufoni,** a mostly Renaissance affair complete with a tower copied from the Palazzo Vecchio in Florence, is now taking American paying guests in six apartments furnished with lovely antiques. You also can stay in the converted hayloft of a farm on the property. Walk the Italian gardens with their lemon trees, and swim in the 14-meter pool. Rates range from $440 per week in October or May for a modest two-bedroom duplex with bath and kitchenette to $1,430 in July or August for a five-bedroom apartment called La Galleria. (You also have to pay 10,000 lire to 50,000 lire for the final cleanup. However, you pay no other taxes or service charges.) To make reservations, contact **Posarelli Vacations,** *180 Kinderkamack Road, Park Ridge, NJ 07656; (201)573-9558.*

Pisa: Tuscany's most famous sight

Pisa, which is famous for its leaning tower, has less-known sights that also are worth seeing: the cathedral, the baptistery, and the Campo Santo. The **duomo** is fronted by white columns that support five tapered arcades. Winged angels peer out from the corners, and mysterious inscriptions can be found on the walls. Inside are Corinthian columns and striped walls. Art in the cathedral includes an ivory Madonna by Giovanni Pisano; Andrea del Sarto's *Sant'Agnese Mourning;* and Giovanni del Biondo's *Flight from Egypt* and *Presentation at the Temple.*

The **baptistery** has gables, arches, and stained-glass windows. A white shaft of light shines through the baptistery dome onto the floor. Sounds echo eerily in the dome.

The **Campo Santo** is a walled cemetery filled with earth brought back from Calvary by the Crusaders. The cemetery walls are covered with terrifying medieval frescoes: the *Triumph of Death,* the *Last Judgement,* and *Hell.* This last is a picture of snakes, skewered corpses, and demons punishing sinners.

Sicily: Italy at its most exotic

Sicily, an island at the southern tip of Italy, is a land unto itself. The least Italian region of Italy, it has been invaded and settled by Carthaginians, Greeks, Saracens, Normans, and Spaniards over the last 3,000 years. And each group has left its mark on the island's culture. In ancient times, Sicily was part of Greece. Later, it became part of the Roman Empire. After the fall of Rome, it was invaded by northern tribes, Saracens, Byzantines, Normans, French, and Spanish. It didn't become part of Italy until 1860.

Sicily's climate is more like that of northern Africa than that of Europe. So the best time to visit is the spring or fall (it is blisteringly hot in the summer).

Best-preserved relics

Some of the best-preserved relics of ancient Greece are scattered across Sicily. Taormina's amphitheater is spectacular, with Mt. Etna smoking behind it. The temple in Segesta (a town in western Sicily) is set on a lonely hill facing a huge amphitheater. In Agrigento, the temples to Juno, Concordia, and Hercules are awe-inspiring. Visit Messina, founded by the Greeks in the eighth century, and Siracusa (Syracuse), which has archeological evidence of the ancient Greeks and Romans.

Europe's highest active volcano

Europe's highest active volcano is in Sicily. **Mt. Etna** rises 9,840 feet. Don't take the organized tour of Mt. Etna—it is a terrible disappointment. The trip takes all day, and you will see nothing but dirt and rocks. The group never goes near the crater.

The least-changed towns

The smaller hill towns in Sicily are some of the least modern in Italy. Donkeys and mules rather than cars and trucks carry loads. Women carry water from wells in jars on their heads. Each morning, a goatherd follows his goats into town. He milks the goats at each door, delivering fresh milk to the residents. Plumbing in some towns in nonexistent, and water is scarce.

Sicily's most charming resort

Taormina is the most charming resort town in Sicily. Set on a ridge with a spectacular view of the bay, its greatest sight is the Greek theater carved out of the hillside, which is still used for productions during summer theater festivals. Palazzo Corvaia, site of Sicily's parliament in the 14th century, is on the Piazza Vittorio Emanuele. Enjoy a glass of wine and a view of the bay from one of the many cafés along the Piazza 9 Aprile.

The best way to get to Sicily

The most beautiful way to get to Sicily is by ferry or hydrofoil from the southern tip of the mainland at Reggio di Calabria or Villa San Giovanni across the Strait of Messina. The crossing is long and often rough, but always lovely. Boats also connect with Naples, Livorno (Leghorn), Genoa, and Cagliari. You also can fly to Palermo and Catania from major Italian cities.

Sicilian cuisine—Italy's most colorful

Sicily is known for its exotic and colorful dishes, which have a slightly Arabic flavor. One typical dish of the region is *pasta con le sarde,* in which pine nuts and currants lend a Middle Eastern touch to *bucatini* (thick, hollow spaghetti) in a sauce of fresh sardines and wild fennel. The combination of pine nuts and currants is common. Eggplant and sun-ripened fresh tomatoes also are commonly used.

La Scuderia, *Viale del Fante 9; tel. (39-91)520-323,* one of the best restaurants in Palermo, serves sophisticated Sicilian cooking. It is expensive by Sicilian standards.

Trattoria Primavera, *Piazza Bologni 4; tel. (39-91)329-408,* also in Palermo, has simple food and low prices. It is closed Fridays.

Best places to sleep in Sicily

Palermo's luxury hotel is the **Grand Hotel Villa Igiea,** *90142 Palermo, Sicily; tel. (39-91)543-744.* Designed to look like a castle, this hotel is right on the sea. It has lovely flower gardens with palm trees and the ruins of an ancient temple. A swimming pool, tennis courts, an elevator, and a bar add to the amenities of the Grand. All rooms have baths. You can have a car sent to pick you up at the train station. Double rooms start at 94,000 lire.

Pensione San Michele in Taormina is inexpensive. The food is lavish. Ask the staff to pack you a picnic lunch, then walk down the steep hill to spend a day at the beach.

Unconquered Sardinia, the wildest region

"Unconquered **Sardinia**," as D.H. Lawrence called it, is the least-tamed region in Italy. It is still the land of the *banditti,* family clans, and blood feuds. It has produced such rebels as Antonio Gramsci, theorist and founder of the Italian Communist Party.

Today, Sardinia also attracts movie stars and royalty. Prince Karim bought 35 miles of coastline and established the most luxurious resort in Italy: the **Costa Smeralda.**

Despite an onslaught of foreign tourists and developers, Sardinia is beautiful—hilly and occasionally tropical. The coast has granite cliffs and long, sandy beaches. The water is the cleanest in the Mediterranean. What's more, Sardinia has fascinating Roman ruins at Nora and Tharros, as well as prehistoric stone towers called nuraghi.

Cagliari, the best bet

Costa Smeralda has become an expensive luxury resort for the jet set. A better bet is **Cagliari,** on the southern coast, which has inexpensive hotels and a charming medieval district called the Castello. Narrow streets and tall towers cover the hills rising out of the harbor. This friendly town is near the nuraghi ruins at Barumini and the sandy beaches of the Costa del Sud. Pink flamingos inhabit the lagoons outside town. The tourist office in Piazza Matteotti can help you find a room.

Cagliari has good seafood restaurants. **Dal Corso,** *Viale Regina Margherita 28; tel. (39-Cagliari)66-43-18,* serves fresh lobster, eel, shrimp, and fish.

Trattoria Gennargentu, *via Sardegna 60,* serves enormous plates of lasagne, shish kebab, and squid for the ridiculously low price of 10,000 lire. The trattoria is comfortable, has plenty of local atmosphere, and serves a good house wine.

A good, cheap place to stay in Cagliari is **Locanda Firenze,** *Corso Vittorio Emanuele 50; tel. (39-Cagliari)65-36-78.* It has clean, pleasant rooms, and the management speaks English. The hotel, which is on the third floor, has no elevator. Doubles are only 16,000 lire to 20,000 lire.

Sardinia's oldest city

Nora, a small city near Cagliari, is the oldest city in Sardinia. Settled by Phoenicians, who left the ruins of their temple behind, it became a bustling Roman town before it died out about A.D. 500. The Roman roads and theater are well-preserved, and the ruins are being excavated. Climb to the Spanish watchtower for tremendous views of the sea, which breaks on either side of the isthmus.

The best beaches

La Costa del Sud, about 31 miles southwest of Cagliari, has unspoiled beaches and hidden coves. The water is turquoise and perfectly clear. Buses run to the coast from Cagliari as far as the beach near the Torre di Chia. But the next beach over, Capo Spartivento, is larger and has two lovely islands that are great for sunbathing.

Sardinia's unique ruins

Don't leave Sardinia without examining its **nuraghi**—ancient stone towers found only in this part of Italy. They were once used as tombs, temples, or forts of refuge. The **Nuraghi of Su Nuraxi** in Barumini, near Cagliari, are the best-preserved in Sardinia. Set on a hill, they are the remains of an ancient village. The huge blocks of stone were designed primarily for defense. The huge central tower dates to about 1300 B.C. The Nuraghi of Su Nuraxi can be visited every day except Mondays.

The town of **Sassari** has the best Sardinian museum, the **Museo Giovanni Antonio Sanna,** *via Roma 64.* See reconstructed nuraghi, Sardinian paintings and costumes, Roman statues and mosaics, and an ethnographic section where Sardinian music is played. Open from 9 a.m. to 2 p.m. Tuesdays through Saturdays and 9 a.m. to 1 p.m. Sundays.

Two good, inexpensive hotels in Sassari are **Albergo Gallura,** *Vicolo San Leonardo 9; tel. (39-79)276-373,* and **Albergo Giusy,** *Piazza Sant'Antonio 21; tel. (39-79)233-327.* The first is well-run and located in the center of town. The second is very comfortable and located at the far end of Corso Vittorio Emanuele.

The best Roman ruins

Near Sassari, **Porto Torres** occupies the site of the Roman town **Turris Libisonis.** Remains of the Roman settlement, including a circular marble altar and the baths of the Palace of the Barbarian King (Palazzo di Re Barbaro), can be seen next to the train station. Seven arches of an ancient Roman bridge span the River Turritano. The Church of San Gavino is one of Sardinia's most notable monuments. Built in the 11th century, it has 28 columns and a wooden truss ceiling.

Sardinia's most beautiful city

Alghero, the most beautiful and best-preserved city in Sardinia, has a Spanish flavor. Sardinia was united with Aragon in 1325, and the Spaniards left their mark on Alghero, which looks somewhat like Barcelona. Alleys are covered with arches, and some restaurants serve *paella.* Starting at the Bastione della Maddalena in the port, walk around the ramparts and the 16th-century Spanish towers to enjoy the view of the shimmering sea.

Outside Alghero are two beaches with clean, clear water—**Spiaggia di San Giovanni** and **Spiaggia di Maria Pia.** Both are crowded. A short boat trip away is the **Grotto di Nettuno,** which puts Capri's Blue Grotto to shame. The large underwater cavern can be visited by boats that leave from docks in front of Bastione della Maddalena.

One of the best restaurants in Alghero is **Il Pavone,** *Piazza Sulis 3/4; tel. (39-Alghero)97-95-84,* which is family-run. The soups, antipastos, risottos, and seafood are recommended. A meal for two is about 60,000 lire. Closed Wednesdays and during January. Reservations are a good idea.

Chapter 6

THE BEST OF WEST GERMANY

Germany is the best all-around travel destination in Europe. As balanced as a fine cuckoo clock, it has something for everyone. Its old cities have museums, concert halls, and gourmet restaurants. Romantic little villages nestle beneath the snow-capped Alps. Its North Sea beaches are edged by 30-foot sand dunes and beautified with goose-pimpled, bronzed (and sometimes nude) bodies. The avant-garde lives side-by-side with folk culture: new wave is popular, but so is oompah music; leather skirts are seen as often as dirndls.

Munich: the most fun-loving city

Munich is Germany's party town. Every season provides an excuse for a party—and in Munich, there are nine seasons: spring, summer, winter, fall, Bock beer time, the opera festival, beer garden days, carnival, and Oktoberfest.

Munich's best party

If you like a good party and crowds, visit Munich during **Oktoberfest** at the end of September. But make sure you have a hotel reservation; the city never has enough rooms for all the revelers. If you can't find a hotel, contact the **Munich Tourist Office (Verkehrsamt),** *Sendlingerstr. 1, 8000 Munich 2; tel. (49-89)23911.* The staff may be able to help you find a homestay.

The first Oktoberfest was in 1810, when 40,000 royal merrymakers celebrated Prince Ludwig's wedding reception. Since then it has been celebrated every year beginning three Saturdays before the first Sunday in October and continuing for 16 days. Festivities start with a parade through the streets of Munich to the Theresienwiese (a meadow named after Prince Ludwig's bride). Here, after horse-drawn beer wagons arrive, the mayor taps the first of more than 700,000 kegs. Thousands quaff Bavarian brew and enjoy brass-band music.

Enormous beer tents, sponsored by Germany's 13 major breweries, are the hub of activity. Stein-serving waitresses in folk costumes weave among wooden tables. Midway rides and sideshows add to the carnival atmosphere.

On the second day of Oktoberfest, from 10:30 a.m. until noon, groups in national costumes parade. After this, it's back to the beer gardens, which remain open from noon until 10:30 p.m. Spend the afternoon drinking and feasting on *Weisswurste* (white sausage made out of veal and pork). By nightfall, you'll be ready to join the rousing, if slightly slurred, renditions of *"In München steht ein Hofbräuhaus."*

Munich's heart

The historic center of the town is around the **Marienplatz,** a huge pedestrian mall surrounded by the new (19th-century) and old (15th-century) city halls. The ringing of the **Glockenspiel** from the new city hall spire is a daily ritual at 11 a.m. Life-size figures enact a knights' tournament, the dance of the coopers, and a medieval royal wedding ceremony.

The highest points in Munich

Although Munich lost many of its old buildings in World War II bombing raids, almost all have been restored. **Frauenkirche,** with its two onion-domed spires, and the 942-foot **Olympic tower** are the most prominent landmarks on Munich's skyline. Take an elevator to the top of the Olympic tower for a breathtaking view of the city.

The world's largest science museum

The **Deutsches Museum,** which takes up an entire island in the middle of the Isar River, is the world's largest science and technology museum. It's great fun for people who love gadgets. Most of the displays involve participation (pushing buttons, turning cranks). Exhibits trace the development of technology and include a turn-of-the-century transformer, antique cars, and glass-blowing demonstrations. You can avoid the crowds by visiting during the week and arriving at 9 a.m., when the museum opens. Almost all the display information placards are now in English as well as German.

The best collection of Dürer and Rubens

Alte Pinakothek (the old art gallery), *Barerstr. 27,* has the most complete collection of Dürer and Rubens paintings in the world, as well as works by many other famous artists of the 15th to 18th centuries, including Rembrandt, Van Dyck, and El Greco. The museum is free on Sundays.

Munich's three top sights

Neue Pinakothek (the new art gallery), which was destroyed during World War II, was rebuilt in postwar years and today is Munich's best modern art gallery. Its natural lighting sets off the paintings well. Sloping ramps lead past artworks hung in chronological order. The collection of works by 18th- and 19th-century masters is especially good—it includes works by Manet, Monet, Dégas, Cézanne, Van Gogh, Gauguin, Klimt, and Goya.

Schatzkammer (Treasure House), *3 Max-Joseph-Platz,* holds the splendid treasures of Bavarian royalty: jeweled crowns and crosses, goblets, medals, swords, dishes, and jewelry. Perhaps the most beautiful object is in the third room: a statue of St. George slaying the dragon made in 1590 and inlaid with precious stones.

Residenzmuseum shares a building with the Schatzkammer. Once the palace of the Wittelsbach kings, it contains rooms from the Renaissance to the baroque to rococo periods. Damaged during World War II, it has been restored. The Ancestors Gallery houses portraits of all the Bavarian kings.

Munich's most inviting park

When you tire of the historic and cultural sights, take a walk through **Der Englischer Garten.** The park was designed by an American Tory named Benjamin Thompson, who was forced to leave America during the Revolutionary War after he was found spying for the British. Thompson hailed from Rumford (now Concord), New Hampshire and was called Count Rumford. He became an advisor to the Bavarian King and in 1795 transformed what had been a royal hunting ground into Germany's first public park.

The park has woods, brooks, and a Chinese tower turned beer garden, which is the best place to drink huge steins of beer, eat Bavarian pretzels and wienerschnitzels, and meet people. It's fun. There's even an area set aside in the park for nude sunbathing. Take an ice-cold dip in the Isar River, an exciting way to end the day.

Munich's oldest church

Alte Peter Kirche (Peter's Church), just off the Marienplatz near the *rathaus,* is often overlooked, although it is the oldest parish church in Munich. Begun in 1050 and finished in 1294, it contains very few of its original furnishings. However, it does still house a macabre relic—a gilded and bejeweled skeleton of the martyr St. Munditia (the patron saint of lonely women). Fake eyes look out of her skull, gems glitter where her teeth should be, and a jeweled coronet balances on her head of fake hair! If you don't mind climbing the 277 steps to the top, you'll have a great view of the Alps from the 300-foot tower of the Alte Peter.

The world's best Kandinsky collection

Städtische Galerie im Lenbachhaus (Municipal Gallery), *Luisenstr. 33,* has the most comprehensive collection in the world of the works of abstract painter Vassily Kandinsky. It also displays works by other Munich artists, including some early Paul Klee paintings. The gallery is in an imitation Italian villa with a small garden. Works by Kandinsky and Klee are housed in the older part of the villa, once the home and studio of Germany's most famous 19th-century portrait painter, Franz Lenbach. His works and collections also are on display. The museum is open every day except Mondays, from 10 a.m. to 6 p.m.

Peerless puppets

The **Munich Municipal Museum,** *Sankt Jakob's Platz 1,* has one of the most extensive displays of puppets and puppetworks in the world. It traces the history of puppetry through time and countries and houses the famous Moiska-Tänzer statuettes, all dancing with bizarre expressions on their faces (they were created in 1480 by Erasmus Grasser for the dance hall of the old *rathaus*). After seeing the exhibits, you can try your hand at puppeteering in the theater.

Other sights in the museum include a beer-brewing exhibit, a musical instrument collection, and displays of children's furniture from times past. The museum is open every day except Mondays from 9 a.m. to 4:30 p.m. and Sundays from 10 a.m. to 6 p.m. (Admission is free on Sundays.)

The best place to buy folk fashions

Loden-Frey, *Maffeistr. 7, 8000 Munich 40; tel. (49-89)236-930,* in Munich's Fussgängerzone (pedestrian precinct), is the best place to buy German folk-style clothing in traditional fabrics. This family-run establishment has been in business since 1842. It was bombed during World War II but later rebuilt in the South German style at its old address.

Climb the store's circular stairway to the third floor. You will find dirndls, hunting and walking wear, sports clothes, and evening wear, all in the traditional style. The staff will welcome you with a Bavarian greeting, *"Grüss Gott,"* then help you find just what you're looking for in Loden or Tracht (traditional costume) for men, women, or children.

You can write the store for a copy of its catalog, issued twice yearly.

Munich's best bargains

An enormous flea market is held on Fridays and Saturdays along **Marsstrasse,** just outside Munich. Disney memorabilia, especially Mickey Mouse T-shirts, can be found throughout the market (the Germans are crazy about Mickey). If you get tired of perusing old junk, stop for a stein in the beer hall here.

Used cars (BMWs, Volkswagens, and Mercedes) are sold by their owners (not dealers) for a good price along **Leopoldstrasse.** They are cheaper than in the United States. One enterprising young American bought a car along Leopoldstrasse, had it inspected and repaired, then shipped it back to the United States, where he sold it for a profit.

The most magnificent sight

Schloss Nymphenburg, outside Munich, is a magnificent 17th-century palace set in a 500-acre park filled with fountains, statues, lakes, waterfalls, and formal gardens. Portraits of the 24 most beautiful women in Europe 200 years ago that were commissioned by King Ludwig hang in the south pavilion.

Also on the palace grounds is the **Marstallmuseum,** one of the finest coach museums in all Europe. Housed here are Ludwig II's ornate carriages and sleds, laden with gold and sculptured cherubs, curlicues, lions, and roses. And don't miss the rococo Amalienburg, built from 1734 to 1739 as a hunting lodge for Electress Amalia. Although its intended use was humble enough, the lodge includes a hall of silver-framed mirrors.

When your feet give out, stop for lunch in the jungle-like palm house, where you can get *Bockwurst mit Senf und Brot* (sausage and mustard on bread) for 6 marks and a beer for 3.50 marks.

To get to the Nymphenburg, take Subway 1 from the Hauptbahnnof, get off at Rotkreuzplatz, and change to Streetcar 12. This sounds complicated, but the total travel time is only 15 minutes.

The darkest side

Munich has its dark side. Outside the city is **Dachau Concentration Camp,** now a memorial to those who died there during World War II. More than 200,000 people, mainly Jews, were labeled undesirable by the Nazis and imprisoned here between 1933 and 1945. The camp is virtually intact. Several barracks can be seen, as well as the morgue, the crematorium, and the Brausebad (where prisoners were gassed to death). Documentary films of the Holocaust are shown, and photo displays are on view.

To get to Dachau, take the S-Bahn 2 (marked Petershausen) from the Munich Hauptbahnhof. Trains leave every 20 minutes except Saturday, when they run every two hours. Then take Bus 722 from the railroad station to the camp.

Munich's best restaurants

The best restaurant in Munich is **Die Aubergine,** *Maximiliansplatz 5, 8000 Munich 2; tel. (49-89)598-171.* The first German restaurant to receive a three-star Michelin rating, Die Aubergine serves French-influenced German nouvelle cuisine based on traditional favorites. Try the venison served with wild berries in season or the lobster fricassée. Die Aubergine is closed Sundays, Mondays, and bank holidays. Make a reservation well ahead, because the restaurant is small.

Altes Hackerhaus, *Sendlingerstr. 75; tel. (49-89)260-5026,* is the best place for Bavarian specialties (if you have the nerve, try the pig's knuckles).

Franziskaner und Fuchsenstuben, *Perusastr. 5; tel. (49-89)231-8120,* serves delicious sausage and *Leberkas,* a kind of meat loaf that is made of ground beef, liver, and bacon and eaten with sweet mustard.

Traditional Bavarian food is served at **Nürnberger Bratwurstglöckl,** *Frauenplatz 9; tel. (49-89)22-03-85* or *(49-89)29-52-64,* near the Dom. The decor here is charming—large prints, arms, and carved woodwork.

The best restaurant in Germany

Weichandhof, *Betzenweg 81; tel. (49-89)811-1621,* in Obermenzing, just outside Munich, is one of the most charming restaurants in Germany. Bavarian and international foods are served in the converted farmhouse. The restaurant is cozy in cold weather, with an open fireplace and a wood stove. During the summer, tables are moved outside under the apple trees. Venison is served in season. Try the Bavarian classic, *Schweinebraten mit Kartoffelknödel* (roast pork with crackling and potato dumplings). You must drive or take a taxi to the Weichandhof; public transportation does not travel there. It is located on the Munich-Stuttgart highway.

The hottest night life

Schwabing, Munich's student district, has more than 200 restaurants and cafés, as well as a myriad of nightclubs and bars. It is the best place to wander if you're looking for a lively night out. Sidewalk artists sell their goods along Blvd. Leopold, and working girls strut their stuff.

The **Park,** at the end of Ludwigstrasse near the Residenz, is a fifties-style lounge that has some of the best new music in Munich. It is *the* place to go.

P-Eins is a small but good disco near the National Museum.

Steamy jazz is played at **Domicile,** *Leopoldstr. 19;* **Musicland,** *Siegestr. 19;* and **J.A.M.,** *Rosenheimerstr. 4,* in downtown Munich. On Sundays, steamy jam sessions are held from 11 a.m. to 3 p.m. at the **Unterfahrt,** *Kirchenstr. 96; tel. (49-89)448-2794.* It opens at 8 p.m. every day except Mondays.

Germany's best beer cellars

Munich is famous for its beer cellars—informal halls where lots of beer is downed at long, friendly tables. The city has 12 historic *Bierkeller,* which serve huge steins of beer along with Bavarian dishes. Sit anywhere, these are friendly meeting places. Often oompah bands play, and patrons sing.

The most famous beer hall is the **Hofbräuhaus,** *Platzl 9; tel. (49-89)221-676.* Although it is touristy, the Hofbräuhaus has such a friendly atmosphere that it's worth a visit. Beer is drunk from one-liter blue-glazed jugs on the ground floor, which is a great vaulted hall, and in the outside beer garden. Upstairs is an enormous banqueting hall.

Across the street is the **Platzl,** which has a floor show with Bavarian skits. The **Mathäser Bierstadt,** *Bayerstr. 5,* is an enormous area with a cavernous beer hall. More locals than tourists drink here. The **Donisl,** *Weinstr.1,* is the oldest of Munich's beer halls, popular since 1715. The **Augustiner Keller,** Neuhauserstrasse, is one of the oldest and nicest of the beer cellars. Two pleasant outdoor beer halls are the **Chinesischer Türm** and the **Aumeister,** both in the English Gardens.

Munich's best hotel

Hotel Vier Jahreszeiten Kempinski, *Maximilianstr. 17, 8000 Munich 22; tel. (49-89)23-03-90,* is the best hotel in Munich. A deluxe, traditional hotel with yellow stucco external walls and blue awnings, the Vier Jahreszeiten exudes Bavarian hospitality. Modern amenities include an indoor pool and sauna. The hotel's Walterspiel restaurant is excellent. Munich's bigwigs come here for lunch. Double rooms range from 365 marks to 495 marks.

West Berlin: the most exciting city

West Berlin, a Communist-encircled capitalist city, has an exciting, devil-may-care atmosphere. Sidewalk cafés, little shops, parks, and offices exist side-by-side with the graffiti-covered Berlin Wall. Armed guards gaze down from their guard posts atop the barbed-wire covered wall, while residents go about their business. Beyond the wall are minefields.

Despite (or perhaps because of) serious political uncertainty, Berlin is a lively city. Its slogan is *"Berlin weil Spass macht"* (Berlin because it's fun). Berlin is a fashion center, known for its chic, quality clothing. It has 5,000 restaurants, cafés, and bars situated along its Kurfürstendamm (the local Champs-Elysées). Unlike bars and restaurants in other German cities, they stay open all night.

West Berlin is larger than you would think—25 miles across and long. Lakes, rivers, and forest cover 35% of the city. The architecture is modern. Berlin is ablaze with neon and gleaming with chrome and glass architecture.

Berlin's most important sights

Only 100 of the original 347 buildings along the Kurfürstendamm (known as the Kudamm locally) survived World War II. Most notable is **Kaiser Wilhelm Gedächtnis-Kirche.** The ruins of the church were left standing as a permanent reminder of the horrors of war. (On a lighter note, the chapel and bell tower, adjacent to the church, are known by Berliners as the lipstick case and the powder box.)

Across the square is the **Europa Center,** much bigger than New York's Rockefeller Center, encompassing five acres of office buildings, shops, restaurants, an ice-skating rink, saunas, and a swimming pool.

The **New National Gallery,** *Potsdamerstr. 50,* houses modern European paintings, including some by German expressionists. This starkly modern building houses changing exhibitions. Its collection includes works by Manet, Renoir, and Monet, as well as Munch, Klee, and Picasso. The gallery is open Tuesdays through Sundays, 9 a.m. to 5 p.m. Admission is free.

Berlin's best museum

The **House at Checkpoint Charlie** displays many of the ingenious, homemade contraptions that have been used by East Berliners to cross the Berlin Wall over the past 20 years. The museum is located in a dilapidated tenement building at Friedrichstr. 44, near the gate between East and West Berlin in the American sector. Displays include a mini-submarine created with a motor taken from a motor scooter; a low-slung sportscar that zoomed beneath the horizontal barrier at Checkpoint Charlie; a homemade ski lift that carried an East Berliner, his wife, and their son to freedom; a homemade bulletproof truck that crashed through the wall; and photos of a 476-foot tunnel that 57 people crawled through to the West.

The world's largest Rembrandt collection

Gemälde Galerie, *23/27 Arnim-Allee, Dahlem,* displays the world's largest Rembrandt collection. The Picture Gallery, which seems to go on forever, also displays works by Dürer, Giotto, Fra' Angelico, Ghirlandaio, Titian, Holbein, Rubens, Van Dyck, Hals, and Vermeer.

The Gemälde Galerie is one of several museums that make up the immense Dahlem museum complex, which includes sculpture, prints, the Ethnographical Museum, the Museum of Far Eastern, Islamic, and Indian Art, and the Botanical Museum. You could spend days here. The Dahlem museums are open Tuesdays through Sundays from 9 a.m. to 5 p.m. Admission is free.

Berlin's most famous work of art

The **Egyptian Museum,** *Schlosstr. 70,* is the home of the most famous piece of art in Berlin—the painted limestone bust of beautiful Queen Nefertiti, created more than 3,300 years ago.

Germany's best park

When you tire of museums, go to the **Tiergarten,** Germany's most inviting park. Originally the royal hunting preserve, it is now one of the world's largest urban parks, dotted with lakes and ponds. At its western edge is Berlin's famous zoo, which has more species than any other zoo in the world. At its eastern edge is the Reichstag, Germany's former parliament building, which burned down in 1933 but was rebuilt after the war. It is used for political meetings—the German parliament now meets in Bonn. The Brandenburg Gate at the eastern end of the Tiergarten marks the border between West and East Berlin (along with rolls of barbed wire).

Berlin's best castle

Schloss Charlottenburg, *Luisenplatz,* is the best example of royal Prussian architecture in Berlin. Begun in 1695, the palace took 100 years to build. The schloss was destroyed during World War II, but it has been restored. You can tour the castle, which is surrounded by lovely grounds and a lake, Tuesdays through Sundays from 9 a.m. to 5 p.m. (the tours are given only in German).

Charlottenburg houses a great porcelain collection, the museum of arts and crafts, and sumptuously decorated royal apartments, including the splendid white-and-gold Rococo gallery. The **Charlottenburg Mausoleum** contains the tombs of King Friedrich Wilhelm III and Queen Luise.

Counterculture bests

For a taste of Berlin's counterculture, visit **Kreuzberg,** West Berlin's answer to New

York's East Village. Art galleries, bookstores, used-clothing shops, high-fashion boutiques, and small theaters thrive in this area. Restaurants offering every imaginable cuisine line the streets. The Berlin Wall, which is covered with colorful graffiti, is the eastern boundary of the neighborhood. A sign here reminds you that you are at the site of Gestapo torture chambers.

The heart of the Kreuzberg is the **Mehringhof complex,** a former factory at *Gneis-enaustr. 2.* It is used by about 30 counterculture organizations, including theater troupes, jazz bands, political groups, a health cooperative, and a bookstore.

The avant-garde of the art world

The most far-out modern art is on display at the **Akademie der Kunste** (Academy of Art), *10 Hanseatenweg,* in the Hansa quarter. Exhibitions on *le dernier cri* in art from all over the world are displayed here. In the evenings, lectures, performances of experimental music, and theater are staged in the Akademie's studio. It is open every day during the summer from 10 a.m. to 7 p.m. Admission to the downstairs section is free; admission upstairs, where exhibitions are larger, is 4 marks.

Most decadent shopping

If the proximity to the Berlin Wall gives you an uncontrollably capitalist urge to shop, stop in at **Kaufhaus des Westens,** known as KaDeWe, Berlin's version of Harrods in London. Located near the Kudamm, it has an enormous selection of clothing, as well as 450 kinds of bread, 1,000 types of sausage, and 1,000 different cheeses.

Best bargains

A much less expensive place to shop is Berlin's flea market, **Die Nolle,** open every day except Tuesdays from 8 a.m. to 7 p.m. It is situated in 16 old subway trains at Nollendorfplatz, a 10-minute walk from Wittenbergplatz, the square near KaDeWe. Old sewing machines, furniture, and antique dolls are some of the good buys. Stop at the little restaurant here, where a hamburger (without a bun) can be bought for 3 marks.

The wildest night life

The **Metropol,** *5 Nollendorfplatz,* in a former theater building, is the largest disco in Germany. It draws 3,000 Berliners a night. By the end of the night, dancers are in an elated frenzy.

The **Riverboat,** *177 Hohenzollerndamm,* is another energetic night spot, where frenetic jazz is played. The building itself is a maze of halls and booths. The Riverboat is closed Sundays and Mondays.

If you are looking for an older crowd (the Metropol and the Riverboat draw young groups), try the **Café Keese,** *Bismarckstr. 108.* This is a large dance hall where women must ask men to dance and it is against house rules for a man to refuse. Men can ask women to dance only once an hour. No admission is charged, and drink prices are reasonable.

All age groups can be seen chugging beer in five-liter steins at the **Wirthaus zum Löwen,** *Hardenbergstrasse.* The dancing here is lively, too. No entrance fee is charged on weekdays.

Jazz concerts are held in the sculpture garden of the **New National Galerie,** *tel. (49-30)2666,* during the summer.

The Berlin Philharmonic is wonderful. Performances, conducted by Herbert von Karajan, are at the **Philharmonie,** *Matthäikirchstr. 1; tel. (49-30)261-4383.*

Top restaurants

Rockendorf's, *Düsterhauptstr. 1; tel. (49-30)402-3099,* is the best restaurant in Berlin. Off the beaten track in the suburb of Waidmannslust, it is an old-fashioned establishment that serves continental dishes and has a good wine selection. It is closed Sundays, Mondays, and three weeks in August. Reservations are preferred. Dinner is 73 marks to 100 marks.

Another little-known restaurant with German atmosphere is the **Blockhaus Nikolskoe,** *Nikolskoer Weg, Am Wannsee; tel. (49-30)805-2914.* Set in the forest high above the Havel River, it was built log-cabin style in 1819 by Prussian King Friedrich Wilhelm III for his daughter Charlotte and her husband, Grand Duke Nicholas (later Russian Czar Nicholas I). Continental cuisine is served. Dinners are 32 marks to 56 marks. The Blockhaus is closed Thursdays and in the winter after 7 p.m. Ask directions when you make reservations, because the place can be difficult to find.

The **Kardell,** *Wielandstr. 24; tel. (49-30)882-7181,* serves mouth-watering leg of lamb and game dishes. Every detail is perfect. It is open every day, but only dinner is served on Saturdays. Dinner is 38 marks to 65 marks.

Conti Fischstuben, *Bayreutherstr. 42; tel. (49-30)219-021,* is the best place to go for seafood. This small restaurant in the Hotel Ambassador is closed Sundays and four weeks in July or August. Dinner starts at 32 marks.

I-Punkt, *tel. (49-30)261-6968,* has a panoramic view of Berlin from its location on the 20th floor of the Europa-Center complex. At night, the city lights are spectacular. The international menu is good. Dinners are 32 marks to 48 marks.

The best hotel

The best place to stay in Berlin is the **Bristol-Hotel Kempinski,** *Kurfürstendamm 27, 1000 Berlin 15; tel. (49-30)881-091.* The sprawling, old-fashioned hotel has been newly renovated and has a sauna. Double rooms are 280 marks to 400 marks.

Close seconds

The **Hotel Ambassador,** *Bayreutherstr. 42; tel. (49-30)219-020,* has a heated swimming pool and serves enormous buffet breakfasts. The views from the rooftop are impressive. Double rooms are 180 marks to 250 marks.

For a taste of the elegance that existed in Germany at the turn of the century, stay at the **Schloss Hotel Gehrus,** *Brahmstr. 4-10; tel. (49-30)826-2081.* Formerly known as the Pannwitz Palast, it was built in 1912-14 to house the art and china collections of the personal attorney of Kaiser Wilhelm II. The immense ceilings are hung with elaborate chandeliers. Antiques and larger-than-life mirrors give the rooms a stately air. Surrounded by a large park, the Gehrus is in the Grünewald, five minutes from the Kurfürstendamm. Double rooms are 110 marks to 385 marks a night.

Hotel Belvedere, *Seebergsteig 4, Grünewald, Berlin 33; tel. (49-30)826-10-77,* is next to a forest and near the Havel. A big, turn-of-the-century villa with gardens, it is peaceful and has antique-furnished bedrooms. Rooms have televisions and telephones. Some have private bathrooms. Double rooms are 75 marks to 115 marks.

Red tape tip-offs

A passport and transit visa are required for any rail, bus, or car travel between East and West Berlin. Visas are issued at the border checkpoints. It is best to get entry and return visas at the same time. (For more information, read Chapter 13, "The Best of Eastern Europe.")

The best of Frankfurt

Frankfurt is the logical center for touring Germany. A number of inexpensive flights land at Frankfurt-am-Main Airport, the largest and busiest of Germany's international airports. (All major trains go beyond Frankfurt's main railroad station to the airport, allowing incoming tourists to make train connections to all parts of Germany—or Europe for that matter.)

A modern, industrial city and Germany's banking and finance center, Frankfurt has a charming old section with good beer halls. The *Altstadt* (old town) is ringed by the *Innenstadt* (inner town), which developed in the 14th century.

Frankfurt's five top sights

Stroll through the *Altstadt* past the **Römer** (the city's town hall), which is made up of a group of eight 15th-century Gothic buildings on Römerberg Square. The Römer is covered with carved decoration and has beautiful courtyards. It houses the ornate Imperial Hall, where coronation banquets were held, and is hung with portraits of the emperors from Charlemagne to Francis I.

Near the Römer is the red sandstone **Dom** (Cathedral) **of St. Bartholomäus.** The 13th-century cathedral was badly damaged during World War II but has been restored. Here Holy Roman emperors were crowned. And a short distance away, at Grosser Hirschgraben 23, is the restored house (now a museum) where the poet Goethe was born in 1749.

On the other side of the Main River is the **Sachsenhausen quarter,** once a fishing village, where pleasant cafés, popular cider bars, and lively taverns line the streets. A riverside promenade called the Schaumainkai borders the Main in Sachsenhausen. The view of the old town from the promenade is beautiful, especially in the evening.

The **Städel,** a museum on the Schaumainkai, houses European paintings from the 14th century to the present day, including Rembrandt's *Blinding of Samson.*

Frankfurt's zoo, *Tiergarten Rhönstrass,* is one of the best in the world. More than 5,000 exotic animals are allowed to roam more or less freely. Rather than fences, ditches and pools of water are used to keep animals confined in large, open areas. One of the best exhibits is the Nocturnal Animals House.

Palmengarten, which is bounded on two sides by Miquelallee, is one of the best and largest botanical gardens in the world.

Frankfurt's best restaurants

Weinhaus Brückenkeller, *Schützenstr. 6; tel. (49-69)28-42-38,* is one of the best restaurants in Germany. The old vaulted cellar is furnished with precious antiques. It is closed on Sundays and bank holidays. Only dinner is served, and reservations are required. Dinner is about 105 marks per person without wine.

Restaurant Français, *Bethmannstr. 33; tel. (49-69)2-02-51,* was awarded one of Michelin's coveted stars for its delectable fare. Its reputation is well-known, so reservations are essential. Dinner is 57 marks to 100 marks. It is closed on Sundays and bank holidays and for four weeks in July and August.

Other good dining spots

German specialties are served at the reasonably priced **Dippegucker,** *Eschenheimer Anlage 40; tel. (49-69)55-19-65.* This *Weinstube* (wine bar) has wood paneling and beams, stained-glass windows, a tiled floor, and tables set in alcoves. The wine of the month is usually a bargain. Try the shrimp served with green sauce on toasted rye bread. Dinner is about 51 marks per person without wine.

The place to go for atmosphere is the **Gutsschanke Neuhof,** *Dreieich-Götzenhain 6072; tel. (49-6102)3214,* a 500-year-old building outside Frankfurt. The low, half-timbered building is surrounded by birches, weeping willows, and carpet-like lawns. The interior is rustic, with a fire in the fireplace during the winter. The mouth-watering specialty is venison served in its own juices. Try the house wine, made by the owner from his own vineyards. Dinner is 38 marks per person without wine.

The two finest hotels

Steigenberger-Hotel Frankfurter Hof, *Kaiserplatz 17; tel. (49-69)2-02-51,* is the doyen of Frankfurt's hotels, having welcomed visitors since 1876. Central and comfortably old fashioned, it has two pleasant bars, three good restaurants, and an outdoor café. Rooms have polished wood furnishings and modern facilities. Double rooms are 280 marks to 430 marks.

Hessischer Hof, *Friedrich-Ebert-Anlage 40; tel. (49-69)7-54-00,* receives the highest possible praise from Michelin for its deluxe accommodations. The hotel restaurant is excellent, too. Rooms are 275 marks to 470 marks.

Frankfurt's best undiscovered hotels

If you don't mind staying across the Main in Sachsenhausen, we recommend the **Hübler,** *Grosse Rittergasse 9, Sachsenhausen, Frankfurt; tel. (49-69)616-038.* This small, family-run hotel has a swimming pool and costs half as much as city hotels.

The **National,** *Baselerstr. 50; tel. (49-69)23-48-41,* is a homey, comfortable hotel with quiet charm and reasonably priced rooms (all profits from the hotel go to an orphanage). Newcomers are often discouraged by the drab exterior of the National—but regulars love its cozy interior. Rooms are furnished with antiques, and many have views of the neighboring park. Service is friendly. Double rooms are about 214 marks.

About seven miles outside Frankfurt is an elegant castle hotel called the **Schlosshotel Kronberg,** *Hainstr. 25, 6242 Kronberg im Taunus, Frankfurt am Main; tel. (49-6173)70-11.* Built in 1888 as the residence of Empress Friedrich, mother of Kaiser Wilhelm II, it became a gathering place for European royalty. After World War I, French Occupation officials took possession of the castle. After World War II, American Occupation forces used it as a club for high officers and civilians. Today, the palace is a hotel with 19th-century furnishings. The cuisine is excellent; guests can use the 250-acre golf course. Rooms start at 170 marks.

The best night life

Frankfurt, surprisingly for a German town, is not a big beer-drinking city. The preferred drinks are hard cider (known as *Appelwein, Appelwoi, Ebbelwoi,* and *Ebbelwei*) and wine (because Frankfurt is so close to the wine-growing Franconia region). Try the cider, which is delicious—but be aware that it carries a much stronger punch than its sweet taste suggests.

Frankfurt is filled with Weinstuben. The **Volkswirt,** *Kleine Hochstr. 9; tel. (49-69)283-419,* is popular among young professionals. It has the greatest wine selection in town. **Peter Dunker,** *Bergerstr. 265,* is a wine bar beneath a half-timbered building. The wine list is long, and the prices are low. **Operncafé,** *Opernplatz 10; tel. (49-69)285-260,* is a trendy place where good-looking young people ogle one another before and after concerts.

Jazz is big in Frankfurt. **Der Jazzkeller,** *Kleine Bockenheimerstr. 18a; tel. (49-69)288-537,* features top performers. And good jazz concerts are staged Sunday mornings in the courtyard of the **Historisches Museum,** *Saalgasse 19; tel. (49-69)212-7599.*

Heidelberg, the most romantic town

Heidelberg is the hub of German Romanticism. Schumann began his career as a Romantic composer in this pretty town, and Goethe fell in love here. Heidelberg is also the oldest university town in Germany and the site of scenes from the movie and opera *The Student Prince.*

The best place to ramble in Heidelberg is the **Haupstrasse,** which is lined with coffeehouses and little shops. Have a drink in one of the cafés beneath the *Rathaus.* Or meander along **Philosopher's Walk,** where Goethe and Hegel wandered. From the path you'll have a bird's-eye view of the city and Heidelberg Castle.

Don't leave town without visiting the **Electoral Palatinate Museum,** where the 500,000-year-old jawbone of Heidelberg Man is kept.

The most beautiful sight

Above town is **Heidelberg Castle,** a magnificent red structure with octagonal towers and ruined belfries. It was the residence of the Wittelsbach family from the 12th to 19th centuries (the Wittelsbachs were a powerful German family that ruled Bavaria and the Rhenish Palatinate). From the castle, you have a panoramic view of the city's red roofs, the spire of the Heiliggeist Kirche, and the Neckar River.

The castle's most awe-inspiring feature is the **Grosses Fass** (Great Vat), a 58,000-gallon wine vat. Local legend has it that a dwarf named Perkeo once drank its contents. The castle also houses Germany's **Pharmaceutical Museum,** which houses a unicorn's horn (so they say) and bizarre body parts.

Weinstube Schloss Heidelberg, the restaurant in the middle of the castle courtyard, has marvelous food. The ceiling is ornately paneled, and the tables are natural wood. The restaurant is closed Tuesdays. Dinner for two is 43 marks to 76 marks.

Heidelberg's best hotels

While **Der Europäische Hof,** *Friedrich-Ebert-Anlage 1; tel. (49-6221)2-71-01; telex 461840,* is the most elegant hotel in Heidelberg, it is also the most expensive. Luxurious and traditional, it charges 260 marks to 340 marks per night.

We prefer **Zum Ritter Sankt Georg,** *Hauptstr. 178, 6900 Heidelberg; tel. (49-6221)202-03.* A cozy establishment in one of Heidelberg's few Renaissance buildings (built in 1592), it has reasonable prices and good service. Rooms are 85 marks to 250 marks (the least expensive rooms don't have private bathrooms). The restaurant, which serves good regional dishes, also can be recommended.

Hamburg: the most worldly

Hamburg, an international port, is Germany's most worldly city. It is known for the steamy sex shows and wild discos along the Reeperbahn in Sankt Pauli. However, it also has a more peaceful section. The lakes at its center are bordered by wide green avenues, opulent shops, and hotels. The old quarter is laced with waterways and has a town hall built on 8,000 piles over marshy ground.

It is difficult to get a handle on the many sides of Hamburg. The best place to take in Hamburg at a glance is from the tower of the baroque Michaelis Kirche . The view of the river, the old section, and Sankt Pauli is panoramic.

The most historic quarter

The most historic section of Hamburg is along **Deichstrass,** near the docks. Many of the 17th-century houses are now restaurants. While you are in the area, visit the **Museum of Hamburg History.**

Germany's best fish market

The best fish market in Germany is held on Sunday mornings in Hamburg. This raucous but fun affair is located by the docks in Altona and begins at 5 a.m.

The largest warehouse complex in the world

You can take a boat tour through the canals of Hamburg's **Warehouse City,** the largest warehouse complex in the world, with buildings dating from the 1800s. Look for the statue of the pirate Klaus Stoertebeker on the Magdeburg docks, where he and 71 of his mates were beheaded in 1401.

The best place to dig up your European roots

Hamburg's Historic Emigration Office is located in the **Museum of Hamburg History,** which has displays relating to Hamburg's history as a harbor town and exhibits dedicated to the emigrants who left for America via Hamburg. If you visit the office in person, you can receive information on your ancestors within one or two hours.

A ship's roster can provide your ancestor's family name and surname (which may have changed upon arrival in the United States; ask your grandparents for the original name); a list of all family members traveling together; place of your ancestor's birth; his marital status, profession, age, and sex; the name of the ship; and the date the ship left Hamburg.

To complete the research, the emigration office needs the name of your ancestor and the year he left Hamburg. The fee for the service is $30 for each year researched, even if the search is unsuccessful. The office is open Tuesdays through Saturdays from 10 a.m. to 1 p.m. and from 2 p.m. to 5 p.m. For more information, contact the **Historic Emigration Office,** *Museum fuer Hamburgische Geschichte, Holstenwall 24, 2000 Hamburg 36; tel. (49-40)300-500-50.*

Germany's sexiest strip

Hamburg's **Reeperbahn** in the Sankt Pauli district west of Hamburg is world famous for its sex shows and wild discos. It's worth a visit, but be careful! This is the territory of criminals, prostitutes, and pimps.

The best strip show is at **Colibri,** *Grosse Freiheit 34.* Live music is played (unlike in many of the bars), and the strippers are young and good-looking. Beer with peppermint schnapps is sold for a reasonable price (you can't get beer without the liqueur).

Moonlight has the raunchiest shows, with sexual acts of all varieties. **Salambo** is salacious. **Erotica**, which has no entry fee, is easiest on the pocket (films are shown rather than live shows).

Hamburg's finest dining

The best restaurant in Hamburg is the **Landhaus Scherrer,** *Elbchaussee 130, Altona; tel. (49-40)880-13-25.* North German cuisine is served at tables overlooking the Elbe. Prices are humble (65 marks to 110 marks), despite the restaurant's Michelin star. And prices are even lower (47 marks to 70 marks) if you eat in the Scherrer's neighboring bistro-restaurant, which serves lunch only.

Schümanns Austernkeller, *Zundseinstiez 34; tel. (49-40)34-62-65 or (49-40)34-53-28,* is another good bet. An elegant Belle Epoque restaurant, it has been in the same family for years. The decor is sumptuous, and the service is first-class. Try the seafood platter (Seezungenplatte), which is delicious. Dinner for two is about 100 marks.

The **Fischerhaus,** *Fischmarkt 14; tel. (49-40)31-40-53,* in Sankt Pauli, serves inexpensive but wonderful seafood. The atmosphere is plain, but the fish isn't. Dinner for two is 34 marks to 60 marks.

Hamburg's best hotel

The best hotel in Hamburg—in Germany for that matter—is **Vier Jahreszeiten,** *Neuer Jungfernstieg 9-14; tel. (49-40)349-40.* This elegant establishment on Lake Alster has a grand white facade rising eight stories and decorated with window boxes. Inside, you will find antique furniture, wood paneling, marble floors, brass trim, and modern facilities. All rooms have telephones, color televisions, private bathrooms with bath, shower, bidet, bathrobes, thermometers, and toiletries.

Founded in 1897, this family-run hotel has an especially comfortable lobby, with leather armchairs, Oriental rugs, wood paneling, and a huge fireplace. Just off the lobby is a lounge with a large stone fireplace, tapestries, and views of the lake. A staff of 450 caters to the requests of guests staying in the 175 rooms. While you are here, you can have your suits mended or altered by the in-house Italian tailor.

The hotel restaurant, **Haerlin,** also is excellent. Vegetables, fruit, flowers, and poultry come straight to the restaurant from the hotel's farm on the outskirts of town. Choose a fine German wine from the hotel's 65,000-bottle cellar.

Double rooms are 400 marks to 445 marks. To make reservations in the United States, contact **Leading Hotels of the World,** *(800)223-6800 or (212)838-3110.*

Charm for less than a fortune

Hotel Abtei, *Nobistor 204, Hamburg-13; tel. (49-40)31-170,* is a small hotel on a shady street in a quiet residential section of Hamburg. Rooms are spacious, bright, and clean. Breakfast is delicious. Double rooms are 180 marks to 230 marks.

Hotel Atlantic, *An der Alster 72, 2000 Hamburg 1; tel. (49-40)28-8001,* is a first-class hotel. Convenient to the center of town, it has a view of Lake Alster. Doubles range from 330 marks to 400 marks.

Hotel Prem, *An der Alster 810, Hamburg 1; tel. (49-40)24-17-26,* is a small, elegant hotel also on Lake Alster. The rooms are large, airy, and filled with flowers. Some look over the lake, others the gardens. Rooms facing the street are noisy. Double rooms are 190 marks to 260 marks.

Bremen, the most beautiful city

Bremen is Germany's most beautiful city and its oldest port. It became a bishop's seat 1,200 years ago and in 1358 joined Hamburg and Lübeck as a leading member of the Hanseatic League, an association of independent merchant towns. Bremen prides itself on its historical buildings. The oldest (some are 800 years old) are grouped around the Markplatz. The Gothic city hall was built in 1405-10.

The oldest building in Bremen

The massive, twin-towered **cathedral,** built in the 11th century, is the oldest building in Bremen. Its cellar contains a mummy. According to the legend, the body of a roofer, who fell to his death in 1450, was put in the cellar for safekeeping but forgotten. When it was discovered many years later, it had been perfectly preserved by the cellar's dry air.

Outside the cathedral stands the famous bronze **statue of Roland,** a Crusader knight.

Germany's best banqueting hall

Grosse Halle in the city hall is one of the largest and most elegant banqueting halls in Germany. A large mural, the *Judgment of Solomon,* hangs on the wall. A richly carved spiral staircase ascends to the upper stories.

Germany's oldest inn

Der Ratskeller, west of the town hall, is one of the oldest and most traditional of Germany's inns. It is known for its huge selection of more than 500 German wines, including a 1653 Rüdesheimer.

The oldest quarter

Schnoor Viertel, Bermen's oldest district and a former fishermen's quarter, has artists' workshops and colorful restaurants and inns. Many of the half-timbered, gabled houses in the quarter are 400 to 500 years old.

Best fish dishes

When you are ready for dinner, stop in at **Grashoff's Bistro,** *Contrescarpe 80; tel. (49-421)14740.* This little restaurant doesn't look like much, but it serves some of the best fish dishes in the region. The haddock in mustard sauce is especially good. Expect to pay 60 marks to 100 marks for dinner without wine. The bistro is closed Sundays. Reservations are recommended.

The best ship museum in the world

Just north of Bremen in Bremerhaven (the most important fishing port in Europe) is one of the best ship museums in the world, the **Schiffahrtsmuseum,** *Columbusstrass,* in the old quarter. The *Seute Deern,* a Hanseatic tall ship wrecked in 1380, is especially impressive.

Bremen's best hotels

Park Hotel, *Bürgerpark; tel. (49-421)3408555,* is Bremen's most prestigious hotel. It has spacious public rooms, a garden terrace, rooms with balconies overlooking a pond, and a fine restaurant. Double rooms are 310 marks to 320 marks.

The **Canadian Pacific Plaza,** *Hillmannplatz 20; tel. (49-421)17670,* is the most convenient hotel in Bremen, just a five-minute walk from the pedestrian area. It is picturesque, located opposite a windmill. Double rooms are 250 marks to 350 marks.

Cologne: best carnival, best churches

If you like churches, you'll believe yourself at the gates of heaven when you reach **Cologne** (Köln). The number of churches marking the city's skyline is remarkable (13 in all). What's more, many of these churches are among the most beautiful in Germany. While some were damaged during World War II, most have been restored to their former beauty and are open to the public.

It's probably a good thing Cologne has so many churches, considering that it also is the site of Germany's wildest carnival season. If you like a good bacchanalia, visit Cologne the week before Ash Wednesday. Carnival begins with Weiberfastnacht, the Women's carnival, held on the Alter Markt. Women choose their dancing partners and dance from morning to midnight. (This custom is said to have its origins in 16th-century pre-Lenten orgies.)

Cologne's beautiful churches

Cologne's famous Gothic **cathedral** is a gigantic structure that can be seen from almost any point in the city. Begun in 1248 and completed in 1880, it houses several great works of art, including the 12th-century Shrine of the Three Magi, a masterpiece of the goldsmith's art created to house holy relics.

Hlg. Maria im Kapitol was the church most severely damaged during the war, but it has been well-restored. Its extraordinary, carved wooden doors, with 26 reliefs illustrating the life of Christ, date back to 1050. A 12th-century sculpture of the Virgin also is on display.

Hlg. Pantaleon, a twin-towered structure with a 10th-century nave and cloister, is the oldest remaining Romanesque church in Germany.

Hlg. Aposteln is the finest example of Rhineland Romanesque architecture. Built between 1192 and 1230, it has a squat nave with ribbed vaults, a trefoil choir, and a tower.

The oldest church in Cologne is **St. Gereon,** *2 Gereonsdriech.* Its walls, crypts, and pillars are from the fourth century.

When you tire of touring churches, visit **Rhine Park.** During the summer, dances and concerts are held here. Concerts begin at 4 p.m.; dancing begins at 8 p.m.

The prettiest part of Cologne is the old section, near the Rhine, where 12th- and 13th-century buildings remain.

Cologne's best restaurant

Seafood dishes and the best German wines are served at **Weinhaus im Walfisch,** *Salzgasse 13; tel. (49-221)21-95-75,* situated in a 350-year-old building. Weinhaus is closed Sundays. Reservations are recommended.

The coziest hotel

The **Hotel Bristol,** *Kaiser-Wilhelm-Ring 48, Köln 1; tel. (49-221)12-01-95,* is a cozy, family-run hotel near the cathedral. Rooms on the lower floors can be noisy. Bedrooms have intricately carved wooden furniture and modern bathrooms. Some rooms have canopy beds. Double rooms start at 155 marks, including breakfast.

Aachen: a history buff's favorite

Aachen (Aix-la-Chapelle in French) is the most historically interesting town in Germany. Located near the Belgian and Dutch borders, Aachen's hot, curative mineral springs were used by the Romans, and remains of their baths and temples can be seen near the cathedral.

Holy Roman Emperor Charlemagne made Aachen a stronghold in A.D. 794. His empire united the people of what later became France and Germany. He died in Aachen on Jan. 28, A.D. 814 and is buried in the town's cathedral. The cathedral also contains parts of the clothing of Jesus, the Virgin Mary, and John the Baptist.

Aachen has seen the crowning of 32 kings. During World War II, most of the town was destroyed, but the important historic buildings have been restored.

Aachen's best dining, playing, and sleeping

The **Schloss Friesenrath,** *Pannekoogweg 46, Aachen-Friesenrath; tel. (49-2408)50-48,* is an elegant restaurant in Aachen's castle. The setting and furnishings are authentic.

After dinner, gamblers (and curious non-gamblers) frequent **Spielcasino Aachen,** *Monheimsallee 44,* where you can play roulette, baccarat, and blackjack. The casino is open every day from 3 p.m. to 2 a.m.; it stays open until 3 a.m. Fridays and Saturdays.

The **Steigenberger Hotel Quellenhof,** *Monheimsallee 52; tel. (49-241)15-20-81,* is the nicest hotel in town. It has well-appointed rooms, an indoor thermal swimming pool, and a sauna. Double rooms range from 248 marks to 318 marks.

A fairy-tale lover's favorite: the Black Forest

If you loved the movie *The Princess Bride* and you know all Grimm's fairy tales by heart, the best place for you is the **Black Forest.** This region has dense pine forests, quaint villages, and lone thatched cottages. Surely, Hansel and Gretel got lost here.

The best drives through this fairy-tale land are along the **Black Forest Crest Road** and **Route 500,** which winds for about 120 miles on its way to Hinterzarten. At an altitude of 3,500 feet and higher, the road rides the summit of a series of steep mountains. Sunlight seeps through the firs in white shafts of light.

The road passes gingerbread villages and serene lakes, eventually coming to an open-air museum just north of Gutach. The museum is a restored town with low-ceilinged houses built into hillsides.

Stop in **Triberg,** where an immense clock sounds the hour every hour and an automatic organ plays the *William Tell Overture.* A figure representing Death rings a bell on one side and an angel rings on the other. The 12 Apostles rotate past a wooden Jesus who raises His arms in blessing.

Another pretty drive is along the shores of **Bodensee** (Lake Constance), which leads past little fishing villages. Near Bodman you'll see Neolithic, Celtic, and Roman ruins. In Unteruhldingen, you'll pass reconstructed thatched dwellings on stilts over the water. Mammoth tusks are on display at the local museum in Überlingen, an ancient walled town on the lake.

Cuckoo favorites

The woods around **Triberg** are known as the home of cuckoo birds, who cuckoo like crazy all day. Known as the cuculus canorus among scientists, the bird is shy and rarely seen (or heard) elsewhere.

If you fail to spot a real cuckoo in the woods, stop in the **Heimat Museum** in Triberg, which houses the largest collection of cuckoo clocks anywhere. And if clocks make you tick, also visit Triberg's **Uhrenmuseum,** which houses an alarm clock made in 1690.

The oldest castle in Germany

Meersburg, an almost vertical village pitched high above a ravine, lies in the shadows of the oldest castle in Germany. Locals claim it was built by Dagobert in A.D. 630. Some of the walls do date back to A.D. 1,000, but most of the building is from the 16th century. The entire castle was restored in 1877. The chapel and the courtyard are especially worth seeing.

Across from the old castle is the ancient residence of the bishops of Constance. Stand on the terrace and enjoy the view.

Meersburg has a marvelous hotel—the stately **Hotel Bad Schachen,** which looks out over Bodensee toward Lindau. Its grand dining room serves delicious meals.

The forest's highest peak

The highest peak in the forest is the **Feldberg.** Take a chairlift to the top. The village of Feldberg at the foot of the mountain was the birthplace of German skiing and is one of the oldest winter resorts in Germany.

Baden-Baden: the world's most famous spa

Baden-Baden, the world's most famous spa, was founded by Roman legionnaires. Located south of Heidelberg in the Black Forest, it is known for its curative waters. The magnificent 19th-century spa (*Kurhaus*) was built directly over the ruins of the ancient Roman baths.

The casino, where Dostoyevsky lost all his money, has attracted royalty for centuries. Massive old hotels line the Oos River.

The best time to visit is the last week in August, **Baden-Baden Week,** when horse races, balls, and receptions are held. While the week is great fun, it is also the most crowded time of year here.

Baden-Baden's best hotel

Brenner's Park-Hotel, *Schillerstr. 6, 7570 Baden-Baden; tel. (49-7221)3530,* is the best hotel in Baden-Baden, and one of the best in Europe. This Edwardian hotel is a traditional part of any visit to the spa. It has large, graceful public rooms, excellent service, an indoor heated pool, a sauna, and a solarium. Take the waters, then see the sights via horse and buggy or have tea while listening to a string quartet. The hotel has views of the park and the river. Double rooms range from 250 marks to 890 marks.

If you'd rather not empty your pockets at the rather expensive Brenner's Park-Hotel, the **Hotel Badischer Hof,** *Langestr. 47, 7570 Baden-Baden; tel. (49-7221)22827,* is a good, family-run alternative. Double rooms are 248 marks to 308 marks.

The coziest shelter in the forest

One of the loveliest hotels in the Black Forest is the **Park-Hotel Wehrle,** *Haupstrasse, Triberg 7740; tel. (49-7722)86020.* It has a swimming pool, a sauna, and an excellent restaurant known for its trout dishes. Double rooms are 93 marks to 153 marks.

The **Buhler-Hohe Hotel,** *Kurhaus-Schloss, 7580 Bühl-13; tel. (49-7226)50,* is a great place to absorb the atmosphere of the forest. It is hidden behind a thick canopy of evergreens and covered with ivy. Originally a hunting lodge, it is now a fitness center.

Bacchus' bests

Germany's 11 **wine-growing districts,** which stretch from the middle Rhine at Bonn south to the Bodensee, produce the lightest white wines in the world. These regions are filled with classic scenery—castle ruins, grand cathedrals, gabled houses, elegant spas, and enchanting little villages.

The world's best Rieslings

The **Rheingau region** on the right bank of the Rhine is the aristocrat of Germany's wine-producing areas. This small region, extending from Hocheim in the east to Lorch in the west, is known for the Riesling grape. A sampling of wines at the local wineries will give you a taste of the best white wines in the world. This is also the place to buy good German wine cheaply. In addition to wine, the Rheingau also is known for its wealth of monuments, monasteries, and wine cellars, some of which date back to the time of Charlemagne.

A good place to sample the local Rieslings is the crowded but energizing town of **Rudesheim.** The Drösselgasse, a narrow, cobblestoned alley, is lined with wine taverns and restaurants. Order a *Römer* (a wine goblet with a green pedestal) of the local wine and watch the crowds. Rudesheim is the site of rousing wine festivals in May and August. One of Germany's best wine museums is in Brömser Castle at the west end of town.

A fine restaurant that features wine tasting is located in the Waldhotel Jagdschloss Niederwald, three miles from Rudesheim. Delicious game dishes are served in season. This **castle hotel,** *tel. (49-6722)1004,* is impressive, set on a hill high above the Rhine. It is closed in the winter.

The best German reds

Stuttgart is the perfect base for touring the Wurttemberg area, which follows the Neckar River south of Baden-Baden. Red wines such as Trollinger and Limberger can be sampled throughout Wurttemberg. (They are rarely exported, so this could be your only chance to enjoy them.)

If you tire of wine tasting, visit the old Renaissance palace or the Staatsgalerie (National Gallery) in Stuttgart, the Roman baths and castle ruins in Weinsberg, or the Palace Gardens of Ludwigsburg.

The best place to sample local Wurttemberg wines is the **Wirtshaus zum Götzenturm,** *Allerheiligenstr. 1,* in the medieval walled town of Heilbronn. The owner of this restaurant also runs the Beichstuhl, a wine cellar around the corner. Both places are closed Sundays, Mondays after lunch, and in August.

The wine cellar of the Holy Roman Empire

The elegant wines of the **Rheinpfalz region,** northwest of Wurttemberg, have been famous since the days of Holy Roman Emperor Charlemagne, when this area was known as the Wine Cellar of the Holy Roman Empire. The picturesque Deutsche Weinstrasse (German Wine Road) runs its length.

Detour if you can to nearby **Speyer** (Spier), where the town's museum houses the oldest wine in the world, dating from the third century. While in Speyer, have a glass of the local wine at **Café Hindenburg**, *Maximilianstr. 91.*

The oldest wine region

Fine wines are produced northwest of Rheinpfalz in the **Moselle Valley**, which has the oldest vineyards in Germany and the steepest vineyards in the world. The Moselle's vines are ancient. The *Neumagen* wine ship in Trier Museum was used by Romans to bring vines to Germany. Timbered houses, old churches, and stately castles cluster along the steep banks of rivers.

Markers along the Rhine describe the wines produced here: Piesporter, Wehlen, Bernkastler, and Graach. The finest Moselle wines are Bernkasteler Doktor and Wehlener Sonnenuhr.

The best place to try the local wines is **Kurtrierische Weinstube zum Domstein,** *Hauptmarkt 5, Trier; tel. (49-657)7-44-90.* This Roman wine cellar serves Moselle wines and dishes prepared according to old Roman recipes.

The most beautiful wine region

The **Ahr Valley,** Germany's northernmost wine region, is the most beautiful. Between Altenahr and Bad Neuenahr, the river forces its way in a rapid, winding course between rugged slate crags. Vineyards climb steep slopes in the shadows of castle ruins. Wine villages are sandwiched by the hills.

Wine has been made here since Roman times, and today the area produces Germany's best reds and bubbling whites. Try the local wines at the **Weinstube Sankt Peter** in Walporzheim or at the lively **Lochmuhle** at Mayschloss. Hikers can follow the 30-kilometer Red Wine Trail through vineyards from Lohrsdorf to Altenahr.

The best rosés

Between Heidelberg and the Badensee is the **Baden region,** famous for producing sweeter whites and Schillerwein rosés. A giant cask holding 52,000 gallons of the region's wine is located in Heidelberg. You can try the local wines at **Perkeo,** *Hauptstr. 75,* a large beer and wine house in Heidelberg. A more scenic place to sample the wines is on the terrace of the **Weinstube im Schloss Heidelberg,** a restaurant in a castle outside Heidelberg.

How to become an expert wine taster

To better understand the wines within each region, enroll in a seven-day English-language seminar offered by the German Wine Academy, which is located in Kloster Eberbach, a former 12th-century monastery near Wiesbaden. Each seminar includes lectures by experts and visits to wine-growing regions, vineyards, cellars, and tastings. The cost is about 1,640 marks per person, double occupancy, including room, board, transportation to Germany, and program fees. For information contact the **German Wine Academy,** *c/o Reisebüro, A. Bartholomae GmbH, Wilhelmstr. 8, D-6200 Wiesbaden, West Germany,* or the **German Wine Information Bureau,** *79 Madison Ave., New York, NY 10016; (212)213-0909.*

The most charming castle hotels on the Rhine

The Rhineland is a fairy-tale region with more than 30 medieval castles. The best way to soak in the atmosphere of the region is to stay in one of the many Rhine castles that have been turned into hotels.

The **Rheinfels,** which is the largest of the Rhine castles, is also one of the best castle hotels: **Schlosshotel auf Burg Rheinfels,** *Schlossberg 47, 5401 Sankt Goar; tel. (49-6721)20-71.* An immense maze of courtyards and towers, the castle was built in 1245. The view of the Rhine Valley from the Rheinfels is panoramic; the castle is perched on a high bluff over the river. If you listen carefully from the terrace, you might hear singing from the nearby Lorelei. The treacherous and craggy 450-foot rock is where ghostly maidens lure sailors to their deaths by singing, according to legend. Some say this is also where the treasure of the Nibelungs (the Burgundian tribe of Wagner's opera *The Ring*) is hidden. Terraces, a fireplace, a chapel, walking paths, a heated indoor pool, and a sauna are some of the hotel's charms. The dining room serves delicious venison. Rooms start at 77 marks.

The **Klostergut Jakobsberg,** *Höhe 318m, 5407 Boppard/Rhein; tel. (49-6742)30-61,* a monastery-turned-hotel, is also near the Lorelei. Built in 1157 by Kaiser Friedrich I, it is situated on a bluff overlooking the Rhine. The monastery was owned by the archbishops of Trier. In 1640 it became the property of the Jesuits, who used it as a university center until the French Revolution. The monastery was later taken over by the Prussians. Today it is a hotel with modern amenities, a good restaurant, and an indoor pool. Double rooms are 100 marks to 160 marks .

The **Hotel Burg Reichenstein,** *6531 Trechtingshausen/Rhein; tel. (49-6721)6117,* has a magnificent view of the Rhine. Its 13th-century Gothic arches and rough stonework remain. Robber-knights once watched the river from the castle's towers. Inside the castle is a museum displaying medieval weapons and armor. Double rooms are 110 marks.

Germany's oldest city

Trier is the oldest city in Germany, founded by the Celts 1,300 years before Rome. Roman relics in Trier include the Porta Nigra, which was the northern gateway to the Roman Empire, Roman baths, and an amphitheater that can hold 30,000 spectators. The 11th-century cathedral contains what is believed to be a piece of Jesus' clothing. Pilgrims from all over the world come to see the tomb of Sankt Matthias at Sankt Matthias Abbey (Sankt Matthias was the only apostle buried north of the Alps). Sankt Maxim Abbey has a register of all the witches in the area during the 16th century—the list includes more than 6,000 names! More recently, Karl Marx was born in Trier. His house is a museum.

Trier's **Petrisberg Hotel,** *Sickingenstr. 11; tel. (49-651)4-11-81,* is a family-run bed and breakfast that has a pleasant atmosphere and serves big breakfasts. Try to get a room in the front of the hotel, where you'll enjoy a balcony and a fine view of the city. A Roman amphitheater is nearby, and town is a 20-minute walk away. Double rooms are 100 marks.

Worms: the strangest history

The city of **Worms** has a strange name and an even stranger history. It was named for a legendary giant worm with fangs and webbed feet that lived in the Rhine and demanded human sacrifices.

Worms was the fifth-century capital of the Nibelungs. The tribe left the area, according to legend, after the wicked Hagen slew their hero, Siegfried, and threw their treasure into the river. A huge statue of Hagen commemorates the story. The town was destroyed in A.D. 436 by Attila the Hun.

In the center of the town's old quarter is the tall, spired Cathedral of Sts. Peter and Paul, built in the 11th and 12th centuries. Worms has a huge statue of Martin Luter, the oldest synagogue in Germany, built in the 11th century and restored in 1961, and the oldest and largest Jewish cemetery in Europe. Tombstones date from the 11th century. The synagogue and the cemetery are among the few remaining traces of pre-World War II German Jewry.

The most disappointing sight in Germany

Lorelei, subject of myth, poem, and song, turns out be something other than a beautiful river nymph whose golden tresses led sailors to their deaths. If you follow the Rhine between Mainz and Cologne through the sharp valley cut by the river between wine-laden hills topped by great castles and picturesque villages, you eventually come to Sankt Goarshausen, south of the only intact castle (Marksburg) on the route. Here, 82 miles south of Cologne and 29 miles from Mainz on the right bank of the Rhine, is the Lorelei, which is nothing but a huge rock overhanging a hairpin bend in the river. What the sailors took for a mermaid was the play of light on the peak—which is not to say that they did not risk drowning as their boats maneuvered the narrow passage between the rocks. On either side are other peaks named by superstitious sailors: Burg Katz (Cat's Mountain) and Teufelstein (Devil's Stone).

Germany's most beautiful islands

Germany has beautiful beaches as well as deep forests and medieval villages. The **East Frisian Islands,** which fringe the North Sea coastline, have long sandy beaches guarded by dunes and frequented by nude sunbathers. The islands have fishing villages, seal-covered rocks, and an ancient language and culture. Five of the seven islands are closed to cars—you can drive only on Borkum and Norderney.

Borkum, the largest island, has particularly salty air because of the heavy surf along the beaches. **Sylt** is the most beautiful island, dotted with traditional fishing villages and dolmens erected by prehistoric man. The islanders' thatched-roof houses are sharply pitched to ward off the cold winds of the North Sea. Spectacular 30-foot dunes are covered with purple heather. But the beaches can be brisk—sunbathers rent wicker protectors or build small walls of sand to protect themselves from the wind. And the water is bracing. The area between Borkum and Sylt is home to herds of seals numbering in the hundreds.

The small islands of **Juist** and **Memmert,** between Ems and Weser, attract hundreds of birds and birdwatchers. **Westerland** has a casino. **Amrum** has high sand dunes—the sites of ancient pagan sacrifices. And most of the islands have resorts with seawater swimming pools (which are a good deal warmer than the sea itself).

For more information on the East Frisian Islands, contact **Fremdenverkehrsverband Nordsee Niedersachsen-Bremen,** *East Frisian Bahnhofstr. 19-20, Postfach 1820, D-2900 Oldenburg; tel. (49-441)1-45-35,* or visit the tourist office in the railroad station in Oldenburg.

Harz: the most bewitching region

According to legend, witches live in Germany's northernmost mountains, the **Harz.** They are said to fly on Walpurgis Night, the last night of April. Residents of the area celebrate Walpurgis Night with more abandon than Germans elsewhere, dressing as devils, witches, and demons. Try to time your visit to the area so that you too can participate in the revelry.

If you can't manage to make it to the Harz for Walpurgis Night, don't despair. The region is bewitching year-round.The mountains are covered with evergreen forests, inhabited by deer, and brightened by waterfalls, ravines, and rocky streams. One of Germany's highest peaks is the Wurmberg near Braunlage in the Harz. Take a cable car to see the top.

The Harz was made famous by the celebrated German poet Heinrich Heine (1797-1856) in *Die Harzreise* (*The Harz Journey*), a cycle of poems set to music by Schubert.

Bavarian bests

Bavaria, which was independent until 1918 (Munich was its capital), is the largest and most visited section of Germany. This southeastern region is touristy, but with good reason—Bavaria is beautiful. You can avoid the masses, by exploring Bavaria off-season in the spring or fall. The Alps stretch along the region's southern border with Austria, offering wooded slopes, flower-filled meadows, lakes, and castles. The mountain-encircled Konigsee is a gorgeous deep-blue lake surrounded by sheer alpine cliffs.

Alpine peaks

The **Alps** stretch along Germany's southern border from the Bodensee in the west to the Watzmann Peak near Berchtesgaden in the east. This mountain range rose from the sea about 80-million years ago. You can find fossils of sea creatures among the peaks. The beautiful lakes in the Voralpenland are remnants of the Ice Age.

Germany's highest peak

The **Zugspitze,** Germany's highest peak (9,840 feet), overlooks Garmisch-Partenkirchen and is part of the Wettersteingebirge, an ancient formation of hard rock. You can take a cable car or train from Garmisch to the summit. Even when clouded over (about 35% of the time), the view is spectacular. You can see the peaks of other mountains rising above the blanket of clouds. Get a beer at the top, or just breathe in the intoxicatingly thin mountain air.

The best skiing

Garmisch-Partenkirchen, the most popular resort in the German Alps, offers Germany's best skiing. The powdery peaks are accessible by an assortment of lifts. Trails are geared toward every level of skier. A pretty town with gaily painted Alpine houses, Garmisch has aprés-ski entertainment, a casino, and concerts. Proximity to the American Army base, however, is causing the town to lose some of its Germanic charm. Nearby are Ludwig II's Linderhof Castle and the domed Benedictine abbey of Ettal.

The best place to stay is the **Schneefernerhaus,** a miracle of engineering perched at 8,692 feet atop the Zugspitze. The view is absolutely incredible, but the hotel is basic and inexpensive.

The best Alpine hikes

The German Alps are crisscrossed by 9,000 hiking trails. They are well-used by the Germans, who consider *das Wandern* (walking, rambling, exploring the world) a way of life.

The most beautiful walking trail in the Alps is along Bodensee between the towns of Friedrichshafen and Lindau. The snow-capped Alps are reflected in the waters of the lake. The walk is not difficult and can be done in tennis shoes. The entire length takes about two days (longer if you stop off in some of the towns along the way). For a map of the trail, stop in at the tourist office in Friedrichshafen or Lindau.

The trail from the town of Füssen to Neuschwanstein Castle is also beautiful. Füssen is a picturesque village in the shadows of the turreted castle. The trail leads past several lakes and into the shadows of the Austrian and German Alps. The walk isn't difficult.

Our third-favorite hike begins at a path leading from the Olympic Ski Stadium in Garmisch-Partenkirchen to the Graseckbahn cable car, which carries you to the Frosthaus Graseck. At the peak is an inviting little restaurant with panoramic views. From the terrace, you can pick up another trail along the spectacular Partnachklamm, a very narrow and deep gorge filled with torrents of water. Hold on to the guardrails along the path, which is narrow and sometimes slippery.

Hitler's favorite hideout

The **Kehlsteinhaus** (Eagle's Nest), perched on a rocky crag above the town of Berchtesgaden, was Hitler's favorite hideout. No wonder—the view from the hideaway-turned-restaurant is exhilarating. Anyone could develop delusions of grandeur here. Alpine peaks rise above cottony clouds at this level. The snow at their summits glistens in the sun. Below, a thick carpet of dark green pines stretches toward the valley.

The road to the Eagle's Nest is so steep and dangerous that cars are not allowed to use it; you must take a special bus from the Obersalzberg-Hintereck parking lot. You can dine in the restaurant from mid-May to mid-October.

The world's best passion play

Every 10 years, the world's most moving passion play is performed in the shadows of the Alps in the little artisan town of **Oberammergau.** From May through September in years ending in zero, local amateur actors put aside their daily professions and devote themselves entirely to the play. Written in the 17th century, it enacts Christ's suffering between the Last Supper and His death. Villagers have performed the play every 10 years since the 17th century, when they vowed they would perform the passion if the black plague ceased. It did, and they have.

Because the text is so old, many consider it anti-semitic. It blames the Jews for Christ's crucifixion.

The picturesque **Passionsspielhaus** (Passion Play Theater) can be visited any time of year. The immense open-air stage holds 700 actors, and the theater's wooden benches hold 5,200 people. You can see the elaborate costumes used during the passion play when you visit. Performances begin at 8:30 a.m. and finish at 6 p.m., with a two-hour break for lunch.

The next passion play will be in 1990. You must make reservations well in advance. For information, contact the **Information Bureau of Oberammergau,** *Verkehrsamt, Schnitzelergasse 8; tel. (49-8822))41-21.*

The best hotel in Oberammergau is the Alois Lang. This quiet place has rooms with private bathrooms and three good dining rooms.

Bavaria's looniest king

Mad King Ludwig, who ruled Bavaria from 1864 to 1886, built the most fanciful and beautiful buildings in Germany, despite (or perhaps because of) his insanity. But his magnificent creations were extremely costly, and his extravagance nearly bankrupted Bavaria. An important patron of the arts, Ludwig was a great fan of Wagner's. He built the Bayreuth Opera House for the composer and lived in a fantasy world based on Wagner's operas.

Ludwig's death by drowning has raised many questions over the years. Some say his madness drove him to suicide; others say it was a fatal accident; and others hold it was murder. Whatever the case, Ludwig died shortly after having been declared insane.

Germany's most beautiful castle

Ludwig created Germany's most beautiful castle: **Neuschwanstein.** The turreted, white castle reaches high into the sky from its perch on a cliff above a valley. Walt Disney liked it so much that he copied it for his Disneyland and Disney World. It looks enchanted, with its mountain backdrop. Inside, the walls are decorated with murals of German heroic sagas. In Ludwig's bedroom, stars in the dark blue ceiling light up to look like the night sky. Ludwig lived at Neuschwanstein for 102 days before he drowned in the waters of nearby Lake Starnberg at age 40.

Germany's smallest castle

The smallest castle in Germany also was the product of Mad King Ludwig's imagination. **Linderhof Castle,** near Garmisch-Partenkirchen, is an ornate, one-man palace designed as Ludwig's personal residence. The mad king preferred to be alone and went to great lengths to maintain his privacy. He had the dining room built directly above the kitchen and installed a dining table that could be lowered into the kitchen, set by the cooks, and lifted back up to the dining room. Thus, he could be waited on at dinner without having to see the servants. Ludwig lived the longest at this castle.

Up the hill from the castle, Ludwig created a grotto. Entered by way of a hinged boulder, the artificial cave is the recreation of Venus Mountain from Wagner's *Tannhäuser*. Inside the grotto is an artificial lake with a waterfall and Ludwig's boat.

The world's best violins

The world's most perfect violins are crafted in **Mittenwald,** a pretty Bavarian town whose buildings are decorated with brightly colored frescoes. The craft has been passed down through generations of local artisans, who make the instruments to order for famous musicians. The meadows, mountains, and village houses around Mittenwald are so typically Alpine that they were used as location sites for the filming of *The Sound of Music*.

The most scenic drives through Germany

A number of beautiful scenic routes wind their ways through Germany. The longest is the Alpen-Ostee, stretching from the Baltic Sea island of Fehmarn to the Bavarian village of Berchtesgaden. The most unusual is the Windmill Road in the marshy area of Minden/Lübeck. The roads overlap in many of the most picturesque places. For instance, the Romantic and the Alpine roads both lead to Mad Ludwig's castle Neuschwanstein.

The Romantic Road

The **Romantic Road** runs from Würzburg in the north to Füssen in the south. The road, which follows a medieval trade route, is about 200 miles long and passes vineyards, ruined castles, and wooded hills.

Begin by heading east from Heidelberg along the Neckar River on the Castle Road (Route 37). At Nedkarelz, turn left on Route 27 and go through Mosbach. Take Route 292 to Bad Mergentheim. Stop in Weikersheim to visit the town's castle, which has a marvelous Hunting Hall and baroque gardens.

The best-preserved walled town

Continue on to **Rothenburg ob-der-Tauber,** the best-preserved medieval town in Germany, with gabled houses topped by steep Gothic roofs. You can walk around the city atop its huge encircling fortress walls. Climb the tower of the *Rathaus* (town hall) for a superb view of the town's fortifications, which are shaped like a wine goblet. Visit the Medieval Crime Museum and stroll the Burggarten, the lovely public gardens.

Don't miss the clock on the 15th-century **Ratstrinkstube** (City Counselors' Tavern). Its mechanical figures re-enact the heroic feat of Burgomaster Nusch, who saved the town from plundering by Imperial forces in 1631. According to legend, Nusch offered the commander of the army a cup of the best local wine, after which the commander agreed to spare the town if someone could down six pints (three liters) of the wine at once. Nusch obliged. You can watch the astonishment on General Tilly's face as Nusch downs the draught seven times a day—when the clock strikes 11 a.m., noon, 1 p.m., 2 p.m., 3 p.m., 9 p.m., and 10 p.m.

Two restaurants with inviting medieval atmospheres can be found in the marketplace. **Baumeisterhaus** is in a 16th-century patrician residence surrounded by a garden that serves German food at reasonable prices. **Ratsstube** is a tavern-restaurant that offers good regional dishes, including sausage with sauerkraut. Dinner is inexpensive, about 34 marks for two.

The best hotel in Rothenburg is the **Eisenhut,** *Herrngasse 3; tel. (49-9861)2041.* This historic inn is actually several medieval patrician houses that have been joined together. It has a much-admired restaurant with a paneled, galleried dining hall and a garden terrace by the Tauber River. Try the trout specialties in season. Double rooms are about 210 marks to 285 marks a night.

The best of Augsburg

Another gem of a town along the Romantic Road is **Augsburg,** founded by the Romans in 15 B.C. Once a medieval metropolis, it has mansions, palaces, Gothic churches, towers, and ramparts. Don't miss the **Fuggerei,** founded in 1519 by the Fugger family (bankers for the Hapsburgs) as a refuge for the old and needy. A town within a town, the Fuggerei has its own church, gabled houses, and courtyards. The needy still live here on the original terms— an annual rent of 2 marks and a daily prayer for the soul of the founder!

Augsburg's cathedral has 11th-century bronze doors, an altar by Holbein the Elder, and the oldest stained-glass windows in Germany (they're from the 12th century). Climb the Perlach tower of the *Rathaus* for a view of the Alps. A yellow flag flies if they are visible.

The best way to go

You can drive the Romantic Road yourself, which gives you the freedom to come and go as you please, or you can take the convenient Europa Bus tour, which is free with a Eurailpass. The 11-hour tour leaves daily from Frankfurt and Munich and visits Wiesbaden, Frankfurt, Rothenburg, Dinkelsbühl, and Munich. You can break your journey anywhere along the road and catch the same bus the next day. The bus company can arrange hotels for you along the route. To make reservations, contact **Europa Bus,** *German Rail, 747 Third Ave., 33rd Floor, New York, NY 10017; (212)308-3100.*

The German Alpine Road

The **Deutsche Alpenstrasse** (German Alpine Road) leads from Bodensee through the Bavarian Alps. It passes Germany's highest peak, the Zugspitze; the limestone massifs of the Alpine National Park; the ski resorts of Garmisch-Partenkirchen; Berchtesgadener Land, where the mighty Watzmann Mountain drops down suddenly to the deep-blue Konigsee; Mittenwald; and the castles of Hohenschwangau and Neuschwanstein, where Mad King Ludwig lived out his fantasies. The natural scenery along the route is consistently awe-inspiring.

The best place to stay along this route is the **Posthotel Partenkirchen,** *Ludwigstr. 49; tel. (49-8821)5-10-67,* in Partenkirchen near Garmisch. This 15th-century family-run hotel overflows with Bavarian atmosphere. The exterior of the three-story building is covered with paintings. Inside are oil portraits, dark wood furniture, beamed ceilings, and wood paneling. Many of the rooms have balconies, and a roof garden affords a view of the Zugspitze. Double rooms start at 142 marks.

The Road of the Nibelungs

The **Nibelungenstrasse** (Road of the Nibelungs) is a favorite among devotees of the Siegfried sagas. (The Nibelungs were an evil family that possessed a magic but cursed hoard of gold, according to German legend. In some stories they are depicted as dwarfs, in others they are Burgundians. They are central to the *Nibelungenlied,* an ancient German epic composed between 1100 and 1300. In the saga, the warrior Siegfried takes the gold and is later murdered.) Wagner used these tales for his *Ring* operas.

The route, which goes from Worms to Wertheim, passes through the Odenwald, an inhospitable forest region in the time of the Nibelungs. Today, the hilly, wooded region is much more welcoming, with a series of health spas (Amorbach, Bad König, Beerfelden, Erbach, and Michelstadt). The **Bergstrasse-Odenwald Nature Park** is a good place to stop and appreciate the rocky forest. The park is covered by an extensive network of footpaths.

Hotel Badischer Hof, *Am Stadttor 4, Amorbach 8762; tel. (49-9373)12-08,* is the best place to stay along the way. This cozy hostelry has been run by the same family for nearly 200 years. After a good breakfast on the balcony, wander through the courtyard, which is filled with flowers. Double rooms start at 70 marks.

The Fairy-Tale Trail

The **Fairy-Tale Trail** leads from Bremen through Hamelin to Steinau, the home of the brothers Grimm. The road leads 360 miles south, through medieval towns and past castles, palaces, and seemingly enchanted forests. It takes you to the 13th-century castle of Neustadt, where Rapunzel was locked in a tower by a witch; the town of Schwalmstadt, where Little Red Riding Hood lived; and Kassel, where the brothers Grimm wrote their first book of fairy tales in 1812.

The most magical place to stay en route is Sleeping Beauty's castle in Sababurg. The Grimm brothers, authors of the tale, visited the castle and made it the setting of the story. Built in 1334 to protect pilgrims heading for Gottsbüren, the castle has two massive towers.

The hotel is closed in January and February. Rooms are 77 marks to 170 marks. To make reservations, contact **Hotel Sababurg,** *3520 Hofgeismar-Sababurg; tel. (49-5678)10-52.*

Chapter 7

THE BEST OF SPAIN

Spain is the most exotic West European nation. Although it is linked to the European continent at the French border, in many ways it feels more like North Africa. Not until the reign of Ferdinand and Isabella in the 15th century did Spain become part of Europe culturally. But when it did finally join hands with Europe, it became a great power, colonizing much of the world.

Although it is no longer mighty, Spain boasts Roman ruins, Moorish fortresses, and early-Christian cathedrals. The landscape is ruggedly beautiful, the traditions colorful, and the art collections among the greatest in the world. A tour of Spain will lead you from Madrid's gigantic Prado Museum, which rivals the Louvre as the best museum in the world, to the rich and elaborate Alhambra, idyllic sandy beaches, and quaint fishing villages.

Madrid: Spain's most cosmopolitan city

Madrid is a cosmopolitan city with museums, elegant restaurants, and trendy discos. It is worth visiting, despite its pollution problem. Situated more than 10,000 feet above sea level, Madrid is filled with trucks and cars spewing hydrocarbons unhindered by any anti-pollution devices.

The most picturesque quarter

The most picturesque section of Madrid is the labyrinth of narrow streets between **Puerta del Sol** and the **Royal Palace.** Each street has a sign depicting an activity that distinguished it in the past. For instance, Pasadizo del Panecillo has a picture of friars distributing bread to the poor. The best way to explore is on foot. You will find Velazquez's grand statue of Philip IV in the center of the Plaza de Oriente, east of the Royal Palace.

Have a glass of sangria in the vast main square of Madrid, the **Plaza Mayor,** near the Royal Palace. You will be surrounded by 17th-century buildings with balconies and arches. Descend the stairway at the southwest corner of the plaza to an area filled with lively bars.

El Prado: the Louvre's greatest rival

El Prado Museum, in the Plaza Canovas del Castillo, is Madrid's number-one attraction. One of the greatest museums in the world, it holds the cream of the collections of Spanish monarchs from the 16th through 19th centuries, including works by Velazquez, Goya, Murillo, El Greco, Breughal, Rubens, and Dürer. The best time to visit the Prado is in the late afternoon, when the sun adds light to the somewhat dim museum.

The most remarkable work at the Prado is *Las Meninas* (*Maids in Waiting*), painted by Velazquez in 1656. This is a painting of the artist painting an unknown subject, probably the royal couple, who are reflected in a mirror behind him. However, the artist appears to be painting the viewer, because of his direct, straight-forward gaze. The artist is surrounded by the royal entourage—the little infanta, *las meninas*, or ladies-in-waiting, dwarfs, and a dog.

The Black Goyas, so called because of their dark backgrounds and tragic themes, are housed in a special gallery within the Prado. The Spanish resistance to Napoleon (1808 to 1814) is their theme.

On the ground floor is a special section with tapestries designed by Goya for the Escorial (see below) and his *Disasters of War* etchings, inspired by his experiences during the war against Napoleon.

Picasso's *Guernica,* the famous anti-war painting, hangs in the **Casa de Buen Retiro,** next door to the Prado. Spaniards consider this work of art a national monument. Hundreds come to see the painting every day. It is kept behind bulletproof glass. (A ticket to the Prado will get you into the Casa de Buen Retiro.)

Madrid's most impressive palace

El Palacio Real (Royal Palace) is a baroque structure created under Charles III in 1764. About 50 of the 2,800 rooms are open to the public. They are filled with chandeliers, floral-patterned wallpaper, and colorful rugs. In one room the walls and ceilings are covered with 400 panels of painted porcelain. One of the strangest sights in the palace is what appears to be a doll in a glass case in the private Royal Chapel. Actually, the glass case contains the bones of St. Felix, a Christian martyr, wrapped in wax and silk and made to look like a small person. The figure was a gift from the pope to Queen Isabella II. Tours of the Palace cost 300 to 400 pesetas.

El Palacio's **Royal Library** houses more than 300,000 books, including 15th-century books, rare manuscripts, and Queen Isabella's prayer book.

You still can see bullet holes and other signs of the bloody civil war of 1936-1938 in the tapestries, frescoes, and furniture at the Palacio Real. The victorious Franco regime decided to keep these as reminders of the civil war (but you won't find this information listed in guide-books).

Madrid's best market

El Rastro, the flea market that starts at the Plaza Mayor and spills down Madrid's streets on Sundays, is a shopper's mecca. Vendors sell fine cotton shirts from India for 1,320 pesetas, Moroccan belts of brass and leather for 770 pesetas, leather bags for 900 pesetas, and alabaster pots for 165 pesetas, as well as bootleg tapes of U.S. musicians, semiprecious stones, fossils, and antiques.

Throughout the flea market are Gypsies who have a talent for spotting unwary tourists. They will pull you aside and offer you watches, jewelry, and electronic equipment at prices that are too good to be true. Be careful. The watch cases are often empty or filled with cheap materials. The jewelry is fake, and the electronics usually don't work. But if they offer you leather goods, you may get a bargain. Look at the items carefully. If they interest you, offer the seller one-tenth of the asking price. Haggle!

The best jogging

Parque del Retiro is a great place to take an early-morning jog. Part of the park is designed to look like the pattern on a blue willow plate. Avoid the places designated "*Zona de perros en libertad*" (Zone of dogs in freedom)! You also can rent a row boat or have a picnic.

The best of the bull

While bullfights may seem barbaric to animal-lovers, the Spanish believe the odds between man and bull are even. They see bullfights as a match between man and the untamed elements. The Spanish sense of fair play in a bullfight can be gruesome to the uninitiated. A recent match pitted a matador against the bull who had gouged out his eye. In the rematch, the bull's eye also was removed. An eye for an eye, so they say! The rematch was one of the most heavily attended events in Spanish history. Incidentally, the matador won.

Bullfights can be seen nearly every Sunday and Thursday from Easter through October at **Las Ventas**, *Plaza de Toros Monumental,* or at the smaller ring, **Vista Alegre.** Tickets can be purchased in advance at a counter at Calle Victoria 9, near the Puerta del Sol. But you usually can get a ticket at the door. Shows generally start at 5 p.m. or 7 p.m.

Tapas—the world's best snacks

Madrileños don't eat dinner until very late—after 10 p.m. It's impossible to order dinner before 8 p.m., which frustrates many foreign visitors. The solution is a little snack called a *tapa*. Madrileños, too, get hungry around 6 p.m., so they nibble on *tapas* (sardines, squid, octopus, olives, fried potatoes, sausage, shrimp, almonds, and any number of other delicious concoctions) and a glass of sherry or sangria in a *tapas* bar.

The most popular *tapas* is *chorizos* (Spanish sausage). The best are those that have been aged in a farmer's well, then cooked to kill the bacterial growth. Foreigners, however, should be careful with such local *tapas*. Build up a tolerance slowly for these new foods and their unusual bacterial elements. (Severe disorders have been reported by people who have overeaten exotic fare on unacclimated stomachs.)

A small version of the *tapa*, a *pincho,* is usually served free with the first drink in any of Madrid's *tapas* bars, known as *mesones* and *tabernas.* The custom is to have only one drink per *taberna,* then move on to the next one. Many of the *tabernas* are located around the Plaza Mayor. Two classics are the Meson de la Tortilla and the Meson del Champiñon, on Cava de San Miguel.

Europe's disco capital

Spain's capital has more discos than anywhere in Europe. They don't get going until midnight. The music tends to be about five years behind what's playing in London and New York.

The leading disco in Madrid is **Pacha**, *Barcelo 11; tel. (34-1)446-0137,* which attracts a rich young set. Dancers are videotaped and come back the following week to see themselves on tape.

One of the most unusual clubs is **Oh Madrid,** outside town. It has a swimming pool and terraces decorated with beach scenes.

If you tire of rock, new wave, and the young set, try **Café Berlin,** *Jacometro 4; tel. (34-1)231-0810,* which has Madrid's best jazz.

La Cúpola, *Fernando de la Hoz 9,* is the hottest meeting place in Madrid. Society types, politicos, and artists table-hop and name-drop here.

Madrid has Las Vegas-style music halls with top-notch entertainers. **Scala Melia,** *Edificio Melia Castilla, Rosario Pino 7,* is the best.

The finest flamenco

Flamenco dancing has evolved into a unique art form in Madrid. Dinner night clubs such as the **Café de Chinitas,** *Torrija 7; tel. (34-1)248-5135,* and **La Maestranza,** *Mauricio Legendre 16; tel. (34-1)231-0810,* have superb shows.

Flamenco nightclubs can be expensive, however (about 6,000 pesetas with drinks). Often you can watch a show for free just by roaming the streets around the Plaza Mayor. Keep your eyes open. You might see an impromptu dance by an Andalusian Gypsy troupe. Often little Gypsy girls will enter into a whirling flamenco with terrific vigor, paced by the insistent clapping of Gypsy boys. Eventually the hat is passed around. A good place to see flamenco dancers is the pedestrian street off Calle Serrano outside the Casa Inglese department store.

The newest thing in Madrid is to do the flamenco, rather than simply watch it. After 1 a.m., you can join in the heel-tapping, castanet-snapping, hand-clapping whirl of energy at **Al Andalus,** *Capitan Haya 19,* or at **El Porton,** *Lopez de Hoyos 9.*

Spain's most luxurious hotel

Hotel Ritz, *Plaza de la Lealtad 5; tel. (34-1)521-2857,* is unrivaled for luxury. The late King Alfonso XIII's pet hotel was built in 1910 to regal standards of luxury. Over the years, the hotel became a bit worn around the edges. But in 1984 it was restored when Trusthouse Forte, a British hotel chain, took over. All the old luxuries are still there (Limoges china, handwoven carpets, silverware) and some new ones have been added, such as individual temperature control for each room. The bathrooms at the Ritz are magnificent. Large bouquets of gladioli or exotic birds of paradise give color to the muted greens and grays of the rooms.

When you stay at the Ritz, you are served a breakfast of fresh croissants, Seville marmalade, and hot tea or coffee, served on immaculate white tablecloths with a little vase of pink carnations, shiny starched napkins, and polished silver.

Twice a day, the splendid bowl of fruit on your dressing table is replenished. It is accompanied by a knife, fork, napkin, and finger bowl in which geranium petals float.

The Ritz is in a splendid location, too. The Prado museums and shops are within walking distance.

A night at the Ritz isn't cheap. Double rooms are 38,000 to 56,000 pesetas, but you're paying for exquisite service and handsome surroundings. **Leading Hotels of the World,** *(800)223-6800,* can make arrangements.

The closest competition

Although topping the Ritz is impossible, Villa Magna and Miguel Angel come closest. Both are expensive luxury hotels with beautiful decor and first-class service.

Villa Magna, *Paseo de la Castellana 22; tel. (34-1)261-49-00,* is quiet, despite its central locale. The hotel's garden is gorgeous, set beneath the balconied, nine-story structure. Rooms are large, with bathrooms, individual thermostats, and huge, comfortable chairs. The hotel is decorated with marble, glass, and stainless steel. The bar is cozy. The hotel also has an elegant lounge, a hairdresser, a sauna, and a shopping area. Rooms start at 37,500 pesetas.

Miguel Angel, *Miguel Angel 31; tel. (34-1)442-00-22,* looks like an ice palace. Enormous chandeliers hang from the ceilings, and the balustrades are crystal. Silk spreads cover the beds, and plush carpet cushions the foot. Perhaps the nicest aspect of the hotel, however, is its marvelous indoor pool surrounded by white furniture. Rooms start at 20,600 pesetas.

Sweet nights at sweet prices

Alcala, *Alcala 66; tel. (34-1)435-10-60,* is one of our favorites. Near the Retiro Park, it is cozy, with a circular iron hearth. Rooms are air-conditioned, and dual-glaze windows keep out the sounds of traffic. Full-length mirrors and walnut-paneled walls grace the bedrooms. The hotel restaurant is very good also, serving Basque specialties. Double rooms are 10,000 pesetas.

Spain's best restaurant

Zalacaín, *Alvarez de Baena 4; tel. (34-1)261-4840,* with its 15 cooks, is one of the finest restaurants in Europe. Michelin was so impressed that it gave the elegant restaurant three stars. The food is imaginative and delicious. Dinner is 4,850 to 7,525 pesetas. Reserve in advance. The restaurant is closed Saturday afternoons, Sundays, Holy Week, and in August.

Spain's restaurant capital

Madrid has become a restaurant capital in recent years. Hundreds of fine restaurants have opened, serving good regional dishes, as well as seafood and international cuisine.

The best Castillian cuisine is served at **Casa Botin,** *Cuchilleros 17; tel. (34-1)266-42-17,* and **Posada de la Villa,** *Cava Baja 9; tel. (34-1)266-18-60,* both in Old Madrid. Castillian cuisine is known generally for its use of garlic, onions, and olive oil. Try the roast baby lamb and suckling pig. Both restaurants are more than 200 years old. Dinner in either is 2,050 pesetas to 4,000 pesetas. The restaurants are closed for dinner Sundays.

Casa Lucio, *Cava Baja 35; tel. (34-1)265-32-52,* is one of Madrid's oldest restaurants. Despite its unpretentious service and surroundings, this cozy establishment has attracted the king and the prime minister of Spain. Dinner is 2,650 to 4,000 pesetas. It is closed Saturday afternoons and in August.

Cabo Mayor, *Juan Hurtado de Mendoza 11; tel. (34-1)250-87-76,* is elegant. One of its best dishes is *ensalada de rape y almejas,* paper-thin slices of raw monk fish and whole clams marinated in lemon, oil, and fennel. The salmon and corn salad is also good. Dinner is 3,150 to 3,800 pesetas. The restaurant is closed Sundays and from Aug. 15 to Sept. 2.

El Amparo, *Callejon de Puigcerda 18, corner of Jorge Juan; tel. (34-1)431-64-56,* in the exclusive residential neighborhood known as Barrio de Salamanca, serves the unique cuisine of chef Ramon Ramirez, French and Basque. The house wines are exceptional and fairly priced. Dinner is 3,150 pesetas to 5,250 pesetas. The restaurant is closed Saturday afternoons, Sundays, Holy Week, and in August.

Horcher, *6 Alfonso XII; tel. (34-1)522-07-31,* one of the most elegant restaurants in Madrid, serves unusual game dishes. Dinner is 3,050 to 7,000 pesetas. The restaurant is closed on Sunday.

Jockeys, *Amador de los Rios 6; tel. (34-1)419-10-03* or *(34-1)419-24-35,* is a fine restaurant that features Spanish and French dishes. Try such innovative inventions as poached eggs in truffle sauce, lobster ragout with pasta, or boned duck with figs. Dinner is 3,950 pesetas to 5,800 pesetas. The restaurant is closed Sundays and in August.

The Spanish passion: *paella*

Paella—a delicious concoction of rice with seafood and spices—is a national passion in Spain. It is generally served in huge, heavy black skillets and comes in two varieties: *valenciana* has chicken, sausage, and seafood; *mariscos* has only seafood, no chicken or sausage.

The place for *paella* in Madrid is **El Pescador,** *José Ortega y Gasset 75; tel. (34-1)401-30-26* or *(34-1)402-12-90,* an informal restaurant in Old Madrid near Plaza del Sol. Long communal tables are shared by diners, who serve themselves *paella* from large pots. If you stop by in mid-afternoon, you will see fishermen with weathered faces peeling freshly caught seafood for the evening's *paella*. Dinner is 2,050 to 2,850 pesetas.

The best way to get around

The best way to get around Madrid is the city's fast and efficient subway. Buy metro tickets at booths and machines in the stations for only 60 pesetas a ride (you can buy 10 tickets for 500 pesetas). Tickets are inserted into electronic turnstiles that let you enter the system. Don't throw away your ticket—you'll need it to get back out again. The subway is open from 6:30 a.m. to 1 a.m.

Spain's most intimidating edifice

El Escorial, on a mountain northwest of Madrid, is the powerful 16th-century monastery-palace that saw many of the horrors of the Inquisition. It was the home of Phillip II, who commissioned the Armada to try to conquer England—and failed. A giant, gloomy building with hundreds of rooms and thousands of windows, it is full of history, art, rare manuscripts, and reminders of the Inquisition. Almost all of Spain's royalty is entombed here, as well as a number of saints, in a cavernous, black-marble room.

Trains to the palace leave 20 times a day from the Atocha station in Madrid. A bus takes visitors from the station to the palace.

Spain's best medieval walled town

Just beyond El Escorial is **Avila,** Spain's most beautiful walled town. Perched on a crest and enclosed within massive 38-foot-high walls, Avila is the highest provincial capital in Spain. Six archways lead into this austere and intimidating town, and 90 towers keep watch over the area. It was also the town of St. Teresa, the 16th-century mystic and reformer.

The town has a handful of main tourist sights: the cathedral, the Convent of St. Teresa, and the Basilica of St. Vincent. Visit these, then explore the streets at random. The best view is from the town walls on the edge of Avila's *parador,* or government-run hotel. Go through the *parador's* garden and climb the flight of stairs to the wall. You will see the River Adaja, the road to Salamanca, and the endless plain. A tourist information office is located opposite the cathedral on the main plaza.

Toledo: the richest history

Toledo, a city rich in history, is an hour's drive from Madrid. In the words of Gerald Brenan in *The Faces of Spain* (1950), "Like Fez it reeks of the Middle Ages; like Lhasa, of monks."

Lording over the city is a fortress called the **Alcazar.** El Cid, the Lord Champion of the 11th century, whose courageous deeds were described in Spain's epic poem, lived here. Destroyed during the Spanish Civil War, the Alcazar has been reconstructed. It houses a museum of the Spanish Civil War.

Ferdinand and Isabella built a cathedral at the heart of Toledo in the 15th century and filled it with art, sanctuaries, and chapels. For a great view of the city and a small adventure, climb the cathedral's tower and examine its 18th-century bell, which is still in use.

El Greco left his mark on Toledo as well. His famous painting, the *Burial of the Conde de Orgaz,* is housed in St. Thomas Church (Iglesia Santo Tome) at Angel Santo Tome. The **El Greco House and Museum** (Casa y Museo del Greco), *Paseo del Transito,* contains paintings and memorabilia of the 16th-century artist.

A 14th-century synagogue called El Transito is down the street from El Greco's house. It was once a house of worship for Jews in Toledo. During the Inquisition, it became a church, and its members were forced either to became Christian or flee the country. A museum containing Sephardic religious articles is located in part of the synagogue.

Don't buy any tourist knicknacks in Toledo. Prices here are almost twice as high as elsewhere in Spain. The merchants stalk gullible foreigners.

The best view of this dramatic city is from the **Circunvalacion,** a road that runs parallel to the Rio Taju.

Outside Toledo are three *paradors.* **El Parador Nacional Conde de Orgaz,** *Cerro del Emperador; tel. (34-25)22-18-50,* is one of the most beautiful in Spain. The two-story hotel has a sweeping view of Toledo. Its restaurant serves Castilian cuisine and international fare. Rooms are air-conditioned, and guests can use the hotel's pool.

Parador Nacional Virrey de Toledo, *Plaza del Palacio in Oropesa, near Toledo; tel. (34-25)43-00-00,* in a restored 14th-century castle was built during the reign of King Pedro the Cruel. It is a favorite among hunters, and the walls are decorated with the curved horns of the rare, local mountain goat. The wood-beamed dining room serves specialties, such as terrine of pigeon.

Request a room on the left as you enter the courtyard. You will face Toledo and enjoy a glittering view at night. During the winter a big fireplace keeps the lounge warm; however, the place has no central heating. Rooms are 7,000 pesetas to 10,000 pesetas.

Barcelona: the most European city

Flower-filled **Barcelona** is sociable, stimulating, and the most European Spanish city. Residents love their town. To them, Barcelona's ancient hegemony over the Mediterranean is only temporarily in eclipse.

The city's Catalan culture, once suppressed by General Franco, is back in full swing—street signs, maps, museum labels, and conversations are again in the distinctive Catalan language.

Adding to Barcelona's charms are low-priced hotels, restaurants, and transportation.

The most interesting quarter

The **Gothic Quarter** (Barrio Gotico), at Barcelona's heart, is filled with shops, bars, nightclubs, and 14th-century buildings. Roman, Gothic, and medieval walls still stand. Wander around—you probably will chance upon crumbling classical arches and statuary.

The barrio's handsome Gothic cathedral is worth a visit, even if you stop in only to see the white geese in the cloister gardens. Interesting contrasts to the medieval buildings are the street lamps, which were designed by Antonio Gaudi, a leader of the art nouveau movement. This quarter is a great shopping area, especially if you're looking for trendy clothes and unusual art.

Barcelona's most entertaining avenues

The first thing to do in Barcelona is stroll along **Las Ramblas.** These wide avenues go from the Diagonal (a wide avenue that cuts diagonally across the center of Barcelona) to the Columbus monument at the harbor. (Although the contiguous segments of Las Ramblas have their own names—Rambla Dels Estudis, Rambla de Sant Josep—they are known collectively as Las Ramblas.)

On Las Ramblas near Placa de Catalunya is Orator's Corner, where men gather to discuss the issues of the day. You'll also find the grand opera house, ornate churches, elegant cafés, as well as Barcelona's intriguing seedy side on Las Ramblas.

This exotic stretch is the place to shop for everything from colorful tropical birds and flowers to postcards showing Barcelona's lewd and kinky night life. A little street called Riera Alta, between Las Ramblas and Calle Ronda San Antonio, hides a wine shop called Bodega. A little old man runs this dark place lined from floor to ceiling with bottles. If you ask for a sample, he will give you a squirt from a wine skin, or *bota.* He squeezes the *bota,* creating an arc of wine in the air, which you must artfully capture in your wide-open mouth. After dark, a parade of colorfully dressed transvestites joins families and tourists strolling along Las Ramblas near the Diagonal.

One note: Be careful when walking along Las Ramblas—about 30 purse snatchings a day take place here. Don't carry anything valuable with you if you go through the seedy Barrio Chino at the lower end of Las Ramblas.

Toulouse Lautrec's favorite brew

An adventure to try in Barcelona is drinking *absenta,* or absinthe, a potent liquor that is illegal in most countries but perfectly legal in Spain. *Absenta* has given a number of writers and artists their inspiration (and probably rotted their brains), including Toulouse Lautrec.

This licorice-flavored alcohol (not to be confused with Pernod, a much milder drink) is sold at the beautiful Antique Bar on San Pau, near Jeronimo, in the Barrio Chino. The bar is old and ornate and has a sign that reads "Prohibited to Sing."

Limit yourself to two shots of *absenta,* at the most. After three, you won't know where you are or what you're doing there! (And you don't want this to happen when you're in the shady Barrio Chino.)

The best of Picasso

Museo de Picasso, *Calle Montcada near the Barrio Gotico,* has one of the world's most comprehensive collections of Picasso's works, starting from his childhood and continuing through his entire life. Few people take advantage of the free guided tour, available in English, so you rarely have to wait and often you can have the guide to yourself.

Gaudi's greatest works

Walking around Barcelona, you can't miss the strangely beautiful works of **Antonio**

Gaudi. The luxury apartment buildings on and around the Paseo de Gracia were designed by the architect. They are distinguished by their asymmetrical shapes and unusual colors.

Templo de la Sagrada Familia is Gaudi's never-completed but extraordinary church. Its stonework resembling an enormous dribbled-sand castle, the structure towers above the Placa de la Sagrada Familia. Climb the tiny, twisting and turning, steep stairs in the church towers to enjoy the view from the top.

Work continues to complete the church whenever a bit of money is collected. (Many Gothic cathedrals took centuries to build, too.)

Gaudi died on the street here. He stepped off the curb into the road to admire his work and was hit by a car.

Park Guell, north of the city, was also created by the imaginative artist, full of wild, beautiful, and sometimes decaying sculptures and objects. The benches and walls are studded with pieces of pottery and glass, and caves are hollowed out of a hill.

Barcelona's tiptop displays

Barcelona lies in the shadows of an intriguing hill, **Montjuïc,** which is topped with the remains of the 1929 World's Fair. It is a pleasant place to visit—during the day. Don't stroll around by yourself, however, as the park attracts its share of strange characters.

The walk to the top of Montjuïc is long and strenuous (but enjoyable if you are in good shape). If you don't feel up to the hike, take the funicular on weekends and holidays from the Parallel metro station or bus 61, 101, or 201.

The most beautiful of the World's Fair pavilions is a starkly modern structure designed by Mies van der Rohe. Reconstructed last year in celebration of the 100th anniversary of the architect's birth, it was the first of its kind, with chrome, glass, reflecting walls, and an exterior that played an important part in the interior design of the building. Van der Rohe designed the building for the German exhibit, using green marble and golden onyx in the construction. Inside, scarlet velvet curtains sweep across glass walls. White-kid covered chairs once served as thrones. George Kolbe's statue *Morning,* a classical nude, is reflected in the interior pool. The pavilion is open during daylight hours; entry is free.

Pueblo Español, also designed as a pavilion for the 1929 World's Fair, is still in operation. Typical buildings from all over Spain were reproduced in this village, designed as a miniature view of Spain. Houses are of stone, stucco, or intricately laid brick, topped with Spanish tiles and embellished with elaborate balconies. Typical wood carving, metalwork, pottery, glass, leather, and crafts are sold in the village's 35 shops. A carved wooden salad bowl sells for as little as 681 pesetas.

Museo d'Art de Catalunya, at the summit of Montjuïc, specializes in Catalan Gothic religious art. The mosaics, frescoes, and artifacts come from isolated churches and hermitages in the Pyrénées. The museum is open Tuesdays through Sundays from 9 a.m. to 2 p.m.

The **Miró Museum** features the work of Joan Miró. Miró, whose paintings were inspired by the art and landscape of Catalonia, is revered by Catalans. His painted-bronze sculptures are displayed on the museum balconies, and his stark, late paintings are in alcoves overlooking the courtyard. Perhaps his best work is *Self Portrait,* begun in 1937 and completed in 1960. He drew himself from a reflection in a convex mirror, creating an enlarged, distorted image. His eyes are star-like. The Miró Museum and Contemporary Art Center is open Tuesdays through Saturdays from 11 a.m. to 8 p.m., Sundays and holidays from 11 a.m. to 2:30 p.m.

Barcelona's best night life

As in Madrid, Barcelona's night life begins well after midnight. Then it rolls on full-steam until sunrise. Hundreds of bars and nightclubs are located all over the city.

The trendiest nightclub right now is the zany **Otto Zutz,** *Lincoln 15,* where you'll see Barcelona's most beautiful and fashionable. The latest music is played, and the decor is ultra-modern: neon, concrete, metal.

Barcelona's jet-set can be found at a new disco called **Up and Down,** *Numancia and Diagonal.*

Two popular bars are **Network,** *Calvo Sotelo,* and **Vaticano,** which was opened by a Catholic priest and plays good music. On the north side of Las Ramblas is the **Born,** named after a huge market surrounded by tiny streets filled with bars, *coctelerias,* and *xampanyerias,* where local wines and champagne are drunk in vast quantities.

Barcelona's best restaurant

The best restaurant in Barcelona is **Neichel,** *Pedralbes 16 bis; tel. (34-3)203-84-08.* Michelin awarded this restaurant two stars. The good news has spread, and reservations are essential. Try the duck paté, the lamb, or the veal with truffle sauce. Closed Sundays, bank holidays, Holy Week, Christmas, and August. Dinner is 3,200 to 5,400 pesetas.

Perfect *paellas*

Barcelona is known for its fish restaurants and its *paella,* made with seafood fresh out of the Mediterranean.

The section of Barcelona between the port and the beach, called Barceloneta, has several traditional *paella* restaurants. One of the best is **Cal Pinxo,** *Final Calle Maestranza.* Have *paella* (with either peeled or unpeeled seafood) and the house wine, which is cheap and good.

Other favorites

Eldorado Petit, *Dolors Monserdá 51; tel. (34-3)204-51-53,* serves only the freshest produce, fish, and meat, and the wine cellar has a huge selection. Try the crayfish and shrimp or the salmon lasagna with asparagus. Dinner is expensive—3,500 pesetas to 5,000 pesetas—but worth it.

Azulete, *via Augusta 281; tel. (34-3)203-59-43,* is a favorite among international celebrities. Nouvelle cuisine and very good seafood (especially the salmon) are served. Dinners are 4,000 pesetas to 5,000 pesetas. Closed Sundays.

El Egypto, *Calle Jersulalen 3; tel. (34-3)317-74-80,* behind the Boqueria Market near Las Ramblas, is a favorite. It has delicious and reasonably priced food but slow service.

La Venta, at the top of Tibidabo, has fabulous views of Barcelona and the Mediterranean. Dinner is served outside in the garden, so you can enjoy the panorama.

Jaume de Provença, *Provenza 88; tel. (34-3)230-0029,* serves delicious fish. Reservations are necessary. Dinner is 2,250 pesetas to 4,450 pesetas.

Reno, *Tuset 27; tel. (34-3)200-91-29,* serves Catalan haute cuisine in an elegant black dining room. Book well in advance if you want to try this well-known, classic restaurant. Dinner is 7,000 pesetas per person.

Best places to sleep

The best hotel in Barcelona is the **Ritz,** *ave. Cortes Catalanas 668; tel. (34-3)318-52-00.*

One of the four original Ritz hotels founded by Caesar Ritz, it has been restored to its 19th-century opulence. Rooms are large, all with private bathrooms, and the atmosphere is elegant. But the real drawing card is the efficient, friendly staff. Rooms are 19,000 pesetas to 29,000 pesetas per night.

Another grand hotel is the **Avenida Palace,** *Gran Via 605-607; tel. (34-3)301-96-00.* Less formal than the Ritz, it has comparable service. The lobby is lovely, with gleaming brass, marble, and wood. Rooms have air conditioning, wood furniture, white chenille bedspreads. However, the dining room is mediocre, and the bar is boring. Doubles are 10,000 pesetas to 19,000 pesetas.

One of our favorite hotels in Barcelona is the relatively inexpensive but charming **Hotel Colón,** *ave. Catedral 7; tel. (34-3)301-1404.* You couldn't find a more scenic location—it faces Barcelona's ancient cathedral in the Gothic Quarter. Despite its medieval surroundings, it offers air conditioning and private bathrooms. The best rooms are on the sixth floor. They have terraces with views of the cathedral and the streets below. Prints and gilded mirrors hang on the walls above velvet chairs. The cellar-restaurant, Carabela, is cozy. Rooms are 7,340 pesetas to 18,575 pesetas.

Hotel Calderón, *Rambla de Catalunya 27, Barcelona 08007; tel. (34-3)301-0000,* has a rooftop swimming pool with a panoramic view and air-conditioned bedrooms with televisions and private bathrooms. Rooms are 13,000 pesetas.

Bests outside Barcelona

A **Benedictine monastery** whose Marian shrine has attracted pilgrims for more than 700 years is located in the Montserrat Mountains 38 miles northwest of Barcelona. The Black Madonna (La Morena)—a 12th-century statue of the Virgin Mary—is the focus of the pilgrims' journey.

Seville's greatest pleasures

Seville is a city of simple pleasures: warm sunshine, brightly colored flowers, an expressive river, fragrant orange groves, rustling palm trees, ancient buildings, and shining white houses with patios, flat roofs, and shuttered windows.

In a sense, Seville is the essence of Spain. It has typically ornate and colorful architecture and warm and friendly people. Located on the left bank of the Guadalquivir River, the city is sunny but surrounded by marshland and swamps.

Seville's history is colorful. The Romans conquered the city in 205 B.C. (when it was known as Hispalis), and it became so Romanized that it produced several Roman emperors, including Trajan and Hadrian. Under the Moors, it became splendid, the subject of poetry. During the reconquest of Spain, it was the capital. It became the headquarters of trade with the New World in the 16th century. Cervantes spent his youth here, and his famous *Don Quixote* was born in a Sevillian prison.

The old quarters of the city, with narrow winding streets and tiny squares, were built in medieval times in a way intended to provide the best shelter from the heat of the Andalusian summers. The twists and turns of the narrow streets lead to surprises and unexpected views. The houses in the old part of the city have white lime-washed fronts and lots of flowering plants on the balconies.

Spain's most graceful bullfights

Even if you're squeamish, you should see a bullfight in Seville, which is famous for its bullfighters. The Sevillian school of bullfighting teaches a graceful style. Andalusian bulls are bred for the fight and show their stuff in the handsome Maestranza bullring.

Seville's top sight

The most outstanding monument in Seville is the **Giralda.** Built on Roman foundations as a minaret in 1184, it is adorned with four huge gilded-bronze apples. In the 1500s, a belfry with 25 bells was added, as well as the enormous statue representing Faith, which serves as a weather vane.

The world's third-largest church

Seville's cathedral was built on the site of one of Spain's largest mosques, destroyed in the 15th century. It is the third-largest Christian church in the world. The Gothic structure has five spacious aisles, and the main chapel is decorated with a magnificent wrought-iron screen. The tombs of King Alfonso X (the Wise) and his mother, Beatrice of Swabia, are here, as well as an urn containing the remains of King Ferdinand.

Many people visit the cathedral without realizing they can enter the crypt below, which contains the royal coffins of King Pedro the Cruel and Doña Maria de Padilla. The cathedral also contains jewels, vestments, and the sword of King Ferdinand. The Sacristy of the Chalices has paintings by Murillo, Zurbaran, and Goya. Before leaving the cathedral, see the Patio de los Naranjos (Orange Court) and the Christopher Columbus Library. The former was originally the *shan,* or courtyard, of the Mosque. The library contains manuscripts by the discoverer of America.

Best Mudejar architecture

The facade of the old **Alcazar** is one of the finest examples of Mudejar art in Spain. (Mudejars were ex-Moslems who remained after the Reconquest.) It was built on the ruins of King Almotamid's palace. After the conquest of Seville, Ferdinand and Isabella and their successors also lived here. Among the remains is the Patio del Yeso.

The Alcazar as it is today was built by King Pedro the Cruel. Moorish master masons, Sevillian craftsmen, and Toledan decorators took part in creating this building.

The prettiest palace

Casa de Pilatos, or Pilots' House, a typical 15th-century Andalusian mansion, was built as a reproduction of the Praetorium in Jerusalem. The patio, with a graceful fountain and two ornamental statues of Minerva, is one of the most beautiful examples of Spanish Renaissance art in Seville.

Seville's best museum

The **Museum of Fine Arts,** located in a monastery, displays Spanish primitives, a magnificent El Greco, and nearly 50 Murillos.

Granada, the most romantic city

Granada is one of those romantic towns that make you feel like you're living a legend or lost in a movie set. It is most famous for its beautiful Moorish palace called the **Alhambra.**

The palace is delicate, with many-colored wooden ceilings carved with stars. Arched windows look out over the water, and private patios open off bathing rooms. The Patio de la Ria and the upper garden are exquisite. The gardens have intricate waterworks, with channels of water that run alongside the steps. Elaborate fountains dance amid the flowering trees.

Patio de los Leones and the adjoining rooms were the heart of the private apartments of the ruler. Light, filtering through the patio, bathes the rooms and glimmers on the patio's fountains and water channels.

Washington Irving wrote *Tales of the Alhambra* from his apartment on the Lindaraja patio, which looks out on tall cypress trees and a gently gurgling fountain.

The Alcazaba was the guardian of the Alhambra. Its watch tower (Torre de la Vela) is the outstanding feature. In moments of danger, bells rang an alarm. Ferdinand and Isabella flew the banner of Castile from the tower when they took Granada on Jan. 2, 1492. From the tower you can see the entire city and the Alhambra.

The ugliest sight in the Alhambra

Charles V decided to plop a huge marble Renaissance palace into the middle of the Alhambra. His imperial majesty felt the Moors' remains were not majestic enough, so he built his monumental palace (now a museum).

A thousand beautiful nights (the most romantic hotels)

Nightingales sing in the gardens of the **Convent of San Francisco,** *tel. (34-58)22-14-40,* a *parador* inside the walls of the Alhambra. One of the oldest buildings in the Alhambra, it was originally a Moorish palace. Rebuilt in the 14th century by Yusuf I, it became a convent under Ferdinand and Isabella in 1492. The monarchs were buried there for some time. The *parador* has an elegant interior, cloisters, arches, towers, and gardens. Make reservations far in advance.

Another nearby hotel is the **Alhambra Palace,** *Penapartida 1; tel. (34-58)22-14-68.*

The most passionate dancing

Outside Granada at **Sacromonte,** the summit of Albaicin, are the famous Gypsy caves, where, to the beating of hands and the sounds of guitars, Gypsies dance the *zambra,* a colorful and passionate dance. The caves sound primitive, but they are warm in the winter, cool in the summer, and often elaborately decorated.

A word of warning, however. You may be harassed for handouts. And many visitors have been known to leave the caves minus wallets or watches.

Salamanca: Spain's intellectual center

Salamanca is the Oxford or Cambridge of Spain. But remember that intellectual life here inevitably is colored by the country's centralization and religious conformity. The **University of Salamanca,** the oldest in Spain, was founded at the end of the 15th century, almost at the same time as the Spanish Inquisition, by Cardinal Cisneros, advisor to the monarchs who financed Columbus. A plaque on the Patio de las Escuelas, the entrance to the campus, honors Ferdinand and Isabella, those most Catholic monarchs. The campus is now split between the seminary to train priests and the secular university—but many figures on the lay side dress in Roman collars, soutanes, monkish habits, wimples, and coifs.

Perhaps the most telling clue to the way the Renaissance was viewed as both a threat and an opportunity is the large sign at the entrance to the university library, threatening with excommunication those who read books without getting permission from the bishop. All the 16th-century bookshelves lock—and this is not in an effort to stop book thieves!

Near the library is the splendid chapel, with a painted Renaissance ceiling, now used for ceremonial occasions. The university buildings are mostly 17th to 19th century, built in tiers around central courtyards. You can visit lecture halls if you enter without disturbing the classes.

Apart from the university, the city also boasts not one but two cathedrals, built partly on top of each other in the local pinkish granite. The older cathedral holds a beautiful retable and the polychrome shrine of Bishop Anaya—both masterpieces.

As is normal in a college town, Salamanca has plenty of cheap eats and cheap digs. If you can't get into the *parador,* do not despair. We have tried the **Alfonso X,** *Tor 64; tel. (34-23)21-44-01,* in the old town, and it is quite delightful—an international-level hotel built into an old townhouse.

Good eating includes the Michelin-starred **Chez Victor,** *Espoz y Mina 26; tel. (34-23)21-31-23,* which features cockles in *noilly prat* on homemade noodles and *isla flotante* (floating island). Chez Victor is closed in August (when the university is closed), Sunday nights, and Mondays.

Valladolid, a best for history and architecture buffs

A busy provincial capital in the heart of the Meseta Central, **Valladolid** has medieval churches, university buildings, and traces of Spain's greatest writers and artists. The view of the city as you arrive from the highway is memorable—the cathedral, the university buildings, and church spires.

Valladolid's two literary giants

Valladolid produced two famous Spanish literary figures: Zorrilla and Cervantes. The house where poet **José Zorrilla** was born, on Calle Fray Luis de Granada, is a small white-washed building that contains his letters, manuscripts, and death mask.

The house of **Miguel de Cervantes** (author of *Don Quixote*), on Calle Miguel Iscar, has been converted into a museum and a public library. The room that Cervantes used as a study is filled with maps and has a painting of the Battle of Lepanto. One of the writer's manuscripts is exhibited, and the furnishings, carpet, and tapestries were his. Two of his works were written here, *El Licenciado Vidriera* and *El Coloquio de los Perros*.

The most important sights

The **College of San Gregorio,** built between 1488 and 1496, is one of the marvels of pre-Renaissance art. It houses the National Sculpture Museum and contains the finest and most valuable carved figures from Castile.

Iglesia de San Pablo, next door, was originally a Dominican monastery built in the 15th century. Inside are two exquisite small doorways and a vaulted ceiling.

La Séo Cathedral is quite impressive. Begun by the medieval architect Juan de Hererra (who also built the Monastery of El Escorial), it was continued in the 18th century but never completed. The interior is sober and grand, with 32 pillars. Next door is a Diocesan Museum, which contains fine images and jewelry.

Spain's castle country

A great number of castles were built outside Valladolid for its defense. **La Mota**, in Medina del Campo, is one of the most beautiful castles in Spain. Built in the 13th century, it was later the home of Ferdinand and Isabella. Over the years it imprisoned Hernando Pizarro, Rodrigo Calderon (the favorite of Philip II), and Cesar Borgia.

Seven miles outside Valladolid stands **Simancas,** originally a bishop's see. It was granted town status in the year A.D. 927. Simanca was a Moorish castle until the 11th century, when it was reconquered by the Christians.

Simancas' cylindrical towers and walls are well-preserved. The inner part of the castle is used as the General Archives of the Kingdom. In its 52 rooms and halls are more than 30-million documents.

Farther down the Douro River is **Penafiel Castle,** a fabulous 14th-century structure that looks down over a historic village. Built in the 10th century, it looks like a huge ship, with 12 buttresses and an interior tower 27 yards high.

Spain's most picturesque city—Cuenca

Cuenca is famous for its ancient hanging houses that jut out over a 600-foot gorge. These *casas colgadas,* as they are called, went unoccupied for 200 years before the government restored them. They date from the 14th century, when they were summer residences of kings and queens. Today they are national monuments.

One of the houses is now a restaurant that serves delicious trout caught from the Huecar River and crayfish from the Jucar River. From the restaurant's balcony you can look down into the gorge and watch swallows swooping from cliff to cliff.

Climb the steep, stony streets to the cobblestoned main square with its wrought-iron window grills. Relax in one of the cafés over a glass of *resoli,* the local liqueur made of pure alcohol, coffee, sugar, orange peel, and cinnamon.

A light flickers in the town's lower gate every night in memory of the victory of King Alfonso over the Moors. According to legend, King Alfonso got his troops through the gate by dressing two soldiers in sheepskin and having them slay the gatekeeper. Alfonso's troops then opened the gates and conquered the town without shedding any Spanish blood. A festival is held Sept. 20 to 22 every year in celebration of the victory.

The town is prettiest at night when it is lit by hundreds of lights that cast odd shadows on the crooked buildings and winding streets.

The best Roman ruins outside Rome

Merida, founded in 25 B.C. as a rest home for retired Roman legionnaires (it was then known as Colonis Emerita Augusta), has the most impressive Roman ruins outside Rome itself—and it beats the Provençal ruins (Orange, Arles, Nîmes) hands down. But while it was on the main Roman road in antiquity, Merida today is a backwater. It is on a road that goes to the Portuguese border, on a river that you can navigate all the way to the sea at Ayamonte—if you have any reason to do so.

Merida's Roman sights include a multitier bridge over the Guadiana River, which carries both traffic (including modern trucks) and drinking water. The city's monumental aqueduct system, built in granite blocks striped with red clay bricks, is Roman and partially still in use.

The city had both a Roman theater (for plays and performances of music for the legionnaires) and a Roman amphitheater (for sports events). The Romans were just like modern soldiers— the sports theater is four times as large as the cultural theater.

The theater was built into a slope of a hill, with seats in a horseshoe facing the stage. The stage was made of brick and decorated with marble pillars and columns two huge stories high. Statues of the Roman gods are visible between the pillars and the wall. Here and there are little doorways cut into the brick, through which entrances and exits were made. In the middle is a two-story doorway used for spectacular effects (deus ex machina, for example). Behind the facade you can see the actors' dressing rooms, built into the brick structure. You enter the theater (as you do the Coliseum in Rome) through arched stairways.

The huge amphitheater held 40,000 spectators. On the hillside where both structures stand were Roman notables' houses, and the mosaics, paintings, and statuary from these houses can be seen in the Museo Arqueologico (you pay only one admission price to view the lot). The bas reliefs in the museum include depictions of a lute player and a tavern keeper drawing wine from a barrel.

As if being a major Roman center were not enough, Merida also was a power center under the Moors. The Moorish fortress by the Guadiana is graced by a lovely colonnaded walk, created of ocher and cream stucco with marble pillars. Even more impressive is the *aljibe,* a set of staircases leading to a bath fed water from the river. Despite the Moslem prohibition against alcohol, the frieze on the entrance to the *aljibe* is decorated with bunches of grapes.

The Romans' greatest engineering feat

The Roman **aqueduct** in Segovia is the most powerful example of Roman engineering and architecture in Spain. After centuries of use, it still carries water from the River Frio to the town. Running across the center of Segovia, it has 118 arches and rises 96 feet. It was built in the time of Trajan of uncemented limestone blocks.

Segovia is a beautiful walled town on a rocky ledge above the Eresma River. A 14th-century alcazar (with 19th-century modifications) dominates the town. But the late Gothic cathedral, which dates from the 16th century, vies for attention.

Just south of Segovia is the bridge described by Hemingway in *For Whom the Bell Tolls.*

The Moors' most beautiful city: Cordoba

Cordoba was the capital of Moslem Spain in the eighth century and one of the major cities of the Moslem world. It once had 500,000 inhabitants and 300 mosques; today 255,000 live there, and most of the mosques are gone.

La Mezquita: a Moorish masterpiece

The city's most amazing monument is **La Mezquita,** a masterpiece of Moorish-Spanish architecture topped by a beautiful cupola and studded with priceless mosaics. Construction of the mosque, which was built on the site of a Visigothic cathedral, was begun in the middle of the eighth century at the orders of Abd-er-Rahman I. Elements of the early cathedral were incorporated into the mosque. Later in the eighth century, Moslems and Christians shared the building, which also was used as a cathedral.

Walk through the Door of Forgiveness into the Orange Tree Patio, an enchanting place with fountains and orange trees. Beyond the patio is a forest of columns—alabaster, jasper, and marble—topped by horseshoe arches. The columns came from North Africa, where they were taken from Roman, Visigothic, and Phoenician ruins.

Christians transformed the mosque into an enormous cathedral after they conquered Cordoba in 1236. But they never really got rid of its Moorish look and feel. The interior is vast, large enough to hold hundreds of Moslems facing east. The ceilings are low, with rounded arches. Striped columns hold up the ceiling. Baroque chapels embellish the edges of the cathedral, trying desperately to make it look Christian. In front of the western wall of La Mezquita is the Episcopal Palace, the residence of the Visigothic governors and later the caliph's alcazar.

Most inviting corners

Outside La Mezquita is **Cordoba's old quarter,** which is filled with inviting nooks and crannies. Look for good buys in filigree silver and Cordoba leather in the quarter's little shops.

The **Jewish quarter** (Juderia), northwest of the Moorish structure, has a 14th-century synagogue, located on Calle Judios. Around the corner, on Calle Averroes and Calle Judios, is a patio where you can watch flamenco dancers.

Glance into Cordoba's patios. You will see white-lime walls draped with trailing plants and embellished with wrought-iron balconies. In the center are wells, marble columns, and fountains surrounded by flowers.

The best hotel in town

The best place to stay in Cordoba is **Residencia Maimonides,** *Torrijos 4; tel. (34-957)47-15-00.* Relatively inexpensive, with rooms from 7,240 pesetas to 11,035 pesetas, it is directly across the street from La Mezquita in the old quarter. It is named after the Medieval Jewish philosopher, the most famous son of Cordoba.

Pamplona: the ultimate machismo

Each July in **Pamplona,** the ultimate display of *machismo* takes place. The townsmen pit their lives against hundreds of bulls set loose in the streets and herded toward the bullring. To display their courage, the men run before the bulls, often injuring themselves.

Festivities begin when a rocket is fired from the town hall. Then bands of *txistularis* and bagpipers march through town announcing the running of the bulls. Young people roam the streets singing, dancing, and drinking. The celebration was made famous by Ernest Hemingway in *The Sun Also Rises.*

All this revelry is in the name of the town's patron saint, San Fermin, a bishop and martyr from Pamplona. Buried in Amiens, France, his body mysteriously disappeared. The body was miraculously found six centuries later, and legend says that, although it was mid-winter, the trees burst into leaf.

Costa del Sol: a people-watching paradise

The **Costa del Sol** is the best place in Spain for partygoers, extroverts, and people-watchers. However, it's the worst place to go if you are looking for a charming getaway. The Costa del Sol is for you only if you thrive on the excitement of crowds and night life. It's overdeveloped and overcrowded. Its long, sandy beaches are lined with beautiful bodies from all over the world, and its discos are filled with fun-loving dancers ready for a good time.

Young Europeans flock to the coast on their vacations the same way American college students flock to Florida on their Easter breaks. The crowd can be an attraction.

Between Malaga and Algeciras are the most crowded resorts—Torremolinos, Fuengirola, and Marbella. Every imaginable language is spoken.

Marbella: the chicest resort

The chicest town on the coast is **Marbella**—it is also the most expensive. Movie stars and oil sheikhs keep prices here high. Puerto Banus has a marina that houses yachts from all over the world. Nueva Andalucia, a community within Marbella, has a fancy casino and chic nightclubs. This is night life at its best

Régine's, *Hotel Puente Romano, Carretera de Cadiz; tel. (34-52)77-01-00,* is the place to find celebrities, including Princess Margaret, Alain Delon, and Gunther Sachs. This basement nightclub is funky and exciting.

Marbella's best hotel

The **Marbella Club Hotel,** *Carretera de Cadiz KM 184; tel. (34-52)77-13-00,* is an expensive but chic jet-set resort. Adnan Khashoggi has an apartment here. The club's Andalusian-style bungalows encircle pools and gardens. Expect to pay 17,000 pesetas to 25,000 pesetas per night.

Torremolinos: the busiest resort

Torremolinos, once a quiet fishing village, is now the busiest resort on the coast. Germans seem to love Torremolinos, flocking there by the hundreds. High-rise hotels and condominiums line the beaches, and restaurants, nightclubs, and boutiques line the streets. The place is packed with tourists all summer long.

The two best restaurants are **El Caballo Vasco,** *Piso 1 (First Floor), Casablanca, La Nogalera; tel. (34-52)38-23-36,* and **El Molino de la Torre, Cuesta del Tajo 8; tel. (34-52)38-77-56.** Dinners are 2,000 pesetas to 4,000 pesetas.

El Torcal—the strangest landscape

When you tire of the beaches, take a trip inland to **El Torcal,** a plain covered with fantastically shaped boulders. The softest parts of the park's limestone rocks have dissolved over the years, leaving the oddly shaped hard sections of rock. You will think you're on the moon.

The Costa Brava—the most beautiful coast

Spaniards who would rather relax on a secluded beach than gaze at masses of bodies head for the **Costa Brava** which stretches from Blanes to the French border. The Wild Coast is known for its ferocious, rugged beauty. Pines fringe the rocky cliffs that drop to the fine, sandy beaches. Little towns are sheltered by the coast's protective coves.

Phoenicians, Greeks, Romans, and Arabs all have taken refuge in the Costa Brava's harbors. Ruins left by these early invaders dot the coast, as do fortified villages from the days of pirate invasions. You'll find Phoenician ruins at Rosas, Greek in Ampurias, and a Moorish fortress at Tossa del Mar.

Gerona is the best town for exploring the coast. It is filled with dungeons and ramparts, medieval walls and paintings. The old quarter is dominated by the majestic cathedral, built in the 17th century above Roman ruins. St. Felix Church, next to the cathedral, contains Roman sarcophagi.

The most popular resort

Tossa de Mar, a shiny white town by the sea, is the most popular resort along the Catalan coast. It has an old quarter that predates even Roman civilization and a Moorish alcazar, and it is surrounded by walls that were built in the 12th century.

El Codolar beach, behind Vila Vella, and Playa Llorell beach are the least crowded.

The lap of luxury

If you're looking for luxury, stay in **S'Agaro.** This contemporary residential community attracts the crème de la crème of European society. Paseo de Ronda, which leads to the beach, is lined with gardens, fountains, and statuary.

S'Agaro's **La Gavina,** *Plaza de la Rosaleda; tel. (34-972)32-11-00,* is the most luxurious beach hotel in Spain. The white, Spanish mission-style building is perched on a cliff above a beach. Guests can swim in the pool or play on the tennis courts. Golf is available, and the restaurant is excellent. Rooms are 17,000 pesetas to 22,500 pesetas.

Dali's favorite town

The Costa Brava attracts artists and writers. **Salvador Dali,** born nearby, was one of the first major artists to live there—at Port Lligot, Cadaques, near the French border. You can visit his estate, which is marked by gigantic egg-shaped ornaments and has a whimsical garden.

Cadaques is a purely Catalan fishing village whose white houses contrast with the dark mountain backdrop. Tourists haven't yet flooded this tranquil town. Mediterranean cooking is served at **Es Baluard,** *Riba Nemesio Llorens 2; tel. (34-72)25-81-83,* a favorite among local artists. The restaurant is closed Oct. 15 to Dec. 15.

Make hotel reservations in Cadaques in advance. The few hotels book up fast. One good place to stay is the **Playa Sol,** *Playa Pianch 5; tel. (34-72)25-81-00.* It has a pool and tennis courts and is reasonably priced—rooms go for 5,000 pesetas to 9,000 pesetas.

The best nude beach

The Costa Brava has a number of lovely secluded beaches perfect for nude sunbathing. Cabo de **Creus** has clean water and little caves hidden among the rocks.

Costa de Almeria: the most peaceful beaches

Spain's most peaceful beaches are along the relatively undiscovered **Costa de Almeria.** Stretching 120 miles between Almeria and Cartagena on the southeastern edge of Spain, the coast retains much of its original charm and still has reasonable prices.

The dry, warm climate and the landscape are somewhat like southern Arizona—with the difference that off the Costa de Almeria's precipitous edges the deep blue Mediterranean gleams. Much of the coastline is dotted with little fishing villages, many still lacking modern facilities—which helps keep the tourists away.

Inland, the rusty brown of the Costa de Almeria's dry, terraced mountains is broken by patches of pear cactus, tidy olive groves, and rows of pine trees. Here and there is a crumbling stone farm building (*cortijo*), its faded tile roof askew. Now and then a flock of sheep or goats shuffles across the picture, herded by a craggy shepherd and a floppy sheepdog.

Hollywood Spanish-style

A short drive north of the town of Almeria is **Mini-Hollywood,** where replicas of American Wild West streets have been built for spaghetti Westerns. *Lawrence of Arabia, The Good, the Bad, and the Ugly,* and *Reds* all were filmed on these incredible sand dunes. Some travelers make a little pocket change by acting as extras in films being shot in the region. To find out which movies are being filmed, stop in at the offices of **Almantur,** *Carretera de Malaga; tel. (34-52)23-48-59,* the tourist promotion board. Staff members there can give you maps showing you film sights.

One of Almeria's best hotels is **El Moresco,** *tel. (34-951)47-80-25,* in a spectacular setting in Mojacar. El Moresco has views in all directions of the mountains, valley, and sea. It also has a roof-top pool. Rooms are 5,000 pesetas to 9,000 pesetas.

The best place to stay in Almeria is the **Gran Hotel Almeria,** *ave. Reina Regente 8; tel. (34-951)23-80-11,* a modern place overlooking the harbor. Among other comforts, it has a pool.

Spain's loveliest cathedral

The largest city in Cantabria is frequently overlooked by travelers, who stick primarily to the coast. **Leon** was the center of the Spanish movement led by El Cid to oust the Moors, as well as one of the great cities along the pilgrim route to Santiago de Campostella.

As you might expect from a city with such important religious traditions, Leon has a splendid cathedral. But you'll be surprised at just how splendid it is. The stained-glass windows here are second only to those of Chartres in France. Because the cathedral was built before the art of using flying buttresses had been mastered, the way the light plays into the Leon cathedral is even more dramatic, being at ground level. The windows are predominantly red and gold (as you might expect in Spain), rather than mostly blue as in Chartres.

In addition to the windows, Leon's cathedral has a beautiful Romanesque cloister with fountains, gardens, and a rood screen by an unknown master, depicting the deposition of the body of Christ.

Leon is the center of the Gallego region, where the people speak a dialect of Spanish closer to Portuguese than Castillian. Leon is not close enough to the sea to provide good fresh fish, and gastronomically it is pretty disappointing.

The best hotel is the **San Marcos,** *Plaza San Marcos; tel. (34-87)23-73-00,* built into the remains of a magnificent 16th-century monastery. This is a rare free-enterprise hotel—most monastery hotels are *paradors.* Prices are high, more than 10,000 pesetas for a bed and breakfast fit for an abbot.

Santiago de Compostela—Spain's pilgrimage center

All roads in northwest Spain (and many roads in France) lead to **Santiago de Campostela,** the greatest pilgrimage center on the Iberian Peninsula. During the Middle Ages, this town was the destination of pilgrims from all over Europe, who came to worship at the tomb of St. James (Santiago), housed in the 11th-century cathedral. Santiago was as important a pilgrimage destination as Rome or Jerusalem.

According to legend, the apostle St. James came to this part of Spain to bring Christianity. He landed at Padron in an estuary of the Ulla River. After his death, his remains are said to have been brought back to Spain, where they were lost during invasions by Barbarians and Moors. In the ninth century, a star is said to have appeared, marking the point where St. James' remains were buried. They were then taken to Santiago and placed in the cathedral.

Another tale says St. James appeared during a battle against the Moors in A.D. 844, dressed in armor and carrying a white standard with a red cross on it. He fought off the infidels and became known as Matamore, or Slayer of Moors. Later, the saint is said to have fled the Moors by swimming across a river. When he emerged on the other side, he was covered with seashells. For this reason, pilgrims wore cockleshells to show they had been to Santiago de Compostela.

Even if you aren't a pilgrim, Santiago is worth visiting. It is especially beautiful at sunset, when its church spires, hospitals, monasteries, and palaces glint with the sun on their roofs.

The town's Romanesque cathedral and old town, where ancient houses and little shops fill the streets, are worth exploring.

The best place to stay in Santiago de Compostela is **Los Reyes Catolicos,** *Plaza de España 1; tel. (34-981)58-22-00.* Built in the 16th century by Ferdinand and Isabella as a hospice for pilgrims, the *parador* is in the form of a cross, with an interior square and four patios. Bedrooms have high ceilings and ornate furniture. The nightclub and grill offer dancing. And the cathedral is just across the square. Rooms are 12,000 to 14,000 pesetas.

San Sebastian: Basque-ing with the best

Beautiful **San Sebastian,** bordered by the Urumea River, Bahia de la Concha, and three hills, is where Europe's wealthiest vacationers play during the summer. Drive to the top of Mt. Urgall for a long vista of the bay and the sea. An even better view of the city, the bay, and the sea can be seen three miles west of the city at Mt. Igueldo.

San Sebastian is known for its Basque cooking with Spanish and French touches and its original use of seafood.

The best restaurant in San Sebastian is **Arzak,** *Alto de Miracruz 21; tel. (34-943)27-84-65.* Chef Juan Mari Arzak won Spain's National Gastronomy Prize for his river crabs with truffles and lobster sauce, his apple pudding with strawberry cream, and his mousse. Arzak specializes in nouvelle Basque cuisine. The restaurant is closed in June and November and on Sunday nights and Mondays during the winter.

San Sebastian's best hotels

The two most elegant hotels in town are **De Londres y de Inglaterra,** *Zubieta 2; tel. (34-943)426-989,* and **Costa Vasca,** *ave. Pio Baroja 15; tel. (34-943)21-10-11.* Rooms from 9,000 to 11,000 pesetas.

Sleeping like a king

El Emperador, *Plaza de Armas, Fuenterrabia; tel. (34-943)64-21-40,* is an elegant *parador* in a massive Gothic castle between the resort of San Sebastian and the French border, in the little fishing village of Fuenterrabia. It was once the stronghold of Charles V, Holy Roman Emperor and king of Spain (1519-1556).

This dreamy inn has thick stone walls and floors, Gothic arches, exposed beams hung with heraldic banners, and winding staircases that lead to the 16 guest rooms. The kitchen serves tasty local Basque dishes. Rooms are 7,000 to 9,000 pesetas.

Galicia—the fishermen's favorite

Galicia, the westernmost coast of Spain, is a land of fishermen and damp, green land-scapes. It has changed little over the centuries and has yet to draw hordes of tourists, probably because of its damp weather. The coastline is beautiful, a great place for romantic walks.

Vigo, the main fishing port

Vigo is the main fishing port of Galicia. Hemingway described this town as "a pasteboard village, cobbled-streeted, white and orange plastered, set up on one side of a big, almost land-locked harbor."

Vigo lies at the end of a swampy river valley. Sheltered bays and quiet inlets surrounding the town produce the shellfish for which Galicia is famous, as well as sardines, tuna, and hake. During the winter, the port is battered by winter gales.

Snug little bars and restaurants can be found on the steep, winding streets of Vigo. Fishermen drink the local wine, *ribeiro,* and chat among themselves in Gallego, the local Spanish dialect, similar to Portuguese. Early in the morning, Vigo bustles. Fisherwomen wearing clogs push cartloads of fish to market.

White sandy beaches called Samil and America stretch south of Vigo. A road, lined by vines that produce *ribeiro,* hugs the shoreline, dipping into tiny hamlets and climbing the hills. Narrow one-lane bridges cross muddy creeks.

The best place to stay on the coast

Conde de Gondomar, *Bayona; tel. (34-986)35-50-00,* is a *parador* in a dizzying location on the northwest Galician coast. Located in an old fortress surrounded by water, this inn stands between the Vigo and Bayona fjords and has spectacular views of the coast. The guest rooms and lounges are decorated with Renaissance furniture and antique tapestries and clocks. Walk along the top of the fortified walls that ring the property. Or enjoy a seafood dinner in the dining room. The inn's facilities include a swimming pool and tennis courts. Rooms are 8,000 pesetas to 12,000 pesetas per night.

The Canary Islands: Atlantis regained

Scattered off the bulge of West Africa, Spain's 13 **Canary Islands** are blessed with 360 days of sunshine. Only on record-breaking days does the temperature dip below 65 degrees Fahrenheit. As a result of this year-round springlike climate, farmers in the Canaries can harvest four crops a year. The Canaries have markets filled with incredible varieties of fruits and vegetables.

According to legend, the islands are all that remain of the lost city of Atlantis. Roman discoverers named the islands Canaria, from *canus,* after the wild dogs that lived there.

Tenerife, the largest Canary

Tenerife, which covers 1,231 square miles, is the largest Canary. Through the center of the island runs Mt. Teide, the highest peak in all Spain, at 12,192 feet.

Throngs of Europeans come here from cold Scandinavia, Germany, and Britain. They romp among the sand dunes and fill the hotels and restaurants all seasons of the year. The burgeoning growth of multistoried highrises and discos and bars and planeloads of tourists make south Tenerife another Costa del Sol. However, the pace of growth is being checked as building requirements become more stringent.

Cosmopolitan Santa Cruz

The most cosmopolitan city in the Canaries is **Santa Cruz,** on Tenerife, the largest port in Spain. The capital city of 200,000 looks for all the world like San Francisco, located at the foot of a gentle slope. It has attractive stores (including designer shops), great restaurants, museums, art galleries, theaters, and even a symphony orchestra.

Shopping in Santa Cruz is a special joy. Because the town is a duty-free port, items can be purchased for prices lower than in their countries of origin. Chinese silks, pearls from Japan, watches, designer clothes, and photographic equipment are some of the best bargains.

Puerto de la Cruz, the prettiest town

On the northwest coast, toward Buena Vista, is the small city of **Puerto de la Cruz.** Built on a rocky coast, it has a 600-acre man-made lake and a chain of natural pools that are terrific for swimming. Yellow and red hibiscus, trailing pink geraniums, 30-foot-tall poinsettias, and other tropical greenery surround the pools, and fountains shoot 20 feet into the air. However, the ocean has no beach.

Perhaps the most entertaining thing about Puerto de la Cruz is its underwater nightclub, where you can sip your drink and look through the water to the stars.

Stroll along the town's pedestrian street to the best ice cream parlor in the Canaries (if not Spain). It has more than 40 flavors and just as many fresh toppings. Imagine cinnamon ice cream smothered in fresh mango and blueberries!

The best times in Tenerife

The two best times to visit Tenerife are July, when a two-week fiesta attracts people from all over Europe, and February, for Carnival.

The island's best hotel

Tenerife's most attractive hotel is **Semiramis,** *Urbanizacion La Paz, Puerto de la Cruz; tel. (34-22)38-55-51,* an imaginatively designed structure overlooking the ocean. Double rooms are 16,000 pesetas a night.

The best of Gran Canaria

Gran Canaria is a mountainous island with banana trees, coffee groves, sugarcane, and almond trees. Along the southern coast, from the tourist-ridden Playa San Augustino to the more quiet and chic Puerto Mogan, is an unbroken chain of serious sunbathers, windsurfers, campers, and other winter refugees from all over Europe.

Las Palmas, the capital of this 922-square-mile island, is a duty-free port and a shoppers' paradise. Although it's difficult to imagine wearing a fur coat in this warm climate, fur coats are a tremendous bargain in the Canaries, where they are available for 30% to 50% less than in European shops. Two good shops are **Kanellopoulos,** *Sagasta 46,* and **Voula Mitsakou,** *Luis Morote 28.*

The most gorgeous resort area in the Canaries is **Maspalomas.** It has long, sandy beaches, lagoons, graceful sand dunes, and enormous palm trees swaying in the breeze.

The Oasis Maspalomas shopping center has boutiques, restaurants, bars, banks, car rentals, and book and trinket stalls. Moroccans and Africans enthusiastically greet you with their wares: camel-skin bags complete with desert aroma, stuffed coiled cobras, and carved ebony elephants. Bikini bottoms are a real buy at $5 each, and the selection includes bright colors as well as leopard and zebra prints. But forget about finding matching tops. Topless is the *moda de la playa*.

The most charming village on the island is **Mogan,** a fishing village that rises from the sea on its natural wall of crags and burned earth. Tanned people chat in a half-dozen languages on the streets here. A village artist portrays flamenco dancers on the outside of his house. And the valley is brightened by flowering almond trees and tropical fruits.

Unsurpassable meals

Gran Canaria is a paradise for food lovers. Most restaurants serve delicious meals in gigantic portions for incredibly low prices. This holds true whether you dine in a tiny beach shack or an elegant restaurant. Two generally can feast for a mere $15.

Choose from a variety of fresh meats and fish, including *chulletas de cordero* (thick, juicy grilled pork chops); *solomillo pimentas* (steak smothered with roasted sweet peppers); *tuna casuela* (home-style tuna steaks baked with garlic, onions, and red and green peppers); and local fish, such as *salmonetta* (red mullet), and sole, all prepared with fresh parsley and garlic. Tiny island-grown potatoes called *papas arrugadas* are steamed with sea salt and served with a spicy dipping sauce (*mojo picon*) made of chopped chili peppers, garlic, and oil. A good wine is the velvety Lanzarote.

Our favorite restaurant on the island is the roof-top **Restaurante Rio** in the town of Puerto Rico. Try the *langosta Americana*—grilled rock lobster with mayonnaise. A Latin band plays, and after your meal you can dance until dawn.

Sleeping in the lap of luxury

Maspalomas Oasis, *Playa de Maspalomas; tel. (34-28)76-01-70,* is a huge resort complex with a nightclub, a golf course, horseback riding, tennis, and a health club. It's expensive and popular. Double rooms are 12,000 to 29,000 pesetas.

Tamarindos, *Playa San Agustin, Las Retamas, 3; tel. (34-28)76-26-00,* is a sophisticated hotel with two swimming pools and a nice beach. A full buffet is set up next to one of the pools. A disco and several bars keep the atmosphere friendly. Double rooms are 23,870 pesetas.

The best of the Balearic Islands

The **Balearic Islands** peek sleepily out of the Mediterranean. Europeans love the islands for their perfect weather, easygoing inhabitants, and lovely beaches. Mallorca, Menorca, Ibiza, Formentera, and scores of rocky islets make up the Balearics, which lie 100 miles southeast of Barcelona. The trip from Barcelona can be made in 25 minutes by air or within nine hours by boat.

The islands have changed a great deal since the days when Mallorcans stoned George Sand for wearing pants. You will see artists and jet-setters, punk rockers and tourists, as well as old women in traditional black.

Mallorca—a jet-set getaway

Mallorca offers craggy mountains, Roman temples, and unspoiled beaches.

The biggest Balearic island with the starkest contrasts, Mallorca has office buildings and windmills, highways and ancient villages. Although tourists sunbathe topless, the natives wear traditional costumes. And children inherit thousand-year-old olive trees when the family farms get passed down.

About half the island's residents live in Mallorca's capital, **Palma de Mallorca.** While in the capital, visit the cathedral, Santa Maria, which boasts one of the world's biggest stained-glass windows. Construction of the cathedral began in 1230 and continued for 300 years.

Perfect pearls

If you are a shopping addict, Mallorca should please you. In **Manacor,** *via Roma 52,* you'll find the most beautiful artificial pearls in the world—strings and strings of almost perfect deceptions. You can tour the factory.

Inca, in the heart of the island, produces inexpensive leather goods.

The prettiest town in Mallorca

The most peaceful town in the Balearics is **Deya,** on the northwest coast. It is a haven for artists and writers who yearn for the romance of the sea yet despair of spending too much time alone with blank paper or canvas. Robert Graves, who wrote *I Claudius,* lived here for years.

A road leads two miles from town through goat fields and over terraces built by the Moors to a beautiful beach. Princess Diana vacations here—but it isn't expensive. For about $350 a month, the aspiring painter can rent a small cliffside dwelling.

George Sand's bitter refuge

Visit the monastery of **La Cartuja** at Valldemosa, where George Sand and the composer Chopin took refuge for three months during the dreary winter of 1839. Sand's book, *A Winter in Mallorca,* talks bitterly of the island's inhospitality. Set high in the mountains on the west coast, the monastery's beauty belies the misery the two artists felt while living there. They were disliked by locals, who were convinced that Chopin had the plague and were offended by the morals of an unmarried couple who refused to attend Mass. Nonetheless, Chopin composed some of his greatest preludes here.

Built in 1311 as a palace for King Sancho, the place was converted into a monastery after his death. By the time Sand and Chopin lived there, it had become an apartment building. Its pale yellow stone contrasts sharply with the deep green of the surrounding mountains and the blue sky above. Chopin's piano remains in one of the cells.

Also at Valldemosa is an old pharmacy with jars whose contents are labeled with descriptions such as "Nail Pairings of the Great Beast."

Mallorca's best hotels

The finest hotel is **Hotel Formentor,** *Playa de Formentor; tel. (34-71)53-13-00,* set in gorgeous hillside gardens. Paths lead down to a private beach. The king of Spain has stayed here, as have other dignitaries. Double rooms are about 15,000 pesetas.

Hostal Fortune in Palma is one of the few hotels open year-round. Built in 1703 around a courtyard, it is modestly priced and offers bedrooms furnished in heavy wood and marbled baths. Room 104 has a colorful ceiling fresco.

The best of Ibiza

The cobblestoned streets of **Ibiza,** decorated with rainbows of flowers, wind through bright white buildings that lead to the sea. Orange and lemon trees climb terraces to sturdy farmhouses on hilltops. A grove of fig and almond trees curtains sandy beaches. In the evening, lovers stroll to Vedra, the Magic Rock, which reflects the moonlight and is washed gently by the sea.

This island off Spain's east coast has been inhabited by Phoenicians, Greeks, Carthaginians, and Romans. Centuries of invasions by Vandals, Byzantines, and Arabs led to the construction of an enormous fortress here. But the forbidding citadel isn't enough to keep the tourists away.

Now is the time to see Ibiza. Despite efforts to enforce zoning restrictions, houses and apartment buildings are going up at a rate that bodes ill for people who like the island's secluded beaches. Already, hotels line some of the island's most languid beach strips. Ancient olive groves are being razed for golf courses. And the visitors' appetites for night life have made clubs and bars materialize in out-of-the-way places.

Of course, all this modernizing has its good points (depending on your point of view). Ibiza was the pioneer of nude beaches in Spain, and Agua Blanca beach is an excellent place to get a full-body tan. Cabo Falcon also has a good nude beach called Es Cavallet.

Comida San Juan is the best and one of the cheapest restaurants in Ibiza. Local patrons swear by it. Grilled trout is only a couple dollars, a fruit plate a few cents. La Marina is almost as good and even cheaper.

El Caliu, a restaurant in a thick-walled farmhouse, has the island's best wine cellar and grilled food. The view of the fields and the sea beyond is lovely. Prices are modest.

The wildest night life in Ibiza is at **QU,** a disco that combines swimming, dancing, and eating. It is the source of many a bawdy tale.

The island's most luxurious hotel is the **Hacienda,** balanced on its own pinnacle at the northern end of the island. It is expensive—more than 8,400 pesetas for a double room.

Cala is a small hotel in Santa Lauria, where the intelligentsia stays. The price is only about 1,650 pesetas per person, even in high season.

Menorca, the most romantic isle

Menorca, the most romantic of the Balearic Islands, is the kind of spot you might want to escape to on your honeymoon, as Princess Grace and Prince Rainier did. Traveling from one end of the island to the other on its narrow, winding roads, you will probably encounter no one, save the unobtrusive sheep on the hillsides. Menorca is lush and hilly, not mountainous.

Menorca is said to have about 120 coves with beaches, mostly unpeopled. The most deserted beach is Sambal, which is four miles long.

Mouth-watering lobster and bouillabaise are served at Espla, a restaurant famous for its breathtaking location on the waterfront. Another good island restaurant is Buccañeros.

The best hotel on the island is **Port Mahon,** *ave. Fort de l'Eau, Paseo Maritimo; tel. (34-71)36-26-00.* It has a pretty view and a swimming pool. Double rooms are 6,600 pesetas to 8,500 pesetas.

The most colorful time to visit Spain: Holy Week

The mysterious religious world of medieval times is resurrected each year in Spain during Holy Week. Candlelit processions mourning the death of Christ file silently through the old quarters of Spain's cities and towns. Statues depicting the life of Christ are carried through the streets. In some areas, residents don the attire of Biblical times and re-enact the life of Jesus.

The biggest Holy Week celebration is in **Seville.** More than 50 orders of priests and laymen march in procession following an ancient route from the Plaza de la Campana along winding Sierpes Street, past the town hall, and through the Gothic cathedral. They end up in front of the Giralda and the baroque Bishop's Palace. *Pasos* (platforms of wood and silver) carry statues of the Virgin. They are covered with carnations and rock gently on the shoulders of the bearers to the rhythm of *saetas,* short and fervent prayers or hymns.

The **Burial of the Sardine** is a nighttime tradition in Murcia that marks the end of Lent. It includes 25 carriages, each with an accompanying group of merrymakers, bands, and *hachoneros,* or men who carry bras. Little toys are thrown to the spectators from the carriages. At the end of the festival a huge papier-mâché *sardina* is burned at the old bridge in Puento Viejo, and fireworks are set off.

The Burial of the Sardine dates back to the 19th century, when university students, who could afford to eat nothing but sardines, would bury some to celebrate their graduation.

Spain's best wines

Spanish wines rival French wines and are half the price of their Gallic counterparts. Spain's champagnes are darn good too.

Of the Rioja wines, the two best are Marques de Murrieta and Marques de Riscal. And the rare Castillo Ygay Reserva, made four times a century, is incomparable. The Riscal clarets are delicious; the best of the Riscal reds is the 1922.

Vega Sicilia, which is aged for 10 years, is the best of the Penedes wines (1966 is the best year). Torres is the best brand; the best Torres is the Gran Coronas Black Label.

Spanish sherry is world-famous, yet underpriced. Barbadillo's Sanlucar Manzanilla is the elegant before-dinner drink in Spain. The best-selling dry sherry in the world is Tio Pepe.

The cheapest skiing in Western Europe

Spain is famous for sunshine and bullfights, not snow-covered mountains and ski slopes. However, the skiing in Spain can be quite good, and it's much less expensive and less crowded than in the Alps.

The most popular ski resort is **Baqueira Beret,** in Lerida province in the Pyrénées. The long ski season here lasts from late November to late April. You can choose from seven slopes of varying difficulty. Facilities include six chair lifts, eight ski lifts, and one baby lift. Ski instruction and equipment rental are available.

Hotels are open from Dec. 1 to May 1. **Hotel Montarto,** *Baqueira Beret, Salardu, Lerida; tel. (34-73)64-50-75,* is comfortable, has spectacular views of the slopes, and is near the lifts. Rooms are 5,400 pesetas to 11,000 pesetas.

Chapter 8

THE
BEST
OF
PORTUGAL

Portugal is the best travel bargain in Europe. As beautiful and historic as neighboring Spain, it is far cheaper and less developed. Don't make the mistake of most foreigners and see only Lisbon. Portugal has much to offer outside this capital city, including quaint old villages surrounded by rolling hills, Moorish cities, long sandy beaches, and mountain vistas.

Portuguese culture has been influenced by the Moors, the Catholic Church, and a seafaring history. The Portuguese sing the fado, a heart-rending, wailing sort of blues. Their unique cuisine includes *bacalhau,* a dried codfish served a different way every day of the year. Portugal has its own sweet wines, Port and Madeira. And the Portuguese have a version of the bullfight gentler than that in Spain. Portuguese matadors wrestle the bull but never kill the animal. At the end of a bullfight, the bull is enticed out of the ring by a cow.

Portugal's cultural center: Lisbon

The capital of Portugal is studded with ancient Moorish buildings and bordered by lovely beaches. Its National Museum of Ancient Art houses one of Europe's best collections. Outside Lisbon are palaces that rival the chateaux of the Loire in France. And at the heart of the city are winding streets that pass medieval churches and inviting cafés.

Built on a series of hills, **Lisbon** has 17 overlooks, called *miradouros,* that offer wide views of the city. The best is at the Castelo de São Jorge, built in the fifth century by the Visigoths and later used as a Moorish stronghold. Another panoramic view is from the top of the statue Cristo Rei, or Christ the King (a smaller replica of the one in Rio de Janeiro), located on the opposite side of the Tagus River from the city. To get there, cross the Ponte 25 do Abril (April 25 Bridge).

Lisbon's seven best sights

Lisbon's most beautiful landmark is the **Basilica da Estrela,** *Largo da Estrela.* Queen Maria I promised God she would build the basilica if he granted her a son. God kept His part of the bargain, and the basilica was built in the late 18th century of luminous pale marble and topped with an enormous stone dome. Maria's tomb is inside. Look for the life-size manger scene carved by Machado de Castro.

The **se** (cathedral), *Largo de Se,* is the city's most imposing structure. The 12th-century cathedral was once a fortress and has battlements, two towers, and massive walls. Behind the austere facade are Gothic cloisters and a burial chapel.

Igreja de São Roque is a Jesuit church with an ornate chapel called São Joao Baptista, which is lavishly decorated with amethyst, agate, marble, and entire columns of Chilean lapis lazuli.

The **Gulbenkian Museum,** *ave. de Berna 45,* houses the huge collection of French furniture, Oriental carpets, and great paintings of the eccentric millionaire Calouste Gulbenkian, as well as Beauvais tapestries.

The **Museu de Etnologia,** *avenida Ilha da Madeira,* has one of the finest collections of African art in the world.

Museu National de Arte Antiga, *rua das Janelas Verdes 9,* contains one of Portugal's greatest treasures, the polyptych of the *Adoration of St. Vincent,* painted by Nuno Gonçalves between 1460 and 1470. The six-panel work surrounds a statue of St. Vincent, patron saint of Portugal.

Igreja da Madre de Deus has Europe's best display of antique tiles, called *azulejos,* which line the 16th-century crypt.

Belem: an area of bests

Belem, an island in the middle of the Tagus, west of downtown Lisbon, is surrounded by museums and monuments. The **Torre de Belem,** a five-story tower, is the most outstanding landmark. Built between 1515 and 1521, cannons on this Gothic structure protected the Tagus for centuries. A statue of *Our Lady of Safe Homecoming* on the tower's peak welcomes sailors home from sea.

In 1502, the profits of the spice trade were used to build the **Mosteiro dos Jeronimos,** a celebration of Vasco da Gama and other Portuguese explorers. This was da Gama's point of return after finding the sea route to India. He is buried in this church, which is backed by a decorative cloister with columns, arches, fountains, and cool stone benches. In front is the *Monument to the Navigators*—erected in 1960 in the shape of a ship's prow.

Belem is also home to the Museum of Folk Art, the National Coach Museum, and the Naval Museum, which houses beautifully restored ships, as well as early airplanes.

Lisbon's oldest quarter, the Alfama

The only neighborhood in Lisbon not destroyed by the great earthquake on All Saints' Day, 1755 is the **Alfama,** whose tiny medieval streets twist and turn between rows of shops and old houses. The violent earthquake, which struck while most of the city's residents were in church, was followed by 40-foot tidal waves and fires that burned for a week. At least 60,000 people died.

The Alfama existed before the Visigoths arrived in the fifth century. It clusters beneath the Castelo São Jorge on one of Lisbon's tallest hills. The cobblestoned streets are so narrow that in some places you must walk single file. Wrought-iron lamps light the streets. Canaries and geraniums brighten the balconies. Laundry waves from lines strung above the streets. Tiles portraying the Virgin Mary, St. Anthony, and St. Martial decorate buildings, some of which date back to the Moors or the Middle Ages.

Walking along **Beco do Mexias,** you pass dozens of tiny shops and come to a doorway that leads to a large fountain where local women do their laundry. Also explore **rua da Regueira,** which is lined with restaurants and shops; and **Patio das Flores,** a little square with houses faced in tile.

Lisbon's most colorful market

Begin your day in Lisbon wandering through the fish market at the foot of the Alfama. Weathered fishermen bring in their catches here, and *varinhas,* or fishwives, march about with baskets of fish on their heads. The *varinhas* wear black skirts with aprons and go barefoot in the summer. Gold hoops dangle from their ears.

Lisbon's best shopping

Veer off the grand avenida da Liberdade onto the rua do Carmo and rua Garrett. This is **Chiado,** Lisbon's shopping district, where you'll find jewelry, Portuguese tiles, leather goods, and wine for reasonable prices.

Lisbon's other main shopping area, **Baixa,** is located between Rossio Square and the river. Here are old bookshops and antique stores. The best place for gold and silver filigree is **Sarmento,** *rua do Ouro 251.* **Por-fi-ri-os Contraste,** *rua da Vitoria 63,* sells the skimpiest bikinis around. **Helio Cinderela,** *rua do Carmo 93,* has good prices on Charles Jourdan shoes and smart leather bags. **Saboia,** *rua Garrett 44,* sells fine men's suits for less than 40,000 escudos.

Brightly colored *azulejos* are sold at **Fabrica Sant'Anna,** *rua do Alecrin 95.*

Where to find a real steal

A cheap, offbeat place to shop is the **Feira da Ladra** (Market of Female Thieves). This 300-year-old market is similar to huge flea markets in Rome and Paris. Originally, it was literally a market of *sovaqueiras,* or female thieves. The *sovaqueiras* hid illegal wares in their armpits and sold them at stalls then located in Lisbon's central Rossio Square. In 1882, the market was moved to the Campo de Santa Clara, in the shadows of the Pantheon of St. Vincent, where the bodies of the kings of Portugal lie. You can buy just about anything you want at this market. Be on the lookout for bronze, copper, and gold—sometimes you can find great bargains. But be wary, because you also can be ripped off. The market is open Tuesdays and Saturdays.

Portugal's liveliest country market

If you're in Lisbon on the first Sunday of the month, take a detour to the country fair at **Vila Nogueria de Azeitão,** 21 miles south of the city. Portugal's liveliest and largest marketplace, the Azeitão offers everything from livestock and household furnishings to clothing and food. If you miss the fair at Azeitão, the nearby villages of Pinhal, Novo, Coina, and Moita have fairs on succeeding Sundays. Prices at these fairs are lower than those in city stores. Haggling is expected.

Best dishes

Lisbon is famous for its seafood, and the Alfama and the Bairro Alto are the best places to dine on the local *camaroes* (shrimp), *langosta* (lobster), *pesca espada* (swordfish), *salmonete* (red mullet), *linguado* (sole), and *bacalhau,* as well as the ubiquitous *sardinas grilhadas* (fresh grilled sardines), which are delicious. If you see *carne de porco com ameijoas* or *ameijoas na cataplana* on a menu, order it. These are uniquely south Portuguese combinations of pork and sausage with clams.

Drink Sumol (lemon or orange soda), Sagres *cerveja* (beer), or the local wine, Dão or Vinho Verde. Most of the gin and whiskey in Portugal is faked.

Best restaurants

The best restaurant in Lisbon is **Tagide,** *Largo da Academia Nacional de Belas Artes, 18; tel. (351-1)32-07-20.* Michelin gave it a star and especially recommends its salmon paté and the pork. It is closed Saturday nights and Sundays. Dinner is 3,000 escudos to 5,000 escudos.

Tavares, *rua de Misericordia 37; tel. (351-1)32-11-12,* is Portugal's most elegant restaurant. Founded in 1784, it serves traditional Portuguese cuisine. The enormous mirrors and magnificent chandelier are trappings of bygone days. A full-course meal, including Portuguese wine, is 2,000 escudos to 5,000 escudos.

Casa da Comida, *Travessa das Amoreiras 1; tel. (351-1)68-53-76,* is a Michelin-star winner with a pretty patio. Meals are 3,000 escudos to 6,500 escudos.

However, the best meal for the best price is at **Conventual,** *Praça das Flores 45; tel. (351-1)60-91-96.* Despite its Michelin star, it charges merely 1,500 escudos to 3,500 escudos for dinner.

Fado: Portugal's saddest music

Fado, which means fate, is as important to Portugal as flamenco is to Spain—although it is more intense and somber. The best fado is played in the Alfama, the Mouraria (another neighborhood with Moorish traditions), the Bairro Alto (the old section), and the Madragoa (the fishermen's quarter). Fado songs range over many octaves, almost always in a minor key. They are usually sung by women dressed from head to toe in melancholy black and carrying red roses. Male fado singers or guitar accompanists wear black monks' robes.

Some of the songs date back to the 13th century; others are influenced by Portugal's Moorish past (and sound atonal) or by Portugal's seafaring tradition (and are reminiscent of sea chanties). Most are about unrequited love.

Recommended fado restaurants include **Cota D'Armas,** *Beco de São Miguel; tel. (351-1)86-86-82;* **Parreirinha de Alfama,** *Beco do Espirito Santo; tel. (351-1)86-82-09;* **Fado Menor,** *rua das Praças 16;* **Painel do Fado,** *rua S. Pedro de Alcantara 65/69;* **Senhor Vinho,** *Meio-a-Lapa 18; tel. (351-1)67-26-81;* **Lisboa a Noite,** *rua das Gaveas 69; tel. (351-1)36-85-57;* and **A Severa,** *rua das Gaveas 51-61; tel. (351-1)36-40-06.* You must make reservations. Go after a late dinner; shows don't start before 10 p.m.

The hottest night life

Lisbon's most popular nightclub, **Bananas,** near the Largo das Fontal, Alcantara, has a membership system (as do many of the city's nightclubs). But couples and single women often can get in without a *cartao,* or pass, by paying a 552-escudo cover charge (the owners like to attract women to the disco).

Two discos that don't require memberships are **Trumps,** *rua da Imprensa Nacional, 104-B; tel. (351-1)67-10-59;* and **Whispers,** *Centro Comercial Imaviz (beneath the Sheraton Hotel), avenida Fontes Pereira de Melo; tel. (351-1)57-54-89.*

If you don't like rock music, try **Pe Sujo,** *Largo de S. Martinho, 6-7; tel. (351-1)86-56-29,* in the Alfama, where soft Brazilian music is played.

The cheapest fun

If you're trying to save money, you still can spend a pleasant evening in Lisbon—by strolling through the old sections. You'll find plenty of free entertainment. Student choral groups dressed in caps and gowns sing traditional college melodies to the accompaniment of Spanish and Portuguese guitars.

Lisbon's best hotels

The most luxurious hotel in Lisbon is the **Ritz,** *rua Rodrigo da Fonseca 88; tel. (351-1)69-20-20,* set on a hill overlooking Parque Eduardo VII. Rooms at the Ritz are decorated in silks, satins, and suedes. The hotel restaurant, the Grill Room, is one of the city's most popular. Rooms are 20,000 escudos to 25,000 escudos.

The **Principe Real,** *rua de Alegria 53; tel. (351-1)36-01-16,* is a tiny, relatively unknown hotel tucked away in the Barrio Alto. It has great charm and is furnished with lovely antiques and good reproductions. Rooms are 8,000 escudos to 10,000 escudos.

The least expensive places to stay are off of the avenida de Liberdade. **Hotel Jorge V,** *rua Silveira 3; tel. (351-1)56-25-25,* has clean, modern rooms and elevators. **Hotel Lis,** *ave. da Liberdade 180; tel. (351-1)56-34-34,* has rooms with private bathrooms for 2,000 escudos to 5,000 escudos, including breakfast.

Best side trips from Lisbon

Queluz, Portugal's version of the Palace of Versailles, is not far from Lisbon. The 18th-century pink rococo palace is filled with Portuguese Empire antiques and surrounded by ornamental gardens. The palace kitchen, Cozinha Velha, is now a famous restaurant.

Cabo Espichel, a windy cape jutting into the Atlantic, is an ancient pilgrimage center. Explore the ruins of the 17th-century baroque church, **Nossa Senhora do Cabo** (Our Lady of the Cape), as well as the arcaded outbuildings that once housed pilgrims. Go around the church to the edge of the cliff, which drops 350 feet into the ocean.

Estoril is a beach resort 13 miles west of the city with a casino that is open from 3 p.m. to 3 a.m. You can take a train to Estoril from Lisbon's Cais do Sodre station. You must show a passport to get into the casino, and men must wear suit coats. The **Hotel Palacio,** *rua do Parque; tel. (351-1)268-0400,* is a gracious old hotel in Estoril near the beach with gardens, a swimming pool, and excellent service. Rooms are 16,000 escudos to 18,000 escudos.

Nearby is a fishing village that has been turned into a sophisticated resort, **Cascais.** A fine sandy beach lines its beautiful bay. Cascais has had an elegant air since 1870, when the court first moved here for the summer. A royal palace was constructed in the former citadel and is still used by the head of state. **Dois Mil e Um** (2001), Cascais' famous disco, offers British and American rock and a good sound system.

Just outside Cascais is one of the strangest sights on the coast—the **Boca do Inferno** (Jaws of Hell). This great hole, formed by the force of the ocean entering under a rock arch, roars when waves crash into it.

Praia do Guincho, five miles west of Cascais, is a long, sandy beach with dunes. Its massive headland is the westernmost point in Europe. It is famous for good fishing and surfing (beware the undertow).

Setubal is a busy fishing port with 16th- and 17th-century churches and a medieval fortress. Inside the walls of the town's castle, São Filipe, is the attractive **Pousada de São Filipe,** *tel. (351-65)23844.* Built in 1590, the fortress is 600 feet above the harbor and has many towers and massive battlements. It is entered via a dark, sweeping stone staircase. Underground tunnels and prison cells are now used as wine cellars and storage areas. The chapel is completely tiled. Rooms in the government-run hotel are 9,500 escudos to 11,000 escudos.

Sintra—the most romantic town

Sintra is the breathtaking mountain resort made famous by the poet Lord Byron, who wrote, "The village of Sintra is the most beautiful, perhaps, in the world." For centuries, Sintra was favored as a summer refuge by Portuguese royalty. It's a 45-minute train ride from Rossio Station in Lisbon.

Once a mountain stronghold of the Moors, Sintra is dominated by a seventh-century Moorish castle. Situated 1,400 feet above sea level, it has crenelated walls and battlements that extend along rocky cliffs. From the walls, you have a view of the cliffs and the sea.

The most romantic sight in Sintra is the **Pena Palace,** a towering pseudo-medieval palace built in the 19th century. From the windows are views of the coast, the cliffs, and the sea. The palace's 500-acre park, which you enter by crossing a drawbridge, has 400 kinds of trees and plants.

Europe's sunniest spot—the Algarve

Spanning 200 miles of Portugal's southern coast, from Sagres in the west to the Spanish border in the east, the Algarve is Europe's sunniest site, with 300 sunny days per year. During the summer, temperatures range from 68 to 86 degrees Fahrenheit. The hottest days are tempered by refreshing breezes off the Atlantic. Spring and fall have warm weather just right for swimming.

Separated from the rest of Portugal by a spine of mountains, the Algarve was once considered a separate kingdom. The Phoenicians, Greeks, Carthaginians, and Romans all traded here before the Moors took over and ruled for 500 years. The Algarve was the last province taken from the Moors by Portuguese kings, and many towns still more closely resemble the villages of North Africa than those of Europe.

Europe's best golf course

The Algarve has the best golfing in Europe, combining emerald greens and perfect weather year-round. And the best of the Algarve's many courses is **Quinta do Lago,** *Almancil, 8100 Loule; tel. (351-89)94271* or *(351-89)94329.* Lush fairways of Bermuda grass invite international golfers. The clubhouse and the pool are both welcoming.

Dona Filipa, *Vale do Lobo; tel. (351-89)94141,* is a grand hotel with views of the greens and the sea. It has a pool and tennis courts for those who tire of golf. Rooms are 22,000 escudos to 28,000 escudos.

Hotel Dom Pedro, *8125 Vilamoura; tel. (351-89)35450,* has a swimming pool and tennis courts. It is popular with golfers. Rooms are 13,000 escudos to 20,000 escudos.

Albufeira—the hottest town

Albufeira, a Moorish town, has the most beautiful bodies and the hottest night life in the region. **Sir Harry's Bar,** an English-style pub on the main square, draws revelers of all ages. But the real action is along rua Candido dos Reis, a cobblestoned pedestrian street that leads from the beach to the plaza. In the evening, the outdoor cafés, the restaurants, and the bars along here are filled. The two most popular bars are **Fastnet,** which is big with the British, and **Twist,** a Scandinavian and German hangout.

The discos in Albufeira get going after midnight. **Sylvia's** is the best, filled with Scandinavians on the prowl and handsome night owls. Across the street is **7 1/2,** which is almost as exciting.

A good, inexpensive place to stay is the **Hotel Rocamar,** where rooms are less than 4,000 escudos a night.

Nature's best show: sea caves and rock formations

Between Albufeira and Portimão, near the cliffside fishing village of Praia do Carvoeiro, nature provides one of its most beautiful spectacles. Drive to the **Nossa Senhora da Encarnaçâo,** a chapel at the summit of a steep hill east of Praia do Carvoeiro. The view of the cliffs and the sea crashing below is breathtaking. Climb down 134 steps through oddly shaped red rocks to see the gaping holes leading into the sea caves, which are engulfed every few minutes by waves. A path leads to a bluff from which you have a clear view of the entrance to an underwater sea cave.

The **Caves of Cape Carvoeiro** are best seen by boat, which you can do during high season. Ask for information at the tourist office in Praia do Carvoeiro.

The best *cataplana* in Portimão

The largest Algarve city, **Portimão** is a fishing port whose quays are lined with seafood restaurants. Try the dish called *cataplana*. A seafood stew cooked in a thick, hinged container, the exact recipe for *cataplana* varies from place to place but always includes clams and usually includes tomatoes, ham, and sausage. The average cost of cataplana is 665 escudos to 1,330 escudos per person.

The best place for this regional dish is **Avozinha,** *rua Capote 7; tel. (351-82)22922,* a family-run restaurant hidden on a narrow cobblestoned street that climbs uphill from the waterfront. The fish is very fresh, brought from the market at the harbor, just 100 yards away. The *cataplana* here is made of tiny clams, onion, garlic, fresh pork, pimiento, and bacon. The price is only 530 escudos.

Another good place for *cataplana* is **O Bicho,** *Largo Gil Eanes 12; tel. (351-82)22977,* a working-class establishment with the freshest seafood in town.

Lagos: the saddest past and the sandiest beaches

Ten miles west of Portimão is the town of **Lagos,** once a center of the African slave trade. The **Praça da Republica** is the site of the first slave market established in Europe. Sections of Roman walls remain in the old quarter of Lagos, and you can walk along the walls of the old fortress that guards the harbor. The 18th-century baroque **Chapel of St. Antonio** is known for its ornate gilded wood carvings.

South of town is Ponta da Piedad, a promontory with fine beaches connected by natural rock tunnels. The scenery is striking—the rocks are a reddish color that contrasts with the green of the sea. The boulders have been carved into strange shapes by pounding waves. From the lighthouse is a lovely view of the coast. Hire a boat in town to take you to see offshore grottoes.

A good inexpensive place to stay is the **Pensão Residencial Iberica,** *ave. Marçal Pacheco 157; tel. (351-89)62027.* Rooms are only 1,260 escudos to 4,480 escudos.

Sagres: the end of the world

Sagres, the most southwesterly point in Europe, is guarded by the fortress of **Prince Henry the Navigator.** His famous navigational device, the **Compass Rose,** is laid out in the stone.

Prince Henry founded his Navigation School here at the beginning of the 15th century. It also was here that he planned his expeditions into Africa and west into the unknown.

Before the great explorations began, sailors believed that **Cabo de São Vicente** (Cape St. Vincent), near Sagres, was the end of the world. The place is marked by a famous lighthouse. Waves crash ferociously on the rocks 250 feet below the lighthouse. If you're going to walk the beaches here, bring a windbreaker. Or buy one of the handsome handmade sweaters Sagres women are famous for knitting.

Pousada do Infante, *Sagres; tel. (351-82)64222,* has views of the coast and the lighthouse on the promontory of Cape St. Vincent. Delicious soups are served in the dining room, including *creme de espinafres* (spinach cream soup) and *sopa do mar* (fish soup). The fish is always fresh and well-cooked, and the wine list is extensive. Rooms are 7,000 escudos to 23,380 escudos.

The best wildlife

Monção is a good base for exploring the **Peneda-Gerês National Park.** The National Forest Department can arrange guided trips through the mountainous 170,000-acre park, where wild horses, stags, and boars roam and where you can spot milestones along the ancient Roman Way. For more information, stop at the tourist office in Monção.

The **Pousada de São Bento,** *Estrada N 304, Vieira do Minho; tel. (351-53)57190,* is a good place to stay if you want to explore the park. A modern hotel with dizzying views of the Minho Valley, it is cozy in the winter, with the atmosphere of a hunting lodge. It has high ceilings, massive rafters, and large picture windows overlooking the mountains. The swimming pool and tennis courts are inviting in warm weather. Double rooms are about 7,300 escudos during the summer.

Oporto—the Port wine capital

Originally a Roman settlement, **Oporto** has many old palaces, convents, and churches (the cathedral is famous for its gilded wood altars and grand organ). But Oporto's true fame comes from Port wine. If you wander along the banks of the River Douro, you will see *rabelos,* or barges, bringing the distinctive Port wine grapes down from the vineyards.

The area upriver from Oporto is the only place in the world that grows grapes for Port, and Oporto is the only place where it is made. You can try Port wine and the local Vinho Verde at any restaurant or café in the city. Or you can visit the **Port Wine Institute,** *rua Ferreira Borges; tel. (351-2)26522,* or the **Port Wine Solar,** *Quinta da Macierinha-R. Entre-Quintas; tel. (351-2)694749.*

Vila Nova de Gaia, on the south bank of the Douro, opposite Oporto, is the center of the Port wine trade. You can sample Port at the wine bodegas here and learn how it is matured for at least 25 years before being sold.

Portugal's saddest love story

The **Santa Maria Monastery** in the town of Alcobaça is the final resting place of the ill-fated lovers **Dom Pedro** and **Ines de Castro**. When Prince Dom Pedro married his beautiful mistress Ines de Castro, his father, King Alfonso IV of Portugal, was so outraged by the unequal union that he had Ines assassinated in 1355. When he succeeded to the throne, Dom Pedro got his revenge. He dressed the body of Ines in royal attire and forced the noblemen who had killed her to pay homage by kissing her decomposed hand. The lovers are positioned in their ornate tombs so that they will face each other on Judgement Day.

Constructed by Cistercian monks in 1178, the kitchen in the monastery was built above a trout stream so the cooks could have fresh water and fish.

The oldest university town

Coimbra, where Princess Ines was murdered, is one of the oldest medieval university towns in Europe. The city's streets are dotted with students wearing traditional black capes. A steep cobblestoned street leads to the university courtyard, where you can join a tour of the old university buildings, including the Manueline Chapel, with its ornate door and 17th-century *azulejos,* and the library, with its carved and varnished wood embellishments.

The Venice of Portugal

Aveiro, at the northernmost tip of the Costa de Prata, is called the Venice of Portugal. It is surrounded by salt flats, beaches, and lagoons and dominated by the Central Canal. Gaily painted *moliceiros* (boats reminiscent of Venice's gondolas) move through the waters gathering algae, which is used as fertilizer.

The best place to stay is the **Pousada da Ria,** *Bico do Muranzel; tel. (351-34)48332* or *(351-34)48334,* located by a lagoon, has bedrooms with views of the water. Eels from the Ria d'Aveiro are the mainstay of the *pousada's* dinner specialties—*caldeirada de enguias* (eel chowder) and *enguias de escabeche* (marinated eels). Rooms are 7,000 escudos to 14,000 escudos.

Buçaco: the most beautiful forest

Buçaco National Park, which has 700 species of trees from around the world, has been considered a holy place for centuries. Benedictine monks built a hermitage here in the sixth century. In 1622, Pope Gregory XV forbade women to enter the oak and pine forest. And the Barefoot Carmelite monks began an arboretum here in 1628.

In 1810, **Buçaco Mountain** was the site of a battle between the combined British and Portuguese forces under Wellington and the French (Wellington's forces won). The Portuguese government took over in 1834 and expanded the arboretum. Today, the park covers 250 acres of woodland.

In the center of the park is the royal hunting lodge built by Carlos I (1888-1907). Today it is the **Palace Hotel,** *tel. (351-39)93101,* an incredibly ornate luxury hotel. Rooms are 10,000 escudos to 24,000 escudos.

Portugal's most spectacular monastery

Portugal's most spectacular monastery is in **Batalha.** King João vowed to the Virgin

Mary that he would build a monastery if she helped him defeat the Castillians. The king's army was indeed victorious against the Castillian army in the Battle of Aljubarrota on Aug. 14, 1385, ensuring Portugal's independence for the next 200 years.

The monastery does justice to the momentous victory, with flying buttresses, turrets, a mass of gables, columns, and elaborate tracery. King João and his wife Philippa of Lancaster are buried here along with their children, including Prince Henry the Navigator.

The **Pousada do Mestre A. Domingues,** *tel. (351-44)96260,* next to the monastery, is a comfortable place to stay, named after the architect of King João. The dining room serves excellent seafood, especially the clams and the shrimp. Rooms are 9,000 escudos to 10,600 escudos.

The prettiest Portuguese town

Obidos, one of the best-preserved medieval fortified towns on the Iberian Peninsula, was traditionally the property of Portuguese queens. It has a feminine look, with tiny whitewashed houses and flower-lined streets. The 12th-century **Obidos Castle** dominates the city. **St. Mary's Church,** where King Alfonso V married his 8-year-old cousin Isabella in 1444, is tiled with blue *azulejos*. The octagonal **Senhor da Pedra Church** has a remarkable second-century stone cross.

The **Pousada do Castelo,** *rua Direita; tel. (351-62)95105,* housed within the castle walls, is furnished with antiques and has excellent cuisine and extensive wine cellars. Because it has only six rooms, early reservations are recommended. Rooms are 12,000 escudos to 16,000 escudos.

The **Estalagem do Convento,** *rua Dom João de Ornelas, Obidos; tel. (351-62)95217,* is a medieval hotel in Obidos furnished with tables and chairs from the days of the knights and crusaders. This is a novel place to stay the night, with little rooms and cobblestoned court-yards. Rooms with showers go for 2,500 escudos to 9,000 escudos.

Miraculous Fatima

The village of **Fatima,** where Catholics believe the Virgin Mary appeared to three shepherd children in 1917, is a major shrine and place of pilgrimage. Special ceremonies are held on the 13th day of each month between May and October. Make reservations well in advance if you plan to visit Fatima during that time—throngs descend upon the town.

The two nicest hotels in Fatima are **De Fatima,** *João Paulo II; tel. (351-49)52351,* and the **Santa Maria,** *rua de Santo Antonio; tel. (351-49)51015.* Rooms at De Fatima are 4,000 escudos to 11,000 escudos; rooms at the Santa Maria are 2,800 escudos to 7,300 escudos.

Portugal's oddest dance

The mountain town of **Miranda do Douro,** perched on a ravine just across the River Douro from Spain, is famous for its *pauliteiros,* who perform a traditional sword dance each year on the Feast of St. Barbara (the third Sunday in August). Dancers carry sticks represent-ing swords and wear kilts, embroidered shirts, and black hats covered with ribbons and flowers. They move in an ancient pattern to the sounds of tambourines and bagpipes. Another regional remnant of bygone eras is Mirandês, a Latin slang that the locals speak among themselves.

The **Pousada de Santa Catarina,** *tel. (351-73)42255,* balanced on the edge of a rocky

The **Pousada de Santa Catarina,** *tel. (351-73)42255,* balanced on the edge of a rocky gorge, has lovely views of the River Douro. Occasionally you'll see a golden eagle. The food, cooked over a wood fire, is good. Try the *guisado de polvo a transmontana,* or octopus ragout.

Evora—the most Roman

Evora, one of the oldest towns on the Iberian Peninsula, has the best Roman ruins in Portugal. Originally a Roman settlement, Evora was later inhabited by the Visigoths. Under the Moors it became a major trade and agricultural center. And during Portugal's heyday in the 15th and 16th centuries, Evora's university was a magnet for the best scholars and writers of the time. Now a public high school, the old university's great hall is covered with 17th-century tiles.

The Roman **Temple of Diana,** dating from the second century, is well-preserved. Before it was excavated in 1870, it was used as a slaughterhouse! The 1975 bloodless revolution was planned beneath its Corinthian columns.

Notice Evora's quaint street designations—streets bear the names of a countess' tailor, a cardinal's nurse, the lisping man, and the unshaven man. And take a look at the macabre **Igreja de São Francisco,** *Praca 28 de Maio.* It contains a chapel built of 50,000 monks' bones. The Franciscans thought this a good way to encourage meditation upon the transitory nature of life. Above the entrance is a warning, "*Nos ossos, que aqui estamos pelos vossos esperamos*"—which means, "The bones here are waiting for yours."

Evora's **Pousada dos Loios,** *Largo Conde de Vila Flor; tel. (351-66)24051,* is one of the best in the country. It faces the Temple of Diana and is located in what was the St. Eligius Monastery, consecrated in 1491. The cloisters have been glassed in to form a dining room, which has a vaulted ceiling, horseshoe arches, and a marble font. The bedrooms are converted monastic cells. One of the suites has a baroque antechamber. Rooms are 12,000 escudos to 20,700 escudos.

Portugal's pottery town

Estremoz has been an artistic center since the 16th century. It is famous for its Alentejo pottery, sold in the main square on Saturdays. Typical wares include narrow-mouthed jars called *barris* and wide-mouthed jars called *bilhas.* Local artists also create clay figurines of people and animals. Local crafts are displayed at the Rural Museum on the main square.

Madeira: the most fruitful island

About 600 miles off the coast of Morocco lies **Madeira,** a garden paradise that belongs to Portugal. The lush, semitropical volcanic island was discovered by Portuguese explorers in 1419 and soon became a regular port of call for seafarers. Ships coming from the New World and Asia stopped here and left behind specimens of exotic plants, which islanders grew in the rich volcanic soil with great success. The result is an island abounding in tropical fruit (including passion fruit, mango, papaw, avocado, banana, and melon), vegetables, and flowers. Madeira's mild temperature ranges from 60 degrees Fahrenheit in winter to 72 degrees Fahrenheit in summer.

The best footin'

The best way to see the interior of the island is to walk along the *levadas,* or footpaths, which follow ancient Madeiran irrigation channels carrying water from high up in the mountains down through the terraced farms to the fields and villages below. The paths are graded 1 to 4, from easiest to most difficult.

For the most difficult walks, you need more than hiking boots—you also need a good head for heights. On one side of the foot-wide paths is the irrigation stream, which may be running 18 gallons per minute, while on the other is a vertical precipice hundreds of feet high. The natives scurry up the paths often carrying huge burdens on their heads.

Portugal's best thrill

If you're brave enough, make time during your visit to Madeira to take an exhilarating ride in a little wicker fruit cart with steel blades from Monte downhill to Funchal, the island's capital. You use levers to control the wooden carts as they roll like bumper cars down the hill. Once used for practical purposes, such as transporting fruits and vegetables, today the carts are used purely as amusement rides. To arrange a ride, visit the **tourist office,** *ave. Arriga 18; tel. (351-91)29057.*

Bacchus' favorite—Madeira

After such an exploit, you probably will need a drink. Try the island's fortified sweet wine, called **Madeira.** According to the legend, when early settlers reached Madeira (which means *wood*), they burned off the thick forests in a fire that raged for seven years. When vines were planted in the resulting soil, so the story goes, the grapes acquired their characteristic smoky flavor.

During the days of the American Revolution, Madeira could be imported to Colonial America in non-British ships, which made it the drink of independence. It was the favorite tipple of the early American revolutionaries.

Tour the wine bodegas in Funchal to see how Madeira is processed and stored. At the end of the visit, you can sample the stuff.

Funchal's best sights

Funchal's most famous sights, the **botanical gardens,** are brightly colored year-round. Against the natural beauty of these gardens, the works of man fade. The churches in Funchal range from the 15th-century **Capela de Santa Catarina** (in the Manueline style, a Portuguese version of Gothic characterized by nautical-inspired stone carving) to the **se** (cathedral), with its carved-wood and gilded altars. Church paintings in Funchal and throughout the island show a strong Flemish influence. The **Palace of the Conde de Carvalhal** is now the town hall.

The island's early houses with black stone trim are made of the volcanic rock of Madeira. The customs house in the harbor (Alfandega) is an often-overlooked site; especially noteworthy are the second-floor carved and painted ceiling and the 17th-century illuminated Bible, on which captains had to swear they had nothing to declare.

The world's second-highest sea cliff

Cabo Girão, on Madeira, is the world's second-highest sea cliff. This promontory has extraordinary views. Go at sunset. (The highest sea cliff in the world is the north coast of East Molokai Island, Hawaii.)

Madeira's best festival

One of the best times to visit Madeira is June, during the **Ribeira Brava Festival of St. Peter.** In celebration of the patron saint of fishermen, residents join in solemn processions, which are followed by dances, including the traditional sword dance.

Madeira's best eats

Good restaurants near Funchal include **A Seta,** which serves barbecued beef and chicken on sword skewers hung from the ceiling, along with mounds of fresh-baked bread and pitchers of red wine.

A Gruta is a particularly inviting outdoor café, where you can sit for hours sipping ice-cold Mateus for about 399 escudos a bottle. The fish is fresh, the bread crusty and warm. Costumed folk dancers sometimes perform. Lunch for two, including wine, salad, fish, coffee, and dessert, is about 1,600 escudos.

In the fishing village of **Camara de Lobos,** perched on a rugged cliff, is **Restaurant Coral.** From the windows you can see brightly painted fishing boats bobbing in the water and children mending fishing nets along the jagged coastline. The cost of a meal, including a bottle of good wine, coffee, and brandy, is about 2,000 escudos.

The most gracious hotel

Reid's, *Estrada Monumental 139, Funchal; tel. (351-91)23001,* is a Madeira's most gracious resort hotel. Set on a cliff overlooking the sea, it has a British colonial flavor. It is surrounded by tropical foliage and flowers and has a private beach, tennis courts, two pools, and boat rentals.

The best hotel prices

Madeira is cheap by Caribbean standards. The top-ranked **Casino Park Hotel,** *Aeroporto, Funchal, Madeira; tel. (351-91)33111,* near the Funchal airport, charges 12,500 escudos for a double room with a mountain view and 14,000 escudos for a double room with a sea view. (The price is for two people, including breakfast, taxes, service, and use of a pool, a sauna, and tennis courts.)

Apartment hotels, such as the **Estrelicia** and the **Mimosa** (same ownership), *Caminho Velho da Ajuda, Funchal, Madeira; tel. (351-91)30131,* charge about 6,000 escudos per day, double occupancy. Cheaper are the **Pensão Astoria,** *rua João Gago 10-3, Funchal, Madeira; tel. (351-91)23820* (2,500 escudos), and the **Pensão Palmeira,** *Porto Santo, Madeira; tel. (351-91)982112* (2,000 escudos).

Portugal's best accommodations: the pousada

The 25 *pousadas* throughout Portugal, many of which already have been mentioned, offer historic accommodations and fine food. They are housed in converted medieval castles or convents in areas of great natural beauty. For more information or to make reservations, contact **Marketing Ahead,** *433 Fifth Ave., New York, NY 10016; (212)686-9213.*

Chapter 9

THE
BEST
OF
SWITZERLAND

Mountainous Switzerland is at the peak of Europe. Its mountains are threatening, yet nurturing, encompassing fruitful farms, lakeside resorts, and picturesque old towns. The Rhine, the Rhone, and the Inn rivers originate in Swiss mountain glaciers. The Swiss Alps challenge the world's best mountain climbers, skiers, and hikers. The famous Matterhorn rises above Zermatt, and the Berner Oberland mountain range guards Interlaken. Davos and St. Moritz sit snugly in their Alpine valleys.

Zürich: best financiers, best fun

Zürich, a prosperous banking town, is a two-sided coin. The seat of the Reformation in Switzerland, it later became a center for Dadaism. While it is the home of staid bankers, its German-speaking people also have a jovial, witty side that is evident during the city's festivals. During **Sechselauten** (Zürich's spring festival, held toward the end of April), for example, Zürich's bankers don costumes and celebrate the end of winter by burning a huge straw dummy named the Boogg.

Zürich has produced writers as well as financiers. Joyce, Mann, Brecht, and Kleist all lived here at various times during their careers.

The cleanest street in the world

The **Bahnhofstrasse,** Zürich's main artery, is the cleanest street in the world. James Joyce once said, "Zürich is so clean that should you spill your soup on the Bahnhofstrasse, you could eat it up with a spoon." The avenue does have its dirty laundry, however. Some of the most powerful bankers in the world, the gnomes of Zürich, work here.

Zürich's best shopping

The Bahnhofstrasse is also known as **Luxury Mile,** because of its expensive, first-class shops. While it's fun to look at 18-carat gold shoehorns and watches, you're better off doing your shopping in Zürich's department stores or along **Marktplatz Oerlikon,** a pedestrian district near Bahnhofstrasse.

Zürich's top sights

On the left bank of the Limmat River is the **Fraumünster,** *Staathousquaistrasse,* an austere Gothic cathedral enlivened with stained-glass windows by Marc Chagall and Augusto Giacometti.

The *Altstadt* (old town), on the right bank of the Limmat River, is a maze of steep cobblestoned streets lined with cafés, sex shops, and nightclubs. A series of 17th- and 18th-century arcaded guildhalls line the Limmatquai and surrounding streets. Inside, the guildhalls are decorated with ornate friezes and ceilings. Most are now restaurants, so you can enjoy lunch as well as the surroundings.

Above it all is Zürich's massive cathedral, the **Grossmünster.** The Romanesque cathedral was a center of the Reformation. Here, Ulrich Zwingli preached against the sale of indulgences, common at that time in the Catholic church.

Zürich's **Schweizerishches Landesmuseum** (Museum of Swiss History), *Museumstr. 2,* behind the railroad station, displays prehistoric artifacts, medieval and Renaissance art, and the richly carved furniture of an old peasant civilization.

The **Kunsthaus** (Fine Arts Museum), *Heimplatz 1,* northwest of the opera house, has paintings, sculpture, and graphic art from the Middle Ages to today. The museum has a strong collection of 19th- and 20th-century works by Monet, Munch, Giacometti, Rodin, and Chagall. The Kunsthaus is a large open gallery that is not divided by floors, walls, or stairs.

The **Rietberg Museum,** *Gablestr. 15,* in the former Wesendonck Villa on the western shore of Lake Zürich, houses Europe's best collection of non-European art. Most of the collection was donated by Baron von der Heydt. Works are mainly Indian, Southeast Asian, Chinese, Japanese, and African. Richard Wagner was often a guest at this enchanting villa, and his love affair with the hostess inspired him to compose *Tristan and Isolde.* A private park surrounds the museum.

Zürich's coziest café

When you tire of sightseeing, stop at the **Café Schober,** *Napfgasse 4,* which serves a scrumptious chocolate cake. Both students and businessmen enjoy the atmosphere (although the two generations ignore one another here).

The best night life

Most of Zürich's night life centers around the **Niederdorfstrasse** and the **Limmatquai,** where you'll find bars, clubs, and street musicians. The nightclubs in Zürich are expensive—a beer can cost as much as 11 Swiss francs. And mineral water is only slightly less expensive. So if you are on a budget, stick to the cafés and bars.

The best restaurants

The best dining in the area is at a restaurant a 20-minute drive from the heart of the city. **Bienengarten,** *Regensbergertr. 9, Dielsdorf; tel. (41-1)853-12-17,* is in an old, half-timbered house. Chef and owner Karl Gut spares no effort to make his dishes exceptional. The eight-course meal must be ordered a day in advance.

The restaurant at the Dolder Grand Hotel, **La Rotonde,** *Kurhausstr. 65, 8032 Zürich; tel. (41-1)251-62-31,* is also superb. Escoffier, one of the first great restaurant critics, praised the cuisine back in 1930. To this day, the restaurant features traditional French cooking of premier quality. The *éminé de filet de veau Zürichoise* (finely sliced milk-fed veal in a white wine and parsley sauce) is one of the many delicious dishes here.

Chez Max, *Seestr. 53, 8702 Zollikon; tel. (41-1)391-88-77,* on Lake Zürich, is famous for its luxurious decor and first-class food and service. The menu includes *soupe de homard glacée* and *salade de foie gras aux truffes tièdes.* The restaurant is closed for lunch Sundays and Mondays and entirely the last three weeks in July.

Kronenhalle, *Rämistrasse 4, 8001 Zürich; tel. (41-1)251-0256* or *(41-1)251-5287,* which was frequented by James Joyce, is more famous for what is on the walls than what is on the tables. Hulda Zumsteg, who ran the restaurant for a half-century, decorated the walls of this brasserie with the works of Braque, Miró, Giacometti, and Leger. You can sit at one of the wide tables designed by Giacometti and enjoy the art while eating a rather overpriced meal. Service is perfect—most of the staff has been here for years.

Kronenhalle has become an institution in Zürich, revered by locals, who favor it as a spot for after-theater and after-work refreshments.

Zeughauskeller, *Bahnhofstr. 28a; tel. (41-1)211-26-90,* a huge restaurant with outdoor dining during the summer, is the best place for traditional Swiss dishes, including potato salad (17 tons of potato salad are sold here every year) and suckling pig. It also has a good selection of local wines. An authentic Zürich guildhouse restaurant, it is cheaper than most Zürich eateries and is popular among business people from neighboring banks.

Au Premier, on the first floor of the Hauptbahnhof, *tel. (41-1)211-15-10,* is an inexpensive restaurant that offers a wide selection of Swiss wines. You can order exactly the amount of wine you want, in carafes of two, three, or five deciliters (called decis). Local dishes, such as *Kalbsbratwurst,* are offered, as well as fancier fare, such as calf's sweetbreads with sherry vinegar or veal steak with morels.

Mère Catherine, *Nagelihof 3; tel. (41-1)69-22-50,* in the city's old town, occupies a long 200-year-old building that has many interconnected rooms. The food is predominately French, and the service is friendly.

Zürich's best desserts

When you crave something sweet, stop by the **Confiserie Sprungli,** *Am Paradeplatz, Bahnhofstr. 21; tel. (41-1)221-0795.* The biggest chocolate maker in Switzerland, it serves delicious fresh white truffles. The chocolate is made with fresh Swiss milk and cream. You can get lunch here, too.

Zürich's best hotel

The **Baur au Lac,** *Talstr. 1, 8022 Zürich; tel. (41-1)221-16-50,* was named the best hotel in the world by *Travel & Leisure* magazine and received a Pomme d'Or for its elegance from travel writer William Chamberlayne. Built in 1830, it is not a glitzy palace but a four-story masterpiece of elegance located on the edge of the Zürichsee, not far from the center of town. The Baur au Lac's restaurant, the **Grill Room,** is one of the best in Zürich.

When you stay at the Baur au Lac, you will be in prestigious company. The hotel's guestbook has included the king of Sweden, Kaiser Wilhelm II, and Margaret Thatcher. The hotel was built by Johannes Baur, who began life as a baker's apprentice. (Baur's son founded the Hotel School of Lausanne, whose alumni include Charles Ritz and other hotel magnates.) Rooms start at 230 Swiss francs.

Other top-notch hotels

Whenever he is in town, Kissinger stays in the **Dolder Grand,** *Kurhausstr. 65, 8032 Zürich; tel. (41-1)251-62-31,* a classic grand hotel. Built in the lavish turn-of-the-century German art-nouveau style Jugendstil, the hotel looks like a castle. Some of the rooms are modern, others are decorated with antiques. Facilities include a pool, jogging paths through the forest, tennis courts, and a golf course. The rooms at the Grand cost about the same as those at the Baur au Lac, but they tend to be slightly more ostentatious—grander, if you like—and to have better views.

A drawback to the Dolder Grand is that it is not in Zürich itself, but a 10-minute drive from the center of the city. And the decor is dark and heavy. Rooms are 220 Swiss francs to 450 Swiss francs.

Waldhaus Dolder, *Kurhausstr. 20, 8030 Zürich; tel. (41-1)251-93-60,* the Dolder Grand's less-expensive sister hotel down the hill, has modern but smaller rooms, as well as a good view, a sauna, and an indoor pool. If you stay at the Waldhaus, you can use the sports facilities at the Grand. Rooms are 150 Swiss francs to 360 Swiss francs.

Hotel Florhof, *Florhofgasse 4; tel. (41-1)47-44-70,* is a pleasant, moderately priced hotel in a 16th-century house with a small garden. It is near the Kunsthaus, and the music conservatory is next door. Service is excellent. Double rooms are 110 Swiss francs to 195 Swiss francs.

Bests outside Zürich

Winterthur, a town north of Zürich that dates back to Roman times, is known for its art collections. Oskar Reinhart, an arts patron who died in 1965, left his comprehensive art collection to the town. His collection is divided between the **Oskar Reinhart Foundation,** *Stadthausstr. 6,* and the **Oskar Reinhart Collection Am Romerholz,** *Haldenstr. 95.* Works by Swiss, Austrian, and German painters from the 18th through 20th centuries can be seen at the Oskar Reinhart Foundation. The Oskar Reinhart Collection, which is housed in the collector's former house, has paintings covering five centuries, including some of Picasso's drawings from his Blue Period. The collection of 19th-century works by Corot, Delacroix, Courbet, Manet, Renoir, and Cezanne is comprehensive.

Winterthur also has a good **Fine Arts Museum,** which displays works of the 16th century, the local schools of the 17th and 18th centuries, and the Swiss and German painters of the 19th and 20th centuries. It also has paintings of the French schools and sculptures by Rodin, Maillol, Haller, Marini, and Giacometti. A private collection of clocks is displayed in the center of town, at the *Rathaus.*

Four miles outside Winterthur is **Kyburg Castle,** a feudal castle built in the 10th and 11th centuries and passed from the counts of Kyburg to the Hapsburgs. Since 1917, the castle has belonged to the canton of Zürich. It has a collection of furniture and arms and a panoramic view of the surrounding countryside. The castle is open from 9 a.m. to noon and 1 p.m. to 5 p.m. (4 p.m. in the winter). It is closed Mondays.

Geneva: where modern history unfolds

Geneva, a French-speaking city on shimmering Lake Geneva, is an international center and the home base of some 200 organizations. This is the best place in Europe to grasp the magnitude of modern history as it unrolls.

The European headquarters of the United Nations is housed in the **Palais des Nations,** *14* *ave. de la Paix, Pregny Gateway.* Built in 1936 as the seat of the League of Nations, the Palais des Nations is situated in the Parc de l'Ariana. Marble of various hues was donated by U.N. member countries to create the Salle des Pas Perdus, which leads into the Assembly Room, where U.N. meetings are held. The walls of the Council Chamber, where the most important conferences are held, are decorated with huge frescoes illustrating the achievements of mankind. From the terrace is a panoramic view of Geneva, the lake, and Mt. Blanc. Guided tours of the palace are conducted from 9 a.m. to noon and 2 p.m. to 4:45 p.m. (5:15 p.m. in the summer) every day except during conferences and the Christmas and New Year holidays.

Not far from the Palais des Nations are the **World Health Organization,** the **International Red Cross,** and the **International Labor Office.** Group visits can be arranged by special request.

The world's tallest fountain

In the center of Lake Geneva is the tallest fountain in the world, the **Jet d'Eau,** which spouts 476 feet. The fountain is striking, backed by the Swiss Alps. For a good view, walk out onto the Quai du Mt. Blanc, near the bridge.

The best of *vieille ville*

Most of Geneva's monuments are in the *vieille ville* (old town). The most prominent among them is **St. Peter's Cathedral.** Built between the 12th and 13th centuries, it was partly rebuilt in the 15th century and has an 18th-century neo-Grecian doorway. The cathedral is huge, but the decor is plain.

St. Peter's has been a Protestant church since 1536, when it became a center of the Reformation. You can see Calvin's seat in the north aisle. And the tomb of the Duc de Rohan, who headed the Reformed Church in France at the time of Louis XIII, is in the first chapel on the south side of the chancel.

The flamboyant Gothic chapel in St. Peter's is more elaborate than the rest of the church. It was built by Cardinal de Brogny in the 15th century and was restored in the 19th century.

Climb the 145 stairs to the north tower of the cathedral. From the top, you have a view of the Jura Mountains, Geneva, the lake, and the Alps.

The **Reformation Monument** was built against a 16th-century rampart of the old town. At the center of the 100-yard wall are statues of the four Genevan Reformers: Calvin, Knox, Farel, and de Beze. The monument was built in 1917 and includes texts that recall the origins of the Reformed Church.

Geneva's **hôtel de ville** (town hall), parts of which date back to the 15th century, has an old courtyard with a cobblestoned ramp once used to carry litters to the upper floors. The Geneva Convention (the first convention of the Red Cross) was signed in the Alabama Room on Aug. 22, 1864.

The oldest house in Geneva is the **Maison Tavel,** *4 rue St. Pierre,* near the cathedral. The first written record of the house is in 1303, but it was built long before then. The Museum of Old Geneva, which has a display of historic engravings, is located here.

Geneva's best museums

The Voltaire Museum, *25 rue des Délices,* is located in Les Délices, where Voltaire lived from 1755 to 1765. It shares the building with the Voltaire Institute, where researchers delve into the life of the famous writer. The drawing room and an adjacent gallery hold

Voltaire's furniture, manuscripts, rare editions, and portraits. Look for the terra-cotta model for Houdon's statue of Voltaire and the portrait of the young philosopher done by Largillière. The museum is open from 2 p.m. to 5 p.m. during the week. It is closed weekends and Christmas week.

Musée d'Art et d'Histoire, *2 rue Charles-Galland,* contains art from ancient Rome, Greece, and Egypt, as well as European paintings from the 15th through 19th centuries. Especially interesting are the prehistoric objects found in Switzerland and the reconstructed rooms of a castle. The most important artwork in the museum is the 15th-century altarpiece by Konrad Witz depicting the miraculous draught of fishes. It is the first exact representation of landscape in the history of European painting. The museum is open 10 a.m. to noon and 2 p.m. to 6 p.m. every day. It is closed Monday mornings, Good Friday, Christmas, and New Year's Day.

Petit Palais, *2 Terrace St.,* features the works of Parisian artists from the time of the Impressionists, including Kisling, Van Dongen, Soutine, Chagall, Utrillo, and Valadon. The crypt displays works by 20th-century naif painters, including Henri Rousseau. The Petit Palais is open 10 a.m. to noon and 2 p.m. to 6 p.m. It is closed Monday mornings, the afternoons of Easter Monday and Christmas, and Jan. 1.

The **Musée de l'Horlogerie** (Watch and Clock Museum), *15 Route de Malagnou,* traces the measurement of time from the Middle Ages to today. On the ground floor are sand timers, sundials, and early watches and clocks. Elaborate, enameled watches from the 19th century, often with musical mechanisms, can be seen on the first floor. Clockmaker Louis Cottier repairs watches in the workshop. The museum is open 10 a.m. to noon and 2 p.m. to 6 p.m. It is closed Monday mornings.

Lake Geneva—the deepest Alpine lake

Lake Geneva—the deepest of the Alpine lakes (1,000 feet)—is 45 miles long, 7.5 miles wide at its widest point, and covers 143,323 acres. The best cruise of Lake Geneva is the "Tour of the Upper Lake," which lasts 12 hours. Official timetables and rates are posted at landing stages throughout Geneva, including Quai du Mt. Blanc, Jardin Anglais, and Eaux Vives, opposite the Parc de la Grange.

Chillon, the most poetic castle

Chillon Castle, perched on a rocky island at the opposite end of the lake from Geneva, inspired the poet Lord Byron to write the lyrical poem "The Prisoner of Chillon."

Francois Bonivard was imprisoned in the castle dungeon for four years for trying to introduce the Reformation to Geneva. The Duke of Savoy, an ardent Catholic, had the prior chained to one of the pillars. If you visit the dungeon, take a close look at that pillar and the floor around it—supposedly, the prisoner's footprints are traced in the rock here. Byron carved his name on the third pillar in Bonivard's cell in 1816.

The fortress was built in the ninth century, but it took on its present-day appearance when it was expanded by the bishops of Sion and embellished by the counts of Savoy from 1150 to the mid-13th century. To get to the castle, you cross a moat on the 18th-century bridge that took the place of a drawbridge.

The Great Hall has an imposing 15th-century fireplace, a large collection of pewter, and 13th-century Savoyard furniture. The Banquet Hall's timber ceiling is shaped like an inverted ship's hull. From the keep, you have a view of Montreux, Lake Geneva, and the Alps.

The best local cuisine

The best restaurants in Geneva tend to be French, but Genevan cooking can be delicious as well. Humble fare, it is generally served in informal places. Fish and cheese are the main ingredients.

Raclette—melted cheese that has been scraped off a chunk of grilled Swiss cheese—is a delicious local meal. You can enjoy it in almost any brasserie in Geneva, served with potatoes and gherkins.

Fondue is another typically Genevan dish. Also a melted cheese, it is more refined—mixed with garlic, white wine, and sometimes kirsch. The best part of the fondue is the hardened brown cheese at the end, known as *la religieuse* or *la dentelle.*

The best place for fondue is **Café Huissoud,** *51 rue du Stand; tel. (41-22)28-25-83,* which is popular with local businesspeople. The setting is rustic—wooden tables and paper tablecloths—but the selection of Swiss white wines is good. The café is closed Saturdays for lunch, Sundays, and evenings from April to October. Credit cards are not accepted.

Lake fish is also prepared well in Geneva. (Unfortunately, it no longer comes from Lake Geneva, which is polluted.) The fish is generally deep-fried, steamed, or baked. A good place to try it is the **Restaurant du Vieux Port,** *132 Route Suisse, 1290 Versoix-Ville; tel. (41-22)55-15-99,* a family-run bistro. The terrine of lake fish is especially good. The restaurant has rustic antique sideboards, beamed ceilings, and a tiny back garden where tables are set in the summer. The restaurant is closed Sundays, Mondays, and Dec. 15 through Feb. 28. Credit cards are not accepted.

The best of the French

Parc des Eaux-Vives, *82 Quai Gustave-Ador; tel. (41-22)35-41-40,* is the most famous French restaurant in Geneva. Located in the park by the same name, Eaux-Vives has splendid views and good classic cuisine. The service is always good, and the wine list is the best in Switzerland. The restaurant is closed Mondays and Jan. 1 to Feb. 15.

La Perle du Lac, *128 rue de Lausanne; tel. (41-22)31-35-04* or *(41-22)31-79-35,* across the lake, is another superb French restaurant with a view of Mt. Blanc. Servings are generous, but the prices are high. The restaurant is closed Mondays and Dec. 20 through Feb. 15. (You may want to try the brasserie next door, which serves the same fare from the same kitchen at one-third the price!)

One of the best restaurants in Geneva is the often underestimated **Bearn,** *4 Quai de la Poste; tel. (41-22)21-00-28,* run by Jean-Paul Goddard. The *rable de lapereau aux basilic et petits légumes* (rabbit fillets served with rabbit's liver and kidneys and young vegetables) is superb. Bankers lunch here on the *repas d'affaires,* which changes daily. The market's seasonal fare (fish and game) is presented, uncooked, on a trolley. The restaurant is closed Saturdays for lunch, Sundays, and July 15 through Aug. 15.

The best country cooking

In the suburbs of Geneva you'll find two charming restaurants in former private houses. **Le Marignac,** *32 ave. Eugene-Lance, 1212 Grand-Lancy; tel. (41-22)94-04-24,* is in a white villa shaded by a weeping willow. Dishes range from country to aristocratic—buckwheat pancakes to caviar. The restaurant is closed Saturdays for lunch, Sundays, Feb. 13 through 20, and Sept. 4 through 18.

Le Vieux Moulin, *89 Route d'Annecy, 1256 Troinex; tel. (41-22)42-29-56,* in a former farmhouse, has a cozy dining room with low-beamed ceilings. The menu is diverse. Try the salmon in tomato, basil, and garlic sauce. The restaurant is closed Saturday evenings, Sundays, April 1 through 15, and Sept. 1 through 15.

Switzerland's best hotel

Hotel Le Richemond, *Jardin Brunswick, 1211 Geneva; tel. (41-22)311-400,* is one of the best hotels in the world. Run by the Armleder family, this imposing, seven-story building has 120 bedrooms that go for 270 Swiss francs to 490 Swiss francs a night. The hotel has two fine restaurants, and the wine cellar contains 80,000 bottles.

Adolphe-Rodolphe Armleder founded the Richemond in the 1870s. What makes staying at the hotel so special are the elegant little touches, such as finding your ties hung in order of color and your clothes perfectly folded. Hotel Richemond has served writers Colette and Antoine de St. Exupery, as well as the Russian delegations of the 1930s and the Chinese delegations of the 1950s.

Other good hotels

Another fine hotel is the **Beau Rivage,** *13 Quai du Mt. Blanc, 1201 Geneva; tel. (41-22)310221,* an immaculate, family-run hotel on the lake. Double rooms are 200 Swiss francs to 450 Swiss francs.

Hotel de la Paix, *11 Quai du Mt. Blanc, 1201 Geneva; tel. (41-22)326-150,* is a five-star hotel on the lake with lovely views. Rooms are 160 Swiss francs to 390 Swiss francs.

A less expensive hotel that comes highly recommended is the **Hotel Les Armures,** *1 rue du Puits-St. Pierre, Vieille Ville; tel. (41-22)28-91-72.* Located on a quiet square near the cathedral, it has one of the oldest restaurants in town. Service is excellent, and the food is good. The building was originally the residence of bishops and counts in the 13th and 14th centuries. The walls are decorated with centuries-old frescoes. But modern amenities have been added. Rooms are 175 Swiss francs to 380 Swiss francs.

Bern—the loveliest city

Switzerland's capital, **Bern,** is one of the best-preserved medieval cities in Europe. It is filled with turreted buildings and has more fountains per capita than any other city on the continent. The Alps surround the city, which is divided twice by the Aare River.

Established in 1191 by the duke of Zahringen, Bern was originally a hunting ground. The duke and his cronies decided that the town should be named after the first animal caught on a particular hunt. The unfortunate beast was a bear (*Bar* in German), so the town was called Bärn (Bern is a corruption). A bear appears on the city's coat of arms, and for centuries mascot bears have been kept in the *Bärengraben,* or bear pits.

The best way to explore Bern is to get a map from the tourist office and follow its walking tour along arcaded, cobblestoned roads and through little squares with fountains past all Bern's major sights.

Bern's five top (and topless) sights

St. Vincent Cathedral is an impressive Gothic church with 16th-century statues depicting the Last Judgment. You'll have an incredible view of Bern and the Alps from the top of the 100-meter tower, but you'll have to climb 254 steps to get there.

The **Kunstmuseum** (Art Museum), *Hodlerstr. 12,* has the world's largest Paul Klee collection (Klee was a native of Bern). Works by Modigliani and Picasso also are featured.

The **Bernisches Historisches Museum** (Historical Museum), *Helvitiaplatz 5,* displays booty from the Burgundian wars, including the tapestries and embroideries of Charles the Bold, duke of Burgundy. The museum also has replicas of rural Swiss rooms and objects dating back to the Stone Age.

Zytglocke, the city's medieval clock tower, rings several times a day to the delight of large audiences. Mechanical bears, clowns, and kings perform at four minutes before every hour.

One of the most popular sights in Bern is the city's beach, lined with topless sunbathers. These free-spirited sun worshippers caused a good deal of controversy when they first disrobed (probably because the beach is right beneath Parliament's windows).

Best table, best beds

The best place to eat in Bern is the **Kornhauskeller,** *Kornhausplatz 18; tel. (41-31)22-11-33,* a huge beer cellar with good Swiss food. It specializes in *Berner Platte,* an assortment of boiled meats and sausage served with sauerkraut. At night, a brass band often plays.

Kings and queens stay at the **Bellevue Palace,** *Kochergasse 3; tel. (41-31)22-45-81.* This expensive but luxurious place has lovely views and a pleasant terrace where you can have a drink.

A much less expensive hotel with more traditional Swiss charm is the **Goldener Adler,** *Gerechtigkeitsgasse 7; tel. (41-31)22-17-25,* in the heart of the old town. A beautiful old inn, it is comfortable and friendly.

Gimmelwald—the most picturesque Swiss town

Gimmelwald (not to be confused with Grindelwald!), a sleepy little town in the mountains near Interlaken, looks like something straight out of *Heidi.* You'll hear cowbells here and see farmers in lederhosen. Cars aren't allowed in Gimmelwald, which explains why it is so peaceful.

To get to Gimmelwald, take the Lauterbrunnen-Grutschalp funicular from Interlaken to Murren, where you'll find several good hotels. You have to hike the rest of the way from Murren.

Once in Gimmelwald, take the cable car to the summit of the Schilthorn, where you can dine in a revolving restaurant with a view across the valley to the German border. This was the setting for a James Bond movie.

Alpine wilderness at its best

The **Swiss National Park** is the best place to enjoy a view of the Alps as God made them, untouched by the hand of man. The Swiss obviously want to keep it this way—fires, camping, pets, and mountain climbing are prohibited, and visitors may not leave designated trails. If you want to sleep in the park, you must stay in one of the designated lodges.

These rules may seem restrictive, but the results are a wonder. The 40,000-acre park is filled with wild valleys of woods and broken by torrential creeks. You'll see deer, ibex, chamois, and marmots—but you won't see any trash dumps or unsightly trailer parks.

Walks through the park are organized at the **Tourist Center,** *Zernez; tel. (41-82)8-13-00.* The Sierra Club publishes a little book by William Reifsnyder called *Footloose in the Swiss Alps* that describes the park's trails and accommodations in detail and is updated every few years.

St. Moritz: the world's most famous ski resort

St. Moritz is the most famous, most elegant ski playground in the world. Tina Onassis, Princess Ira von Furstenberg, and Gunther Sachs are among the celebrities who ski here. And it's easy to understand why—the five mountains at St. Moritz have great slopes. However, as you might expect, skiing here in peak season is expensive.

St. Moritz has the most treacherous toboggan run in the Alps, the 101-year-old **Cresta Run,** which is for men only (the British invented it). It is also the only place where you will find polo played on a lake. Ponies are equipped with spikes.

Most people don't realize that St. Moritz is also a spa. The town is divided into two sections, on two sides of the sky-blue St. Moritz Lake. **St. Moritz-Dorf,** the ski resort, has the world's oldest ski school, dating to 1927. The only vestige of the original village here is the leaning campanile. **St. Moritz-Bad** is the spa quarter. Its curative mineral waters have been sought after since the Bronze Age.

Badrutt's Palace, *tel. (41-82)21101,* is the finest hotel in town. In February, the most elite skiers stay here. It has its own ski school and a private rail link. Rooms are 340 Swiss francs to 1,250 Swiss francs.

Less glamorous, less expensive, and more charming is the **Hotel Chesa Sur L'En,** *St. Moritz-Bad; tel. (41-82)3-31-44.* A Swiss chalet surrounded by pines, it has a massive front door, a stone-flagged entrance hall, and a richly paneled ornate main hall. You can sleep in the watch tower, if you are a real romantic. King Faroukh stayed here during his exile. Rooms are 146 Swiss francs to 226 Swiss francs.

The best place to have lunch is **La Marmite,** at the top of Corviglia. Chef Hartley Mathis prepares haute cuisine for weary skiers. Try the Lady Curzon soup and the truffles. Make reservations. And keep an eye out—you might spot Princess Caroline.

The two best night spots are **Kings' Club** at Badrutt's Palace and **Gunther Sachs' Dracula Club.**

The prettiest ski resort: Zermatt

Zermatt may be the most desirable piece of real estate in the world. It is a small, automobile-free village with a picture-postcard tangle of stately hotels. The Matterhorn dominates the town, which has very good skiing. But in season, the queues for the ski lifts are daunting. The hotels and restaurants, too, are crowded.

Zermatt's winter lifts reach as high as 11,500 feet, offering some of Europe's highest slopes and a whopping vertical drop of 6,300 feet. Zermatt's summer skiing is also Europe's best. The most popular run is down to Cervinia on the Italian side, which any strong interme-diate skier can do in a morning.

Zermatt is also the best place in Europe for heli-skiing. The best hotels are the **Mont Cervin** (French for Matterhorn), which has an indoor pool, a sauna, and day-care facilities, and the **Zermatterhof,** a modern hotel with a swimming pool, saunas, and a fitness center. Both are expensive.

Hotel Alex, *tel. (41-28)67-17-26,* run by former Matterhorn guide Alex Perren and his wife Gisela, is the center of social life in the winter. Facilities include an indoor swimming pool and indoor squash and tennis courts. Rooms are 202 Swiss francs to 420 Swiss francs.

The **Hotel-Garni Metropol,** *tel. (41-28)67-32-31,* in the center of town on the banks of the Vispa River, has fabulous views. The Taugwalder family, which runs the hotel, recently bought a meadow opposite the hotel so that the views won't be spoiled. Each room has a private bathroom and a balcony facing the Matterhorn. The best are on the south side of the hotel. Rooms are 94 Swiss francs to 196 Swiss francs.

The Matterhorn: the most daunting peak

The Killer Alp, as the **Matterhorn** is known, was scaled for the first time July 14, 1865. Four men were killed in the process. A young British illustrator named Edward Whymper arranged the climb. He, three British friends, a guide from Chamonix, and two guides from Zermatt first reached the peak.

On the return journey, one of the men slipped, dragging three of his fellow climbers with him to their deaths, 4,000 feet below. After the fall, Whymper and his two Swiss guides, the Taugwalders, father and son, reported seeing two crosses shining in a great arc of clouds in the sky.

The Matterhorn (14,688 feet) is intimidating, but you don't have to be an experienced mountain climber to scale its sides. You can climb the daunting mountain with the help of a Zermatt guide. At the Matterhornhutte, the cost of the guide and accommodations is about 452 Swiss francs. It takes three to five days to hike the easiest trails. Information on hiking the Matterhorn is available at the **Mountaineering Office,** *tel. (41-28)67-34-56,* near the tourist office.

The best Swiss train ride

A more comfortable and relaxing way to climb the Alps is aboard the **Glacier Express,** which runs from Zermatt to St. Moritz. This train leisurely crosses 291 bridges, passes through 91 tunnels, spans the valleys of the Rhone and Rhine rivers, stops in typical mountain villages, heads into the wild, barren Gotthard region, and then climbs the 6,706-foot Oberalp Pass. The grand finale of the trip is a series of spectacular loops and tunnels that ends at St. Moritz.

The trip takes seven hours and costs $48 one way second-class, $72 one way first-class. For more information, contact **Swiss Federal Railways,** *608 Fifth Ave., New York, NY 10020; (212)757-5944.*

Switzerland's most beautiful waterfalls

Near Interlaken, in the village of Lauterbrunnen, is the **Staubbach Waterfall,** which plunges 1,000 feet and then dissolves into a fine spray. Lord Byron described the falls as the "tail of the pale horse ridden by Death in the Apocalypse."

Not far away are the **Trummelbach Falls,** which leap and boil, forcing their way through a series of eroded potholes.

The most spectacular views of the Alps

The most spectacular view of the Alps—indeed one of the most incredible mountain views in the world—is from **Kleine Scheidegg,** a peak near Interlaken. Take a train from Interlaken to Grindelwald, then catch another train to Kleine Scheidegg—or even higher to Mannlichen.

Kleine Scheidegg has a lodge and an outdoor restaurant, where you can watch mountain climbers dangling in the distance. You can hike back to Interlaken through the Lauterbrunnen Valley if you have the energy. Or you can take a train from Wengen to the valley floor.

The pearl of the Swiss lakes

The pearl of Swiss lakeside resorts is **Montreux,** with its six-mile promenade lined with palm trees and tropical flowers on the shores of Lake Geneva. The climate here is the mildest on the north side of the Alps and produces fig trees, almond trees, cypresses, magnolias, and bay trees.

Montreux is famous for its international music festivals, especially the jazz festival in July, the International Choral Recitals the week after Easter, and the Musical September concerts.

Eden au Lac, *11 rue du Theatre; tel. (41-21)963-55-51,* a turn-of-the-century hotel on the lake in Montreux, is the best place to stay. Lunch is served in the hotel garden, right on the lake. Rooms are 150 Swiss francs to 240 Swiss francs.

Le Château, *1844 Villeneuve, VD1820 Montreux; tel. (41-21)960-13-57,* a towered 17th-century building at the foot of a mountain, was once the residence of the Bouvier family (related to the House of Savoy). Today, it is a hotel. Wood-beamed ceilings and other antique touches add charm. The restaurant is a rotisserie and has an outside terrace. The famous Castle of Chillon is nearby.

The best local specialties are served at **La Vieille Ferme,** *tel. (41-21)64-64-65,* a rustic restaurant outside town in Montreux-Chailly. The *raclette* is good, as is the country music. The restaurant is closed Mondays.

The best of Lausanne

Lausanne, another resort on Lake Geneva, is a French-speaking city and a university center. Its universities date back to the 16th century, but its students keep the atmosphere young. Excavations in Lausanne have uncovered Neolithic skeletons and a section of a Roman road where the Geneva-Lausanne highway now comes into town.

The best place to begin exploring Lausanne is **place de la Palud,** in the old town. This square is bordered by the Renaissance facade of the town hall and centered around the 16th-century Fountain of Justice.

Behind the fountain is an unusual covered staircase that leads to the town's 12th-century cathedral, one of the finest Gothic buildings in Switzerland. It shelters one of the last night watches in the world, whose duty it is to call out the hour during the night. The south door of the cathedral, known as the Door of the Apostles, is covered with 13th-century sculptures. A 700-year-old rose window illustrates the elements, seasons, months, and signs of the zodiac. Climb the 232 steps to the top of the tower for a view of Lake Geneva and the Alps.

Switzerland's best restaurant

Lausanne boasts the best restaurant in Switzerland (and most of Europe): **Girardet,** *1 Route d'Yverdon, Crissier; tel. (41-21)27-01-01.* Chef Fredy Giradet does amazing things with fish and fresh produce. He is precise, yet inventive. Try the chocolate soufflé. Make reservations far in advance. Dinner is 110 Swiss francs to 140 Swiss francs.

Lausanne's most romantic hotel

The most romantic place to stay in the region is **Chateau d'Ouchy,** *2 place du Port, VD-1006 Lausanne; tel. (41-21)26-74-51.* This 12th-century stronghold of the bishops of Lausanne is on Lake Geneva. It was the site of the Louis de Savoie Treaty in 1300 and became a government custom house in the 1700s. A hotel was built around the castle in 1884, and the Lausanne Peace Treaty was signed here in 1923. The Salle des Chevaliers hasn't changed in 800 years. The hotel offers dancing, tennis, and excursions. Rooms start at 180 Swiss francs.

Lugano: the best Italian town

Lugano's language is Italian and its atmosphere Mediterranean. It was ceded to Switzerland by Milan in the early 16th century. Gardens bloom year-round.

A mini-Louvre exists in this lakeside town, housed in a gorgeous villa in Castagnola surrounded by gardens and statues. The **Villa Favorita,** *6976 Castagnola; tel. (41-91)521-741,* houses one of the finest private art collections in the world, collected by Baron Heinrich Thyssen-Bornemisza. It includes works from the 16th century through the end of the period of the French Impressionists. Among the museum's many treasures are the painting of Henry VIII by Hans Holbein and Claude Monet's *Dejeuner sur l'Herbe.*

The finest hotel in Lugano is the five-star **Hotel Splendide Royal,** *Riva A. Caccia 7, 6900 Lugano; tel. (41-91)54-20-01.* Efficient and luxurious, it overlooks Lake Lugano and has a pool, a sauna, a casino, and plush rooms. A tribute to the belle epoque, it opened in 1888 and is the inn of choice among the world's rich and royal. Request a room in the old section; while the new wing is nondescript, rooms in the old section are high-ceilinged and furnished with antiques. Bathrooms are tiled in Italian marble. Rooms are 220 Swiss francs to 317 Swiss francs.

Chapter 10

THE
BEST
OF
AUSTRIA

Austria—the land of Mozart, Strauss, Schubert, and Mahler—is the music capital of Europe. Instead of Muzak, classical music is played in elevators and offices. School children learn to play musical instruments at an early age. And Austria's yearly classical music festivals draw music lovers from around the globe.

Vienna alone supports four major symphony orchestras, two opera houses, and a host of theaters.

The world's best music festivals

The world's biggest and most famous music festival is the **Salzburg Festival.** Other important Austrian melomanic delights include the **Haydn Festival** in Vienna and the **International Chamber Music Festival.** Tickets to the festivals are cheapest if you buy them in Austria. *Tickets for Events in Austria,* an information sheet, is available from the **Austrian National Tourist Office,** *500 Fifth Ave., New York, NY 10110; (212)944-6880.*

The best of Vienna

Vienna, the capital of the Hapsburg empire for 600 years, is one of the loveliest cities in the world. Magnificent palaces, theaters, and ballrooms from its days of glory remain throughout the city. The best way to explore Vienna is on foot, and the place to begin is the **Ringstrasse,** affectionately known as the Ring. One of the most beautiful avenues in the world, the Ring circles Vienna's old quarter. Most of Vienna's major sights line this shaded, tree-lined boulevard created by Emperor Franz Joseph in December 1857.

You can walk the most picturesque section of the Ring in 45 minutes. (You can walk the entire Ring in two hours.) Begin at the 600-year-old Vienna University, near the Schottentor (Scottish Gate) and work your way around the Ring past the Stadtstheater, Europe's leading German-language theater; the neo-Gothic *Rathaus;* the Greek-style parliament building; the Hofburg Palace; the Natural History Museum; and the Art History Museum. Then continue past the great opera house, the Imperial Hotel, and the town parks (as well as the airline bus terminal).

Vienna's number-one attraction

The most important sight in Vienna is the **Hofburg Palace** (known as the Hofburg), once the winter residence of the Hapsburgs. Built in the 13th century, it has been embellished with every architectural style up to the modern day. More a city than a palace, it is now filled with government offices and museums.

The great entranceway to the Hofburg, the **Michaelertor,** is on the Michaelerplatz flanked by two grand fountains. On the left as you enter are the Imperial Apartments, where you can see the exercise equipment of Emperor Franz Josef's beautiful, reclusive wife Sisi, who was obsessed with her figure.

Beyond the courtyard to the left is the gateway to the **Schweizerhof,** the original nucleus of the Hofburg. The 13th-century Schweizerhof was named for the Swiss Guards who watched over the ruler. The **Hofburgkapelle** (the chapel), where Mozart and Schubert played, is in the courtyard of the Schweizerhof. Today, the Vienna Boys' Choir sings here on Sundays during the summer and on holidays.

The Hofburg also contains the **Imperial Treasury,** where you can see the ancient Imperial Crown, encrusted with gems and dating back to A.D. 962; objects said to be made of unicorn horn; the elaborate cradle designed for Napoleon's son; and an agate bowl, once thought to be the Holy Grail.

In the Augustinerkirche of the Hofburg is the **Chapel of St. George.** The crypt of the chapel contains 56 urns holding the hearts of the Hapsburgs. However, the chapel is not just a place of death. Maria Theresa and Francis of Lorraine were married here, as was Napoleon, by proxy, to Marie Louise.

The world's best horsemanship

The 400-year-old **Spanish Riding School,** located in the Hofburg Palace, trains the noble white stallions that descend from the Spanish horses imported to Austria by Emperor Maximilian II in the 16th century. The horses dance to Viennese music, guided by expert riders wearing the traditional gold-buttoned brown uniform and gold-braided black hat.

Performances are held at the school most Sunday mornings at 10:45 a.m. and Wednesday nights at 7 p.m. from March to June and September to December. It's difficult to get tickets; write six months in advance to the **Spanische Reitschule,** *Michaelplatz 1, A-1010 Vienna, Austria; tel. (43-222)533-9031.*

Gothic at its best

The most important Gothic structure in Austria is the early 12th-century **St. Stephen's Cathedral.** Most of the Gothic touches were added in the 14th and 15th centuries. Climb the 345 steps to the top of the 450-foot church spire for a view of Vienna.

Inside, the black marble baroque altar is carved with illustrations of St. Stephen being stoned to death. The pulpit, designed by Anton Pilgram between 1510 and 1515, is carved with the heads of the early fathers of the church (Augustine, Gregory, Jerome, and Ambrose), as well as animals symbolizing the sins. Pilgram's own face peers out from the stairs.

Another masterpiece is contained in the theater: the tomb of Frederick III, created by Nikolaus of Leyden from 1467 to 1513. It is covered with carvings representing good and evil and topped with a marble statue of the emperor in his coronation robes.

Beneath the cathedral in the catacombs are the internal organs of 56 Hapsburgs minus the hearts (the bodies are in the Imperial Burial Vault at the Church of the Capuchin Friars). You also can see the foundations of the original basilica, which burned in 1258.

Maria Theresa's favorite palace

Schönbrunn Palace, west of town, was the summer home of the Hapsburgs from 1695, when it was built, to 1918, when the last Hapsburg emperor, Charles I, abdicated. Maria Theresa ruled Austria from here while raising 16 children (Marie Antoinette was one of them) and fighting a war for her right to the throne. She redesigned the palace and today it is much as she left it.

Often compared to Versailles, the Schönbrunn has 1,441 rooms (45 can be visited) and a vast baroque garden. The rococo palace theater, once the stage for Max Reinhardt's famous acting school, still houses a drama school. See the collection of royal carriages; the room where Napoleon stayed; the Millions Room, a highly ornate rococo room with gold-framed mirrors and Indian paintings; and the Great Gallery, with its frescoed ceilings. The Schönbrunn is also home to the oldest zoo in Europe, designed in 1752 by Jadot. It is probably the only baroque-style zoo in the world.

The favorite park of the Viennese

Prater Park, across the Danube River, is famous for its Ferris wheel, the Riesenrad (the best view in Vienna is from the top). The park was the royal hunting ground until 1766, when Emperor Joseph II opened it to the public.

The three-mile-long Hauptallee leads through the center of this garden-filled park. Lined with chestnut trees, this road is a great place to bike ride. Avoid the Krieau section, where thieves are said to lurk.

Austria's greatest museum

If you see only one museum in Vienna, make it the **Kunsthistorisches Museum** (Art History Museum), which is across the Ringstrasse from the Hofburg. The greatest museum in Austria, it houses the paintings, sculptures, jewels, and bibelots collected by the Hapsburgs from 1500 to 1918.

The Kunsthistorisches Museum looks more like a palace than a museum, with its columned windows, enormous doors, broad central staircase, heraldic patterns, painted ceilings, and high cupola. Spread through seven buildings, it can be confusing, and the easiest way to see it is to ramble. Be sure to see the works of Pieter Brueghel the Elder in Gallery X; Albrecht Dürer's works in Room 15; Giuseppe Arcimboldi's surreal works in Room 19; the Titians in Gallery I; the Tintorettos in Gallery II; the Raphaels in Gallery III; and Vermeer's works in Gallery VIII.

Vienna's other top museums

The **Osterreichische Galerie** (Austrian Gallery), *Prinz Eugenstr. 27,* contains modern, baroque, and church art. Located in the baroque Belvedere Palace, which was built by Hildebrandt between 1714 and 1723, the gallery is divided into three parts. Modern artworks are kept in the Upper Belvedere. Look for the works of Gustav Klimt (1862-1918), many of which are embellished with gold. The Lower Belvedere, where the beloved Prince Eugene (who protected his country from the Turks) once lived, is now the Museum of Austrian Baroque. The orangery houses the Museum of Medieval Austrian Art.

The **Graphische Sammlung Albertina** (Albertina Graphic Arts Collection), near Augustinerbastel, has the greatest collection of drawings by old masters in the world. The etchings of Albrecht Dürer are the biggest attractions. Also here are works by Rubens, Watteau, Fragonard, and other masters. (Reproductions are usually on display, for conservation reasons.)

The **Naturhistorisches Museum** (Natural History Museum), across the street, houses the world's oldest-known sculpture, the *Willendorf Venus,* created in Moravia about 29200 B.C. You'll find this ancient fertility figure in Room 11. The five-inch limestone carving of a plump woman represents the mother goddess.

The **Akademie der Bildeden Kunste** (Academy of Fine Arts), near Getreidemarkt, is the respected art school that rejected the young Adolph Hitler after he failed the entrance exams. Some say this rejection fueled Hitler's anti-semitism (he claimed Jewish professors kept him out). Established in 1692, the academy houses the impressive triptych the *Last Judgment* by Hieronymus Bosch.

Neue Hofburg, a wing of the Hofburg, has a collection of Roman sculptures from the ancient city of Ephesus, which were found on the western coast of Turkey. The museum also houses musical instruments, including the pianos of Beethoven, Schubert, and Mahler.

The world's best boys' choir

The world-famous **Vienna Boys' Choir** performs every Sunday and religious holiday from Jan. 1 to late June and from mid-September to Dec. 31 at the Imperial Chapel of the Hofburg Palace. High Mass begins at 9:15 a.m. The choir sings from the loft of the church and can be heard (although usually not seen) from all seats. Tickets ordered in advance cost from $3.85 to $9.25. Order tickets (well in advance) from **Verwaltung der Hofmusikkapelle,** *Hofburg Schweizerhof, A-1010 Vienna, Austria; tel. (43-222)533-9927.* Tickets sometimes can be obtained at the last minute from local ticket agents. Get to the chapel early if you want a seat.

A musical extravaganza

The finest musical experience in Austria is a night at the **Staatsoper,** *Opernring 2; tel. (43-222)514-440.* This opera house is considered the most beautiful in Europe. The Vienna State Opera, one of the world's finest opera companies, is accompanied by the Vienna Philharmonic, one of the world's finest philharmonics.

If you plan to attend the Vienna Opera in June, September, October, or May, play it safe by ordering your tickets two to three months in advance from **Bundestheaterverband,** *Goethegasse 1, A-1010 Vienna, Austria.* Don't send money; you pay for the tickets when you arrive in Vienna. Take your passport and a copy of your confirmation letter when you pick them up. Do so no earlier than four days and no later than one day before the performance.

If you haven't ordered tickets in advance, go to the ticket office a few minutes before 9 a.m. to see what is available for the next four days. A bulletin board lists the performances. The cheapest tickets are sold at the ticket booth an hour before the performance. The 567 standing-room-only seats are only about $1.

Café culture at its coziest

The Viennese have gotten the café down to an art. Cafés have been a way of life in Vienna since the Turks retreated in 1683, leaving their sacks of coffee beans outside the walls of the city. People spend hours in cafés sipping coffee and talking or reading newspapers (cafés usually supply an assortment of international newspapers).

Café Hawelka, *Dorotheergasse 6; tel. (43-222)512-8230,* is a dark café with black chairs, coatracks, upholstered seats in red and brown stripes, and heavy curtains. It draws students, old people, artists, and businessmen. Caricatures and drawings paper the walls of this café, once frequented by Trotsky and his contemporaries. Orson Welles came here to soak up atmosphere and prepare for his role in the film *The Third Man.* English and American newspapers are available. Try friendly Frau Hawelka's freshly baked *Buchteln* (a sort of doughnut) with a pear brandy.

Café Central, *Herrengasse 14; tel. (43-222)66-41-76,* is another cozy place that was an intellectual hangout at the turn of the century. It is decorated with frescoes, marble columns, and fountains and is in an enclosed courtyard. It serves the best *Topfenstrudel* in Vienna.

Café Schwarzenberg, *Kaerntner Ring 17; tel. (43-222)52-73-93,* is a 117-year-old café with oak-paneled walls, mirrors, and a white tile ceiling. The pianist draws crowds. This café stays open until 6 a.m. during the Christmas season.

Vienna's best restaurants

Gottfried, *Untere Viaduktgasse 45, Maxgasse 3, A-1010; tel. (43-222)73-82-56 or (43-222)13-82-56,* received a Michelin star for its good food. The specialties of the house are fish and *Rohe Rinderfiletscheiben mit Rührei und Schalottenrahm* (raw beef with scrambled eggs and shallot-flavored whipped cream). Meals are 400 Austrian schillings to 745 Austrian schillings per person. Make reservations in advance. The restaurant is open for lunch only on Saturdays; it is closed on Sundays.

Hauswirth, *Otto-Bauer-Gasse 20, A-1060; tel. (43-222)587-1261,* is another good restaurant. Try the *Roulade von der Bachforelle* (baked trout), *Kalbsbriesrose mit Gänseleber im Blättereig* (sweetbreads and goose liver in puff pastry), or *Rehrückenfilet im der Semmelhülle auf Wacholdersauce* (venison in juniper sauce). Meals are 315 Austrian schillings to 495 Austrian schillings. Reservations are required. The restaurant is closed on Sundays and bank holidays.

Mattes, *Schönlaterngasse 8, A-1010; tel. (43-222)52-62-75,* is a cozy restaurant with good house specialties. Try the *Kalbsbriessuppe mit Gänseleber* (soup with goose liver), *Ravioli von Jakobsmuscheln im Basilikumsud* (basil-flavored mussels in pastry), *Taübchenbrüstchen im Salzteig* (breast of pigeon cooked in salt). Dinners are 380 Austrian schillings to 630 Austrian schillings per person. Reservations are necessary. The restaurant is closed Sundays, holidays, in August, and Dec. 22 to Jan. 2.

Sacherstube, the Hotel Sacher's restaurant, *Philharmonikerstr. 4; tel. (43-222)51-45-60,* is a pleasant surprise to those who assume that hotel restaurants are just so-so. The food is good, and the ambience is inviting. Opera-goers dine here after shows. Save room for the sinfully rich chocolate *Sachertorte* for dessert. Meals are 335 Austrian schillings to 620 Austrian schillings. Wear a tie and make reservations.

Zu den Drei Husaren, *Weihburggasse 4; tel. (43-222)51-21-092,* is the essence of old Vienna, serving superb hors d'oeuvres and desserts. Opened by three veteran hussars of Kaiser Franz Josef more than 50 years ago, the restaurant is decorated with stag horns, antique busts, Gobelin tapestries, and old portraits. It serves imaginative specialties, such as zucchini-garnished *Lammruchen in Strudelteig* (saddle of lamb in strudel pastry). Save room for the *Preiselbeeren* omelette with praline sabayon, the dessert to end all desserts. The restaurant's guestbook, filled with the names of dignitaries, celebrities, and royalty, reads like a Who's

Who. Dinners are 400 Austrian schillings to 750 Austrian schillings. Reservations are necessary.

The world's best pastries

Vienna's *Konditoreien* (pastry shops/cafés) produce the world's most delectable pastries—seductive arrays of tempting cakes, dripping with icing and whipped cream. Imagine a horseshoe-shaped *Kipferl* with shredded almonds or a *Schifferl,* shaped like a small boat, with tiny strawberries as passengers. Sugar lovers can be spotted on any afternoon lingering in *Konditoreien* over savory confections and a cup of coffee or tea.

Vienna's *Konditoreien* are as colorful and varied as the pastries they serve. **Demel's,** from its exalted position on the Kohlmarkt, calls itself *K.K. Hofzukerbäckerei* (imperial and royal sugar baker). **Gerstner,** with its enviable position overlooking the Kaerntnerstrasse, also claims royal recognition: Emperor Franz Josef prophetically remarked more than 100 years ago, "Gerstner will have a great future." Another landmark, famous for its dainty china and delicious cakes, is **Heiner's,** with *Konditoreien* on both the Kaerntnerstrasse and the Wollzeile.

The best Viennese night life

The **U4,** *XII Schoenbrunnerstrasse; tel. (43-222)85-83-07,* is our favorite nightclub in Vienna. So named because it is downstairs from an elevated subway stop on the U4 line, it is popular with a mature, sophisticated clientele.

Queen Anne, *Johannesgasse 12; tel. (43-222)512-0203,* is the most popular disco in town.

The best place to go for jazz is **Jazzland,** *I Franz-Josefs-Kai 29; tel. (43-222)63-25-75,* which has a smoky, funky atmosphere. Famous bands sometimes play here.

The place popular among young professionals is the **Reiss Bar,** *Marco d'Aviano Gasse; tel. (43-222)512-7198,* near the Karntnerstrass. A wide selection of champagnes is served in this art-retro spot, where executives hobnob.

Griechenbeisl, *Fleischmarkt 11; tel. (43-222)533-1941,* claims to be the oldest tavern in Vienna, dating back to 1500. It has good local food and live music in the evenings. You can get Austrian wines and Pilsner beer on tap.

Vienna's best hotel

The **Imperial,** *Kärntner Ring 16, A-1015; tel. (43-222)651-7650,* is a deluxe hotel located in a former palace. Built in 1869 for the duke of Württemberg, it was turned into a hotel in 1874. Wagner lived here for two months during the productions of his operas around the corner. Elizabeth Taylor stayed here with her three dogs and two cats, her mother, and her servants. Other noted guests have included Ormandy, Nureyev, Fonteyn, Domingo, and Carreras. During World War II, the Nazis used the Imperial as a guesthouse, and Hitler stayed here several times. When the war was over, the hotel served as the Russian headquarters.

Rooms at the Imperial are furnished with antiques and have wall safes. The magnificent central staircase of red, yellow, and black marble is supported by reclining gods and goddesses. Gobelin tapestries and portraits of Emperor Franz Joseph and Empress Elizabeth hang on the walls. The hotel has a staff of 252 employees for the 160 rooms. Rooms are from 1,700 Austrian schillings to 4,440 Austrian schillings.

Three top-rung hotels

The **Bristol,** *Kaerntner Ring 1; tel. (43-222)51-51-60,* is a luxurious, traditional hotel across the street from the opera house. It has large, beautifully furnished bedrooms and one of the best hotel bars in Europe. The Bristol's restaurant, the **Korso,** received a star from Michelin for its terrific food. Rooms are from 1,820 Austrian schillings to 3,940 Austrian schillings.

The **Sacher,** *Philharmonikerstr. 4; tel. (43-222)5-14-56,* is a first-class place with lovely rooms that are furnished with antiques. Musicians and music lovers stay at this hotel, which is next door to the opera house. The concierge is said to be able to get tickets to almost any of Vienna's musical events—for a handsome fee, of course. Rooms are 1,150 Austrian schillings to 3,700 Austrian schillings. Credit cards are not accepted.

The **Hotel im Palais Schwarzenberg,** *Schwarzenbergplatz 9; tel. (43-222)78-45-15,* is in a converted 17th-century baroque palace in a quiet location. Its restaurant has a Michelin star. Once a palace, it has ceiling frescoes and elaborate chandeliers and is furnished with antiques. Surrounded by a 37-acre park in the center of Vienna, the hotel has very good service. Rooms are 2,200 Austrian schillings to 3,500 Austrian schillings.

Bargain hotels

Amadeus, *Wildpretmarkt 5, A-1010; tel. (43-222)63-87-38,* is a consistently good, centrally located hotel with private baths and telephones. It is closed Dec. 22 to Jan 6. Rooms are 890 Austrian schillings to 1,680 Austrian schillings.

Kaiserin Elisabeth, *Weihburggasse 3; tel. (43-222)51-52-60,* is a charming hotel in a 14th-century building that is centrally located. Double rooms with bathrooms are 792 Austrian schillings to 1,100 Austrian schillings, including breakfast.

The baroque **Römischer Kaiser,** *Annagasse 16,* was built in 1684 as the private palace of the imperial chancellor. It has been a hotel since the turn of the century. Double rooms with bathrooms are 825 Austrian schillings to 1,100 Austrian schillings, including breakfast.

The **Ring,** *Maria am Gestade 1; tel. (43-222)63-77-01,* is an inexpensive hotel at the foot of a staircase leading to a Gothic church. The rooms are small but comfortable, with private bathrooms. The restaurant serves Viennese cuisine and has a wine cellar. Double rooms are about 800 Austrian schillings.

Best bet for *The Sound of Music* buffs

North of Vienna is the **Schlosshotel Martinschloss,** *Martinstr. 34-36, Klosterneuburg bei Vienna; tel. (43-2243)7426,* where the Von Trapp Family Singers once lived. You can spend the night in this castle, made famous by the movie *The Sound of Music.*

The Russians occupied the baroque castle after World War II. Today, it is decorated with antiques, including an arms collection that dates back to the original owners. Many of the artifacts were hidden in the depths of a 130-foot cistern during the German Occupation. Wild boar and deer can be hunted on the grounds. Rooms are 750 Austrian schillings to 1,800 Austrian schillings.

The most tragic site: Mayerling

A chapel in **Mayerling,** in the middle of the Vienna woods, marks the spot where Crown Prince Rudolf, son of Emperor Franz Joseph, and his lover Baroness Mary Vetsera committed double suicide. The emperor had refused to allow Prince Rudolf to end his unhappy marriage.

Heurigen, or little wine bars, are located in Grinzing and other villages in the woods. A sprig of pine above the door of one of these bars means the new wine, less than a year old, is ready to be drunk.

Innsbruck: the prettiest Alpine city

Innsbruck, the capital of Tyrol, is one of the most beautiful cities in the world and one of the biggest ski centers in Europe. The towering Alps can be seen from nearly every street corner. The **Nordkette,** a steep Alpine headwall, is the closest and most dramatic of the mountains that surround the city. **Maria-Theresien-Strasse,** the main street, has an especially inspiring view of the mountains.

Miles of free cross-country ski tracks can be found outside Innsbruck, as well as Olympic legacies, including the Olympic bobsled run (which tourists can ride), a ski jump, and a large ice-skating and hockey arena.

Gothic architecture (the pointed, arched, and vaulted style prevalent in Europe from the 13th to 15th centuries) can be seen throughout 800-year-old Innsbruck. Much of it was built by order of Empress Maria Theresa and Emperor Maximillian I. Gothic arcades, forerunners of modern malls because they kept shoppers out of the weather, can be found off Herzog Friedrichstrasse.

Innsbruck's treasures

The **Goldenes Dachl** (Golden Roof) is the symbol of Innsbruck. The ornate Gothic balcony, built in 1500 by Maximilian I to commemorate his wedding, was used by the royal couple to watch armor-clad knights jousting below. The regal balcony has sculpted crests and heroic wall paintings. A roof made of 2,657 gold-plated tiles tops the balcony.

Next to the Golden Roof is the **Goldener Adler** (Golden Eagle Inn), the oldest hostelry in the city. Andreas Hofer, the leader of the Tyrolean uprising against Napoleon, gathered his small and poorly armed troop of volunteers here. His troops, despite their poor state, managed to defeat the well-equipped French and Bavarian armies in three battles.

Hofkirche (the court church), on the Renweg, is known as the Tyrolean Westminster Abbey. It was commissioned by Emperor Ferdinand I as a cenotaph dedicated to his grandfather Maximilian I (who is buried at Wiener Neustadt). Built from 1553 to 1563, it contains a white marble tomb with a monumental bronze statue of the kneeling Maximilian on top. Standing vigil are 28 enormous bronze statues of royal figures. It also contains the tomb of Andreas Hofer.

Across the Inn River is the **Hungerburgbahn** (a funicular) that will carry you to the peaks with the best views of Innsbruck. It crosses the Inn and ascends the mountainside to Hungerburg, a lofty section of the city. An aerial tram continues from here to Seegrube and Hafelaker, breathtaking overlooks on the Nordkette.

Downhill from here is the **Alpine Zoo,** which contains species already extinct in the Eastern Alps, as well as rare animals and birds seen only by hunters in the high mountains. Wildcats, wolves, bears, bison, otters, beavers, griffons, vultures, owls, and eagles are kept in surroundings as similar as possible to their natural habitats. The zoo is open every day from 9 a.m. to 6 p.m. You can get here from Innsbruck via Bus Z.

The best way to explore the mountains

Club Innsbruck arranges daily hikes and ski trips in the mountains outside Innsbruck. You don't have to be a member; you get a Club Innsbruck card when you register at a hotel in town for at least three nights. Sign up for Club Innsbruck's programs at information centers or your hotel before 4 p.m. the day before you plan to participate.

From June to September, the club offers daily guided hiking tours, with a free loan of hiking boots and a rucksack. Bus transportation to the starting point of each day's tour and back from the end point, as well as the services of experienced, licensed guides, are free.

During the winter, the club provides free ski buses to the five main ski areas surrounding Innsbruck and a daily cross-country ski bus. Winter hiking trips with guides are scheduled Mondays through Fridays. If you would rather hike on your own, buy the map called "Innsbruck und Umgebung." Many of the best trails start at Hungerburg. The blue trails can be followed in good walking shoes, but don't try the red ones without sturdy climbing boots.

The best summer skiing

For a real thrill, try summer skiing on the **Stubai Glacier,** 25 miles from Innsbruck. You can get there via Post Bus or bus line ST from Stubaitalbannhof. A round-trip ticket is 130 Austrian schillings. A day's skiing is 275 Austrian schillings.

Innsbruck's best inn

The 600-year-old **Goldener Adler,** *Herzog-Friedrichstr. 6; tel. (43-5222)26334,* in the heart of the old town, is the best inn in Innsbruck. Request a room with antique trappings. Double rooms are 400 Austrian schillings to 1,360 Austrian schillings, including breakfast.

The best of Salzburg

Mozart's birthplace, dominated by a 12th-century fortress called the Hohensalzburg, is a baroque city surrounded by mountains. The Salzach River divides **Salzburg** into two worlds. On the left bank are narrow streets and ancient buildings that date back to the 13th to 15th centuries. The right bank is a modern city in the shadows of the Kapuzinerberg Mountain.

The Salzburg Music Festival

The best time to visit this musical town is during the **Salzburg Festival,** held from late July to August. Advance ticket sales usually end by mid-May.

For information on the Salzburg Festival or other festivals in Salzburg, contact **Austrian National Music Festivals,** *20th Floor, 500 Fifth Ave., New York, NY 10110; (212)944-6880,* or the **Ticket Office of the Salzburg Festival,** *Festspielhaus, A-5010 Salzburg, Austria.*

The old quarter

The best place to begin your exploration of Salzburg is the **old quarter.** In the shadows of the castle, it is a maze of winding old streets with little shops, medieval wrought-iron signs, and fountains. Explore on foot—cars are banned here.

The main thoroughfare, Getreidegasse, leads into **Judengasse,** once the Jewish ghetto. Today, it is a picturesque neighborhood with five- and six-story houses. Continue on to the **Alter Markt** (Market Square), where flower stalls scent the air and a 16th-century fountain splashes.

Salzburg's top sights

Mozart was born at *Getreidegasse 9* in 1756, and he lived here for his first 16 years. Early editions of his works (he began composing when he was 5) and models of sets of his most famous operas are on display at the house, which is open every day. (The house where Mozart lived from 1773 to 1787, on the other side of the river at *Makatplatz 8,* is open during the summer only.)

The **Dom** (cathedral), with its two towers, marble facade, and massive bronze doors, is also in the old quarter. Look for its blue terra-cotta dome. Consecrated in 1628, the early-baroque structure was modeled on St. Peter's in Rome.

Across from the cathedral is the **Residenz,** a series of buildings that once comprised the palace of the prince-archbishops. On the first floor are 15 staterooms decorated with frescoes and paintings. A gallery of European painting from the 16th through 19th centuries on the second floor contains works by Rembrandt, Rubens, and Breughel.

The **Glockenspiel,** in front of the Residenz, is a 35-bell carillon constructed in the 18th century. The bells are played every day at 6 and 11 a.m. and 7 p.m.

The magnificent **Mirabell Palace,** with its elaborate formal gardens, is on the other side of the river. Built in 1606 by Archbishop Wolf Dietrich for his mistress (and the mother of his 12 children), it is known for its grand ceremonial staircase, which is decorated with marble angels, and its Marble Hall. The gardens are filled with statues, pools, and flowers of every shade and variety. Candlelight chamber music concerts are held here.

Guarding Salzburg from a great rock 400 feet above the city is the **Hohensalzburg,** a fortress built between 1077 and 1681. This stronghold of the bishops of Salzburg is filled with Gothic wood carving, coffered ceilings, and intricate ironwork. To get to the fortress, which offers the best view of the city, walk or take the funicular from Festungsgasse, near St. Peter's Churchyard. Tours of the castle are scheduled every 15 minutes.

Outside Salzburg is the 17th-century **Hellbrunn Palace,** built by the archbishop and prankster Markus Sittikus. Hidden nozzles in the benches, walls, sculptures, floors, and ceilings were used by the archbishop to spray unwary guests. The palace is open to the public every day from April through October.

The best eating in Salzburg

The two best restaurants in the Salzburg area are **Weisses Kreuz,** *Bierjodlgasse 6; tel. (43-662)845641,* and **Eschlböck-Plomberg,** five miles northeast of Salzburg in Mondsee, *tel. (43-662)31660.* Weisses Kreuz offers garden dining. It is closed in the winter and Wednesdays and Thursdays for lunch. Meals are 290 Austrian schillings to 520 Austrian schillings per person.

Eschlböck-Plomberg, which is located on a beach, also serves meals on the terrace. It is closed Mondays during the winter. Meals are 400 Austrian schillings to 850 Austrian schillings per person.

Stiftskeller Sankt Peter, *1 St. Peters Bezirk; tel. (43-662)841268,* near the cathedral, is a 16th-century wine cellar that serves wines from its own vineyards. Divided into eight rooms, it also serves traditional Austrian dishes at reasonable prices.

Salzburg's best affordable hotels

Hotel Schöne Aussicht, *Heuberg 3, Salzburg 5023; tel. (43-662)78226* or *(43-662)78449,* is a chalet hotel on a hill with a view of Salzburg and the Alps. It has a pool, tennis courts, a sunny terrace, and a cozy, beamed bar. Some of the rooms have balconies. Service is friendly, and fresh flowers decorate the rooms. However, the walk from the bus stop is up three steep hills, so it's best to have a car if you stay here. Double rooms are 800 Austrian schillings to 1,100 Austrian Schillings.

The **Hotel Kaserbräu**, *Kaigasse 33, Salzburg 5020; tel. (43-662)842445*, is a small hotel in the shadows of the Hohensalzburg. The building dates back to 1342, and some of the rooms have been furnished in baroque style. Others are furnished in pinewood. Rooms are 400 Austrian schillings to 700 Austrian schillings.

The **Hotel Elefant**, *Sigmund Haffnergasse 4, Salzburg 5020; tel. (43-662)843397*, is a medieval townhouse in the historic heart of Salzburg. The tall, narrow building is on a quiet pedestrian street five minutes from the opera house. The public rooms have inlaid furniture and old paintings. The floors on the first floor are marble, and the rooms are decorated with antiques. The upper floors are less elegant; some of the rooms are small and plain. About half have private baths. Double rooms are 840 Austrian schillings to 950 Austrian schillings a night.

Salzburg's castle hotels

Gastschloss Monchstein, *Monchsberg 26, A5020 Salzburg; tel. (43-662)858555*, parts of which date to 1358, is a many-tiered, ivy-covered castle on a mountaintop above Salzburg. Once a guesthouse for archbishops, it became a retreat for scholars from the University of Salzburg in 1654. Today, it is a hotel. You can take an elevator to the castle from the streets below. Half the rooms have private bathrooms. Double rooms are 1,800 Austrian schillings to 3,000 Austrian schillings a night. The hotel is open March through October.

Schloss Haunsperg, *tel. (43-6245)2662*, is a 14th-century castle hotel just south of Salzburg. The spacious rooms are furnished with antiques, and guests can use the tennis courts on the grounds. The castle is near the Autobahn that runs south from Salzburg past the airport; exit at Hallein and follow the signs to Oberalm and the castle. Double rooms are 590 Austrian schillings to 990 Austrian schillings a night.

The world's best salt mines

The salt mine at **Hallein**, 10 miles south of Salzburg, is a bit like a roller coaster. To get around inside the tunnels, you slide down a series of long wooden chutes at 40 miles per hour. To visit, you must put on a special uniform, which consists of baggy white overalls with a white hood and a leather backside.

The mine contains sketches of the 1,000-year-old body of a man found in 1666 perfectly preserved in salt. And at mid-level is a salt lake, which, during the off-season, you can raft across to see a cathedral-like cavern 270 feet long and 150 feet wide.

Europe's highest waterfall

Krimml Waterfall (the highest in Europe) splashes down 1,250 feet through the mountains 30 miles east of Innsbruck. You know when the fall is close; it fills the valley with mist.

The highest Austrian village

The highest village in Austria, **Obergurgl** (6,320 feet), is where Professor Auguste Piccard landed his famous hot-air balloon in the 1930s. Nearby is a little ski settlement called Hochgurgl, where you can catch a chair lift to a year-round ski area.

Austria's strangest tradition

The little mountain town of **Landeck** has a fascinating tradition. Each year at Christmas, young men from town climb to the top of the rocky crags that loom above Landeck. Here, they light huge bonfires that can be seen for miles. Then they set fire to circles of wood dipped in tar and roll them down the hill. The blazing circles are quite a sight against the black night sky. Finally, the daredevils ski downhill, racing the fiery disks at breakneck speed!

Austria's best skiing

The **Arlberg** region of Austria is the best place in the world for skiing. It offers a combination of features not duplicated anywhere else: a high altitude, which guarantees good snow; slopes for skiers of all levels of experience; interconnected villages that range from quaint to crowded to exclusive; serious ski instruction; and a cheery dose of *Gemütlichkeit,* or camaraderie. Some of the villages are large, such as Lech or St. Anton; others, including Zürs, are small and exclusive.

Kitzbühel, the prettiest ski town

A treasure of a ski village is **Kitzbühel,** a friendly, uncrowded town with slopes for skiers of all experience and enough activity to keep even snow-haters happy. This is the place to go to avoid irritating crowds and the ridiculously high prices often found in the Alps. It has well-groomed slopes, a casino, and plenty of night life.

Kitzbühel is worth visiting even if you don't ski. An ancient walled town, it has crooked, narrow streets and Tyrolean architecture, with gabled stone-and-stucco houses that date back to the Middle Ages.

The skiable part of the Kitzbühel Alps reaches as high as 7,750 feet. The greatest vertical drop here is 4,150 feet. These heights may seem small compared with those at other Alpine resorts; however, the smooth pastures of these mountains require less snow for good skiing than the rockier slopes of other ski areas. And the weather is milder than in other areas. Kitzbühel's 60 ski lifts and trails provide an overwhelming choice of trails, all accessible with a single ski pass called the Kitzbühel Ski Circus.

The best place to stay in Kitzbühel is **Schloss Lebenberg,** *Lebenbergstr. 17, A6370 Kitzbühel; tel. (43-5356)4301.* Situated on a hill overlooking the valley and the mountains, the castle was built in 1540 by the dukes of Lebenberg. The hotel's 11 guest rooms are all furnished with antiques. Rooms in the newly added chalet-wing have private baths. Other modern additions include health facilities, a heated pool, a sauna, and tennis courts.

The best ski school

St. Anton is the best place to go for ski instruction, thanks to tradition and the city's 300 instructors. This is the cradle of modern skiing, where Hannes Schneider began teaching the now-accepted Arlberg School ski technique. The runs from the top of the Galzig and the Valuga (9,216 feet) are superb—as are the views.

St. Anton is also a good place to go for night life. The Hotel Hospiz has a fine restaurant. And the Krazy Kanguruh is a hopping nightclub.

Zürs, the most exclusive ski resort

Zürs, a first-class ski resort where tour groups are discouraged, is for skiing purists who also like fine living. The city has one ski instructor for every 10 beds, and most of the instructors give only private lessons. And in Zürs it's common for the ski instructor to come to the hotel to pick up his class.

All the hotels in Zürs are first-class or better. The **Zorserhof,** *Zürs am Arlberg, Austria,* is an expensive five-star deluxe establishment that regularly attracts celebrities, such as King Hussein of Jordan. It may be the best ski hotel in Austria.

Chapter 11

THE BEST OF GREECE

Greece is a breathtaking country of mountains and islands and sea. Its special light gives a clarity to the blue sky above and the colors below—colors that include a profusion of wildflowers in early spring. When you visit Greece, forget the packaged tours. This is a do-it-yourself country that should be experienced outdoors. Camp out under Greece's stars to best experience the country. Travel light and be prepared to follow the impulse of the moment. You'll find anything you need along the way, at throw-away prices.

Athens: the birthplace of modern civilization

Athens—the birthplace of Western democracy, poetry, drama, art, and philosophy—is no longer at the center of the world it nurtured. A decaying, polluted city, it has a Third World flavor. Nonetheless, Athens merits more than a quick visit. It has the world's largest and most remarkable collections of ancient ruins, including the ancient Parthenon and one of the world's finest archeological museums. And beyond these archeological wonders is an exciting night life and a unique lifestyle, part European, part Middle Eastern.

The Acropolis: the heart of ancient Athens

You shouldn't miss the **Acropolis** and the ancient city. You couldn't miss the Acropolis even if you tried—it stands in full view on a hill above Athens, adding a majestic dignity and beauty to what otherwise would be a shabby city.

Buildings in Athens are subject to a height limit so that the **Parthenon,** the most important structure of the Acropolis, remains visible from most points in the area. Dedicated to the goddess Athena, the Acropolis was the religious center of the ancient capital. It was reconstructed in the fifth century B.C. by Pericles.

Acro means *top,* and *polis* means *city.* Together they mean the highest point, or citadel, of the city—which also means a stiff climb. Wear walking shoes. It is best to visit the Acropolis at dawn or in the late afternoon, because of the play of light. In summer, midday temperatures are too intense.

To the right of the entrance to the Acropolis is the **Temple of Athena Nike,** built to commemorate the victory of the Athenians over the Persians. At the top of the hill is the beautiful Parthenon, temple of the goddess Athena. Also on the hill is the **Acropolis**

Museum, which houses some of the Acropolis' statuary pieces (some older than the Parthenon) to protect them from the city's pollution. The Acropolis is open from 8 a.m. to 5 p.m. weekdays; from 11 a.m. to 5 p.m. Tuesdays; and from 8 a.m. to 5 p.m. Sundays. The museum is closed Tuesdays. The entrance fee is 500 drachmas.

Just beneath the Acropolis on the southern slopes are two ancient amphitheaters. The **Theater of Dionysos,** where the first Greek tragedies were performed, dates back to the sixth century B.C. The **Odeion of Herodes Atticus,** which dates to A.D. 161, is the site for performances of theater, opera, ballet, and music during the Athens Festival held between July and September each year. The amphitheaters are open from 8 a.m. to 7 p.m. weekdays; they are closed Sundays.

The ancient **agora,** or marketplace, is on the eastern slopes of the Acropolis hill, on the north end of the Plaka. Now a major archeological excavation site, this was the downtown area of the ancient city and the main crossroad for routes to other major towns, such as Piraeus. Here you will find the **Stoa of Attalus,** a trading center built in 20 B.C.; the **Roman Forum,** begun during Julius Caesar's reign; the **Kerameikos,** the ancient city cemetery; and **Hadrian's Library,** built in the second century. A museum houses artifacts found during excavations. The museum is open from 8 a.m. to 8 p.m. weekdays and from 10 a.m. to 4:15 p.m. Sundays; it is closed Tuesdays.

The oldest section of Athens

When evening begins to fall, head for the **Plaka,** where hanging lights twinkle in the dark and you'll hear the sounds of *bouzouki* music. Have supper at an outdoor table along one of the narrow streets. Although most of Greece is crime-free, this area of Athens is the one place where you may encounter it.

The Plaka is the oldest part of Athens. The earliest Athenians lived on the hill of the Acropolis. Later the top of the hill was reserved for worship and civic functions, and the citizens moved down from the summit to dwell on the slopes surrounding it, the Plaka. It wasn't until the Turks left Greece in the 1800s that the city began to expand beyond the Plaka.

The world's finest sculptures

The **National Archeological Museum,** *1 Tossitsa St.,* has the finest collection of sculptures in the world. Treasures include giant figures of Greek gods and men, a world-renowned collection of Greek vases, pieces of ancient Cycladic art, and magnificent frescoes from the Minoan sites of Knossos on Cyprus and Akrotiri on Santorini. The gold Mycaenean death mask here is reputed to be that of Agamemnon, the ancient Greek king of the *Illiad.*

Athens' main square

Syntagma Square (Constitution Square), the heart of the business district, is Athens' main square. A favorite pastime of both visitors and native Athenians is to sit at one of the square's outdoor café tables and watch pedestrians walk by. The 3,000 chairs in the square are arranged so that they all face the sidewalk for a better view. Have a coffee, beer, or ouzo and Greek *meze* (snacks) while you watch.

The grand dame of the city's hotels, the **Grande Bretagne,** is on the north side. Watching the wealthy, famous, and sometimes outlandish-looking people step from limousines and taxi cabs to be ushered into the elegant old hotel by fancy-dressed doormen is part of the fun of a long sit in the square.

Many of Athens' most important sights and monuments border Syntagma Square. The **National Parliament Building** faces the square on the east side. The changing of the palace guards takes place here 20 minutes before the hour each day. On Sundays at 11 a.m. the ritual of the evzone, when the guards dress in kilts, white tights, and turned-up shoes, is accompanied by a regimental brass band.

Benaki Museum, *Syntagma Square,* to the left of the Parliament Building, is an old private house crammed with clothes, furniture, and photos dating from Byzantine times to the present. The museum is open from 8:30 a.m. to 2 p.m.; it is closed Mondays. Admission is 70 drachmas (free on Sundays).

Byzantine Museum, *22 Vasilissis Sofia,* in a villa not far from the Benaki, is the best place to see Greek icons. Two rooms are replicas of Byzantine basilicas of the 5th and 11th centuries. The museum is open from 9 a.m. to 3 p.m. weekdays and from 9 a.m. to 2 p.m. Sundays; it is closed Mondays. Admission is 100 drachmas (free on Sundays).

The **Arch of Hadrian,** located near the square in the direction of the Acropolis, was erected by the Romans in A.D. 132 to mark the boundary of the ancient city. One side of the arch bears the inscription, "This is Athens, ancient city of Theseus." The other side of the arch says, "This is the city of Hadrian and not of Theseus."

The largest Greek temple

The **Temple of Olympian Zeus** stands directly behind Hadrian's Arch. Also built by Hadrian during the third century (on foundations laid 700 years earlier by the Greeks), this is the largest temple in Greece. It is open from 9 a.m. to 3:15 p.m. weekdays and from 10 a.m. to 2 p.m. Sundays.

The trendiest neighborhood

Kolonaki Square, a 10-minute hike up the hill from Syntagma Square, is trendy, with boutiques and Greek outlets of expensive international shops, such as Laura Ashley. Rub elbows with young Athenian professionals, the occasional Greek movie star, and stylishly dressed teenagers who stake out the tables of little sidewalk cafés.

The best view of Athens

Lykabettos, a hill northeast of the Acropolis and behind the fashionable homes of Kolonaki, has a spectacular view of Athens, the Acropolis, Pireaus, and the Saronic Gulf. Take a funicular ride 910 feet to the top (board at the end of Ploutarhou), where you'll find a small church and a café. The trip back down through the wooded slopes to Kolonaki is more romantic on foot.

Athens' best shopping

The Plaka, where you can buy any kind of handicraft made in Greece, is the best place for shopping. However, if you're heading out to the islands, where goods are cheaper, wait.

Monastiraki, better known as the Athens Flea Market, is a special part of the Plaka. It runs from Monastiraki Square to Ifestou Street and includes shops of both antiques and old junk. The best time to visit is Sunday mornings.

Kolonaki has posh boutiques, modern art galleries, expensive antique shops, and good dress designers.

Omonia Square is where the locals shop. The Greek-style department stores here offer better prices than in Kolonaki. Goods are sensible rather than stylish.

Pandrossou, the Street of Shoes, also has shops selling brassware, peasant costumes, Greek dolls, and good imitation antiques (you can't take real ones out of the country).

The **National Archeological Museum** sells copies and castings of Greek museum pieces.

The **National Organization of Hellenic Handicrafts,** *9 Mitropoleos; tel. (30-1)322-1017,* the **YMCA,** *28 Omirou St.; tel. (30-1)362-6970,* and the **YWCA,** *11 Amerikas St.,* the **Ethniki Pronia Institute,** the **Ikotechnia** of the Greek Lyceum, and the **Ergastirion Aporon Gynekon** all sell popular arts and crafts.

Athens' best food and drink

The best guide to eating, drinking, and current events in Athens is the English-language *Athenian* magazine, which not only lists every restaurant and bar in the city, but critiques them, too.

Piccolino's, *Moni Asteriou,* between Hatzimichali and Kydathinaion, has the best Greek-style pizza in town.

The old **Xynos Taverna,** *4 Agg. Geronda; tel. (30-1)322-1065,* serves Greek wine from the barrel and features guitar music.

Five Brothers, *Aiolou Street,* off the square behind Hadrian's Library, is inexpensive.

For late-night reveling, try the **Erotokritos,** *16 Lyssiou St.,* which presents musicians in national costume.

Athens' most elegant (and among its most expensive) restaurants are **G.B. Corner,** *Syntagma Square,* at the Grande Bretagne Hotel; *tel. (30-1)323-0251;* **Ta Papakia,** *tel. (30-1)721-2421,* near the Hilton in the American Embassy area, located in what was once a private home with a tree-filled courtyard; the **Balthazar,** *27 Tsoha; tel. (30-1)644-1215;* the **Dyonissos,** *Dyonyssiou Areopagitou Avenue; tel. (30-1)923-3182,* a first-class restaurant across from the Acropolis; and **Gerofinikas,** *10 Pindarou St.; tel. (30-1)362-2710,* which has good Greek and Oriental food.

The best fish restaurants are in Pireaus and along the coast from Glyfada to Sounion. The fish restaurants with the most atmosphere (but also the most expensive prices) are located in the yacht harbor known as Mikrolimano. In Glyfada, try the **Psaropoulos,** *2 Kalamou St.; tel. (30-1)894-5667,* which has a view of the yacht marina.

Athens' *ouzeries* are a dying tradition. Take the time to visit one, where you can sample Greek hors d'oeuvres and the national Greek licorice drink in the company of Greek intellectuals. Stop in at teatime or late in the evening.

The most famous *ouzerie* is the **Orfanides,** *7 Panepistimiou,* in the same block as the Grande Bretagne Hotel. The **Apotsou,** *10 Panepistimiou; tel. (30-1)363-7046,* is the oldest *ouzerie* in Athens; it opened in 1900.

Mezodopolieon are restaurants that serve only appetizers, which the Greeks call *mezes.* **Savories,** in the arcade at *10 Panepistimiou 10,* off Syntagma Square, is a good place to sample a selection. The **Salamandra,** *3 Mantzarou and Solonos Street,* has *bouzouki* music at night. One of the most famous and unusual *mezodopolieon* is the **Vasilena,** *72 Aitolikou, Piraeus; tel. (30-1)461-2457.* At this seemingly ancient restaurant located in an old grocery store, you pay a set price and are served about 20 varieties of *mezes.*

Bouzoukia concentrate more on music than food. Most of these Greek-style nightclubs are located in an area along the seafront between Athens and Piraeus known as **Tzitzines.** Ask your hotel which clubs are in at the moment. It usually depends on the artists playing.

The best places to sleep in Athens

The **Grande Bretagne,** *Syntagma Square; tel. (30-1)3230-251,* is located at the heart of things and, as mentioned above, is touted as one of the world's greatest hotels. Although it's crumbling a little around the edges now, the old hotel retains an air of 1920s splendor. It has been welcoming guests since 1862. Rooms are spacious, and those in the front have balconies looking out at the Acropolis. The public rooms have baroque furnishings. This hotel is a favorite among celebrities. Rooms are 30,218 drachmas to 147,905 drachmas.

Meridien, *Vas. Georgiou, Syntagma Square; tel. (30-1)3255-301,* is a good second if the Grande Bretagne is booked up. Because it is newer, its physical amenities are more modern. Rooms are 16,000 drachmas to 20,000 drachmas.

St. George Lycabettus, *2 Kleomenous; tel. (30-1)7290-711,* is less expensive and has more atmosphere. Its hilltop location gives it views of the city and the sea. It's not quite as convenient as hotels in the heart of things on Syntagma Square, and the rooms are only adequate, not particularly praiseworthy. But a swimming pool adds a point to its scorecard. Rooms are 16,000 drachmas to 20,000 drachmas.

For atmosphere, stay in the Plaka. Hotels here are among the least expensive in the city. Two charming ones are **Hotel Phaedra,** *6 Herephodos, Adrianou St.; tel. (30-1)323-8461,* in a quiet part of the old section; and **Clare's House,** *tel. (30-1)922-2288,* a lovely old mansion with a garden and huge rooms.

The best side trip from Athens

Cape Sounion, which is about 40 miles from downtown Athens, is crowned with the magnificent, white-columned, wind-swept **Temple of Poseidon,** standing alone on the point of the cape and looking out over the sea. From here, you can see all the way to Piraeus.

The solitary temple is most beautiful at sunset when its white luster turns pink against the green pine trees and blue sea beneath it. Take your bathing suit—two fairly unpolluted beaches are nearby: Vouliagmeni and Varkiza. The temple is open from 11 a.m. to sunset; it is closed Tuesdays.

If you want to get the full benefit of sunrise and sunset at this impressive site, spend the night at the **Cape Sounion Beach Hotel,** *tel. (30-1)39-391.*

The best of the Byzantine

The Greeks claim the sixth-century **Dafni** (Daphne) **Monastery,** five miles west of Athens, is their most important surviving Byzantine monument, famous for its mosaics. The nearby **Kaesariani Monastery** was built in the 11th century near the ruins of a temple to Aphrodite.

Each year from June 29 to Sept. 29 the Greeks hold a wine festival at the Dafni Monastery (the entrance fee is about 250 drachmas). You can sample a large variety of Greek wines free and participate in dancing, singing, and contests.

The best of northern Greece

Northern Greece is the home of the country's tallest mountains, including the magical Mt. Olympus, as well as the Macedonia of Alexander the Great, and Thessaloniki, the only other city in this essentially rural nation. The farther north you go, the thicker the woods and the more Balkan the atmosphere.

Mt. Athos: a misogynist's best

The large Greek Orthodox complex perched on the rocky cliffs of **Mt. Athos,** at the end of the Chalkidiki Peninsula overlooking the Aegean, is one of the major wonders of the Christian world. The only self-governing monastic state in Europe, it is made up of about 20 monasteries, many of them individual walled towns.

Only adult males are allowed to visit this impressive Byzantine fortress-state. All others are considered temptations. Admission rules, issued by Emperor Constantine Monomachos of Byzantium in 1060, forbid women, children, and female animals within the complex. To this day, ships with women on board may not come within 500 meters of the shores around Mt. Athos.

Even a man must obtain a permit to enter the complex. He must get a letter of recommendation from a diplomatic or consular officer of his own country and then apply for a permit from the **Greek Ministry of Foreign Affairs,** *Directorate of Churches, 3 Academia St., Athens; tel. (30-1)362-6894,* or the **Ministry of Northern Greece,** *the Directorate of Civil Affairs, Platia Diikitiriou, Thessaloniki; tel. (30-31)270-092.*

The best underwater diving

The **Eagle's Palace Hotel and Bungalows,** not far from Mt. Athos, is an outstanding (and expensive) resort with the best underwater diving in Greece. Tennis, sailing, and boutiques are available. What's more, women are allowed!

Mt. Olympus: the home of the gods

Mt. Olympus is the home of the gods of Greek legend. It's easy to see why this huge, impressive mountain looming above in the clouds, which cut off its tip, captured the imagination of the ancient Greeks.

With an altitude of 9,620 feet, Olympus invites skiers in winter (through May) and mountain climbers and hikers in summer. Hotels in the area include the **Markessa,** halfway between the mountain and the Aegean, the **Olympios-Zeus,** on the beach at the foot of the mountain, and the government-run **Xenia,** a small hotel with views of both the mountain and the sea. All are moderately priced.

The best Greek cave

The **Petralona Cave** on the Halkidi Peninsula is 30 miles from Thessaloniki. A Neanderthal skull was found here in 1960, and the site appears to have been inhabited a half-million years ago.

The world's best fur bargains

Kastoria, in western Macedonia, is the center of the Greek fur industry and offers some of the best fur bargains in the world. Craftsmen here have been expertly sewing together the scraps from fur cutters around the world since the 15th century. You can get a coat for as little as 14,000 drachmas.

The best buy on handwoven rugs

Trikala is a small village in the mountains of northern Greece. This is where the famous shaggy Greek *flokati* rugs originated, thanks to the local sheep population and the crystal-clear mountain streams that are necessary for the manufacturing process. Villagers have been handweaving the rugs, now considered an art form, for 700 years. They hang them on their walls to keep out winter cold and damp.

The rugs available in Trikala are less expensive than those you'll find elsewhere. A five-foot-by-seven-foot rug is 9,975 drachmas to 13,300 drachmas. Stay away from the dyed ones.

The best of central Greece

Most of Greece's highest mountains are in the center of the country, where all points are within a few hours of Athens.

Mt. Parnassus: the best skiing

About an hour and a half from Athens stands **Mt. Parnassus** (8,059 feet), where Greece's most serious skiers spend their winters. For overnight stays, book Hotel Anemolia in Arahova, which is high up on the mountain, a hotel in Delphi, or a government ski hut.

Delphi: the most sacred sight

Just a short drive down from the ski area of Mt. Parnassus is one of Greece's most important and impressive ancient sacred sites, **Delphi,** where Apollo was worshipped, Greek games were held, and the famous oracle was consulted about matters of great significance by pilgrims from throughout the ancient world. Both the ruins and their setting on the steep side of Mt. Parnassus are magnificent.

The **Vouzous Hotel,** *tel. (30-265)82233,* built into the side of a mountain, is the best place to stay in Delphi. Its rooms have spectacular, if dizzying, views of the Gulf of Corinth. **Grigoris Taverna** offers dramatic vistas over a cliff and serves delicious charcoal-grilled food.

Meteora: the best monastery

More accessible than Mt. Athos is the monastic complex of **Meteora,** perched on the summits of some precipitous rocks above the valley of the Pineios River, about five miles from Kalambaka. The monasteries here were built in the 14th century. In all, 33 monasteries and cells still stand, but only 4 are now occupied. In these are housed rare manuscripts, icons, miniatures, and ecclesiastical objects of Byzantine art.

The Peloponnese: the most beautiful islands

The **Peloponnese** is a lovely, wild place covered with wildflowers in spring. You will never feel you've wandered long enough among its mountains, rolling plateaus, and numerous ruins. More major archeological sites are located in the Peloponnese than anywhere else in Greece.

Among the must-see ruins are the city of **Corinth,** known for its luxury and decadence during Roman times; **Mycenae,** the main attraction, site of some of the best archeological finds in the world, including the tombs of Agamemnon and Clytemnestra; **Nafplion,** a pretty town that is the site of a Venetian fortress; **Epidaurus,** where Greek plays are performed in an ancient theater every summer; and **Olympia,** site of the ancient games.

Five miles from the site of ancient **Sparta,** where only a few stones are left, is the pretty

Byzantine town of Mistra, once known as the Florence of the East. Its steep, winding streets are full of churches, old mansions, a monastery, a citadel, and fragrant flowers.

The best music and drama festival

The **Summer Festival of Music and Drama** at Epidaurus is one of the world's most exciting performing-arts events. The ancient theater holds 14,000 people, and its famous acoustics system enables each of them to hear the tiniest whisper from the stage.

The best hotels in the Peloponnese

The **Xenia Palace,** *4 Stadiou St.; tel. (30-752)3254722,* situated inside the walls of the old Venetian fort in Nafplion, is the best of the government-run hotels. Situated on the bay, it has gorgeous views all the way to Mycenae. It is expensive.

La Petite Planete, *Christou Tsounda Avenue; tel. (30-751)66240,* in the village near Mycenae, is a small, inexpensive hotel with lovely views of the orange groves.

The best eating in the Peloponnese

The fish *tavernas* along the waterfront in **Nafplion** are recommended as much for their views as for their fresh fish and wine served straight from the barrel.

Roadside stands between Corinth and Nafplion sell the Blood of Hercules, the rich red wine famous here.

The Cyclades—the most visited

The **Cyclades Islands** are the most visited of Greece's island groups. They offer dramatic beauty and a civilization within a civilization. The Cycladic culture was a subculture of the ancient Mediterranean civilization led first by the Minoans, then by the Mycenaeans.

About 17 of the islands are suitable for vacationers. The most famous members of the group are Mykonos, Santorini, and Delos. Others often visited by tourists are Tinos, a destination for pilgrims of the Greek Orthodox faith; Los, with a dramatic setting and a town built on the side of a mountain; and lovely Paros, where you can get away from it all. The island of Kithnos has one of the best government-run **Xenia** hotels, *tel. (30-Kithnos)31-217,* situated in a renovated building dated 1840, near spas recommended for rheumatism and gynecological disorders.

Mykonos: the island for the jet set

Mykonos, a favorite spot among the jet set, has a reputation for being both wild and flashy and quaint and romantic. It is more open, vivacious, and relaxed than other Greek spots, with a philosophy of live and let live. It is a place where people are allowed and encouraged to do their own things, and where lovers of all persuasions are tolerated—and hardly even noticed. The Greek community itself is more tightly knit and warmer here than perhaps anywhere else in Greece.

Like other Cycladic Islands, Mykonos is dry, with few trees, but beautiful in a dramatic way. Its whitewashed windmills are its trademark. Mykonians are almost compulsive about the spotlessness of their white houses and cobblestones, which offset nicely the beautiful colors of the potted flowers growing everywhere.

Mykonos' little houses, inns, hotels, and restaurants are hidden in a maze of tiny winding streets. It takes about a week to decipher the layout of the alleyways. Legend has it that the citizens of Mykonos purposely designed their streets in a random pattern to confound pirates.

Mykonos' beaches, by the way, particularly Paridis, Superparadis (predominantly gay), and Ilia, are covered with nude sunbathers.

The best clothes shopping

Mykonos' alleyways are filled with quaint boutiques and handicraft shops offering some of the finest-quality clothing in the country. This is the best place in Greece to buy hand-knit sweaters, from heavy fishermen's knits to stylish mohair and cotton creations.

An enclave for artists, many shops in Mykonos offer special designs and one-of-a-kind fashion experiments. Fur stores here offer good bargains, too.

The island's best photographs

A Greek-American photographer, Bo Patrick, sells lovely artistic photographs, as well as his book called *Whitewash and Pink Feathers,* a story about Mykonos for children. White-wash refers to the locals' habit of whitewashing their houses and the cobblestoned lines on their sidewalks each Friday. The paint is not whitewash but something called *asbesti,* used to kill insects. Pink feathers refers to Petros the Pelican, a living character of local fame you'll see standing by the small fishing boats tied up on the waterfront. Bo's shop is in Little Venice, the quaintest part of town.

Wining and dining in Mykonos

Niko's, just off the harbor, is the best restaurant in Mykonos, with good prices and fresh fish. It is the favorite among local fishermen, who dock their tiny boats a few yards away in the harbor every evening.

Little Venice is the most charming area to eat, with outdoor *tavernas* on the water's edge looking out on a gorgeous view.

The hottest night life

Remezzo, at the end of the harbor nearest the ferry landing, is the most famous nightclub in town. Greek celebrities often congregate here. The **Mykonos Disco Bar** is the place to see Greek dancing. Get here about midnight.

Staying in Mykonos

Although the town is full of quaint little alleyway inns, some of the better places to stay in Mykonos are situated on the hillside overlooking the town. Even though staying at the top of the hill means a steep 5- to 10-minute climb home, the view is worth it—as are the lower prices. The stepped paths up the hill pass windmills, flowers, and sometimes a goat or two.

The best of the in-town hotels include the **Leto,** *tel. (30-289)22207* or *(30-289)22918,* right on the harbor (3,720 drachmas for a double), and **Kouneni,** *tel. (30-289)22301,* with a lovely little secret garden (2,390 drachmas for a double).

Hotel Aphroditi, *tel. (30-289)71367,* located on remote Kalafati Beach, is a beautiful place to hide away. Rooms are like bungalows, built in levels stepped up the hill along cobblestoned alleyways behind the main building. Each has a balcony. In the beflowered central patio is a large warm salt-water swimming pool, just a few yards from the white sandy beach across the driveway. The Aphrodite has a small disco, a nice restaurant, and a couple of private little *tavernas* at the end of the beach. Double rooms are 2,390 drachmas.

Delos: Apollo's birthplace

An excursion you must take from Mykonos is to the tiny island of **Delos,** now an archeological park. The god Apollo was born on this sacred island. You can visit this beautiful and eerie island via tour boat from Mykonos, a half-hour away. In spring, wildflowers grow among the impressive ruins.

Agents at Mykonos harbor offer tours to Delos on alternate mornings for about 1,330 drachmas, but a regular ferry goes every morning at 9 a.m. for only a few drachmas. Once on Delos, you'll be charged a few drachmas to enter the park. The island has no refreshment facilities, so take a canteen.

Climb the centuries-old stone steps up the small mountain in the center of the island for a memorable view of what was once the center of the Mediterranean world.

Santorini: the best sunsets

Santorini is a volcanic island. Its towns of Oia (on the northeastern tip) and Thira (the capital—also known as Fira) are situated way up in the clouds, looking down on a dramatic harbor shaped like a huge cauldron. In the evening, people gather along the mountain to watch the magnificent colors of Santorini's sunset.

Ferries pull in at one of two jetties. If you are lucky, your ferry will pull in at the one just below town, giving you the opportunity to be transported to the center of town by donkey. Akrotiri, at the southeastern tip of the island, is one of Greece's most perfect excavations of a Bronze Age town, thought by many to be the legendary lost Atlantis.

Things to see on Santorini include churches in Thira; Oia, known for its antiques; the beaches of Kamari, Monolithos, and Perissa (black sand) on the southwest coast; the island's castles; and the active Nea Kaimeni volcano on the small island in the harbor (tour boats are available to take you there).

Buses are the least expensive way to tour the island. You also can rent a car or a moped and go it on your own. Santorini has great out-of-the-way country restaurants and isolated beaches.

Best beds on Santorini

Hotel rooms are a little hard to come by in Thira—if you insist on a room overlooking the harbor. If you do find one, you'll pay dearly for it. The **Atlantis,** *26 Amalias Ave.; tel. (30-286)322-9456,* is the nicest hotel, but it is expensive. The **Panorama,** *tel. (30-286)22479,* is touristy but affordable. It is less expensive to stay on the other side of town, away from the harbor.

The most unusual place to stay on the island—and one of the most unusual in all Greece—is the government-renovated traditional settlement at Oia. Fifteen old Greek houses, complete with kitchens, patios, and gardens, are for rent. Oia, like Thira, is perched high on the cliffs overlooking both sides of the island. Rates are about 1,330 drachmas per bed per night. The largest house has three double beds and three singles. The smallest has one double and one single. Contact the **Greek National Tourist Organization** (EOT in Greek), *Dieftynsi, Ekmetalefseos, 2 Amerikis St., Athens 10564, Greece,* for reservations.

The best of the Dodecanese Islands

Situated near the Turkish coast, the **Dodecanese Islands** have a more Turkish atmosphere than other Greek islands, because they recently were ruled by Turkey. Rhodes was a major trade hub of the ancient world. Patmos is considered one of the most beautiful. Kalymnos offers both a busy harbor town and quiet countryside.

The best island for golfers and gamblers

Rhodes is a favorite among European tourists. It has a more sophisticated atmosphere than other Greek playgrounds. The city is located in and around the walls of the medieval **Fortress of the Knights of St. John.** Wandering among the shops and restaurants inside the fortress is like visiting Disneyland. Its amusements include an evening sound-and-light show best seen from a boat off the harbor, costumed Greek dances at the summer wine festival, painting and handicraft exhibits, and an aquarium and a small zoo.

Outside the fortress walls is the **Rhodes Casino,** *tel. (30-241)24458* or *(30-241)24450,* open from 7 p.m. to 4 a.m. An 18-hole golf course is located at Afandou. The archeological site of Lindos is about an hour's drive from town.

Rhodes' most tempting shops

Rhodes is a free port with numerous shops selling Greek handicrafts and high-fashion European goodies. Gucci, Yves St. Laurent, and other top European designers have shops here. Exquisitely crafted modern gold jewelry is available.

Rhodes' hottest nights

Casa Castellano, *35 Aristotelous St.; tel. (30-241)28-803,* in a 15-century building with a garden full of flowers, is the island's most romantic place to have dinner.

Kontiki, *Limin Mandrakiou; tel. (30-241)22-477,* is a houseboat nightclub with a close-up view of the harbor.

The best places to stay

Luxury hotels with huge swimming pools are common on Rhodes: the **Belvedere,** *tel. (30-241)244-71,* the **Grand,** *1 Akti Miaoui; tel. (30-241)26284,* and the **Miramare Beach,** *tel. (30-241)24251* or *(30-682)2662.* The Rhodes Bay Hotel is the most luxurious, set against a cliff, on the top of which you can rent a bungalow situated among flowers and trees. Rooms are 16,000 drachmas to 22,000 drachmas.

Patmos: the holiest island

St. John the Divine is said to have written the last book of the New Testament in a mountain cave on **Patmos.** A huge 11th-century monastery atop the rocks marks the spot.

The best of the Sporades Islands

These pine and olive tree-covered islands are among Greece's most beautiful. Reached by plane or boat from the mainland port of Vollos, Skiathos is the major destination. Only three other of the Sporades Islands receive attention from tourists: Skopelos, Ilonissos, and Skyros, all quieter versions of Skiathos.

Skiathos: the best beaches

Skiathos has the best sand beaches (most beaches in Greece are pebbly) and a charming old town. Not as tourist-trodden as the other, more well-developed islands, such as Corfu,

Rhodes, and Mykonos, Skiathos is said to be the Greeks' favorite island. Its large British expatriate community colors its cultural atmosphere. A few of the resident artists are British. English pubs are sprinkled among the alleyways of the old town.

Vacation amenities include water skiing, windsurfing, and boating; yet those who want to get away from it all will find a sense of privacy. Small boats gather on the town waterfront each morning to offer tourists excursions to nearby islands, beaches, and the Kastro, a castle ruin on the other side (the tour here costs about 670 drachmas). The best organized trip is to an uninhabited island across from the town, which has a beautiful beach with flowers growing in the sand and a myriad of butterflies.

The best places to stay

The **Skiathos Palace,** on Koukounaries beach, *tel. (30-Skiathos)22242*, is the most luxurious hotel on the island—but it's a bit too perfect and not very Greek.

The government-run **Xenia,** also on Koukounaries, *tel. (30-Skiathos)22041,* has more charm if you want to stay on the beach. You'll find more atmosphere at a room in town or in a villa along one of the beach roads. Tourist agents can find you a room in just about any price range.

Savoring Skiathos' cuisine

Skiathos' seafood restaurants offer some of Greece's best meals, prepared with more European subtlety than elsewhere. You can't go wrong at any of the outdoor *tavernas* along the harbor in town. For the best lunch, go where the local fishermen eat—it's a plain establishment, right in the middle of the row of *tavernas* at the bottom of the hill.

Skopelos: the most beautiful island

Skopelos is an unspoiled Greek gem smothered in plum trees, where traditional Greek costumes are still the everyday dress. The lack of tourist buildup is what makes this island so inviting.

The most Turkish islands: the northeast Aegean

Less visited than others, these seven, which include Lesbos, Samos, and Chios, are the most Turkish of Greece's islands.

Lesbos: the prettiest in the group

The large, tree-covered island of **Lesbos** is one of the prettiest in this group. It has a Genovese castle in the northern town of Molyvosa and a petrified forest. The ancient castle above the lovely harbor town of Mytilani is the site of summer concerts performed by international artists each summer. The island's sardines, wine, and locally made ouzo are excellent. The best place to stay is the government-run **Xenia,** *tel. (30-251)22713,* with its pool that looks out toward Turkey. Double rooms are 3,720 drachmas.

Samos: the best red wine

Dominated by 5,000-foot Mt. Kerketeos, **Samos** has been famous for centuries for its dark red wine. It was considered by the ancients to be the birthplace of Hera, Zeus' wife. The human immortals Pythagoras and Epicurus were born here. The island is popular among Germans and Scandinavians.

Chios: the most inviting

This island's main attraction is a government-run guest settlement, a renovated 14th-century Genoan village. On a small island off Chios is another guest settlement built in an old church cloister that is both cheap and charming. Reserve with the **EOT**, *address above.*

Corfu: the most beautiful island in Greece

Northern **Corfu** is said to be the most beautiful island of Greece—which is saying something. (Corfu has recently gotten some bad press, however, because of trash left by hordes of tourists each summer.) Covered with lemon, orange, cyprus, fig, and olive groves, it is a lush place. Many of the island's beautiful villas belong to British expatriates. The main port, Kekira, is a town of Venetian elegance, more Italian than Greek. Corfu offers shops, hotels, restaurants, and night life.

The southern and western coasts of Corfu have the most striking scenery. Eight miles south of the port is the impressive **Achilleion Palace,** once a summer residence of Kaiser Wilhelm II of Germany, now a gambling casino. The jet set hangs out in **Paleokastritsa,** on the west coast. The north coast is the most touristy area, with several resort towns. **Kassiopi** is one of the least spoiled and most reasonable places to stay.

The best shopping on Corfu

One of Greece's best shopping sites is on Corfu. The island's specialties are woolen items, woodwork, jewelry, and embroidery. The island also has an artists' colony that produces paintings and sculptures. The best shopping is in **Hora,** in the center of town.

Corfu's best hotel

Cavalieri Corfu, *4 Kapodistriou St.; tel. (30-Corfu)30485,* an elegant Venetian mansion, was King George II's summer residence in the 1920s. It is expensive but not the highest-priced place on the island.

The best eats on Corfu

Corfu food is a combination of Greek and Italian. The island's wine is said to be among the nation's best. (Try the Hyma, local unbottled wine.)

Paliokastritza is a world-renowned eating spot. After lunch, swim in this beautiful cove where Odysseus is said to have washed ashore.

Crete: the most Eastern of the islands

Crete, the most Mideastern of Greece's islands, is a mini-country with its own lifestyle. A huge island of more than 5,000 square miles, it really warrants a separate trip. Unless you are planning an extended stay, do not try to visit Crete and the rest of Greece on the same trip.

Crete has some of the world's most impressive ruins. Rent a car to see the island. Camping is also recommended here.

The most important sight

The major attraction of Greece and one of the most important archeological sites of the Mediterranean world is the ancient capital of Minoan civilization, **Knossos.** If you're only in port for a day, you can sign up for tours to Knossos in Iraklion. However, the public bus, which leaves from Venizelou Square, is more economical.

The tourist belt

To the east of Iraklion is the tourist belt of Crete, with beaches and hotels. The most popular area is near **Elounda.** Nearby is the ancient city of Hersonissos; Gournia, a completely preserved Minoan town; and Zakros, another Minoan palace.

The least developed coasts

The southern and western coasts of Crete are the least developed. The interior is virtually unspoiled. Phaistos Palace is inland from the central-southern coast. Gortys, an old Roman town, is nearby, and Agia Triada, another Minoan site, is on the coast to the west. Limnes, a picturesque fishing village, and Matala, which has ancient cave tombs overlooking a beach, are modern-day resort areas near the ruins.

Europe's most beautiful gorge

The natural wonder of the island is the **Samarian Gorge,** located in central-western Crete. It is the largest—and many think the most beautiful—gorge in Europe and a popular jaunt for hikers. Buses leave from Hania early in the morning and drop hikers off at the top. The walk down takes about five hours. The gorge exits onto a beach, where you can stop for a swim.

Hania, the capital

Hania, the capital of Crete, has a picturesque Venetian harbor and narrow streets. Although not particularly beautiful, it has a special charm. Visit the Venetian quarter.

Accommodations are easy to find and reasonable. Among the best hotels are two old mansions: **Hotel Doma,** *124 Venizelos St.; tel. (30-821)217723,* once the British Consulate, and the **Contessa,** *15R Theofanous, Palia Limani; tel. (30-821)23966,* a bed-and-breakfast establishment by the harbor.

The best hotel

The **Elounda Beach Hotel,** *tel. (30-821)414123,* one of the world's best hotels, was designed by one of Greece's great architects, Spiro Kokotas. It is on a beautiful beach, set off by lots of flowers. The adjoining Elounda Mare has bungalows with private swimming pools. Terrific service, food, and amenities make this resort outstanding. It is pricey.

Best travel tips

Unless you come in July or August, when bookings are tight, wait until you arrive in Greece to arrange your itinerary. The local prices for tours, cruises, transportation, and hotels are much better than those of the agents at home.

The first thing to do when you arrive in Athens is visit the **EOT,** *address above.* The office is open from 8 a.m. to 9 p.m. Mondays through Fridays. Here you can pick up free publications describing the sites throughout the country. You also can pick up ferry and train schedules, change your money, and get directions.

Europe's cheapest cruises

You can spend several thousand dollars to sail the Greek islands for a week or two on a passenger liner. Or you can spend just a few dollars to do the same thing on a ferry. Greek ferries are incredibly inexpensive. A six-hour ride from Athens to Mykonos, for example, is only 150 drachmas deck class. In addition, with ferries you have the flexibility to stay in a port as long as you choose—and the opportunity to participate firsthand in Greek life.

Connections among the islands are numerous, and part of the adventure of ferry travel is finding out when you arrive on an island what the next possible connections are. (Inquiring about ferry, bus, train, or plane connections should be the first thing you do when you arrive at any Greek destination—they may not be daily.)

When you disembark, you'll be met by people wanting to rent you rooms. Most will have photo albums showing their accommodations. These rooms are much cheaper than hotels (although they usually don't have private baths). If the pier where you disembark is not in the middle of a fishing village, buses and taxis or donkeys will be waiting to get you where you want to go.

For information on ferry schedules, call the **Piraeus Authority,** *tel. (30-1)451-1311,* or the **Volos Port Authority,** *tel. (30-421)20-115.* To make ferry reservations by telephone, call *(30-294)22-700.*

The best way to see the mainland

Renting a car is the best way to see the mainland, especially in the Peloponnese. Rental cars are available from **Avis,** *tel. (30-1)322-4951;* **Hertz,** *tel. (30-1)994-2850;* **Budget,** *tel. (30-1)92-14771;* **Thrifty,** *tel. (30-1)922-1211.* Daily rates range from 1,996 drachmas to 2,660 drachmas. Weekly rates range from 19,285 drachmas to 62,510 drachmas.

Should you have car trouble while driving through Greece, the **Automobile and Touring Club of Greece** (ELPA in Greek) provides assistance to tourists for free. For emergency medical service on the mainland, dial *104.*

The best way to fly

Domestic air service in Greece is dirt cheap. **Olympic Airways,** *6 Ophonos St; tel. (30-1)961-6161* or *(30-1)92-92111,* provides the only domestic service in the country, offering numerous flights among the islands and to mainland destinations. Reserve as far in advance as possible—it's not easy to book on whim.

Flights from Athens to almost any of the islands cost about 8,400 drachmas. All domestic flights in Athens go through the domestic airport—not the international airport. Be sure to specify to your taxi driver which airport you want. On most islands, bus service between the village office of Olympic and the airport is available (for a minimal charge, sometimes free).

The worst way to travel

Although train travel in Greece is cheap, it is painfully slow. One line runs from Athens to encircle the Peloponnese, with offshoots to Kalamata and Kiparissia; another runs from Athens to Thessaloniki and onward to a dead end at the Turkey-Bulgaria border. First- and second-class season tickets allowing unlimited travel for a specified time are available at reduced rates. Round-trip tickets are 20% cheaper than one-way tickets.

Sailing: the best way to travel

Renting your own boat is the best way to explore the islands. You can rent a bareboat or a crewed luxury yacht with either sail or motor. Prices range from 11,970 drachmas to 931,000 drachmas per person, per day, including fuel and other supplies. Hiring a skipper costs an additional 4,655 drachmas. A cash deposit of 53,200 drachmas to 119,700 drachmas, depending on the size of the boat, is required before you can board.

To charter a bareboat, the charterer and at least one member of the crew must have a certificate or a letter of recommendation from a recognized sailing club.

To rent a boat, contact the **Yacht Brokers and Experts Association,** *34-36 Alkyonis St., Paleo Faliro; tel. (30-1)981-6582.*

Marina charges range from about 300 drachmas for three days to 5,500 drachmas for a month, depending on the marina and the length of the boat. You'll find more than 10 yacht repair yards along Greek shores.

How to get good hotel prices

The only time it makes sense to make hotel reservations from home is if you'll be arriving in Greece in July or August. To reserve hotel rooms directly, contact the **Hellenic Chamber of Commerce,** *24 Stadiou; tel. (30-1)323-6962.*

Your best bet, however, is to wait until you arrive and stop by the hotel reservation desk at the airport.

If you have the time and energy, shop around. Offer about 200 drachmas less than the going rate. The Greeks always say their bottom price is a hundred or two more than yours. You can get rooms on the islands for as little as 1,995 drachmas in the spring and fall. Prices rise by about 30% in July and August.

The Greek government has begun a program of restoring traditional Greek homes around the country for tourist rental. The village of Oia on the island of Santorini is one. Another is at Mesta on the island of Chios.

EOT-run campsites are located in some of the most picturesque parts of the mainland. One is at the foot of the legendary Mt. Olympus. Charges for using the campsites are 240 drachmas to 400 drachmas for adults and 120 drachmas to 220 drachmas for children over 10. Children under 10 can stay for free. You have to pay additional fees for vehicles and electricity. If you're traveling without a tent, you can rent a hut with two to four beds for 1,500 drachmas to 2,000 drachmas.

Chapter 12

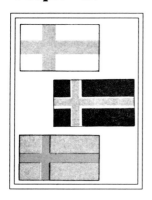

THE BEST OF SCANDINAVIA

Summer, when the sun hardly sets over Scandinavia, is the best time to visit this northern land. After months of darkness, Scandinavians come out of hibernation to celebrate the golden months of June and July with parties that would go on until dawn—except dawn never comes.

Scandinavia—for our purposes Denmark, Norway, Sweden, and Finland—has both cosmopolitan cities and the most enormous wilderness area in Europe. Lapland, which crosses Norway, Sweden, and Finland, is a stunning region with glittering glaciers and bright blue skies. Lapps herd their reindeer across the tundra as they have for centuries. The region's parks offer well-marked trails and huts, where hikers can sleep in comfort.

The best way to explore Scandinavia is with the **Scandinavian Rail Pass,** which allows unlimited travel in Scandinavia for 21 days. First-class passes are $320; second-class passes are $210. For information contact the **Scandinavian National Tourist Office,** *655 Third Ave., New York, NY 10019; (212)949-2333.*

Denmark: the most accessible country

The southernmost of the Scandinavian countries has a romantic landscape crisscrossed by waterways and dotted with thatched-roof houses. It is easy to imagine the trolls, werewolves, and sorcerers of Danish legend; Hans Christian Andersen was inspired by these legends to write his famous fairy tales.

Denmark, the most accessible of the Scandinavian countries, is the only one attached to mainland Europe. North of Germany and south of Sweden and Norway, Denmark is made up of the Jutland Peninsula, which shares a border with Germany, and two major islands, Zealand and Funen. Altogether, the Danish islands number 480. Most are uninhabited.

The best way to meet the Danes

Through the **Meet the Danes** program, you can spend an evening in a Danish home in any of eight cities: Århus, Aalborg, Esbjerg, Fredericia, Lønstrup, Odense, Roskilde, or Skive. Local tourist offices can arrange the visit if you give them 24 hours notice. For more information, contact the **Danish Tourist Board,** *75 Rockefeller Plaza, New York, NY 10019; (212)949-2333.*

Copenhagen: the best fun

Copenhagen (København), on the east coast of the island of Zealand, is a city dedicated to entertainment. What other capital city revolves around an amusement park such as **Tivoli Gardens**? Merrymaking Danes of all ages scream with fear and excitement aboard Tivoli's rides. (The best is Det Flyvende Taeppe, or The Flying Carpet.) The famous Ferris wheel has a far-reaching view.

Built in 1843 on 20 acres in the heart of Copenhagen, Tivoli is more than just an amusement park. It has gardens, lakes, theaters, dance halls, games, bars, and scores of restaurants to suit every budget. At night Tivoli is illuminated by 100,000 colored lights, and you can enjoy vaudeville acts, concerts, music, and dancing.

Stroget: the best place to stroll

The longest pedestrian thoroughfare in the world, the **Stroget** (Strolling Place) meanders through the heart of Copenhagen. This mile-long stretch is lined with cafés, banks, department stores, and boutiques selling everything from cheap T-shirts to fine Icelandic sweaters and expensive watches. The most elegant shops are clustered at the eastern end. The **Sweater Market,** *Frederiksberggade 15; tel. (45-1)15-27-73,* sells hand-knit designer sweaters.

The Stroget is actually an area made up of five streets: Frederiksberggade, Nygade, Vimmelskaftet, Amagertorv, and Ostergade. It is between the city's two main squares: Raashuspiadsen and Kongens-Nytorv. All this is made more confusing by the fact that "the Stroget" isn't marked as such on city maps.

The two best museums

Copenhagen has 40 public museums and galleries, most within easy walking distance of the Stroget. The largest is the **Nationalmuseet** (National Museum), which has the best display of Viking artifacts in the world. It is behind the Christiansborg Palace, where Parliament meets.

Nearby is **Ny Carlsberg Glyptotek,** which has extensive collections of Roman, Etruscan, and Egyptian art, as well as a respectable number of Impressionist paintings. Its arboretum is a tranquil place where you can sit beneath immense trees and listen to a Gregorian chant.

A beer-lovers' best

If you love beer and don't mind crowds, visit the **Carlsberg** and **Tuborg breweries.** The tours and beer are free, and it's always a good time—especially after a few tastes.

Copenhagen's two castles

Rosenborg, *Øster Voldgade 4A,* a 17th-century castle, houses the crown jewels and the royal treasures of the Danes. **Amalieborg Castle,** *Amalieborg Square,* is the residence of the royal family. Witness the changing of the guard daily at noon.

Capital night life

Copenhagen's chic set frequents **Annabel's,** *Lille Kongensgade 16; tel. (45-1)11-20-20.* Fashions straight out of Paris' finest boutiques hang on the bodies here. Officially, Annabel's is a private club, but if you look terribly chic you'll probably get in.

Montmartre, *Nørregade 41; tel. (45-1)11-46-67,* is Copenhagen's largest nightclub, attracting the best jazz bands of Europe. The music is terrific, but it's too crowded to enjoy the dance floor.

Vin & Olgood, *Skindergade 45; tel. (45-1)13-26-25,* is a rowdy beer-drinking joint with live oompah bands and busty waitresses in leather aprons serving beer in large steins. All age groups can be seen at the trestle tables, arms locked and voices harmonizing (or disharmonizing) in song. No one is left out; this is a good place to go if you're out on your own.

Avoid the bars in the much-touted **Nyhavn,** or sailors' district. They attract rowdy drunks and can be rather depressing.

The best legal sins

Prostitution is legal in Denmark, and bodies of all kinds are for sale. The traditional sex clubs aren't particularly exciting, but the unique sauna clubs, escort services, and massage parlors are a different story. Services cater to women as well as to men, and escorts are screened for diseases. The top sex clubs and escort services are the **VIP Club,** *Nygade 3; tel. (45-1)11-46-01;* **Rendezvous,** *tel. (45-1)37-05-65;* **Venus,** *tel. (45-1)39-98-93* or *(45-1)85-92-41;* and **Exclusive Escort,** *tel. (45-1) 86-00-32.*

The cheapest way to go

The major problem with Copenhagen is that it is expensive. The best way to cut costs is by buying the **Copenhagen Card,** available from the **tourist office,** *22 H.C. Andersen Blvd.,* train stations, Copenhagen's hotels, and travel agents. You can buy cards good for one to three days. They allow entry to 36 museums, unlimited travel on buses and trains within the city, and a 50% discount on the ferry crossing to Sweden. The one-day card is about $12; the two-day $20; and the three-day $25.

The best eating

The most elegant restaurant in town is **Belle Terrasse,** *Tivoli; tel. (45-1)12-11-36,* which has lush gardens and live music. While it is romantic, it is also expensive. Reservations are necessary.

Another good restaurant in Tivoli is **Faergekroen,** *tel. (45-1)12-94-12,* a rustic inn on the lake. Try the Danish specialty called *hvid skieperloen sobs,* a sort of meat-and-potato shepherd's pie.

Fiskehusets Restaurant, *Gammel Strand 34; tel. (45-1)14-76-30,* across the canal from Christiansborg, is the best seafood restaurant.

The best hotels

D'Angleterre, *Kongens Nytorv 34; tel. (45-1)12-00-95,* is the oldest and most fashionable hotel in Copenhagen, located near the activity of Nyhavn. Built in 1795, it has old-fashioned wood-paneled rooms. It also has a good French restaurant and a popular nightclub. Double rooms start at $250 a night.

Another fine hotel is the **Plaza,** *Bernstorffsgade 4; tel. (45-1)14-92-62,* where rooms are filled with antiques and paneled with mahogany. Double rooms start at $200 a night. Reserve months in advance.

The **Hotel Capriole,** *Frederiksberg Alle 7; tel. (45-1)21-64-64,* is a lovely old two-story building shaded by big trees. Rooms are quaint, furnished in unpainted wood, and cost $70, including breakfast.

Hotel Sankt Joergen, *Julius Thomsensgade 22; tel. (45-1)37-15-11,* is a comfortable hotel with brass doorknobs and wall-to-wall carpeting. Rooms are $65, including breakfast.

Roskilde: the first capital

The ancient city of **Roskilde,** west of Copenhagen, was the capital of Denmark until 1445. It is also the site of the first Danish church, built in A.D. 960. Members of Denmark's royalty are buried in marble and alabaster tombs in the 12th-century cathedral (known as the Westminster Abbey of Denmark), including Harald the Bluetooth, a 10th-century king; Queen Margarethe, once queen of Scandinavia; and Christian X, the Danish king during World War II who wore a yellow star to demonstrate his sympathy for the Jews.

The **Vikingeskibshallen** (Viking Ship Museum) at Havnen displays five Viking ships painstakingly pieced together from hundreds of pieces of wreckage. An amazingly well-preserved seagoing cargo ship from A.D. 1000 sits in the main hall.

Lindenborg Kro, *Holbaekvej 90; tel. (45-2)40-21-11,* just outside Roskilde, is one of the most pleasant inns in Denmark. The original inn, built 300 years ago, burned in 1967, but a new one was built on the site. Double rooms are $65 and $75 a night, including breakfast.

Denmark's best castles

If you see only one castle in your lifetime, it should be **Frederiksborg.** This 17th-century treasure trove in Hillerod is surrounded by a moat and has an ornate, gilded chapel with a rare 1610 Compenius organ. Here, Danish kings were crowned. The castle houses the most important national history museum. Every square foot is covered with art and antiques, including four-poster beds, ebony cabinets, coats of arms, and tapestries.

Kronborg Castle at Elsinore is the bleak and imposing castle where Shakespeare set *Hamlet.* It has secret passages and turrets, exactly as you would imagine. Built in 1574 and restored in 1629, it now houses the Danish Maritime Museum.

Nyborg Castle, on the island of Funen, is the oldest royal castle still standing in Scandinavia and is believed to have been built in the 12th century. Until the 15th century, the moated castle guarded one of the most strategic spots in the country. Be sure to see the knight's hall and the old *danehof,* which was used by the medieval parliament, an uneasy alliance between noblemen and clergy. Nyborg can be reached by ferry from Zealand.

Egeskov, near Odense, is the best preserved moated castle in Europe. A Renaissance structure with magnificent gardens, it was built in 1554 on oak pillars in the middle of a small lake. Legend tells of a maiden who bore an illegitimate child to the young nobleman of the castle and was locked in one of the castle towers from 1559 to 1604. The landscaped gardens are open to the public every day. But the castle itself is a private home and can be visited only during chamber music concerts, which are held in the castle's great hall during the summer.

Denmark's best bike route

The **Haervejen** (pronounced Hairvine), a marked bike trail, follows an ancient military road along Denmark's spine. It leads through the center of Jutland past menhirs (large monumental stones erected by prehistoric Danes), barrows (mounds of earth or stones over burial sites), runestones etched with characters from the ancient Scandinavian alphabet, and churches built by the first Danish Christians.

Haervejen runs 170 miles from Viborg in central Jutland south to the Eider River in Germany. For centuries, it was the only road connecting Scandinavia with continental Europe. The official start is at the corner of St. Jørgensvej and Lille St. Mikkelsgade.

Every year a full-scale week-long group trek along the Haervejen is organized the first weekend in July. For more information on the Haervejen, contact the **Danish Tourist Board, *655 Third Ave., New York, NY 10017; (212)949-2333,* or Dantourist,** *Hulgade 21, DK-5700, Svendborg, Denmark; tel. (45-9)21-07-41.*

The two prettiest Baltic islands

Aerø, a tiny island in the Baltic, is the best place to get a glimpse of the traditional Danish seafaring life. A five-hour trip from Copenhagen by train and then ferry, it is one of many Danish islands in the archipelago north of the German coast.

Brightly painted little fishing villages fringe this 22-mile-long island. Its picturesque beaches are occasionally dotted with nude sunbathers. Inland, thatched-roof farmhouses break the rolling hills. The villages are tiny, but they usually have hotels and bakeries.

Aerøskøbing, on Aerø, is Denmark's most carefully preserved medieval village, dating from the 13th century. Its narrow cobblestoned streets are lined with gingerbread houses roofed with round tiles and painted blue or red. They were once the homes of Aerø's sea captains.

Bornholm, a Danish island between Sweden and Poland, has the world's finest-grain sand and is known for its grandfather clocks and smoked herring. The island's towns balance on sloping rocks. The ruins of a 13th-century castle can be explored at Hammershus Slot. And half-timbered houses and ancient round churches, once used as protection against pirates and enemy armies, still stand here. The greatest round church is in Ølsker. Built in 1150, the structure is literally round.

The best natural sight on the island is at **Rø**—a 72-foot rock formation filled with columns, caves, and crevices. Its name means Sacred Thing. The most beautiful beach is in **Dueodde** on the south coast, where the sand is incredibly fine, dunes rise 45 feet, and there is a 145-foot lighthouse. If you tire of the sea, explore Bornholm's forest, **Almindingen,** the third largest in Denmark.

Norway: the most rugged

Norway, with the second-lowest population density in Europe, is the most rugged Scandinavian country. It has deep-gouged sharp mountains rising from the jagged coastlines and frigid glaciers glittering beneath the midnight sun. Grass-thatched houses occupy little patches of land on steep hillsides. This is a country that challenges the sportsman, with superb skiing, hiking, sailing, hunting, and mountain climbing.

Oslo: the world's most forested capital

Oslo, the capital of Norway, is the most heavily forested capital in the world—it encompasses farms as well as nightclubs. The 175-square-mile city was founded in the 11th century by Viking King Oslo. Because it was completely destroyed by fire in 1824, little medieval architecture remains. The finest residences that survived are along Radhusgate.

Oslo's most dramatic sight

Akershus Castle, the ancient protector of the city, looms from atop a cliff that juts out into the eastern half of the harbor. The well-preserved medieval structure (built in 1300 by King Haakon V Magnusson) was an impregnable fortress and royal residence for several hundred years. Although it suffered through nine battles, it was never conquered and eventually was transformed into a Renaissance palace by Danish-Norwegian King Christian IV.

Today, the castle is used by the government for state occasions. The bastions offer tremendous views of Oslo. Inside, some of the works of Expressionist painter Edvard Munch are on display.

Scandinavia's oldest church

The oldest church in Scandinavia, **Gamle Aker Kicke,** *Akersbakken 26,* is still in use after 888 years. Daily services are held May 15 through Sept. 10, and Sunday services are held year-round (at 11 a.m.). You can visit the church with an appointment on Tuesdays and Thursdays. The tour is free.

Top sights

Next to Akershus Castle is **Norsk Hjemmefrontmuseum,** Norway's Resistance museum, which documents World War II and Norway's resistance to the Nazis.

Domkirken (Oslo's cathedral), *Stortorvet,* built between 1694 and 1699, has its original altarpiece and pulpit. The stained-glass windows were created by the well-loved Norwegian artist Emanuel Vigeland (the younger brother of sculptor Gustav Vigeland). The bronze doors and ceiling decorations are also impressive, and the cathedral's organ rises five floors. Sunday services are at 11 a.m. and 7:30 p.m.

Rådhuset, Oslo's City Hall, completed in 1950, was embellished in a collective effort by Norway's greatest artists and designers. Inside are more than 2,000 square yards of bold, colorful murals, including Munch's *Life.* The walls are a rainbow of colorful stones and woods.

The **Nasjonalgalleriet** (National Gallery), *Universitetsgaten 13,* has paintings by Norwegians, including works by romantic landscape painter John Christian Dahl, statues by Gustav Vigeland, and a wing devoted to Edvard Munch.

The best place to see works by Munch, the Expressionist painter who died in 1944, is the **Munch Museum,** *Toyengate 53,* filled with 1,000 paintings, 4,500 drawings, 15,000 prints, and notes, letters, and sketches by the artist.

Norway's most memorable sculptures are at **Frognerparken,** a 75-acre park behind the Royal Palace devoted to the works of Gustav Vigeland. In 1921, the city gave the sculptor free rein in the park. The result: a 1,150-piece collection of huge, writhing nude figures illustrating the human struggle. The works were once the subject of much controversy.

The best of the Vikings

Three Viking burial ships excavated on the shores of the Oslo fjord, whose clay had preserved them since A.D. 800 and A.D. 900, are kept at the **Vikingskiphuset** (Viking Ship House), *Huk Aveny 35; tel. (47-2)43-83-79,* on the Bygdoy Peninsula. The most spectacular is the *Oseberg,* a 64-foot dragon ship with animals carved on its prow. It is believed to have been the burial ship of Harald Fairhair's grandmother and her slave, who were buried in it along with 15 horses, an ox, 4 dogs, and some artifacts.

The greatest Norwegian adventure

The balsa-log raft *Kon Tiki,* on which Norwegian scientist Thor Heyerdahl sailed 5,000 miles in 1947, is kept at the **Kon Tiki Museum** on the Bygdoy Peninsula. The *Kon Tiki,* designed according to specifications for early Peruvian boats, sailed from Callao, Peru to Raroia, Polynesia to prove that pre-Inca Indians could have crossed from South America to populate Polynesia.

The museum also houses the papyrus *Ra II,* in which Heyerdahl crossed the Atlantic from North Africa to Barbados in 1970, and artifacts from Heyerdahl's voyage to Easter Island.

A close-up view of folk life

Historic buildings from all over Norway have been transported to the **Norsk Folkemuseum** (Norwegian Folk Museum), a 35-acre area on the Bygdoy Peninsula. Sights include: Raulandstua, one of the oldest wooden dwellings in the country; a hand-built wooden stave church that dates back to 1200; 150 historic log cabins; Lapp artifacts; and a reconstruction of the last apartment of Norwegian playwright Henrik Ibsen.

The highest lookout in Scandinavia

For a dizzying view, climb to the lookout tower at **Tryvannstarnet.** To get there, take the Holmenkollen subway near the National Theater in Oslo to the end of the line. From there, a 30-minute ride by street car takes you to Voksenkollenn. Then it's a 15-minute walk uphill to Tryvannstarnet, the highest lookout in Scandinavia.

Another 20-minute walk down the hill leads to the **Holmenkollen ski jump,** one of the most famous in the world and the site of Olympic competitions in 1952. At the base of the jump is the **Ski Museum,** which displays 2,500-year-old ski equipment and equipment used on polar explorations.

Holmenkollen has the widest network of ski trails in the world—more than 1,300 miles of them. The best skiers in the world gather for the Holmenkollen Ski Festival each winter to compete in downhill, slalom, cross-country, and ski jumping competitions, drawing thousands of spectators.

The best way to make friends

The **Know the Norwegians** program, sponsored by the **Oslo Travel Association,** *Raadhusgate 19,* and the Lions Club allows you to visit local English-speaking families. Invitations are not arranged during July and August.

Eating well

Norwegian cuisine consists primarily of fish. The smoked salmon and mackerel are delicious. However, the meat, especially during fall hunting season, is equally good—try a reindeer or moose steak. The Norwegian *koldtbord* is a buffet that includes everything from herring to roast beef.

The best seafood restaurant in Oslo is **La Mer,** *Pilestredet 31; tel. (47-2)20-34-45.* It is open every day except Sundays after 4 p.m. Meals are about $25.

Molla, *Sagveien 21; tel. (47-2)37-54-50,* a fish and game restaurant in an old textile mill on the banks of the Akerselva River, was the setting for Oskar Braaten's novels about factory workers at the beginning of the century. It is open daily except Sundays after 3 p.m. Reservations are necessary.

Etoile, *Karl Johans Gate 31; tel. (47-2)42-93-90,* on the top floor of the Grand Hotel, has a beautiful view and serves savory French and Norwegian food. It is open daily from noon to midnight.

Tostrupkjelleren, *Karl Johans Gate 25; tel. (47-2)42-14-70,* is a basement restaurant popular with politicians, journalists, and business people. Meals are about $50.

Noberto, *Majorstuveien 36; tel. (47-2)46-02-02,* has gotten rave reviews from food editors. Meals range from $12 to $25.

Oslo nights

Oslo doesn't have enough hotels to house all its tourists, so make reservations well in advance, especially if you are visiting during the summer. The **Oslo Travel Association,** *address above,* can make reservations for you if you send $2.09 per person plus $12.51 advance deposit with a self-addressed international-reply envelope at least two weeks ahead of your stay.

The **Holmenkollen Park Hotel Rica,** *Kongeveien 26, Holmenkollasen; tel. (47-2)14-60-90,* has cozy rooms with views of the city. The public salon has a huge fireplace, and the restaurant serves Norwegian specialties. Rooms are $103 to $142 a night.

The **Scandinavia,** *Holbergs Gate 30; tel. (47-2)11-30-00,* is Norway's largest hotel. Located near the Royal Palace, its rooms have views of the city and the fjord. It has a pool, five restaurants, and several bars. Rooms are $198 to $271 a night.

Sta Katarinahjemmet, *Majorstuveien 21B; tel. (47-2)60-13-70,* is run by Dominican sisters and is quite inexpensive. Every room has hot water and a balcony, but showers and bathrooms are shared. Doubles are $35 to $40.

Best sights outside Oslo

Fredrikstad, a fortified town with ramparts, a drawbridge, and a moat, has a flourishing artists' colony. The cobblestoned streets are lined with 18th-century houses and artisans' workshops. You can take an hour-long guided tour of the workshops weekdays between 9 a.m. and 3 p.m. for about $2. Outside town is the 17th-century **Kongsten Fort,** which has secret passages and dungeons.

Tønsberg, Norway's oldest town (founded in A.D. 870), is where Norwegian kings were once crowned. The **Vestfold Folk Museum** at the town's entrance contains relics of the once-mighty whaling industry and of Viking chieftains. A trip to Tønsberg can be combined with a trip to **Sandefjoord,** once a great whaling town. This summer resort is just two hours by express train from Oslo. Old whalers work as guides in the **Whaling Museum,** relating stories about the whaling days and explaining the sights.

A 13th-century Norwegian stave church is located in **Heddal,** southwest of Oslo. Only 32 of these tiered timber churches with their pointy shingled roofs are still standing.

Bergen: a music-lovers' best

If you like Grieg's music, you'll love **Bergen.** The city's native son left traces wherever he went. And you can hear his music at the ultramodern **Grieg Hall,** which seats 1,420.

Grieg's music also is played during the international arts festival held in Bergen during the last week in May. (The festival also features opera, ballet, and folklore.) Details are available from the **Festival Office,** *Grieghallen, Lars Hilles Gate 3A; tel. (47-5)230-010.*

Climb up to **Troldhaugen,** the summer villa of the composer in Hop, outside Bergen. The Victorian house contains Grieg's Steinway grand piano (which is used for concerts given at the house during the annual festival). The composer created many of his best works in a cottage on the estate. Grieg and his wife are buried in a cliff grotto here.

Bergen was the seat of the Viking kingdom of Norway until the 14th century and was a member of the Hanseatic League, which linked free towns in northern Germany and adjacent countries for trade and protection. Most of ancient Bergen was destroyed by a fire in 1702. A row of Hanseatic timbered houses, rebuilt along the waterfront after the fire, is all that remains. This area, called **Bryggen,** houses the **Hanseatic Museum,** which illustrates commercial life in Bergen hundreds of years ago.

The oldest building in Bergen, dating back to the 12th century, is a Romanesque church called **St. Mary's.** The baroque pulpit, donated by Hanseatic merchants, is covered with carved figures symbolizing the Virtues. Visit during one of the free organ concerts held at 8 p.m. on Thursday evenings in the summer.

The **Fantoft Stave Church,** built in 1150, is covered with both pagan and Christian designs—serpents, dragons, and crosses. It was built to withstand the winter wind and has overlapping roofs and interlocking gables.

The best of Sweden

Progressive, wealthy **Sweden,** the fourth-largest nation in Europe, is sparsely inhabited. This California-sized country is made up of wheat plains, pine forests, thatched and timbered villages, cosmopolitan cities, historic islands, mountains, waterfalls, 95,000 lakes, and miles of rugged coastline. Best of all, it is the least-traveled (therefore, the least-crowded) European capital.

Stockholm: Mother Nature's favorite

While **Stockholm** has museums and fine old buildings (nearly all the same size and painted mustard yellow), the city's real attractions are natural: the waterways, the beaches, the parks, and the 24,000 little islands of the archipelago that lead to the Baltic Sea (most of them uninhabited). The city is built on 14 islands in Lake Malaren, and, believe it or not, the waterways are clean enough for swimming.

The heart of the city

Founded 700 years ago, Stockholm's roots are visible in the twisting streets of the medieval old town, **Gamla Sta'n.** At the heart of the area is the **Stortorget** (the old market-place), surrounded by little streets lined with thick-walled, crooked buildings, boutiques, galleries, and inexpensive restaurants.

The old town is dominated by the 18th-century **Royal Palace.** (During the summer you can see the changing of the guard here at noon on Mondays through Saturdays and at 1 p.m. on Sundays.) Parts of the palace can be visited, including the king's throne room, the chapel royal, the royal treasury, and the apartments of state, which have magnificent baroque ceilings and fine tapestries. Look for the crown jewels or the silver throne.

The royal burying ground

On the small island of Riddarholm, next to the old town, is **Riddarholm Church,** the burial place of Swedish kings and queens. Queen Desideria (Désirée), the childhood sweet-heart of Napoleon Bonaparte, is buried here in a green marble sarcophagus. Born Bernadine Eugénie Désirée Clary (but known simply as Désirée), she married Marshal Jean Baptiste Bernadotte after Napoleon married the sophisticated Josephine. Bernadotte was elected king of Sweden in 1818 (he took the name Carl XIV) and later took part in the battle against Napoleon at Leipzig. Désirée hated the long Scandinavian winters and longed for her native Paris until her death in Sweden in 1860.

Top sights

To the east of Gamla Sta'n is **Djurgården** (Deer Park), a lake-encircled forested park. Stockholm's great estates and gardens are located here, as well as the Royal Flagship *Wasa,* a man-of-war that sank 20 minutes into its maiden voyage in 1628.

Skansen, an open-air museum on Djurgården, displays more than 150 18th- and 19th-century buildings from all over Scandinavia, including windmills, manor houses, workshops, and a complete town quarter. At the old workshops you can see how early printing, silversmithing, glassblowing, and leather making were done. During the summer, chamber music concerts are held at the Skogaholm manor house. At night you can dance in the outdoor pavilion.

The **Nordiska Museet** (Nordic Museum), also on Djurgården, is the world's best museum on Scandinavian life, with tools, clothing, and furnishings illustrating life from the 1500s to today.

The **Nationalmuseet** (National Museum of Art), at the tip of a peninsula on Sødra Blasieholmshamnen, has works by Rembrandt and Rubens and a rare collection of Russian icons, most from the 1400s. Room 45 features the works of Rembrandt, including *Portrait of an Old Man* and *Portrait of an Old Woman.*

Stadshuset (city hall), on the island of Kungsholmen, designed by Ragnar Ostberg, is one of the finest examples of modern architecture in Europe. The poet Yeats said of the building, "No architectural work comparable to it has been accomplished since the Italian cities felt the excitement of the Renaissance." Completed in 1923, the city hall is dominated by a lofty tower topped with three crowns, the symbol of the defunct Scandinavian Union. Its Golden Hall is decorated with 19-million pieces of pure gold mosaic. Banquets following the Nobel Peace Prize ceremony are held here. Climb the tower for a view of Stockholm's islands and waterways.

Drottningholm Palace, on Queen's Island in Lake Mälaren, is the French-style, 17th-century palace of the royal family, surrounded by fountains and parks. The **Drottningholm Court Theater,** the best-preserved 18th-century theater in the world, is located on the palace grounds. Each summer, operas and ballets are staged with full 18th-century regalia. For reservations, contact the theater, *P.O. Box 27050, S-10251, Stockholm.*

The **Moderna Museet** (Museum of Modern Art), on the island of Skeppsholmen, has works by Andy Warhol, Salvador Dali, Picasso, Braque, and Leger.

The best nights out

If you're interested in meeting someone of the opposite sex, the place to go in Stockholm is the **Café Opera,** located in the same building as the national opera across from the Grand Hotel and directly across the bridge from the Royal Palace. The Café Opera has a dance floor, a bar, and a casino, where men toss away thousands of krona playing roulette while some of the most beautiful unattached females in the world dance with one another or sit lingering over drinks.

For a different kind of fun, stop by **Grona Lund's Tivoli** (not to be confused with Tivoli in Copenhagen). Enjoy the amusements and go up to the top of the revolving tower for a wide view of Stockholm. Tivoli is open April to September from 2 p.m. to midnight. **Jump In,** a disco in the park, attracts a lively crowd and is open from 8 p.m. to midnight.

Stockholm's best hotels

Nobel Peace Prize winners usually stay at Stockholm's finest, the **Grand Hotel,** *Sodra*

Blasieholmshamnen 8; tel. (46-8)221020. It is the best hotel in Sweden and one of the best in the world. The staff is intelligent, thoughtful, and prompt. This luxurious, expensive establishment faces the Royal Palace and has two restaurants and a bar. Ask for a room facing the water.

Runners up to the Grand are the **Sergel Plaza,** *Brunkebergstorg 9; tel. (46-8)226600,* and the **Royal Viking,** *Vasagatan 1; tel. (46-8)141000.* Another well-regarded hotel is the **Malardrottningen,** *Riddarholmen; tel. (46-8)243600,* across from the old city.

The **Diplomat,** *Strandvagen 7C; tel. (46-8)63- 58-00,* at the edge of the diplomatic quarter, is a small, sophisticated, expensive hotel furnished with antiques. It has a cocktail bar and an elegant teahouse.

Lady Hamilton, *Storkyrkobrinken 5, 2-111 40; tel. (46-8)234-680,* in the old town of Stockholm, has rooms furnished with nautical antiques. Nearby church bells mark every quarter-hour, but you get used to them after a couple of nights. Double rooms are 700 Swedish kronor per night.

If you are looking for a bargain that's full of charm, try **Hotel Anno 1647,** *Mariagrand 3, on the Island of Sodermalm; tel. (46-8)440480.* The old brick building that dates (surprise) to 1647, was originally the home of a tailor who achieved a senior position in his guild. It has a fine view of Gamla Sta'n.

How to sleep like a king

If you don't mind staying outside Stockholm, you can sleep like a king in the home of one of Sweden's aristocrats. Sprawling country estates are now open to paying guests on a limited basis. These are not hotels; they are private homes, subject to the whims of owners who may be ambivalent about having guests at their hearth. The following country estates take guests (they charge about $100 a day):

Johannishus, *37205 Johannishus; tel. (46-455)33011,* near the southern town of Karlskrona, is surrounded by 18,000 acres of woods. Contact Count Hans Wachtmeister.

Orbyhus, *74060 Orbyhus; tel. (46-295)11061,* north of Upsala, is the home of the Duchess d'Otrante. Contact Birgitta Tragardh.

Trollenas, *24100 Eslov; tel. (46-413)45100,* southwest of Sweden, is a 400-year-old castle on a sprawling estate. Contact Baron Nils Trolle.

Best restaurant, best wine cellar

The Swedes like to eat, which is why Stockholm has so many first-class restaurants.

Ulriksdals Wärdshus, *Erlichstals Slottspark 1, 17171 Solna; tel. (46-8)850815,* located on the grounds of a royal park a few miles outside Stockholm, has a sweeping view of gardens stretching down to the water. This might have been the setting for the movie *Elvira Madigan.* The current owner, Lauri Nilsson, is the ninth restaurateur to have run an establishment on this spot.

Nilsson has the best—and best engineered—wine cellar in Scandinavia. Press a button, and things happen. A tour takes you from one automated passage to another and finally into the inner sanctum, a kind of bacchanalian boardroom, where Sweden's most posh wine-tasting club gathers to chew bread and spit Mouton Rothschild into crystal bowls. At the center of the room is the pièce de résistance, a high-tech wine spittoon that seems to be a combination of a pagan baptismal and some cruel machine you would find in a dentist's office. The queen of Sweden comes here to taste champagne.

The food at Ulriksdals Wärdshus is superb. Chef Carl-Heinz Krucken specializes in preparing a butterfly of chopped avocado with Swedish caviar and chopped onions. For the main course try the noisettes of reindeer with raisin and green peppercorn sauce. The cloudberry mousse dessert is delicious.

Close seconds

The **Operakallaren,** *Operahuset; tel. (46-8)24-27-00* or *(46-8)11-11-25,* prepares state banquets for the Royal Palace. Rooms are enormous, with high ceilings, carved oak paneling, and fine paintings. The smorgasbord is excellent. Reservations are necessary.

Another good restaurant in Stockholm is the **Coq Blanc,** *Regeringsgatan 116153,* a spacious and comfortable restaurant decorated with what seem to be thousands of chickens and eggs in various forms of artistic torment. The food is good, especially the morel-stuffed filet of sole and the fried filet of turbot in vermouth sauce.

Wedholms Fisk, *Nybrokajen 17; tel. (46-8)104874,* has a gray and rather forbidding interior but serves excellent food. Specialties include marmite of fish, shellfish soup, and fricassee of turbot, sole, and salmon with vegetables in champagne sauce.

Caesar, *Fredrikshovsgatan 4; tel. (46-8)60-15-99,* a small neighborhood restaurant, rivals many of the better restaurants in the city. The chef is creative, and prices are reasonable.

Fem Sma Hus, *Nygrand 10; tel. (46-8)10-04-82,* is a maze of five interconnected buildings and a medieval cellar with vaults, arches, and alcoves. Try the Swedish specialties: reindeer and salmon. Reservations are recommended.

Don't bother looking for a giant smorgasbord. You may find one at Sunday lunch; otherwise, this famous feature of Scandinavian cuisine hardly figures at all in Stockholm's best restaurants. Ditto for Swedish meatballs.

Best side trips from Stockholm

Sigtuna, founded at the beginning of the 11th century on the shores of Lake Mälaren, is Sweden's oldest town, containing remnants of Vikings and early Christians. Low-timbered buildings line Storagatan. Sweden's first cathedral, St. Peter's, is here, along with the 13th-century Monastery of St. Maria.

Uppsala, Sweden's major university town, has a famous 15th-century cathedral and a 16th-century castle. The first Swedish university was founded here in 1477. (The university at Uppsala remains a well-respected institution.)

Walpurgis Eve, April 30, is the best time to visit Uppsala. Alumni and students wearing white caps celebrate the rebirth of spring and the death of winter with a torchlight parade and festivities until dawn. Thousands gather to join in hymns to spring and to hear speeches about the end of winter.

Walpurgis Eve, according to folklore, is when witches ride. It is the night before the birthday of St. Walpurgis, the medieval protectress against magic.

Gamla Uppsala (the old quarter of Uppsala), two miles north of Uppsala, was once a sacred grove, where animals and people were sacrificed to Norse gods. The Viking burial grounds date back to the sixth century. Nearby, on the site of an old pagan temple, is a 12th-century church. An open-air museum illustrating the life of peasants is open June to August.

While you're in the area, visit **Odinsborg,** an old wooden inn where you can drink mead from silver-tipped ornamental ox horns—as the Vikings did centuries ago. Waitresses wear Viking breastplates over provincial dresses, old murals adorn the walls, the corner fireplace has copper kettles, and the main room is decorated with crude furniture.

Midsummer magic at its best

Dalarna Province in the heart of Sweden has preserved the rites of midsummer (with a Christian touch, these days) as they were celebrated centuries ago. On **Midsummer Eve,** young people race through forests gathering birch boughs and wildflowers for the maypole. Once the pole is raised, villagers dance around it until dawn, weaving long ribbons that hang from the top.

In the morning, the townspeople go to church in rowboats decorated with greenery. A young girl will dream of her beloved on Midsummer Night if she places a bouquet containing seven wildflowers under her pillow. And if she looks into a reflecting pool on Midsummer Day, the next man she sees will be her loved one. The morning dew supposedly cures all ills.

The most colorful midsummer celebrations are in the villages around Lake Siljan: Rattvik, Leksand, and Tallberg. In Siljansnas, a church boat race is held on Midsummer Day. In Hjortnas, traditional dancing takes place on the jetty the Saturday night following midsummer.

Two simple but comfortable hotels in the region are **Hotel Langbers,** *79303 Tallberg; tel. (46-247)50290,* and **Romantik Hotel Tallbergsgarden,** *79303 Tallberg; tel. (46-247)50026.*

The world's biggest cross-country ski race

The town of **Mora,** about four-and-a-half hours north of Stockholm by car, is a peaceful place that comes alive suddenly once a year on the first Sunday in March. This is the day of the **Vasaloppet**—the world's biggest and oldest cross-country ski race. As many as 12,000 cross-country skiers race along the course, fueled by the blueberry soup, lime juice, and Swedish meatballs offered by spectators. If you are brave, a good skier, and in good condition, enter the race. For application forms contact **Vasaloppet,** *Vasagatan 19, S-792 00 Mora, Sweden; tel. (46-250)16000.* Arrangements also can be made through major travel agencies.

The rest of the year, you can cross-country ski more peacefully. Rentals are about $10 a day, and exquisite trails run along the frozen rivers and fields. Situated on the shores of Lake Siljan, Mora guarantees snow in the winter. It is about as far north as Anchorage.

The **Mora Hotel,** *tel. (46-250)117-50,* is the best place to stay. On weekends, rooms are $60 to $95 per night, including dinner and breakfast. The hotel has a swimming pool, a sauna, a solarium, and a good restaurant called Terrassen.

Visby: the best medieval town

Sweden's best-preserved medieval town, **Visby,** on the country's largest island, Gotland, is protected by a massive, two-mile wall and 44 towers. Punctuating its skyline are 100 churches, 91 of which were built before 1350. Known as the City of Roses, Visby is filled with the sweet-smelling flowers. Nearby are beautiful sandy beaches that are remarkable for their marine stacks, piles of oddly shaped rocks sculpted by wind and water.

The best Swedish boat trip

The best trip through Sweden is a 3-day, 322-mile ferry ride from Stockholm to Gothenberg (Göteborg) through the **Göta Canal** aboard a century-old ship. You can get off the boat at various spots to explore hinterland towns.

The drawback of the trip is cramped quarters; two people can't stand in a stateroom at the same time. And there is only one toilet per deck and one shower per boat.

The cruise, which runs from May to September, is $150 to $300 per person. Contact **SCANWORLD,** *12444 Ventura Blvd., Studio City, CA 91604; (818)506-4114.*

The cheapest way to go

The **Swedish Budget Hotel Cheque,** a hotel plan offered by the **Swedish National Tourist Board,** *655 Third Ave., New York, NY 10019; (212)949-2333,* allows you a choice of hotels for $17 to $30 per person, double occupancy, including breakfast, not including private bathrooms.

Finland: the least spoiled

Finland is an unspoiled land with the cleanest air in Europe. Its historic towns and cities are simple, elegant, and brightly colored, and its countryside is covered with virgin forests and 62,000 freshwater lakes. Although the population is less than five million, this is the fifth-largest nation in Europe. The lengthy coastline is marked by coves and framed by 20,000 small islands. During the summer, Finland is basked in perpetual sunshine.

Finns are known as great sailors and great magicians. Their language is not related to other Nordic tongues, except Lappish. The Finno-Ugric language family is more similar to Hungarian, Turkish, Estonian, and even Eskimo than to Swedish, Norwegian, or Danish. However, Finland has a Swedish-speaking minority, and most Finns have studied English.

Helsinki: where East meets West

The capital of Finland is located halfway between Russia and Sweden and shows signs of both Eastern and Western influences. It has been ruled by both over the centuries. The skyline is marked by the domes of the Lutheran cathedral and the Russian Orthodox Church.

A light-colored city built of white granite and surrounded by water on three sides, Helsinki is carefully laid out, with 240 parks and scores of modern buildings, such as Temppeliaukion Church, an underground church blasted from solid rock and decorated with purple wood and copper.

The city's most imposing sight

The approach to Helsinki by sea is guarded by the 18th-century **Suomenlinna Fortress.** You can walk the fortress' old ramparts, visit its gardens, and have lunch in its open-air cafés.

A bit of the East

In front of the cathedral is **Senaatintori** (Senate Square), which is so reminiscent of Leningrad that many movies set in that city have been shot here, including *Reds.* The square even holds a statue of Czar Alexander II, a Russian ruler of Finland who is fondly remembered for allowing the Finns some independence. Also on the square is the oldest building in the city: the Sederholm residence, built in 1755.

The best picture of Finnish history

Finnish history is long and involved. A good place to begin absorbing it is the **Suomen Kansallismuseo** (National Museum), which has relics of the seafaring life of Viking times and the migration of the Finnish people northward 1,300 years ago. Located in a 200-year-old wooden building on Mannerheimintie, the city's main artery, the museum was designed by Eeno Saarinen. Opposite the museum is the ultramodern cultural center, **Finlandia Hall.**

World's best fur bargains

Furs are well-made and inexpensive in Finland, the world's biggest seller of farmed furs. Furriers there say you can easily buy a coat and pay for your trip to Finland for what it would cost to buy a similar coat in the United States. Mink coats start at about $5,000; mink jackets at $2,000. In Helsinki, the best places to look are along the Pohjoisseplanadi, the city's main shopping street, and in the shops at Station Tunnel and Hakaniemi Market Hall.

A sacred tradition: the sauna

Don't miss the chance to enjoy a Finnish sauna, a 2,000-year-old tradition that will make you feel euphoric. You take a sauna in a wood-lined room with layers of benches that climb toward the ceiling (the hottest are at the top). A stove heats the room to about 200 degrees Fahrenheit, and water is thrown on a layer of stones on the stove to produce steam.

Finns consider the oldest saunas the best. Built by early Finno-Ugric tribes, they were log cabins with earth floors, a pile of rocks above a fire, and no chimney.

Most saunas are built by the water—not surprising considering Finland has 188,000 lakes. Country saunas are stoked for hours, until the stones of the hearth are red-hot and the log walls have absorbed the heat and reflect it back.

If you're lucky, you'll be invited to take a sauna at the house of a native, which is a sign of hospitality. Because a sauna involves certain rules of etiquette, you should imitate your host. Allow him to create the first *loyly,* or vapor, by pouring water on the stove. Always ask other bathers if they are ready for a new cloud of steam before taking it upon yourself to create one.

If you're on your own (nearly every hotel has a sauna), take off your clothes and sweat. Then brush yourself lightly with birch branches. When you've had enough, dive into the frigid waters of a lake, roll around in the snow, or take a cold shower. (If you have a heart condition, you should skip that last step.) The ritual can be repeated three or four times. After the last sauna, soap the perspiration off your body.

Don't take a sauna for at least one hour after a meal, and don't drink alcohol before a sauna—it strains the heart. Remove all jewelry, including rings and pierced earrings, because metal gets hot and can burn you.

The best saunas in Helsinki are at the Palace Hotel, the Kalastajatorppa, and the Hesperia. You don't have to be a guest, but you must book in advance.

Best side trips

One of Finland's greatest surviving castles is the citadel at **Hämeenlinna.** Built over a long period of time and used for many things, including a prison, it displays a collection of Finnish art. Composer Jan Sibelius was born in this town; his house is a museum displaying his violin, his family's piano, and photos. One of the town's centuries-old wooden buildings houses a historical museum.

Operas are staged in the courtyard of **Olavinlinna Castle** in Savonlinna each July by the Finnish National Opera. Begun in 1475, the castle stands on a small island in a passage connecting two large lakes. Tickets to the operas are about $30 and should be ordered as early as the preceding October. You can stop by the festival **ticket office,** *Puistokatu 3; tel. (358-*

57)244-84, about 4 p.m. the day of the performance to see if tickets are available.

In **Kerimaki,** near Savonlinna, is the largest wooden church in the world. The 150-year-old church seats 3,600 people. Strange, considering the town's population is 2,900. According to legend, the builders were tipsy when they began working on the church. They misread centimeters as inches, making the structure 2 1/2 times the size planned by the architect.

Lapland: Europe's last wilderness

Lapland, where the tundra never completely thaws and the winter darkness is broken only by the glimmering aurora borealis, stretches across the northern halves of Norway, Sweden, and Finland. This is Europe's last true wilderness, suffering long, cold, dark winters. During the summer, however, it is eerily beautiful under the Midnight Sun, reflected by glaciers, waterfalls, rivers, lakes, and mountains. For six weeks in June and July, the sun never sets.

This is the land of the Lapps (or Sami as they call themselves), a nomadic group that herds reindeer for a living and retains old traditions long forgotten elsewhere in Scandinavia. Some Lapps still wear the traditional costume of blue felt with contrasting bands of red, yellow, and green, often decorated with embroidery. Men wear the "caps of four winds," with four floppy points. Women wear red felt bonnets with flaps over the ears.

Try the Lapp specialties: *poro* (reindeer meat), *lohi* (salmon), and *siika* (whitefish). Also taste the local liqueurs and desserts made from Arctic cloudberries.

The northernmost point in Europe

Nordkapp, Norway's North Cape, is the northernmost point in Europe, the place where the sun doesn't sink below the horizon from May 14 to July 30. This mountain plateau rises 1,000 feet out of the ocean—a bleak but beautiful black cliff. In August, when the sun dips below the horizon for a few minutes, the sky is lit by the Northern Lights, a rainbow of spectacular colors. Even though most people come in July to see the Midnight Sun, this is still the best time to visit. The North Cape is snowbound until early June.

Nordkapp is on Mageroy Island, about 15 miles north of **Honningsvag,** the northernmost village in the world. During the summer, a Lapp camp with reindeer herds is usually set up at Nordmannset, a little more than a mile outside Honningsvag.

The northernmost hotel in this northernmost region is the **Sas,** *tel. (47-84)72331,* in Honningsvag. A modern place, it has great views and rooms for $117 to $134. Make reservations well in advance.

To fly to the North Cape, take SAS from Oslo to Tromso or Lakselv, then take Wideroe's Airlines to Honningsvag. Regular bus service runs between Honningsvag and the North Cape.

Norwegian Lapland

Several towns bring civilization of a sort to **Finnmark** (Norwegian Lapland). **Tromsö** is the base for trappers, whalers, and sealers (as well as Greenpeace, the international volunteer organization that crusades for the environment). Polar explorers also set out from here.

The **Arctic Church,** one of the most impressive pieces of modern architecture in the world, is in Tromsö. Built across the longest suspension bridge in Scandinavia (1,100 yards), it is shaped like an iceberg and made of aluminum that reflects the Midnight Sun.

Live like a local

You can rent a fisherman's cottage in the summer on one of the **Lofoten Islands** near the town of Bodö. Edgar Allan Poe spent several months here writing *A Descent into the Maelstrom*. During the summer, the cottages are empty (winter is the fishing season). Built on piles, they are usually next to piers, and they are always on the beach. The timbered structures often can accommodate 8 to 10 people. Most have running water, but not all have indoor toilets. Prices range from $20 to $30 a night per cabin. For more information, contact **Tourist Information,** *P.O. Box 128, 8301 Svolvar, Bodö, Norway.*

The best way to visit the Lapps

The town of **Alta** in Finnmark is the best base for excursions into Lapp country. Most Lapps live on the tundra south of here. In Masi, about 44 miles from Alta on the main road to Finland, they wear traditional costumes, although many have taken up a modern way of life.

During the winter, the Lapps live inland. In May and June, they migrate to the coast as they have for centuries, herding thousands of reindeer across rivers and fjords—a spectacular sight. Colorful reindeer roundups usually take place between September and February.

The **Alta Gjestestue,** *tel. (46-84)35-336,* in Alta is an inviting guesthouse with double rooms for $70, including breakfast.

Swedish Lapland

Norrland, the Swedish word for their Lapland, covers half the area of Sweden. One-quarter of the country is north of the Arctic Circle and about 10,000 Lapps live here. It is easier to reach than you might imagine. Trains come here from Stockholm. Postal buses continue even farther north and connect with smaller villages and settlements. You can fly to the airports at Umeå, Luleå, and Kiruna. Or you can drive there on Road E4.

Arvidsjaur is modern but has an old Lappish center, with well-preserved, cone-shaped huts. Reindeer are rounded up here in June and July. Pine forests surround the town.

Norrbotten is a Lapp trading and cultural center. A market is held here the first week of February, when traditional Lapp handicrafts (delicately carved wooden utensils, silver jewelry, colorful and elaborate woven fabrics) are sold.

Kvikkjokk is the gateway to Sarek National Park, the largest wilderness in Europe. There are no roads or trails in the park.

The best hiking trails

Svenska Turistföreningen, the Swedish Touring Club, *Stureplan, Stockholm; tel. (46-8)22-72-00,* maintains hotels and marked hiking routes for hundreds of miles through Lapland. About 80 huts are available with beds and bedding, cooking utensils, and firewood. The huts can be used for one or two nights only. Huts are about $11 for members, about $12 for non-members (if room is available).

Swedish hikers prefer the **Kungsleden,** or Royal Trail, the longest marked trail in the world, leading from the resort of Abisko to Jakkvik, a total of 210 miles. Huts are spaced a day apart along the trail, which follows the old nomadic paths of the Lapps.

The National Swedish Environmental Protection Board owns several huts in **Padjelanta National Park,** where you can stay for about $7 a night. The mountain's park is known for its unusual flora and many lakes.

Finnish Lapland

Finnish Lapland, the largest and most northerly of Finland's provinces, occupies one-third the area of Finland and lies almost entirely above the Arctic Circle. It adjoins the Lapland districts in neighboring Norway and Sweden, but the landscape contrasts sharply. Some parts are barren, others are covered by vast forests of pine and spruce and watered by rushing rivers. There are only about four people per square mile.

About 3,500 Sami, or Lapps, live in the northernmost parishes: Utsjoki, Enontekiö, Inari, and Sodankylö. Until the seventh century, Lapps inhabited all of Finland. After the arrival of the Finns from the Volga, they retreated to the north, where they continue their traditional ways.

Finland's best hiking

In the summer, hiking expeditions are led through Lapland by experienced guides. Don't attempt an independent excursion unless you really know what you're doing. And bring the right equipment—boots, protective, warm clothing, and maps, which can be obtained from the **Map Department of the National Board of Survey,** *Maanmittaushallitus, Karttamyynti, Etelaesplandi 10, 00130 Helsinki 13.*

A marked 49-mile hiking trail called **Karhunkierros** (the Bear's Ring) runs near Kuusamo, about 124 miles from Oulu, just south of the Polar Circle. You don't need a guide to follow the clearly marked trail, which passes the most dramatic scenery in the area. You can spend the night for free in huts along the trail. However, in July and August, it is a good idea to carry a tent in case the huts are full. Bring food and mosquito repellent as well. Traveling the entire circle takes four to six days (shorter trails are also marked).

The capital of Lapland

Rovaniemi, the capital of Lapland, is a good base for explorations. This modern town five miles south of the Arctic Circle is easy to reach by train or plane from Helsinki. **Lapin Matkailu,** *Maakuntakatu 10, Helsinki; tel. (358-0)17201,* has a reservation service.

The best place to stay in Rovaniemi is **Rantasipi Pohjanhovi,** *Pohjanpuistikko 2; tel. (358-60)313-731,* located next to the river Kemijoki. It has two dining rooms, saunas, a swimming pool, and entertainment. Cross-country ski tracks pass right by the hotel. A double room with a bath is about $147, including breakfast.

The **Hotelli Ravintola Oppipoika,** *Korkalonkatu 33; tel. (358-60)991,* is a modern hotel. A single room with a bath is $70; a double room with a bath is $87.50.

The best adventure: Lapland in winter

If you like romping in the snow, you'll love Lapland in the winter. Days and nights are spent cross-country skiing, taking reindeer rides, and whizzing across the powder in snow-mobiles. Light from the stars and moon reflects off the snow, providing enough visibility for these activities 24 hours a day.

The terrain makes for some of the finest cross-country skiing in the world. Competitive skiers come here from around the world to train. Lapland offers a vast network of maintained ski tracks. Seasoned skiers can book a cabin in one of the fell regions and take on the un-marked countryside. Caution! If you are going out into the wilderness, hire a guide. This is a wild, isolated, and frozen netherworld, and you could easily become lost forever. Arrange guides through the **Finnish Tourist Board,** *655 Third Ave., New York, NY 10019; (212)370-5540.*

A reindeer safari is a great way to discover the land. On a guided trip, you are given a sled (a canoe-shaped contraption of wood planks) and a reindeer. The reindeer wears a harness, which is attached to the sled with a colorful braid. Tucked into blankets, you control the critter with a single rope.

A reindeer safari can last from 20 minutes to an entire week—it's up to you. The longer excursions are definitely for the hardy—you sleep in a tent or cabin and eat reindeer meat cooked over an open fire (which can be tough).

To explore Lapland at a faster pace, take a snowmobile safari. You wear enormous Arctic overalls, sled shoes, gloves, and a hat. The cold, dry air is exhilarating as you fly through the forests and across the frozen lakes.

Chapter 13

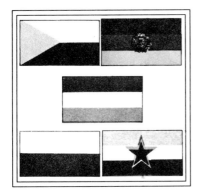

THE BEST OF EASTERN EUROPE

Eastern Europe is the least-discovered corner of Europe. While Western Europe is overrun with tourists vying for hotel space and flocking to the same crowded museums, Eastern Europe is spared the camera-toting masses.

Europe beyond-the-curtain offers as many culture-filled cities, medieval towns, snow-capped peaks, and sandy beaches as its capitalistic neighbor. Yet its hotels and restaurants are cheap, and its people are still curious about Americans. While amenities haven't caught up with those in the West, neither have crowds and high prices.

Hungary: the most unusual nation

Hungary is a world unto itself. While it is at the very heart of the European continent, its language, food, and music are not like those of any other country. Its people are unique as well.

Hungarians, or Magyars, are descendants of fierce horsemen from the Ural Mountains, who terrorized much of Europe until the ninth century. Hungarians still speak Magyar, which is distantly related to Finnish and Estonian. Their folk music is passionate; strains of the old tunes can be heard in the works of Liszt, Bartok, and Zoltan Kodaly.

Budapest: Eastern Europe's loveliest city

The capital of Hungary is one of the most beautiful cities in the world. Its 15th-century streets lead past Renaissance houses that hide pretty interior courtyards. At night, delicate neon signs glow from the old stone facades of the buildings. Budapest has more museums per citizen than any other city in the world.

Budapest is made up of two sections: **Buda** and **Pest,** which are divided by the Danube River. Once two separate cities, they were united in 1873. Buda, dominated by the spires of the 13th-century Matthias Church, has medieval cobblestoned streets, centuries-old houses, and steep little stairways that climb to the castle. Pest, centered around the neo-Gothic parliament building, is the flatter, modern business section of the city, with grand 19th-century monuments and memorials.

The best way to get to Budapest is aboard the hydrofoil that glides from Vienna down the Danube and around Czechoslovakia, reaching Budapest at sunset.

Top sights

Buda Castle, *Szent Gyorgy Ter 2,* tops Castle Hill on the Buda side. Generations of Hungarian kings were crowned at this castle, which is embellished with elaborate reliefs. Demolished during bombing raids in World War II, it has been carefully rebuilt. From the courtyard is a splendid view over the Danube. The castle houses the Historical Museum of Budapest, which contains archeological remains of the old town and exhibits on the history of the palace, and the National Gallery.

However, the most fascinating part of the castle is underground. Labyrinths running below the castle were used to house troops and a hospital during World War I. The tunnels are now a wax museum depicting Hungary's history: the early Roman settlers; the invasion of Attila the Hun and his horsemen from Mongolia in A.D. 430; the Turkish domination of Hungary from 1526 to 1686; the Austrian rulers; and modern history.

Kings Charles and Matthias were crowned at **Matthias Church,** *Szentharomsag ter 2,* as were Empress Maria Theresa and Emperor Franz Josef. High Mass is celebrated every Sunday at 10 a.m., and organ concerts are held in the church on Sunday afternoons.

The **Houses of Parliament,** *Kossuth Square,* across the Danube in Pest, are a grand imitation of the Houses of Parliament in Westminster (except they are topped with a red star). Built 100 years ago, the neo-Gothic buildings are the seat of the Hungarian National Assembly and are used for state receptions.

Also in Pest is the **Hungarian National Museum,** *Muzeum Korut 14-16,* which features a permanent exhibit called "The History of the Hungarian People from the Magyar Conquest to 1849." One room displays a large, lavishly decorated Turkish tent, captured in 1686 when Buda was liberated from the Turkish occupation. Another room shows paintings and sculptures by Hungarian artists from the Middle Ages to the present.

Across from **Heroes Square,** where you'll see a statue commemorating Attila the Hun (a Hungarian hero, believe it or not) and Hungary's 1,000 years as a nation, is the **Museum of Fine Arts,** *Dozsa Gyorgy ut 41.* The museum has more El Grecos than any institution outside Spain, as well as three Rembrandts and major works by Goya, Raphael, Rubens, Franz Hals, Monet, Renoir, and Cézanne. (It also may have a Leonardo sculpture, depending on whether you listen to the Hungarians or the Italians.)

The world's best Gypsy music

Every February in Budapest, the **Gypsy Music Festival** is held. However, you can hear Gypsy music year-round at some of the best restaurants in the city, including Feher Sandor, Lakatos Sandor, Lakatos Gyorgy, Kallai Kis Erno, and Voros Kalman. The best Gypsy music while you dine is at the restaurant called Matyaspince. Ask the concierge at your hotel or a local office of IBUSZ where the Gypsies are playing.

Budapest's best markets

Not far from the Matthias Cathedral, heading toward the river, a lively gypsy market is held on weekends. Gypsies in Hungary deal in secondhand goods and crafts. Among the bargains are leather clothes (jackets, skirts, and tops), embroidery (clothing and tablecloths), and jewelry. Offer to pay half the price they ask in dollars.

The Hungarian state stores carry many of the same handicrafts as the Gypsies, but their selection is limited. One of our editors found a lovely embroidered felt suit in the **Vaci Utca Handicrafts Shop** run by Intourist. It cost only 1,125 forints ($25), but was available in only one color (red) and only one size (40, or about a U.S. 12). Her companion found a beautiful blue-suede suit with knee breeches for 1,575 forints ($35). It was half-price because it was soiled. Even after the cost of dry cleaning, it was a great bargain.

The **Tolbuchin Indoor Food Market,** *Tolbuchin Korut 1-3,* an enormous emporium of glass and iron, sells delicious sausages, salami chunks, and smoked meat, with thick slabs of bread and pickled peppers—all for about 25 cents.

Best restaurants and cafés

The best restaurant in town is **Gundel,** near Heroes Square in Pest, *tel. (36-1)221-002,* which sets the standard for fine dining in Hungary. Expect to pay 500 forints for dinner.

Our favorite restaurant is **Alabardos,** *Orszaghaz Utca 2,* which not only offers luxurious dining, but it is also cheap. Dinner for two with wine is less than 450 forints ($10)! Guests are seated in a huge Gothic room with a vaulted ceiling; in the summer you can sit at tables in the cobblestoned courtyard.

Other top-drawer places include **Hungaria** (formerly New York), a café-restaurant at Lenin Korut, by the train station, and **Feher Galamb** on Castle Hill.

The smartest café in Budapest is **Gerbeaud** on Budapest's equivalent of Fifth Avenue, Vaci Utca. Order *dobos* cake, with its many chocolate layers and a hard caramel hazelnut topping.

The **Hungaria** in Buda and **Angelika** in Pest also have mouth-watering pastries.

Best digs

Hungary is one of the few East European nations with a flourishing private sector in bed-and-breakfast accommodations for tourists. You can make arrangements for this through **IBUSZ,** *630 Fifth Ave., New York, New York 10111; (212)582-7412.*

If you want something more elegant than a bed and breakfast, Hungary offers that, too. Budapest has one of the most stunning hotels of any city in the world: the **Budapest Hilton,** *I, Hess Andras ter 1-3; tel. (36-1)885-35-00,* which is built into the ruins of a 13th-century abbey on top of a hill in Buda. It is next to Matthias Church and has views of the city and the river.

The **Duna-Intercontinental,** the **Atrium-Hyatt,** and the **Forum** are beautifully designed palaces all on the Pest side of the Danube. The Duna has river views but is a bit too big. The Atrium has a glass-covered central court through which glass-sided elevators soar. The Forum, a four- rather than a five-star hotel, is a little cheaper.

Budapest's incomparable spa hotel, the **Hotel Gellert,** *Szent Gellert Ter 1,* is famous for its spring-fed baths. Guests are supplied with thick bathrobes and can take an elevator directly to them. The radioactive pools (which are supposed to be good for you) are located in mosaic-decorated art-deco halls with ornate balconies, massive columns, and skylights.

The **Thermal Hotel,** *Margitsziget, Budapest 1138; tel. (36-1)32-11-00* or *(36-1)11-10-00,* on Margaret Island in the middle of the Danube, treats rheumatic ailments. The hotel's restaurant is excellent and inexpensive. A three-course dinner is less than 450 forints ($10). Doubles are about 3,600 forints ($80). The hotel has swimming pools, tennis courts, riding trails, and medieval ruins, as well as medicinal waters.

Hungary's Versailles

Not far from Budapest, in Fertod, is **Esterhazy Palace,** the 18th-century home of Prince

Nicholaus Esterhazy the Magnificent, who ruled at the height of the Hapsburg monarchy. Haydn was concertmaster here.

The palace, which was looted by Soviet troops during World War II, has been restored recently and is open to visitors. Nicholas modeled the palace after Versailles, which he had visited on a diplomatic trip.

Hungary's largest cathedral

Esztergom, a town on a narrow side channel of the Danube, contains the largest cathedral in Hungary, built between 1822 and 1856. However, the 19th-century marble cathedral pales in comparison with the Primate's art collection in the attached museum. The Renaissance chapel adjoining the cathedral houses a 13th-century gold cross, upon which Hungarian kings took their oaths. Marcus Aurelius wrote *Reflections* in this town, which was once an important Roman outpost. It was the seat of the Magyar kings in the 12th and 13th centuries and the center of the Hungarian Catholic Church.

Central Europe's largest lake

Lake Balaton, Central Europe's largest lake, is 48 miles long and 36 feet deep in some places. It is known for its sandy beaches, its warm water (you can swim here from spring through late fall), its resort hotels, and its fine fishing (Lake Balaton has 42 kinds of fish). The tastiest is the giant pike-perch *(fogas)*.

Lake Balaton served as a line of defense against the Turks for centuries. The remains of border castles can be seen in Tihany, Nagyvazsony, Szigliget, and Fonyod.

The most popular resorts are on the south shore of the lake, where the water is warmer and the beaches have a softer grade of sand. The north shore is relatively undiscovered and a good place to get away from the crowds. But the water is colder, and the beaches aren't as nice.

Siofok, the largest town on the southern shore, is also the most crowded. The **Hotel Balaton,** *Petofi setany 9; tel. (36-84)10-655,* is the best place to stay, with reasonable prices and a private beach for guests.

Siofok has several three-star restaurants: **Europa,** *tel. (36-84)11-400;* **Lido,** *tel. (34-84)10-633;* and **Hungaria,** *tel. (36-84)10-677.*

The best restaurant on the lake is just outside Siofolk. **Menes Csarda,** *15 Apaczai Csere J., Szantodpuszta; tel. (36-84)170-803,* serves food cooked according to local custom—very spicy. The restaurant is in a restored stable and is decorated with antique art.

The healthiest place along the lake is the small spa town of **Balatonfured,** on the northern shore. It has 11 medicinal springs that are supposed to be good for the heart and the nerves. This hilly old town is covered with twisting streets. At its center is **Gyogy Ter** (Spa Square), where the waters of volcanic springs bubble under a pavilion.

The most charming hotel in Balatonfured is the old-fashioned **Arany Csillag** (Golden Star), *tel. (36-84)40-323,* a four-story hotel in a small grove of trees. It doesn't have a view of the lake or private baths, but the rooms are airy and clean.

Also in Balatonfured are three one-star hotels: **Annabella,** *tel. (36-80)40-110;* **Margareta,** *tel. (36-80)40-821;* and **Marina,** *tel. (36-80)40-810.*

Nearby Zichy Castle hosts the annual **August Horse Show.** This is the best place to observe top riders and horses—Hungary is famous for its equestrian traditions. Riders dress in medieval costumes. For more information, contact **IBUSZ,** *address above.*

You can bathe in a warm-water lake surrounded by rose-colored Egyptian lotus plants in **Heviz,** a town near Lake Balaton. Fed by a thermal spring, the temperature of Heviz Lake varies from 82 to 100 degrees Fahrenheit. In cool weather, the warm lake steams, giving it a mysterious air. The mud from the bottom of the lake is also therapeutic. It is dried and exported for mud packs. Cemeteries dating back to Roman times have been found along the lake.

The best hotel in town is the new and luxurious **Thermal,** *Margitsziget; tel. (36-1)321-100,* which has a gambling casino.

Yugoslavia: the best beaches

Yugoslavia has a spectacular coastline with long sandy beaches, secret coves, and dramatic cliffs. Why battle the crowds and spend a fortune to lie on the beach in Greece, when you can enjoy almost the same Mediterranean sun and sea for half the price in Yugoslavia?

Dubrovnik: Yugoslavia's most beautiful city

Dubrovnik, on the Dalmatian Coast, is a medieval walled city so perfectly preserved that it has been declared a national monument. George Bernard Shaw wrote in 1931, "Those who seek Earthly Paradise should come and see Dubrovnik."

Once a city-state and a rival of Venice, Dubrovnik is filled with Renaissance palaces and churches. Especially beautiful are the **Doge's Palace, Onofri's Fountain,** and the **Church of St. Vlaho.** Car ferries link Dubrovnik to Italy's coast, making it convenient to visit along with southern Europe. The best time to visit is during Dubrovnik's summer festival of music, drama, and ballet, which is held from July 10 to Aug. 25.

As you walk along the city's battlements, you will have a view across red-tiled rooftops to the blue Adriatic Sea beyond.

Europe's oldest pharmacy

Off the Stradun, also called Placa, is the 14th-century **Franciscan Pharmacy.** One of the oldest on the continent, it is still in operation. Today, its ancient weighing scales and ceramic jugs are used as decoration.

Europe's third-oldest synagogue

Zudioska Ulica (Jew Street), near the Ploce Gate, has a 14th-century synagogue, the third oldest in Europe. It is on the second floor of a Gothic building. In the early 14th century, large groups of Jews found sanctuary in Dubrovnik from persecution in Spain and Italy.

Best sunset, best swimming

The prettiest place to spend the evening in Dubrovnik is the west end of the city, near the **Fortress of St. Ivan.** Young men often gather by the Porporela jetty below the fortress, where three huge iron spikes jut out from the stone wall. To prove their manhood, they swing from one spike to the other and finally drop into the sea. According to a saying in Dubrovnik, a boy has become a man when he has "passed three spikes."

Dubrovnik's two best nightspots are **Arsenal,** in the old city, and **Lazareti,** outside the old city. Both have good dance floors.

The best place to swim is at the western end of the city, by **Fort Lovrijena.** Jacques Cousteau called the water here the purest in the Mediterranean. Offshore is the island of Lokrum, known for its nudist beaches and good swimming.

Dubrovnik's best restaurant

Ragusa, *Prijeko Street,* the best restaurant in the city, serves good seafood and Dalmation specialties, which are distinguished by heavy use of olive oil and garlic. Upstairs is an arbor-covered terrace. Try the risotto and the local white wine, called Posip.

Good Dalmation cuisine is also served at **Jadran,** *P. Milicevica 1; tel. (38-50)23547,* and **Domino,** *od Domina 3; tel. (38-50)32832,* where a meal of squid costs about 6,500 dinars ($5) and a small lobster about 11,700 dinars ($9).

Yugoslavia's finest restaurant

The **Orsan Restaurant,** *T. Kikelja 2,* a 15-minute drive from Dubrovnik, is the finest in Yugoslavia. Located in an old stone peasant house, it specializes in seafood. Ask at your hotel for directions.

Dubrovnik's best hotel

The only hotel within the town walls is the **Dubravka,** *tel. (38-50)26-319,* which is a former convent. Because it is the most convenient place to stay, it is usually fully booked. Local specialties and fish are served in the dining room. Prices are reasonable.

The best hotel near Dubrovnik is a little place called **Villa Dubrovnik,** *P. Bukovca 8; tel. (38-50)22-933.* Perched on a cliff, this modern hotel has views of the walled town and of the harbor. Pine trees and flowers scent the air. In warm weather, you can dine outdoors on the terrace. It's worth the extra cost to get a room facing the sea. The hotel motorboat can take you into town, which is a 20-minute walk away.

The Slovenian Riviera

The **Slovenian Riviera**—the area from the Italian border to the end of the Istrian Peninsula's west coast—is the most glamorous stretch along Yugoslavia's coast. It feels like Italy.

Izola and **Piran** are attractive resort towns along the Slovenian Riviera—both look very much like old Italian resorts. **Portoroz,** a more modern resort, is the most expensive.

Porec, farther down the peninsula, is the most pleasant town in the region. Located near spectacular fjords, it has narrow cobblestoned streets and a maze of red-roofed stone houses. Galleries and studios fill the medieval towers.

The Riviera is the place to stay, and Club No. 1, a small, chic club with surrealistic paintings, is the place to do the town. You can bathe nude at the giant nudist complex south of Porec called FKK Koversada, located at the entrance to the Lim Fjord. Hotels, camping, and nightclubs here require no clothes. Day visitors can enjoy the beach for a few dollars (groups of men might be barred entry).

The most picturesque town along the coast is **Rovinj,** an artist colony near Porec. This little town, which has a beautiful old church, is built into a hill. Outdoor cafés and restaurants line the harbor. Monte Bar in the old city serves good Istrian cuisine. The Hotel Eden has an informal casino and several discos.

The best place for peace and privacy is **Rab,** a lush town shaded with evergreens. Located south of the Istrian Peninsula, it has deserted coves where you can swim undisturbed.

The residents are friendly. Spend an evening listening to a live band on the terrace of the Hotel Imperial.

Yugoslavia's best beach

The nicest beach on the entire Yugoslavian coastline is at the south end of the island of **Krk,** a half-hour boat ride from Rijeka. Krk is a strangely beautiful place with a barren valley surrounded by stern, stony hills. The island has a small hotel.

The Dalmatian Coast

Stretching from Zadar to Dubrovnik is the **Dalmatian Coast,** where people are loud and friendly. The best beaches along this stretch are between Sibenek and Split.

The most beautiful place along the Dalmation Coast is the island of **Hvar** (which means *sun*). Above its harbor, the town spreads across a hill crowned with figs, oleanders, and purple bougainvillea. At the water's edge, a promenade is lined with kiosks that sell seafood and hand-woven rugs. Dazzling white stone covers the grounds of the marketplace. You can rent a boat for about 26,000 dinars ($20) a day and explore the beaches.

Hvar attracts a good-looking young crowd, which keeps the night life lively. The **Tvrdava Disko,** which is located in the castle, can be seen from a distance—its lights flash from its perch on a hill. From the outdoor dance floor you have a view of the town.

Montenegro: the least known

Montenegro (Black Mountains) is the least-known and most southern of Yugoslavia's coasts. It follows the Adriatic Sea for 200 miles, from Kotor south to Albania. The scenery is dramatic, varying from high mountains to flat meadows to coastline beaches. The drive down the Old Post Road (now the coastal highway) to Dubrovnik is especially beautiful.

Herceg Novi, in the north, is the oldest town along the coast. It was founded 600 years ago by Tvrtko, the first Bosnian King. The old part of town has ramparts and towers that contrast sharply with the new villas and hotels. Herceg Novi is known as the rainiest spot in Europe. The Topla is a good place to stay.

The area around **Risan** is filled with bays and waterfalls. It is said that Illyrian Queen Teuta, after valiantly trying to fight off the invading Romans in 228 B.C., drowned herself here rather than surrender.

Sveti Stefan: the most exclusive resort

Off the coast at Montenegro is the island of **Sveti Stefan** (St. Stephen), a 15th-century fishing village that became an exclusive resort in 1960. The original fishermen's cottages have been preserved intact, but the interiors have been renovated in luxury. Flower gardens add color to the stone surroundings. The Duke of Bedford came here on his honeymoon; Adlai Stevenson, Kirk Douglas, and Princess Margaret also have been among the resort's guests.

The 118 rooms at the resort's hotel vary widely in price. Modest doubles are $45 to $70, including breakfast; luxury suites are $80 to $110; and a private villa is available for $600 a day (Sophia Loren slept here). You can choose your meals, which are served on a huge terrace, from a 25-page menu. The wine cellar also offers a good selection.

If you're looking for night life, the island has four small bars and a casino.

For reservations, contact the resort at *81315 Sveti Stefan; tel. (38-86)41-333* or *(38-86)41-411.*

Plitvice Lakes: nature at its best

The **Plitvice Lakes National Park,** halfway between Zagreb and the coast, has been classified by UNESCO as one of the unique natural wonders of the world. Here, 16 magnificent blue-green lakes merge one into the other in a chain of waterfalls that rushes into the Korana River. The highest waterfall is 247 feet. The lakes are surrounded by walking paths, deep forests, beaches, and hotels.

The best hotel in the area is the **Hotel Jezero,** perched in the mountains overlooking the largest of the lakes, Kozjak. The hotel has a large indoor pool, and two ski lifts are located only a mile away. Room and board during the summer is 53,300 dinars ($41) a night. During the winter this drops to 15,600 dinars ($39) a night.

The best of Czechoslovakia

Czechoslovakia, at the heart of Europe, has suffered the blows of almost every power to hit the continent. As a result, it is rich in history and culture and filled with 40,000 monuments and 3,000 castles. Its capital, Prague, is one of the most beautiful cities in Eastern Europe, outdone only by Budapest.

Czechoslovakia is an outdoor-lovers' paradise. The Tatras Mountains are dramatic, rising out of the plains to provide excellent skiing and hiking. The 1,000 lakes and ponds that dot Czechoslovakia are chock-full of fish. And the deep, wildlife-filled forests attract campers, backpackers, and hunters.

Czechoslovakia's most beautiful city

Prague, described by Goethe as "The most precious stone in the stone crown of the world," is one of the most beautiful cities in Eastern Europe.

The best way to see Prague is on foot. Start by climbing the 186 steps to the top of the **Prasna brana** (Powder Tower), in the old town. You'll have a panoramic view of the city from the top. A remnant of the old city fortifications, it was built in 1475 and rebuilt in the 19th century.

Old town's best treasures

Stare Mesto (the old town) dates to 1120. Celetna Street leads from the Powder Tower through the heart of the old town. It passes the **Tyl Theater,** where Mozart's *Don Giovanni* premiered in 1787 and where scenes from the movie *Amadeus* were filmed. Then it skirts the **Church of Our Lady at Tyn,** once a center of early Protestantism, whose twin spires dominate the skyline.

The street empties into **Staromestske namesti** (the old town square). A medieval astronomical clock has kept time here since 1490. On the hour, figures of Christ and the 12 apostles appear at two little windows above the clock face. Then the skeleton figure of Death, below, tolls the bell.

The **town hall,** built in 1338, stands above dungeons. Its 15th-century council chamber, decorated with the shields of Prague's medieval guilds, is still used.

Novelist Franz Kafka (1883-1924) was born in the painted house next door to the town hall.

Betlemska kaple (the Bethlehem Chapel), *Betlemske namesti 5,* is a reconstruction of the Gothic chapel where the reformer Jan Huss preached his revolutionary ideas from 1402 to

1415. Huss, who was burned at the stake for his views, became a symbol of freedom to the Czech people.

The most beautiful bridge

The most beautiful bridge in Eastern Europe connects Prague's old town and Mala Strana (Lesser Town). The **Charles Bridge**, built in 1357 by Charles IV, is lined with baroque statues. The bridge is especially lovely at night, when it is illuminated.

The best of Lesser Town

Lesser Town, despite its modest name, contains many of Prague's best sights. Much here is baroque, even though the town was founded in 1257. Arcades and 16th-century houses surround **Malostranske namesti** (the Lesser Town square), which is dominated by **Kostel sv. Nikulase** (St. Nicholas Church), a Jesuit church with a beautiful dome, belfry, nave, and ceiling frescoes.

Nerudova ulice (Neruda Street) is the most beautiful street in Lesser Town. The baroque buildings here are identified by signs (a red eagle, for example), as was the custom before numbered streets were introduced.

The magnificent **Valdstejnsky palac** (Wallenstein Palace), *Valdstejnske namesti,* built in 1624 by Italian architects for the Hapsburg general, Albrecht Wallenstein, now houses the Ministry of Culture. Concerts are held here during the summer.

New Town bests

Prague's **New Town** is not new by American standards—it was established in 1348. At its heart is **Vaclavske namesti** (Wenceslas Square), marked by a statue of King Wenceslas and filled with shops, restaurants, and hotels. Prague's best craft shop, **Slovenska Jizba,** located on the square, sells handmade jewelry, glass, porcelain, and folk art.

The **Narodni muzeum** (National Museum), also on Wenceslas Square, displays neo-Renaissance paintings, artifacts from Czech history, historical and archeological collections, and a famous mineral collection.

Prague's oldest pub, **U Fleku,** *Kremencova 11,* has been in existence at least since 1499. A huge place, it is filled with people singing and drinking its good dark beer.

Karlovo namesti (Charles Square), the biggest square in New Town, is named for Charles IV, who planned the city. Located in this square is the **Novomestska radnice** (town hall), which was the government center from 1398 to 1784. Antonin Dvorak's mementos are housed in the **Dvorak Museum,** *Ke Karlovu 20,* near Charles Square. During the summer, Dvorak's music is played in the sculpture garden behind the 18th-century house.

The best-preserved ghetto

Jewish merchants settled in the area north of the old town hall as early as the ninth century. As the area grew, it became a center of Jewish culture. The well-preserved Prague Ghetto is now the **State Jewish Museum.**

The **Altneushul** (Old-New Synagogue), built in 13th-century Gothic style, is the oldest surviving synagogue in Europe. Beside it is the old **Jewish Cemetery,** which holds 12,000 graves piled in layers. Tombs date from 1439 to 1787. If you lay a pebble on a grave here, it is said your dreams will come true.

The most visited tomb is that of the 16th-century scholar **Rabbi Loew,** who created the mythical, magical being called Golem. Today, visitors place scraps of paper with wishes on them in the crack in Loew's tomb. During World War II, Jews hid their valuables in the tomb's cracks before they were transported to concentration camps.

Franz Kafka is also buried in the cemetery. When the Nazis occupied Prague, they sent Kafka's three sisters to a concentration camp, where they were killed. And they destroyed most of Kafka's letters and manuscripts. However, his diaries were overlooked and are now housed among the treasures of the State Jewish Museum.

Klausen Synagogue, *U stareho hrbitova,* has a moving collection of drawings done by Jewish children in concentration camps.

The names of 77,700 Czechoslovak Jews murdered by the Nazis are inscribed on the inside walls of nearby **Pinkas Synagogue.**

Hradcany, the royal quarter

The **Hradcany Quarter** grew up around Hradcany (Prague Castle), the former residence of the kings of Bohemia and today the seat of government. A city within a city, it holds some of Prague's best treasures. The president of Czechoslovakia lives here, in a well-guarded section.

Three walled courtyards open into each other, progressing in architectural design from medieval to 20th century. Off the first courtyard is the former chapel, which houses the treasury. Inside are gold, crystal, and jewels.

The Hradcany also houses the **National Gallery,** which is divided into three chronological sections. The earliest and best, in the former Convent of St. George, houses the state collection of Bohemian Gothic paintings and sculpture.

The third courtyard of the castle contains **Katedrala sv. Vita** (St. Vitus' Cathedral), the mausoleum of Czech kings, which holds the crown jewels (including the crown of St. Wenceslas, decorated with a thorn, supposedly from Christ's crown of thorns). The cathedral is closed for restoration until late 1989.

Behind the Hradcany is **Golden Lane,** once the residence of alchemists. The beautiful cobblestoned street, with its small houses, great palaces, and shops, brings the Middle Ages to life.

The bookstore at Number 24 was the residence of Franz Kafka in 1917 (he lived here just after he wrote *The Trial* and before he wrote *The Castle*). Ironically, the bookstore sells no books by Kafka, who has been largely ignored by Czechoslovaks.

Nearby is **Strahovsky Klaster** (Strahov Monastery), which houses a museum of Czech literature and beautifully preserved ancient manuscripts and Bibles from all over the world, is one of the most impressive libraries in Europe. The **Theological Hall,** a vaulted gallery built in 1671, is lined with 17th-century bookshelves. Its white stucco ceilings are embellished with frescoes.

The **Loretto,** another monastery, was founded in 1629 by Princess Lobkowitz. It centers around a replica of the Santa Casa in Loretto, Italy. Paired half-columns and relief panels add to its beauty. Its treasury contains saints' crowns and religious objects made of gold and precious stones.

The oldest fortress

Vysehrad Fortress, believed to have been founded in the ninth century, looms above Prague from sheer cliffs facing Hradcany. The Hussites destroyed much of it—apart from the walls, all that remains are an 11th-century rotunda and the Church of St. Peter and St. Paul.

Many of Czechoslovakia's greatest heros and artists are buried in Vysehrad's cemetery, including Dvorak, Karel Capek, Jan Neruda, and Bedrich Smetana.

The world's best crystal

Czechoslovakia is known for its Bohemian crystal. **Moser,** *na prikope 12,* is the best place in Prague to shop for crystal. You can order through the store's catalog, which lists sets ordered by the world's royalty.

Best restaurants

Opera Grill, *Divaeelmin ulice; tel. (42-2)26-55-08,* is Prague's finest restaurant. An elegant establishment decorated with antique Meissen candelabra, it serves French cuisine. After dinner, brandy is served in giant crystal snifters. The restaurant is closed weekends. Make reservations in advance.

The **Zlata Praha** (Golden Prague), *Curieovych namesti; tel. (42-2)28-89,* on the eighth floor of the Prague Inter-Continental, has a lovely view of the castle. National specialties— roast duck, sauerkraut, and dumplings—are well-prepared.

Svata Klara (St. Klara), *Prague 7, U. Trogskeho Zamku 9; tel. (42-2)84-12-13,* the former wine cellar of Count Vaclav Vojtech, is now a first-class *vinarna* (wine restaurant) that offers a good selection of Moravian wines. You can enjoy dinner in front of a fireplace.

Best hotels

U tri pstrosu (Three Ostriches), *Drazickeho namesti 12; tel. (42-2)53-61-51,* is the most charming hotel in town. Located in a 16th-century house at the Lesser Town end of the Charles Bridge, it has an excellent restaurant. Reservations must be made at least one month in advance. Doubles are $70 to $90.

Pariz, *U Obecniho domu 1; tel. (42-2)232-20-51,* is a recently reopened art-deco hotel with double rooms for $40 to $70. The hotel's café and restaurant are decorated with blue mosaic tile.

Best night life

If you're looking for some insight into how local Czechs spend their evenings out, try **U Fleku** (Fleku's Inn), *Kremencova 11.* Or you could stop in for a beer at **U Kalicha** (The Chalice), *Na Bojisti 12; tel. (42-2)29-60-17.* Both these beer halls are lively places to meet people. **Slavia Café,** *Narodni 1,* on the embankment opposite the National Theater, is where local artists and intellectuals hang out.

For Western-style entertainment, try **Night Club,** on the ninth floor of the Intercontinental Hotel; **Est Bar,** in the Hotel Esplanade, *tel. (42-2)22-25-52;* or **Lucerna,** *Stepanska 61; tel. (42-2)24-61-53.* All these places offer dancing; some also have cabaret shows.

Avoid the **Lanterna Magika,** *Narodni 40; tel. (42-2)26-00-33.* The only people you'll meet here are tourists. This corny extravaganza includes live actors, mimes, films, music, magic, and dance. The price is unbeatable, though—only $3.

Bohemia's three best castles

Of Czechoslovakia's 3,000 castles, the best are in Bohemia. **Hazmburk,** near Ceske Budejovice in the north, is surrounded by a 30-foot-high wall and guarded by two observation towers. (Peregrine falcons have taken up residence in one of the abandoned towers.) The ruins rise out of sheer rock and are surrounded by a valley filled with wheat fields and plum orchards. Be careful—no railings protect you from the 700-foot drop from the ruins to the valley below. You can take a day trip to this castle from Austria or Southern Germany.

Spilberk Castle in Brno, built in 1287 to fend off invaders, was later used by the Hapsburgs to lock up their opponents. During World War II, the Nazis also used the dungeon as a prison. Take a look at the castle's hair-raising instruments of torture. The castle has a good restaurant that serves game dishes along with Moravian wines.

The little town of **Hluboka** has a wedding cake of a château, gleaming white with high, crenelated towers. It is a replica of Windsor Castle in England. Brussels tapestries, fine paintings, glassware, china, antique furniture, and medieval weapons can be seen here.

The best East European skiing

Czechoslovakia has Eastern Europe's best ski area: **Stary Smokovec,** a national park in the High Tatras with jumps, slalom runs, and long cross-country trails. You won't find the crowds and frenzy of St. Moritz here.

In addition to being the best place to ski, Stary Smokovec, which lies in the shadows of the peak called Slavkovsky, is the oldest community in the High Tatras. The first tourist buildings here were built in the late 18th century. The two best hotels in town are the Grand and the Parkhotel.

Romania, the most romantic nation

Romania is a land for romantics. More Gypsies live here than anywhere else in the world (they call themselves Romany). Romanians claim to be descendants of a lost Roman legion. If you remember any of your Latin, you can get by on it in some of the country's small towns.

The Roman poet Ovid was exiled here, on a lagoon north of Constanta. And Vlad the Impaler—the man behind the myth of Dracula—led his bloody life in Transylvania.

Bucharest: the Paris of Eastern Europe

Thousands of years ago, a little Stone Age settlement was established on the trade route that crossed the forest-covered Romanian plains. Today, that settlement is Bucharest, the capital of Romania, and the trade route is the chain of grand boulevards that earned the city the title, the "Paris of Eastern Europe."

The boulevards—N. Balcescu, 1848, Magheru, and Ana Ipatescu—are lined with restaurants and brasseries. Along their southern stretch is the **Princely Palace,** which is surrounded by the trading quarter called **Lipscani,** where narrow medieval streets wind past little shops. The palace, which is now the National Art Museum, was inhabited by the notorious Vlad in the 14th century.

The most beautiful hotel in Bucharest is the **Hanul Manuc.** The Russian-Turkish Peace Treaty of 1812 was signed here. **Stavropoleos,** a nearby church built in 1724, has superb wood and stone carvings.

Calea Victoriei, Bucharest's most famous street, passes many of the city's major sights. Starting at the **Operetta Theater,** *Piata Natiunile Unite,* it leads north past Stavropoleos Church to the History Museum of Romania in the former post office. The museum displays the 42-pound golden Hen with Golden Chickens, a fifth-century treasure made of 12 gold pieces.

Like Paris, Bucharest has a triumphal arch. Built in 1922 to celebrate the Allies victory in World War I, it is located on the wide avenue of Soseaua Kiseleff.

Bucharest's best restaurants

Capsa, *Canea Victoriei 30; tel. (40-0)13-44-82,* is the traditional meeting place for Bucharest's artists. It offers a choice of local or continental cuisine and excellent desserts. A three-course meal for two here (and in most good restaurants in the city) costs about $12.

Pescarus, *tel. (40-0)79-46-40,* serves international cuisine on a terrace overlooking the lake in Herastrau Park.

Bucharest's best hotels

The newest deluxe hotel is **Bucuresti,** *Caleca Victoriei 63-81; tel. (40-0)14-21-77* or *(40-0)15-58-50,* in the center of town. It has 800 rooms, two restaurants, two swimming pools, a sauna, and a gym. Rooms are $65 to $100 per night.

Athenee Palace, *Str. Episcopiei 1-3; tel. (40-0)14-08-99,* a prewar grand dame, has a slightly faded grandeur. It has two restaurants and a good pastry shop.

Dracula's castle

While in Brasov, make a day trip to the town of Poiana Brasov (Sunny Glade) to see **Bran Castle,** the legendary home of Count Dracula. The prince of Wallachia, he repelled a Turkish invasion by impaling hundreds of his countrymen on tall stakes and lining the route of the enemy's march. The Turks, frightened by the brutal display, avoided the region. In truth, Dracula stayed at this castle only occasionally.

Poles: the warmest people

Poland doesn't have the tourist amenities of Western Europe, but it does have the Polish people. Self-effacing and fun-loving, they are the warmest people in the Eastern bloc. If you get lost in Poland, a Pole is likely to take you out for dinner and drinks as well as point you in the right direction.

Nature, too, welcomes visitors to Poland. The country's 12 natural parks and 500 wildlife preserves contain animals that have disappeared elsewhere in Europe—bison, chamois, bear, moose, and tarpan (small horses). Poland's 325-mile Baltic seacoast is lined with long, sandy beaches.

Warsaw: worst destruction, best restoration

Warsaw has had the bloodiest history of any Polish city. Hitler ordered that not one stone be left standing in the city following the 63-day Warsaw Uprising against the Nazis. As a result, more than 200,000 people were killed, and the city was razed. Between 1940 and 1945, a total of 750,000 of the city's residents died.

The Nazis weren't the first to demolish Warsaw. In the 17th century, the city was razed by the Swedes. It was sacked again in the 18th century. In 1795, Warsaw was given to Prussia. Napoleon took the city in 1806. And the Russians claimed it in 1813.

Although most of Warsaw's old buildings and monuments have been destroyed, most have been beautifully rebuilt. The old town was reconstructed after the war according to prints and old family photographs. It looks much as it did before, with narrow houses, winding streets, and Gothic churches. The district is closed to all traffic except horse-drawn buggies.

At the heart of the old town is **Market Square,** surrounded by re-created baroque houses, shops, and cafés and filled with flowers. The **Negro House,** Number 36 on the square, was once a center of the slave trade. It is marked by a bust of a black man. It is now the home of the **Warsaw Historical Museum,** where chamber music concerts are held on Tuesdays. The oldest house on the square is the **House of the Mazovian Dukes,** or St. Anne's House, at Number 31. It has the greatest number of Gothic details.

The **Royal Castle,** blown up during the war, is the most beautiful in Poland. Built between the 14th and 18th centuries, it was restored after World War II. It can be seen from Zamkowsky Square along with **King Sigismund's Column,** a symbol of Warsaw. The slender column was the first monument rebuilt after the war. Originally built in 1644, it honors King Sigismund III, who made Warsaw his capital in the late 16th century.

The old walls surrounding the city and a 16th-century tower called the **Barbican** also have been reconstructed. You can see fragments of the old defensive walls along Kamienne Schodki Street. They are defended by the statue of Syrena, a mermaid with a raised sword. According to legend, the mermaid rose out of the Vistula River and told two children playing on the banks to found the city. Their names were Wars and Szawa, hence the Polish name for the city, Warszawa.

The most frightening sights

The horrors of World War II are evident throughout Warsaw. The most frightening reminder is **Pawiak Prison Museum,** *Ul. Dzielna 24/26,* where 35,000 Poles were executed and 65,000 imprisoned.

The walled Jewish ghetto called **Muranow** was flattened by the Nazis. Today, Spartan modern apartments stand in its place. The Monument to the Heroes of the Ghetto stands on a small square at Zamenhofa and Anielewicza streets, once the heart of the ghetto. It is a slab of dark granite with a bronze bas-relief.

The **Jewish Historical Institute,** *Swierczewskiego 79,* has exhibits of the ghetto uprising. The **Mausoleum to Struggle and Martyrdom,** *Armii Wojska Polskiego Street,* is located at the former gestapo headquarters and prison.

A less obvious memorial to the war is a manhole cover at the intersection of Dluga and Miodawa streets. Here, 5,300 insurgents left the sewer canal through which they escaped from the old town during the Warsaw Uprising in September 1944. The horrors of their journey through Warsaw's sewers are graphically depicted in Wajda's film *Canal.*

Poland's prettiest palace

Lazienki Palace and Park is among the most beautiful in the world. In 1766 King Stanislas Poniatowski bought the neoclassical castle, which stood on an island in the middle of a lake, and had it enlarged and remodeled. The grounds also contain the Myslewicki Palace, the White Cottage, an old orangery, a baroque bathhouse, and a theater by the swan-filled lake, complete with artificial ruins.

The Polish Versailles

Wilanow Palace and Park, called Warsaw's Versailles, was built in the late 17th century by King Jan III Sobieski. The building is crowned with parapets, and the facade is carved with deities symbolizing the virtues of the royal family. Inside is the gallery of Polish portraiture and the world's first poster museum.

Warsaw's most famous residents

Stop by the often-overlooked **Maria Sklodowska Curie Museum,** *Ul. Freta 16.* Madame Curie was born here. The scientist was twice awarded the Nobel Prize for her discoveries of the radioactive elements polonium and radium.

Another little-known treasure is the house where **Chopin** was born in 1810. Set in a park in Zelazowa Wola, 33 miles west of Warsaw, the ivy-covered cottage is now a museum. A black Steinway grand piano stands in the corner of the music room. A 19th-century upright grand, which looks something like a harp, stands in another room. Framed musical compositions hang on the walls along with poems Chopin wrote as a boy for his parents. During the summer, Chopin concerts are held here on Sundays.

Best restaurants

The best restaurant in Warsaw is **Bazyliszek,** *Old Town Market Square 5/7,* a wood-beamed restaurant decorated with Hussar armor. Wild game is served. According to legend, a monster who could kill with a deadly glance once lived in the vaulted cellars. A shoemaker's apprentice did the ogre in by wearing a mirror-covered suit. The monster saw himself and died. Dinner for two costs about 7,500 zloty to 10,500 zloty ($25 to $35).

Karczma Slupska, *Czerniakowska 127,* features traditional Kashubian (northern Polish) fare in a comfortable setting. Try the nut soup and boar paté. Expect to pay about 4,500 zloty ($15) for two.

The bar at Karczma Slupska is also worth a visit—patrons sit on carousel horses that move up and down and are controlled from behind the bar.

Krokodyl, *19/21 Old Town Market Square,* is a favorite of Fidel Castro, who donated a large stuffed crocodile to the restaurant.

Best hotels

Victoria Inter-Continental, *Ul. Krolewska 11; tel. (48-22)27-54-64* or *(48-22)27-92-71,* is Warsaw's top hotel. Its 410 rooms go for about 19,500 zloty to 27,000 zloty ($65 to $130) per night. The hotel restaurant, Canaletto, specializes in Polish dishes.

Orbis-Europejski, *Ul. Krakowskie Przedmiescie 13; tel. (48-22)26-19-23,* is a grand four-story building more than 100 years old. It has a delightful café that overlooks the Saxon Gardens and the Monument to the Unknown Soldier. Doubles are about 19,500 zloty ($86) per night.

Cracow: the only unscathed Polish city

Cracow is the only Polish city that escaped demolition during World War II. Most of its buildings date from the 15th century. The city is dominated by **Wawel Hill,** with its fortified castle and Gothic cathedral. UNESCO described the castle, now a museum, as one of the most beautiful in the world. Poland's kings lived here until 1609, when the royal court moved to Warsaw. Even after the move, Polish kings continued to be crowned here.

Wawel Castle looks like a movie set, with gargoyles hanging from walls, elaborately carved doorways, columns, and brightly painted roof tiles. The castle museum contains the "Szczerbiec," a 13th-century sword used in coronation ceremonies, and the world's largest collection of tapestries—356 in all. The 71 rooms of the castle are richly decorated—one is covered entirely in embossed, hand-painted Spanish leather.

Czartaryski Palace (the National Museum) has collections of tapestries, pottery, weapons, and paintings by masters, including da Vinci and Rembrandt.

The **cathedral** on Wawel Hill contains the elaborate tomb of St. Stanislaus, Poland's patron. Lovely 15th-century frescoes decorate the cathedral's **Chapel of the Holy Cross. Sigismund Chapel,** an 11th-century crypt, contains red marble tombs of royalty, bishops, and national heroes.

Mariacki (the Church of the Virgin Mary) is famous for its bugler. Seven-hundred years ago, a bugler in the church tower was sounding an alarm when he was stopped mid-toot by a Tartar's arrow. Today, a bugle sounds every hour on the hour. The call is cut off suddenly, just as it was centuries ago.

The church also is famous for its 500-year-old altarpiece with life-size figures in gold raiment depicting the assumption of the Virgin Mary.

You enter Cracow's old city via the **Florian Gate,** which is next to a round fort called the Barbacan whose walls are 10 feet thick and pierced by 130 peepholes. Pedestrians can climb medieval staircases here and view the gargoyles. This area is the site of one of the world's oldest universities, **Jagiellonia University,** which was founded in 1364 and counts Copernicus among its alumni. Today it has 16,000 students.

All streets in the old city lead to **Rynek Glowny** (the main marketplace). Once the largest municipal square in Europe, it is the site of political rallies, festivals, and public performances. Hundreds of pigeons share the square with crowds of people.

Zakopane: Poland's best ski resort

Zakopane, in the Tatra Mountains near the Czech border, is the top ski resort in Poland. At 2,625 feet, it has good ski conditions from November through May. A funicular takes you to the top of Gubalowka, a peak above town. And a cable car takes you to the top of Kasprowy Wierch, at nearly 6,514 feet.

The place to stay in Zakopane is **Orbis Kasprowy**, a 300-room hotel with a restaurant, a nightclub, an indoor pool, a sauna, an ice-skating rink, and a mini-golf course. All rooms have private baths.

Czestochowa, a Czech mecca

Every year on Assumption Day (Aug. 15), hundreds of thousands of pilgrims come to the drab little town of **Czestochowa** on the Warta River to pay homage to a portrait of the Madonna, said to have been painted by St. Luke. The Madonna's cheeks are marred by two slashes that, according to legend, were made by an enraged Tartar who felt the painting getting heavier and heavier as he tried to steal it.

The portrait is kept in a huge monastery called **Jasna Gora** (Hill of Light), founded in 1382 by Paulist monks. Swedish armies were halted here in 1655 and driven out of Poland.

Central Europe's last primeval forest

Bialowieza National Park, the last primeval forest in Central Europe, covers 480 square miles, half in Poland, half in the Soviet Union. A thick wall of 1,000-year-old oaks, pines, and spruce trees, it is home to Europe's only wild bison, as well as moose, lynx, wild tarpans, bears, foxes, deer, and wild boars. You can explore the forest on four-hour horse-drawn excursions.

East Germany: the starkest contrast

The contrast between Eastern and Western Europe is most startling in East Germany (more formally known as the German Democratic Republic, or the GDR), because of its proximity to prosperous West Germany. Germany beyond the Berlin Wall is rich in culture and perfectly preserved historical treasures that contrast starkly with the Spartan lifestyle and severe political system of an East bloc country.

Berlin: the closest point

The easiest way to experience the two faces of Germany is to cross the Berlin Wall from West to East for a day. Drive through at Checkpoint Charlie or take a bus or subway across to Friedrichstrasse in East Berlin. Visas good from 8 a.m. to midnight are issued by border guards. The process takes five minutes to an hour and costs about $2.75. You must change 25 marks into East German currency (although this sounds like a small sum for a day of shopping and restaurants, you will have trouble spending it all).

The best view of Berlin

Fernsehturm (the television tower), between Alexanderplatz and Marx-Engels-Platz, offers the best view of Berlin. Rising 1,209 feet, the slender spire is Europe's second-tallest tower. You can have a meal or a cup of coffee in the revolving sphere that tops the tower at 655 feet. But keep in mind that you have only one hour to eat. When the revolving sphere completes its 60-minute circuit, you will be asked to leave.

The tower is open every day. You can spot it from almost any section of town.

East Germany's crown jewel

Museumsinsel (Museum Island), surrounded by the Spree River and the Spree Canal, is one of the world's largest and most magnificent museum complexes. It includes the Pergamon, the Bode, and the Altes museums, as well as the the National Gallery, the Berlin Cathedral (Deutscher Dom), and several ruins.

The magnificent **Pergamon** is the most important of the complex's museums. Everything here is on a giant scale. The huge **Ishtar Gate** was transported centuries ago stone by stone from ancient Babylon.

The museum has an extensive collection of ancient art, including artifacts from 200 B.C. Far Eastern, Near Eastern, and Islamic Art also also featured. The beautiful **Pergamon Altar** is one of the Seven Wonders of the Ancient World. Originally part of a temple complex to Zeus, it was brought from Turkey and reconstructed here.

The neoclassical **Altes Museum** houses contemporary paintings and 135,000 prints by 15th- to 18th-century masters, including Botticelli's illustrations of Dante's *Divine Comedy*.

The **National Gallery** has a comprehensive collection of 19th- and 20th-century art from the Soviet Union and other East bloc countries. The **Bode Museum** has an outstanding collection of Egyptian, early Christian, and Byzantine art.

The museum complex shares the island with Berlin's **Lutheran Cathedral,** built from 1894 to 1905 and recently restored; the **French (Calvinist) Cathedral;** and ruins of the former main synagogue, which was destroyed by Nazi vandals and by bombings during World War II. Designed by the architect Knoblauch and built from 1859 to 1866, it is a curious combination of Western and Moorish influences.

Berlin's top sights

Die Deutsche Staatsoper (the opera house), *Unter den Linden 7; tel. (37-2)205-4556,* seats 1,500 people and hosts some of the finest opera performances in the world. It was built in 1743 but burned down 100 years later. The rebuilt facade is modeled on the original.

Hegel, Max Planck, and Einstein taught at **Humboldt University,** *Unter den Linden 6.* And Marx and Engels studied here. The largest university in East Germany, it was built in the mid-18th century. The palace of Emperor William I, built in 1836, is now part of the university. The emperor spent the last 50 years of his life here. **Die Alte Bibliothek** (the Old Library) also is part of the university. Formerly the Prussian State Library, it is set back from Unter den Linden, on Bebelplatz. The Nazis burned books here in 1933.

Zeughaus, *Unter den Linden 2,* is a baroque structure housing the Museum of German History. It is worth visiting to see a Marxist view of history. The museum is closed Fridays.

Just south of the rathaus is the ornate **Sankt Nicholas Church,** the oldest in the city, begun in 1230. You have a splendid view of the city from the tower.

Marienkirche (St. Mary's Church), Berlin's second-oldest church, near Museumsinsel on Karl-Liebknechtstrasse, was built in 1240. It is one of the few Gothic buildings in East Berlin.

Berlin's best restaurants

Muggelsee-Perle, *Am Grossen Muggelsee; tel. (34-2)652-10,* is the best restaurant in Berlin, and one of the best restaurants in East Germany. The fish, fowl, and game dishes are delicious. While dining, you can enjoy a view of the city's largest lake, Grosser Muggelsee. Dinner for two is about 27 marks.

Ermeler Haus, *Märkisches Ufer 10-12; tel. (37-2)279-4036,* a continental restaurant in a baroque building, serves good food in a romantic ambience. Reservations are suggested. Dinner for two is about 26 marks.

Stockinger, *Schönhauser Allee 61; tel. (37-2)448-3110,* is a simply furnished restaurant that serves good traditional German dishes. The Oriental dishes aren't as good as the local fare. Dinner for two is about 43 marks.

Best places to sleep

The best hotel in East Berlin is the **Metropol,** *Friedrichstr. 150-153; tel. (37-2)2214250,* a modern high-rise hotel built by a Swedish firm (perhaps the reason it features saunas). Rooms are luxurious and the service good. Doubles start at 220 marks.

Palast, *Karl-Liebknechtstr. 5; tel. (37-2)2412100,* is another luxury hotel with first-class service. The rooms are attractive and have views of the city. The hotel restaurant is good. Double rooms start at 230 marks.

Dresden: fine porcelain and restoration

Dresden, known in the United States for its fine porcelain, is also known for the beauty of its now-restored buildings. During World War II, the city was fire bombed by the Allies, and 80% of it burned to the ground. It has been beautifully reconstructed. Linden trees line the banks of the Elbe River, and the city has some of the best museums in Germany.

Stroll along **Pragerstrasse,** once one of Dresden's most fashionable streets. It is lined with apartments and shops and embellished with fountains and benches. This street connects the new section of Dresden with the old quarter.

Frauenkirche (Church of our Lady) has been left in ruins purposely as a memorial to the city's bombing.

Dresden's best

Zwinger Palace, and the portrait gallery it contains, is Dresden's drawing card. Carefully restored following the bombings of World War II, it retains much of its original structure, including a majestic courtyard where fountains play in the summer. Built as a fortress in the 18th century, it houses Raphael's *Sistine Madonna,* as well as a dozen Rembrandts, 16 Reubens, and several Tintorettos. The bells in its carillon tower are made of Dresden china.

Music-lovers' favorite

Dresden's second jewel is the **Semper Opera,** where Wagner and von Weber conducted and Richard Strauss' operas premiered. The opera house was designed by architect Gottfried Semper and completed in 1850. After 1945, it was restored based on original drawings. The building was immortalized in a painting by the 18th-century artist Canaletto.

Dresden's best art museum

The 16th-century glass-domed **Albertinum** contains the state collection of 19th- and 20th-century paintings, including many works by French Impressionists. The museum's **Grünes Gewolbe** (Green Vault) displays works of goldsmiths and jewelers from the 15th to 18th centuries. The collection once belonged to the kings of Saxony, whose capital was Dresden. The museum is closed Thursdays.

Best restaurants

Aberlausitzer Topp'l, *Strasse der Befreiung 14; tel. (37-51)5-5605,* serves the hearty fare of the Lusatia area, home of the Sorbs, a Slavic people of Eastern Germany numbering 100,000 and speaking a language related to Polish. (Lusatia is a rural area along the Spree River.) The dark beers served here are excellent. Reservations are suggested. Dinner for two is 35 marks to 51 marks.

Secundogenitur, *Bruhlische Terrasse; tel. (37-51)49-51-435,* serves a set meal each day, and it's always outstanding. Dinner for two is 35 marks to 50 marks.

Meissener Weinkeller, *Strasse der Befreiung 1B; tel (37-51)55814* or *(37-51)55928,* on the Elbe, has a comprehensive list of East German wines and very inexpensive meals. The view from the terrace is lovely. Reservations are suggested.

Best hotels

Astoria, *Ernst Thalmann-Platz; tel. (37-51)47-51-71* or *(37-51)485-6666,* is a small, comfortable hotel in the heart of the city. The service is friendly, and the prices are good— about 120 marks a night. Not every room has a shower or bath.

Königstein, *Pragerstrasse; tel (37-51)4-8560,* on the main shopping street, is pleasant but not luxurious. All rooms have private baths. Double rooms start at 160 marks.

East Germany's most beautiful palace

Potsdam (where the 1945 Potsdam Agreement was signed by Truman, Stalin, and Churchill, allowing Soviet forces to remain in control of East Germany) has East Germany's most beautiful Rococo palace. **Sans Souci** (literally, without worry) was built by Frederick the Great in imitation of the French Versailles in 1745. You must wear felt-soled slippers when you visit, to protect the beautiful floors. Voltaire, the French philosopher admired by Frederick, lived here for a time. Paintings by Rubens, Van Dyck, and Caravaggio hang in the palace galleries.

Interhotel Potsdam, *Lange Brücke; tel. (37-33)4631,* is one of the most prestigious hotels in East Germany. It has a sauna, shops, dancing, entertainment, a restaurant, and a bar. Double rooms in this large, high-rise hotel are 160 marks to 200 marks a night.

Buchenwald—the blackest memory

Just north of Weimar is the infamous **Buchenwald Concentration Camp,** where 56,000 people died in World War II. The camp and its museum of torture and extermination devices are chilling. Even in spring the site is so cold and bleak that you cannot imagine surviving a winter in the scanty barracks. Outside the camp is a memorial to the victims.

If you visit, be prepared to be showered with pro-communist, anti-American rhetoric likening the evils of fascism to modern-day capitalism. A film showing the horrors of Buchenwald ends with a shot of an American soldier holding the body of his Vietnamese victim.

THE BEST OF ASIA

For many Americans, Asia is an enormous, incomprehensible, mysterious mass on the other side of the earth visited only by the Marco Polos of the world. Quite the contrary, Asia is not the moon and can be enjoyed by Westerners.

China recently opened its doors to American tourists and has attracted many more visitors than in the past. The Japanese, too, encourage Americans to come to their land. And India, despite internal turmoil in certain areas, has the most varied landscape of any country in the world. Asia is filled with wonders that just can't be experienced anywhere else on earth.

Chapter 14

THE BEST OF CHINA

The **People's Republic of China** (PRC), with the largest population in the world, is as big as all the countries in Europe combined. Its civilization flourished when the Occident was struggling its way out of the Dark Ages. Lying on the world's largest continent, China faces the world's largest ocean, the Pacific. It has the world's tallest mountains, the Himalayas, and the world's biggest city, Shanghai; and it controls the world's highest city, Lhasa, in Tibet.

Although 98% of China's population is made up of Han people, the remaining 2% contains nearly 50-million members of minority groups. Tibetans, in their land of monasteries above the clouds, consider the Dali Lama the head of the Buddhist religion; Mongolian horsemen roam the Gobi Desert; Chinese Muslims (Hui) live in the north; the Miao and Dai people in the south are related to hill tribes of Southeast Asia.

(Note: The telephone numbers listed in this chapter may have changed by the time this book is published. China is planning to revamp its telephone system. Prices, too, may be different, because prices in China today are fluctuating drastically.)

The best of Beijing

Beijing (Peking), one of the oldest cities in the world, has been the capital of China for 700 years. People have been living in this area for at least 50,000 years. Peking Man, a fossil found in 1918 in a village southwest of Beijing, is one of the oldest relics of early man yet found.

Situated at the end of the route followed by camel caravans for centuries, Beijing is the site of many cities that have come and gone. Kublai Khan built his palace here and called the city Ta-tu (Great Capital). The northern part of the city has remnants of the old Mongol town visited by Marco Polo.

Beijing houses some of the greatest man-made wonders in the world. The Emperor's Forbidden City in the heart of Beijing and the Great Wall on the outskirts of the city are the most notable attractions.

The Forbidden City

The **Forbidden City,** where the emperor of China once lived, is no longer barred to common man. Hundreds pass through the palace museum every day, gaping at the royal opulence. Surrounded by red brick walls and guarded by tile-roofed towers, the palace was built by Ming Emperor Yung Lo in the early 15th century and covers nearly 250 acres. For five centuries, China was ruled from here by the emperor, who was considered the son of heaven. His every wish was granted. His meals were prepared by 5,000 to 6,000 cooks, and concubines, eunuchs, court favorites, and entertainers were kept here.

Surrounded by 35-foot walls and a wide moat, the city contains six palaces, all roofed in yellow tile (yellow was the imperial color), and many gardens and pavilions. See the apartments of the emperor, the empress dowager, and the concubines; the halls of Supreme Harmony, Perfect Harmony, and the Preservation of Harmony; the temples; the libraries; and the art collection. Altogether, the rooms number 9,000.

The best way to prepare yourself for touring the palace is to see Bernardo Bertolucci's film *The Last Emperor,* which tells the sad story of China's last ruler, who was, as a child, virtually a prisoner in the palace.

The world's largest public square

Tian'anmen Square (the Square of Heavenly Peace), where Mao Zedong proclaimed the People's Republic of China in 1949, is the largest public square in the world, covering 100 acres and capable of holding one-million people. As they have for centuries, the Chinese people come to hear government proclamations and to rally and demonstrate.

The square is bounded to the west by the Great Hall of the People, which contains a 328-foot-long marble hall and reception rooms where diplomatic meetings are held; to the east by the Museum of Chinese History and the Museum of the Chinese Revolution; to the north by the Tien'anmen Gate to the Imperial City, built in 1417 and hung with a portrait of Mao Tse-tung; and to the south by the Quianmen gate, built in the 15th century. In the center is the 120-foot Monument to the People's Heroes, an obelisk depicting scenes from the revolution and inscribed with quotations by Mao Tse-tung and Chou En-lai.

Kite-flying in the square is a popular pastime and a good way to meet locals. You can buy a colorful Chinese kite in any Friendship Store (government stores for tourists)—an exotic souvenir, unless it gets tangled in the gates to the Imperial Palace.

The most beautiful temple

The blue **Tiantan** (Temple of Heaven), built in the 15th century, is the finest example of Chinese architecture. Actually a complex of buildings, the temple is surrounded by a walled park. The most beautiful building within the complex is the Qi Nian Dian (Hall of Prayer for Good Harvest), set on three marble terraces, each with a 36-foot balustrade, and connected by eight flights of stairs. Supported by 28 columns and topped by 50,000 glazed blue tiles, the 123-foot hall was built of wood with no nails. Blue-roofed pavilions flank the temple.

Nearby is the **Huan Qiu Tan** (Round Altar), where each year for centuries on Dec. 20 (the day before the Winter Solstice), the emperor made a mysterious animal sacrifice that determined the destiny of the nation. The altar is made up of three terraces, each surrounded by a white marble balustrade with 360 pillars.

Beijing's best park

The most famous of Beijing's many parks is **Beihai,** or North Lake, which has pagodas, formal gardens, and three lakes. Created in A.D. 300, the park is the best-preserved ancient garden in China. Young people row on the lakes and whisper sweet nothings on the shores.

Closed during the Cultural Revolution, the park reopened 10 years ago.

In the middle of Beihai is an island called **Qionghua,** which is crowned by a Tibetan-style white dagoba (a shrine for sacred relics) built in 1651 to commemorate the visit of a Dalai Lama. The view from the dagoba takes in the park and most of the city. The beautiful **Zhichu Qiao** (Bridge of Perfect Wisdom) leads to the island.

The empress dowager's favorite palace

Yiheyuan (the Summer Palace) on the outskirts of Beijing was the extravagant summer retreat of the infamous Empress Dowager Ci Xi. Located in the Haidian district and surrounded by a walled 692-acre park, the palace was built in 1888 to replace an older and supposedly more beautiful palace that was destroyed by British and French troops in 1860. (All that remains of the original are a marble arch, pillars, and a wall.) The existing palace, too, was burned by Western troops, during the Boxer Rebellion in 1900, but it was restored a few years later.

Stroll along the **Long Corridor,** bordering the lake and exquisitely painted with scenes from Chinese mythology. Visit the royal apartments, which contain jewel-encrusted furniture and beautiful works of art. Climb **Longevity Hill,** at the heart of the palace.

Best undiscovered sights

The **Gulou** (Drum Tower), *Drum Tower Street,* near Shichahai Lake in northern Beijing, is a 15th-century structure in brick and wood, so named because a drum was beaten here to summon officials to audiences with the emperor. For some unknown reason, it is seldom visited by tourists.

Just 100 yards behind is the **Zhonglou** (Bell Tower), similar in design, built about 1745. The nightwatch announced the hour from here until 1924.

Between the two towers is a charming maze of residential streets that feel like they belong more in a small village than a large city. The stone houses here are tightly packed, topped with tiled roofs, and entered through doors that are thick, old, and decorated with iron. Clay walls surround courtyards that are broken by doors at irregular intervals. From time to time you will see a woman with tiny, bound feet, a remnant of the days before the revolution. The area is safe at any hour, but you may get lost and have trouble finding someone who speaks English and can set you back on the right trail.

Another neighborhood worth exploring is a tangle of streets off **Wangfujing,** one of the main shopping streets, where Manchu nobility once lived. The formidable Empress Dowager Ci Xi was raised in one of the mansions on Xila Hatung. Another landmark in the neighborhood is the **East Church,** built in 1666 by the Jesuits. Pao Fa Hatung is lined with remnants of the **Fa Hua Si Temple** (Temple of Buddha's Glory), built in the 15th century. You can see the original walls, entry gates, and a small antechamber. The rest is gone.

Beijing's best shopping

The easiest place to shop in Beijing is the government-run **Friendship Store,** *Jianguomenwai Avenue,* the largest in China. It has just about anything you could want (jade, ivory, silk hangings, furniture, paintings, cloisonné, carpets, and handicrafts). It is the only place in Beijing that will take care of shipping (which is expensive) and customs.

However, it is more fun to shop at Beijing's **street bazaars.** The most famous is **Donghuamen,** *Wangfujing Street,* behind the Beijing (Guoji) Hotel. Near the Temple of

Heaven is the Tan Chiao Bazaar, where fresh fish and vegetables are sold to throngs of people while storytellers, musicians, and street performers entertain.

Wangfujing, around the corner from the Beijing Hotel, is the city's main shopping district. In addition to **Baihuo Dalou,** the main department store, *255 Wangfujing St.,* which is the largest and best-stocked store in Beijing, the neighborhood has scores of little specialty shops.

Zhongguo Pihuo Fuzhuangdian (the China Fur and Leather Clothing Store), *192 Wangfujing St.,* has ready-made fur and leather coats, jackets, hats, and gloves and will make clothing to order as well. **Capital Medicine Shop,** *136 Wangfujing St.,* sells traditional Chinese medicines.

Chinese wind instruments are sold at the **Musical Instruments Store,** *231 Wangfujing St.,* and personalized Chinese stone seals are made at **Wangfujing Kezi Menshibu** (the Wangfujing Seal-Engraving Store), *261 Wangfujing St.* Chinese scrolls and tomb rubbings can be purchased at **The Arts Store,** *265 Wangfujing St.*

Buying antiques in China is a tricky business. Government regulations are strict. Only those items with proper invoice papers and red government seals of approval can be taken out of China.

If you feel up to dealing with the red tape, quite a few shops in China carry fine antiques. In Beijing, the best shops are on **Liulichang,** especially numbers 70 and 80. Here, collectors can find fine porcelain, jade, and wood carvings.

The Great Wall

Forty-six miles from Beijing is the **Great Wall,** stretching nearly 4,000 miles through the hills of northern China. It is the only man-made structure that the astronauts have been able to see from the moon. Construction on most of the wall began in 403 B.C. and continued until 206 B.C. Thousands of men, many political prisoners, carried the stones and dirt that make up the gigantic defense. Some of their bodies are buried inside. Once 6,000 miles long, much of the wall has been destroyed.

The section most visited is at **Badaling,** northwest of Beijing, which was constructed during the Ming Dynasty (1368-1644). You can walk along the top—it is 18 feet wide and 21 feet tall. Look through the slots in the wall along the top and imagine the terrible battles that once raged against the barbarians from the north. Special trains and buses connect Beijing and the Great Wall.

To avoid all the tourists who gather at Badaling, go a bit farther afield to **Mutianyu,** where a newly restored section of the wall opened in 1986. A great fort with 22 watchtowers was built along this stretch. From the top you'll have a view of the surrounding mountain slopes, forests, and the town of Mutianyu. To get to Mutianyu, hire a car or take the Dongzhimen Long Distance Bus Line (tickets must be purchased one day in advance).

The Ming tombs

On the way to the Great Wall are the **Ming tombs,** where 13 of the 16 Ming emperors chose to be buried. **Shisanling,** the peaceful valley where the tombs are located, was chosen by the rulers because the winds and the water level ensured that only good spirits wandered the area.

The road to the tombs, known as the **Sacred Way,** is lined with 24 immense statues: 12 animals, real and mythical, and 12 Mandarins in ceremonial dress. One of the Qing emperors is said to have wanted to take the statues to line the road to his own tomb. He abandoned the plan after dreaming that the statues are forever loyal to the Ming Dynasty and that if he should move them an evil wind would blow across the capital.

Only two of the tombs have been excavated, those of Chang Ling and Ding Ling. The best-preserved and largest tomb is that of Chang Ling (the burial name for Yong Le), who died in 1424. It is entered through a red gate that opens into a courtyard. Another gate leads into a second courtyard, where the marble **Lingendian** (Hall of Eminent Favors) is supported by 32 giant tree columns. To get to the sepulcher, you must continue into a third courtyard.

The tomb of Ding Ling (the burial name for Emperor Wan Li) was the first to be excavated. A deep marble vault four stories underground contains the coffins of Ding and two of his wives, who were buried here in 1620. A bronze lion and gigantic marble doors guard the tomb. Inside are the three coffins and 26 chests filled with jewelry.

Beijing's best restaurants

Fang Shan (Imitation Imperial) is the restaurant in Beihai Park. The goal of the chefs, who are said to have studied with the last empress' chefs, is to recreate dishes served to the royal families of the past. The restaurant is set on the shores of North Lake. It can be difficult to get reservations.

On the grounds of the Summer Palace, on Longevity Hill overlooking Kunming Lake, is **Tingliguan** (Listening to the Orioles Pavilion). This restaurant features dumplings, velvet chicken, and other northern dishes. The **Sick Duck,** *13 Shuaifuyuan* (1 block off Wangfujing), takes its name from a nearby hospital, not from the condition of its poultry. It is comfortable and close to the Beijing Hotel.

Beijing's best hotels

The **Beijing Hotel,** *East Chang'an Avenue and Wangfujing Street; tel. 5007766,* takes the honorable first position. Not too long ago, it was the only good place in Beijing, and it's still the most exclusive. Foreigners cannot book rooms directly—you must go through an influential Chinese contact. Rooms are modern and spacious, many with color televisions, radios, and refrigerators. Some have balconies with views of the Forbidden City.

Xiang Shan (the Fragrant Hills), *Xian Shan Park; tel. 285491,* a 40-minute drive outside town and halfway to the Great Wall, was designed by the famous Chinese-American architect I.M. Pei. Jackie Kennedy was one of the hotel's first guests.

A grand, white fortress of a place, Xiang Shan has beautifully landscaped gardens and skillfully lit rooms. Double beds (an unusual feature in Chinese hotels), an outdoor swimming pool, and a health club are special features. While the Fragrant Hills is not conveniently located if you want to visit Beijing every day, it is surrounded by lovely countryside and situated near little-known shrines and monuments. For this reason, it may be the best place to stay on your *second* trip to Beijing.

Zhu Yuan (Bamboo Garden Hotel), *24 Xiaoshiqiao, Jiugulou Street; tel. 444661,* in an attractive residential neighborhood in the northern section of the city, has bamboo gardens, rookeries, air conditioning, and color televisions. It is near the Drum Tower and was once home to Kang Sheng, one of the Gang of Four.

The **Holiday Inn Lido Beijing,** *Jichang and Jiang Tai roads; tel. 5006688,* is Beijing's version of an American resort hotel. It has a bowling alley, restaurants and lounges, a health club, a swimming pool, and rooms with air conditioning, private bathrooms, color televisions, and direct-dial telephones. While it is comfortable, the Lido is outside town on the road to the airport. Whoever chose the color combinations must have been color blind (mustard yellow and pea green).

The best of Guangzhou

Still known to most English-speaking people as Canton, **Guangzhou** is a popular point of entry for foreign tourists—it is only three hours from Hong Kong by train or hovercraft. (By the way, you can buy lovely pure silk Chinese scarves on the Guangzhou train from Shenzhen, port of the ferry from Hong Kong, for a mere $2!)

Unlike the rest of China, which stayed free of outside influence until well into the 19th century, Guangzhou began dealing with foreign traders in A.D. 714. Thus, a foreigner has never been much of a rarity here. In fact, when considering the deference shown visitors elsewhere in China, some foreigners have found Guangzhou less than hospitable.

Early on, the Chinese government thought it best to canton the barbarians, as foreign traders were known, so they wouldn't corrupt the rest of the kingdom—hence, the name Canton. Arab, Portuguese, English, French, and American traders who sailed up the Pearl River were isolated and cantoned in their own areas. After their victory in the First Opium War, the Europeans were given an island in the Pearl River off Canton's waterfront, called **Shamian.** French and Victorian buildings still can be seen here.

Another result of foreign influence: Guangzhou has one of China's largest Muslim communities and the nation's oldest mosque, dating from A.D. 627.

This old city remains a trading capital, and the mixture of local and foreign influences is as exotic today as it must have been to residents and traders of the Middle Ages.

Top sights

Zhenhailou (Tower Overlooking the Sea), a five-story red pagoda built in 1380 on the highest hill in Yuexiu Park, was originally a temple. Today it is the Guangdong Historical Museum—fitting, considering the pagoda's involvement in Guangzhou's history. It served as a watch tower during the Opium War, when it was seized by French and British troops, and again during the 1911 Revolution.

If you climb all the way to the top of the tower, you will be rewarded with a cup of green tea and a view of the park and the city. The museum's exhibits are displayed in chronological order from prehistoric times to the modern day.

The graceful **Five Goats Statue,** a reminder of Guangzhou's mythical beginnings, is also in Yuexiu Park. According to legend, the city was founded by five gods who rode to earth on five goats bearing a stalk of rice, a symbolic promise that the city would never go hungry. (That promise wasn't kept.) Guangzhou is still known as Yangcheng, or Goat City.

Cultural Park, near the Pearl River, covers 20 acres and includes an aquarium, an opera house, and a concert hall; seven exhibition halls, three television screens for the public, and two open-air theaters; a roller-skating rink, a teahouse, and a ping pong area; and flower gardens.

Chen Clan Academy, a 19th-century compound, is one of the best examples of late imperial southern Chinese architecture. The roof and walls are decorated with terra-cotta sculptures, and the windows, doors, columns, and roof beams are carved. This family-run school of Confucian studies was built around an ancestral temple, where you still can see an altar and a shrine.

The **Jade Carving Factory** is open to visitors, who can watch workers carving and polishing the glowing green stone.

China's largest garden

The largest garden in China, **South China Botanical Gardens,** is just northeast of Guangzhou. Covering 750 lush acres, it has one of the best botanical collections in the world.

Oldest mosque, best cathedral

Foreign visitors brought foreign religions to Guangzhou, and, as a result, the city has two buildings that may seem out of place in a country with a Buddhist history and a communist present. On Zhongshan Road, near the intersection with Haizhu Road, is the **Huaisheng Mosque,** the oldest in China. It was built in A.D. 627 by an uncle of the prophet Muhammed, who is said to have brought the first Koran to China. It is now the mosque of China's largest Muslim community, which is estimated at 4,000. On the Yide Road, near the popular Renmin Daxia Hotel, is a Gothic-style cathedral that was designed by the French architect Guillemin and built in 1860. During the Cultural Revolution, this building was used as a warehouse; however, it was renovated and reconsecrated in 1979 and now holds regular Sunday services.

The best shopping

International traders still flock to Guangzhou for the **Chinese Export Commodities Fair,** held Oct. 15 to Nov. 15 and April 15 to May 15 in the big exhibition hall near the Dong Fang Hotel.

If you are interested in more modest retail purchases, wander along **Renmin Road,** home of the Nanfang Department Store, the biggest in the city. Number 8 is a well-stocked poster store; Number 14 is a tea shop; Number 20 is a housewares store; and Number 60 is a barber shop that brings a bit of the American West to Southeast Asia. You can unearth fine antiques on **Hongshu Road,** in an antiques warehouse that has just about anything you could want.

While shopping, stop for a snack at the most popular dumpling shop in town, the **Nanfang,** *Number 35.*

The most exotic market

The **Quingping Market,** just over the bridge from Shamian Island, has an incredible assortment of animals intended for the table. (The Cantonese will eat anything.) Dogs hang from hooks. Kittens are sold by the pound. Dead rats are sold as food. Wild boars are caged. Owls, mice, and snakes await slaughter.

Some of the beasts at this market are seen in the West only in zoos. The pangolin, for example, is on the endangered species list. Small, Bambi-like deer are slaughtered before your eyes. And internal organs you have never heard of are for sale.

China's best food

Guangzhou's cuisine is the best in China and the best-known in the West, where Cantonese restaurants are common. However, exported Cantonese cuisine is not the real thing. In Canton, the ingredients are exotic, including snake, dog, frogs, and rats. The people of Guangzhou have an expression that explains, "The things flying in the sky, except the planes, can be eaten. The things on the ground with four legs, except the tables, can be eaten."

If you are feeling adventurous enough to try monkey brain (more power to you!), try **She**

Canguan, *41 Jianglan Lu; tel. 83811.* Guangzhou's most palatable contribution to the world is *dim sum,* or *dyan syin,* a Chinese brunch that consists of a long series of small courses (sometimes 10 or more), served in the course of one or two hours. Most of the dishes are different varieties of dumplings filled with pork, seafood, or vegetables.

Banxi, *East Xiangyang Road,* is Guangzhou's biggest and best *dim sum* restaurant. **Yuyuan,** *90 S. Liwan Road,* is also good.

Guangzhou, *2 Wenchang Nan Lu,* is open late—which in this city means until 9:30 p.m. Try the chicken steamed in Maotai and the crab-paste dumplings.

Nanyuan, *120 Qianjin Road,* offers dining in a splendid garden. The **Pan Xi,** an old teahouse on a lake, has a tiled roof, garden walkways, and footbridges.

The best hotels

The **White Swan Hotel,** *1 South St., Shamian Island; tel. 886968,* is China's only five-star hotel. Rooms are decorated in jade-colored silk and filled with walnut furniture. The hotel opened in early 1983 and quickly distinguished itself with its many guest services (including a 24-hour laundry), its 30 dining rooms, its trilingual staff, and its astounding variety of fitness activities (including skydiving lessons).

The lobby is one of the most beautiful anywhere. And the hotel has reasonably priced shops selling Chinese silk rugs, handpainted screens, gigantic carved jade boats, and silk paintings. The building is situated on Shamian Island in the Pearl River, where a legendary hero is said to have been spirited away by a white swan. Free shuttle service is available to the hotel from the train station.

The most romantic temporary address in Guangzhou is the **Dong Fang Hotel,** *Xicun Highway; tel. 32644*—not so much for its appearance, which is strictly Soviet revival, but for its inhabitants. Journalists, consular personnel, and powerful international businessmen have stayed in its rooms. The dining room serves everything from Wiener Schnitzel to Indian curries, Japanese tempura, and American apple pie.

A small, reasonably priced hotel downtown is **Renmin Daxia** (People's Mansion), *207 Changdi Road; tel. 661445.* Located in a 14-story mansion built in 1936, it has spacious rooms with private bathrooms and simple furnishings.

Two of China's most luxurious hotels are outside Guangzhou, on the slopes of Baiyun (White Cloud Mountain): the **Shanzhuang** and the **Shuangxi.** Guests stay in large villas with sunken baths, private gardens, and lovely sitting rooms. Chinese government officials and high-ranking foreigners stay here.

The best side trips from Guangzhou

Nine miles from Guangzhou is **Baiyun,** which rises 1,400 feet and has a panoramic view of the city, the countryside, and the river. At the top are teahouses and pavilions, where you can recover from the six-hour climb. Don't stray from marked paths—the government doesn't want Americans to get too close to the nearby defense installations.

China's best mineral springs are in **Conghua,** 50 miles north of Guangzhou. The eight springs are about 104 degrees Fahrenheit and are said to cure chronic ailments. They are worth visiting even if you feel fine—they are surrounded by mountains, lichee orchards, plum trees, and bamboo groves.

Zixingyan (Seven Star Crags) is a series of natural rock towers connected by arched bridges and little pathways. Five small lakes and several caves lie in the shadow of traditional pavilions, which provide shelter. You can get to Zixingyan by bus or taxi in three hours.

Shanghai: the largest city in the world

Shanghai was the most powerful city in China before the Communists took over in 1949. Merely a fishing village in the 17th century, it gained its wealth from trade as a treaty port opened by the Europeans during the Opium Wars. Controlled by the British from 1842 to 1949, Shanghai still has a Western air and has been compared to New York and Rome. Before the Chinese Revolution, Shanghai had a lively stock market and great wealth.

Today, Shanghai is the largest city in the world and China's most important city economically. Covering 2,355 square miles, metropolitan Shanghai has a total population of more than 11 million. The trend-setter for China, Shanghai is in the forefront of the nation's drive to modernize. Billboards advertise Japanese as well as Chinese products. Many of the people are fashionably dressed, with Western hairstyles.

In the past, too, Shanghai set the pace in China. The Communist Party of China formed here, and this was the city where 800,000 workers rose against the rulers in 1927. The Gang of Four was most powerful here in 1965.

The prettiest neighborhood

Shanghai's most charming corner is the **old town,** the Chinese ghetto during the British Occupation. Between Jinling, Renmin, and Zhonghua roads, are narrow streets, thatched huts, tiny shops, and outdoor markets with piles of fresh produce. In the northeast section of the old town is a bazaar where you can buy beautifully carved walking sticks and traditional Chinese handicrafts. A little farther north are the Temple of the Town Gods and the Garden of the Purple Clouds of Autumn. Be careful, it's easy to get lost in this maze.

Forget the fancy restaurants and eat in the old town's little food shops. (But don't drink the water.) Chinese lunchtime fare is cheap and fun to eat.

Opium dens and brothels

Until 1949, the area west of People's Park, off Fuzhou Road, was the heart of Shanghai's world-famous red-light district known as **Blood Alley.** Before it was cleared out, it was inhabited by thousands of opium addicts and prostitutes. Liberation Lane alone, then known as Meet-With-Happiness Lane, had 34 brothels worked by more than 1,000 women. From 1949 to 1954, the brothels and opium dens were closed, the prostitutes given new work and new identities, and the addicts detoxified.

Yu Yuan: the happiest garden

At the heart of the old town is **Yu Yuan Garden** (Garden of Happiness), built in 1577 by a city official as a peaceful retreat for his aging father. It includes more than 30 halls and pavilions, all with charming names: Pavilion for Paying Reverence to Weaving, Fairyland of Happiness, Tower for Observing Waves, Tower for Appreciating the Moon. A tall, white brick wall topped with stone dragons divides the garden into three separate areas. Each section is designed to create the illusion of space and depth using artificial hills, ponds, bridges, and miniature gardens. A small lake at the center of the garden is crossed by zigzag bridges and bordered by teahouses and pavilions. The scene inspired the famous blue willow china pattern.

When you tire of the crowds in the Yu Yuan, take a break at **Wuxing Ting** (Five-Star Pavilion), a teahouse just opposite the garden.

The Temple of the Town Gods

Not far from the Yu Yuan is **Cheng Huang Miao** (the Temple of the Town Gods), devoted, as its name implies, to the ancient town gods. Once, every Chinese town had such a temple. This is one of the few that remain. Behind the temple is a garden with a lake, pavilions, and artificial hills. **Qiu Xia Pu** (the Garden of the Purple Clouds of Autumn) was laid out during the Ming Dynasty.

The liveliest promenade

The most delightful place to stroll in Shanghai is **Wai Tan** (the Bund), the area around Zhongshan Park, Zhongshan Road, and the Wusong River, near the old town. The park is green with shade trees and decorated with rock and flower gardens. During the British Occupation, the Chinese were forbidden in this area. The tall buildings that line the Bund once housed international banks and corporations; now they house the Bank of China and government offices.

Evening is the best time to stroll along the Bund, when city lights reflect in the water. If you are energetic, come here in the morning and join the locals in their daily Tai Chi Quan exercises.

China's best art collection

The three stories of the **Shanghai Museum of Art and History,** *Henan Road,* house the finest art collection in China. The first floor has bronzes from the Shang and Western Zhou dynasties (1523 B.C. to 771 B.C.) The most interesting objects are the instruments of torture. The second floor has ceramics from the Neolithic era to the present, including life-size terracotta statues of warriors and a horse from Emperor Qin Shi Huangdi's tomb in Xi'an. Scrolls from the Tang, Song, Yuan, Ming, and Quing dynasties are kept on the third floor, where good reproductions are sold.

The best Buddhas

The **Jade Buddha Temple,** in northwest Shanghai, has two statues of Buddha, each carved out of a single piece of white jade. They were brought by a monk to China from Burma in 1890. Several other statues fill the halls of the temple. Twenty-four monks still live here.

The oldest and biggest temple

Shanghai's oldest and largest temple is **Longhua,** in the southern suburbs. Built before A.D. 687, it has four main halls, drum and bell towers, and a seven-story pagoda next door. The best time to see the temple and pagoda is early spring, when the peach trees blossom.

The best way to meet the people

If you wander the back streets of Shanghai and take public transportation rather than taxis, you will get a glimpse of the lives of the locals. The masses of Shanghai live in tiny, unheated one-story apartments. It's common for a middle-class family to live in two rooms and share cooking and washing facilities with six other families. Because their homes are so small, most people's daily lives take place outdoors, regardless of temperature: morning ablutions in icy water; Tai Chi Quan exercises; cooking; haircuts; ping pong; and card games.

The best entertainment

The **Shanghai Acrobatic Theater,** *400 Nanjing Xi Lu; tel. 564051,* presents highly skilled and exciting shows every day except Tuesdays.

Exotic foods

Food is sold helter-skelter on the streets of Shanghai. Shortly before New Year's, the sidewalks are piled with carcasses of pigs ready for the butcher. The below-freezing temperatures keep the meat from spoiling. At New Year's, men sell pancakes cooked over barrel stoves in the streets and set out chickens in cages or baskets of eggs.

Snake is a specialty. Customers choose their favorite snakes from squirming masses on the snakemongers tabletops. Restaurants devoted exclusively to this delicacy are located throughout Shanghai.

The best Shanghai cuisine

Shanghai has more than 600 restaurants serving 14 kinds of regional foods. The best place to look for restaurants serving regional specialties is along **Nanjing Dong Road.**

The best place for authentic Shanghai cuisine is **Lao Fandian Restaurant,** *242 Fuyou Road; tel. 289850.* In the heart of the old city, this is a good place to stop after a day's sightseeing. Another good place for local fare is **Laozhengxing** (Old Prosperity) **Restaurant,** *566 Jinjiang Road; tel. 222624,* a small, well-respected place famous for its turtle, crab, and fish.

If you tire of the exotic fare, take refuge at the Peace Hotel's dining room, which has the best cream puffs in China.

The best hotels

The **Heping** (Peace) **Hotel** (formerly the Cathay), *Nanjing Dong Road near the Bund; tel. 211244,* is the aging bastion of the cosmopolitan life Shanghai once enjoyed. Its high ceilings, spacious 1930s-style suites with attached servants' rooms, and gilded dining room once hosted Chinese and European guests. The eighth-floor dining room, which has a view of the harbor, is one of the best in the city.

Another old hotel, the **Jinjiang,** *59 Maoming Road; tel. 582582,* is in a group of mansions surrounded by a wall in the French Quarter. The grounds are beautifully landscaped. This is where Richard Nixon and Zhou En Lai signed the Shanghai Communiqué in 1972, opening the door between the West and China.

While the rooms at the **Shanghai Mansions Hotel,** *20 Suzou Bei Road; tel. 244186,* are nothing special, the suites are spectacular, some with grand pianos and private balconies. The view from the rooftop terrace is panoramic. The one drawback is that at night the horns of river barges can be startling.

Hangzhou: the best silks and embroideries

Hangzhou, which lies on the startlingly beautiful Xi Hu (West Lake), is known for its silks, embroideries, tea, and gourmet restaurants. You can watch silk being made at the Hangzhou Silk Dyeing and Printing Mill, where nearly 5,000 workers produce silk by reeling fibers off silkworm cocoons and then print designs on the finished fabric. Mulberry trees, where silkworm cocoons are found, grow in profusion in the surrounding countryside.

Longjing (Dragon Well) tea is picked and dried at **West Lake People's Commune,** where you can watch the work or try your hand at tea-leaf picking.

Four islands with pavilions and temples float in West Lake. The largest and most beautiful is **Gu Shan** (Solitary Hill) in the northwest. The second largest, **Three Pools Mirroring the Moon,** is beautiful on moonlit nights, when the pagodas along the water, lit with candles and sealed with thin paper, look like moons on the water.

Suzhou, the Venice of China

With its maze of canals bordered by small whitewashed houses and weeping willows, **Suzhou** is the most romantic town in China. Venetian Marco Polo felt at home here. And China's most famous romantic novel, *The Dream of the Red Chamber,* is set in a Suzhou mansion. Gnarled sycamore branches bend low over the town's narrow cobblestoned streets, where high walls shield private gardens.

Suzhou's other claims to fame are its gardens—150 in all. The two loveliest are **Zhuozhengyuan** (the Humble Administrator's Garden) and **Liuyuan** (the Tarrying Garden), both of which have all the elements of traditional Chinese gardens: pavilions, ponds, bridges, rock sculptures, and temples. They are two of China's four nationally protected gardens (the other two are the Summer Palace in Beijing and the Imperial Mountain Resort in Changde).

Suzhou is also famous for its silks. You can buy some of the finest silk items in China or tour the bustling silk factories for a closer look.

Most of Suzhou's shops are grouped close together in the downtown area. The best outlet for visitors is the Friendship Store, which caters exclusively to foreigners. Here you find a large and varied selection of silk, dry goods, and clothing. Collectors will drool over the extensive selection of unusual Chinese antiques. Local handicrafts also are featured, including fragrant sandalwood fans and double-faced embroidery.

The best place to stay in town is the **Suzhou Hotel,** *115 Shiquan Jie Road; tel. 24646,* near the Lingering Garden. It is set in the old section of the city, near farmhouses, and has a walled garden.

Guilin and the Li River: beauty defined

The sharp peaks so often depicted on Chinese scrolls exist in **Guilin,** known for its magnificent natural beauty. Set in the Karst Hills of southern China, Guilin has shrouded limestone peaks and subterranean caverns.

You can visit some of the spectacular caves in the hills around Guilin. Reed Flute Cave in the northwest suburbs was once a refuge for villagers escaping enemy armies and bandits. Inside is a grotto, **Shuijinggong** (Crystal Palace), that holds 1,000 people. A trail leads through the cave past stalactites and stalagmites, ending at a terrace with a view of the mountains, farms, and Li River.

A Stone Age matriarchal people lived in **Zengpiyan Cave,** where 14 human skeletons were found, as well as skeletons of elephants, boar, and deer. It is open to tourists.

Seven Star Park contains six caves. The most famous is **Longyindong** (the Dragon Refuge Cave), whose walls are carved with ancient inscriptions.

Li River Cruise

The best way to see this region is to take a cruise on the **Li River.** As you float down-river, look for Elephant Trunk Hill, Old Man Mountain, Folded Brocade Hill, and Crescent Moon Hill. They look like their names.

You will pass lush tropical scenery—fruit trees, bamboo groves, sugarcane, and rice paddies—and your boat probably will stop so you can look at a 1,300-year-old banyan tree.

Boats leave at 8:30 a.m. and sail for five hours, docking for a time at a small village called Yangdi, at the base of two mountains. This is a good place to look for shopping bargains. Local peasants meet the boat, anxious to sell their produce and handicrafts.

For more information on boat cruises, stop by the **tourist office,** *14 Ronghu Bei Road, Guilin.*

The best of the black market

Because of the increasing number of tourists, Guilin is the heart of a flourishing black market in currency, one that is rapidly spreading to every corner of the PRC. This black market is a boon to travelers who, in many cases, are required to pay a higher rate than the locals for the same transportation and lodging.

Zhongshan Lu, Guilin's main commercial thoroughfare, provides a substantial sidewalk trade in Foreign Exchange Certificates (FEC), which are bank notes given to foreigners when they convert their home currencies. The whole dual-currency phenomenon is the result of the government's Friendship Stores, which accept only FECs. The Chinese currency, the Ren-minbi (RMB), is literally "people's money," the official coin of the realm. RMBs are nego-tiable everywhere except Friendship Stores.

To purchase rationed items, the Chinese are eager to sell their RMBs for FECs at a premium. The usual premium is 20%, but foreign students from the Beijing Language Institute report 50% premiums offered around the institution's gates, practically around the clock. On the streets the operation is fronted by "change-money" women, who approach anyone who looks like a Westerner, a Japanese, or an overseas Chinese with offers of *"fifaty-siksaty"* for FECs.

A word of caution: While selling FECs is a great way to stretch the budget, it's illegal. A little discretion will prevent hassles later. Everyone entering China is required to complete a customs declaration form stating the amount of hard currency brought into the country. On leaving China you can convert any unused FECs and RMBs to foreign currency. But don't exchange more RMBs than you have vouchers to show for FECs. In other words, you can't show a profit.

Xi'an: once the world's largest city

Once the largest city in the world, **Xi'an,** in north central China, is filled with archeologi-cal wonders. The most famous is the recently discovered tomb of China's first emperor, Qin Shi Huangdi, which is guarded by 8,000 life-size terra-cotta soldiers.

Chang An, as the city was known in ancient times, was the capital of 11 dynasties, and the hills to the north of the city are filled with ancient tombs. Qin Shi Huangdi, who com-pleted the Great Wall in the third century B.C., chose Xi'an as his capital. Under the Tang Dynasty, from the 7th to 10th centuries, it became the largest city in the world, with a population of about one million.

Today, the masses are returning to Xi'an, this time as tourists. In fact, more foreign visitors are appearing in the city than at any time since the eighth century.

While Xi'an is an industrial city congested with throngs of bicyclists, remnants of the city's loftier past remain. A medieval city wall can be seen in places. Two pagodas, Big Wild Goose and Small Wild Goose, watch over the city from a distance. (The view from the top of Big Wild Goose takes in the city and the green fields beyond.) And the city museum has the Forest of Steles, 1,000 standing stone tablets inscribed with ancient poems, essays, and images.

Xi'an has a large Muslim population and a functioning **Great Mosque,** *Huajue Xiang Road,* founded in A.D. 742. This, too, is a remnant of the city's past, when trade routes from all over the world led here. Arab traders brought Islam. The best time to see the mosque is on Fridays, when about 2,000 Chinese Muslims arrive to pray in the splendid Ming Dynasty prayer hall.

The best collection of ancient artifacts

The **Shaanxi Provincial Museum,** in a former Confucian temple in the south of the city, has the best collection of ancient artifacts in China. It is made up of three main buildings and three annexes and can hold 4,000 separate exhibitions. The Forest of Steles mentioned above is the museum's most important display. Also important is the stone menagerie, a collection of gigantic statues of real and imaginary animals that once guarded royal tombs.

Xi'an's top sights

At the center of Xi'an is a Ming Dynasty bell tower that provides a convenient vantage point when scouting out street routes. Within sight is Xi'an's drum tower (inside is the city's best antique shop), marking the city's Hui, or Chinese Muslim, neighborhood. The aquiline features and bearded faces of the men here bear witness to their Arab ancestry. Arab and Persian merchants and mercenaries came to Chang An during the Tang Dynasty (A.D. 618 to A.D. 907). The men of this neighborhood often congregate on the tranquil grounds of the Chinese-style mosque.

Throughout old Xi'an are many small shops offering handmade products. Follow the hammer taps to the tinsmith. Simple enamelware, army canteens, straw hats, oilcloth umbrel-las, and chopsticks are some of the souvenirs you can buy here. Roast chicken is sold by Hui street peddlers, whose lamp-lit stands dot the street corners in the evenings.

Stop at the **Hua Xing Hot Springs,** outside town, where, according to a local joke, Chiang Kai Shek left his dentures when running from the Chinese Red Army. (He was arrested here in 1936.) The lush oasis was popular with the Chinese emperors, who bathed in the hot springs with their concubines and built a number of palaces in the area. After the court moved from Xi'an, the palaces were turned into a Taoist monastery.

Today, some of the buildings are used as a spa. The springs, discovered 2,800 years ago, have a temperature of 110 degrees Fahrenheit and are said to be curative.

The **Xing Jiao Temple,** located southeast of Xian, is the burial site of a Tang Dynasty monk, the patron saint of the Silk Route. Xuan Zhuang traveled to India and back in A.D. 627 on a quest for Buddhist scriptures.

China's greatest archeological find

The 8,000 life-sized terra-cotta warriors found in Lingtong County, 20 miles east of Xi'an, are the 20th-century's most exciting archeological find. In 1974, a group of well-diggers accidentally unearthed the ancient figures, which had stood guard at the tomb of Emperor Qin Shi Huangdi for 2,000 years.

The first emperor of China, Qin Shi Huangdi united warring states and completed the Great Wall against northern barbarians. His tomb is divided into three vaults. The first contains the infantry, each statue with an individualized face. The second and third contain an additional 2,000 figures of men, horses, and chariots. The emperor himself is buried a distance away, hidden in a maze of corridors and gates.

The emperor began to build the army of life-sized soldiers when he came to power at age 13. Over a period of 36 years, Qin conscripted three-quarters-of-a-million countrymen to build 6,000 figures and ordered the statues to guard his tomb (the model soldiers acted as substitutes for real soldiers, who in earlier times would have been buried with their emperor).

The figures have stood for centuries 20 feet underground in an area the size of a football field. Most are lined up in marching positions as they would have been on a military campaign, while others are being pulled in chariots by teams of horses. The painted soldiers are modeled after Qin's live honor guard and carry real swords, spears, and crossbows, set to be triggered by invaders. Despite the decoys and booby traps, however, looters raided Qin's tomb four years after he died.

The best food and spirits

Sichuan Restaurant, *Jiefang Lu, near the train station; tel. 23184,* is Xi'an's most inviting restaurant. No less than 125 varieties of *jiaozi* (Chinese ravioli) are served here, with names such as Buddha's Claw and Make Money. Try the local liquor with your dinner, a pale spirit with the unappetizing name Yellow Osmanthus Thick Wine (Kueihua Chen Chew). This sweet but potent brew has a way of obliterating your memory.

China's best hotel

The two-year-old **Golden Flower Hotel,** *8 Chang' an Road W., Xi' an, Shaanxi, China; tel. 32981,* offers rooms that are vast by present-day standards in China, well-lit, tastefully decorated, and equipped with two queen-sized beds, televisions, and video machines. The staff is well-trained and speaks English.

Facilities at the Golden Flower include secretarial and translation services, money changing, and a gift shop. The hotel runs tours and a fleet of taxis, and the concierge can negotiate restaurant reservations, prices, and menus. The hotel restaurant offers Sichuan and Shaanxi food. Double rooms are $135 a night (lower rates are available out of season).

The most exotic destination: the Silk Route

The legendary **Silk Route** is far from silken. Ancient caravans following the route braved trackless deserts, towering mountains, and staggering distances to barter with foreign merchants or to spread new religions. Although some of this terrain is paved today, it remains a difficult passage. However, the payoff for undertaking the trip is great: the stark beauty of the landscape; the friendly, freedom-loving Uygurs; the colorful bazaars; and the incomparable religious art.

This 3,720-mile network of routes has spanned Eurasia since the second century B.C. Beginning at China's ancient capital Chang An (modern Xi'an), it snakes to Kashgar in western China, then splits. The main route climbs the Himalayas and continues west to Samarkand (now in the southern Soviet Union), Persia (now Iraq and Iran), and Rome. One alternate route dips down to Pakistan.

The Chinese leg of the route is long enough for most travelers. Guided tours are practical for those with limited time, tolerance, or language skills.

Making the best of it

The first leg of the Silk Route is a 13-hour train journey from Xi'an to Lanzhou. This ordeal is more palatable if you make a reservation in hard-sleeper, the class between hard-seat and soft-sleeper. You will have your own berth, but you won't be secluded from the other passengers. Bring food, tea, and a lidded tea-cup; attendants will provide hot water.

The best place to stay in Lanzhou is the megalithic Chinese-built **Friendship Hotel,** *14 Xijin Xi Lu; tel. 33051.* Rooms, which are comfortable, if cavernous, with well-worn, deep-seated armchairs with lace arm covers, fragile pink lampshades, and heavy velvet curtains, cost a mere $15 and have attached bathrooms.

Just across the road from the hotel is the Provincial Museum, which has magnificent pieces of decorated pottery dating back 6,000 years. The most important is the 1,800-year-old "Flying Horse of Gansu," which really looks as if it is flying.

Buddhist bests

Twenty miles from Lanzhou are the **Bilingsi Buddhist Caves,** which are definitely worth visiting. China International Travel Service (CITS) arranges inexpensive tours to the caves, which were dug into the face of a 180-foot cliff about 1,500 years ago by Buddhist monks. They are full of Buddhist statues, sculptures, and murals. From here, the Silk Route crosses the Wei River Valley into the arid province of Gansu, where it flanks the Great Wall for 700 miles. Eventually, it comes to **Jiayuguan,** a fortress built by Min Dynasty rulers in 1372 as their western outpost.

Northwest of Jiayuguan are the **Thousand Buddha Grottoes** at Dunhuang, an oasis stuck in the middle of the Gansu Desert. In the old days, this dusty little place was a vital staging post for camel caravans going east and west—here the northern and southern branches of the Silk Route met. Only 40 of the 500 cave temples are open to the public. Each enshrines superb paintings and sculptures that were commissioned over a period of 1,500 years by rich and pious pilgrims and merchants as gestures of thanks for a safe journey on the Silk Route. Bring a flashlight to see the details of the works.

The best of the desert

The **Taklamakan Desert,** which the route follows on the southern border, translates from Uygur to mean, "Once you go in, you never get out." The desert is haunted not by the specters that the ancients feared but by atomic tests (one as recently as the spring of 1987). A long, parched trip via bus and train will lead you out of the desert and into Turpan, a cultural oasis where grape arbors shade courtyards.

Friendliest folks

Descendants of the Uygurs make up the region's largest ethnic group (besides the Han Chinese). Their language is Turkish, their religion Islam. Cool evenings, when the people are outdoors, are the best times to meet the Uygurs. Invitations to their adobe huts are not unusual.

Past present

Nearby ruins of two ancient Silk Route cities still have recognizable streets, town walls, and buildings. **Gaochang,** the larger of the two cities, was the capital of the Uygur kingdom in the ninth century. It once hosted Marco Polo and is a vast and slightly terrifying place.

Jiaohe, perched above a river bed, was a Chinese garrison until it came under local control. Its main road is still clearly visible.

Join with other travelers and hire a mini-bus to take you to the ruined cities. With 12 people, it costs about $4 per person.

The Silk Route's best guesthouse

The best place to stay in Turpan is the **Turfan Guesthouse,** *not* the garish new Tourgroup Hotel up the road. The guesthouse is one of the great joys of the Silk Route. Plan to stay several days. Relax on the vine-covered verandas, sipping cool beer, snacking on grapes, and contemplating the past splendors of the Silk Route.

China's least-desirable digs

The **Turfan Depression,** which surrounds the town of Turpan, has been called one of the strangest places on earth. It lies nearly 500 feet below sea level and can get so hot in the summer that people live in the underground cellars of their houses. An underground irrigation channel was built 2,000 years ago to bring melted snow from the Tian Shan Mountains in the north (hence, the profusion of well-watered melon and grape crops in the middle of the desert).

Ugliest city, loveliest carpets

A few hours beyond Turpan is **Urumchi,** one of the ugliest, most polluted cities in China. One thing saves this industrial city—it has the best carpet market. To find it, go to the **Hua Qiao Hotel** (popular with overseas Chinese), *Xin Nan Jie Lu,* head toward the city center, and turn into the fourth lane on the right. At the end is a bustling little market with noodle restaurants, kebab stalls, teahouses, clothes shops, and a magnificent array of carpets.

Switzerland in the desert

Once you have visited the market, head out of town toward **Heaven Lake,** a bit of Switzerland halfway up Bogda Shan (the Mountain of God). The trip takes four hours.

Deep-blue Heaven Lake is surrounded by pine forests and snow-capped peaks. The Kazakhs, herders and horsemen (not to be confused with the Russian Cossacks), set up their yurts (dome tents) in the cool meadows here during the summer.

If you can't face returning to Urumchi, you can rent a yurt from a Kazakh nomad for less than $1 a night per person. Or you can stay at the Heavenly Lake Hotel, on the shore of the lake, for $12.

Best horsing around

While in Urumchi, you may be invited to see the *boz kashi,* a contest of horsemanship. Riders must carry a headless goat or lamb from one end of a field to another. Apparently lacking a referee or rules, it's best to view this feat from a safe perch.

China's westernmost city

From Urumchi, you can fly to **Kashgar,** China's westernmost city and the end of the

Chinese portion of the Silk Route. (If you continue on from here, you will end up in Pakistan.) But taking the three- or four-day bus trip in the company of Uygurs, Mongols, Tibetans, and Han Chinese better duplicates the Silk Route sojourns of long ago. The buses make frequent stops that allow you to sample the area's plentiful melons.

They say Kashgar is farther from the sea than any other town on earth. When you get there, you'll believe it. The streets are narrow and dusty, lined with adobe houses. You will hear muezzin cries and smell the smoke-filled kebab markets. Kashgar has been around for 2,000 years and is one of the most important cities on the Silk Route, at the borders of Russia, Afghanistan, India, and Pakistan.

One thing above all must be seen in Kashgar: the **Sunday Market.** When you plan your trip, make sure you will be in town on a Sunday. Hundreds of thousands of people (mostly Uygurs) swarm to an area on the outskirts of town, where they buy and sell everything you can imagine—and much you can't. The most exciting part of the market is where Kazakh horsemen test-ride horses in an enclosure full of donkeys, sheep, goats, cows, and camels.

Near the market is **Id Kah Mosque,** one of the largest in China. Built in 1442, it domi- nates the old town and draws thousands of worshipers on Fridays.

When you tire, relax over a meal at the **Tian Nan Restaurant,** tucked behind the hotel of the same name, 300 yards east of the imposing Mao statue. The food is excellent (which is evidenced by the number of Han Chinese who crowd the restaurant).

The best hotel in Kashgar is the **Kashgar Guesthouse,** *tel. 2387,* on the eastern edge of town. It is comfortable, but a bit too far from the center of things. Double rooms are $17.

The **Seman Hotel,** *Seman Lu; tel. 2129,* is more central. Its old wing was once Kashgar's Russian Consulate. Little seems to have been repaired since the Russians left in 1949, but the dilapidated rooms are rather charming. They have the biggest and best bathtubs you'll find within 1,000 miles! What's more, you'll be provided with plenty of hot water. Rooms in the older wing are $8; rooms in the newer wing are $20.

For information on booking a tour along the Silk Route, see "The cheapest way to get to China" at the end of this chapter.

Dali—China's newest vacation spot

One of the most popular new destinations in Yunnan Province, which only recently opened to tourists, is the town of **Dali,** a handsome historical city in a spectacular setting. Look one way and you see the snow-capped Cangshan (White-Haired Mountain); look the other way and you see the blue Erhai (Ear Lake). Between the mountain and the water are well-irrigated green fields dotted with villages.

The majority of Dali's natives—about 80%—are of Bai nationality. For hundreds of years, they formed a kingdom independent of China that flourished until conquered by Kublai Khan in 1253. A stone tablet commemorates the event.

The Bai people are extremely friendly and will greet you constantly with "hi." Women wear traditional colorful clothing, including ornately decorated backpacks for carrying small children.

When Chinese emperors moved the provincial capital to Kunming, Dali sank into oblivion. Because of this, the town is well-preserved, with narrow cobblestoned streets and old buildings of wood, plaster, and stone. A short walk takes you down the main street from one Ming Dynasty gate to the other. The gates have been impressively rebuilt, but most of the wall that surrounds Dali is now little more than earthworks with rice planted on the top.

You can buy colorful clothing at the marketplaces in and around Dali. The largest is held every Monday at **Shapin,** on the north side of the lake, about 18 miles from Dali. In addition to pigs, seed, and farming tools, you can buy coins, handkerchiefs, and fabrics. Tailors in Dali can stitch up clothing to order.

Beyond the wall, two competing entrepreneurs rent out bikes for less than $1 a day. The bikes are crude one-speeds, and the roads are very bumpy.

Finagle a boat ride across the lake and watch the fishermen with their nets. Hike up the mountains, where many old temples are still in use. To relax your tired muscles, get a vigorous massage at Dali's public bathhouse.

Plans are under way for an airport and a luxury hotel, but until these plans are finalized, Dali is a place for the rugged. At present, accommodation in Dali is limited to the **Number Two Hotel,** which offers rooms for $2 to $4—adequate, but not luxurious.

Food in Dali is cheap and good. The **Peace Café,** next to Number 2 Hotel, caters to travelers. The **Garden Café,** a family restaurant, serves locals as well as visitors. Late at night, three generations of the owner's family gather in the back room to eat, squabble, watch television, and make a lot of noise.

April is the best time to visit Dali, when the town holds its **Third Month Fair,** an annual festival that dates back 1,000 years. People come from miles around for their once-a-year trip to town.

Getting to Dali involves a nine-hour bus ride from Kunming, the capital of Yunnan Province. Flights to Kunming depart from Hong Kong, Beijing, Guangzhou, Shanghai, and Rangoon.

Xishuangbanna: tropical China

The southernmost region of China's Yunnan Province, **Xishuangbanna,** is more like Thailand than China. Bordering Burma and Laos, this is a lush, tropical land with hillside tea and rubber plantations, markets full of exotic fruit, and coconut palm-shaded villages where women dress in brilliantly colored sarongs.

The liveliest time to visit is during the **New Year Water Splashing Festival** (celebrated according to the Buddhist calendar in mid-April). Festivities in Jinghong, the capital, include dragon-boat races on the Mekong River, Dai music and dancing, bamboo rockets, and a riot of water splashing. If you plan to visit during the festival, make reservations far in advance. Both flights from Kunming to Jinghong and accommodations become scarce.

A better time to visit is off season, when you can enjoy the tranquil countryside and the gentle ways of the attractive Dai people (one of Yunnan's largest and most prosperous minority groups).

Jinghong is a small, sleepy town of broad streets bordered by palm trees. Buddhist monks in saffron robes bicycle slowly along the streets, while Dai women carrying pretty parasols congregate in the open markets. If you are lucky, one of the Dai will present you with a sticky cake of glutinous rice wrapped in palm leaves, a common sweet snack in Xishuang-banna.

About 35 miles west of Jinghong lies **Menghai,** one of the great tea regions of China and home of the most famous temple site in the province: the **Octagonal Pagoda.** This tiny gem of intricate architecture was built in the 17th century.

Far to the south, five miles from the Burmese border, lies **Damenglong,** a village with a 13th-century White Pagoda and a lively Sunday market. Here you can see a panoply of other minority people, who come to trade with the local Dai: Lahu women in brightly colored bodices; Bulang with colored tufts of wool for earrings; and women of the Hani and Aini tribes (who are similar to Thailand's Akha people) bedecked in breastplates and headdresses of silver and metal coins, embroidered black leggings, belts of cowrie shells, and short black miniskirts that have an alarming tendency to fall off.

Another market is held at **Menghan,** southwest of Jinghong, which you can get to by slow boat on the brown Mekong River. It's a one-hour trip downstream, with stops to pick up villagers. Women can be seen on the river's edge panning for grains of gold.

The life of the Dai in these villages is slow and traditional. They live along the northern shore of Menghan's Virtuous Dragon Lake in large wooden houses built on stilts. You can see men making bamboo baskets and girls weaving cloth. In the Buddhist temple, boy monks learn their sacred texts. Chickens and pigs roam the dusty village paths, and buffalo plow the fields. Inside the thatched-roof wood and bamboo houses, gold-toothed Dai women prepare banquets: purple rice, spiced zucchini, sesame beef, and fried bumblebees.

The easiest way to reach Xishuangbanna is to fly from Kunming to Simao (75 minutes) and then take a bus or taxi the 100 miles to Jinghong. You'll pass spectacular scenery, including rice plains, hillsides of tea and rubber, and dense jungles.

Accommodation in Jinghong is at the **Banna Guesthouse,** a villa complex adorned with flowering bougainvillea. Double rooms are about RMB 40 per night.

Hainan, the Red Hawaii

Hainan Island off the coast of China is slated to become the Hawaii of the Far East. The island is off the southernmost part of China, not far from Vietnam, and is nearly as big as Taiwan. Recently, it was made a separate province (it had been part of Guangdong).

Despite its coconut groves and pristine golden beaches, the island has a few problems. Telephones are unpredictable. The only airstrip on its south coast is a military field, and the new airstrip originally scheduled to open in 1985 is now promised for 1989—if then. Passengers are ferried in venerable Russian planes. Sanya, slated to be the tourist center, has only 500 hotel rooms, none with private baths.

Lhasa: the world's highest capital

Lhasa, Tibet, at 12,087 feet above sea level, is the world's highest capital. Set in royal blue skies above the clouds, it is so high that tourists are given oxygen bags when they arrive. Unfortunately, the monks here and the Chinese police have been coming into confrontation. The city is closed to individual travelers and can be visited only by groups.

When the political problems subside, make your way to this autonomous region of China. The City of the Sun, as it is known, is high in the Gyi Qu Valley, just 100 miles north of India. Summers here are hot and humid, winters bitingly cold. The best times to visit are spring and fall.

The former seat of the Dalai Lama, the head of Tibetan Buddhism, Lhasa is filled with palaces and temples. Behind these grandiose man-made monuments are towering snow-covered mountains that make the Rockies seem mundane.

The **Potala,** where the Dalai Lama lived until he was ousted by the Communists in 1959, is an enormous 17th-century edifice that dominates the entire valley. The 13-story, 1,000-room palace is a museum today. Inside are gigantic, bejewelled Buddhas, murals illustrating Buddhist legends, and solid gold crypts containing the remains of former Dalai Lamas. The

10,000 chapels are decorated with human skulls and thighbones. Beneath the palace are torture chambers, where criminals and dissidents were kept in dungeons or eaten alive by scorpions.

The **Deprung Monastery,** which is about three miles outside Lhasa, is where lesser religious leaders lived. The stone building, constructed in 1416 and set precariously against a mountainside, was once the largest cloister in the world. Although thousands of monks once lived here, the monastery is now inhabited by 300.

The **Jokhang Temple** houses two enormous gold and bejewelled Buddhas. Built 1,300 years ago, it is still visited by pilgrims who can be seen prostrate in front of the temple at dawn and dusk. Beautiful from the outside, the temple is smelly inside, because of the fermented butter burned by monks as part of their religious ceremonies.

The best hotel in Lhasa is the **Lhasa Hotel,** *1 Minzu Road; tel. 22221.* Rooms are air-conditioned and are equipped with televisions, telephones, and oxygen tanks. Prices are high, as all supplies must be transported by truck for miles up the mountain.

The cheapest places to stay are two dormitory-style hotels: the **Banak Shol** and the **Snowlands,** both in the old section of town near the Jokhang Temple. Bathrooms are primitive, but the price is right—5 yen to 10 yen.

The best way to travel

If you have the time, boats are the most pleasant way to travel through China. If you're making the circuit of major Chinese cities, you can choose from several boat routes. One goes from Guangzhou to Wuzhou, a small town en route to Guilin, in 20 hours. The price, including a seven-hour bus trip to Yangshuo, is less than $10.

Everyone on these boat trips gets his own berth, either an upper with a window view of the Pearl River or a lower with easier access. No one sits in the aisles. Thick mats and quilts are provided in the dormitory-like setting. You'll enjoy lovely views and ample people-watching opportunities.

The cheapest way to get to China

Hong Kong is often the cheapest place to buy a package tour to China. You can save a few thousand dollars by flying to Hong Kong on your own and joining a tour group heading for China there. A flight from Los Angeles or San Francisco to Hong Kong can cost as little as $599 round trip with **TFI Tours International,** *(212)736-1140.* The best bet is to book through bargain travel agencies run by Chinese-Americans in San Francisco; they generally can find the cheapest fares. Try **U.S. China Travel,** *(415)398-6627.* Bargains are also available for departures from New York. **Travel Wholesalers' Club,** *(212)685-2503,* offers a $875 fare.

The least expensive direct flights to China are offered by China's CAAC Airlines from the West Coast to Shanghai for $1,124 round trip.

CITS, which has offices at *77 Queens Road, Central District, Hong Kong Island; tel. (852-5)259-121,* and *Alpha House, 23-33 Nathan Road, Kowloon; tel. (852-3)667-201,* is among the agencies that sponsor tours from Hong Kong to China. Make sure that the Hong Kong agent you deal with is officially authorized to issue you a visa. Tours offered recently by CITS have included: a Guangzhou three-day excursion for $232 round trip; a Beijing-Xi'an-Shanghai nine-day excursion for $1,260 round trip; and a Beijing-Xi'an-Chongquing-Yangtse River-Wuhan-Shanghai 13-day excursion for $1,590 round trip.

Low-cost tours using rail connections, charter flights, and budget hotels are available through two operators: the **Hong Kong Student Travel Bureau,** *120/2 Des Voeux Road, Tai Sang Bank Building; tel. (852-5)414-841;* and **China Youth Travel,** *151 Des Voeux Road; tel. (852-5)410-975.*

Some of the least expensive Silk Route tours also are arranged in Hong Kong. Typically, such tours cost $2,200 and last two weeks. The trips usually depart from Hong Kong and include stops in Beijing, Xi'an, Lanzhou, Dunhuang, Turpan, and Urumqi. Check with CITS for prices.

Chapter 15

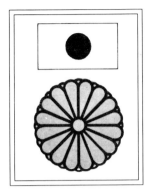

THE BEST OF JAPAN

J apan is at once the best-known and least-understood country in Asia, a unique combination of Eastern and Western cultures. The Japanese go to great lengths to provide Western travelers with American-style hotels and modern amenities; yet, the Westerner may be excluded from a geisha club or a traditional Japanese inn. In the space of a few miles, you can race with the dizzying traffic of Tokyo's Ginza district and take in the purifying silence of a remote Buddhist temple.

An ancient country, Japan is also the most modern nation in Asia. It is at once tranquil and chaotic, trend-setting and traditional. Young people wearing the latest fashions share sidewalks with elderly people in traditional costumes. Japanese businessmen taking the international market by storm also take time to meditate in centuries-old temples.

The best of Tokyo

Japan's capital and largest city is the most expensive city in the world. Tokyo is not known for its beauty. Indeed, the central districts are an architectural study in neon and chrome. But the city has hidden temples and flower gardens that preserve the serene, traditional side of classic Japanese culture.

The metropolis of Tokyo sprawls to the horizon, covering 800 square miles and comprising 26 cities, 6 towns, 9 villages, and several islands. Curiously, this industrial city also has 346,000 farmers.

The best ways to travel

The subway system in Tokyo is excellent. Its routes are color-coded, and most stations are marked in Roman letters. The bus network is efficient as well, but information is printed only in Japanese. Taxis are luxurious, many with television sets and doors that open and close by remote control.

Despite all this, walking is the best way to see Tokyo. Even at night, the streets in this virtually crime-free city are safe. However, many of the streets are not named, and buildings aren't always numbered, so it is easy to get lost. If you're going to get lost, do it on a weekday between 9 a.m. and 5 p.m. or Saturday between 9 a.m. and noon. During those times, you can stop by a police box and call the **Tourist Information Center,** *tel. (81-3)502-1461.* A member of the English-speaking staff will be able to help you.

The number-one sight

At the heart of Tokyo is the **Imperial Palace,** a 28-acre retreat surrounded by a moat where swans glide soundlessly. The palace stands on the site of Edo Castle, built in the 15th century by Lord Dokan Ota. From the 1500s to 1868, when it was the residence of the Tokugawa Shoguns, it covered 608 acres and was defended by a 10-mile wall with 111 gates, 20 turrets, and 30 bridges. The city of Tokyo grew around the edifice, which has been destroyed and rebuilt several times.

Emperor Hirohito and his wife live in the palace today. Behind its walls are a silkworm farm, rice paddies, and a mulberry field. Visitors can enter the palace only twice a year: Jan. 2 and the emperor's birthday, April 29.

You can visit the **Imperial Palace East Garden** any day except Mondays and Fridays from 9 a.m. to 3 p.m. A stroll in this garden, with its perfectly kept hedges and swans, will make you think you are in the Shoguns' Japan, not a modern city. You still can see four of the gates that once led into ancient Edo Castle. The Kitakibashimon, the entrance to the castle tower, is the most imposing, its stone bulwarks reflected in the deepest part of the moat.

The **Kitanomaru Koen** and **Chidorigafuchi Suijo Koen** parks are open to the public year-round. The Kitanomaru Koen Park contains the National Museum of Modern Art; the Crafts Gallery, located in the former headquarters of the Old Imperial Palace Guard; the Science and Technology Museum; and the Nippon Budokan (built for the 1964 Olympics), a concert hall that looks like a Buddhist temple but hosts concerts by rock stars such as Rod Stewart.

The Imperial Palace is encircled by a 4.6-mile bike trail. Five-hundred free bikes are available at the police station in the Imperial Palace Plaza if you'd like to make the *tour du palais*. Or you can join the locals in a jog around the palace's perimeter. The Imperial Hotel provides its guests with complimentary running gear and shoes for this purpose.

For the best view of the palace and its gardens, have lunch or dinner in the 10th-floor restaurant at the nearby Palace Hotel. Another good view is from the 36th floor of the Kasumigaseki Building, southwest of the palace. On a clear day you can see all the way to Mt. Fuji.

The loveliest shrines and temples

Beyond the palace grounds and up a hill is the **Yasukuni Shrine,** *3-1-1 Kudan Kita, Dhiyoda-ku,* dedicated to the souls of those who have fought and died for Japan, including those who fought against the United States. Surrounded by parklike grounds, its entrance is marked by a huge, yoked wooden gateway called a torii. Walk through the maze-like shrine, with its many pillars. Toss some coins in the box by the door, clap your hands to awaken the spirits within, and say a prayer. Flocks of doves seem somehow symbolic. Inside the shrine is a museum containing war memorabilia.

Asakusa Kannon Temple, at the heart of the Asakusa neighborhood, is dedicated to Kannon, the Buddhist goddess of compassion. According to legend, the temple was built in A.D. 628 by three fishermen who had discovered a statue of the goddess in their fishing net. It is marked by a 10-foot red paper lantern that weighs 220 pounds. An enormous incense vat sends sweet-smelling smoke into the air from the courtyard in front of the temple. When cupped in one palm and patted on the body, the smoke is said to cure ailments. The flocks of doves that fly around the temple are considered sacred messengers of Kannon. Many of Tokyo's temples hold annual festivals, but the one held here May 16 to 18 is the largest in the city.

Hie Shrine, *2-10-5 Nagata-cho, Chiyoda-ku; tel. (81-3)581-2471,* is dedicated to Oyamakuni, the monkey god, who grants fertility and good relationships and wards off evil. The best time to visit the shrine is every other June, during the Sanno-sai Festival, when miniature shrines are carried through the neighborhood.

Meji Shrine, *Shibuya-ku,* is one of the most popular Shinto shrines in Tokyo. Founded in 1920, it is dedicated to the Emperor Meiji (1868-1912), who ended the 600-year rule of the shoguns and opened Japan to the West. The shrine is surrounded by a 180-acre garden and before it stands Japan's largest torii. The shrine's best feature is its Iris Garden, which bursts into color in June and July. Horsemen wearing samurai costumes compete in the yearly archery contest held here.

Sengakuji Temple, *Takanawa,* is the burial site of the 47 samurai of Asano Naganoni, Lord of Ako. They died for their master after avenging his death. Naganoni had made the mistake of drawing his sword when the court chamberlain insulted him. As punishment, he was forced to commit suicide. His faithful samurai then cut off the head of the chamberlain, for which they too had to commit suicide. Their story is re-enacted in the Kabuki play *Chushingura.* The faithful still come to lament the death of the samurai by lighting joss sticks on stone memorials in the temple gardens.

The Zen Buddhist **Sengakuji Temple** was founded in 1612 and has been reconstructed in recent years.

Tokyo's best park

On weekends, Tokyo residents flock to busy **Ueno Park.** Weekdays are less crowded. If you want to see every level of Tokyo society, visit the park during the Cherry Blossom Festival, from late March through mid-April, when the trees are breathtaking.

Ueno Zoo is worth visiting, if only for its pandas. Also visit the **Shitamachi Museum,** at the far end of the park, featuring everyday objects donated by Tokyo residents.

Ginza: Tokyo's best shopping

The **Ginza district,** southeast of the center of the city, is world-famous for its enormous department stores and exclusive little shops. Cars and trucks are barred from this district on weekends, when shoppers take over the streets and merchandise is moved onto sidewalks. Ginza (which translates as Silver Mint), is named for the Japanese mint, which was once located south of Kyobashi bridge.

In addition to the usual fare, Takashimaya, a department store in the Ginza, has restaurants, tearooms, boutiques, a kimono department, and an art gallery that exhibits shows from top international museums. The best time to experience the formal hospitality of this store is at 10 a.m., when it opens and the salespeople line up and bow to you.

For an experience in high-tech shopping, visit **Seibu.** In addition to designer clothes and imported ice cream, Seibu has 177 closed-circuit televisions that entertain shoppers with rock music videos, breaking waves, and cherry blossoms.

The most colorful place in the Ginza is the **Tsukiji Fishmarket,** a 50-acre stretch of wholesale fish stalls. This is a great place to take photos. You will see all the fish that make their way into Tokyo's sushi bars, some familiar, some not. Wear waterproof shoes.

The Ginza, which is filled with restaurants, nightclubs, cafés, and hostess bars, is also a good place to go at night. In the early evening you can see hostesses, dressed in kimonos, on their way to work.

The most memorable neighborhoods

Shinjuku, around the busy Shinjuku Station, is a maze of small alleys crammed with bars, restaurants, and coffee shops. It is popular with the student crowd. An interesting contrast to these energetic, off-beat establishments is Shinjuku Central Park, a peaceful wooded area with gardens, the largest manmade waterfall in Japan, and a clear view of Shinjuku.

On the west side of the city is the **Harajuku district,** a prime spot for people watching, especially if you want to watch Tokyo's youth wearing the latest fashions. At the heart of Harajuku is Omotesando Street, lined with fashionable boutiques, restaurants, and cafés.

You can buy anything, from a tape recorder to a stuffed peacock, at **Asakusa,** a bustling shopping and entertainment area made up of dozens of cross-hatched alleys and covered passages, for less than elsewhere in Tokyo. The western end of Asakusa has theaters, burlesque shows, bathhouses, and restaurants. A large boulevard on the edge of the area is home to the Kokusai Theater. Tickets to plays here are inexpensive, despite the extraordinary sets. Surprisingly, behind the glitz, Asakusa is also one of Tokyo's most traditional areas.

Japanese baseball (*besuboro*)

One of the most popular destinations in Tokyo is in the Korakuen district, southwest of Ueno Park: the **Korakuen Baseball Stadium.** With 2 baseball leagues and 12 teams, the Japanese are passionate *besuboro* (baseball) fans, and the stadium is often sold out through the entire season (the Japanese baseball season is roughly equal to ours). To see a game, make arrangements well in advance through the **Japan National Tourist Organization,** *(212)757-5640.*

Traditional Japanese theater

The three traditional forms of theater in Japan are Kabuki, No, and Bunraku, all of which can be seen at their finest in Tokyo. The **National Theater of Japan,** *4-1 Hayabusa-cho, Chiyoda-ku; tel. (81-6)212-2531,* is the best for Kabuki and Bunraku. It was designed by Hiroyuki Iwamoto based on a centuries-old design for Kabuki theaters. No plays are better done in small No theaters.

Kabuki plays have fantastic plots, elaborate costumes, a lot of action, and singing. All parts are played by men, and performances go on for hours. (You don't have to sit through an entire performance. It is acceptable to leave or arrive in the middle.) Musicians are seated on stage, and stage hands wearing black hoods bring actors their props during performances.

The largest Kabuki theater in Tokyo is **Kabukiza,** in the Ginza (however, as mentioned above, the best place to see Kabuki is at the National Theater, because performances are translated and explained via earphones).

Bunraku—puppet versions of Kabuki—are heroic tales of samurai enacted by life-size puppets. A small theater in the National Theater is designed especially for Bunraku.

No plays, which date back to the 12th century, are highly stylized and symbolic dramas. The stage is bare except for a backdrop showing a huge pine tree. Actors wear masks and speak in falsetto voices. You can see No plays at **Ginza Nohgakudo,** *6-5-15 Ginza, Chuo-ku;* **Kanze Kaikan,** *1-16-4 Shoto, Shibuya-ku;* and **Hosho Nohgakudo,***1-5-9 Hongo, Bunkyo-ku.*

The world's best flower arranging

Ikebana, the Japanese art of flower arrangement, follows strict aesthetic and philosophical principles. Flowers are placed to symbolize heaven above, earth below, and man in the middle. Ikebana was developed in the eighth century, when it was practiced at the Imperial Court. Today, the art can be seen in every temple and many households throughout Japan. The **Ohara School of Ikebana,** *5-7 Minami-Aoyama, Minato; tel. (81-3)499-1200,* offers a two-hour course in traditional Japanese flower arranging, Monday through Friday mornings.

Tea ceremony secrets

The Japanese make even the English look careless when it comes to making tea. O-cha (green tea) is served ceremoniously on important occasions, at the beginning of conversations, at temples, and at the end of meals. The many details of the ceremony have been carefully preserved throughout the centuries. Tea is served without sugar in small cups without handles as participants sit silently in a circle. The tea is ground into a fine powder, then, after steeping, whisked until it foams. The cups are held and contemplated before the tea is sipped. Every movement has a symbolic significance.

You can take part in a Japanese tea ceremony at the **Tea Ceremony Service Center,** *Mejiro; tel. (81-3)951-9043.* Demonstrations are held Thursdays and Fridays from 11 a.m. to 4 p.m. You also can participate in a tea ceremony at the Okura, Imperial, and New Otani hotels, the tearoom of Suntory, and the tearoom of the Yamatane Museum of Art.

Super sumo wrestling

If you're interested in sumo wrestling, visit the Ryogoko district in northeast Tokyo, where you'll find more than 30 stables for the immense wrestlers who wander the streets dressed in kimonos and topknots. You can watch them competing (wearing slightly less) at the new sumo stadium called New Kokugikan.

Sumo tournaments take place mid-January, mid-May, and mid-September. If you can't make it to the tournaments, have your hotel call a stable to ask permission for you to watch a morning practice session. Two stables you might try are **Kasugano-beya,** *1-7-11 Ryogoku, Sumida-ku; tel. (81-3)631-1871;* or **Takasago-beya,** *1-22-5 Yanagibashi, Taito-ku; tel. (81-3)861-3210.*

Bathing at its best

In Japan, a bath is not just a bath. It is a ceremony. Tokyo has 2,700 public *sento* (bathhouses)—which indicates the importance of the bath to the Japanese. Sixteen of the baths are fed by natural hot springs. You can enjoy one for 200 yen ($1.60)—but you must follow the rules.

Shoes are left in lockers by the front door, and clothes are exchanged for small towels, with which you attempt to cover yourself as you walk to the communal bath (men and women bathe separately). Before climbing into the steaming water, wash yourself with soap and water using your little towel. Little stools are lined up in front of a row of faucets near the pool. This is where you soap up. Remember to rinse yourself thoroughly—it is a terrible faux pas to get soap in the clear water of the bath. Once you are clean, climb into the *furo* (tub) and soak. Be prepared for some scrutiny. After all, not many Westerners are seen here. One good bathhouse is Azabu Onsen, in the Juban district near Roppongi.

Best restaurants

Chinzanso, *10-8 Sekiguichi 2-Chrome, Bunkyo-ku; tel. (81-3)943-1111,* is an enormous restaurant set in a magnificent garden. Dinners are about 5,000 yen ($40).

Kushi Hachi-ten, *10-9 Roppingi, 3-Chrome, Minato-ku; tel. (81-3)403-3060,* was Jimmy Carter's favorite restaurant when he passed through Tokyo. Dinners are about 5,000 yen ($40).

Iseju, *14-9 Kodenmacho, Nihonbashi; tel. (81-3)663-7841,* the oldest restaurant in Tokyo, established in 1869 by the Takamiyama family, serves the world's best sukiyaki.

Hundreds of restaurants in Tokyo are named **Yabu-Soba,** but the one at *2-10 Kanda Awaji-cho, Chiyoda-ku; tel. (81-3)251-0287,* is the best. *Soba* is the traditional noodle soup eaten by everyone in Japan with astonishing speed and slurping noises. Try the *mori-soba* with wild vegetables. Dinners are about 2,000 yen ($16).

Sushi is also found everywhere and is eaten as often for breakfast as for dinner. Tokyo's best sushi is served at **Kyubei,** *8-5-23 Ginza, Chuo-ku; tel. (81-3) 571-6523.* Warning: The prices match the quality. Dinners are about 5,000 yen ($40).

The best place for eel is **Chikuyo Tei,** *8-14-7 Ginza, Chuo-ku; tel. (81-3)542-0787.* The eel, grilled (*kaba-yaki*) or cooked with a sweet sauce (*shiro-yaki*), is served in a teahouse atmosphere—you sit on the floor on tatami mats. Well-prepared eel is one of the most expensive meals in Tokyo. Expect to pay about 10,625 yen ($85) for a meal for two.

The lantern-lit **Goeimen,** *2-39-14 Hakusan, Bunkyo-Ku; tel. (81-3)821-0111,* serves homemade tofu. Reservations are recommended. A meal costs about 5,000 yen ($40).

For a good Western meal, try **Maxim's,** *Sony Building, 5-3-1 Ginza, Chuo-ku; tel. (81-3)572-3621.* This replica of the Paris restaurant is staffed by Paris-trained cooks and waiters. This is the best French restaurant in Japan; it's also one of the most expensive. Meals are up to 20,000 yen ($160).

Asia's most dangerous food

If your culinary curiosity is stronger than your common sense, try fugu (poisonous blowfish), considered the greatest Japanese delicacy. The meat is fine, but the innards are deadly (about 30 Japanese per year die eating fugu). The fish is served as *fuguashi* (raw flakes eaten with a soy, orange, and chive sauce), *birezake* (sun-dried fins dipped in hot sake), and *fuguchiri* (*fugu* soup). You should eat fugu only during a month with an R in it (as with oysters) and only when prepared by a licensed fugu cook.

Sake at its best

Tokyo has a number of *nomiya* (sake houses), where you can sample this peculiarly Japanese brew. **Sasashu,** *2-2-2 Ikebukuro, Toshima-ku; tel. (81-3)971-9363,* is the best, serving little goodies along with the warm white wine. **Chichibu Nishiki,** *2-13-14 Ginza, Chuo-ku; tel. (81-3)541-4777,* is the most attractive sake house, a historic building filled with antiques.

Tokyo's best (and most traditional) hotels

Don't visit Japan without staying in a *ryokan.* These traditional Japanese inns can be found throughout the countryside and even in the heart of Tokyo. They are virtually unchanged since the times of the samurai, with translucent paper windows, sliding doors, mat floors, alcoves, polished wood, and intricate gardens. They also have electricity, running water, and modern toilets.

When you arrive at a *ryokan*, you are greeted at the entrance (where you leave your shoes), then escorted to your room, served tea, and given a freshly laundered cotton kimono. The rooms are furnished with tatami mats, cushions, and scrolls. Sliding-glass walls usually overlook Japanese gardens. After the ritual bath in a sunken wooden tub, dinner is served in your room by a maid in kimono, who later prepares your futon bed.

Ryokans in Tokyo vary widely in price. **Fukudaya,** *6-12 Kioi-cho, Chiyoda-ku; tel. (81-3)261-8577,* is expensive, starting at 25,000 yen ($200) per person. **Atamiso,** *4-14-3 Ginza, Chuo-ku; tel. (81-3)541-3621,* is moderately priced. **Tokiwa Ryokan Shinkan,** *7-27-9 Shinjuku, Shinjuku-ku; tel. (81-3)202-4321,* is relatively inexpensive.

A slightly cheaper but less intimate version of the *ryokan* is the *minshuku*. These inns are frequented primarily by vacationing Japanese. You are not always given a kimono or served your meals in your room, but a night in one of Japan's 27,000 *minshuku* costs only about 5,000 yen ($40) a day per person, including two meals. For reservations, contact the **Japan Minshuku Center,** *Kotsu Kaikan Building, 2-10-1 Yuraku-cho, Chiyoda-ku, Tokyo 100; tel. (81-3)216-2501;* or the **Japan Minshuku Association,** *Nogiku Building 505, 1-29-5 Taka-danobaba, Shinjuku-ku, Tokyo 160; tel. (81-3)232-6561.*

Tokyo's top Western-style hotels

Hotel Okura, *10-4 Toranomom, 2 Chome, Minato-ku; tel. (81-3)582-0111,* next to the American Embassy, offers both Western- and Japanese-style suites, the latter with tatami mats, futons, and shoji screens. The hall is brightened with enormous, elaborate flower arrangements. Shops, restaurants, and a swimming pool are available to guests. Service is impeccable. Double rooms begin at about 25,000 yen ($200).

The **Imperial Hotel,** *1-1-1, Uchisaiwai-cho, Chiyoda-ku, Tokyo 100; tel. (81-3)504-1111,* is next door to the Imperial Palace, overlooking its grounds and Hibiya Park. Dating back to the Meiji era, it is now a thoroughly modern building that comprises some of Tokyo's best shops and restaurants. Double rooms begin at about 28,125 yen ($225); suites are about 62,500 yen ($500).

The **Keio Plaza,** *2-2-1 Nishi Shinjuku, Shinjuku-ku, Tokyo 160; tel. (81-3)344-0111,* was the first high-rise in Tokyo and has magnificent views. The hotel restaurant, Ambrosia, features performances by a harpist. Double rooms are usually 21,250 yen ($170), but special deals are available.

Gajoen Kanko, *1-8-1 Shimo-Meguro, Meguro-ku; tel. (81-3)491-0111,* is an old-fashioned hotel with ornate doors and 1940s decor. Double rooms are 12,500 yen ($100).

The **Hyatt,** *2-7-2 Nishi Shinjuku, Shinjuku-ku; tel. (81-3)349-0111,* overlooks Shinjuku Central Park and has views of Mt. Fuji. Live music is played in the lobby every night. Double rooms are 21,250 yen ($170).

Romance with a twist

Just outside Tokyo are **Rabu Hoteru** (Love Hotels), where you can choose from rooms with exotic themes: waterbeds that look like space shuttles; revolving roulette-wheel beds; or beds built into copies of the Sphinx. Most rooms have mirrored ceilings and large television screens. Rooms are about 2,500 yen to 3,750 yen ($20 to $30) an hour (they're cheaper after 10 p.m.). For more information, contact the tourist office.

Night life

Tokyo's liveliest night life is in the **Roppongi district,** where clubs stay open until 6 a.m. Wandering the maze of streets, you'll find everything from intimate jazz cafés to huge hostess clubs. The nightclub hostess, although often clad in a kimono, is not to be confused with the geisha, who presides only at private parties, usually to entertain businessmen.

Geishas undergo intensive training in the arts of dance, music, and song. They serve at parties as entertainers, waitresses, and witty conversationalists. Hostesses, on the other hand, are employed by nightclubs to pour sake, provide conversation, and sometimes serve as dance partners. Neither the geisha nor the hostess is a prostitute.

Tokyo's hottest disco is **Lexington Queen,** *B1, Third Goto Building, 3-13-14 Roppongi, Minato-ku; tel. (81-3)406-1661,* which attracts celebrities such as Sylvester Stallone, Stevie Wonder, and Rod Stewart. It is big with the fashion and film crowds. The cover charge is 3,000 yen ($24).

Two other good discos are **Le Rat Mort,** *Ginza; tel. (81-3)571-9296,* and **May Flower,** *Ginza; tel. (81-3)563-2426.*

At **Club Fontana,** *Roppongi; tel. (81-3)584-6758,* you can listen to a pianist and a vocalist. The entrance fee is 7,000 yen ($56).

For more chic dancing and drinking, visit the **Potato Club,** *Akasaka; tel. (81-3)583-1348,* which has live music. An evening here is 10,000 yen ($80).

Akasaka is another good district for nightclubs. This is the home of the **Mikado,** *2-14-6 Akasaka, Minato-ku; tel. (81-3)583-1101,* an enormous club with a waterfall, a moving stage, and more than 500 hostesses. The entrance fee, including drinks, is about 4,500 yen ($36); 9,375 yen ($75) with a hostess.

Also in Akasaka is **Club Charon,** *tel. (81-3)586-4480,* which is inexpensive. Although it's crowded, it's a good place to enjoy live jazz and mingle with Tokyo's artistic circles.

The seediest side

The seedy side of Tokyo's night life is in the **Shinjuku district.** The streets here are crammed with neon signs for X-rated movie theaters, brothels, often called Turkish baths, and little local bars, where *mama-san* will serve you cheap *miziwari* (watered-down whiskey).

These local bars are also the places to experience *karaoke,* or well-whiskied customers with microphones and accompanying tape recordings who entertain the bar with their favorite love songs. Talent is of little consideration in these late-night shows. What counts is volume (*karaoke* has been forbidden in many residential areas).

Yoshiwara, known as the Turkish massage district, is Tokyo's lust-ridden den of iniquity.

Mt. Fuji: the world's best sunrise

Those who have seen the sun rise from the top of **Fuji-san** (Mt. Fuji) claim it is a mind-altering experience. Mt. Fuji, which the Japanese consider a goddess, hides its dazzling beauty in a cloak of clouds most days. When the cloak is lifted, the 12,390-foot peak glitters white. You can climb the mountain only from the end of June through the beginning of September. Six trails lead to the top.

A short train or bus ride from Tokyo brings you to **Fuji-Hakone-Izu National Park.**

Although the climb takes four to six hours, most of the trails are easy to hike, and the view is spectacular. Fellow trekkers, who sport everything from the latest fashions to the long white robes of religious pilgrims, are interesting additions to the view.

You can spend the night in communal stone huts along the way and wake up in time to see the sunrise. Or you can begin hiking at night and reach the peak above the clouds just as the rising sun illuminates the sky. Wear sturdy shoes or boots and bring along warm, waterproof clothing and a flashlight. It is windy at the summit.

Kyoto: Japan's most beautiful city

For more than 1,000 years, **Kyoto** was the political, cultural, and religious capital of Japan, and the city's heritage is still evident in its 1600 temples, 200 shrines, and well-preserved traditions of architecture and craftsmanship. After trying to make your way through Tokyo, you'll find Kyoto's grid-like street plan a pleasure. While Kyoto is only three hours from Tokyo, it merits a visit of several days. The city's treasures are many.

Kyoto's most important sights

The **Imperial Palace** and its 220-acre park are the city's central attractions. Built by Emperor Kammu in A.D. 794, it has been destroyed several times by fire, but the existing building follows the original design. To visit the palace, you must get a pass at least 20 minutes and sometimes up to two weeks in advance. Register for a pass at the **Imperial Household Agency,** *Kyoto Gyoen, Nai Kamigyo-ku; tel. (81-75)211-1211.*

The **Heian Shrine,** with its impressive torii gate, was built in 1895 to commemorate the 1,100th anniversary of Kyoto's founding. The shrine itself is a replica, 12 times reduced, of the original Chinese-style Imperial Palace, set in Kyoto's most beautiful gardens. In the spring, you can walk among weeping cherry trees and azaleas; in the fall chrysanthemum displays decorate the stepping stone pond. The shrine is a favorite spot for weddings, and often you will catch a glimpse of a bride and her party, all dressed in kimonos.

Kinkaku-ji (Temple of the Golden Pavilion), in the northwest corner of the city, is Kyoto's prettiest. Surrounded by a lake, its exterior walls are gilded. The existing temple is a reconstruction of the original one, built in 1397. Trees shade the structure, and you can see mountains in the distance.

Southwest of Kinkaku-ji is **Ryoanji** (Temple of the Peaceful Dragon), founded in 1473. Its famous stone garden is simple yet thought-provoking. Stones are raked in Zen patterns (the sea, the desert, or the mountains), which are said to aid meditation.

The **Kyoto National Museum,** *527 Chayamachi, Higashiyama-ku; tel. (81-75)541-1151,* houses an impressive collection of Chinese paintings from the Ming and Ch'ing dynasties, as well as treasures from Buddhist temples and Shinto shrines.

Toji Temple, which is five stories and 183 feet, has the tallest pagoda in Japan. The temple's stone house (*azekura*), built of wood without using nails, houses an unrivaled collection of art treasures. On the 21st of each month, the Toji Flea Market, where you'll find everything from household items to miniature bamboo cages with singing crickets, is held here.

Nijo Castle, situated on 70 acres and surrounded by stone walls and a moat, was built in 1603 as the Kyoto residence of Lcyasu, the first shogun of the Tokugawa Family. Of the palace's five buildings don't miss the Ohiramai and its Great Hall, decorated with paintings by Tanyu Kano. Corridors in the Imperial Messenger's Chamber are constructed so that anyone stepping on the floor will trigger a sound resembling the song of the Japanese bush warbler, warning guards of approaching intruders. The shogun's apartments, in the fifth building, contain hidden chambers, where samurai guarded their master out of sight of palace guests.

Sanjusangendo (Temple of 33 Niches), a few blocks east of Kyoto Station, founded in 1132, is a national treasure. It is so-named because the facade is divided into 33 niches, one for each of the goddess Kannon's 33 personifications. The goddess is embodied here in a 10-foot statue, the *Thousand-Armed Kannon.*

Saiho-ji (Moss Temple), founded in 1339, is an incredible green. Its pond is shaped like the Chinese character for heart and mind.

The **Katsura Villa** is widely admired as the crowning achievement of Japanese architecture. Begun in 1590 by Kobori Enshu for the military dictator Hideyoshi, it is silent, austere, and perfectly balanced.

The **Shugaku-in,** a villa in the foothills of Mt. Hiei, has three large stepped gardens. Built in 1629 as a retirement home for Emperor Gomizuno-o, the buildings are fragile, simple, and airy.

The craft quarter

Kyoto's old **Nishijin district** is the place to buy famous Nishijin silk brocade, which is still handwoven. You can hear the sounds of silk looms along the narrow back streets. Displays of the district's handwork can be seen at the **Nishijin Textile Museum,** *Omiya Imadegawa, Kamigyo-ku.*

Another Kyoto specialty is Kiyomizuware pottery, produced by a 16th-century technique. Kiyomizuware is sold everywhere in Kyoto, but a concentration of particularly good shops is located along Teapot Lane near Kiyomizu Temple.

A good place to watch a variety of craftsmen at work on damascene metalware, woodblock prints, dolls, and porcelain is the **Kyoto Handicraft Center,** *Kumano Jinja Higashi, Sakyo-ku.* You'll also see painters, weavers, and goldsmiths here. The restaurant on the top floor has a good view of the city.

Yuzen cloth, decorated using a special 300-year-old dying process, is another Kyoto specialty. To achieve its perfect color, the cloth must be washed in the cold running waters of the Kamo River. Walk along the river between the Nijo-dori and Shijo-dori bridges for a good view of this activity.

The world's best knives

Aritsugu, *Gokomachi Nishiiru, Nishikkoji-dori, Nakagyo-ku; tel. (81-75)221-1091,* in the heart of the market district in central Kyoto, has been supplying Japan with swords and knives since 1560. Fujiwara Aritsugu, who began the family business, was the sword maker to the imperial household and supplied feudal warriors with their weapons.

Today, cooking knives, which are direct descendants of the original Aritsugu swords, form the core of the business. The assortment is bewildering: the *deba-bocho,* for slicing through fish, meat, and bones; the *usuba* and the *nakiri,* for chopping and slicing vegetables; knives with rosewood or black synthetic composition handles; and knives banded with buffalo horn to help prevent cracking.

Aritsugu's knives range from 4,375 yen ($35) for a *deba-bocho* with a five-inch blade to more than 12,500 yen ($100). Terakubo Wasaburo, the director of the shop, can instruct you on the proper care and storage of your knives.

Kyoto's best restaurants

Kyoto's restaurants tend to be smaller, more old-fashioned, and more intimate than those in Tokyo.

Sagano, *45 Susuki-No-Banba, Saga-Tenryu-ji; tel. (81-75)861-0277,* which offers 10 kinds of tofu dishes, is unknown to non-Kyoto residents. Dinner is served overlooking the garden. This restaurant is particularly cozy in the rain.

Another excellent tofu restaurant is **Okutan,** *Nanzen-ji; tel. (81-75)771-8709,* where you are served by kimono-clad waitresses. Order the *yudofu* or the *shojin-age* for deliciously prepared Zen-style vegetables.

Junidanya, *Shijo Hanami Koji; tel. (81-75)561-0213,* is also small and intimate. If you can't read the Japanese menu, you can order in English.

Good places to look for a restaurant are the English-language *Kyoto Restaurant Guide,* published by the Kyoto Restaurant Association, and the *Kyoto Gourmet Guide.*

Japan's best hotel

The **Tawaraya,** on a quiet back street in Kyoto, *tel. (81-75)211-5566,* is a Japanese paradise. Dim and cozy, it has 19 rooms that are booked year-round. You must remove your shoes at the door, where you are welcomed with a warm washcloth, tea, and a *yukata,* a light, cotton version of the kimono (your street clothes are neatly packed away).

Bedrooms at the Tawaraya open onto a wooden platform overlooking the garden. Guests sit on *zabuton,* square cushions placed on the tatami mats that cover the floor. The bathroom looks out onto its own garden. All utilitarian items, such as televisions, telephones, and tea-making sets, are hidden. There are no room keys, and futons are kept in the closets. You're served eight-course dinners on a lacquered table. A staff of 38 keeps things running smoothly.

You must make reservations at least six months in advance. (You can make reservations from the United States through the **Ryokan Reservation Center of Pacific Select Agency,** *(800)722-4349* or *(212)972-8748,* or a travel agent.)

The best Western-style hotels

The most luxurious hotel in Kyoto is the new **Takaragaike Prince Hotel,** *Takaragaike, Sakyo-ku; tel. (81-75)712-1111,* in the northern suburbs.

Two other good Western-style hotels are **Miyako,** *Sanjo Keage, Higashiyama-ku; tel. (81-75)771-7111,* and **International Kyoto,** *284 Nijo, Abura-koji, Nakagyo-ku; tel. (81-75)222-1111.* Both are opposite the Nijo Castle.

Three hotels with both Western- and Japanese-style rooms are the **Kyoto Royal,** *tel. (81-75)223-1234,* the **Fujita,** *tel. (81-75)222-1511,* and the **Kyoto,** *tel. (81-75)211-5111.*

The hottest night life

Gion is Kyoto's answer to Tokyo's Asakusa district. The city's best nightclubs are located here, including the Gion, Onsome, and Bel-Ami.

Gion is also the best place to attend a geisha party. Make arrangements through your hotel or travel agent. Settle on the price beforehand—these are usually costly evenings.

Gion Corner, *Yasaka Kaikan,* was established by the Kyoto Visitors Club. Classes here teach various aspects of Japanese traditional arts. In two evening shows, demonstrations are given of the tea ceremony, flower arrangement, Bunraku puppet plays, *kyomai* (Kyoto-style dance), court music, and *koto* music, which is played on a 13-string instrument.

Nihon Seibukan presents an evening martial arts exhibition, a fast-moving, hour-long performance of karate, kendo, and judo. Geisha dances are performed during April and May at the **Pontocho Kaburenjo,** the **Kitano Kaikan,** and the **Gion Kaburenjo** theaters. You can watch Kabuki performances at **Minami-za;** No performances are staged at **Kanze Kaikan,** *Oe-Nogaku-do.* Call the **Kyoto Tourist Information Center,** *tel. (81-75)371-2108,* for exact dates and times.

Osaka: bests beneath the grime

Osaka, the industrial center of Japan, seems an ugly city at first glance. But if you look behind the city's utilitarian facade and grime, you will discover its traditional temples and shrines, secluded in their gardens, a mighty castle, and two good museums.

Visit the 10th-century **Temmangu Shrine** on July 24 and 25, when the annual Tenjin Festival is held. On these nights, the normally solemn shrine to Tenjin, god of learning, is transformed, as lantern-lit boats sail down Osaka's canals accompanied by a fireworks display.

The 16th-century **Osaka Castle,** located southeast of Temmangu Shrine, was built by the warlord Hideyoshi, who ordered huge stones for its construction, some of which are still in place. One of the stones, called Higo-ishi, is 47 1/2 feet long and more than 19 feet high.

Tennoji Park, in the southern part of the city, contains a zoo, botanical gardens, the Shitennoji Temple, and Keitakuen, one of the best examples of a Japanese strolling garden.

Two excellent museums of Chinese and Japanese art are the **Fujita Art Museum,** *10-32 Amijima-cho, Miyakojima-ku; tel. (81-6)351-0582,* and the **Masaki Museum of Art,** *2-9-26 Tadaokanaka, Tadaoka-cho, Senboku-gun; tel. (81-72)521-6000.*

Tree-lined **Mido-suji** is Osaka's best street for strolling and window shopping, but for serious shopping you're better off in one of the city's shopping districts and arcades. An underground labyrinth of stores is located in Kita, near Umeda Station. Shinsaibashi-suji is another well-known shopping street. Also visit the shopping arcade between Shinsai-Bashi- Suji and Ebisu-Bashi- Suji.

Osaka's best restaurants

For luxury dining with some unusual surprises, visit **Wakatake,** *60 Higashi-Chimizu-cho, Minami-ku; tel. (81-6)271-0005.* Service is irreproachable, and the food is excellent, but the main attraction is the garden, which has a large sculptured *lingam* (holy penis), as well as more traditional pavilions and a bathhouse.

Naniwa, *Nakano-cho 3, Daihoji-machi, Minami-ku; tel. (81-6)271-8646,* is a pleasant restaurant specializing in *udon,* Osaka's thick, white noodles. A meal for one costs about 2,500 yen ($20).

For Osaka's best eel, try **Hishitomi,** *53-9 Soemon-cho, Minami- ku; tel. (81-6)211-1159.* Order the *unagi-teishoku.* Dinner is about 5,625 yen ($45) per person.

For local atmosphere and good grilled specialties, try **Goenya,** a chain of 12 inexpensive restaurants. The best in Osaka is at *30 Sennen-cho, Minami-ku; tel. (81-6)5731.* The place stays open until 3 a.m., and a meal costs less than 1,250 yen ($10).

The best accommodations

Two deluxe hotels in Osaka are the **Royal Hotel,** *Nakanoshima; tel. (81-6)448-1122,* which has double rooms for 22,500 yen ($180), and the **Miyako Hotel Osaka,** *Minami; tel. (81-6)773-1111,* where double rooms are 16,250 yen ($130). The **Hotel Do Sports Plaza,** *tel. (81-6)243-3311,* is centrally located and inexpensive, with double rooms for 11,250 yen ($90). It has its own athletic facilities.

The liveliest entertainment

Kokuritsu Bunraku Gekujo (National Puppet Theater), *1-12-10 Nihonbashi, Minami-Ku, Osaka; tel. (81-6)212-2531,* is considered the original home of the 300-year-old art of puppeteering. The best Bunraku shows in Japan are presented here. Bunraku is not just for children. The stories are colorful and exotic, designed for adults.

Kabuki performances are given in the five-story **Shin-Kabukiza,** *4-3-25 Namba Minami-Ku, Osaka,* in the southern part of the city. The Takarazuka all-girl's revue, Japan's most famous girl's opera, performs at the Grand Theater in Takarazuka City, 40 minutes by train from Osaka.

The best bars and nightclubs can be found in Sonezaki Shinchi in Kita, near the Umeda arcade.

Hiroshima: the world's most sobering city

Hiroshima, the site where the first atomic bomb was dropped in 1945, is a sobering site. Heiwa O-dori (Peace Boulevard) leads to the **Hiroshima Peace Memorial Museum,** *1-2 Nakajima-cho, Naga-ku; tel. (81-82)241-4004,* south of Peace Park. The center features the Peace Tower and a museum of objects left after the explosion, as well as photographs of the bombed city and its victims.

The Industrial Promotion Hall, the building believed to have been directly below the center of the blast, also is located here. It has been left standing, gutted from the explosion, as a reminder of the bomb. On Aug. 6, the day of the bombing, Hiroshima holds its annual Peace Festival in the Peace Memorial Park.

You can reach the city of Hiroshima, set on a bay of the Inland Sea, by a two-hour bullet train ride. The stretch between Okayama and Hiroshima (when traveling from Osaka or Kyoto) is considered the most beautiful train ride in Japan.

The best place for singles

A worthwhile excursion from Hiroshima is to the island of Miyajima to see the Shinto shrine **Itsukushima,** known among the Japanese as one of Japan's Three Great Sights. (The other two are Amanohashidate and Matsushima.) The island is dedicated to a Shinto goddess, who, according to legend, is extremely jealous. For this reason, married couples might want to think twice about visiting the shrine. Singles can take the train or bus from Hiroshima to Miyajimaguchi, where a ferry takes you to the island. Offshore stands the red painted torii, the gate of the Shinto shrine.

The shrine itself and its smaller galleries are on stilts above the water—when the tide is high, both the shrine and the torii appear to be floating on the water. The sight is most spectacular in April, when the cherry blossoms are out, and in the fall, when the maples turn glowing red. These are also the most crowded times.

For an incredible view of Hiroshima surrounded by mountains and the Inland Sea, take the ropeway from Momiji-dani Park behind the Itsukushima Shrine to the highest peak on the island, Mt. Misen. From this height you also can see the ninth-century Gumonjido Temple.

Hiroshima's best hotels

The three best Western-style hotels in Hiroshima are the **Hiroshima Grand,** *4-4 Hatchobori, Naka-Ku; tel. (81-82)227-1313,* which has double rooms for 15,000 yen ($120); the **Hiroshima Kokusai,** *3-13 Tate-Machi, Naku-Ku; tel. (81-82)248-2323,* which has double rooms for 10,625 yen ($85); and the **Hiroshima River Side,** *7-14 Kaminoboicho, Naka-Ku; tel. (81-82)227-1111,* which has double rooms for 9,375 yen ($75). The best *ryokan* is **Mitakiso,** *1-7 Mitaki-Machi, Nischi-Ku; tel. (81-82)237-1402,* which charges 18,750 yen ($150) per person, including two meals.

Nagoya: Japan's best pearls

Japan's best pearl farms are in **Nagoya,** between Tokyo and Kyoto. You can get from Tokyo to Nagoya Station in just two hours on the super-express trains on the Shinkansen Line. The station is the commercial center of the city, with stores and restaurants located in the network of underground passageways that connect to neighboring buildings.

The heart of the pearl industry is just south of Nagoya in Ago Bay and five other bays off Ise-shima National Park. To learn about the process of pearl cultivation, visit Toba, where pearls are developed, harvested, and prepared for sale. *Ama* (women divers), ranging in age from adolescence to their early 40s and dressed in white cotton body suits, face masks, and caps, collect the oysters, making six or seven dives an hour to depths of up to 100 feet. The oysters are then seeded and suspended in cages from bamboo rafts. More than 200-million pearls each year are harvested after about six months, sorted, and polished.

Ama demonstrate their diving methods at the Toba Aquarium and on Irukajima, also in Toba Bay. Nearby Pearl Island has a model pearl farm that you also can visit.

Nagoya's two most important sights are its castle and the Atsuta Shrine. **Nagoya Castle** is topped by a famous pair of golden dolphins and crowned with a five-story inner tower. The grounds are lovely.

Atsuta Shrine is considered one of the most important Shinto shrines in Japan, housing the **Kusanagi-no-Tsurugi** (Grass-mowing Sword), one of the nation's Three Sacred Treasures. (The other two are the Sacred Jewels at the Imperial Palace in Tokyo and the Sacred Mirror of Ise Grand Shrines.) Nagoya also claims one of the largest zoos in the Orient, in Higashiyama Park.

Nagoya's best Western-style hotels are the **Meitetsu Grand,** *1-2-4 Meieki, Nakamura-Ku, Nagoya; tel. (81-52)582-2211,* which has double rooms for 12,500 yen ($100); **Nagoya Castle,** *3-19 Hinokuchicho, Nischi-Ku; tel. (81-52)521-221,* which has double rooms for 17,500 yen ($140); **Nagoya Kanko,** *1-9-30 Nishiki, Naka-Ku; tel. (81-52)231-7711,* which has double rooms for 12,500 yen ($100); and **Nagoya Miyako,** *4-9-10 Meieki, Nakamura-Ku; tel. (81-52)571-3211,* which has double rooms for 12,500 yen ($100).

Japan's strangest festival

Japan's strangest festival is the **Konomiya Naked Festival,** held Jan. 13 in Inazawa City, near Nagoya. This festival, first held in A.D. 780 to ward off the plague, is still thought to drive out devils. Each year, one man is chosen to act as a divinity who takes on the sins of others and purges them. The divine man appears naked before a crowd of naked men at the Owari Okunitama Shrine and exorcises spectators' demons. The male worshippers surge forward to touch the holy man and transfer their sins to him.

Best fishing and parasols

The most colorful fishing spectacle in Japan takes place in **Gifu,** 30 minutes by train north of Nagoya. From mid-May to mid-October, cormorant are fished at night along the Nagara River. Boats are hung with fire baskets to attract ayu, a kind of river smelt. The fishermen then command large tame birds, tied to long leashes, to dive in and retrieve the fish from the illuminated river.

Gifu is also famous because it contains one of the few remaining *bangasa,* or Japanese parasol factories, where you can watch paper and silk dancing parasols being made and individually painted. If you buy one, the factory will take care of shipping it home for you.

Kyushu: Japan's best seaside resort

Kyushu, the southernmost of Japan's islands, is a popular summer resort for Japanese vacationers. Because few Western visitors make their way here, it is a good place to sample Japanese culture as well as sandy beaches. Stay in a *ryokan* in one of the remote towns in the area and explore the secluded coves at your leisure.

Kitakyushu, the largest city on the island, is a good place to find a hotel and make travel arrangements. The island's nicest drive is from Kitakhushu to Fukuoko, which takes you along the coast and through Genkai-Quasi National Park. En route are oddly shaped rock formations and pine groves that dot the white sand beaches.

At the southernmost tip of the island is **Ibusuki,** a popular seaside resort. The **Ibusuki Kanko Hotel,** *3755 Junicho, Ibusuki, Kagoshima Prefecture; tel. (81-9932)2131,* a Western-style hotel facing north to Mt. Sakurajima, is a good place to stay. You can lie by the pool in the shade of banana trees and dine in hotel robes and slippers in the Jungle Theater restaurant. Double rooms are 10,625 yen ($85).

Another good restaurant is the **Ibusuki Royal Hotel,** *42-32-1 Junicho, Ibusuki; tel. (81-9932)32211,* with double rooms for 12,500 yen ($100).

Ibusuki's seawall is lined with small *ryokan.* The beaches cover underwater hotsprings, and in certain spots attendants will dig holes so you can immerse yourself from toe to chin in warm sand.

The best of **Fukuoko's** many parks is **Ohori,** a large open parkland surrounding a tidewater lake formed from the moat of an old castle. Bridges link the surrounding park with smaller island parks in the lake. In the background is a forest with remnants of the stone walls of Fukuoko Castle.

Nagasaki: Japan's first open door

Curving around the mouth of the Urakami River, **Nagasaki** is considered Japan's first open door. This was the first major port to trade with the Portuguese and Dutch in the 16th century. European influences are still visible in the city's old forts, brick buildings, and cobblestoned streets.

Nagasaki was also the first place in Japan to accept Christianity. However, in the 16th to 17th centuries, the Christian communities here were forced underground. Monuments to martyred Christians can be found throughout the city. The most impressive is **Oura Catholic Church,** built in 1865 to commemorate 26 Christians who were crucified here in the 16th century. Oura is the oldest example of ecclesiastical Gothic architecture in Japan.

Glover Mansion is the house where Madame Butterfly (from the opera of the same name) waited for her lover's return. Set on a hilltop, the house has a panoramic view over the harbor.

Nagasaki is also known as the second city on which the Americans dropped the atomic bomb. Peace Park and the Atom Bomb Museum are monuments to the horror.

Good Western hotels in Nagasaki are the **Nagasaki Grand,** *5-3 Manzai-Machi, Nagasaki; tel. (81-958)231-234,* which has double rooms for 12,500 yen ($100); **New Nagasaki,** *tel. (81-958)266-161;* **Nagasaki Tokyu,** *1-18 Minamiyamate-Machi; tel. (81-958)251-501,* with double rooms for 15,625 yen ($125); and the **New Tanda Hotel,** *2-24 Tikiwa-Machi; tel. (81-958)276-121,* where double rooms are 12,500 yen ($100).

Suwa-so, on a hillside overlooking the city, is a *ryokan* often visited by Japan's royal family.

The most threatening volcano

A short ride by bus or ferry from Nagasaki brings you to the active volcano **Mt. Aso** in Aso National Park. A toll road leads most of the way up the side of the volcano. You can reach the rim by foot or ropeway, unless the area has been closed by volcanologists. Standing at the rim, you will see white smoke and gases spurting from the bottom of the crater and feel the ground rumbling.

Hokkaido: Japan's best skiing

The 1972 Winter Olympics were held in **Hokkaido,** Japan's northernmost district. It was then that the world discovered the region's ideal skiing conditions.

Skiing in Japan is luxurious. Everything is civilized and efficient. And après-ski, try a relaxing *o-furo* (hot bath) with a massage and hot sake.

The two best places to ski are **Teine,** good for slalom skiing, and **Eniwa,** good for downhill skiing. **Mt. Moiwa,** 30 minutes southwest of the city by bus, is also popular, overlooking the capital and the Sea of Japan.

The region's biggest city is **Sapporo,** which has a wide choice of hotels, as well as taxis and buses to take you to the slopes.

The **Akakura Kanko Hotel,** *Myoko-Kogen, Naki-Kubiki-gun; tel. (81-255)87-2501,* in Niigata Prefecture, is one of the best in Sapporo, with an excellent restaurant. Tables are set with crisp white linen and sparkling crystal and silverware. You can ski right from the back door, and a connecting system of lifts and slopes extends for miles through the mountains. Double rooms are 22,500 yen ($180).

Three other good ski hotels are **Yamagata Grand,** *1-7-42 Honcho, Yamagata 990; tel. (81-236)41-2611,* with double rooms for 12,500 yen ($100); **Sapporo Park,** *3-11 Nishi Minami-10, Chuo-ku, Hokkaido 64; tel. (81-11)511-3131,* with double rooms for 18,750 ($150); and **Sapporo Grand Hotel,** *4 Nishi Kita-1, Chuo-ku, Hokkaido 060; tel. (81-11)261-3311,* with double rooms for 22,500 yen ($180).

Numerous lodges and *minshuku* (guesthouses) are located throughout Japan's ski country. They cost about 3,750 yen to 6,250 yen ($30 to $50) a night per person, including breakfast and dinner. Accommodations are Japanese-style—which means you sleep on a futon and share a room with three or four other people. Rooms are heated and often have televisions. Baths are communal, and toilets are down the hall. The food, Japanese country cooking served boarding-house style, is plentiful and good.

You can rent ski equipment at most Japanese resorts. The selection is good at larger establishments. Boots are the main worry for Americans; few Japanese wear size 10, for example. A set of equipment (boots, skis, and poles) rents for about 3,750 yen to 4,375 yen ($30 to $35) a day. Lift passes cost 3,125 yen to 3,750 yen ($25 to $30).

It's easy to book a ski trip once you're in Japan. Trains depart for snow country from Tokyo's Ueno Station every half-hour during ski season (reservations are necessary). The closest slopes are three to four hours north.

Hokkaido's minority

Hokkaido is also known as the home of the **Ainu,** a fast-disappearing people originally from Honshu who have been forced north into the mountains. The Ainu are Caucasians, who, unlike other Japanese, have light skin and hairy bodies. The men often have thick beards, and the women have blue tattoos around their mouths. The best place to see their huts and their rituals of worship—the Ainu practice a form of nature worship influenced by Shintoism—is the small colony in **Asahikawa,** Hokkaido's second-largest city. You also can visit a display village in **Shiraoi,** near Noboribetsu Spa on the south coast.

Karuizawa: the best mountain resort

Karuizawa, two hours north of Tokyo, is the mountain escape of Japan's powerful elite who come here to play tennis, golf, horseback ride, and sail on the lakes. Since Prince Akihito met and married the untitled Michiko Shoda at the Karuizawa Kai tennis club in the late 1950s, Karuizawa has been seen by many as a fairy-tale town where you can do anything—even marry a prince.

The countryside is embellished with waterfalls and streams and dotted with elegant villas. In the summer, classical music concerts are staged outdoors.

Generally, the hotels in Karuizawa have great restaurants. The Kuruizawa Prince complex holds about 13 restaurants, including an informal Japanese grill and an excellent French restaurant where diners eat overlooking a pond while being entertained by a harpist. The Suehiro (a steakhouse) is a favorite, as is the Akasaka Hanten, a Chinese restaurant with a pleasant garden.

The elegant **Karuizawa Prince,** *Karuizawa, Karuizawa-machi, Kitasaku-gun, Nagano Prefecture 389-01; tel. (81-267)46-1111,* offers three types of accommodations: the original hotel, log cabins, and a fancy new annex overlooking a pond and a golf course.

Hoshimo Onsen Hotel, *2148 Oaza Nagakura, Karuizawa-Machi, Kitasaku-gun; tel. (81-287)45-5121,* has hot springs as well as comfortable rooms.

Tsuruya Ryokan, *678 Kyu-Karuizawa, Karuizawa-machi, Kitasaku-gun, Nagano Prefecture 389-01; tel. (81-263)93-2331,* is a cozy little Japanese inn.

Asia's most alluring women

Geishas are highly talented entertainers, well versed in all the traditional arts of Japan. They are not prostitutes. They are good conversationalists who serve food and drinks and provide high-caliber singing and dancing. Geisha parties, often organized by Japanese businessmen, feature pretty entertainers dressed in kimonos, elevated clogs, white face makeup, and elaborate hairdos. Generally these parties are for men, but women can be included.

The Akasaka district in Tokyo has a concentration of exclusive houses where geishas perform. Company presidents and others who can afford the high cost frequent these places.

You can see young apprentice geisha, called *maiko,* near Gion Corner and Ponto-cho in Kyoto. The young women appear at 6 p.m., dressed in their colorful costumes, and shuffle in tiny steps from their residences to their places of work.

Your travel agent can arrange for you to attend a geisha party in Kyoto or Tokyo. Expect to pay at least 10,000 yen per person.

Chapter 16

THE BEST OF HONG KONG AND MACAO

Hong Kong, the pearl of the Orient, is the most dynamic city in the world. The bustling colony is as hectic as New York, but it doesn't have the crime or the unemployment. It is a thriving financial center, a shoppers' paradise, and a gourmets' delight. Everyone works in this city, where fortunes are still made and lost overnight and almost anything can be bought—at a bargain price.

Hong Kong is a unique mixture of British and Chinese cultures. A British Crown Colony and a free market port, it is a gateway between worlds: Eastern and Western, ancient and modern, communist and capitalist, poor and wealthy.

In 1997, Hong Kong will revert to Chinese sovereignty. However, in an agreement signed in 1984, the Chinese government pledged to allow Hong Kong to continue its economic system and way of life until 2047. So you still have plenty of time to see it.

Hong Kong has more people per square mile than any other spot on earth (and more Mercedes, too). And most of its six-million people are crammed into tall buildings in an area just a few miles wide and long. However, despite its claustrophobic urban crowds, Hong Kong has more open space than cities half its size. You can travel easily from the city to the rural countryside, where the dramatic terrain is inspiring.

The best view of Hong Kong

One of the world's greatest views is that of **Hong Kong Harbor** from **Victoria Peak.** Guarded by a tall fortress of mountains, behind which looms the awakening giant China, Hong Kong Harbor is alive with ships and boats from every corner of the earth. Rimmed by skyscrapers, the harbor is dotted with picturesque Chinese junks, hydrofoils, Russian cargo ships, big navy vessels, and the tiny sampans of those who make their livings from the sea. Some of these boats carry people who have never stepped foot on land.

Out in the water beyond the traffic jams of the central harbor rises a large emerald mountain called **Lantau Island.** And if you look hard or get up very high, you'll see 236 other such islands floating in the South China Sea.

You can take a trolley up to Victoria Peak, or, if your legs are up to it, make the trek on foot. The mile-long Governor's Walk takes you through jungle-like growth around the top of the mountain.

The biggest bazaar in the world

Hong Kong is the biggest bazaar in the world. With no import duties on anything (except cigarettes, liquor, automobiles, and cosmetics), the city has some of the best prices in the world. Clothes, electronic gadgets, watches, cameras, jewelry, and Chinese goods should be at the top of your shopping list. Anywhere you stay will be surrounded by shops (hotel shops tend to be the most expensive).

Have a suit made—in a day

Hong Kong's major industry is textiles, so clothing is a good buy. This is the best place in the world to have a suit made. Tailors here are world-famous for their inexpensive, quality work—overnight, if you like. However, it is better to allow time for at least two fittings. If you have no particular tailor in mind, begin by approaching tailors who display the HKTA logo (a red junk in a circle).

Name brands at bargain prices

Silks, cottons, linens, furs, and jeans are also great buys. You can buy jeans on the street for one-third the price you'd pay in the United States. One of Hong Kong's best-kept secrets is its factory outlets, which carry overruns or rejects of items with well-known labels manufactured originally for export to the United States or Europe. The merchandise is available for a fraction of what you'd pay in the United States.

Two well-known outlets are **Oriental Pacific,** *Room 601-6 6/f, Sands Building, 17 Hankow Road, Tsimshatsui,* and **Safari Shopper's World Ltd.,** *Room 104, Pedder Building, Pedder Street, First Floor, Central.*

The greatest outlet is **Four Seasons Garments,** *Kaiser Estate, Phase II, 1/f, G1, 51 Man Yue St., Hunghom, Kowloon.* Also known as the Silk Factory, this place sells every kind of glamorous silk item imaginable.

Linen, imported from China and exquisitely embroidered, is a bargain at Stanley Market and China Arts & Crafts stores.

Affordable furs

If you want to buy a fur coat, do it in Hong Kong, where prices are competitive. **Jindo,** in the Kowloon Hotel shopping center, claims, "We make the world's finest furs rather more affordable." The store's March 1988 price list included a silver fox half coat for US$3,710 and a full-length mink for US$2,300. (Silver fox has replaced mink as the ultimate status symbol in Hong Kong and is reportedly favored by local film stars.)

Chinese goods

For anything Chinese, shop at one of the Chinese Arts & Crafts stores, which you'll find throughout Kowloon and Central (one is located at the Star House by the ferry terminal in Tsimshatsui). Don't be put off by the department store atmosphere. You can't bargain here, but you'll find many high-quality Chinese goods, including art, crafts, jewelry, clothing, carpets, furniture, porcelain, silk, furs, leather, watches, cosmetics, shoes, cameras, electric appliances, and Chinese medicines. Chinese-style dresses, made in Western proportions, are a particularly good deal.

Stanley Village Market

The most famous of Hong Kong's many street markets is the **Stanley Village Market,** on the south side of the island. Stanley is an old fishing village with a large expatriate community. Silk dresses, sunglasses, fresh fruits, rattan furniture, porcelain ware, shoes, and luggage are all available for incredibly bargain prices.

Camera equipment

The best places to shop for camera equipment are along Lock Road and lower Nathan Road in Tsimshatsui and along Hennessy Road in Causeway Bay. The best selection is at **Goodyear Company Communications & Electronics,** *22 Hanoi Road, Tsimshatsui; tel. (852-3)684395.*

Eyeing the best buy

Hong Kong is the best play to lose your eyeglasses. Friendly, efficient opticians have offices throughout the city that display the HKTA logo. Competition makes for better prices on lenses and frames.

Antique bests

Shop for antiques on **Hollywood Road,** about two streets up from Queen's Road in Central. This picturesque area has the atmosphere of a Chinese city from the 1930s. Follow the road around the hill to the old Cat Street quarter, where you can browse through the **Cat Street Galleries,** *Lok Ku Road.* Antique porcelain, traditional Chinese furniture, wall scrolls, old Chinese photographs, jade, ivory, carved wood, vases, and curiosities fill the crowded stalls. Remember to get a red wax seal if you plan to export any antiques you buy.

Ivory buys

Ivory has been carved in China for 3,000 years, and in Hong Kong you will find ivory in both modern and traditional designs. Each province has its own style of carving.

Rickety stairs lead to the ivory factories lining Hollywood Road and Tsimshatsui. At the tops of the stairs are rooms where Chinese sit carving ivory. In the showrooms are shelves upon shelves of ivory statues, jewelry, chopsticks, and ornaments. Intricately carved balls are the most popular items.

Shopping for gems

Hong Kong boasts more jewelry shops per square mile than any other city in the world, and it is the world's third-largest diamond-trading center. Because you pay neither sales tax nor import duty on gems or jewelry, you'll find good buys not only on diamonds, but also on gold, pearls, emeralds, sapphires, coral, jade, and lapis lazuli. You can bargain, too. Stick to shops displaying the HKTA logo in their windows.

The world's most famous jade market

The **Jade Market,** located at the end of Reclamation across Kansu Street in the Yuamati section of Kowloon, is the heart of the world's jade trade. You'll recognize the big-time dealers—they're the Chinese with newspapers covering their hands. They bargain by tapping each other's hands beneath the papers, which keeps competitors from seeing what the bids are. You're not likely to get a bargain here unless you know a lot about jade.

Asia's biggest computer center

Asia Computer Plaza, *in the Silvercord Building, Canton Road, Tsimshatsui,* is devoted solely to the computer and associated gadgets. Vendors sell personal and small-business computers, as well as peripherals, spare parts, software, and information services. For more information, and up-to-date product listings, call *(852-3)734111.*

The best Buddhas

The **Temple of Ten Thousand Buddhas** actually contains about 12,800 of the statues. **Yuet Kai,** the gold-plated monk on exhibit, is actually a mummy, sealed in gold leaf and serenely dressed in his saffron robe. Also look for the scarlet Buddha, a bright red statue of the philosopher. The temple is near the train station at Shatin.

The best place for bird lovers

Bird Street, a small alley in Kowloon, is where the Chinese buy birds. Hundreds of them—whistling, singing, talking, screaming—are for sale, along with elaborate bamboo cages and live insects (bird food). The street's real name is Hong Lok Street. It is a few blocks west of the intersection of Argyle Street and Nathan Road.

The best place for a workout

Bowen Road is a quiet, tree-shaded path about 400 feet above sea level on Hong Kong Island. Along it you'll see people jogging, playing badminton, and performing the tai chi. Following the path as it winds around the island, you'll hear (and maybe encounter) bands of monkeys playing in the subtropical forest.

The world's most noteworthy new building

If you are interested in architecture or money, visit the **Hong Kong & Shanghai Bank,** *1 Queen's Road, Central.* This high-tech edifice, built of steel, glass, and aluminum, cost $641 million. Rather than resting upon the framework, each section is suspended from it. Only the supports and service shafts touch the ground. What normally would be the ground floor is open space, connected to the bank by twin escalators—the longest freely supported escalators in the world. They look like ramps reaching down from a spaceship and are sealed off when the bank closes by means of a sliding glass underbelly.

The best time to visit

The best time to visit Hong Kong is during **Chinese New Year,** at the end of February. Or you may want to schedule your visit to coincide with the **Dragon Boat Festival** or the **Cheung Chau Island Bun Festival,** when special buns are distributed to ensure good luck and prosperity.

The most tranquil escapes

If you're looking for relief from the frantic pace of the city, retreat to Hong Kong's quiet coves, beaches, and small villages. You can reach them by ferry from the city center. Lantau, Lamma, and Cheung Chai islands have beautiful beaches and seafood restaurants. **Lamma** is the best getaway spot—it has no cars or motorcycles, and its villages have no more than a few-hundred inhabitants. It is known as Hong Kong's Stone Age Island.

The world's best Chinese food

Hong Kong, not China, has the world's best Chinese food. The best Chinese cooks fled here in 1949.

The finest Cantonese restaurant is the **Man Wah,** *Mandarin Hotel; tel. (852-5)220-111.* Another excellent restaurant is **Tan Wong Kok,** *Carpo Commercial Building, 18-20 Lyndhurst Terrace, Central; tel. (852-5)413-071-3.*

The most delicate Chinese food is the bite-size *dim sum,* served for breakfast or lunch in steaming bamboo baskets. The **Luk Yu Tea House,** *Stanley Street, Central,* an old restaurant decorated Chinese-style, is one of the best places to eat *dim sum.* Elderly Chinese men dressed in long gray robes sit for hours over tea, reading Chinese newspapers and choosing from the delicacies brought around on *dim sum* carts.

The world's oldest eggs

The oldest eggs in the world are served in Hong Kong. *Pay daan,* known as 1,000- or 100-year-old eggs, are actually only about three months old. *Pay daan* are buried in dung, and their whites turn to a clear, gel-like substance. Despite their odd name and dirty appearance, many find them quite good.

Hong Kong's best seafood

The freshest seafood dinner can be had at **Lei Yu Mun,** a fish market on a tiny peninsula in east Kowloon. You take a ferry over to an enclave of fish stalls, where you can wander among hundreds of tanks and tile pools filled with fish, crabs, multicolored lobsters, prawns, eels, scallops, and a myriad of other live sea animals. Watch your dinner flop on the floor as you bargain with vendors, then make your way to one of the 20 restaurants around the market, where you can have your seafood cooked to order for a reasonable charge.

The most romantic dining

Dining afloat is one of Hong Kong's most novel gastronomic experiences. You can have a meal on one of the big floating restaurants in Aberdeen or on board a tiny sampan with room for six to eight people. Sampans are for rent at the Causeway Bay Typhoon Shelter. They will pull alongside the dock to cook your meal, serve your drinks, and even serenade you. All this is not cheap, of course.

The best of the West

Some of the 20,000 restaurants in Hong Kong serve exceptionally good Western-style food. The two best are **Gaddi's,** *Salisbury Road, Tsimshatsui; tel. (852-3)666251,* in the Peninsula Hotel, and the **Plume,** *Salisbury Road, Tsimshatsui; tel. (852-3)721211,* in the Regent Hotel. The Plume has an extraordinary view of the harbor and about 10,000 bottles of wine in its cellar—which probably qualifies as the best wine cellar in Asia.

The best hotels in the world

Service is what sets hotels in the Orient apart from those in the rest of the world—and in

Hong Kong you'll find the world's best hotels. The **Peninsula,** *Salisbury Road, Tsimshatsui; tel. (852-3)666-251,* is a unique establishment, reminiscent of the best days of the British Empire. The **Regent,** *Salisbury Road, Tsimshatsui; tel. (852-3)271-211,* is an expensive and luxurious hotel with a commanding view of the harbor.

The **Mandarin,** *5 Connaught Road, Central; tel. (852-5)220-111,* is cited by businessmen as the best hotel in the world, with a reputation for personal, discreet service.

The **Hong Kong Hilton,** *2 Queen's Road, Central; tel. (852-5)233-111,* is an elegant, well-run hotel in a superb location right in the heart of the business district between the Hong Kong & Shanghai Bank and the new headquarters of the Bank of China.

Hong Kong's hotspots

Hong Kong's night life is varied. Posh hotel nightclubs offer sophisticated music and dancing, while the **Poor Man's Nightclub,** in a parking lot near the Macao ferry, offers street entertainment for a fraction of the cost of one drink in some clubs. When all the cars are gone at 8 p.m., you can eat at the noodle stalls, toss a coin to the singers and dancers, and have your fortune told.

For the best Western-style entertainment, visit **Lan Kwai Fong Street,** in the heart of Central, where *gweilos* (Westerners) abound. One of the hottest nightclubs here is **1997,** *9 Lan Kwai Fong; tel. (852-5)260303,* which has a restaurant, an art gallery, and a brasserie, as well as a dance club.

The easiest place to get to in Asia

You won't have any trouble getting to Hong Kong. All the world's major international airlines fly into the city or have offices there, and about 1,000 flights go in and out of Kai Rak International Airport each week. The airport has a great location, right in the middle of Kowloon, which makes for dramatic landings, particularly at night.

Hong Kong's airline, Cathay Pacific, is one of the best in the world. U.S. airlines with routes to Hong Kong include Pan Am and Northwest. Flights are about $1,000 from the East Coast, about $850 from the West Coast. Charters can be as low as $700 round trip (from New York).

The world's best cheap transportation

The **Star Ferry** is the best way to cross Hong Kong's harbor. At HK$.70 for a first-class fare (about 8 cents), it's one of the cheapest and most scenic journeys in the world. In the eight minutes it takes to go from Central to Tsimshatsui, you'll experience the essence of Hong Kong. Twilight is the best time to take the ride.

The best way to see Hong Kong

The best way to see Hong Kong is on foot. Driving is too hectic. Besides, Hong Kong is so compact and its transportation systems are so good that you'll have no trouble traveling around the city and exploring the countryside.

After you go through customs at Kai Tak Airport, pick up a free Hong Kong Tourist Association (HKTA) map at one of the stands outside the customs area. The street names are in English and Chinese, and the map indicates hotels, office buildings, markets, and important sights.

Taxis are metered and inexpensive. The first two kilometers are HK$5.50 (US$.70); every .25 kilometers after that are HK$.70—a real bargain.

The **Mass Transit Railway** (MTR) is fast, efficient, clean, and cheap. Most trips cost HK$2 to HK$2.50. You can buy an MTR Tourist Ticket (HK$15) at any MTR station or HKTA information center, which saves you the trouble of buying a ticket for each journey.

Macao—Asia's oldest European colony

Macao is one of the last remnants of the 16th-century Portuguese empire, renowned for its gourmet food, exotic setting, and outrageous gambling. Officially a Chinese territory under Portuguese administration (until it reverts to China in 1999—two years after Hong Kong), Macao has a tangible sense of history that is preserved in its beautiful colonial buildings.

For centuries, it was a place where smugglers, pirates, prostitutes, drug lords, sailors, flesh merchants, and Catholics made their homes. Today, Macao is a refuge from the hustle and bustle of Hong Kong. However, Macao, too, has an exciting night life, with a flavor all its own.

The best gambling tables in Asia

Macao is famous for its casinos. The biggest is the **Casino de Lisboa,** *Avenida da Amizade,* in the Lisboa Hotel. The Lisboa is probably the ugliest hotel in the world, designed to look like a roulette wheel, which it wears like a crown upon its head. The **Macao Palace,** known as the Floating Casino, is a more exotic place to gamble. This red and gilded Chinese boat is moored on the inner harbor off Avenida de Almeida Ribeiro.

Games include both those familiar to Westerners, such as blackjack, and Chinese games, such as *dai-siu* and keno. Slot machines are known locally as "hungry tigers."

The best place to honeymoon

Macao's **Pousada de São Tiago,** *Avenida da Republica, Macao; tel. 78111*, became a hotel only recently—it was built 350 years ago as a fortress (the Fortaleza da Barra). Every historical feature was preserved during the transformation, including the Portuguese marble, hand-painted tiles, ancient stone walls, gentle cascades, hand-carved mahogany, and even the trees that shade the multilevel terraces.

Overlooking the South China Sea, enveloped in warm, salty breezes, the *pousada* is an ideal romantic hideaway, perfect for a honeymoon. You could have your wedding here, too—small weddings can be arranged in the chapel (which holds only 15 people). The *pousada* is complete with restaurants, gardens, a pool, and reading rooms—you'd never need to venture beyond its grounds.

The *pousada* has 20 rooms and 3 suites, starting at about $100 per night.

Macao's most memorable monument

The ruins of the **Church of St. Paul** are Macao's most memorable monument. Built by the Jesuits in 1602, the beautiful church was mostly destroyed by a typhoon-fanned fire in 1835. All that remains is its baroque facade, covered with Catholic saints, Chinese dragons, and a Portuguese caravan. It is an imposing sight, with a broad granite stairway.

The oldest shrine

The **A Ma Temple** is the territory's oldest temple, built before the Portuguese came to Macao. According to legend, A Ma, the goddess of fishermen, was the sole survivor of a fishing boat caught in a severe storm.

The temple is a series of shrines built at various levels on the Barra hillside and linked by winding paths and steps. The shrine has a mysterious religious atmosphere, with its painted rocks, prayer sticks, tiny shrines, and statue-filled pavilions. Keep a close eye on your purse or wallet. Beggars congregate here, and signs warn against pickpocketing.

The best place to get away from it all

Take a day to visit Macao's two outlying islands, **Taipa** and **Colonne.** These quiet retreats offer tree-shaded lanes, wide sandy beaches, small Chinese villages, and lush forests. Both islands are easily accessible, connected by a causeway to Macao City.

Macao's best hike

The **Rua da Praia Grande** is a lovely promenade alongside the South China Sea—a great place to stroll at night. Along the elegant walk you'll see the pink Government House, a typical example of colonial Macao architecture. You'll also see benches where you can rest beneath huge banyan trees.

If you are feeling adventurous and fit, follow one of the steep paths leading up to the lighthouse. Birds, frogs, and dogs will greet you as you climb the hill. At the top, you'll have a bird's-eye view of the city, with its bright lights and neon far below.

Macao's best restaurant

The best restaurant in Macao, if not all of Asia, is **Pinocchio's,** *4 Rua do Sol, Taipa Island; tel. 27128.* This garden restaurant off the main street of Taipa village draws crowds from Hong Kong on weekends. Try the superb roast quail, chili crab, prawns, roast suckling pig, and baby lamb.

Macao's oldest restaurant

Fat Siu Lau, *64 Rua da Felicidade; tel. 573585,* is the oldest restaurant in Macao (opened in 1903). It serves excellent Macanese cuisine, an exotic mixture of Chinese and Portuguese food and wines. The fresh seafood dishes are exceptionally good.

The best way to get to Macao

Because Macao doesn't have an airport, you can get to it only from Hong Kong or the People's Republic of China. The **Far East Jetfoil** from Hong Kong is the best option. Tickets cost about $7.30 one way, and the trip takes about an hour. Hovercraft, hydrofoil, and ferry services also run frequently between Hong Kong and Macao. Make reservations in advance, especially on weekends and holidays.

The best time to go

The best times to visit Macao are spring and fall. Unless you want to see the territory when it is jam-packed with people, avoid the Chinese New Year and the November Grand Prix. For more information, contact the **Macao Tourist Information Bureau,** *3133 Lake Hollywood Drive, Los Angeles, CA 90068; (213)851-3402.* In Macao, contact the **Department of Tourism,** *Travessa do Paiva, No. 1, Macao; tel. 77218.*

Chapter 17

THE BEST OF INDIA

India is an exotic, ancient, multicolored land covering an area of 1,261,597 square miles. The size, variety, and grandeur of this country make it a feast for visitors. Every region is different. The bordering Himalayas contain the highest peaks in the world, including Mt. Everest. The Ganges Plain is one of the world's greatest stretches of flat land—as well as one of the world's most densely populated regions. There are towns dating back to 3000 B.C. and mosques that draw pilgrims by the thousands. The country's diverse population of 683 million shares the land with elephants, tigers, camels, and millions of sacred cows.

The religions of India are as varied as its climate. You'll find Hindus, Muslims, Sikhs, Buddhists, Jainists, Jews, Christians, Zoroastrians, and former headhunting tribes. The different groups are lively and colorful, each with its own festivals, dances, cultures, and cuisines. Each has left its artistic mark on India—ancient, elaborately carved temples are located throughout the country.

We will explore India counter-clockwise, beginning with Delhi and moving southwest toward Bombay, southeast to Madras, northeast to Calcutta, and finally to the farthest corners of India for a look at the continent's least-known regions.

Delhi, the oldest Indian city

When Bombay and Madras were mere trading posts, Delhi was the capital of a 500-year-old empire. India was ruled from Delhi by various Hindu dynasties, then the Moguls, and finally the British. And it was here that India was granted its independence.

Eight cities have flourished on the site of Delhi. And each of the city's rulers has left his mark architecturally.

Modern-day Delhi is divided into two cities: Old Delhi, once the Mogul capital, which is filled with ancient forts, temples, and monuments; and New Delhi, the present capital, which has wide boulevards, modern office buildings, parks, and hotels.

Tour Delhi from south to north, because growth has been steadily northward. Bring sweaters if you plan to be here during the winter, when it gets to be about 40 degrees Fahrenheit.

The Seventh Wonder of Hindustan

Ten miles south of Delhi is **Qutb Minar,** a 234-foot victory tower known as the Seventh

Wonder of Hindustan. One of the earliest monuments of the Afghan period in India, built on a site of pre-Muslim Delhi, it has stood for 800 years. You can climb the 11th-century tower via a spiral staircase.

At the foot of the tower lies the **Quwwat-ul-Islam Mosque.** The first mosque built in India, it was erected in the 12th century on the foundations of a Hindu temple. The mosque contains the **Iron Pillar,** which has remained rust free for more than 1,500 years.

Delhi's top sights

East of the Qutb Minar is the fortress and tomb of the first Tughlaq king (1230 to 1400), Tughlaqabad. A seven-mile, inwardly sloping wall guards the tombs of the founder and his son, mosques, palaces, and hundreds of residences. The fortress has a panoramic view of the surrounding countryside.

Two miles south is the Suraj Kund, the largest Hindu monument near Delhi. It is believed that a sun temple once stood here.

Following the road back toward Delhi you'll come to the **mausoleum of Emperor Humayun,** erected in the 16th century. This was the precursor of the Taj Mahal, with rose-colored sandstone walls inlaid with white marble and surrounded by gardens. Opposite the tomb is a place of pilgrimage, the **shrine of Nizam-ud-din,** which encloses a mosque with a fine Byzantine dome.

A few minutes away is the **Purana Qila,** a fort standing on the site of Indraprastha, a mythological Delhi of prehistoric times. The present fort, built in the 16th century, frames one end of the two-mile vista leading to the Presidential Palace.

Pass through the **War Memorial Arch,** a memorial to the Indian soldiers who died in World War I. This leads to the fabulous **Rajpath,** the broadest avenue of Delhi, lined with government buildings. **Parliament House** is a huge circular structure with an open colonnade. The **Presidential Palace,** built in this century, has 340 rooms and covers 330 acres.

The strange **Jantar Mantar Observatory,** *Parliament Street,* was built in 1725 by Maharaja Singh II of Jaipur to observe the sun, moon, and stars. Every year on the March 21 and Sept. 21 equinoxes, the sun shines through a narrow slit in the wall.

Jama Masjid, India's largest mosque, has three white marble domes and two 134-foot minarets. Typical of Mogul architecture (it was built in the 17th century), its 450-square-foot courtyard is paved with marble.

Facing the mosque is the **Red Fort,** the finest example of Mogul architecture, built in 1648 behind red sandstone walls. Once the imperial palace of Emperor Shah Jahan (1627-1657), today it houses the Museum of Archeology. It is open to the public during daylight hours.

Rajghat (Shrine of Mahatma Gandhi), southeast of the Red Fort, is where Gandhi was cremated in 1948 following his assassination. A black marble slab in the garden is inscribed with the leader's last words, "Oh, God."

Delhi's best shopping

Chandni Chowk, the city's marketplace, is a web of narrow streets that surround the Red Fort. Here you will find astrologers, shoemakers, barbers, cows, pungent Oriental spices, jewelry, ivory carvings, and rich brocades.

The best zoo in India

Delhi Zoological Park, next to Purana Qila on Mathura Road, is home to rare white tigers. Magnificent gardens brighten the park, which has an especially extensive collection of birds.

India's most colorful festival

Try to time your visit to Delhi to coincide with **Ram Lila,** when gigantic effigies of Ravana and his minions are burned on the last day of the 10-day **Dussehra Festival** to symbolize the destruction of evil. According to Indian mythology, the evil Ravana kidnapped the wife of Lord Rama, who was good. Remembering the story of Lord Rama, Ram Lila is one of the biggest events in Delhi.

Dussehra usually falls in October and includes colorful dramas and dances enacting the stories of gods and demons.

The best dancing

The **Bhangra Dance** of the Punjab, a community dance marked by its energy and hilarity, can be seen in Delhi. Men dance in a line on one side, wearing brightly colored turbans, vests, and pants, while women dance on the other. For specific information on when and where performances are held, contact the **Government of India Tourist Office,** *30 Rockefeller Plaza, Room 15, North Mezzanine, New York, NY 10020; (212)586-4901.*

The best hotels in Delhi

The **Ashok,** *50-B Chanakyapuri,* is a modern hotel with a pool, miniature golf, gardens, tennis courts, an art gallery, and an open-air theater that features performances by a highly rated Indian contemporary dance company. Theater seats are RP30. Double rooms at the hotel are RP1,000.

The **Imperial,** *Janpath,* at the edge of town, is surrounded by a palm garden. Rooms are large, with private bathrooms and air conditioning. A pool and tennis courts are open to guests. The restaurants are good.

Oberoi Maidens, *7 Sham Nath Marg,* is a gracious old hotel with colonial-style bedrooms and private baths, a swimming pool, tennis courts, and gardens. The hotel disco, Sensation, is a good place to go at night.

Kapur House, *C-1/5 Safdarjung Enclave, Mahrauli Road,* is a pleasant guesthouse with inexpensive rooms. The family that runs Kapur House offers free yoga classes to guests.

The Taj Mahal—one of the world's seven wonders

South of Delhi, in the town of Agra, lies the **Taj Mahal,** one of the world's seven wonders. Built in white marble by Emperor Shah Jehan as a mausoleum for his queen, Mumatz Mahal, it is most beautiful at sunset and under moonlight.

Twenty-two years went into the construction of this palace, which was completed in 1652. Beautiful formal gardens and a reflecting pool lead to the arched entrance. An enormous dome, accompanied by two smaller domes, tops the structure, and four minarets mark the corners. It is said that the architect's right hand was cut off upon the completion of the Taj Mahal so that he could not duplicate his creation.

Rajasthan: India at its most traditional

Southwest of Delhi is a desert land broken occasionally by jungle. Here are some of the most ornate temples in India. **Rajasthan,** which translates as Abode of Kings, is the home of the Rajputs, an ancient people whose mythology includes tales of chivalry and romance. You can recognize Rajputs by their colorful clothing: the men wear pink and yellow turbans, and the women wear full skirts and half-bodices and wrap themselves in long mantles.

Jaipur: rose-colored glasses not necessary

The buildings of **Jaipur,** the capital of Rajasthan, are made of rose-colored stone. Founded in 1727 by the brilliant Maharajah Jai Singh II, who built an observatory with a remarkably accurate 90-foot gnomon (an object whose shadow serves to indicate time), Jaipur is protected by a crenellated wall with seven gates. The city's spacious streets are filled with exotic animals: peacocks, elephants, buffalo, and camels.

The most beautiful building in Jaipur is the **City Palace,** which is now a museum housing rare manuscripts, arms, and paintings. The loveliest structure within the palace walls is the lofty **Chandra Mahal,** a seven-story building with a view of the city. Also visit the **Jantra Observatory,** constructed in 1718.

Next to the palace are the **Jai Niwas Gardens,** filled with fountains, statues, and artificial lakes where well-fed crocodiles swim.

Hawa Mahal, with its delicate overhanging balconies and perforated windows placed one above the other in symmetrical pattern, is another important landmark in Jaipur. While it looks like a palace, it is actually a facade behind which women of the court could watch processions without being seen themselves.

Guarding the city from the hills above is **Nahargarh,** or Tiger Fort.

Amber: a little-known treasure

The 17th-century palace at **Amber** stands high above a lake, its towers and domes reaching to the sky. An arched gateway leads into the courtyard, where a broad flight of stairs climbs to the royal apartments. Inside are Persian mosaic walls, filigree doors, fountains, aqueducts, and high ceilings covered with mirrors. Beneath the palace are vaults said to hide the treasures of Jaipur.

You can visit the palace astride an elephant. Musicians play as you make the slow climb to the palace apartments.

Mt. Abu—India's most beautiful sunset

While **Mt. Abu** is most famous as an archeological and religious landmark, you should come here for another reason as well: the sunset. From **Sunset Point,** you can see much of Rajasthan illuminated by the pink glow of the setting sun.

Mt. Abu, which is due south from Jodhpur, was originally a center of the cult of Siva. The Jains (a Hindu sect that abhors killing animals) still make pilgrimages to this mountain, which was known in Hindu legend as the son of the Himalayas. Between Abu's peaks are five Jain shrines, the most beautiful of which was built of pure white marble by Vimal Shah in the 11th century. Inside, marble elephants carrying statues of Vimal Shah and his family climb from the pavilion to the domed porch, which is intricately carved and supported by eight sculptured columns.

Udaipur: India's most romantic city

Udaipur, known as the City of Dreams, is the most romantic city in India. Founded in the 16th century by Maharana Udai Singh, supposedly a descendant of Sri Ram (the hero of the Ramayana epic), Udaipur is protected by a bastioned wall; you enter through five spiked gates. Inside the walls are whitewashed houses painted with murals.

The ruler of the city, known as the Maharana, or Sun of the Hindus, lives in a sparkling palace surrounded by a lake. Amber, jade, and colored glass sparkle on the palace pinnacles. Inside are ivory doors, marble balconies, stained-glass windows, and mirrored walls. You can visit every day between 9:30 a.m. and 4:30 p.m.

Udaipur's second most beautiful sight (after the palace) is **Sahelion-ki-Bari Park,** one of the best examples of Hindu landscaping. The park is filled with ornamental pools, fountains with water coming from elephant trunks or bird beaks, and black stone monuments.

How to travel like a maharajah

Maharajah's Palace on Wheels, a reincarnation of the elegant train that once carried maharajahs and viceroys, is the most pleasant way to travel through Rajasthan. The plush cars have been restored, and each coach is equipped with individual sleeping cabins, bathrooms, showers, a kitchen, and an attendant dressed in traditional Rajasthani clothing. The train has two dining cars and a library/bar.

The trip takes eight days and seven nights and includes stops at Jaipur, Udaipur, Jaisalmer, Jodhpur, the Taj Mahal, and the bird sanctuary at Bharatpur. The train leaves from Delhi Cantt Station Wednesdays at 10:45 p.m.

For more information, contact the **tourist office,** *address above,* or **Tours of Distinction,** *Central Reservations, Rajasthan Tourism, Chandralok Building, 36 Janpath, New Delhi; tel. (91-11)321820.*

The best of Ahmedabad

Founded in 1411, **Ahmedabad** was once considered the finest city in India. Of the many Muslim monuments here, the finest is **Ahmed Shah's Masjid Mosque,** which contains his colored marble tomb, 250 massive pillars, carvings, and inscriptions. The shah's queens lie in ornate tombs across the street.

Another Muslim architectural feat is the Haibat Khan Mosque, built in the 16th century by the Rani, one of the two wives of Mahmud Begara, after her son was executed for "misbehavior."

Also see the stone carving of a slave of Ahmed Shah in the **Mosque of Sidi Sayvid** and the **Mausoleum of Shah Alam** at Batwa.

The **Sun Temple of Modhera,** 60 miles northwest of Ahmedabad, is the best of the many temples built by the Solanki kings of Anhilwad Patan. The grandeur of this temple is enhanced by its wide steps and pillared porch. The shrine was designed so that the image of Surya (the sun god) is struck by the rising sun and the equinoxes.

Kashmir: India's most beautiful region

North of Delhi, wedged between China and Pakistan, is the most beautiful region in India, the **Vale of Kashmir.** At 5,200 feet, it is completely circled by mountains (the Himalayas to the southwest, the Karakoram range to the north). It feels as if it is cut off from the rest of the world. Snow-capped peaks appear to float above the clouds. Houseboats and lotus leaves bob on the area's spring-fed lakes. Flowers fill the meadows. The fair-skinned residents look surprisingly European, despite their veils and nose rings.

Mogul emperors (descendants of Genghis Khan) were partial to Kashmir and built lavish palaces and gardens in the valley. In the colonial days, this was one of the few places in India where Europeans were not allowed to build (they resorted to living in houseboats instead of houses). For centuries, caravans from China and elsewhere passed through Kashmir on their way to the southern reaches of India, giving it an international flavor.

The best time to visit Kashmir is April or May, when the spring flowers are in bloom. But every time of year has its charms. The leaves turn scarlet in the fall, and the fields are lush during the summer. Winter brings deep snows and good skiing conditions.

Srinagar, the capital of Kashmir

Srinagar, the capital of Kashmir, has flowering rooftops (the roofs are made of earth, which bursts into bloom in the spring). Painted shutters and dyed-wool doors brighten the brown houses that line the river. Houseboats with canopied roofs sail the river toward the Dal and Nagin lakes, where they anchor. The men wear fur caps, the women veils to cover their hair. Turbanned old men smoke hookahs on the sidewalks.

Sringar's most important landmark is a small **temple to Siva** at the peak of a 1,000-foot hill, which can be climbed by steep stone steps. The view from the top takes in the town, the river Jhelum, and Dal Lake.

The **Palace Hotel,** *Boulevard,* overlooks the lake. Its rooms have lovely furnishings. A 100-acre terraced garden surrounds the hotel, which also has a golf course. The restaurant and bar are good.

Broadway, another good hotel in Srinagar, has a swimming pool and a good restaurant.

Shahenshah is a reasonably priced hotel in Srinagar with a pool, a garden, and a good restaurant.

Garden paradises, beautiful lakes

The Dal and Nagin lakes are bordered by two beautiful gardens: the **Shalimar Bagh** (Garden of Love), which was designed 400 years ago by one of the Great Moguls for his queen; and the **Nishat Bagh** (Garden of Pleasure), which has terraces of flowers and avenues of cascades.

Lake Manasbal, also in this area, is covered with lotus blossoms. **Lake Wular** is the largest lake in the region.

The holiest spot

In the mountains above the Liddar Valley is the sacred cave of **Amarnath,** reached by steps cut into the rock by pilgrims. Situated at 13,000 feet, the cave is surrounded by snow and ice most of the year. The night of the full moon in the month of Sravan (July or August) is considered the luckiest time to visit.

The world's highest golf course

The highest golf course in the world is at **Gulmarg** (8,700 feet), once a summer hill station popular with British colonialists. (A hill station was a mountain village where Europeans took refuge during the hot season.) Gulmarg's seven-mile Circular Path offers a dizzying view of the Vale of Kashmir and Srinagar.

India's best (and only) skiing

Kashmir has beautiful, pristine ski slopes—but its facilities, including the number of lifts and T-bars and the selection of rental equipment, is limited, which can be frustrating to good skiers. However, it does offer heli-skiing, a great adventure.

Kashmir's first and only ski resort is **Highland Park Lodge** in Gulmarg. The rustic lodge is comfortable, and you can hire a Sherpa to keep the children amused all day for less than RP50. For more information, contact the **tourist office,** *address above.*

The best of Bombay

Bombay is India's most modern, prosperous, and cosmopolitan city, an industrial metropolis, and one of Asia's busiest seaports. Despite its industry, Bombay is also a beautiful city, hugging the Arabian Sea and backed by mountains. Hilly islands dot the harbor.

The best introduction to Bombay is a drive along **Marine Drive,** also known as the Queen's Necklace. Tracing the coastline, it is the city's main boulevard and offers views of the sea and the Bombay skyline.

Wander Bombay's intriguing neighborhoods on foot. Venture beyond the Colaba market—a village of the Kolis, one of the original fishing tribes of the region. Old traditions are maintained here, and the women dress in colorful saris and flowers.

Chowpatty Beach with its statue of Tilak, a great political leader of this century, is the political center of Bombay. This meeting place by the sea is always crowded with people fishing, playing, and eating at food stalls. The entertainment here is free: yogis buried in the sand, soap-box orators, fishermen hauling in their nets. The fortune-tellers here are said to be disconcertingly good.

Not far from the beach is **Mani Bhavan** (the Mahatma Gandhi Memorial), which has photographs of the master of passive resistance along with books he wrote.

The **Prince of Wales** in Fort Bombay has a good collection of Nepalese and Tibetan art, as well as 18th-century miniatures, jade, crystal, and china. It is open every day except Mondays from 10 a.m. to 6:30 p.m.

The **Hanging Gardens,** where you can find respite from the noise of the city, has a beautiful view of the city. Here you can walk among bushes cut to look like elephants, monkeys, cows, oxen, or giraffes.

The greenery on the left as you go beyond the gardens is part of the **Parsee Towers of Silence,** the place where the dead are disposed of. The area is concealed by a park surrounded by a high wall. Bodies are carried to the top of towers, where they are left to be devoured by vultures. The Parsees came originally from the city of Pars in Persia, 1,300 years ago. Today they are a key part of the fabric of life in Bombay.

In Byculla, an old residential area, is **Veermata Jijabai Bhonsle Udyan** (the Victoria Gardens), a park with a profusion of trees and plants. The park also includes the city zoo, the Victoria and Albert Museum, and a gigantic statue of an elephant that once guarded the Elephanta Caves outside Bombay. Compared with the noise and crowds of most of Bombay, this is a peaceful place to escape to for a while.

Juhu Beach, 12 miles northwest of Bombay, is the best place to cool off after wandering through the city. To get to the lake, you cross **Mahim Creek,** a fishing village with ancient boats. After your swim, you can watch the performing monkeys.

If you'd really like to relax, stay a few nights at the **Juhu Hotel,** which has secluded cottages shaded by tropical trees and bushes. It also has a restaurant and a beach terrace.

Bombay's best buys

Bombay's shops display beautiful pure silk saris for RP400 to RP500 and silver earrings for $15. Bargain for the best price.

The city's two most colorful markets are **Mahatma Jyotiba Phule Market** (Crawford Market), *Dadabhai Naoroji and L. Tilak roads,* and **Thieves Market,** near Mohammed Ali Road. The first is a good place to buy fruits and vegetables, cotton, animals, and flowers. It is also a great place to take photos. Thieves Market is a junk-lovers delight, selling everything from old car parts to fine antiques.

The best time to visit

The best time to visit Bombay is during **Ganesh Chaturthi,** a reverent festival that glorifies Ganesh, the god of good omens. Hindus worship models of the deity, which are later sunk into a lake. A spectacular procession follows. The festival is usually held in September.

Eating well

The best restaurant in Bombay is the Indian restaurant in the Taj Mahal Hotel, a five-star establishment with a good $10 curry. **Woodlands Café,** *Nariman Point,* has delicious *thalis* and South Indian desserts.

Delhi Darbar, near the Regal Cinema, *Colaba,* has Bombay's best Mughlai (Muslim/Indian) foods. Try the mutton.

Khyber Restaurant, *145 Mahatma Gandhi Road,* offers continental dishes as well as Indian, vegetarian, and Mughlai fare. It is open until midnight. **Sri Ratan Tata Institute,** *30 S. Patkar Marg,* features Parsee foods and tempting pastries. It is open from 9 a.m. to 6 p.m.

Satkar Caterers, *Indian Express Building,* is a favorite with locals, serving vegetarian dishes, South Indian specialties, and Punjabi dishes. The patio is pleasant.

Berry's Restaurant and Bar, *Veer Nariman Road,* near Churchgate Station, has been awarded for its good food. The Indian specialties are good. The restaurant is open until midnight.

Bombay's best hotels

The finest hotel in Bombay is the **Taj Mahal Intercontinental,** *Apollo Bunder, Colaba.* Old World charm is combined with modern amenities at this waterfront hotel. Rooms, which are decorated with antiques and artwork, have views of the city and the harbor, air conditioning, and private baths. French, Chinese, and Indian foods are served in the hotel's four restaurants.

Oberoi Towers, *Nariman Point,* is a luxurious hotel with fountains, marble walls, a health club, a swimming pool, six restaurants, and a shopping arcade.

Less ostentatious is the **Grand,** *17 Sprott Road, Ballard Estate.* The rooms are spacious, with private baths and air conditioning. The Grand has a cozy, old-fashioned air about it, and it is popular with European travelers.

Hotel Nataraj, *135 Netaji Subhash Road,* was once a private club. Today it is a homey hotel near the sea. Rooms have attached bathrooms and air conditioning.

The Elephanta Caves

The most important side trip from Bombay is to the island of **Elephanta,** six miles across the harbor, where five cave temples carved into rock centuries ago have been excavated. No one knows who carved the caves, which were created between the fifth and sixth centuries.

The caves contain beautiful, life-size sculptures of Hindu gods. The most impressive is a 15-foot sculpture of three-headed Mahesamurti, a trinity made up of the gods Brahma, Siva, and Vishnu. Outside the main cave is an enormous columned veranda, approached by steps and sculptured elephants. To best appreciate the subtleties of the religious statues and carvings here, read up on Hindu mythology before going—and bring a flashlight.

The holiest village

Mahabaleshwar, a tiny village nine hours south of Bombay by bus or train, was once considered so holy that Englishmen were not allowed on any part of the hill. (In 1824, General Lodwick broached it anyway.) Five streams of water representing the sources of five holy rivers flow through the Krishnabai Temple. They combine and travel through a cow's mouth into two cisterns where Hindus take holy baths. Mahashivaratri, a festival of Siva held in February or March, brings throngs of pilgrims here.

Climb to nearby **Pratapgarh Fort,** built in 1656, for a view all the way to the coast. On the western side of the fort a precipice drops 2,000 feet to the Konkan plain below. Prisoners once met their deaths here.

The **Frederick Hotel** is the nicest in town, with private bathrooms, tennis courts, and a golf course.

Little Portugal: Goa

South of Bombay is **Goa,** a Portuguese colony from 1510 to 1961. It has a mixture of local and Portuguese charms and some of the most beautiful beaches (ocean and river) in India. In addition to all this, Goa has perfect weather (except during monsoon season, June to September). Whitewashed houses and Catholic churches give Goa a European look. Traders first traveled to Goa seeking Indian spices.

St. Francis Xavier came here in 1540 and converted many of the people to Catholicism. Although he died in China, his body was returned to Goa. His embalmed remains lie in a silver, gem-encrusted casket in the **Basilica of Bom Jesus** in Panaji. Once every 10 years the saint's body is displayed. If you look closely, you will notice that his big toes are missing— they were bitten off by religious fanatics. His arm, too, is gone—it was sent to the pope. Built in 1593, the basilica is Goa's primary example of Portuguese architecture.

Nearby is the magnificent all-white *sé* (cathedral), noted for its five bells. Its Golden Bell is the largest in the world. A small chapel in the back of the cathedral contains a crucifix on which a vision of Christ is said to have appeared in 1919.

Goa's delights are physical as well as spiritual. The silvery beaches along the Malabar Coast are incomparable. The best are near Panaji, the capital. **Dona Paula** is the most chic. Across the Mandovi River from Panaji is **Calangute Beach,** which is spectacular. **Colva Beach,** on the south coast near Margao, is also beautiful. Some of Goa's beaches are spoiled by fierce undertows. Ask around before you test your strength against the sea.

The best place to stay if you are a beach lover is **Holiday Village,** run by the Taj Group, on Calangute Beach. You can sleep in a cottage near the sea, use the sports facilities, and lounge around in hammocks on the beach. Restaurants and bars are part of the resort.

If you would rather stay in Panaji, try the **Fidalgo** or the **Mandovi,** both reputable hotels with good prices.

The world's oldest Buddhist sculptures

The Buddhist caves of **Ajanta** were carved into the face of a 259-foot rock cliff 2,000 years ago and contain the oldest Buddhist art in the world. Acres of frescoes cover the walls, ceilings, and pillars of the 25 monasteries and 5 temples here.

The **Ellora Caves** form another fantastic complex of Buddhist, Jain, and Hindu temples carved side by side from rock. The 34 elaborately carved and frescoed caves were constructed between A.D. 600 and A.D. 1200. The Hindu temple Kailasa is the most beautiful, with enormous pillars, painted ceilings, and grand statues. It took 100 years to quarry the three-million cubic feet of rock here.

Aurangabad is the best base for visiting the caves. Stay at the **Rama International Hotel,** where prices are reasonable and the staff is efficient. The manager personally meets guests at the airport.

Daily flights run between Bombay and Delhi via Aurangabad. By train, you can get to Aurangabad aboard the Punjab Mail and the Panchavati Express from Bombay to Manmad. Daily bus service connects Aurangabad with Ellora, Ajanta, and Jalgaon.

Bus tours to the Ellora Caves from Aurangabad are conducted by the Maharashtra Tourism Development Corporation. Tour guides will pick you up at Aurangabad Railway Station at 9 a.m. and return you there at 6:30 p.m.

The Maharashtra Tourism Development Corporation also provides four-day excursions to Ajanta-Ellora-Aurangabad from Bombay. The cost is less than RP1,000, including transportation, guides, and accommodations. Buses leave daily.

The most sacred Jain hill

Shatrunjaya (the Place of Victory), a hill on the river of the same name, is the most sacred of five hills considered holy by the Jains. It is covered by 863 Jain temples. You must remove all leather before you can climb the hill. To see the temple jewels or to take photos, you must ask permission from the Munimji, Anandji Kalyanji Trust, in Palitana. The temples are closed in the monsoon season (the summer months) and after dark.

The best place to stay while visiting the hill is the nearby town of **Palitana,** due south of Ahmedabad in the province of Gujarat. **Hotel Sumeru** is pleasant, with a pretty garden and good vegetarian food.

The best lion viewing

The **Gir Forest,** on the coast of the Arabian Sea in Gujarat, is the last stronghold of the Asiatic lion (only about 200 remain). The best time to see the king of beasts is during the hot months, from March through May, when they can be seen at watering holes. However, the forest is open to the public from December until June.

To make arrangements to visit the forest, contact your travel agent or the **Regional Manager,** *Gir Tourism Development Corporation, Rang Mahal, Diwan Chowk, Junegadh.* Gir Tourism Development Corporation offers two-day trips for about RP950, including jeeps, binoculars, guides, and accommodations. You cannot shoot the lions, but you can hunt the other game in the area (blue bull, spotted deer, gazelle, and antelope).

Splendid ancient ruins

The empty shell of the once-courtly kingdom of **Malwa** sits atop a plateau in Mandu, northeast of Bombay. Once known among Muslims as the City of Joy, today it is a ghost town. Raj Bhoja first noticed the charms of the location, which is cut off from the world below, and built a retreat here in the 10th century. The Muslims took over in the 13th century and expanded the city until it covered eight square miles, the whole surrounded by massive walls.

The oldest monument is the mosque, which is to the right as you enter the grand Delhi Gate. The most beautiful is the tomb of Hoshang Shah (1405-1432), a white marble structure with a great dome and four turrets. The buildings are divided into three main groups: the Royal Enclave, the Village Group, and the Reva Kund Group.

You can stay overnight at the modern **Travellers' Lodge,** which has eight rooms with attached bathrooms, or at **Taveli Mahal,** once the royal stables.

Little-known Buddhist caves

A drive through the jungle from Mandu will bring you to **Bagh,** where sixth-century Buddhist caves rival those at Ajanta (but they're not as crowded). Sadly, the beautiful wall paintings have been damaged somewhat over time.

The river Bagmati flows in front of the humid sandstone caves. Because of the pythons and tigers here, the foliage has been cut back.

Only four of the nine caves have survived. Hewn from solid rock, each has a veranda, a large central hall, gloomy monks' cells, and a prayer hall. The second cave has a maze of passageways and hidden chambers. It contains larger-than-life sculptures of the Buddha and his disciples and paintings of animals and flowers. The most beautiful paintings are in the fourth cave, Rang Mahal, which has a mural of life-size figures on its veranda.

Sanchi—the best Buddhist art

Northeast of the Bagh Caves, near the ill-fated Bhopal, is **Sanchi,** one of the world's most important centers of Buddhist art. Emperor Asoka built his most beautiful monuments here on a hilltop overlooking the forest. (The emperor's son, Mahendra, left Sanchi for Sri Lanka, where he spread Buddhism.) After the decline of Buddhism in India, the town lay forgotten until 1818, when it was rediscovered. Restoration was begun in 1912 by Sir John Marshall. Of the eight stupas (sacred mounds) originally built on the hill, only three remain.

What catches the eye first in Sanchi is the **Great Stupa,** a 106-foot second-century round burial mound with elaborately decorated gateways. Balustrades encircle its roof and base, and it is surrounded by a fence with four ornate gates. The bas-reliefs on the yellow stone gates are the most beautiful early Buddhist works of art that exist today. Don't expect to understand the elaborate religious illustrations—one archeologist published three enormous volumes on Sanchi.

The **Travelers' Lodge** is a pleasant little inn near the caves with eight rooms and a restaurant.

India's greatest man

If you head south from Sanchi through the jungles, you will come to the tiny town of **Sevagram,** where Mahatma Gandhi established his ashram (retreat) in 1933 and began putting his doctrines into practice. The Hindu leader established a self-sufficient community, with a dairy, a tannery, and a cloth-weaving industry. He eradicated the caste system, with its untouchables and unclean occupations. His simple hut is preserved exactly as he left it. At the

Nai Talimi Sangh School in Sevagram, students continue to follow Gandhi's way of life, growing their own food and weaving their own cloth.

The best place to stay (if you share Gandhi's values of simplicity and modesty) is the guesthouse at the ashram, where food is served communal-style. The price is certainly right. For reservations write to **Sarve Seva Sangh,** *Sevagram, Wordha, Maharashtra.*

If you prefer creature comforts, stay at **Mt. Hogel,** *Commercial Road, Nagpur,* 50 miles away. (Nagpur is known for its fragrant orange groves.)

Madras—the most traditional city

The state of **Tamil Nadu,** at its southern tip, is more traditional than the rest of India. Because it is so far south, this region was untouched by the many invaders who assailed the north. Founded by the Dravidians more than 5,000 years ago, Tamil is the home of India's oldest sculptures.

The capital of the region, **Madras,** is as colorful as the cotton cloth it is famous for producing. The fourth-largest city in India, it sprawls across 68 square miles.

India's best beach

Hugging the coast of the Bay of Bengal, Madras has one of the most beautiful beaches in India, if not the world: **Marina Beach.** The second-longest beach on earth, it has fine sand and is lined with walkways and gardens.

The best sights

Fort St. George, built in 1640 by the British, is the best place to begin a tour of Madras. Twenty-foot walls loom over the city, which acts as the government center of Tamil Nadu. Inside is **St. Mary's Church,** the oldest Anglican church in Asia, built in 1680. The **Fort Museum** contains memorabilia of the East India Company, as well as costumes, coins, and china.

Madras National Art Gallery houses the famous 10th-century bronze statue of Nataraja-Siva dancing and rare Mogul, Rajput, and South Indian paintings.

Next door is the **Government Museum,** which has the best bronze collection in India, as well as rare second-century Buddhist sculptures.

Madras Snake Park and Conservation Center in the beautiful **Guindy Deer Park** is home to cobras, pythons, and other exotic reptiles. The surrounding Deer Park shelters black buck and spotted deer.

Tradition says that the apostle Thomas (Doubting Thomas) came to Madras as a missionary and was martyred on St. Thomas Mt. in A.D. 78. The **Cathedral of St. Thome**—the first Christian church in India—is a Gothic structure built on the site of a chapel said to have held the remains of St. Thomas.

Kapaliswarar Temple, dedicated to Lord Kapaliswarar (Siva), was built by the Dravidians. It was destroyed in 1566 during a war but rebuilt 300 years ago. Its gopura (pyramid-shaped entrance) marks the city's horizon.

Madras is home to the world headquarters of the **Theosophical Society,** an international organization promoting the inter-play of religion, science, and philosophy. The banyan tree in the garden of the society's building is the oldest in India, shading 40,000 square feet.

The best dancing

Madras is the best place to see the classic **Bharata Natya** dance, in which dancers exhibit perfect control over every muscle in their bodies—they actually can move their necks while keeping their heads motionless. Originally a temple dance, this is the most ancient dance form in India. It is performed to the accompaniment of musical instruments and singing.

The beauty of the Bharata Natya lies in the grace of its symmetrical patterns and the emotions portrayed by the elaborate gestures and facial expressions of the dancers. Check the local newspapers—*The Hindi* and *Indian Express*—for show listings. You can watch Indian dancing every night during tourist season in the Mysore Room of the Taj Coramandel (during the summer, performances often are canceled).

Madras' most important side trips

The ancient city of **Mahabalipuram** has the world's largest bas-relief: *Penance of Bhaghirata,* an 80- by 20-foot fresco in stone. The city's other claim to fame is its group of seven pagodas, which look like flat-topped pyramids and are guarded by statues of an elephant, a lion, and a bull. The walls of the pagodas are illustrated with events from Hindu mythology.

Mahabalipuram was once the main harbor of the Pallava empire, which died out about 1,200 years ago. Hindu sculpture can be found in the cave temples carved from the rock here. When you tire of the ancient works of art, relax on Mahabalipuram's gorgeous beach.

Kanchipuram, the capital of the ancient Pallava empire, has 1,000 temples and 124 shrines. It is an important place of pilgrimage for Hindus. The **Kailasanatha Temple,** believed to be 1,200 years old, contains excellent seventh- and eighth-century paintings. Smaller but prettier is the **Varadarajaswamy Temple.** The best Hindu murals, which illustrate various wars, are in the **Vaikunthanatha Perumal Temple.**

One of the oldest cities in the south, **Kumbakonam,** on the banks of the Cauvery River, has 18 temples decorated with lively Hindu sculptures. Once every 12 years pilgrims invade the city for the bathing festival.

A half-hour away is **Thanjavur,** lying at the foot of India's greatest temple, **Brihadiswara,** whose tower rises more than 200 feet. The crowning dome of the tower rests on an 80-ton block of granite brought in from a village four miles away.

Forty miles south of Madras is the breathtaking ninth-century **Temple of Nataraja** at Chidambaram. Two of the temple's four granite gopuras are covered with sculptures illustrating the 108 positions of Natya Sastra, the Indian science of dancing. No one knows how the granite was brought to the temple—there is no granite for 50 miles around.

India's most elegant hill station

Ootacamund, recently renamed Udhagamandalam (but still affectionately known as Ooty), is a small, elegant hill station in the Nilgiris, the famed Blue Mountains of southern India. Situated nearly 8,000 feet above sea level, Ooty appealed to the royalty and the wealthy of many cultures, each of which left its imprint, but none more indelibly than the British. English is the major tongue here, and Ooty feels for all the world like a Victorian town in the heart of England.

The best way to reach Ooty is to rent a car and driver and travel through the Mudamalai jungle along the intricate hairpin turns that wind through parrot-and-monkey-crowded bamboo jungles. It is a dramatic surprise to make the last turn and find yourself in a bit of

England. Ooty's flowers are celebrated throughout India. Garden clubs present a floral spectacle each May, mingling familiar English varieties with exotic blooms.

Less than 50 miles away is a large wild-animal sanctuary. Not far from the hill station, entire families of monkeys scamper about panhandling from passers-by, running off with fruit from trees or market stalls, and gazing at humans as intently as the humans stare at them. Now and then you'll catch a glimpse of an elephant, and everywhere you'll see birds.

An excellent and inexpensive place to stay is the **Savoy Hotel.** Faded but still elegant in its full Victorian regalia, the Savoy is a treasure. Its gardens are famous throughout India.

Orissa: India in a nutshell

For a capsule view of India, visit the state of **Orissa,** on the Bay of Bengal. You can explore mountains, jungles, valleys, plains, tribal villages, coconut groves, and 250 miles of beach in this area of 60,000 square miles.

The recorded history of Orissa begins in 260 B.C., when the edicts of the Emperor Asoka were carved in rock in Dhauli, five miles from Bhubaneswar, the capital. The peak of Orissan civilization was reached between the 4th and 13th centuries, when thousands of temples and monuments were built. The British took over in 1803.

The **Adivasi,** a tribal group in Orissa, are descendants of the inhabitants of Orissa before the Aryan invasion 3,000 years ago. Over the centuries they have been pushed into the heart of Orissa, the least fertile section of the state. Now they are protected by the government.

Orissa's main sights

Bhubaneswar is a picturesque town with a myriad of temples, some dating back to 300 B.C., covered with spirals, turrets, decorations, and sculptures depicting good and evil, morality and immorality. The **Great Lingaraj Temple,** built in A.D. 1000, is the finest Hindu temple in India, with a tower that can be seen for miles. Outside town are Udayagiri and Khandagari hills, where caves were carved by Jain monks as far back as the first century B.C.

Konarak (the Black Pagoda), outside Bhubaneswar, is one of the most beautiful sights in India. More than 1,000 workers took 12 years to build the 100-foot-high temple. Dedicated to the sun, the 13th-century Konarak is built on a base of 24 wheels pulled by 7 horses. The roof is topped by a three-tiered spire. The entire temple is covered with carvings and sculptures.

Puri, the site of Hindu pilgrimages, is one of the four holiest places in India. Hindus believe that if you stay here for three days and three nights, you will attain eternal life. The enormous **Jagannath Temple,** dedicated to the Lord of the Universe, was built in the 12th century. While non-Hindus are not allowed to enter the structure, you can get a good view inside the 20-foot temple walls from atop the neighboring Raghunandan Library.

The most colorful (and most crowded) time to visit Puri is June, during the **Rath Yatra Festival,** when the image of Lord Jagannath is taken from its temple and carried in a canopied car by thousands of pilgrims to Gundicha Mandir, the God's Garden House.

Puri is also a great place to shop. If you know how to bargain, you can get good buys on statues, toys, and shoes.

The place to stay in Puri is the **South Eastern Railway Hotel,** which is near the beautiful but polluted beach.

Incredible Calcutta

Calcutta is incredible—a huge and growing industrial metropolis inhabited by the

Bengalis, an emotional and artistic people who produce many of the best books, dramas, and films in India. The city is a convenient base for exploring the Himalayas and the temples of Orissa, Bhutan, and Sihkism. No one can claim to really know India without visiting Calcutta.

If you arrive in Calcutta by train, you will see families camping on the platforms of Howrah Station, water vendors, newsboys, rice peddlers, tea-serving waiters, running children, and shouting porters.

When you leave the station and cross the **Howrah Bridge,** you will encounter cars, bicycles, cows, rickshaws, oxcarts, trucks, and crowds of people. Below the bridge, on the banks of the Hooghly River, live Calcutta's masseurs and barbers.

Calcutta's best sights

On the other side of the Howrah Bridge (the third-largest single-span bridge in the world) is **Old Calcutta,** the core of the city, which grew out of three tiny villages: Sutanati, Govindpur, and Kalikata (Anglicized as Calcutta). Kalikata was a sacred spot with two temples. However, aside from the temples, the area is unsavory.

Victorian Calcutta developed around **Fort William,** built in 1780. At the south end of Maidan Park in front of the fort is **Victoria Memorial,** completed in 1921 and filled with relics of British rule in India.

North of **Dalhousie Square** (now called B.B.D. Bagh)—and surrounded by busy bazaar streets—is the **Nakhoda Mosque,** which holds 10,000 people.

The **Indian Museum,** *Chowringhee Road,* is the oldest in India and one of the most comprehensive in the Orient. The archeology section in this museum is the largest in Asia and one of the most important in the world, with a large and representative collection of antiquities illustrating the cultural history of India from prehistoric times to the Muslim period. The museum also has a fine collection of Indian coins, gems, and jewelry.

Parasnath Jain Temple, *Badris Temple Street,* built by the court jeweler in 1867, glitters with crystals and precious stones. A French crystal chandelier hangs above the gleaming mosaic tile floor. The temple lamp has burned continuously for 112 years. A landscaped garden surrounds the structure.

Calcutta has a fabulous **zoo** with white Bengal tigers, monkeys, reptiles, and white peacocks, among other exotic beasts and birds.

The **Botanical Gardens** cover 273 acres with mahogany trees, Royal Cuban palms, an orchid house, and other exotic flora. Its crown jewel is its banyan tree, the largest in the world, with a circumference of 1,000 feet. The garden was established in 1786 by the East India Company.

In the evening, stroll along **The Maidan,** a two-mile stretch of green lawn bedecked with statues of Indian heroes. When the sun sets, the locals use this as a rendezvous point. If you feel lucky, try out the Maidan Racetrack.

Calcutta's best shopping

New Market, *Lindsay Street,* is one of the largest markets in India, with 2,500 stalls selling everything from cheap tin pots to fine silks. The market's real name, the Sir Stuart Hogg Market, is (not surprisingly) seldom used. The market was built in 1874. It is closed Saturday afternoons and Sundays.

Best restaurants

Vineet Restaurant, *1 Shakespeare Sarani,* has live Indian music between 7:30 and 11 p.m. Vegetarian Indian, South Indian, and continental foods are served.

Peter Cat Restaurant, *18 Park St.,* is a peaceful, pleasantly decorated place that serves Indian and continental food from 10 a.m. to midnight.

Shenaz Restaurant and Bar, *2 A Middleton Row,* is a romantic little place with good *tandoori* and Indian specialties. The restaurant is open from 10 a.m. to 11:30 p.m. Make reservations.

Abhinandan, *24 Park St., Second Floor,* is a vegetarian restaurant with live music. It is open noon to 11 p.m. weekdays and 9 a.m. to 11 p.m. Sundays and holidays.

Gay Rendez-Vous, *17 Strand Road,* has a lovely view of the Hooghly River and serves both Indian and Western cuisine. It is open from 10:30 a.m. to 9 p.m.

Mocambo Restaurant, *25 B Park St.,* has good *tandoori* dishes and dancing. It is open from 10 a.m. to midnight.

A word to the wise: Don't expect to be served meat or alcohol on Thursdays in Calcutta.

Calcutta's finest nights

Calcutta's best hotel is the **Oberoi Grand,** *15 Jawahar Lal Nehru Road,* which is centrally located and has rooms with beautiful private baths and refrigerators. Guests may use the swimming pool, health club, in-house astrologer, and disco. The hotel has four restaurants and a shopping arcade.

New Kenilworth Hotel, *1 Little Russel St.,* is more affordable. A fine old hotel, it has marble floors, a well-kept lawn, and rooms with private baths and air conditioning. The garden bar is pleasant, and the two restaurants are good.

Make hotel reservations in advance, especially if you plan to visit between October and March.

The most sacred river

The **Ganges River,** considered sacred by Hindus, is believed to originate in the hair of the god Siva. Regardless of its origins, the water is indeed pure, running downhill from the Himalayas.

Hindus believe that bathing in the Ganges washes away sin. The holiest place to bathe is **Allahabad,** where the Ganges and the Yamuna (or Jumna) rivers meet. This is also considered the holiest place to scatter the ashes of cremated loved ones.

The **Magh Mela,** India's biggest religious bathing festival, is held at Allahabad in the spring. During the festival, pilgrims stay in tents along the river, holy men lie on thorns and give sermons, barbers shave the heads of those who intend to bathe in the river, and women throw rose petals and marigolds into the water. The fair has a commercial aspect as well. Food stalls appear on the banks of the river, along with little booths selling souvenirs and religious pictures.

If you decide to join the pilgrims in their holy bath, you can't just walk into the water— the river has no beaches. You must take a boat to the middle of the river and dive in from there.

The bathing festival is largest every 12th year, when millions join here to celebrate the **Kumbh Mela,** the most important religious ceremony.

The area's three best hotels are the **Yatrik, Barnetts,** and **Vishram.**

Darjeeling: for the most daring

The train ride to **Darjeeling** is spectacular and dizzying. The 52-mile trip begins at New

Jalpaiguri, near Bagdogra, which is a 55-minute flight from Calcutta, and takes about six hours. For the first few miles, the train rushes through dense jungle. Then the steep climb begins. The train chugs through lush tea plantations, clinging to the mountainsides. When it passes through the center of Kurseong, children jump the running boards and make faces at passengers.

From there the train climbs to Ghoom, at 8,000 feet, the site of a Tibetan monastery (this is about as close to Tibet as Westerners are likely to get from India). Monks here worship a 15-foot image of the Coming Buddha and fly prayer flags.

Darjeeling, which lies four miles farther north and about 1,000 feet lower, has an absolutely amazing view of the Himalayas. **Kanchenjunga Mountain** is especially awe-inspiring; the Hindus believe it is the god Siva lying down.

Darjeeling is built in a series of steps. At the top are hotels, cafés, and shops. Halfway up are smaller hotels, Indian restaurants, and more shops. The people of Darjeeling live at the bottom. Nepalese, Tibetans, and Lepchas, in their colorful tribal costumes, crowd the bazaars and markets. Women wear nose ornaments and huge necklaces.

At the center of the town is **Observatory Hill,** where the Mahakala Cave is located. The view is beautiful. Also visit the **Lloyd Botanical Gardens,** which are devoted to the flowers of the Himalayas, and the **Bhutia Busty Tibetan** and the **Aloobari,** two Buddhist monasteries.

Darjeeling also boasts the smallest and highest **racetrack** in the world, where ponies run the course three times before finishing a race. Seven miles from Darjeeling is **Tiger Hill** (8,482 feet), from which you can see Mt. Everest on clear days. The best time to see the mountain is sunrise, when the white mountain peaks turn rose.

You can learn to mountain climb in 40 days at the **Himalayan Mountaineering Institute** in Darjeeling. The instructor climbed Mt. Everest with Sir Edmund Hillary in 1953. The institute has a museum that displays climbing equipment.

India's most exotic areas

India's most exotic and remote areas, **Assam** and **Nagaland,** in the extreme northeast corner of the country, are off-limits to non-Indians. However, if the Indian government lifts the travel restrictions, take the opportunity to visit. These are the most fascinating places in India, inhabited by little-known tribes, some of whom were headhunters a generation ago. This is a paradise for wildlife enthusiasts, hunters, and fishermen. The region has incredible waterfalls, high peaks, and wild rivers.

The **Kaziranga Wild Life Sanctuary** is the best place for big-game hunting in India, if not the world. Because the grass here is 16 feet high, the only way to see the sanctuary is astride an elephant. The sanctuary protects several species of deer, birds, wild boars, jackals, buffaloes, elephants, and tigers.

If the travel restrictions are lifted, you will be able to make arrangements to visit the sanctuary by applying to the **Divisional Forest Officer,** *Sibsagar Division, Jorhat,* three weeks in advance. This allows enough time for reservations to be made for rooms and elephants. It's a two-hour flight from Calcutta to Jorhat, where the Forest Department car meets visitors to take them to Kaziranga, 40 miles away. By road, it's a tough 135-mile ride from Gauhati. Don't wear white or bright colors, which frighten the animals.

The best travel planning

India is immense, so it is important to plan your trip carefully. Bombay, Delhi, Calcutta, and Madras are the best places to begin your travels.

Americans entering India *must* have a visa. Applications for visas should be made from the United States before you leave, on prescribed visa application forms, and should be accompanied by a valid passport. They are valid for three months.

Foreign visitors receive special assistance and concessions in India. Booking and information sections for foreigners, which are located in railway stations and the major offices of Indian Airlines, enable you to jump the long waiting lines. Concessions can greatly reduce the costs of transportation throughout India. In states where alcohol is banned, you can quench their thirst by getting a liquor permit. The Indian government is anxious to promote tourism.

Keep in mind that certain parts of India, which are politically sensitive or strategic, are designated by the government as "restricted or protected areas." Foreign tourists can enter them only with special permits.

You need a permit to visit Darjeeling. Apply to one of the Foreigners' Regional Registration Offices (they are located in Bombay, Calcutta, Delhi, and Madras).

You also need a permit if you plan to stay more than 15 days in the Andaman Islands. These usually can be obtained either through local travel agents in Calcutta or directly from **Home Ministry,** *North Block, New Delhi.* Punjab also is restricted. Check in New Delhi. To visit Bhutan, you need a permit from the Bhutan Government.

You can visit Sikkim for four days with a permit issued by the **Deputy Secretary Ministry of Home Affairs,** *North Block, New Delhi.* It will take about six to eight weeks to process the permit, so make your plans well in advance.

Permits also are required to photograph railway stations and trains.

The best way to travel

Traveling by air can save a lot of time and irritation in India, which is, after all, a subcontinent. **Indian Airlines** has been building up its services and is now one of the largest domestic carriers in the world. More than 240 flights daily from 73 cities are served from the four major bases of Delhi, Bombay, Calcutta, and Madras. Air travel is relatively inexpensive.

The best deal for foreigners is Indian Airlines' $375 **Discover India ticket,** which allows unlimited travel for 21 days. The ticket can be purchased when you book your trip to India. If you buy it on arrival, you must pay for it with foreign currency.

The best time to go

The best time to go to India is between November and the end of March, avoiding the rainy season. You can escape the severe heat of October and April in northern India or the hill stations of southern India. It's wise to choose good weather for your travels, because making your way through India demands tremendous energy.

If you are able to plan your trip and make reservations well in advance, you might try timing your visit to India to coincide with one of the colorful Hindu festivals, some of which are described above.

Diwali, held in October and November throughout the country, is the Hindu new year. Every town glimmers with flickering oil lamps, and fireworks explode in the skies.

THE BEST OF THE MIDDLE EAST

The Middle East, which includes Southwest Asia and part of Northeast Africa, was the site of great ancient civilizations thousands of years before the birth of Christ. Archeologists have found remains of 5,000-year-old settlements between the Tigris and Euphrates rivers, a region known as the cradle of civilization. Three of the world's most important religions—Judaism, Christianity, and Islam—were born here.

The importance of the Middle East is not solely historic. Today, this region is the scene of political turmoil and warfare. The problems have affected the entire world: terrorists have curtailed travel, oil prices have risen, and the United Nations is divided in its support of various factions. The Middle East is also one of the wealthiest areas of the world, with much of the world's oil reserves and many strategic trade routes.

Despite tensions, this is a region worth visiting. Israel is an important place of pilgrimage for Jews, Christians, and Muslims. Egypt has the world's most astonishing ancient monuments: the pyramids and the Sphynx. And the area as a whole has a natural beauty found nowhere else—stark, wide-open deserts; lush oases; the Dead Sea; the Great Rift Valley; and the mysterious Nile.

Chapter 18

THE
BEST
OF
ISRAEL

The Land of Milk and Honey holds a special place in history. A professor at the Hebrew University wrote a study comparing Israel to a newborn child that has emerged from a centuries-old womb. Israel is a 20th-century country built on a 4,000-year-old prophecy; even the modern high-rise buildings carry a history of conflict.

A war-torn desert nation, Israel is thriving. Bordered by four seas, the promised land has dozens of uncrowded beaches and a fertile Mediterranean coast that rivals the French Riviera. The country's three largest cities offer night life and historical landmarks.

The national *aliyya* (settlement) programs attest to Israeli concern for growth and building; however, this dedication has not come without problems. Israel is bordered to the north by Lebanon and to the east by Jordan, its enemies since the country was established in 1948. The Golan Heights and Jericho, for example, are Israeli-occupied territories.

Israel is small—about the size of Rhode Island—but it offers a diversity of terrain, weather, and people. You can ski the slopes of Mt. Hermon, swim in the Mediterranean, and hike in the desert all in the course of one day. Yemenite, American, South African, Ethiopian, and Moroccan Israelis mingle with each other and with one-million Arab Israeli citizens.

Jerusalem, the eternal capital

Israel is best visited in two trips: one to see **Jerusalem,** and one to see the rest of the country.

The capital city has been the center of both conflict and faith for 3,000 years. Divided by Israel and neighboring Jordan for 20 years, the city was reunited after the 1967 war. It is the largest city in Israel. Expansion and construction mark the New City, inside Old Jerusalem heavy industry is banned and archeological research continues.

To commemorate your visit to Jerusalem, make arrangements with the Keren Kayemet Le'Israel (JNF) to plant a tree with your own hands.

Jerusalem's heart: the Old City

The 40-foot-high crenellated wall encircling the Old City is surrounded by a belt of grass and bushes. Most of Jerusalem's sights are inside this wall, which has eight gates. **Golden Gate** is thought to lie over the Closed Gate of the First Temple, the entrance through which the Jewish Messiah is expected to pass. **Jaffa Gate** is the most convenient entrance to the New City and houses a helpful tourist center. At **Damascus Gate** you can buy a ticket (about $1) to ascend the rampart onto the top of the wall, where you'll have a view of the entire Old City.

Among the Old City's attractions are the Dome of the Rock (Mosque of Omar), the Church of the Holy Sepulcher, and the Via Dolorosa (Way of the Cross). The **Dome of the Rock,** an ornate shrine standing on Temple Mount, is usually filled with Muslims facing Mecca and praying. Inside is the rock from which Mohammed is said to have ascended to heaven. The **Church of the Holy Sepulcher** contains the tomb where Christ was laid to rest after the crucifixion, as well as the tomb of Joseph of Arimathea.

The **Via Dolorosa** is the path along which Jesus walked from the court of Pilate to the hill of Golgotha. You can retrace His steps; the 14 stations, or places of devotion, where Jesus rested along the way, are marked. Not far away is the **Coenaculum,** the room of the Last Supper, and to the east stands the Garden of Gethsemane, where Christ prayed the night before his crucifixion.

The **Wailing Wall**, the western wall (and sole remains) of the Second Temple, is the holiest structure in Judaism. Jews have gathered here for centuries to pray and bemoan the temple's destruction. If you write a prayer on a scrap of paper and slip it between the stones of the wall, it is said God will hear you more quickly. Jewish boys' Bar Mitzvahs are held here nearly every day. And at night, floodlights cast shadows on the ancient stones, and you can hear old men murmuring in prayer.

The nearby **Mt. of Olives** has a famous Jewish cemetery, and the Greek Orthodox Church there houses the **Tomb of the Virgin Mary.** According to Christian tradition, the mount was the site of Jesus' Ascension; according to Jewish tradition, the Mt. of Olives is where the Messiah will resurrect the dead. At dawn, **Temple Mount** has a golden glow.

Near the Old City walls is **Mt. Zion,** the site of King David's tomb (it's a bare room).

More interesting is **Hezekiah's Tunnel,** built about 1000 B.C. so water could be brought in when the city was under siege. Begin at the **Gihon Spring,** and slosh through the tunnel all the way to the **pool of Shiloah.**

The **Museum of the Potential Holocaust,** *31 Usishkin St.,* displays contemporary anti-Semitic works from groups such as the American Nazi Party and the Klu Klux Klan.

The Hadassah Hebrew University Medical Center and its synagogue are decorated with stained-glass windows designed and painted by Marc Chagall.

The best of the New City

The first thing to see in the New City is the **Knesset,** Israel's Parliament, which has mosaics by Chagall. Expect to be searched thoroughly when you enter. You can catch a lively debate (in Hebrew) when the Knesset is in session Mondays through Wednesdays, beginning at 4 p.m.

Two blocks away is the **Yad Vashem**, a monument honoring the six-million Jews killed in World War II. The photos and documents trace Hitler's rise and focus on those who fought back, particularly the Warsaw Ghetto.

Walk through the picturesque **Yemenite Moshe Quarter,** which has been renovated into residential and artists' neighborhoods. The nearby village of En Karem is the birthplace of John the Baptist. Take note of the beautiful Church of St. John, with its soaring tower.

The **Rockefeller Museum,** *Suleiman and Jericho roads,* displays Mideastern artwork from the last two millenia. The Billy Rose Sculpture Garden contains works by Picasso and Degas, as well as Israeli artists. The **Israel Museum,** *tel. (972-2)698-211,* which incorporates the Bezalel Museum, has a large collection of Jewish folk and ceremonial art. Main areas devoted to archeology, Judaica, and Israeli painting mix with major exhibits from abroad. The Dead Sea scrolls are displayed here, at the Shrine of the Book.

The best entertainment

While in Jerusalem, try to attend a performance of the Israeli Philharmonic, which stages winter concerts at **Binyanei Haoma,** *Yafo Street,* or the popular Jerusalem Dance Company. A less-known dance troupe is Kol U'Demama (Sound and Silence), an art-dance ensemble with both hearing and deaf dancers. It is the only group of its kind in the world. The **Cahanna Ticket Agency,** *tel. (972-2)222-831,* can provide tickets to most cultural events.

Dig for a day

For a firsthand look at the city's history, participate in the **Dig For a Day Program,** a one-day seminar/dig at various archeological sites in and around Jerusalem. You attend a morning seminar, do about three hours of excavation work, then tour the entire site. For more information, contact **Archeological Seminars Inc.,** *POB 14002, Jaffa Gate, Jerusalem 91 140; tel. (972-2)273-515.*

The most festive times to visit

In the summer, musicians, dancers, and actors from around the globe converge on Jerusalem for the **Israel Festival of Music and Drama.** The holiday of Simchat Torah, which usually falls in early October, is marked by **Hakafot** ceremonies—which consist of singing, dancing, and parading the Torah through the streets. In Jerusalem, Hakafot festivities take place in the Liberty Bell Garden area, located on Recham HaMelekh (King David) Street. (The Liberty Bell was set up to fête the U.S. Bicentennial.)

Christmas and Hanukkah are special times in Jerusalem. Christmas is marked by a week-long festival of choral music called the **Liturgica,** and Hanukkah begins with a public candle-lighting ceremony at the Western Wall. The largest Christmas tree in the city is set up and lit at the West Jerusalem Y.M.C.A. Eastern Orthodox Christmas celebrations include a parade with bagpipers. On Dec. 24 at 12:30 p.m., people gather at Jaffa Gate for the Procession of the Latin Patriarch, commemorating the journey of the Three Wise Men. Anyone can join the procession, which winds its way from the Old City to Bethlehem, about seven miles south. Once in Bethlehem, choirs accompany the priest into St. Catherine's Church for High Mass. If you're thinking of spending Christmas in the holiest of cities, make reservations months in advance, and don't even think of staying in the King David Hotel.

Jerusalem's best bargains

The **Arab bazaar** in the Old City offers Jerusalem's best bargains. (Haggling is the rule.) Throw rugs and Bedouin-style dresses are among the most popular items. A good buy for a dress is $25. You can get a *keffiyah* (Arab head scarf) for about $4.

The best jewelry shop in Jerusalem is **Tarshish,** *18 King David St.,* where you can get intricate Yemenite jewelry. For handcrafted jewelry made with malachite and Israeli glass, go to the jeweler/artisan Uri Ramot. Ramot and other jewelers and weavers display their goods along the **Khutsot Hayotser** (Arts and Crafts Lane) just outside the Jaffa Gate.

The best dining

For Mideastern cuisine, go to the **Caravan,** located about a half-mile before the entrance to Bethlehem along the road from Jerusalem. Chef Abu-Isaac's succulent *mezze* (appetizers), cubed shashlik, and lamb kabobs stuffed with onions are delicious and inexpensive. Don't try making reservations; the restaurant has no telephone.

The **National Palace Restaurant,** in the National Palace Hotel, *tel. (972-2)282-139,* is another good place to get an Arabian meal. Ask your waiter what he recommends—this is considered proper. Order a selection of *mezze*—you'll be served a plate of appetizers ranging from olives to brain salad (it's good). The shish kebab and the grilled mutton marinated in yogurt are delicious. Before your meal, try a glass of arrack, an anise-flavored brandy mixed with water and ice. Dinner for two is about $25, including drinks and tip.

Good Yemenite food is served at **Ruchama,** *3 Yavetz St.; tel. (972-2)246-565.* The outdoor patio is pleasant during the summer; the inside rooms are cozy in bad weather. Try the house specialty: *melawach,* a pastry filled with chopped meat and served with chopped tomatoes.

Caty's Restaurant, *16 Rivlin St.; tel. (972-2)234-621,* popular with the smart set, has first-class French food plus some North African specialties. Brooke Shields has eaten here.

Ticho House, *Abraham Tich Street; tel. (972-2)245-068,* part of the Israel Museum, is a pleasant café in the former home of artist Anna Ticho, whose works are on display. The villa has a Persian garden and a collection of Hanukkah lamps. The kitchen is kosher and serves good crêpes, soups, and salads.

In Jerusalem, a restaurant doesn't have to be expensive to be good. The **Poire et Pomme**, at the Khan Theater, *tel. (972-2)719-602,* serves quiches, salads, and hearty soups by the fireplace for less than $15. **Hashoshana,** *3 Yanai St.; tel. (972-2)228-898,* has similar prices.

Middle Eastern food sold by street vendors is even cheaper. For less than $2 you can fill up on *felafel, mezze,* and *fuul* (beans).

Sublime hotels

The city's premier hotel is the **King David,** *King David Street; tel. (972-2)221-111,* famous for its celebrity guests. Considered one of the classic hotels of the Middle East, the King David has more than 250 rooms, air conditioning, tennis courts, a pool, and a sauna. A double room goes for $100 to $175. Make reservations far in advance.

The **American Colony Hotel,** *P.O. Box 19215, Jerusalem 97200; tel. (972-2)282-421,* once the home of a Turkish Pasha, is a luxurious hotel walled off from the hectic streets of Jerusalem. Rooms have gold and blue ceilings, antique Arab and Turkish furnishings, and modern bathrooms. Archeological finds are displayed in the lobby. The garden and the swimming pool are inviting. Ask for a room in the old building; the new building is not as interesting. Double rooms are about $85 to $130 a night, including breakfast.

Overlooking the Old City is the **King Solomon Sheraton,** *32 King David St.; tel. (972-2)241-433,* with more than 100 rooms and great service. A double room is $100 to $150.

Less expensive is the **Windmill,** *tel. (972-2)663-111,* a peaceful hotel with air-conditioned rooms. Double rooms are about $54.

Babylonian night life

For a good time in Jerusalem, go to **Herod's Bar,** *28 King David St.,* which has a young crowd and, occasionally, belly dancing. The **Jerusalem Khan** is an entertaining nightclub. The **Taverna,** *Nuzzeha Street,* is another good club with a floorshow. The **Goliath Bar,** *10 King David St.,* is a pleasant piano lounge. The cellar bar at the **American Colony Hotel** has good jazz bands.

Most of the city closes down on Friday afternoons (Friday is the Muslim Sabbath, and Jewish shopkeepers must begin to prepare for their Sabbath). But you can catch an earful of jazz on Fridays at 1:30 p.m. at the **Pergod Theater,** *94 Bezalel St.; tel. (972-2)231-765.* And the **Tourist Bureau,** *tel. (972-2)282-295,* conducts synagogue tours on Friday afternoons.

For more information, contact the **Jerusalem Tourist Information Center,** *24 King George St.; tel. (972-2)241-281* or *(972-2)241-282.*

The best side trips

Outside Jerusalem is the intercultural village **Neve Shalom** (Oasis for Peace), an experiment in peaceful coexistence among Arabs, Christians, and Jews, which has received several Ford Foundation grants. Visit Neve Shalom's School for Peace and the educational center for intergroup relations. Few tourists know about the village.

A visit to **Hebron** is a good day trip (if the West Bank is quiet). Egged (a cooperative bus company) buses 34, 440, or 443 (which you can catch at the Jerusalem Central Bus Station) will take you to Hebron's main square, outside the Cave of Machpelah, where the three patriarchs—Abraham, Isaac, and Jacob—arc buried with their wives (except Rachel). This is a major shrine for Jews and Muslims. The large, fortress-like synagogue above the cave opens to a long hallway. On the right is the tomb of Jacob and Leah. Across the courtyard is a tomb covered with calligraphy commemorating Abraham and Sarah. The Machpelah is closed to non-Muslims on Fridays.

Bethlehem: Christianity's birthplace

Bethlehem, the birthplace of Jesus and King David, is only seven miles south of Jerusalem. This town of 25,000 is so touristy that post offices stay open on Christmas day so visitors can mail postcards. On the road from Jerusalem is the **Garden Tomb,** where, according to the Gospels, Christ was buried.

The frenetic heart of Bethlehem is crowded **Manger Square.** On the east side of the square is the imposing **Church of the Nativity** (the oldest church in Israel, built by Constantine in A.D. 326), which you enter through a low doorway designed to stop visitors on horseback. Twelve pillars decorated with images of the apostles hold up the oak ceiling. Armenian, Greek, and Franciscan priests take care of the church. Descend into the cave beneath, where Jesus was born. The manger is holy to both Christians and Muslims.

Other important sights are the **Milk Grotto,** where the Virgin Mary is said to have dropped milk when nursing the baby Jesus, miraculously turning the cavern rocks white; **Rachel's tomb,** a small domed shrine built in 1860 and visited by Muslims, Jews, and Christians; and **Shepherds' Field,** just outside town off Shepherds' Street, believed to be the place where shepherds were told by angels that Christ had been born.

The colorful souk (market) is crowded, but worth a trip just to visit **Barakat Antiques,** *4648 King David St.; tel. (972-2)284-256,* the finest antique shop in Israel.

The **Casa Nova Inn,** *tel. (972-2)282-791,* just east of Manger Square, is a newly renovated pilgrims' inn. Rates begin at only $25 for a comfortable room with a private bath. This includes not only a Continental breakfast, but also a five-course afternoon dinner and a late supper. This hotel and the area surrounding it have yet to be discovered by tourists.

Tel Aviv: Israel's busiest city

Tel Aviv is Israel's bustling metropolis, the fastest growing city on the Mediterranean coast. Most countries have their embassies here. Established in 1909 as a suburb of ancient Jaffa, Tel Aviv has become a second capital. It is situated conveniently, only an hour's drive from both Haifa and Jerusalem.

Tel Aviv's top museums

Tel Aviv Museum, *27 King Saul St.; tel. (972-3)257-361,* houses a comprehensive collection of art, a sculpture garden, and a children's wing. The museum is open Sundays, Mondays, Wednesdays, and Thursdays from 10 a.m. to 5 p.m.; Tuesdays from 9 a.m. to 1 p.m. and 4 to 10 p.m.; Fridays from 10 a.m. to 2 p.m.; and Saturdays from 7 p.m. to 11 p.m.

Diaspora Museum, *Beit Hatefutzot, on the campus of Tel Aviv University; tel. (972-3)425-161* or *(972-3)412-844,* uses films, computers, and audio-visual displays to trace the history of the Jewish people and the birth of Israel.

The **Ha'Aretz Museum** (Museum of the Land), *Ramat Aviv; tel. (972-3)415-244,* displays glass, coins, ceramics, and other archeological finds. It is open Mondays through Thursdays from 9 a.m. to 4 p.m.; Fridays from 9 a.m. to 1 p.m.; and Saturdays from 10 a.m. to 2 p.m.

The tallest tower in the Middle East

The **Migdal Shalom** (Shalom Tower), *Allenby Road,* is the tallest structure in the Middle East. Its 34th-floor observation terrace provides a bird's-eye view of the city.

Israel's Miami Beach

Tel Aviv's sea front smacks of Miami Beach. It is lined with tourist hotels, outdoor cafés, shops, and restaurants, especially in **Kikar Namir** (Namir Square).

Tel Aviv's best park

HaYarkon Park, an urban oasis in the northern part of the city, can be reached by Egged buses 1, 4, or 5. From 9 a.m. to midnight you can rent a rowboat on the HaYarkon River; contact **Irgun HaYarkon,** *tel. (972-3)448-422.*

The best shopping

Tel Aviv's main streets, Allenby, Ben Yehuda, and Dizengoff, are lined with cafés and boutiques. A connoisseur's choice of Israeli handicrafts, including chunky silver jewelry, pottery, and embroidered caftans, is available at **Maskit,** *Ben Yehuda Street.* Dizengoff Street, lined with trees and cafés and bistros that rival those of Paris, is where you buy high fashion and diamonds (cut and polished in Netanya, 19 miles to the north).

Israel's best night life

Tel Aviv's discos are the best in the country. Try **Colosseum,** *Kikar Atarim.* Tel Aviv's answer to Studio 54 is **Sirroco,** *44 Emek Yisrael,* where the trendy crowd begins to arrive after 2 a.m.

Music and theater flourish in Tel Aviv. The 3,000-seat **Mann Auditorium** is the home of the world-famous Israeli Philharmonic, which gives 180 concerts a year, often with such acclaimed Israeli-born musicians as Itzhak Perlman and Pinchas Zuckerman. Habimah, the famous repertory group, and the Cameri Theater offer first-class productions of classical and contemporary drama. The ticket office is at *93 Dizengoff St.;* plan ahead—concerts and plays are often sold out in advance.

Delicious dining

The best restaurants in Tel Aviv can be found along the old port. **Restaurant Yamit,** *18 Kikar Kedumim; tel. (972-3)825-353,* has an outdoor terrace with a view of the sea and serves good drinks. A good place for Yemenite food is **Zion Restaurant,** *28 Peduyim St.; tel. (972-3)658-714.* Dizengoff Street cafés remain open on the Sabbath. Especially recommended is **Cherry's,** *Ben Gurion Street.* You also can get a great meal on Saturdays at the **Taj Mahal,** *tel. (972-3)821-002.*

The best hotels

Considered by many to be the best hotel in Israel, the **Tel Aviv Sheraton,** *115 Hayarkon St., Tel Aviv 63573; tel. (972-3)286-222,* has spacious, air-conditioned rooms, restaurants, discos, and shops. It is within walking distance of the beach and Dizengoff Street shops. A double room is $104, not including breakfast.

Others consider the **Dan Hotel,** *99 Hayarkon Street; tel. (972-3)241-111,* the best in Israel. On the beach close to the city, it is one of the oldest hotels in Tel Aviv. A double room is $115 to $135.

More modestly priced accommodations include **Hotel Tamar,** *8 Gnessin St.; tel. (972-3)286-997,* where a clean, rather Spartan room goes for $18. Slightly better is **Hotel HaGalil,** with double rooms running $17 to $20. **HaGalil,** *tel. (972-3)655-036,* is near Souk HaCarmel and offers rooms with private balconies. The **Greenhouse,** *tel. (972-3)235-994,* the best hostel in Tel Aviv, has double rooms and private apartments for $16 to $24. **Immanuel House Christian Hospice,** *Jaffa; tel. (973-2)821-459,* is a cheaper hostel. A quiet, friendly place built by Peter Ustinov's father, it has double rooms for $14;

Jaffa: an offbeat best

Jaffa, the Biblical port town, is now part of Tel Aviv. Its winding lanes are filled with shops, restaurants, and nightclubs. The reconstructed Old City houses an artists' colony, private and public art galleries, and studios. Shops and boutiques here remain open until midnight. The flea market off Aleystion Street is where everyone ends up; it is as colorful as it is inexpensive.

Old Jaffa, with its intimate restaurants and romantic cafés, is a splendid counterpoint to the dangerous and rocky coastline on its border. **Toutoune,** *1 Simpat Mazel Bagim; tel. (972-3)820-693,* is an outstanding restaurant that serves excellent French cuisine on the roof of an old Turkish house. It is rivaled only by **Via Maris,** *6 Kikar Kdumim; tel. (972-3)828-451,* where you can sit on a vine-covered terrace and enjoy delicious seafood and a view of the floodlit town.

Jaffa comes alive at night, especially on Hayarkon Street near the old port and in the new cafés and restaurants around city hall. The **Omar Khayyam,** *tel. (972-3)825-865,* has the most famous floor show in town, set dramatically in a 500-year-old Arab stone building. **Michal's Aladdin,** *5 Mifratz Shlomo,* is a popular club in an 800-year-old Turkish bath.

Sunday nights at 8 p.m. you can take an Israeli folk-dancing class at **Hamlin House,** *30 Weitzmann Blvd.*

Ashkelon: defying fate

Located on the Mediterranean coast 30 miles south of Tel Aviv, **Ashkelon** is a flourishing port city—despite the Biblical prophecy that "Gaza shall be deserted, and Ashkelon shall become desolation" (Zephaniah 2:4). In response to the prophecy, the center of town is named Zephaniah Square.

Ashkelon, associated with Samson and his battles with the Philistines, is one of the three famous Philistine city-states. The seaside National Antiquities Park here has ancient ruins, including pillars and walls dating back to Canaanite times. The most extensive ruins are Roman, and the haphazard collection of columns, statues, and capitals is highlighted by the Boulouterion, the third-century square filled with marble statues of Atlas, Nike, and Isis.

You can camp at the park for $10 to $12 per person. Trailers can be rented year-round. For information, contact the campground, *P.O. Box 5052; tel. (972-51)36777.*

Ashkelon is big on tennis. Its tennis center has 17 courts, and the Ashkelon Tennis Tournament plays to a crowd of 2,000. For more information, contact the **Ashkelon Tourist Center,** *tel. (972-51)32-412.*

The world's best spa: the Dead Sea

The greatest natural wonder of Israel is one of the healthiest as well. At 400 meters below sea level, the **Dead Sea** region is the lowest point on earth. As a result, it has one of the driest climates in the world, and its pure and pollen-free air is especially good for those with allergies or respiratory problems. (People with skin disorders also come here for the therapeutic ultraviolet rays.) Because this region has the highest atmospheric pressure on earth (which reduces the danger of sunburn), it is one of the most relaxing places to sunbathe—and it has more than 300 cloudless days a year.

The main wonder is the sea itself, with 10 times as much salt as any ocean in the world. The surface of the calm brown water is periodically broken by the green-white salt mounds. It is considered the only sea in which you cannot drown, because the salt-laden water makes you float like a cork. Don't try to swim if you have cuts—the salt will irritate them.

The shores of the sea are lined with resorts and historic sites—few tourists realize just how lively the Dead Sea is.

Mezad Zohar, near Jericho on the Dead Sea coast, is an ancient stronghold surrounded by fantastic rock formations. Natural freshwater bathing pools mark green oases.

Ein Gedi, about 11 miles north of Masada, is the oasis where David hid from King Saul. Now a kibbutz facing the Dead Sea, it contains waterfalls, a nature reserve, hot springs, and an archeological site.

A revitalizing visit to the **Dead Sea spa** is one way to get back into form. Spend a week at the five-star Moriah Spa Hotel enjoying Dead Sea hydrotherapy and treatment in pools and mud. When you are fed up with the brackish water, you can swim in fresh water, indoor or out, or hit the tennis courts. The program costs $769 per person, double occupancy, including accommodations, all meals, and a medical checkup. For more information, contact **Isram,** *630 Third Ave., New York, NY 10017; (212)661-1193 or (212)477-2352.*

If you're going to the Dead Sea, also visit **Arad.** Located a half-hour from the Dead Sea, but 3,500 feet higher, Arad sits on a plateau overlooking an ancient Roman fort. This Biblical city renovated in the 1960s is a mixture of old and new. The nearby Tel Arad excavations include a temple dating back to King Solomon and a fortress that was rebuilt six times before Julius Caesar was born.

Best Dead Sea digs

The best areas to stay while visiting the Dead Sea are En Boqeq and Arad. The **Masada,** *P.O. Box 62, Arad 80700; tel. (972-57)957-140,* is a resort with a bar, a nightclub, a bridge club, and a cinema hall. Rooms are $40 to $60, including breakfast. The **Margoa Arad,** *P.O. Box 20, Arad 80700; tel. (972-57)957-014,* is slightly less expensive. It has a nightclub, a cinema hall, and a private pool. Rooms are $34 to $48.

The two outstanding hotels in En Boqeq are **Ein Bokek,** *Dead Sea 86930; tel. (972-57)84-331,* with a pool, tennis courts, and a nightclub (double rooms are $57 to $70), and the **Moriah Dead Sea,** *Dead Sea 86930; tel. (972-57)84-221,* a five-star hotel with an outdoor pool, an indoor seawater pool, a private beach, and a famous spa fed by waters of the Zohar Hot Springs (double rooms are $88 to $115).

The **Ein Gedi kibbutz,** *Dead Sea 86910; tel. (972-57)84-757,* has a reasonably priced guesthouse. The 92 rooms have televisions and radios and cost only $43 to $50 per person, including two meals.

For more information on hotels in the area of the Dead Sea, contact the **Arad Tourist Information Office,** *tel. (972-57)98-144.*

Masada—the most dramatic

Masada, the famous hilltop fortress built by King Herod, is one of Israel's most important sights. Commanding a view of the pink mountains of Moab, Masada was the last stronghold of the Jews when Rome invaded the country. In 73 B.C., after three years of fighting, the Romans finally broke through Masada's defenses only to find that the 960 rebels had committed mass suicide rather than surrender to slavery. Built on a cliff that drops 1,300 feet, Masada is dramatic in history and appearance.

The peak can be reached either by foot (follow the Snake Path) or by cable cars, which run every 15 minutes from the eastern side of the mountain. The bathhouses, storehouses, water cisterns, and Herod's three-tiered palace have been restored. See the mosaics in the lavish palace halls; the world's largest collection of first-century Roman and Jewish coins; the world's oldest synagogue; and the Mikvot, the world's oldest extant ritual immersion baths, predating baptism by 100 years.

Jericho: the world's oldest city

Jericho, the world's oldest city, was a walled community as early as 7000 B.C. According to the Old Testament, Joshua toppled Jericho's walls with trumpet blasts. Since then, the city has been rebuilt and destroyed several times. Lush scenery surrounds this oasis. Explore the many levels of the ruins and the remains of the magnificent palaces.

Haifa—the prettiest city

Although **Haifa** is heavily industrialized, it is one of the most beautiful cities in Israel. The nation's third-largest city and main port, it has been compared to San Francisco. Hugging a beautiful bay on the Mediterranean, it encompasses the hilly suburb of Mt. Carmel.

Israel's biggest museum

The **Haifa Museum Complex,** *26 Shabatai Levi St.; tel. (972-4)523-255,* is one of the largest in Israel, with three separate exhibits: Israeli modern art; ancient art; and Jewish folklore and ethnology. Also visit the **Haifa Illegal Immigration and Naval Museum,** *204 Derech Allenby; tel. (972-4)536-249,* which illustrates the history of Jewish migration to Palestine when it was under British mandate. Although the British outlawed further migration, Israelis managed to smuggle their relatives in for another 20 years.

Highest tech in the Middle East

The **Technion** (Israel Institute of Technology), *Neve Sha'anan; tel. (972-4)230-111,* is the university that makes Israel the most technologically advanced nation in the Middle East. Covering 300 acres and including 50 buildings, it has a panoramic view of the city, the bay, and, on clear days, Lebanon. Students from all over the world can be seen strolling the campus lawns. Stop by the Coler-California Visitor Center on campus, where a robot welcomes you and a free film is shown about the technological discoveries made here.

The world's Baha'i center

Haifa is the world center of **Baha'i,** a religion that broke away from Islamic mysticism in the 19th century. The Baha'i believe in the unity of all religions and advocate an international language and government.

Few travelers visit the beautiful gold-domed **Baha'i Shrine and Gardens,** halfway up Mt. Carmel (you can get here via Bus 23 from Hanevi'im Street). The Bab, the herald of the primary Baha'i prophet, Bahaullah, is buried in the shrine. (Bahaullah is buried a few miles north of Haifa in Akko.) You must remove your shoes to enter the shrine. The gardens are filled with statues of animals and graceful cypress trees. You can visit from 9 a.m. to noon.

The **Baha'i International Archives** and the **Baha'i Universal House of Justice** are also located in Haifa. The archives were modeled after the Parthenon, and the House of Justice is noted for its 58 marble columns and hanging gardens. Neither is open to tourists.

Israel's largest national park

Mt. Carmel, the site of Elijah's confrontation with the priests of Ba'al, is the site of Israel's largest national park, with 25,000 acres of eucalyptus and cypress forests, picnic areas, and a restaurant. At the peak of the mountain are hanging gardens. Beautiful homes cling to the slopes. Mt. Carmel also has some of Haifa's best hotels. Climb the mountain just before sunset, when the sun is a flaming red ball, dipping below the horizon.

The best restaurants

Haifa's speciality is seafood. The two best places to enjoy it are downtown: **Neptune,** *19 Pinhas Margolin St.; tel. (972-4)535-205,* and **Misabag,** *29 Pinhas Margolin St.; tel. (972-4)524-441.* Or try **Zvi,** *Kikar Paris; tel. (972-4)668-596.*

The best place for a traditional home-style Jewish meal is **Shmulik & Dany,** *7 Habankim St.; tel. (972-4) 514-411.* This popular establishment papers its walls with rave reviews and fine paintings. Try roast duck, the house specialty. The restaurant is open 11:30 a.m. to 4 p.m. daily except Saturdays.

Peer, *1 Atlit St.; tel. (972-4)665-707,* is a good Arabic restaurant.

For European food, try **Bankers Tavern,** *2 Habankim St; tel. (972-4)528-439.*

Haifa's best hotels

Haifa's best hotel is the five-star **Dan Carmel,** *85-87 Sderot Hanassai; tel. (972-4)86-211,* with the most luxurious rooms and the best view of Haifa Bay in the city. Double rooms are $95 to $150.

Almost as good and less expensive is **Yaarot Hacarmel,** *Mt. Carmel; tel. (972-4)229-144,* which has rooms for $40 to $52.

Nof, *101 Sderot Hanassai, Carmel; tel. (972-4)88-731,* has a panoramic view and luxurious rooms. The restaurant serves excellent kosher food. The price is right—double rooms are $75.

Another good hotel in Carmel is the **Shulamit,** *15 Kiryat Sefer St.; tel. (972-4)242-811.* Rooms are $52 to $65.

Highlights near Haifa

Ten miles south of Haifa is **En Hod,** a famous artists' colony that is open to the public. It is situated on Atlit Beach, where a crusaders' castle juts up from the water. This was the site of the crusaders' last stand before they were expelled from the Holy Land.

Nahariyya, a half-hour north of Akko (Acre), is an old-fashioned village where horse-drawn carriages are still the mode of transportation. This friendly town is a popular Israeli honeymoon resort. A small stream flows through the center of town into a wide beach, where legend has it that man first learned to make glass. Sailors made a huge bonfire on the sand, so powerful and hot that it turned part of the beach into glass.

Israel's best beach

Akko is one of the oldest (it existed more than 3,500 years ago) and most picturesque cities in the world. Surrounded by thick sea walls on the tip of a point of land, the city is fringed with palm trees and punctuated with minarets. Only 14 miles north of Haifa, it was an important Phoenician port and later served as a capital for the crusaders.

On the southern edge of Akko is the **Argaman,** or purple beach, the most beautiful on the coast, with crystal-clear water.

Akko was the site of the largest prison break in history. On May 4, 1947, 251 prisoners were freed from the prison known as the Fortress by Jewish underground fighters. The movie *Exodus,* which is about the escape, was filmed here. Part of the prison, known as the Museum of Heroes, contains Jewish memorabilia and the cell where Bahaullah was imprisoned in the 1860s. The other part of the prison is a mental hospital.

Most of Acre's sights are in the Old City, including the remains of an underground crusader town, Al-Jazzar Mosque (the third largest in Israel), caravansarais, and Oriental markets. If you admire architecture, you will be dazzled by the ramparts, minarets, spires, and domes. The city's high walls, alleys, and stairways are thick with fragrances from the Arab market.

Akko is considered the holiest place on earth by people of the Baha'i faith. Their prophet, Bahaullah, is buried here, at the shrine at Bahji. He was brought to the Ottoman-Victorian house here to die after spending two years in the Fortress. His ornate tomb is covered with flowers and gold designs. The house (now his shrine) contains memorabilia of the leader. The surrounding gardens are lush and peaceful.

Concerts are held from time to time at Knights' Hall in **Crusader Castle.** The Haifa

Symphony Orchestra performs here, 10 feet belowground because of the good acoustics. During mid-October, the Knights' Hall hosts the **Akko Theater Festival.**

The **Argaman Motel,** *P.O. Box 153, Akko Beach; tel. (972-4)916-691,* has one of the most beautiful views of the sea in Israel, with the walls of the Old City in the foreground. Rooms are spacious, with air conditioning, balconies, telephones, and modern bathrooms. Double rooms are $50, including breakfast.

Caesarea—built to rival Baghdad

South of Haifa is **Caesarea,** built by King Herod in the first century B.C. to rival Baghdad. Once the port could hold an entire Roman fleet. Today, it is an impressive recreation center, with horseback riding, swimming, and one of the few 18-hole golf courses in Israel. Concerts, both classical and rock, are held in the Roman amphitheater.

The extensive historical remains in Caesarea include a Roman hippodrome, part of the Roman harbor and aqueducts, and the remains of a crusader town, walls, and moat. Archeological digs continue constantly in Caesarea.

The beach in Caesarea is pleasant. The famous Sharon Coast runs from Caesarea down to Tel Aviv—this is where the lilies of Sharon bloom in the sand during the fall.

If you stay in Caesarea, your best bet is the **Dan Caesarea Golf Hotel,** *tel. (972-63)62-266,* which has three restaurants, a pool, tennis courts, a sauna, and a Turkish bath. The beach and shops are nearby. Double rooms are about $100, including breakfast.

Galilee: pastoral perfection

Galilee, in northeast Israel, is a green region dotted with small cities and world-famous historical sites. It borders the **Sea of Galilee,** which is also called Lake Kinneret (which translates as violin-shaped harp), because of its shape.

Greatest knowledge, best baths

Tiberias is the largest city on the shore and a good base from which to tour the area. This holy city, full of synagogues and churches, was founded 2,000 years ago in honor of the purity of Caesar Tiberias (who turned out to be an extremely decadent ruler). For 200 years after the fall of Jerusalem, it acted as the center of Jewish learning, and it was here that the books of Jewish law, the Mishnah and the Gamorah, were written.

Tiberias is also a winter resort, where foreigners and natives have traveled for hundreds of years to enjoy the therapeutic hot springs. After wandering through the city's bazaars, shops, and monuments, a visit to the health resort Hamme Teverya will limber up your aching muscles.

The best restaurant in Tiberias is the little-known Lido. Located right on the water, it serves delicious Near Eastern food. Try the grilled St. Peter fish.

You won't find much in the way of night life in Tiberias. However, across the Dead Sea the En Gev Music Festival is held every year during Passover.

In the footsteps of Jesus

Outside the city are numerous landmarks easily reached by bicycle, taxi, bus, or boat. **Capernaum** (Kefar Nahum) was the site of Jesus' first miraculous cures, as well as where He found His first disciples. Nearby is the **Mt. of Beatitudes,** where Jesus delivered the Sermon on the Mount. **Qursi,** on the opposite side of the lake, has the remains of a beautiful church and monastery built on the site where Jesus drove the devils out of a possessed man and into a herd of swine.

Tabgha, traditional site of the miracle of loaves and fishes, has an ornate church with a Byzantine mosaic floor. And in nearby **Hittim** is the Nebi Shueib, the Druze holy place. **Jethro,** the father-in-law of Moses, is buried here.

Near the sea is **Kafr Kanna,** with its impressive Fransiscan and Greek churches. Have a glass of wine here; this is where Jesus performed His first miracle, changing water into wine.

To complete your religious/historical tour of Galilee, visit **Nazareth,** just to the south. The childhood home of Jesus is filled with shrines, including Mary's Well, the Church of St. Joseph, and the Basilica of the Annunciation. Completed in 1966, the basilica is an ornate shrine to which almost every church in the world contributed.

A good place to lunch in Nazareth is **Abu Nassr,** *Casanova Street,* an English/Arab pub. After lunch, visit the markets and bazaars.

Safed: mysticism and magic

Take a short trip north to the intriguing hillside town of **Safed** (Zefat), one of the Four Holy Cities of Israel. Jewish refugees expelled from Spain took refuge in this town, which clings to the steep slope of Mt. Canaan, in 1492, and Safed became a center for the study of Cabala—Jewish mysticism and magic. (Cabala is so arcane that men may not study it until they are 35 years old and married.)

Six of Safed's old synagogues are named after the city's most learned rabbis of Cabala. The most famous of these is the **Ha'Ari Synagogue,** traditionally guarded by the ghost of Rabbi Luria. (Luria developed a branch of mysticism in the 16th century now known as Lurianic Cabala. The people of Safed named him Ha'Ari, or the Lion.)

Explore the Synagogue Quarter on foot—the streets are too narrow for automobiles. Safed was the site of the first printing press in Israel in 1563. The former Arab Quarter houses a thriving artist's colony, where, among the winding lanes, dozens of painters and artisans work in the sunshine as it glares off the white stone. Most artists open their studios daily to visitors.

Safed's **Ramon Inn,** *tel. (972-69)30-665,* off the standard tourist route in the artists' quarter, has secluded rooms with spectacular views. Double rooms are $75, including breakfast.

For information about walking tours, contact the **Safed Tourist Information Center,** *23 Jerusalem St.; tel. (972-6)930-633.*

The best horsing around in Galilee

Kfar Hittin Ranch, *Shadmot Dvora, Galil Hatchton 15240; tel. (972-67)67-085,* offers a horseback-riding tour of Galilee. You follow a trail that leads to a lookout on Ginossar Hill, an ancient synagogue near Zukei Arbel, the Ginossar Valley, and through a riverbed to the Sea of Galilee. You'll have a breathtaking view of the Jordan River.

Eilat: the world's best scuba diving

During the winter, fashionable Israelis flock to this port town at the southernmost tip of Israel, on the coast of the Red Sea. You'll see lots of tanned bodies on the beach, but you'll also see marine life that exists nowhere else—tropical fish whose origin is lost in time. The

Red Sea is part of the African Rift, which runs through East Africa to the gold mines of the Rand in South Africa. **Eilat** has marvelous facilities for skin and scuba diving. One of the best places to rent gear is Lucky Divers' Eilat Scuba Center.

Eilat has one of the best underwater observatories in the world for viewing exotic aquatic life. In spring, the city becomes a birdwatchers' paradise, as dozens of migrating species make a stopover here. The colorful annual festival at Eilat (usually held in March) is marked by water sports and moonlight pageants.

If you're a nature lover, explore the Eilat zoo and **Hai-Bar,** a wildlife preserve where animals from Biblical times are being returned to their natural habitats. Hai-Bar also contains the ruins of Nabataean cities (Nabataea was a small kingdom from 200 B.C. to 300 B.C.) and remnants of the oldest Christian churches in the world. For more information on the nature reserve, call *(972-59)76-018.* Visiting hours are early morning to early afternoon.

Neviot, Israel's nude beach, about 30 miles south, is generally less crowded than Eilat's beaches.

The best food and lodgings

The most elegant restaurant in the city is **La Coquille,** *tel. (972-59)73-461,* expensive but luxurious. Located on the North Beach, it offers the finest French food on the Red Sea.

Two good seafood restaurants are **La Bohème,** *Aimog Beach; tel. (972-59)7422,* and the **Last Refuge,** *Hof Aimog Jetty; tel. (972-59)724-37.*

The best hotel is the **Aviya Sonesta,** *Eilat Taba; tel. (972-59)79-222,* with a tennis court, a pool, and a private beach. Double rooms are $126 to $150, including breakfast..

The **Red Sea,** *HaTmarim Boulevard; tel. (972-59)72-171,* is an excellent little hotel with a pool. A double room is $30 to $40.

Hotel HaDekel, *L'Hativat Hanegev Street; tel. (972-59)73-191,* offers comfortable rooms for $30 to $35.

The disco at the **Americana Hotel,** *tel. (972-59)75-176,* is fun. The liveliest and most international nightspot is the **Peace Bar,** a popular pub at the corner of Almogim and Agmonim streets.

The Golan Heights

The Israeli-occupied **Golan Heights** is a tension-ridden area, where Palestinians and Israeli soldiers eye each other. Yet, this northwestern region has some of the most interesting archeological treasures of the Middle East. You can visit the area with a private guide.

Although rusty tanks and occasional passing soldiers color the sandy landscape, **Qazrin,** the municipal center of Golan, is an attractive town. The helpful **Golan Field School,** *tel. (972-67)61-352,* can answer your questions and, when space provides, will give you a lift in one of its buses. Located at the north end of town, the **Golan Archeological Museum** is well laid-out and has informative displays.

If you can't get a ride with the Golan Field School, Egged runs a $22 tour of the Golan area. It departs Tiberias on Tuesdays, Thursdays, and Saturdays. This area is one of the few places where a rented car will come in handy.

Hazor: Israel's biggest archeological site

Hazor, about 10 miles north of the Sea of Galilee, is the biggest excavated archeological site in Israel. The original city, which served as the capital of Biblical Canaan, dates back to

2500 B.C. Centuries after Joshua and the Israelites leveled the city, Solomon rebuilt it. The excavations at Hazor span 4,000 years of history and 22 cities layered one atop the other.

The Hykssos (Hittite) fortress, palaces, tablets, and chariot remains on display show the cruelty of this people, who led the way in using chariots and became the first conquerors in history. You are welcome to explore the city.

Getting around Israel

Inland air travel is possible through **Arkia Israel Airlines,** *88 Ha' hashmonim St., Tel Aviv; tel. (972-3)971-2555.* Short flights between Jerusalem, Tel Aviv, Haifa, and Eilat are popular.

The most common mode of transportation is the bus, either in cities or between them. Bus service is regular, and fares are reasonable. The national bus company, **Egged,** *tel. (972-3)251-333,* operates services almost everywhere.

Train travel is also easy. The **Israel Railway** runs a scenic route from Nahariyya to Tel Aviv to Jerusalem, and all passenger trains have a buffet car. Bus and train service is discontinued on Saturdays (the Sabbath) and Jewish holidays. Hitchhiking is another good way to get around the country—it's common and safe. In most cases, it is not advisable to rent a car, unless you know the country well.

Flying into Israel, you will land at the Ben-Gurion International Airport in Lod, about 11 miles from Tel Aviv. To get from Ben-Gurion to Tel Aviv, your best bet is the El-Al airport bus, which departs every hour from dawn until midnight. Egged buses run from 5 a.m. to 11:30 p.m. (Tel Aviv buses leave every 15 minutes and buses to Jerusalem or Haifa every 20 minutes).

When it's time to return to the airport for your flight home, take an Egged bus (these buses travel from Jerusalem and Haifa to Ben-Gurion) or a limousine.

The best travel tips

As a result of the past 40 years of conflict, Israelis have a mixed attitude toward foreigners. On one street, you may be regarded suspiciously, while on the next you may be invited home for dinner.

Most native Israelites understand and like to speak English. To keep up with current events, pick up a copy of the *Jerusalem Post,* a national English-language newspaper. Remember that politics is a topic to be avoided in this part of the world.

Bring light clothing, because the temperature rarely goes below 60 degrees Fahrenheit. Suits are seldom worn; in winter Israeli men wear turtleneck sweaters. Because of the substantial Arab presence in the country, avoid clothes that might offend them. When not on the beach, women should dress modestly; in some parts of old Jerusalem, a miniskirt will get stones thrown at you. Sunglasses and a hat are always recommended.

It sounds hokey, but the **Folklore Program,** which "portrays the spirit of ancient and modern Israel," is an enjoyable evening of song and dance. Folklore evenings are presented regularly in Jerusalem, Tel Aviv, Haifa, and Tiberias. For more information, contact the tourist offices in those cities.

One of the most famous aspects of Israeli life is the **kibbutz,** a collective settlement (agricultural and technological) that is unique to Israel. In a kibbutz, all property is jointly owned through a cooperative, and members receive medical care, housing, and educational services from a common budget. More than 250 kibbutzim, with some 115,000 participants, form the backbone of Israel's agriculture. Many kibbutzim host folklore evenings and musical ensembles. Several programs are available that allow you to spend a month or more working on a kibbutz. For more information, contact **Kubbutz Aliya Desk,** *(212)255-1338,* or **Volunteers for Israel,** *(212)608-4848.*

For a firsthand look at Israel's history and a fascinating change of pace from sightseeing tours and beachcombing, volunteer at a dig for a week to a month. You can help dig, shovel, haul baskets of earth and clean pottery shards. No experience is necessary, but the labor is difficult and sometimes tedious and recommended only to those in good physical shape.

Some sites provide free housing and meals, while others require up to $1,000 for registration, room, and board. In addition to short digs around the country, the continuing excavations in the Negev and the Judean hills always need volunteers. You can get a full listing of available sites from the **Israel Department of Antiquities and Museums,** *Ministry of Education and Culture, 91-004 Jerusalem; tel. (972-2)278-603.*

Hostels are located around the country. Contact the **Israel Youth Hostel Association,** *3 Dorot Rishonim St., Jerusalem; tel. (972-2)222-708.*

The Israeli economy is so sick that one of the only ways a citizen can hold on to his money is if he keeps it in dollars. However, this is illegal in most cases. Non-citizens can hold dollars, though, and Israelis love them for it. Americans are likely to be approached by Israelis willing to buy dollars for a good price—so good, in fact, that many people make a living on the black market buying and reselling dollars.

For more information about Israel, contact the **tourist office,** *350 Fifth Avenue, New York, NY 10118; (212)560-0650.* Tourist Information desks also are located at **Ben-Gurion Airport,** *tel. (972-4)663-988,* and at the **Haifa Port,** *tel. (972-3)971-485* or *(972-3)971-487.*

Chapter 19

THE BEST OF EGYPT

For 4,000 years, the pharaohs of Egypt reigned over a civilization with a stability and technology that has not been duplicated in all history. Recently, a team of Japanese engineers tried to build a pyramid just 35 feet high using the ancient Egyptian methods. They couldn't finish it. Thus, the pyramids of Egypt are eternal reminders of the lost wisdom of a great civilization.

A few days among the tombs and temples of Egypt will convince you that the pharaohs had something we have now lost. But a few days among the guides and poor asking for baksheesh (tips) may also convince you that what the pharoahs intended to build was merely a nation of the greatest tourist attractions known to man.

While Egypt is largely a desert nation, most of its people live on the water—along the banks of the Nile, by the Red Sea, or on the Mediterranean. So one of the best ways to see this country is by boat. One of the country's geographic peculiarities is that the southern half is known as Upper Egypt; the northern half is Lower Egypt.

Cairo: the great paradox

Founded in the 10th century by invading Muslims, this noisy, crowded city thriving in the shadow of the pyramids is one of the most intriguing capitals in the world. **Cairo's** mixture of poverty and riches exemplifies the paradox of the Middle East, which is made up of nations straddling the Third World and the Western world. Minarets rise imperiously from 10th-century mosques; cars hurtle recklessly down narrow streets; poor families live in the grave-yards of wealthy relatives; and merchants crowd the bazaars selling Arabian Night perfume and "genuine" Pharaonic scarabs.

Metropolitan Cairo, jam packed with one-quarter of Egypt's population, is split by the Nile into two districts: Cairo on the east bank and Giza (a suburb on the edge of the Giza Plateau) on the west. In between are two small islands: Zamalek and Roda. Zamalek (also called Gezira) lies across from the northern, more upscale New City, where you can wander through Tahrir Square—Cairo's downtown—or walk east into the Islamic section and the tourist bazaar of Khan el-Khalili. Roda is parallel to the southern, somewhat squalid Old Cairo, which includes the Coptic neighborhood bordered by the Fatimid Wall built in 1087.

The best view of Cairo

Most people come to Cairo to see the pyramids, and in the process they miss the city itself. The best place to get your bearings is atop the 600-foot **Cairo Tower** in Zohria Garden on Zamalek. The view from the observation deck stretches to the pyramids. (Skip the mediocre restaurant here.)

Cairo's two best museums

Two museums on the island provide views of modern Egypt: the **Mukhtar Museum** shows the works of Mahmud Mukhtar, the father of modern Egyptian sculpture; and the **Gezira Museum** displays rare paintings, sculptures, and Islamic and Coptic artifacts.

The most fashionable neighborhood

Walk around the fashionable neighborhood of **Heliopolis** in the New City, where Egyptian President Mubarak lives. Buildings here mix Western and Islamic architecture. Notice especially the Palace of Prince Husayn, the arcades on Abbas Boulevard, and the Palace of Empain, a copy of a Hindu temple with an electronically controlled tower that rotates to follow the path of the sun.

In search of the *Arabian Nights*

Islamic Cairo, with its magic lanterns and flying carpets even better than those of Baghdad, has preserved the atmosphere of the *Arabian Nights*. It takes several mornings of walking to really see the area. Visit some of the 500 mosques here—remember that not all of them are open to non-Muslims and that you won't be allowed to enter any mosque until after prayer.

When visiting a mosque, dress conservatively and don't draw attention to yourself; women should cover their heads. You must remove your shoes at the door (give the man who watches them 25 piastres). Anyone who opens special doors or explains things in detail also should be tipped. Some mosques charge an admission in Egyptian pounds.

The world's oldest university

Cairo's most famous mosque is certainly **Al-Azhar Mosque**, on the corner of Al-Azhar and Al-Muizz streets. Built in A.D. 972, it was the world's first university, and today it serves more than 90,000 Muslim students. Restored in bits and pieces, the mihrab in the center aisle is from the 10th century. You can take photographs here, as in any mosque, as long as you don't focus on any one person.

The holiest mosque

Across the street from Al-Azhar Mosque is **Sayiddna al-Husayn,** Cairo's most venerated Muslim shrine. It is closed to non-Muslims, but you can examine the finely decorated exterior walls. Inside rests the head of al-Husayn, grandson of the prophet Muhammad (transported to Cairo in a green silk bag from Iraq).

Westernization has hit even Sayiddna al-Husayn. Just inside the door is a green neon light reading "Allah."

The Citadel

South of Al-Azhar is the **Citadel,** a monolithic complex that dominates Cairo's skyline.

Built in the late 12th century by Salah al-Din on the Mokattam hill range, it has a strategic view of the capital.

The 19th-century ruler Muhammad Ali added a mosque to the Citadel, one of the great features of Cairo. The silver domes and marble and alabaster decorations are rivaled only by the building's vast interior.

The Citadel houses the Mostafa Kamel Museum and the Military Museum.

Cairo's oldest mosque

Southwest of Salah al-Din Square is the city's oldest mosque: **Ibn Tulun,** *Calen el-Salikban Street.* It was built in A.D. 879 by Ibn Tulun, who seceded from the Islamic Empire and built himself the largest mosque in Egypt, decorating it with sweeping contours and intricate inscriptions. The mosque's courtyard covers almost seven acres, and the building's lacy stuccowork surrounds inscriptions from the Koran. Climb the external staircase to the top of the tower, from which you have a view of the city and the pyramids to the west. You can visit Ibn Tulun from 8 a.m. to 6 p.m.

The most beautiful windows

The mausoleum complex of **Qalaun,** *Gonar al-Qaid Street,* in northern Sharia al-Muizz, is famous for the colors in its stained glass windows. During the times of the Crusades, Egypt was the world's center of glasswork, and the incredible craftsmanship of these windows set a standard for all Islamic tombs and Gothic churches in Europe.

The best Islamic art

The **Museum of Islamic Art,** off Ahmad Maher Square at the corner of Port Said and Muhammed Ali streets, is an overlooked treasure. This museum houses a little of everything, from Persian carpets to Islamic glassware to Kufic script wood carvings. Because most visitors to Egypt dwell on Pharaonic art, the Museum of Islamic Art is rarely crowded. The exhibits are arranged by craft, so it's easy to trace stylistic developments over time, giving yourself a mini-art history course. Don't miss the Koran engravings. The museum is open Saturdays through Thursdays from 9 a.m. to 4 p.m.

Giza Square: the road to the pyramids

Giza Square, in the heart of Cairo's Giza District on the west bank, marks the beginning of Pyramids Road. Cross Al-Gamaa Bridge to get to the Al-Urman Botanical Garden and the Cairo Zoo. To the north is Dokki, Giza's fashionable residential neighborhood, which contains several embassies and two good museums.

The **Museum of Modern Art,** *18 Ismail Abu'l-Futuh St.,* exhibits postwar Egyptian art and has an excellent sculpture garden. The **Agricultural Museum,** at the western end of the 6th of October Bridge, contains the only remaining mummified bull.

The best of Old Cairo

South of Tahrir Square is **Old Cairo,** which surrounds the old Roman fort Babylon outside Fatimid Wall. You'll find evidence of Greco-Roman culture and early Christianity throughout the quarter. From the time of the last pharaoh to the first mosque, Egypt was part of the Greco-Roman world and Christianity, which in Egypt emerged as the Coptic Church.

The world's finest Coptic art

The **Coptic Museum**, built on the site of the Roman fort in Qasr al-Shama, has the finest Coptic art collection in the world. The buildings, courtyards, and gardens of the museum tell the story of early Christianity from the third through the seventh centuries. See the intricately woven robes and curtains for which the Copts were renowned. The museum is open Saturdays through Thursdays from 9 a.m to 4 p.m.

The most beautiful Coptic church

In front of the Coptic Museum are the remains of the fort that took invading Muslims seven months to overpower. The **Church of al-Muallaqa** was built atop the gate of the fort, giving it the name the Hanging Church. Also known as the Church of St. Mary, this is the most beautiful of Cairo's Coptic churches. The pointed arches and carved relief are interesting changes from the Gothic style commonly associated with Christian churches. Climb the 24 stairs to see the interior. The famous pulpit stands on 13 slender columns (symbolic of the 12 apostles and Jesus, with the black column representing Judas).

Unlike in mosques, baksheesh is not paid in churches. Photographs are prohibited.

Three charming churches

North of al-Muallaqa, on Mari Girgis Street, is the **Church of Mari Girgis** (St. George), noted for its fine stained-glass windows. To the left of the church is a staircase descending into an old alley, at the end of which is the elegant Church of Abu Serga. The crypt below is supposed to be where Joseph, Mary, and baby Jesus stayed during their flight to Egypt (the crypt is now flooded and closed to the public).

To the right of Abu Serga is the **Church of St. Barbara**, an ornate structure with striped-marble steps. According to legend, the order was given to destroy one church and restore the other, but the caliph's architect couldn't decide which to destroy. He paced back and forth between the two buildings until he died of exhaustion—so the caliph restored both churches.

Egypt's oldest synagogue

Near the Church of St. Barbara is the **Ben Ezra Synagogue**, the oldest in Egypt. The interior is beautifully decorated, and the custodian is a humorous, talkative fellow. You can follow the steps to the spot where the pharaoh's daughter is said to have found the infant Moses.

The Cities of the Dead

The vast and forbidding **Cities of the Dead,** where thousands live in and around grave-yards, are to the northeast and south of the Citadel. The poor use parts of mausoleums as their homes and parts of tombs as clotheslines or soccer goals.

Wealthy citizens are buried in the northern cemetery, and their graves are marked with elaborate tombs. Especially fine is the tomb of Umm Ahuk. The many-ribbed dome caps an ancient pointed archway.

The most impressive monument in the southern cemetery is the **mausoleum of Imam Al-Shafi'i,** *Imam Al-Shafi'i Street.* Built in 1211, the mausoleum contains an 800-year-old carved cenotaph. The nearby tomb of Shagarat al-Durr was built for Shagarat, the Muslim queen who poisoned two husbands and her son to remain in power. The mausoleum is decorated with Kufic carvings and a mihrab with Byzantine glass mosaics.

Egypt's most important museum

The **Egyptian Museum,** like the British National Museum and the Smithsonian, exhibits an entire culture on several carpeted floors. Located in Tahrir Square just down the road from the enormous Ramses Hilton, the Egyptian Museum (commonly called the Cairo Museum) is the world's unrivaled warehouse of pharaonic art. More than 100,000 pieces are crammed together with little order; the most exquisite are not always highlighted. The famous mummy room has been closed for religious reasons; however, the museum has enough ankhs, scarabs, and statues to fill several days of exploring.

The second floor houses the treasures found in Tutankhamon's tomb, the only one that escaped plundering, because of its hidden location. When viewing the incredible gold statues, alabaster lamps, and general ostentation, remember that Tutankhamon died young and his treasure was comparatively small.

The Cairo Museum is always crowded but less so when the tour groups break for lunch. It is open daily from 9 a.m. to 4 p.m. Cameras are prohibited.

The most colorful markets

In Cairo, you can buy not only an aphrodisiac, but also an anti-aphrodisiac, made from baby crocodiles. The two Arabic phrases you'll want to know when shopping are *"Bikam hadha?"* (How much does this cost?) and *"Hatha Kathir"* (That's too expensive). The main shopping areas are **Zamalek, Dokki** (in Giza), and **Heliopolis** (northeast of the New City).

Khan el-Khalili is the largest bazaar in Egypt, with hundreds of shops grouped by trade: gold merchants, silversmiths, and spice sellers. The 14th-century courtyards buzz with the sounds of haggling. You will find the best buys on *galabiyyas,* full-length cotton robes worn by Egyptian men, and local crafts. **Nassar Brothers,** *tel. (20-2)907-210,* is the best place for precious and semi-precious stones, and **Zaki and Botros,** *tel. (20-2)809-651,* is the best place for woodwork.

Every Friday morning a camel market is held in **Imbaba** (on Zamalek Island). Traders sell and swap hundreds of Sudanese camels, horses, sheep, and goats, as well as food, wagons, jeans, and baskets. (You can buy a camel for about 204 Egyptian pounds, or $450.) The sights and smells are strong: you may witness a camel giving birth or a goat being butchered and skinned for immediate barbecue. Remember to bargain. And don't pet the camels—they spit and bite.

The **Bab Zuwayla district** of Old Cairo teems with people and livestock. Peddlers transport their goods by bicycle and truck and on foot. Saffron, cumin, coriander, and hibiscus perfume the air. Along the Street of the Tentmaker, men sit crosslegged, plying their needles in the traditional art of appliqué stitchery. Also to be found are food, silk carpets, gold jewelry, clothing, ceramics, baskets, and two fez factories. Bab Zuwayla is more commercialized than **Khan el Khalili,** which is across the street, but just as colorful.

Cairo's best cuisine

In a city where butchers slap flies off pieces of meat to show them to customers, only certain restaurants can be trusted. However, if you're willing to venture beyond the hotel restaurants, you will find that the food in Cairo is exotic and inexpensive. Typical Egyptian dishes include *mulokhiya,* a gelatinous soup made with a spinach-like herb; *fool,* a big brown bean; *feteer*, which resembles pizza; *taboula*, ground wheat and parsley salad; and *kofta*, tiny grilled meatballs.

Andrea, *Teret el-Mariottia; tel. (20-2)851-133,* an outdoor farm restaurant near the pyramids, serves delicious grilled chicken and some of the best *mazza* (a collection of appetizers) in Cairo.

Nearby **Felfela Village,** off Pyramids Avenue; *tel. (20-2)854-209,* offers fine Egyptian cuisine and occasional folklore shows. Dinner here or at Andrea costs 1.8 Egyptian pounds ($4).

Abu Shakra, *69 Kasr el-Nil St.; tel. (20-2)848-811,* specializes in shish kebab and *kofta.* Two can dine for less than 4.5 Egyptian pounds to 7 Egyptian pounds ($10 to $15).

A full-course Egyptian meal is best at **Aladin,** *26 Sherif St.; tel. (20-2)755-694,* in the Immobilia Building, a watering-hole popular among foreign journalists. Kebabs, barbecues, and *om ali*—a spicy bread pudding—are tasty and filling.

The best seafood restaurant in Cairo is **Hag Mohammed el-Samak,** *Abdel-Aziz Street; tel. (20-2)901-337,* across from the Omar Effendi department store. The grilled fish is good at this restaurant, which is decorated with art-deco furnishings.

The most romantic meals in Cairo are served on Nile boats. The food is a little more expensive (about 7 Egyptian pounds, or $15, a meal), but the atmosphere is worth it. The two best floating restaurants are **Scarabee,** opposite the Shepheards Hotel; *tel. (20-2)680-549,* and **Pharaoh,** *31 Nile Ave.; tel. (20-2)726-713.* Both have floor shows and large crowds, so make reservations.

Recommended hotels

Maintaining its 20-year reputation as the best hotel in Cairo is the **Nile Hilton,** *Corniche El-Nil, Tahrir Square; tel. (20-2)750-666* or *(20-2)740-777.* Across the street from the Egyptian Museum, it is well-run and elegant. It has luxurious rooms and the best pool in the city. Rooms start at 32 Egyptian pounds ($70).

Located at the northern tip of Roda Island, the **Meridien Hotel,** *Corniche El-Nil, Garden City; tel. (20-2)845-444,* is quieter but also first-class. All rooms have Nile views.

Nearby is the world-famous **Shepheard's Hotel,** *Corniche El Nil, Garden City; tel. (20-2)355-3900* or *(20-2)355-3800,* which has developed a reputation as a hideaway for international spies.

The Club Med, *Em Manial Palace, Kasr Mohommed Aly; tel. (20-2)844-083* or *(20-2)846-014,* in nearby Mena, is outstanding.

Good hotels need not all be five-star. **The President Hotel,** *22 Taha Hussein St.; tel. (20-2)3416-751, (20-2)3413-195,* or *(20-2)3400-718,* in the residential section of Zamalek, is spacious and clean. The rooftop restaurant has an extensive wine cellar. Double rooms are 29 Egyptian pounds to 36 Egyptian pounds ($64 to $80).

The best night life

At night, when the temperature drops, Cairo's night life gets hot. Discos are crowded, especially on Thursday nights. The popular ones include **After Eight,** *6 Kasr El Nil St.; tel. (20-2)983-000,* and **Rasputin,** *Grenn Pyramids Hotel; tel. (20-2)856-778.* **Atlas Hotel,** *El Gomhouria Street,* has good rock'n'roll music. **Al-Capo,** *22 Taha Husayn St.,* is a great place for live music. **Al-Sokkareya,** *Abd'l-Hamid Badawy Street, Heliopolis,* has singers and musicians, a penny arcade and fortune-tellers, good drinks, and the popular *sheesha* (water pipe), all in an Egyptian garden.

Surprisingly, night life in Cairo can be liveliest during Ramadan, a month-long holiday during which devout Muslims fast from sunrise to sunset. After dark, however, they indulge in large meals and take to the streets around al-Azhar and the Nile, where you'll find street theater performances, magic shows, and noisy crowds.

The Nile Hilton, Marriot, and Sheraton hotels have casinos, where gambling takes place in American currency.

If you want glitzy belly dancing, try the **Belvedere** in the Nile Hilton, *tel. (20-2)740-777,* or the **Two Seasons Supper Club** in the Ramses Hilton, *tel. (20-2)744-400.*

More authentic floor shows can be seen at the clubs along Pyramids Road, which cater to Egyptians. The best of these are the **Auberge des Pyramids,** *tel. (20-2)851-713,* and **Elleil,** *tel. (20-2)854-252.*

The popular folk-dancing Rida Troupe performs at the **Balloon Theater,** *El-Nil Street, Agouza; tel. (20-2)711-718.*

If you'd rather spend a peaceful, romantic evening, take a felucca (small sailboat) on the Nile. Feluccas can be rented just south of the Kasr El-Nil Bridge on the east bank for about 2.7 Egyptian pounds ($6) an hour. Across the corniche from the Shepheards Hotel, boats are available from midnight to dawn for 3.6 Egyptian pounds to 4.5 Egyptian pounds ($8 to $10). It's felucca etiquette to bring food for a picnic to share with your navigator.

Getting around Cairo

Getting around Cairo is simultaneously easy and bothersome. Overcrowded buses (commonly called VOAs, for Voice of America—they were bought with American aid) are cheap and run everywhere, but they can be recommended only to the most adventurous. They don't stop—they only slow down for you to jump on or off.

The newly built metro offers fast, inexpensive service, but only in the southern area of the city. The happiest traveler is the one who has mastered the art of Cairo taxis, which come either metered or unmetered. Either bargain the cost before you get into a cab or at the end of the ride pay the driver a fair amount—usually between 1 and 2 Egyptian pounds within the city and between 4 and 5 Egyptian pounds from downtown to the pyramids.

Chaffeured cars can be hired for the day outside either Hilton. You also can rent a car to drive yourself around. This may be practical in the rest of Egypt, but in Cairo it's dangerous. The famous race-car driver Mario Andretti said that the one place he'd never drive is Cairo. Traffic lights here were built to be ignored. Cars speed through intersections, slowing only momentarily to warn pedestrians by honking their horns or flashing their headlights.

Giza: the best and the tackiest of Egypt

Not five miles west of Cairo, the pyramids of **Giza** are easily reached via Pyramids Road by taxi or buses 8 and 900. The best route is through Mena village. Toward the southern edge of this town is a broad plaza where tourist buses park. Here, clear of buildings, you have an uninterrupted view of the Sphinx with the pyramids behind and overhead.

The best time to visit Giza is at dawn, when sunlight makes the area glow and you feel the power that overwhelmed even Napoleon. If you show up before the tourists arrive, you can try to climb the outside of the Great Pyramid. It's necessary to hire a guide to take you up, and then pay him again to take you back down. Although this is technically illegal, it is one of the advantages of Egypt's baksheesh-oriented system—it's done all the time.

The Great Pyramid

The tallest pyramid in Egypt, the **Pyramid of Cheops** (or the Great Pyramid), was finished in 2690 B.C. and stands 448 feet tall. It contains 2.3-million separate blocks of stone, each weighing 2.5 tons. Millions have visited and climbed Cheops, from French novelist Gustave Flaubert to a Parisian wallpaper manufacturer, who left an advertisement on the top.

Scientists believe that Cheops (or Khufu) built the pyramid for some reason besides pure ostentation. Theories that the ancient Egyptians knew the earth was round and calculated the circumference are supported by the pyramid. Measurements taken in the 1930s revealed that the proportions of the Great Pyramid are the same as the proportions of the earth's Northern Hemisphere. Scientists don't know whether this information was used in ancient navigation and astronomy, but it suggests an advanced culture.

The Grand Gallery of Cheops, with its 28-foot ceiling, is unusually devoid of decoration. It provides one of the major factors of the pyramid controversy—it is the largest chamber in Cheops but contains absolutely nothing to suggest worship or religion.

The gallery leads to the King's Chamber, which contains the bottom half of the sarcophagus (a lid was never found). The king was never buried here, because the passages in the pyramid were too narrow for the sarcophagus to be brought in after the pyramid was completed.

The most beautiful pyramid

Next to Cheops is the **Pyramid of Chepren** (Khafre), Cheops' son. This pyramid is actually about 10 feet shorter than the Pyramid of Cheops, even though it seems taller because it's on higher ground. Its construction is not symbolic—only the Great Pyramid is thought to have any astronomical significance.

Chepren, however, is the most beautiful of the pyramids, because part of its limestone casing remains. The interior is spacious, and the ornate sarcophagus sinks into the floor up to its lid.

The least-crowded pyramid

The **Pyramid of Mycerinus** (Menkaure) is a 15-minute walk south of Cheops and Chepren. Because it is "only" 210 feet tall, it attracts relatively few tourists. Mycerinus, Chepren's son, began the pyramid about 2472 B.C. but died before the outermost stones were placed.

The world's oldest boat

Next to the northern face of Cheops is the museum housing the *Solar Barque*, the oldest boat in the world. Discovered in 1954, the 128-foot-long boat is presumed to have been built to carry Cheops to the Underworld.

The boat's construction is ingenious. Its hull is made from hundreds of jigsaw-like pieces of wood that were fitted then sewn together with rope. When the hull was put into water, the wet wood swelled while the rope shrunk, creating a watertight fit.

The riddle of the Sphinx

Northeast of the Great Pyramid crouches the most famous statue on earth: the giant **Sphinx.** Carved out of a single ridge of rock, it has the head of a man and the body of a lion and measures 240 feet long and 66 feet high. The face is missing its nose and beard, because the statue was used for target practice during the Turkish Occupation in the 1700s.

Because it is commonly believed that the face of the Sphinx represents Chepren, some conclude that the statue is 4,500 years old. Other scientists, however, believe it is much older. Geologists have concluded that the severe erosion of the body could not have been caused by wind and sand. Water, they say, must have been the cause. Egypt was flooded at the end of the last Ice Age, about 10,000 B.C.; therefore, the Sphinx must have been built prior to that time, which is thousands of years before mankind is thought to have had tools.

The Sphinx continues to crumble—it recently lost a chunk of its shoulder. Scientists are debating how to save it. See it while you can.

Also explore the **Valley Temple of Chepren** at the foot of the Sphinx. The core contains limestone blocks, each weighing more than 100 tons; the method used to lift these huge blocks into place is unknown. The floors of the temple are made of slabs of alabaster. Though small, the temple is well-preserved, and its construction is unique in all Egypt.

The most romantic views

Perhaps the most romantic thing to do in Egypt is to ride Arabian horses around the pyramids at dusk. Two stables near the Sphinx rent and lease good horses. Rates are 4.5 Egyptian pounds to 9 Egyptian pounds ($10 to $20) an hour, depending on how well you bargain.

The hokiest show

At night you can attend a sound-and-light show on the Giza Plateau. The pyramids and Sphinx are illuminated as the narrator tells the story of Egypt. It's as hokey as you'd expect, but few people regret attending. Admission is 4 Egyptian pounds to 6 Egyptian pounds. The English shows are held at 6:30 p.m. Mondays, Wednesdays, and Fridays.

The best hotels in Giza

Most people stay in Cairo and visit the pyramids from there; however, waking up to see the Great Pyramid catch the first rays of dawn outside your window is a special pleasure.

The best hotel in Giza is the **Mena House Oberoi,** *El-Ahram Street, Giza; tel. (20-2)855-444,* which is within walking distance of the pyramids. It was once a Khedivial weekend palace, then a meeting place for Churchill and Roosevelt. Since 1973, it has been a luxury hotel. The management has kept the old wooden balconies and added air conditioning, restaurants, bars, and a swimming pool. Double rooms are 29 Egyptian pounds to 38 Egyptian pounds ($65 to $83).

A less expensive hotel is the **Holiday Inn Sphinx,** *Alexandria Desert Road, Giza; tel. (20-2)854-700.* It sounds like a motel that has fake pyramids in every room, but it's actually the most reasonably priced place to stay in Giza. The rooms are new and pleasant and almost every one has a view of the pyramids. Rooms begin at 23 Egyptian pounds ($50)

Saqqara: the world's oldest stone complex

Saqqara, a necropolis 24 miles south of Cairo, is the oldest stone complex in the world, dating back to 2611 B.C. Although they'd never before worked with stone on such a grand scale, the Egyptians created a masterpiece here. As Egyptologist John West put it, "Starting architecture off with Saqqara is like starting automobiles off with the 1984 Porsche." The complex was designed by the legendary Imhotep, an Egyptian Leonardo.

The most important sight at Saqqara is the **pyramid complex of King Zoser,** which contains the world's oldest pyramid. Predating the Great Pyramid by a century, the 200-foot **Step Pyramid** was built of six mastabas (traditional rectangular tombs) of diminishing size. Inside are religious inscriptions.

The complex often uses stonework to imitate organic material; the ceiling of the entranceway to Zoser, for example, simulates a roof of split logs. And the colonnade contains columns that look like they're made of papyrus stalks (these may be the first stone columns ever built). The colonnade leads into the Great Court, where Zoser and his successors ran races as part of a ritual physical fitness test called *heb-sed.*

To the south of the complex are the ruins of the **Pyramid of Unas.** The dilapidated outer stones make you wonder at the people waiting in line to get in. However, once you're inside, you'll understand—the interior is decorated with the finest hieroglyphic reliefs in Egypt. The **Pyramid Texts,** as they're known, tell the story of—and give advice concerning—the trip to the afterlife. Carved delicately out of slabs of white alabaster, the outstanding hieroglyphs in the tomb chamber are highlighted in blue paint dating back to 2330 B.C.

Surrounding the Pyramid of Unas are shacks covering stairways to the Persian tombs. (During Persian rule, mummies were buried in shaft tombs to prevent robbery.) See the Tomb of Ti, with its unusual wall decorations, and the Serapium, an ornate monument where the Persians buried sacred cows.

You can catch a minibus in Cairo to take you to Abu Sir in Giza Square at 6 a.m.; it drops you off about a mile from Saqqara. Or you can take a taxi directly to the site for about 2.3 Egyptian pounds ($5).

Luxor: ancient Thebes and modern city

Built on the site of ancient Thebes, **Luxor** remains one of Egypt's most popular cities. As in most Egyptian cities, the grand sights here are crowded with natives looking to hustle naive tourists.

Ancient Thebes was the capital of Egypt during the Middle Kingdom, when Amon was the most popular of the Egyptian gods. Today the metropolitan area comprises the east bank (Luxor) and the west bank (Thebes). Luxor is small enough that you can see it on foot. The three main thoroughfares are Sharia Al-Mahatta, Sharia El-Nil, and Sharia Al-Karnak.

The Temple of Karnak

The principal sight in Luxor is the **Temple of Karnak.** Noble is the only word that aptly describes this gigantic building. Its unusual design stems from its history: From the beginning of the Middle Kingdom until the time of Alexander the Great, each pharaoh added something new to the temple's architecture. A double row of ram-headed Sphinxes guards the entrance to the Great Court, the temple's largest room, built about 1000 B.C.

Pass through the mighty outer pylon (an entranceway between two flattened pyramids) into the corner of the Great Court, which is surrounded by huge columns and flanked by the Triple Shrine of Amon on one side and the Temple of Ramses III on the other.

Continue on through Hypostle Hall, which features the Obelisk of Queen Hathsheput, carved from exquisite pink granite, and enormous columns that have been imitated in several Egyptian temples. Next is Transverse Hall, with 134 monolithic columns.

Pass the southern buildings and pylons to the sanctuary. Filled with carved reliefs covering the mammoth stone blocks, this is the heart of the Karnak Temple. Past this are rooms, sarcophagi, and a sacred lake that is overshadowed by an enormous stone scarab. Take all afternoon to appreciate this.

The Temple of Luxor

The Avenue of the Sphinxes (which, as its name suggests, is lined with sphinxes) leads from Karnak to the most unusual temple in Egypt: the **Temple of Luxor.** Built with virtually no right angles, Luxor's rooms are set crookedly against one another. Six giant statues of Ramses II mark the main doorway, which is cut into the 80-foot Pylon of Ramses. Carved reliefs on the pylon illustrate Ramses' battle with the Hittites (tribes from Asia Minor who battled Egypt for control of Syria). Beside the pylon is a huge granite obelisk whose twin stands in the Place de la Concorde in Paris.

Inside the temple court is the **Mosque of Abu el-Haggag,** a small building contrasting oddly with the general splendor of the temple. You'll pass the Colonnade of Amenhotep III, with its 14 pillars, on your way to the Sanctuary of Alexander the Great, which contains bas-reliefs of Alexander worshipping Amon.

A banana best

In the late afternoon, take a felucca to **Banana Island,** a palm-studded islet three miles upriver from Luxor. Here you can indulge in all the oranges, lemons, and, of course, bananas you can eat for 1 Egyptian pound.

Luxor's best hotels

One of the two best hotels in Luxor is **Etap,** *Corniche, El Nil Street; tel. (20-95)821-60,* where every room has a Nile view. A double room is 11 Egyptian pounds ($25). The other best hotel is the **New Winter Palace,** *El Nil Street; tel. (20-95)2222,* where double rooms go for 19 Egyptian pounds to 26 Egyptian pounds ($41 to $58).

The **Luxor Hotel,** *Maabed El Karnak St.; tel. (20-95)82400,* is cheaper. It's decorated with bizarre Egyptian art-deco prints. Double rooms are 16 Egyptian pounds ($36).

Luxor's best restaurant

The best restaurant in town is **Mont Azza,** overlooking Luxor near the Winter Palace.

The greatest collection of tombs

Across the Nile, in **Thebes,** is the greatest collection of tombs on earth. You can reach the hills of the west bank from Luxor via two tourist ferries. Once in Thebes, your best bet is to hire a taxi for about $11 (plus baksheesh). Or consider a donkey. Thebes is too big and too hot to visit on foot. A donkey is certainly slower than a taxi, but it is also less than half the cost and it can take you through areas too narrow for cars. The trail from the Valley of the Queens over the ridges to the Valley of the Kings makes an especially fun donkey trip.

The best way to see the Valley of the Kings

Some 64 rulers are buried in the **Valley of the Kings.** Because the locations of the graves were selected haphazardly, a little effort is needed to see the seven most impressive tombs in chronological order.

Begin with the **tomb of Tuthmosis III,** the walls of which are covered with the complete text of the *Book of the Duat,* the most important guide to the afterlife. Next is the **tomb of Amenhotep II.** The walls here are covered with glare-producing glass.

You can skip the famous **tomb of Tutankhamon.** Although its discovery in 1922 was front-page news (and the mysterious deaths of the exploration team started the Curse of the Mummy lore), it is the smallest and plainest of all the tombs—all the treasure was moved to the Cairo Museum. In addition, this tomb is always ridiculously overcrowded.

Next are the Ramses tombs. The **tomb of Ramses I** is followed by the **tomb of Seti I,** which is possibly the best-preserved on the west bank. The lower section of the burial chamber displays an incredible vaulted ceiling decorated with the 12 signs of the zodiac.

The **tomb of Ramses III** contains 10 unusual side chambers that show scenes from daily life (these are not found in other tombs). The artwork in the **tomb of Ramses VI** is more garish and fantastic than that in earlier tombs—Ramses VI ruled during the decadent XXth dynasty. This tomb also is noted for its ancient Greek and Coptic graffiti. One marking translates roughly as "Hermogines of Amasa was here."

The best of the Valley of the Nobles

The **Valley of the Nobles** is divided into five ticket regions. To see the best tombs, buy tickets six, seven, and eight. The **tomb of Khaemet** has some of the best detail. The **tomb of Ramose** shows the radical departure Egyptian art took under Akhnaten. Reliefs show the pharaoh in scenes from family life, displaying affection, and showing his physical deformity.

The **tomb of Nakht** contains well-preserved paintings, some biographical, some inexplicable. The **tomb of Usheret** is notable for the female figures, defaced by a Christian monk who lived in the burial chamber in the seventh century. The **tomb of Intefoger** has strangely insulting portraits. One shows an adult yelling at a child, "Your mother was a female hippopotamus!"

The Ramasseum

The **Colossi of Memnon,** two 70-foot statues, guard the **Temple of Ramses II,** also known as the Ramasseum. The temple contains the fallen Colossus of Ramses, which the poet Shelley described as "two vast and trunkless legs of stone, half sunk, a shattered visage." However, even the ruins are impressive—one ear measures 3.5 feet. The rest of the Ramasseum is in better condition, with relics depicting the Battle of Kadesh, astronomical charts, and rituals.

The tomb of the eight primordials

According to legend, beneath the **Temple of Medinet Habu,** which contains temples of Ramses III and Thutmose III, are buried the **eight primordials**—the Egyptian gods that existed before creation (as did the Greek gods Rhea and Kronos). Ramses' temple has pictures chiseled eight inches into the stone.

"The Most Splendid of All"

North of the Ramasseum is the cliffside Temple of Hatsheput, known in Arabic as **Deir El-Bahari,** which translates as "The Most Splendid of All." Considered one of the most important architectural wonders of the world, Deir El-Bahari is the only monument to have been built partly against the cliff and partly into it. This is also the only temple in Egypt, and the first building in history, made to blend with and complement the landscape.

Hatsheput (circa 1473 B.C.) was the only queen to dare crown herself pharaoh. The temple's broad walkway, the chapels to Anubis and Hathor, and the inscriptions here depict her descent from the god Amon.

Hathor: the magnificent temple

About 35 miles north of Luxor lies Dendera and the magnificent **Temple of Hathor** (the cow goddess and deity of healing), built about 200 B.C. A massive gate leads into the great courtyard of the temple, where the ceilings are decorated with the signs of the zodiac. Pass into the column-filled Hypostle Hall, the walls of which are covered with reliefs carved by priests seeking to preserve secret texts when Egyptian culture fell to the Roman Empire. The results are hieroglyphics so complex that archeologists cannot decipher them. A staircase leads to two rooftop chapels. One contains the famous circular zodiac.

The Mysterious Corridor surrounds the sanctuary, opening off into 11 chapels, one of which has a small opening in the floor that leads to the crypts. The purpose of this subterranean hallway is unknown, but its highly stylized reliefs are fascinating. If the crypts are closed, a guard will open them for you if you offer baksheesh.

While visiting Dendera, you can stay in Luxor or get a room at Qena, about six miles away, for 1.8 Egyptian pounds ($4). The **New Palace Hotel,** *tel. (20-6)2509,* is opposite the train station in Qena. Or try the **Aluminum Hotel,** *Naga' a Hammadee; tel. (20-2)757-947.* Double rooms are 10 Egyptian pounds to 11 Egyptian pounds ($22 to $25).

Abu-Simbel: the most remote temple

At the far end of the Nile, 150 miles south of Aswan in the Nubian Desert, is an awe-inspiring temple that seems to rise out of nowhere. Four 65-foot colossi of Ramses II guard the entrance to the structure, which was originally cut out of a cliff. Between and beside his legs are smaller statues of his queens and daughters.

As remarkable as the temple itself is the fact that it was taken apart and moved. In the 1960s, it was dissected stone by stone and moved by archeologists after they learned it would be flooded by the new High Dam at Aswan. The still beautiful temple lost some of its magnitude with the move. Formerly, it was part of a cliff overlooking the roaring Nile. Today, it is set beside calm Lake Nasser.

Scientists took great pains to place the temple exactly as its original builders did so that during equinoxes the rising sun shines directly through the entrance, lighting statues 180 feet back in the sanctuary. Unfortunately, the statues have been badly mutilated (no one knows by whom).

Travel like Cleopatra

The best way to explore Egypt is aboard a felucca, the traditional sailboat that glides along the Nile. Because the river cuts through most of Egypt's towns and villages, following it gives you a complete view of the country. As you bob along, you'll pass women doing wash in the river, fishermen pulling in their nets, and children playing along the river's bank.

Between Aswan, where most felucca journeys begin, and Luxor, where most of them end, the Nile passes many of Egypt's most important ancient monuments and temples. During this 140-mile sail, a felucca stops at one monument a day.

Of course, on a felucca journey, you must be prepared to rough it. Usually, you have no bathroom facilities—other than the Nile. And meals, while hearty and usually tasty, are prepared over a campfire. Your bed is on board, beneath the stars.

Spring and fall are the best times to sail. Be sure to bring sun screen, a hat, toilet paper, and a flashlight. Women should not wear bikinis or skimpy bathing suits—they cause problems in an Islamic country. It takes about three weeks to cruise the entire length of the Nile. However, the Aswan-Luxor stint takes only about five days.

Feluccas can be cheap or expensive. Shop around, and don't be afraid to bargain. If you arrange the trip yourself in Egypt, plan to spend about 2.3 Egyptian pounds ($5) per person per day, plus .90 Egyptian pounds ($2) per day for food, permits, and tips.

Feluccas line the riverfront in Aswan and Luxor. Ask around on the waterfront at the Cataract Hotel in Aswan. Hotel clerks often can recommend a place to rent a boat. It is a good idea to get references.

Making arrangements ahead of time is easier, but considerably more expensive. Two U.S. groups that arrange Nile cruises are **Overseas Adventure Travel,** *6 Bigelow St., Cambridge, MA 02139; (617)876-0533* ($990), and **International Travel Planners,** *21 E. 26th St., New York, NY 10010; (212)683-4854* ($629, including inter-Egypt air fare).

Alexandria: the least Egyptian city

Alexandria was a very un-Egyptian city when it was founded by Alexander the Great in 330 B.C. It flourished as the cultural center of the world for 300 years, until the great library accidentally burned down under Julius Caesar, destroying more than a half-million irreplaceable manuscripts. Modern Alexandria is an international city, small and clean and known for its Greco-Roman relics and its sandy beaches.

The **Greco-Roman Museum,** *Sharia el-Mathaf,* houses a collection of artifacts from the days of Greek and Roman rule, including bas-reliefs, pottery, statues, jewelry, and marble pieces. Don't miss Room 9, which displays relics of the cult of the crocodile god Pnepheros, including a mummified crocodile. The museum is open daily except Fridays from 9 a.m. to 4 p.m.

At the western end of town are the **catacombs of Kom el-Shoqafa,** burial chambers carved into rock 100 feet belowground. Built in the second century for a wealthy family that still practiced the ancient religion, the catacombs represent the last burst of native Egyptian sacred art. However, because the artisans were trained in Italy, the Egyptian gods have unmistakably Roman bodies. Reliefs depict a Roman-style Osiris making an offering to the deceased. Lesser gods hold bunches of grapes and Medusa heads. One statue of Anubis is even dressed in Roman armor. The museum is open daily from 9 a.m. to 4 p.m.

Near Nasr Station is a beautifully preserved white marble **Roman amphitheater,** the only known Roman era amphitheater remaining in Egypt. Behind it lie a cistern and Roman bath. In 1963, when construction workers were building the foundation of an office building, the ruins were unearthed; archeologists continue to uncover artifacts here.

A relatively modern attraction in this ancient city of Alexandria is the 19th-century summer residence of the Egyptian royal family, **Ras el-Tin Palace.** King Farouk forfeited its Throne Room, Gothic Hall, and Marble Hall when he abdicated in 1953 for a life of exile in Italy.

The **Fine Arts Museum,** *18 Menasha St.,* contains both a collection of modern Egyptian art and Alexandria's public library. Not far from the Mosque of Abul Abaas, along the corniche, it is the largest Islamic building in the city and has a beautiful courtyard. According to legend, the priest Abul Abaas rose from his tomb here to catch bombs falling on Alexandria during World War II.

At the western end of the corniche, where the Lighthouse of Pharos (one of the original Seven Wonders of the World) once stood, is the **Fort of Qait Bay.** Built by Sultan Bay in the 15th century from the remains of the lighthouse, the fort commands a sweeping view of Alexandria. Inside are a scale model of the 400-foot lighthouse and a naval museum.

The best case of mistaken identity

A 98-foot granite column erected in Alexandria in 297 A.D. was named **Pompey's Pillar** by Crusaders during the 13th century. Actually, the rose-colored column is a monument to the emperor Diocletian that was built by his troops. The most famous monument of ancient Alexandria, the pillar sits in a small public park on a hill where Diocletian once had a temple dedicated to the bull god Serapis.

Getting to Alexandria

Located 110 miles north of Cairo, bordering the Nile Delta, Alexandria can be reached easily by bus, plane, train, or car. For about 2.3 Egyptian pounds ($5), Golden Rocket buses carry you between Cairo's Giza Square and Alexandria's Zaghloul Square. Make reservations if you plan to use the daily air-conditioned trains that travel between Cairo's Ramses Station and Alexandria's Masr Station (the cost is 1.8 Egyptian pounds to 2.3 Egyptian pounds, or $4 to $5). Shared taxis take the same route, but they cost about $1 less. EgyptAir's flight from Cairo departs daily (the price is 11 Egyptian pounds).

The Egyptian Riviera

In the summer, Moslem Egyptians crowd Alexandria's beaches, where the temperature is an average 15 degrees cooler than in Cairo. The beaches are beautiful and the water clear, but Egypt's **Riviera** is crowded and cluttered. And remember, this is a Muslim beach, so don't wear a bikini or a daring swimsuit.

Corniche, the 15-mile road along the coast, is lined with houses, hotels, shops, and palm trees. At the eastern tip of Alexandria's stretch of beaches is the **Montaza Palace and Gardens,** a huge complex that includes gardens, beaches, and hotels. Just east of Montaza is **Ma'amura,** a cleaner, relatively isolated beach where the people have more Western tastes in swimwear. However, true beach lovers will best enjoy Egypt's beach resorts along the Sinai and Red Sea.

Dining in Alexandria

Alexandria has several excellent restaurants. **Morgan,** *El-Gueish Boulevard; tel. (20-3)61-184,* is an elegant seafood restaurant on the shore.

Lord's Inn, around the corner from the San Stefano Hotel, offers Continental cuisine in a gourmet setting.

For the best Pakistani food outside Pakistan, try **Tikka Grill,** located on the waterfront near the Abul Abaas Mosque.

Expensive by Egyptian standards, meals at Lord's Inn or Tikka Grill run 7 Egyptian pounds to 11 Egyptian pounds ($15 to $25) for two.

Santa Lucia, *40 Safia Zaghoul St.,* is a good French restaurant. **Restaurant Elite,** *43*

Safia Zaghoul St., has inexpensive pizza and strong espresso. Ignore the menu and opt for the daily specials, which are written on the wall.

Egypt's best seafood restaurant

For the best seafood in Egypt, drive to the small town of Abu Kir, about 10 miles east of Alexandria. Here, four blocks from the central mosque, is a famous restaurant called **Zephyrion,** *tel. (20-3)860758.* In business since 1929, Zephyrion has fresh fish, large salads, imported beer, and succulent shrimp.

Alexandria's best hotels

The best hotels in Alexandria are 25 Egyptian pounds to 39 Egyptian pounds ($55 to $85) a night. You won't have as great a choice as in Cairo, but you won't have to fight the crowds either.

Ramada Renaissance, *544 El Gueish St., Sidi Bishr; tel. (20-3)866-111,* has a pool, great views, and air conditioning. Double rooms are 30 Egyptian pounds to 34 Egyptian pounds ($67 to $75).

Two rival beachfront hotels are the **Sheraton Montazah,** *Corniche Road, El Montazah; tel. (20-3)969-220* (double rooms are 31 Egyptian pounds to 38 Egyptian pounds, or $68 to $84), and the **Palestine,** *Kasr El Montazah; tel. (20-3)861-799* (double rooms are 25 Egyptian pounds, or $55).

More modest accommodations can be had at **Alamein,** *Sidi Abdel Rahman; tel. (20-3)491-5476.* It's not on the beach, but a double room costs only 17 Egyptian pounds ($37). **Al Haram,** *tel. (20-3)964-574,* is in a nice old stone building. Rooms are 11 Egyptian pounds to 16 Egyptian pounds ($25 to $35) a night.

It isn't wise to stay too cheaply in Egypt; budget hotels must be chosen carefully. **Hotel Marhaba,** *10 Orabi Square; tel. (20-3)800-957,* is quiet and immaculate and charges only 3.6 Egyptian pounds ($8). Another cheap place is **Hotel Leroy,** *25 Talaat Harb St.; tel. (20-3)4833-439,* located on the top floors of an office building. Rooms are clean; some have breezy balconies. Double rooms are 4 Egyptian pounds ($9).

Sinai: the most unusual landscape

Four wars have been fought between Israel and Egypt on the **Sinai Peninsula.** As of 1967 it was Israeli territory, but the Sadat-Begin Treaty returned it to Egypt in 1982. You now can enter the southern Sinai Peninsula, which, with its high granite mountains and deep chasms, has some of the most unusual landscape in the world. It's also the site of two popular beaches and one of the most famous mountains in history.

The Sinai is heavily militarized. Police want you to keep to the main roads, but you can obtain permission to visit parts of the desert interior with a Bedouin guide (you might even catch a glimpse of military exercises). The Sinai heat can be unbearable, sometimes reaching 110 degrees Fahrenheit.

You can't make direct telephone calls in Sinai—you must go through the operator at **Al-Arish,** *tel. (20-68)0100.*

Buses are the most affordable way to get to the Sinai. They cost 2.3 Egyptian pounds to 7 Egyptian pounds ($5 to $15), and they depart Abassiya Station in Cairo for St. Catherine, Nuweiba, and Dahab. Most stop at Sharm El Sheikh, the southernmost town on the peninsula, where you won't find anything much to do or see.

A car allows you more flexibility when exploring the Sinai. The main roads are well-maintained, but the drive from Cairo to Nuweiba is a good seven hours—and you won't find anywhere to stop for gas or water.

Flying is fastest and easiest. **Air Sinai,** *15 Kasr El Nil St.; tel. (20-2)750663 or (20-2)760-948,* flies from Cairo to St. Catherine for 20 Egyptian pounds ($45) or to Sharm El Sheikh for 26 Egyptian pounds ($57).

Dahab: a golden town

When the Israelis occupied this town, they named it **Zahav** (Gold). It is split into two parts: a terrific beach and a Bedouin village of thatched huts and palm trees. The beach is never crowded and almost always sunny. In town you can rent scuba gear for exploring the coral reefs.

Villagers usually will allow you to stay with them in their huts for as little as 2.3 Egyptian pounds ($5). This is a great way to get to know the people and to experience firsthand their lifestyle. But remember, the huts have neither toilets nor running water, and Bedouins are superstitious about having their pictures taken.

More luxurious accommodations are available at the **Dahab Holiday Village,** where air-conditioned beachfront rooms cost 8 Egyptian pounds ($18) a night. The hotel restaurant serves dinner for about 1.36 Egyptian pounds ($3).

Nuweiba: the best beach

Nuweiba, a tourist village about 10 miles north of Dahab, has an even better beach. That's good, because this town doesn't have much else to offer, and the nearby Bedouin villages don't invite visitors. The bus to Nuweiba lets you off at the **tourist office,** *tel. (20-66)768-832.*

You can rent scuba gear or sailing equipment at the Sailing Club. The best reefs are along the southern part of Nuweiba's beach. For more secluded diving, walk a quarter-mile south to what the locals call the Stone House. Rental prices are good—for 10 Egyptian pounds ($22) you get gear, a boat dive, and a guide.

The best camel treks

Bedouins from Dahab run camel treks into the desert. If you bargain hard, 12 Egyptian pounds will get you a one-day journey to the oasis Wadi Gnay.

Mt. Sinai: the most commanding mountain

God gave Moses the Ten Commandments atop **Mt. Sinai,** a remote mountain in the Sinai Desert. A religious landmark, the mountain is dotted with tents and small chapels.

The most interesting and difficult route to the 7,000-foot peak that the Arabs call Gebal Musa is up the 3,500 **Steps of Repentance,** supposedly carved out by just one monk to fulfill his pledge of penitence. An easier way to reach the peak is to take the camel path that begins directly behind the monastery. When the path and steps meet, look down at the 500-year-old cypress tree that marks Elijah's Hollow, where the prophet Elijah heard the voice of God (there are now two chapels in the hollow). At the mountain's summit is a small church, usually surrounded by dozens of tourists and pilgrims in sleeping bags.

You, too, can bring a sleeping bag and sleep on the mountain (but remember—it gets chilly). When you awaken, you'll see both Africa and Asia from the peak.

More comfortable places to stay include the monastery's hostel (1.36 Egyptian pounds, or

$3, a cot) and **St. Catherine Salam,** *tel. (20-10)240-28-32,* a hotel in town with rooms for 8 Egyptian pounds ($17) and up. A national tourist office is located in this hotel.

A Byzantine best

At the base of Mt. Sinai is **St. Catherine's Monastery,** the oldest unrestored Byzantine complex in the world. Emperor Justinian had it built in 342 A.D. on the site of the Burning Bush, where God first recruited Moses to lead the Hebrews out of Egypt.

Fortress-like walls protect St. Catherine's Monastery (named after the saint martyred in Alexandria). Inside are jewel-studded crosses, hand-carved furniture, and the Chapel of the Burning Bush. The monastery's library contains enough early-Christian manuscripts to rival the Vatican, and the marvelous mosaic of the *Transfiguration of Christ* is one of the great treasures of early sacred painting. Don't miss the Ossary, a separate building containing the bones of all the monks who have died at St. Catherine's over the centuries.

The best snorkeling in the Middle East

The best snorkeling in the Middle East is at **Yemenieh Reef,** off Aqaba, a Jordanian town just across the gulf from Nuweiba. Here, you can see 40 kinds of coral not found anywhere else in the world. Scuba and skin divers commonly cross the gulf to Aqaba (captured from the Turks in 1917 by the legendary Lawrence of Arabia), which has beautiful beaches and an excellent aquarium in its Marine Research Center. Ferries depart daily from Nuweiba for Aqaba at 11 a.m. and 3 p.m. for 27 Egyptian pounds ($60) round trip. You'll need a passport, of course.

The **Nuweiba Holiday Village,** near the ferry terminal, has comfortable lodgings for 18 Egyptian pounds ($40). Farther south is a cheaper, nameless hotel that charges 11 Egyptian pounds ($25) for a double room. Next door is a set of bungalows, where you can stay for 1.8 Egyptian pounds ($4) per person (up to three people to a bungalow).

Hurghada: Egypt's best coral reefs

The sleepy little town of **Hurghada** is one of the best places in the world for unspoiled scuba and snorkeling expeditions. The coral reefs here are the most beautiful in Egypt, and dozens of boats are available to take you to any one of the tiny reef islands. At **Giftun El Saghir**, a small island off Hurghada, the water is so clear that you can see 100 feet down to the rocky bottom. At the offshore island of **Shaab Um Qamar,** divers sometimes catch lobsters at night with their bare hands.

Hurghada lies 240 miles south of Suez and about 350 miles from Cairo. It is separated from both by desert. **EgyptAir,** *tel. (20-62)407-88,* has daily flights out of Cairo for about 22 Egyptian pounds ($50). Or, if you don't mind an eight-hour bus ride, you can make reservations a day in advance for the bus that departs Himli Station in Cairo. The bus leaves at 7 a.m. and travels across to Suez and then down the coast to Hurghada. The trip costs about 6.8 Egyptian pounds ($15).

Everything in Hughada centers around two landmarks: **Al-Dhar Mosque** and **Ugly Mountain,** which is, indeed, ugly.

Hurghada is a good place to fish, teeming with barracuda, swordfish, sailfish, and tuna. You can rent bikes for a few dollars a day from a shop just north of Al-Dhar Mosque. And about two miles north of that is the Red Sea Museum, which has a large collection of sea life, including sharks and sea lions.

The most comfortable place to stay in Hurghada is the **Hurghada Sheraton,** *(800)325-3535,* which has air-conditioned double rooms for 18 Egyptian pounds to 32 Egyptian pounds ($40 to $70) a night.

What the cheaper places lack in air conditioning they make up in personality. At **Hurghada Happy House,** between Al-Dhar Mosque and the main avenue; *tel. (20-62)405-40,* Captain Muhammed Awad rents beds for .90 Egyptian pounds ($2) a night and tells the best fishing stories in town. For 1.4 Egyptian pounds ($3) more, the captain will take you on his boat to the House of Sharks, a reef pulsating with lionfish, sharks, eels, and other sea creatures.

Tips on baksheesh

Baksheesh is a way of life in Egypt. Although only a minority of Egyptians pester foreigners, those who do expect baksheesh for the slightest things—opening a door, for example—and even more baksheesh for doing nothing. In a bazaar, you will be followed by a half-dozen children with outstretched palms.

You always should travel with a pocketful of loose change and 1-pound notes. However, give baksheesh only for services rendered. In most cases, 25 piastres will do, but in rare instances, such as being shown a sight after hours, 1 Egyptian pound is proper.

Two useful terms concerning baksheesh are *"Shukran"* (Thanks) and *"Emshee!"* (Get lost!).

THE BEST
OF AFRICA

Africa is a continent of contrasts: snow-covered
mountains and harsh deserts; palm-shaded beaches and
impenetrable jungles; arid plains and rushing rivers and
waterfalls. Skeletons of the earliest identifiable human
beings were found here. And this is the land where
untamed wild beasts are still king: the lion, the leopard,
the hyena, the crocodile, and poisonous snakes. Here, too,
the primates live in the wild: the gorilla, the baboon, the
chimpanzee. Not to mention animal curiosities, such as
the giraffe, the rhinosaurus, the hippopotamus, the
elephant, and the zebra.

From the tall, thin, and noble Masai warriors in
Kenya to the diminutive pygmies of Burundi, Africans are
a hodgepodge of shapes and sizes. Literally thousands of
languages are spoken in Africa, and the number of
religions practiced is overwhelming.

The culture of Africa is mysterious, in part because
so little of it was written down before the Europeans and
Arabs brought writing skills to the area below the Sahara.
Storytellers were the keepers of tradition until that time.
And although writing did not develop (except in little-
known tribes scattered around the jungles of the west
coast), African culture was highly developed. Africans
have been skilled in metallurgy, sculpture, weaving, and
jewelry making for centuries.

However much they would like to, today's neo-
explorers cannot ignore the troubled nature of the African
countries by immersing themselves in the romance of the
land. Drought, poverty, inefficiency, hunger, corruption,
and political turbulence are characteristic of many African
nations, earning many of them (Mozambique, Chad,
Sudan, Mauritania, Angola, Burkina Faso, Ethiopia, and
Niger) the lowest ratings in the world in our Quality of
Life Index (see Section 1).

Chapter 20

THE BEST OF EAST AFRICA

T he east coast of Africa has the most beautiful and varied wildlife in the world. Kenya, Tanzania, and Zimbabwe are safari lands, where lions roam the plains and exotic animals can be spotted at watering holes. This section of Africa was settled by the British, making it an easy place for Americans to travel—English is generally spoken. You can even have tea if you tire of roughing it! Arabs influenced the coastal areas of East Africa, where women are veiled and mosques are more common than churches.

The world's best safaris

East Africa, one of the last strongholds of the lion, the elephant, the gorilla, and other exotic beasts, is the best place in the world to go on safari. Enormous national parks, where the great beasts roam freely, uninhibited by the progress of mankind, have been established throughout the region.

Kenya and Tanzania are the best countries for viewing wildlife. They offer comfortable accommodations and have mild climates with warm, sunny days and cool nights. Hunting is now banned in Kenya, but you can arrange a viewing safari through a travel agency. To avoid the rainy season, plan your safari for July through March.

Zambia and Zimbabwe are also good safari destinations; they are less known by Westerners and therefore less spoiled. Zambia is the only country where walking safaris are still common. And Zimbabwe is one of the few countries where hunting safaris are still in order.

Your first step when planning a safari should be to read up on the subject. William Collins Sons & Company, Ltd. of London publishes an excellent guide entitled *A Field Guide to the National Parks of East Africa*. Michael Tomkinson's *Kenya, A Holiday Guide* is available through Ernest Benn Ltd. of London. Both also are available in American travel bookstores.

The most accessible game park is **Masai Mara,** on the border between Kenya and Tanzania, in the Rift Valley. It has the largest diversity of game, rolling hills dotted with herds of elephants, antelopes, baboons, and lions. Masai tribespeople, who wear beautifully colored cloth garments, live here.

The Ngorogoro Crater and the Serengeti Plain in Tanzania have the largest concentrations of game in the world.

How to choose a safari

A myriad of tours are available in East Africa. The best visit the Masai Mara, the Serengeti Plain, Hwange National Park, the Ngong Hills, the Amboseli National park, the Athi Plain, and the Ngorongora Crater. The cost of a safari varies widely, so shop around.

The least expensive prearranged safaris leave from London. **Pinja Travel,** *tel. (44-1)499-7203,* offers a 10-day safari for £850 ($1,547), including air fare from London to Nairobi. **Holiday Planners,** *tel. (44-1)439-7755,* offers a 10-day safari to the Masai Mara and Amboseli National Park for £1,000 ($1,820), including air fare from London to Nairobi.

U.S. firms also offer safaris. **Saga Holidays,** *Boston, Massachusetts; (617)482-0085,* offers a 22-day safari for $2,500, including air fare. **Unitours,** *(312)782-1590,* has a 10-day safari for $825, land only; $1,332, including air fare from New York.

The cheapest safaris are arranged in Kenya. For less than $275 you can go on a five-day camping safari. You will travel in a Land Rover, sleep in a tent, and enjoy good food. Tour agents are located along the main streets of Nairobi. (Camping safaris are not always advertised, so you might have to ask for the information.)

Try **Atkin Tours & Travel Ltd.,** *IPS Building, Kimathi Street, P.O. Box 43987, Nairobi, Kenya; tel. (254-2)333669* or *(254-2)331667,* or **Inside Africa Safaris Ltd.,** *Lower Kabete Road, Westlands, P.O. Box 59767, Nairobi, Kenya; tel. (254-2)743413.*

One of the best Kenyan tours is the "Out of Africa Safari," which takes you to the estate of Baroness Karen Blixen (site of her book and the movie *Out of Africa,* which probably spearheaded the current tourist boom), the Athi Plain, and Masai Mara. The cost is $3,525 from the East Coast, $3,801 from the West Coast. Contact **Milt Griffith,** *61478 Longview St., Bend, Oregon; (503)388-3594.*

EcoSafaris Ltd., *146 Gloucester Road, London SW7 4SZ; tel. (44-1)370-5032,* arranges safaris designed to avoid the typical tourist destinations. The 17-day "Zambia Safari" includes walking tours of Luangwa Valley, which has the best unspoiled parks in Africa, as well as a visit to Victoria Falls. The price is £1,350, including air fare from London.

If you'd rather plan your own safari, compare prices and accommodations. Some hotels and tented camps cost more than $100 a night, while other accommodations can be as low as $3. Some are luxurious, with pools, restaurants, and waiters; others offer just the basics. If you're an independent soul, you can rent a vehicle on your own, which allows you the freedom to see what you want and to get closer to the animals. Game reserves hire out rangers for $1.25 a day.

Kenya: the most inviting country

Kenya's 225,000 square miles of mountains, plains, and coastline provide an extraordinary variety of terrain. This country is beautiful and—once you have arrived—inexpensive. Kenya is perhaps the most inviting country in Africa—it is English-speaking, politically stable, and easily accessible.

In Kenya, you can experience both the sophistication of the big city and the savage excitement of the bush country. The population of this nation defies generalization, composed of British colonial descendants, black Muslims with a Middle Eastern culture, Luo and Kikuyu farmers, Somali nomads, and tall, inscrutable Masai warriors. The majority of the population is Christian—but this general category comprises extreme Pentacostalism and mélanges of Christianity with indigenous religions as well as traditional Roman Catholicism and Episcopalianism.

Before a Kenyan football team will play a game, a witch doctor must be hired to set up fetishes around the goal posts to stop the opposing team from scoring any goals. In 1987, Kenyan courts were hearing a case involving a widow's suit against her brothers-in-law, who wanted to bury her late husband according to tribal ritual. Had they buried their brother under the Luo ritual, the dead man's property would have gone to the tribe—and not his family. Even among modern city families, the Kikuyu custom of female circumcision (excision of the woman's clitoris) is tolerated.

Swahili, the official language of Kenya, combines African grammar with Arabic words. Because it is the language of trade, you will hear it in the markets and on the streets of Kenya. However, English is spoken by government officials, bankers, and international businessmen.

Africa's metropolis: Nairobi

"Nairobi is the Paris of the East African coast," said Negley Farson in *Behind God's Back* (1940). The towers of the city shine in the hot noon sun and stand guard in the cool, fresh night air. The harsh contours of modern office buildings are camouflaged by cascades of bougainvillea, clumps of carnations, and banks of orchids. Residents harmonize with this tropical gaiety in brightly printed and tie-dyed garments.

Kenya's best museum

The **National Museum of Nairobi,** on Museum Hill in Snake Park, has the world's foremost collection of fossils of human evolution. The museum houses many of the archeological discoveries of the late Dr. Richard Leakey, as well as 184 watercolor paintings by Joy Adamson, author of *Born Free*. Children can enjoy a special "Please Touch" exhibit. Admission is $1.80 for adults, 60 cents for children. The museum is open daily from 9:30 a.m. to 6 p.m.

Snake Park also is of interest to nature enthusiasts, containing more than 200 species of snakes.

The best dancers

You can watch a troupe of 80 perform tribal dances in a life-size thatched village in the **Bomas** of Kenya. The Bomas are miniature replicas of Kenya's 40 tribal villages, located seven miles outside Nairobi on Langata Road. Craftsmen offer bargains on wood carvings. Admission is $3.60 for adults, $1.80 for children.

Kenya's best art gallery

Paintings, sculptures, batik, and photos by the best artists in Kenya and other African countries can be seen at **Gallery Watatu,** *Consolidated House, Standard Street; tel. (254-2)28737*. The gallery displays and sells works Mondays through Fridays from 9 a.m. to 5 p.m. and Saturdays from 9 a.m. until 12:30 p.m.

The best animal viewing

A visit to the Animal Orphanage in **Nairobi National Park** five miles outside town is a good preview to the wilderness safari. The orphanage is most famous for its lion and leopard cubs, which are as endearing as kittens—as long as they are tiny.

Nairobi's best shopping

In the center of Nairobi is the **Nairobi City Market,** where you can barter for animal carvings and usually come out ahead. The **African Heritage Shop,** *Kenyatta Avenue,* sells animal carvings, textiles, and jewelry. **Colpro Outfitters,** *Kenyatta Avenue,* is the place to go for safari gear.

The best way to send a message

At the **Thorn Tree Message Center** in Nairobi you can leave a message for anyone anywhere in the world for free. By the sidewalk café at the **New Stanley Hotel,** *Kenyatta Avenue,* is a thorn tree with bulletin boards affixed on four sides. You can fill out blank message forms with personal messages, advertisements, or announcements. The service is free.

Exotic meals in Nairobi

In this city, food is a bargain. Foods of all nationalities are served, as well as local specialties, such as *ugali,* a corn and bean dish, and *ino,* a mixture of seeds. The best place to try traditional Kenyan foods is **African Heritage Ltd.,** *Kenyatta Avenue and Muindi Mbingu Street.* Among the specialties served in the rear garden are grilled whole tilapia fish and roast lamb for $2.50 each; beef kabobs with salad are $2.75.

The best restaurant in town is **Carnivore,** where the specialty is—you guessed it—meat. You can try an unlimited amount of exotic skewered meats (anything from antelope to zebra) for $8.50.

The **Mt. Kenya Safari Club,** where a meal of pan-fried Nile perch, potatoes, and salad costs $5.50, is the most elegant place to dine.

Good Indian curry, made with African ingredients, can be found in restaurants throughout Kenya. Many of the Indians in Africa, who were imported by British colonialists as administrators, originally were Muslims, which is why the curries are made with beef (Hindus are not allowed to eat beef). Try Kenya colonial curry (which probably will be cooked by an African rather than an Indian, because many Indians emigrated to England after Kenya gained its independence). Curry is usually served with a proliferation of accompaniments: chutneys and fried and roasted breads as in India; bananas, coconut, mango, and other fruits; hot red pepper sauce; peanuts; and even soy sauce.

The best revolution

The revolving restaurant at the top of the **Kenyatta Conference Center** (the highest building in Nairobi) has a spectacular view of the city, particularly at sunset.

The best Java

Kenya produces the best coffee in the world and is one of the world's leading exporters of Arabica coffee. The **Coffee Board of Kenya,** *Mama Ngina Street,* serves the most tempting coffee in town, as well as light snacks. Coffee, *mandazi* (fried dough), and *samosa* (meat pie in the Indian fashion as interpreted by Kenyan cooks) is only 20 cents.

Coffee was introduced to Kenya by the French Holy Ghost Fathers (who liked a good cup of coffee) in the 1890s. It was developed in the region north of Nairobi. African farmers were forbidden to grow coffee until 1954. It is now Kenya's main export crop (which causes problems when the coffee crop fails). The berries are hand-picked twice a year.

The second-leading export crop is tea—another crop that was not allowed to African growers. Today, the region around Limuru supports more than 100,000 African small-holders, who grow enough tea to make Kenya the third-largest producer in the world, after India and Sri Lanka. Kenya has 61 tea factories, where tea is dried and processed. Unlike coffee, tea is a slow crop and produces leaves ready for picking only 3 1/2 years after planting.

Nairobi's best beds

Nairobi's best hotel is a remnant of the colonial days called the **Norfolk,** *Harry Thuku Road, P.O. Box 40065; tel. (254-2)335422.* It is a Kenyan version of the famous Singapore Raffles Hotel, with individual bungalows in a tropical formal garden. Double rooms are 584 schillings to 654 schillings.

Another good place to stay—if you can get invited—is the private **Muthaiga Club,** whose members can arrange accommodations for their friends.

In general, accommodations in Kenya are expensive, but you can find lodgings at reasonable rates if you look hard enough. The InterContinental's **Nairobi Hotel,** *Uhuru Highway, P.O. Box 30353, City Hall Way; tel. (254-2)33-55-50,* charges about $65 for a double room; the **Mt. Kenya Safari Club** charges $65 for a double room; and (if you can stand the name) the **Hotel Comfy** can put you up in a double room for $23.

The least expensive place to stay is the **Hotel Ambassader,** *Moi Avenue, P.O. Box 30399; tel. (254-2)336803,* which provides bed and breakfast for two for about $36. The hotel also has a fine Indian restaurant called Safeer.

The loveliest drive from Nairobi

If you have the time and money to rent a car, you should strike out from Nairobi to see the region's most important sights comfortably and at your own pace. Here is an itinerary recommended by an old Kenya hand. Drive three hours north of Nairobi to **Nanyuki,** stopping along the way to see the grave of Lord Baden Powell, founder of the Boy Scouts, in Nyerere. On his tomb is a circle with a dot in the middle, the scout symbol for "gone home."

Nanyuki is situated 8,000 feet high on the slope of snow-topped Mt. Kenya, which sits smack on the equator. Once you have become acclimated to the altitude, you will find this an ideal base for observing Kenya's wildlife.

Try to stay at the **Sportsman Arm's Club** or the **Mwingo Gate Hotel** (formerly the Safari Club). Visit Africa's most exciting racetrack.

From here head north to **Archer's Post,** a spring in the middle of the desert. If you are traveling independently, this is the last spot in the Northern Frontier District you may visit— beyond this point, the road is closed (to keep tourists from wandering into the desert and getting into trouble).

However, if an organized trip is available, join it, and continue north to **Marsabit,** a tree-covered mountain in the middle of the Kaisul Desert, where game animals come to drink during the dry season.

Backtrack to Nanyuki, then take the road to **Nakuru,** which runs along the edge of the Rift Valley. You will see flamingoes, mountains, and the plain. This is where early traces of man were discovered.

En route to Nakuru, stop at **Nyahururu Waterfall** (formerly called Thomson's Fall). Stay at the **Thomson's Fall Lodge,** a bit of old England, where you can take English tea on the lawn while watching the water course down. A few miles away is the courthouse where Jomo Kenyatta, leader of the independence movement, was tried.

A birdwatchers' best

Lake Nakuru Park, 100 miles northwest of Nairobi, is the habitat of more species of birds than all the British Isles. It attracts millions of pink flamingos. **Lake Naivasha Hotel,** *Blocks Hotels, P.O. Box 47557; tel. (254-2)335807,* is a collection of cottages on the lakeshore with private verandas overlooking the water.

The best of Kenya's beaches

Kenya has 300 miles of glorious beaches along the Indian Ocean. The Swahili, a people of Arab and African ancestry and culture, live along the coast and for centuries have been astute traders.

The white sand beaches are protected from pollution and sharks by reefs and are edged with palms. Beyond the palm trees is the forest, inhabited by leopards, Colobus monkeys, and brightly colored birds.

Mombasa: the gateway

Mombasa, the gateway to the coast, is Kenya's second-largest city, combining African, Indian, and Arab cultures. Its narrow side streets, impassable by car, are lined with houses that have deeply carved wooden doors and latticed balconies, as well as Indian temples and bazaars. Curry scents the air, and Muslim women walk the streets veiled in black *buibuis.*

While in Mombasa, stay at the **Castle** in the old town or the **Outrigger** by the yacht club. To make reservations, contact **Alliance Hotels,** *College House, University Way, P.O. Box 49839, Nairobi, Kenya; tel. (254-2)33-75-01.*

Not far from town is a different world, a string of modern oceanfront hotels with swimming pools and top-notch restaurants. An eight-mile ribbon of tropical beach at **Diani** draws many visitors.

The best way to get to the beach

Although it is possible to fly to **Mombasa,** the gateway to Kenya's gorgeous coastline, via Kenya Airways, old-timers prefer to take the overnight train from Nairobi. This train offers a well-served meal, a private sleeper, and a porter who wakes you up at 6:30 a.m. with a delicious cup of locally grown tea or coffee.

Malindi: a beachy best

Malindi, an island 74 miles north of Mombasa, is known for its modern hotels, lively nightclubs, and ocean sports, including big-game fishing, sailing, waterskiing, skin and scuba diving, and underwater photography. It also has a half-dozen nature preserves; the Malindi Marine National Park, where you can see technicolor fish, the moray eel, and octopus; and the ruins of Gedi, an abandoned Islamic settlement in a thick tropical inland forest.

The best hotel in Malindi is **Lawford's,** *P.O. Box 20, Malindi, Kenya; tel. (254-123)6157,* which has two restaurants and two swimming pools.

Flying to Malindi is the recommended way to go—taxis are expensive and buses are interminably slow.

The least developed islands

From Malindi, you can take a boat to the out islands of **Manda, Kiwayuu,** and **Pate.** Pate

Town can be reached only if the tide is right. Faza and Siyu, also on Pate Island, are more accessible.

The out islands are sparsely developed. Suggested hotels are the **Ras Kitau Beach Hotel** on Manda and the **Kiwayuu Island Lodge** on Kiwayuu.

The most exotic island

The island of **Lamu** is a perfectly preserved 18th-century Swahili town, where men and women still wear the traditional dress—the women are veiled, and the men wear *kofia,* little white embroidered caps. Lamu's artistic triumphs are its intricately carved wooden doors.

Don't expect to tour Lamu by car. The only car in town is reserved for use by the government representative. A good alternative is a dhow tour of the coast.

The islanders are obviously Islamic. The island has outdoor Koran schools and 29 mosques. People may not be photographed, because photography is a violation of the Orthodox Muslim religious injunction against graven images, but objects, such as the intricate plasterwork and courtyards of the city's grand mansions, may.

Africa's deepest valley

The **Rift Valley,** a geological fault that originates in Syria and runs to South Africa, is best seen in Kenya. Sheer cliffs several thousand feet high rise above the valley floor, which is 50 miles wide in places. Changes in climate and topography when descending the valley slopes are abrupt. Coffee plantations are everywhere. Large herds of relatively tame animals graze along the valley's edges.

Kenya's best watering holes

Throughout Kenya, comfortable (luxurious, in some cases) lodges have been built near the watering holes where animals come to slake their thirst. They are a good alternative to the more stressful safari, eliminating the strain and sweat of an uncomfortable ride across rough terrain. The most important piece of equipment to have at a watering hole is a pair of binoculars. At these lodges, you can sit back and watch elephants, lions, hippos, and monkeys as you sip a gin and tonic.

The best watering hole is **Kilaguni,** 200 miles south of Nairobi in the giant Tsavo National Park. Animals can be viewed day and night, game drives and walks around Mzima Springs are available, and camping facilities are available for true adventurers.

Kilguni Lodge, *P.O. Box 30471, Mtito Andei, Kenya,* has a swimming pool, safari vehicles, and a restaurant and bar that overlook the watering hole. A double room and full board are $93.

The most famous of the watering holes is the original: **Treetops,** *P.O. Box 23, Nyeri,* which is 80 miles north of Nairobi in the Aberdares Mountains. You climb (slowly if need be) to cedarwood huts, where you are welcomed by servants, who look after you, and by baboons, who will pester you if you don't shut the window. As night falls, wild animals visit the watering hole below. The scene is periodically flood lit.

This tame version of safari was being taken by then Princess Elizabeth and her husband when her father died and she became queen—which is one reason Treetops is so famous.

At Treetops you can view elephants, lions, and antelopes from the bar, dining room, or terrace. Treetops is Kenya's most expensive watering hole, charging $149 per person, including full board.

The **Ark,** *P.O. Box 59749, Nairobi,* near Treetops, has comparable food and accommodations, but is much cheaper—$113 per person, including full board. A tunnel here leads you to a hide next to the watering hole.

The best place to see the black leopard

According to our Africa hand, the best place for game viewing is **Nanyuki** (an expensive, luxurious lodge built by actor William Holden in Mt. Kenya National Park). The second-best spot is **Aberdare National Park,** which passes through the central highlands of Kenya. It is the least settled, least accessible, and loveliest of Kenya's parks. Here you can see the black leopard and its favorite prey, the black serval (a wild black hog).

The best job opportunity for Americans

If you are an American college graduate, you are eligible to teach in Kenya. The **Harvard WorldTeach program,** *Phillips Brooks House, Harvard University, Cambridge, MA 02138; (617)495-5527,* offers high school teaching assignments for a minimum of one year. You don't need any teaching experience or knowledge of Swahili (English is widely spoken). Small salaries cover daily expenses, and housing is provided. A fee of $3,100 includes air fare, health insurance, and training.

Africa's peak experiences

Kenya has the most spectacular mountain peaks in Africa: **Mt. Kilimanjaro** and **Mt. Kenya** (also called Nyandarua by the Kikuyu). The eternal snows of these equatorial peaks seem like the stuff of legend, even after you climb them.

Mt. Kilimanjaro, the more challenging of the two, can be climbed from either the Tanzanian or the Kenyan side of the border. The **Uhuru Peak** (20,000 feet) can give climbers quite a rush of success.

Tourist agencies in Tanzania organize climbs of the mountain. The least expensive package is offered by the YMCA ($200 per person). Each group of hikers has its own A-frame hut and cook, but several groups share a large dining hall. You can hire a guide for $150 and rent boots and warm clothing at the park gate. No climbing is allowed during the rainy season (April and May).

In the language of the Masai, who live in its shadow, Kilimanjaro means White Mountain. The Masai climb only to an altitude of 10,000 feet, where the air gets thin. It's another 9,340 feet from there to the top. The climb to the peak can be done, thanks to an easy trail, encouraging Tanzanian guides, and comfortable Norwegian huts.

The standard hike to the top takes five days. From the park entrance at 6,000 feet, the first day's hike is along a gently rising trail for three to four hours until you reach Mandara Hut. Tropical forest animals inhabit this lower altitude.

After five to seven hours of walking, you come to Horombo Hut at 12,000 feet. It has one notable difference from the first hut: the view of the snow-capped Kibo Peak above and the ocean of clouds washing the base of the mountains below.

The third day demands a climb to 14,000 feet over a stream marked "Last Water" and across wind-blown dusty terrain. It takes another three hours to climb to 15,600 feet, where the cold, dark, and uncomfortable Kibo Hut awaits.

By tradition, you must reach the mountaintop in time to see the sunrise. So at 1 a.m. you will be awakened to trudge to Uhuru Peak. You will feel nauseous, lethargic, and sore. But when you see the sunrise from the mountain's peak, it will all seem worthwhile.

Mt. Kenya, a snow-covered peak on the equator, is more scenic and easier to climb than Mt. Kilimanjaro, due to the lower altitude (17,000 feet). Both are volcanoes, but unlike its southern neighbor, Mt. Kenya's fires have long been extinct. The two highest peaks—Batian at 17,058 and Nelion at 17,022 feet—are named after 19th-century Kenyan medicine men. They stand like huge black tombstones and are the domains of technical climbers of rock and ice. The average climber takes an easier route to Mt. Lenana at 16,355 feet.

From the entrance gate at 9,500 feet, another 500-foot ascent brings you to the hut at Met Station Lodge, where a troop of Sykes monkeys entertains.

Before passing the tree line the next morning, you might see black and white Colobus monkeys flinging themselves madly through the trees overhead. At an area called the Vertical Bog, from 11,000 to 13,000 feet, the serpentine trail is covered with soggy peat. This trail leads eventually to the foot of the glacier.

You sleep in the Kami Hut, made of corrugated iron, until 4 a.m., when you begin the trek across ice-coated boulders using flashlights to light the way. A guide is essential to chop steps with an ice ax. By dawn, you will reach the top.

Hikes of Mt. Kenya must be arranged through the **Naro Moru River Lodge,** *P.O. Box 18, Naro Moru, Kenya; tel. (254-Naro Moru)23.* Three- to seven-day trips can be arranged for $50 per person, per day. At the lodge, you can rent any equipment you will need.

Tanzania: the best of the wild

Tanzania is Kenya's southern neighbor. This country is the result of the fusion of the offshore island of Zanzibar, once an Arab stronghold, and the mainland (called Tanganyika in colonial days), inhabited by the Bantu and other African ethnic groups. The political unrest this fusion created was complicated by the country's adoption of Ujamaa, a form of socialism promoted by President Julius Nyerere. Tanzania is still suffering economic woes from its turbulent past; the country is desperately poor, hungry for tourism, and cheap.

Because it is so inexpensive (guides can be hired for $1.25 a day), Tanzania is beginning to draw tourists to its enormous game parks. This is really the place to go to see things in the wild. The famous **Serengeti Plain,** where you can witness spring wildlife migration every year, has the largest concentration of game in the world.

Seronera Wildlife Lodge, *P.O. Box 3100, Arusha, Tanzania,* in the center of the park, has an airstrip and a swimming pool carved from natural rock. **Lobo Wildlife Lodge,** *P.O. Box 3100, Arusha, Tanzania,* is an entire building carved from natural rock.

One of the undiscovered wonders of Tanzania is **Selous,** the largest game reserve in the world. This unspoiled, undeveloped wilderness is populated by more than one-million animals, including Africa's greatest elephant and lion populations. Despite their numbers, the animals here are less visible to visitors than in other parks, because of the immense area of the reserve.

Luxury accommodations are available in Selous at **Mbuyu Safari Camp,** *Bushtrekker Safaris, P.O. Box 5380, Dar es Salaam,* a hotel constructed around a baobab tree.

Be cautious when visiting **Dar es Salaam,** Tanzania's capital, a city rife with criminals who prey on tourists.

And before you enter Tanzania, ask government officials for exact information on how much currency you must exchange. The rules are complicated and strict. The black market exchange rate in Tanzania is much higher than the official rate.

Zimbabwe: best hunting, best waterfall

Zimbabwe (formerly Rhodesia) is the best place to go on a hunting safari (you must have a hunting license). Peaceable safaris are also offered.

Victoria Falls, located on the border with Zambia, is more than a mile wide. The **Zambezi River** falls 300 feet here, creating a spray visible for miles. Spectacular rainbows arc over the cliffs.

Rwanda: the best place to observe gorillas

Perched high in the Rift Valley Mountains west of Tanzania, tiny landlocked **Rwanda** is the best place in the world to see mountain gorillas.

To visit the heart of gorilla country, you must hike through dense bamboo forests to an altitude of 10,000 feet. Professional guides lead small groups and carry rifles to protect against wild buffalo, elephants, stray leopards, and poachers.

The hour-long trek begins easily, taking you through fields of flowers and potatoes before entering the forest, where the trail becomes steep, narrow, and slippery. Just when you're out of breath, the path ambles across flat mountain meadows—but not for long before making another jungle climb.

It takes a while to find the gorillas. They roam over a wide area and move more easily than humans through the dense vegetation—their physiques are better suited to bending and swinging than ours.

When the guide sights a troop of gorillas, he motions the group to hurry forward quietly. You can hear the gorillas snorting and cracking the vegetation beneath them. The guide makes low vocalizations to assure the gorillas' leader that the troop is in no danger, then he decides if the great apes seem willing to allow visitors. If so, you can crouch silently within feet of the primates for about 60 minutes. You are warned not to stare at the 500-pound creatures; they interpret this as a sign of aggression. In the unlikely event of an attack, the best defense is no defense—just lie flat.

The best ways to travel

Direct flights from Belgium, France, and Kenya are available to **Kigali,** the capital of Rwanda. There, you can rent a car or take an inexpensive but crowded bus to the gorillas' habitat, **Virunga Volcanoes National Park.** The most picturesque town to stay in is **Gisenyi,** which is on Lake Kivu, an hour's drive from the park.

To minimize disturbance to the gorillas' habitat, tour groups are restricted to six people. You can book tours through the Rwandan Office of Tourism and National Parks in Kigali, and there is a 10- to 20-day waiting list. You also can book a half-day or two-day tour from the United States with Jim Papineau, **Hotel Meridian,** *Chicago, Illinois.*

The cost is approximately $80 per person, not including the customary 10% tip to porters. Bring your own food, water, and camping equipment from Kigali.

With fewer than 250 of these gorillas in the wild, they are listed as an endangered species. Because gorillas are susceptible to human diseases, a visitor with even a bad cold may not be allowed to visit the troop. Children under 15 may not participate.

The Seychelles: paradise found

Some say the **Seychelles**—an island country 1,000 miles east of Kenya in the Indian

Ocean—were once the Garden of Eden. The Seychelles are some of the least spoiled islands on earth, because of the government's strict environmental guidelines. Tall palms line these sandy beaches, which stretch along the pale-blue Indian Ocean. The people are an exotic mixture of African, Arab, French, British, Indian, and Chinese.

Ninety percent of all Seychellese live on the island of **Mahé.** The high mountain peaks at **Morne Seychellois National Park,** in the center of the island, offer views of the other islands.

Authors Somerset Maugham, Ian Fleming, Alec Waugh, and Noel Coward have been lured by the beauty of the Seychelles, especially Mahé. Most of them stayed at the **Northolme Hotel,** *Mahé, Glacis, P.O. Box 333.* The original hotel building is no longer in use, but guests can visit it and see the rooms labeled with names of former guests. Today's visitors are housed in a new building patterned in the old style but equipped with modern conveniences. The Northolme has a good French and Creole restaurant. A double room is RP995.

Another hotel on Mahé is the **Coral Beach,** *Beau Vallon Beach.* This bed and breakfast has double rooms for RP770.

The second-largest island of the Seychelles, **Praslin,** is home to the rare black bulbul parrot and the Coco-de-Mer palm, which produces a large double coconut shaped somewhat like a woman's derriere and said to have special fertility powers. **Vallée de Mai** on Praslin is the best place to glimpse rare birds and see the Coco-de-Mer, and **Anse Lazio** is the Seychelles' most spectacular beach. **Baie des Chevaliers** is more secluded and can be reached by boat or airplane (Air Seychelles charges RP270 round trip).

The best place to stay on Praslin is **Maison des Palmes,** a guesthouse on Grande Anse beach with individual cottages that have private baths and terraces. Twin rooms are RP410 a night, including breakfast.

The forests of **Silhouette Island** contain plants and animals found nowhere else in the world. And the island's beaches are ideal for swimming and snorkling. The 250 islanders raise cattle, goats, coconuts, sugarcane, cinnamon, vanilla, and fruit. The island has no roads, only paths. The **Silhoutte Island Lodge,** *P.O. Box 608, Victoria,* which has thatched bungalows from RP860 to RP1,180, is a good place to stay.

The most picturesque and expensive of the Seychelles is the coral **Denis Island,** only 30 minutes by plane from Mahé (Air Seychelles charges RP990). You can stay in thatched cottages by the sea at **Denis Island Lodge,** *P.O. Box 404, Denis Island,* for RP1,355 to RP1,500. Creole food is served at the buffet.

Banyan trees surround the **Plantation House** on **Fregate Island,** *P.O. Box 459, Fregate.* Double rooms at this colonial inn near an orchard and a beach are RP500, including meals.

The least developed of the inhabited Seychelles is **La Digue,** with no cars but plenty of bicycles. Enormous boulders and tall palms edge the surf. And 30 pairs of rare paradise flycatchers live in the Indian almond trees. If you like to snorkel or scuba dive, contact **Gregoire's Watersports,** *Gregoire's Island Lodge, La Digue.* You can stay at **La Digue Island Lodge,** *Anse Lou Reunion, La Digue,* right on the beach, for RP900 to RP995, including full board.

Cousin, Bird, and **Aride** islands draw flocks of rare birds. More than a million sooty terns nest on Bird Island from May to November every year. The endangered bush warbler lives on Cousin. Aride is home to the world's largest colonies of lesser noddy and roseate terns.

Bird Island Lodge, *P.O. Box 404,* has cottages with private baths and terraces for $150 per day, including English breakfast, Creole lunch, and European dinner.

Chapter 21

THE BEST OF WEST AFRICA

W hile East Africa is the best place in the world for animal watching, West Africa is the best place for people watching. Much of West Africa was colonized by the French, who left behind their language, their affection for stylish clothing and good food, and a dash of their culture. West Africa is a land of beautiful women dressed in vibrant colors and coiffed with multicolored bandannas. The food is a spicy combination of French and African. And the wood carvings and handicrafts are superb.

Before you begin your travels through Africa, prepare yourself for an astonishing level of corruption. (The local term for bribes is dash.)

Senegal: a French holiday favorite

Senegal is a paradise of European sun seekers, who make up the majority of visitors to this West African country. Americans have yet to discover Senegal, although it is the African country geographically closest to the United States, a mere 6 1/2-hour flight from New York. The Senegalese government is working to attract more American visitors by expanding the recently denationalized tourist industry.

Senegal offers 350 miles of beach, two national game parks (open seasonally), a bird reserve, sailing, and fishing—as well as history and a pleasant climate (for West Africa). Because it juts out into the Atlantic, the country is wafted by pleasant breezes, and the heat is less unpleasant than in neighboring countries.

Senegal's Dance Troupe is world-acclaimed, and the local handicrafts are beautiful: precious jewelry crafted by hand; printed and woven fabrics; and snakeskin and crocodile leather goods.

The three negative aspects of this African country are the panhandlers, the dangerous ocean currents, and the unpleasant creatures of the surf, including sharks and jellyfish.

Dakar: the Paris of Africa

Several cities claim to be the Paris of Africa, but **Dakar** best fits the description. Good restaurants and outdoor cafés can be found throughout the French-speaking capital. The architecture shows signs of French influences, including wrought-iron balconies and little courtyards. But mosques also punctuate the cityscape, and little dirt streets weave between the grand boulevards.

The best of Senegalese art

The best place to see the art of Senegal is the **Musée d'Art Nègre-Africain** (African Art Museum), *place Tascher; tel. (221)21-40-15*. The entire first floor of this museum is devoted to Senegalese culture, displaying clothing, furniture, jewels, costumes, and instruments. The museum is open Tuesdays through Sundays from 8 a.m. to noon and 2 p.m. to 6 p.m. and Mondays from 8 a.m. to noon.

Local galleries also exhibit the works of contemporary Senegalese artists. The best is **Galerie 39,** *avenue Pompidou,* which displays paintings, drawings, and textile work.

The most important monuments

Dakar's two greatest architectural monuments are its cathedral and the Grand Mosque. The **cathedral,** *boulevard de la République and avenue du Président Lamine Gueye,* is one of the finest examples of Senegalese architecture. The **Grand Mosque,** *Allée Coursin,* is one of the largest mosques in Africa (you must be content to view it from outside, because visitors are not permitted to enter).

An international shopping experience

Dakar is filled with fascinating markets that combine African, Arab, and European traditions. The one drawback is that all the city's markets are expensive.

The most colorful market is **Sandaga,** an enormous place covering several city blocks with little stalls selling everything from fruit and meat to cloth and sandals. This is where the locals shop—it is about as authentic as you'll get. Another typical market is **Marché de Tilène,** *avenue Blaise Diagne.*

Local designers create garments decorated with batik and embroidery, then sell their clothing in boutiques throughout the city. Recommended boutiques include **Fara,** *rues Assane N'Doye and Wagane Dioul,* and **Deco Shop,** *rues Carnot and Blanchot.*

Marché Kermel, *near place de l'Indépendence,* is Dakar's European-style market, where you can buy high-quality imported goods, as well as clothing and souvenirs. Haggling is not recommended here. The market is open daily until 1 p.m.

The **Mauritanian Silver Market,** *69 ave. Blaise Diagne,* is a good place to go for jewelry. In addition to silver, filigree work in gold also is available. Although it is quite expensive, gold in Senegal is 22 karat or finer, making the quality superior to what is commonly sold in the United States.

Caritas Tissage Traditionnel, *Route de Ouakam,* is a weavers' workshop that sells belts, bedspreads, purses, and clothing. Prices are reasonable. Again, haggling is not recommended.

The best digs in Dakar

Novotel Dakar, *avenue Sarraut, B.P. 2973; tel. (221)23-10-90,* which belongs to the French Novotel chain, boasts two restaurants, two bars, a swimming pool, and tennis courts.

La Croix du Sud, *20 ave. Albert Sarraut; tel. (221)21-29-27,* has a view of the flower market.

Dakar's best cuisine

Senegalese food tends to be spicy, often garnished with *sauce piment* (hot pepper sauce). Most entrées consist of rice combined with meats and sauces. French cuisine is also available in Dakar. Because alcohol is forbidden to Muslims, only non-alcoholic beverages—mostly teas—are served in restaurants.

La Région du Fleuve, *15 rue A. Le Dantec; tel. (221)21-29-14,* operated by a French-woman and her African husband, is decorated with African masks and textiles and serves African fare. Meals are inexpensive. The restaurant is closed Wednesdays.

La Croix du Sud, *20 ave. Albert Sarraut; tel. (221)21-02-73,* is an elegant but expensive French restaurant. All produce for the meals is imported from France. The restaurant is closed Sundays.

Candi, *avenue Roume,* is Dakar's most inviting café, serving baked goods, ice cream, crêpes, omelets, and quiches.

The best entertainment in Dakar

The Senegalese National Theater Company and the Mudra Dance Group, in addition to many other groups, appear at the **Sorano** (the National Theater), *Daniel Sorano Building, boulevard de la République; tel. (221)21-31-04.*

For authentic Senegalese popular and folk music, spend an evening at **Les Toundes** (The Caves) nightclub.

The darkest history

Just 20 minutes from Dakar is the Island of **Gorée,** once the most important transit center for slave traders, who bought Africans for shipment to America. It was from this appalling place that hundreds of thousands of shackled prisoners were loaded onto ships for the so-called Middle Crossing. The first crossing carried rum from the American colonies to Africa to pay for black gold; the final crossing was of sugar to New England to make rum. A small museum on the island has chilling displays of shackles, chains, and other unpleasant instruments of the trade.

Senegal's best beach

Cap Skirring in Joal is an unspoiled, dazzling white beach fringed by coconut trees. **Club Med,** *tel. (221)91-10-43,* has a highly recommended outpost here. Watch out for sharks (not just the human kind).

The least expensive place to stay is **le Campement,** a government-run accommodation made up of little concrete huts on the water. For a few dollars you can spend the night on foam pads under clean sheets and enjoy good local food.

The best seashells

The **Island of Fadiouth,** 60 miles from Dakar, is so covered with seashells that the populace uses them as building material. Everything here is made of shells: a cemetery, a church, granaries built on stilts. Natives follow a traditional, self-sufficient, African lifestyle, making their own cloth and growing their own food. You can reach the island from the mainland region of Joal via the wooden bridge or in a pirogue (a wooden canoe).

The best place to view game

Basse Casamance, a 12,350-acre game park near Ziguinchor in southeast Senegal, has thick forests inhabited by 52 species of mammals and 172 species of birds. You can visit on guided boat or car tours. A limited number of guests can spend the night in the park at Impluvium Lodge, where light meals and drinks are served.

The best bird sanctuary

One of the most important bird sanctuaries in the world is the 25,000-acre **Djoudj Park,** in the Saloum Delta, where you can see 180 species, including pelicans, herons, flamingos, and egrets. You can observe from a miradour without scaring the birds away.

Mauritanian Blue People camp on the edge of the park from time to time, providing a rare opportunity to see these Berbers.

You, too, can camp here, in the Campement de Djoudj, which provides inexpensive huts without air conditioning.

The best duck hunting

Less benevolent bird watchers prefer **Maka Diama** (150 miles north of Dakar), a paradise for duck hunters, who from Dec. 15 to April 15 are licensed to shoot here. In addition to ducks, bags include fancolin, guineafowl, hare, and quail.

Togo: a microcosm of Africa

Togo, a small west coast country, is sub-Saharan Africa in miniature, with plains alive with game; plantations fertile with crops of cocoa and coffee; and mud-brick villages where the old traditions remain unchanged.

Originally a German protectorate, and then a French colony, Togo is now an independent country. **Lomé,** the capital, offers a wide choice of restaurants, and the coast offers idyllic beaches.

In Lomé, women hold powerful economic and political positions, and every village has a women's union. Powerful Nana Benz—matronly merchants—wield considerable force in the politics of this country (and have overthrown at least one government). They sell everything imaginable in the marketplace—from a fully equipped Mercedes Benz to a pair of plastic slippers. Many of the older Nana Benz are illiterate—but they can calculate their margins and execute foreign-exchange transactions in their heads. Although the language of Togo is officially French, the people also can converse in Pidgin English.

Where to go in Togo

The best way to get a taste of native life in Togo is to visit **Le Grand Marché** in the center of Lomé, where the smells of roasting meats and tangy spices permeate the air and tie-dyed caftans and printed pagnes are sold. These colorful swaths of cloth are used to make the dresses, shirts, and headdresses worn by West Africans, but they also can be used as unique tablecloths, draperies, or sheets back home. Look for the textiles on the second floor of the market.

For an in-depth look at Togo's culture, visit the **National Museum,** housed in the headquarters of Togo's only political party, the Rassemblement du Peuple Togolais (R.P.T.), a building decorated with reliefs sculpted by a leading Togolese artist. Museum exhibits include shells (which were formerly used as currency), pottery, musical instruments, and ceremonial relics. Admission is free.

The **Kloo Craft Center** attracts the best of the country's traditional wood carvers. The center also has a selection of macramé, batik, fiber, and clay works.

The best place to settle a score

Voodoo is practiced in **Bé,** a residential area on the east side of Lomé. At **Bé Market,** near the Hotel de la Paix, you can buy unusual charms—bones, little figurines, skulls—from both pagans and Muslims. The charms are said to bring success or money, to defeat a rival in love, or to attract a lover.

Togo's most interesting village

Deep in the **Tamberma Valley** live the Tamberma people, who continue a lifestyle unchanged by the passage of time. Famous for their masonry, they live in cool *tata* dwellings constructed by hand from clay and wood. The houses are situated in a compound that is surrounded by a circle of conical towers connected by a wall. The towers are used primarily to store grain.

The Tamberma spend most of their time outdoors on patios—they even do their cooking outdoors. They wear little clothing and smoke long pipes. The women are marked by scars in intricate patterns; they are tattooed when they are eight-days-old to protect against miscarriages and stillbirths.

The best hotels in Togo

The best hotel in Togo is the **Hotel du 2 Fevrier,** *B.P. 131, Lomé,* which rivals any posh American hotel. The 36 stories of this glass building include two restaurants, two bars, a nightclub, and a casino. Double rooms are $66.

Hotel Sarakawa is a favorite of the French, a five-star hotel with restaurants, a disco, and recreational facilities. Double rooms are $50 a day; suites are $75.

Less expensive is the **Hotel Benin,** where double rooms are $30 to $35. This hotel is Togo's training ground for restaurant personnel—the dining room serves fine cuisine for low prices.

Nigeria: the most populated African country

Don't spend much time in Nigeria's capital, **Lagos.** It is an appalling place. Built on a lagoon, the city has a mushrooming population, but it lacks the infrastructure to deal with it. Roads, sewage, garbage collection, and water are all becoming problems. The results are a perpetual traffic jam and generally unpleasant conditions. Telephones seldom work, and electricity is erratic. Most of the Westerners in Lagos are diplomats and businessmen, who leave for the country as quickly and as often as they can.

In the days of high oil prices, Lagos was the most expensive city in Africa; now it is cheap—the one point in its favor. Cars and airplane tickets, however, have become more expensive (this is helping to lessen the congestion on the highways and at the airport).

Lagos has some good restaurants. Dinner at one of the nicer restaurants is about 120 Naira per person. Recommended are **Antoine,** *61 Broad St.,* which serves continental food; **Bagatelle,** *208/212 Broad St.,* which serves Lebanese and continental cuisine; and **La Brasserie,** *Adetokunbo, Ademola Street, Victoria Island,* which serves Indian food upstairs, continental downstairs.

Federal Palace Hotel, *Victoria Island; tel. (234-1)610030,* is the best place to stay. It has a good restaurant/nightclub called the Atlantic that serves Italian food.

Nigeria has much more attractive cities, notably Ife, Ibaden, Jos, Onitsha, and Kano. And a new capital is being built in Abuja, which is roughly the geographic center of the country.

Kano: the best place to explore Islamic history

In the Old City of **Kano,** an oasis on the edge of the Sahara Desert, you can step back into the Islamic past. A mud wall inscribed with Islamic scriptures and Hausa engravings protects against intrusion from the outside world. Livestock wander freely through the streets, along with men and women in flowing, Islamic robes and headdresses. Camel caravans of the nomadic Tuareg, dressed in immaculate sheaths and tall turbans, roam the streets.

Men in pastel *baba riga* robes and women in drab wrapper dresses trot freely with goats and lambs along winding footpaths in a maze of mud huts. The only modern addition to the Old City is the heavily guarded electric gate built into the mud wall surrounding the centuries-old Emir's Palace.

The towering 40-foot Nassarawa Kofar mud gate connects the Old City with Kano's hastily constructed replica of a Western commercial center, where business is transacted but aesthetics are forgotten.

Climb to the top of the Dalan or Goren Dutse hills for a view of the city skyline against the Sahara Desert.

The drawbacks

Kano has been the center of much of the political turmoil that has wracked Nigeria since it became an independent country. From this city, Muslims waged holy war against rival groups for control of the country, which has the largest population in Black Africa.

Perhaps this history explains the terrible delays and red tape at Kano's international airport. Soldiers toting submachine guns guard the hangar-like terminal, where a sea of scuffling, sweating bodies crashes against two tiny immigration desks. One correspondent reported waiting six hours to get out of the airport after landing. She finally had to pay a bribe to get through.

Water is scarce and must be boiled, strained, and purified. Sometimes running water is not available.

The best Hausa food

If you enjoy sampling unfamiliar foods, try local *sire* or *souya,* sold every evening at dozens of food stands all over town. Watch at dusk for small flaming fires where chunks of meat, tomato, onion, and pepper roast on skewers.

You can enjoy authentic tribal food at restaurants throughout Kano. The best places are **Akesan Restaurant** and restaurants in the Ikeja, the Usman Memorial, and the international hotels. Restaurant prices are generally expensive, but the meals are worth it.

Hotels: smaller is better

The cost of a hotel room in Kano is usually not worth the price. The major hotels are no better than any of the smaller hotels in town (except that they usually have recreational facilities), and they are twice the price. All hotels are subject to water, electricity, and food shortages, but the smaller ones are cleaner and offer more courteous service.

Two good hotels in Kano are the Daula and the Central. The key to getting a room at a hotel is often a small bribe, not a confirmed reservation.

The best side trips

If you want to shake the dust of Kano off your shoes for a few days, visit one of the three ultramodern spa resorts an hour south of the city. The **Baguada** and **Tiga Lake** resorts and the **Rock Castle Hotel** offer iced drinks under the palms.

Or take a trip to **Daura,** a town two hours north of Kano, where the nomadic desert culture that once dominated the Sahara continues unchanged.

Kano is an excellent base for safaris. The **Yankari Game Reserve** is a four-hour drive due south in Bauchi State. East of Yankari is the **Jos Zoo.** Both nature reserves offer safaris that take you to see thousands of native species.

Yoruba: best markets, best art

Yoruba cities, such as **Ibaden,** which is as large as Lagos but much nicer, are the African cities most welcoming to tourists. Ibaden boasts the best market in Nigeria, called Dugbe, and has a large Lebanese population made up of Middle Easterners who came to Africa to trade and stayed to open restaurants.

Benin City, the Yoruba capital, boasts the best market for souvenirs in Nigeria. Its other claim to fame is **Oba's Palace,** which is difficult to get into—you must apply for permission in advance. (An oba is a Yoruba ruler.)

Far more accessible is the public **Ife Palace complex,** another former home of a Yoruba ruler. Ife is the center of a flourishing art colony, where printmakers have adapted skills once used on cloth to produce gorgeous woodcuts. One of the best wood carvers is Gabriel Alaye, who works at the St. Joseph's Workshop in Inisha (a suburb).

Top travel tips

Nigeria doesn't have to be the bureaucratic nightmare it is often reported to be. You just have to be prepared. Before arriving at the international airport in Lagos, make sure you have a visa, a passport, a yellow fever vaccination certificate, and a return ticket. You must change $100 into naira on arrival; keep the yellow form showing you did so, you'll need it when you leave. (Remember that in Nigeria, only banks—not hotels or stores—may accept U.S. traveler's checks.)

You will need 50 naira for the airport tax when you leave the country (and you may not take more than 20 naira with you when you go).

The Côte d'Ivoire: the richest African country

The **Côte d'Ivoire** (Ivory Coast) has the highest standard of living in sub-Saharan Africa, and it is one of the continent's most politically stable nations. Originally a French colony, the Côte d'Ivoire (the government refuses to answer to the English name Ivory Coast) is now an independent democratic republic (although it retains a strong French influence).

You can examine Ashanti and Senoufu art at the National Museum, observe wild animals at West Africa's largest game reserve, and bathe in the sun and water of the African Riviera. The Côte d'Ivoire also boasts Africa's only ice-skating rink.

Yet another Little Paris

In **Abidjan,** the capital of the Côte d'Ivoire, splendid African ladies dress in brightly colored long dresses and headwraps and carry baguettes fresh from the bakery—on their heads. This metropolis is reminiscent of European cities. Unfortunately, the beauty of the city has been diminished by recent downtown development. But beautiful sites remain along the lagoon, by the seashore, and in the suburbs.

The **Musée National,** *boulevard Nangui-Abrogoua,* houses more than 20,000 works of art, including jewelry, statues, ritual costumes, and furniture. It is open Tuesdays through Sundays from 9 a.m. to noon and 2:30 p.m. until 6 p.m. and Mondays from 9 a.m. to noon.

Le Marché Sénégalais, *boulevard de la Règublique,* sells art and handicrafts from all areas of Africa. It is open every day. The **Treichville Market** is a treat for veteran shoppers who know how to bargain. The second floor of the market features special regional textiles. It is open daily from 7 a.m. until 2 p.m.

A forest reserve called **Banc National Park** is just within the city limits. Its 7,500 acres are scored with trails that lead past exotic—and labeled—flora.

The best local dishes

Most Ivorian cuisine is based on the plantain, which looks like a banana but isn't, and the yam, which looks like a sweet potato but isn't. From both, the Ivorians make a stew called *foutou,* a mush covered in a nut or palmseed sauce. *Aloco,* fried plantains, are another specialty. Drink specialties include *bandji,* made with palm extract, and *lemonroudji,* a concoction of lemon and ginger. Meat and fish are usually fresh and grilled on outdoor barbecues. Have fresh fruit for dessert.

The best African restaurants are in the Treichville section of Abdijan: **Aboussouan,** *avenue Delafosse and boulevard Giscard d'Estaing; tel. (225)22-37-14,* and **Chez Mamie Arras,** *ave. 38; tel. (225)33-24-93.*

The best native dances

A troupe of 35 dancers performs the ritual dances of the Côte d'Ivoire at **Le Wafou,** *blvd. de Marseille 7km; tel. (225)35-98-93),* an expensive nightclub on the lagoon.

The best night life

Treichville has the best discos in Abdijan. Try **l'Acetylène,** *tel. (225)32-50-24,* **Treich Can-Can,** *37 blvd. Delafosse; tel. (225)32-17-91,* and **Zorba le Grec,** *tel. (225)22-66-29.* (These places have a fast turnover, so they may be gone by the time you read this.)

The best places to stay in Abdijan

Hôtel Ivoire, *08 B.P. 001, Abidjan 01, boulevard de la Corniche, Cocody; tel. (225)44-10-45,* is an immense luxury hotel that houses 14 boutiques, 5 restaurants, 5 bars, a supermarket, a cinema, a concert hall, sports facilities, a man-made lake, and the only ice-skating rink in Black Africa.

Le Forum Golf Intercontinental, *boulevard Lagunaire, Cocody, 08 B.P. 18; tel. (225)43-10-44,* on the banks of the lagoon, has a nightclub, a pool, a restaurant, and, of course, golf facilities.

Relais de Cocody is a hotel made up of little bungalows clustered around the edge of the Cocody golf course.

The best place to view wildlife

Comoe National Park, 440 miles north of Abidjan—a comfortable distance only by air—is a government wildlife reserve where you can see buffalo, antelope, wild boar, baboons, and a very few lions. The reserve is open December through May. Food and drink are expensive.

The best place to stay is the **Comoe Safari Lodge Hotel,** *tel. (225)32-25-83,* which has a restaurant, a bar, a pool, and organized excursions. Traditional dances are performed on the premises.

The best place to buy textiles

A modern textile center is located in the provincial town of **Bouaké,** 235 miles from Abidjan. Here, the area's oldest textile factory, **Ets. Gonfreville,** manufactures cotton goods. **Solinci,** a lingerie factory, is also located in town. Both are open to the public on Thursdays. But any day of the week you can buy seconds from the factories at the **Bouaké Market.** Look the goods over carefully, but usually they have been rejected only for minor flaws. Among the goodies are household linens.

In Bouaké stay at the **Hôtel du Centre,** *B.P. 54; tel. (225)63-32-78.* Although the hotel's rooms are simple and plain, its location is excellent; next to the hotel is the **Artisan's Center,** where you can buy leather crafts, cane furniture, ivory sculpture, jewelry, and Baoulé masks (the Baoulé are a traditional carving tribe, whose work is less known than that of peoples elsewhere in Africa). Traditional masks are used in initiation ceremonies and to ward off misfortune.

THE BEST OF AUSTRALASIA

Australasia—which includes Australia, New Zealand, the islands of the South Pacific Ocean, and New Guinea—boasts some of the most dramatic scenery on earth. The largest monolith in the world—a gigantic red rock considered sacred by the aborigines—lies at the heart of Australia's vast, dry desert. The finest surf in the world crashes against Australia's golden shores, attracting the world's most agile surfers. Spectacular waterfalls rush down ravines in New Zealand near lush sheep farms more beautiful than those in Scotland. The towering snowy mountain peaks of New Zealand rival those of the Alps and the Rockies in grandeur.

Australasia also has spectacular man-made sights. Sydney, for example, has the world's most architecturally interesting opera house.

Chapter 22

THE BEST OF AUSTRALIA

Located on the other side of the earth, Australia is a looking-glass land, where things are off-center, not quite the same as back home. While we are suffering through winter, Australia is sweating out summer. Like North America, much of Australia was colonized by the British—but they were convicts, not Puritans. The accents Down Under are flat corruptions of early British—like ours, only different. Australian cowboys call themselves stockmen and dress like Crocodile Dundee, not Roy Rogers. And the original inhabitants of Australia, unlike American Indians, are short and black. They speak a language that includes clicks.

The world's oldest and smallest continent, Australia offers something for everyone. Nature lovers are fascinated by the Outback, with its rugged terrain and unusual animals. Divers explore the Great Barrier Reef, the largest coral reef in the world, stretching 1,260 miles along Australia's northeast coast. This coast is also the place to enjoy the world's best surfing. Sydney and Melbourne have big-city restaurants, night life, and shopping. And enormous ranches cover the interior of the country.

Australia is the world's most isolated country. Because of this, animals, birds, insects, and plants unknown to the rest of the world have evolved here. Nowhere else will you see kangaroos and koala bears, for example. Also because of the country's isolation, the aborigines, who have one of the most intriguing and ancient cultures in the world, were able to continue their way of life—living in harmony with nature—for thousands of years before Europeans arrived. Still largely uninhabitable and unexplored, this continent's vast desert heartland, known as the **Red Centre,** is made up of four great deserts that together occupy 1.2-million square miles.

Australia was formed when Europe and North America were still evolving. The last great geological shifts here took place 230-million years ago. However, some places in Australia date back 1,000-million years. Ancient artifacts are stored in the **Great Western Plateau,** at the heart of Australia. A rock found near Marble Bar contained the remains of 3,500-million-year-old organisms, the oldest forms of life yet discovered. And a dinosaur left his footprint in the rock near Broome.

Only slightly more than 15-million people live in this area roughly the size of the continental United States. Yet this is one of the most highly urbanized nations in the world—

almost 85% of all Australians live in or around the cities. And Australia has one of the world's highest standards of living.

Sydney: the number-one sight

Sydney—a huge city sprawling across 670 square miles and housing 3.5-million people—is the largest, oldest, and most cosmopolitan city in Australia. Sydney is also naturally beautiful, built around a harbor and cradled by hills.

Light-colored buildings and red-tile roofs stand out against the blue water and sky. Flowers bloom year-round. And the ocean laps at 150 miles of shoreline.

Life revolves around the harbor and the sea, where thousands of boats vie for space. Scantily clad sun worshippers flock to the city's 30-odd beaches, where topless bathing is the norm (three beaches also allow nude bathing). But Sydney's beaches are never as packed as those at U.S. resorts.

During the Australian summer (from November through February), the city is hot, and the humidity is suffocating—which is fine if you intend to spend all your time on the beach but uncomfortable if you are want to explore the city. Sydney's many hills, combined with the heat, are hard on visitors who aren't familiar with the transport system. However, during the winter, Sydney is mild and pleasant.

The summer heat brings Sydneyites outdoors and forces them to shed their clothes. At night, the streets of Sydney are overflowing with people, who eat outdoors under palm trees, then wander until dawn.

The best view of Sydney

The best view of Sydney is from the 48th-floor, glassed-in skywalk at the **Australia Square Tower,** which is the tallest building in the Southern Hemisphere. You'll be able to see the entire city, the Blue Mountains, and Botany Bay. What's more, the tower (which isn't square, but round, constructed of steel, cement, and glass) has the fastest elevators in the Southern Hemisphere.

While you are in the building, stop off at the sixth-floor **Opal Skymine,** where you can see films about life in the Australian opal mines and supposedly buy gems at field prices.

If you can afford it, lunch at the **Summit Restaurant,** on the 47th floor, the largest revolving restaurant in the world. Needless to say, the view is superb—even if the fare isn't.

The world's best opera house

When work began on Sydney's ultramodern winged **opera house** in 1957, local residents, who called it the New South Whale and the Operasaurus, said it wouldn't fly. Much to its critics' chagrin, the opera house turned out to be the most beautiful in the world, praised from London to Hong Kong.

Designed by Danish architect Jorn Utzon, the $140-million structure on Bennelong Point, surrounded by Sydney's harbor, is topped by interlocking wing-shaped roofs that glitter with more than one-million Swedish ceramic tiles. The acoustics are the best in the world.

Take a A$3 tour of the building to see the treated timber panels, the tinted glass through which you have a view of the harbor, and the bright blue curtains. The opera house has a total of 980 rooms, 4 of which are performance halls, where concerts, operas, ballets, plays, and recitals are held. Rock'n'roll groups perform as well as symphony orchestras.

Sydney's oldest quarter

The **Rocks,** a renovated area on the west side of Circular Quay, was notorious for its rough residents in the mid-1800s. Convicts, sailors, prostitutes, soldiers, whalers, and gangsters gathered on this rocky ridge, known as the Cradle of Sydney. For a map of the no-longer-seedy area, visit the **Information Center,** *104 George St.,* near the Overseas Passenger Terminal.

At the heart of The Rocks is **Argyle Place,** a peaceful park surrounded by pastel houses dressed with wrought-iron grills and balconies. The **Church of the Holy Trinity,** better known as the Garrison Church, was built in 1840. The second-oldest church in Sydney, it is the earliest example of Gothic architecture in Australia, with Gothic arches, mullioned windows, and a red cedar pulpit.

Sydney's oldest house, **Cadman's Cottage,** built in 1816, is just off Argyle Street. Circular Cove once came nearly to the door of this little homestead, built by John Cadman, superintendent of government boats.

The **Argyle Arts Centre,** *18 Argyle St.,* was built in 1820 by convicts as a three-story warehouse. Today the sandstone building houses craft shops and antique stores. Notice the hand-hewn timber (convict labor came cheap). You can buy hand-blown glass, beeswax candles, and pottery here.

From Argyle Street, take the **Argyle Cut,** a dank 300-foot tunnel hollowed out of solid stone by prisoners 140 years ago. It leads to Miller's Point.

Best picnicking

The best places to get away from the cement and steel that make up Sydney are the Domain and the Botanic Gardens, separated from each other by a highway. The **Domain** is a park with an emerald lawn perfect for picnics and naps. Soapbox orators harangue crowds here with their personal views of the world. The **Botanic Gardens** are known for their exotic flora, including giant Moreton Bay fig trees and hothouses filled with orchids and ferns.

Australia's best art gallery

Near the Botanic Gardens is the **Art Gallery of New South Wales,** divided into two sections, one housing Renaissance to 20th-century art, the second housing impressionist and modern works. The new wing, with its angled white walls and views of the harbor, is more attractive. Look for works by Australian artists William Dobell, Sidney Nolan, and Russell Drysdale.

The Southern Hemisphere's best private gallery

Holdsworth Galleries, *86 Holdsworth St.,* is the biggest art gallery south of the equator, with the best collection of contemporary Australian artists. Among the displays are paintings and sculptures by Sidney Nolan, Sali Herman, Margaret Olley, and Arthur Boyd. The gallery is as lovely as the works it contains. Admission is free. The gallery is open daily until 5 p.m.

The world's most beautifully situated zoo

Taronga Zoo, on a peninsula jutting into Mosman Bay, has the most beautiful setting of any zoo in the world. It offers a view of the harbor (**Taronga** means *water view* to the aborigines) and 75 acres of bushland. Among other strange creatures, you can see koala bears, emus, platypuses, dingos, kookaburras, and wombats. A special underground part of the zoo houses nocturnal animals, which you can see under red light. The rain forest aviary is also worth seeing.

The worst prison

Fort Denison, on a little island in the harbor, was known as Pinchgut among Australia's early convicts, because of the starvation rations meted out here. The fort was never actually used to protect Sydney, although that was its original purpose. You can still see cannons and cannonballs in the round Martello Tower, which is used as a tidal observation station. Tours of the fort depart Wharf Two on Circular Quay three times a day Tuesdays through Sundays. Call a half-day in advance to make reservations, *tel. (61-2)240-2036.*

Sydney's best beach

Sydney has 34 ocean beaches, each with its own style. If you are looking for peace and quiet, try Whale, Avalon, or Bilgola. But if you want to see a Sydney beach at its best—filled with perfect bodies, sun-streaked blonds, surf bums, and joggers, all in a sunny mood—go to Bondi.

Bondi (pronounced Bond-Eye) has produced many world-champion surfers. The half-mile crescent of sand and surf is filled from dawn to dusk with surfers, sunbathers, and swimmers. Snacks and drinks are available at Bondi Junction, near the beach.

Bondi's neighbor, **Tamarama Beach,** is smaller, prettier, and more peaceful.

Sydney's best shopping

Paddington, or Paddo as it is called, is the best place to shop in Sydney. The area is much like Washington, D.C.'s Georgetown, with restored townhouses and colorful little shops.

The major draw is the **Village Bazaar,** held each Saturday from 9 a.m. to 4 p.m. on the grounds of the Uniting Church in Australia. The bazaar feels for all the world like California in the 1960s, filled with lots of long-haired youths. But look closer, and you also will see busy matrons searching for dinner. More than 120 stalls sell handicrafts, antiques, clothing, imported goods, and art. This is one of the best places in Australia to find authentic Australian-made goods at bargain prices.

Although the bazaar can be a shopping spree in itself, it should be considered only the starting point of a shopping journey through Paddington. Along Oxford Street, the main thoroughfare, and its side streets, you will discover antique shops, boutiques, art galleries, bookstores, craft shops, jewelers, and record shops.

Paddo's best shops include: **Jack O'Beans,** *264 Oxford St.,* an elegant antique store; **Australian Centre for Photography,** *257 Oxford St.,* for Australian and international photo art; **Game Birds,** *108 Oxford St.,* for made-to-order leather and lace fashions; **Coo-ee Australian Emporium,** *48 Oxford St.,* for custom-designed jewelry; and **Angelo's,** *112 Oxford St.,* for handmade boots and shoes.

Sample homemade Russian chocolates at **W. Pulknownik's,** *Oxford and Elizabeth streets.*

To get to Paddington from downtown Sydney, take Bus Number 380 from Circular Quay to Oxford Street or Bus Number 378 from Railway Square.

The best time to visit

A festival is held in Sydney almost every month. The entire month of January is one big festival, with plays, exhibitions, operas in the parks, sailboat races, and food and wine fairs. Then come the Royal Sydney Easter Show, which is a huge country fair with animal exhibitions; Royal Gardens Week; Carnivale; and the Blessing of the Fishing Fleet.

Sydney's favorite pastimes

Surfing (which many schools teach as a physical-education course) and wind surfing are the passions of Sydneyites. A sign on trains admonishes, "Surfers, be considerate. Don't block aisles with your boards."

Australia's best restaurant

Outside Sydney is **Berowra Waters Inn,** *Berowra Waters, NSW 2082; tel. (61-2)456-1027,* the finest restaurant in Australia. Chef Gay Bilson produces innovative Australian dishes. Unfortunately, you can't get here by road; you must fly or take a boat.

Sydney's best dining bets

Sydney's best restaurant is **Oasis Seros,** *495 Oxford St., Paddington; tel. (61-2)333377,* a simple but stylish place that serves light food made from fresh ingredients. The china, crystal, and cutlery are elegant, and an enormous bouquet of flowers adorns the mantelpiece.

A small Italian restaurant known as **No Name,** *tel. (61-2)357-4711,* has delicious food, an unpretentious atmosphere, and low prices. It's located in a little house on Chapel Street, a short street in East Sydney near the intersection of Crown and Stanley streets.

The best place for seafood is **Doyle's on the Beach,** *11 Marine Parade, Watson's Bay; tel. (61-2)337-2007.* The battered fish is served in enormous platefuls. And the setting is lovely—a sandy beach lined with little boats. The only drawback is that the restaurant's charms are known, and it's crowded. On weekends, Doyle's provides customers with a free motorboat ride from Circular Quay to and from the restaurant.

Also at Watson's Bay is the **Fisherman's Lodge,** a pleasant restaurant housed in a 19th-century mansion. The **Endeavor at Mosman,** across the Harbor Bridge, is in an old ship.

Bellevue Hotel, *159 Hargrave,* in Paddo, has a back-garden barbecue and live entertainment.

Madame DeFarge, *107 Queen St.,* also in Paddo, has a prix-fixe dinner for A$8. The a-la-carte menu includes succulent prawns in caviar mousse. **Captain Cook Hotel,** on Flinders, serves steak Diane with three fresh vegetables for about A$3.

Sydney's top hotels

Sydney's finest hotel is the **Regent,** *199 George St.; tel. (61-2)238-0000.* Overlooking the Opera House and the harbor, it has luxurious rooms and an attentive staff. Rooms are A$225 to A$320. Make reservations through **Leading Hotels of the World,** *(800)223-6800.*

Three close seconds are the **Sheraton-Wentworth,** *tel. (61-2)230-0700;* the **Inter-Continental,** *17 Macquarie St.; tel. (61-2)230-0200;* and the **Parkroyal Hotel,** *tel. (61-2)977-7666.* The Sheraton and the Manly Pacific have views of Manly, a surfers' beach.

Outside the business district, near King's Cross, is the discreet and elegant **Sebel Town House,** *23 Elizabeth Bay Road, Elizabeth Bay; tel. (61-2)358-3244* (also represented by

Leading Hotels of the World). This place is popular among celebrities, whose signed photographs paper the walls at the bar.

Another attractive small hotel is the **Russell,** *143a George St.; tel. (61-2)241-3543,* where Rachel Ward stays when she's in town.

The hottest night life

Although Sydney's drinking laws are strict, the local residents manage to have a rowdy good time anyway. Bars close at 11 p.m. during the week, after midnight on weekends and holidays (depending on the area). But many Sydneyites belong to private clubs, where you can get beer into the wee hours of the morning. The clubs often have live shows, slot machines, and food.

Sydney's chic set—good-looking models, visiting rock stars, and well-dressed socialites—makes a point of being seen at **Arthur's Bar and Restaurant,** *155 Victoria St., Potts Point; tel. (61-2)358-5097;* **The Cauldron,** *207 Darlinghurst Road, Darlinghurst; tel. (61-2)331-1523;* and the **Hip Hop Club,** *11 Oxford St., Paddington; tel. (61-2)332-2568.*

If you'd like to barhop, but you don't want to drive or risk getting lost, go to the **Holiday Inn Menzies,** *14 Carrington St.,* where 20 pubs share 1 roof. Each has its own character and clientele, from snooty and expensive to cheap and blue-collar.

The liveliest neighborhood at night is **King's Cross,** a combination Greenwich Village and red-light district, where Darlinghurst, Potts Point, and Elizabeth Bay meet. Darlinghurst Road and Macleay Street are the main thoroughfares. Sydney's best bar is here, the **Bourbon and Beefsteak,** *Darlinghurst Road; tel. (61-2)357-1215.* The piano bar provides entertainment in the early evening, and jazz combos jam later on.

Sydney's oldest pub is the **Hero of Waterloo Hotel** in The Rocks. Built in 1804 as a jail, it became a rousing pub in the rip-roaring 1800s. Today it is a peaceful place to have a drink while sitting beside a fireplace.

Wine bars are a popular part of Sydney night life. The **Great Escape,** *McMahon's Point; tel. (61-2)929-6268,* is well-known and has good food.

The **Manzil Room,** *15 Springfield Ave., King's Cross,* has live music until dawn seven nights a week.

The bluest mountains

The **Blue Mountains** really are a vivid blue. Oil released by the mountains' eucalyptus trees reflects the blue light rays of the sun. The saw-toothed peaks are just 50 miles from Sydney, a day's journey. Head for **Katoomba,** where you can take the Scenic Railway, the steepest in the world, up the mountains. Or you can ride the Scenic Skyway, a cable car dangling above a deep chasm. Nearby are the enormous Jenolan Caves and the giant waterfall at Govett's Leap, near Blackheath.

Australia's best skiing

The **Snowy Mountains,** 300 miles southwest of Sydney, are much higher than the Blue Mountains. Covered with snow from June to late August, they are a great place to ski. Australia's highest peak is here, **Mt. Kosciusko** (known as Mt. Kozzie locally), which rises 7,314 feet.

Although skiing in Australia is as spectacular as skiing in the Alps, it is much less expensive. An all-inclusive six-day ski package can cost as little as A$500. And it's one big party. Aussies drink until dawn, then manage to ski the 25 miles of trails flawlessly.

The Snowy Mountains are worth a visit off-season as well, when prices are even lower and you can take a 1 1/2-mile chair lift to the top of Mt. Crackenback. The fishing, swimming, and hiking can't be beat.

Capital Canberra

Canberra, the national capital, is a city-planner's dream. Designed to function expressly as Australia's capital, it is free of traffic and unsightly shopping malls. At its heart is a large man-made lake. Throughout the city are parks, and the broad avenues are lined with trees. An American named Walter Burley Griffin designed the city in 1913, after winning an international competition for the job. However, parliament didn't actually meet here until 1927.

While it is not on the coast and doesn't have sunny beaches, Canberra is fast becoming an artistic and intellectual enclave. It boasts the new National Gallery, one of the finest art museums in Australia, and great restaurants and bars.

Canberra's top sights

The city's best-known landmark is the **Captain Cook Memorial Water Jet,** which shoots 6 tons of water 450 feet into the air from 10 a.m. to noon and 2 p.m. to 4 p.m. every day. Part of the fountain is a nine-foot globe illustrating the routes followed by Captain Cook.

More important, however, is the **Australian War Memorial,** on Anzac Parade, a beautiful structure honoring the 100,000 Australians who died fighting in the world wars. Bronze panels inscribed with their names cover two enormous walls. The memorial contains excruciatingly realistic paintings of the wars, as well as old biplanes, tanks, and bombs.   The **Australian National Gallery,** on the shores of the lake, has an outstanding collection of works by both Australians and foreigners. It also has a good restaurant with a lovely view of the lake.

Canberra's **Carillon** is one of the largest in the world, with 53 bells, the largest weighing more than 6 tons. A gift from Britain, the tall white pillar stands at the northern end of the Kings Avenue Bridge. Recitals are given on Sundays and Wednesdays.

The **Institute of Anatomy** on the campus of the Australian National University has a good museum illustrating the culture of the aborigines and the natives of New Guinea.

The **Botanic Gardens,** *Clunies Ross Street,* is a maze of footpaths and bridges that guide you over little ponds and through gardens with carefully labeled Australian plants and flowers.

For a glimpse of Australia's early pioneer life, visit **Blundell's Farmhouse,** *Wendouree Drive,* off Constitution Avenue. Built in 1858, the cottage's three rooms are filled with pioneer furnishings.

Twenty-five miles southwest of Canberra is the 12,000-acre **Tidbinbilla Nature Reserve,** where you can see local flora and fauna and feed the kangaroos. This unspoiled bushland is open from 9 a.m. to 6 p.m.

The best eating and sleeping

Charlie's, *Bunder Street; tel. (61-62)488338,* is an elegant restaurant with French cuisine and especially good soups. Politicians eat here when parliament is meeting.

Rascals, *Petrie Plaza,* is a restaurant with the atmosphere of a disco. A good place for after-theater supper, it stays open until 2 a.m. The decor is pleasant, with low ceilings and stained-glass windows. Prices are moderate.

Gus' Café, *Bunda Street,* is a tiny place with a pleasant outdoor terrace surrounded by flower boxes. You can linger over a meal here, reading Gus's selection of magazines and newspapers. Save room for the cheesecake, which is out-of-this-world.

Tall Trees, *21 Stephen St., Ainslie; tel. (61-62)479200,* two miles from Canberra, is an inviting lodge named for the tall trees that surround it. All rooms have views of the gorgeous gardens and are supplied with electric blankets (it gets cold here during the winter). The lodge has a laundry room and a lounge with a television and tea-making equipment. Double rooms are A$27.

Chelsea Lodge, *526 Northbourne Ave.,* is a bed and breakfast in a villa with a pleasant veranda. Breakfast is good. All rooms have televisions; two have private bathrooms. Expect to pay A$13 per person for a room without a shower, A$18 for a room with a shower.

The best of Melbourne

Melbourne rivals Sydney as Australia's most attractive city. Both coastal cities have three-million residents. However, Melbourne has fewer tourists and lower prices.

Melbourne's weather is less pleasant than Sydney's. It rains more frequently, and winters can be grim, drizzly, and gray, without even the excitement of snow.

While Sydney's beauty is natural, Melbourne's is man-made. Because it is a planned city, Melbourne's road network forms a grid pattern, making travel within the city easy. The city's architecture is sophisticated, especially along wide and gracious **Collins Street,** the banking capital of Australia. Lush parks and the Yarra River add greenery to the cityscape.

Although Melbourne was founded in 1835 by a group of Tasmanian entrepreneurs, it didn't actually take off until 1851, when it became the center of Australia's biggest and longest gold rush. A product of the time, Melbourne is mostly Victorian in appearance.

Melbourne's must sees

The National Museum, Science Museum, State Library, and LaTrobe Library are combined in one huge, interconnected complex between Swanston and Russell streets. The strangest sight in the entire complex is the stuffed body of the well-loved Australian race-horse, Phar Lap, which died a mysterious and shady death in the United States. Also look for Australia's first car and first airplane.

Melbourne's creepiest sight is the **Old Melbourne Gaol,** *Russell Street.* Built in 1841, it was used as a prison until 1929. More than 100 prisoners were hanged here. The somber building is now a museum, with death masks of notorious criminals and records of the early convicts transported to Australia from Britain. (Some were exiled for incredibly minor crimes.)

The **National Gallery,** housed in the Cultural Centre Complex on St. Kilda Road, has a good art collection and exhibits from overseas. The Great Hall has a beautiful stained-glass ceiling, and fountains fill the central courtyard. The gallery is closed Mondays.

King's Domain is an enormous park that houses the Shrine of Remembrance, a World War I memorial; Governor LaTrobe's cottage, the original Victorian government house prefabricated and sent from England; and the Sidney Myer Music Bowl, an outdoor concert hall.

The **Royal Botanic Gardens,** also within King's Domain, are the most beautiful in Australia. Laid out beside the Yarra River, they include lakes, a rainbow of flowers, and a surprising number of wild animals, including water fowl, cockatoos, and possums. You can have tea and scones by the lake.

The best shopping

Melbourne's center for shopping buffs is located between Swanston and Elizabeth streets, on Collins and Bourke. This is where you'll find Myers, Australia's biggest department store. Bourke Street is a pedestrian mall, but be careful; trams pass through here at alarming speeds.

Aboriginal Handicrafts, *Ninth Floor, 125 Swanston St.,* is the best place for honest-to-goodness handicrafts made by Australia's oldest residents.

The best bets for fitness freaks

On weekends, you can rent a bicycle at the Botanical Gardens and Como Park, then bike the miles-long trail along the Yarra River.

If canoeing is more your style, you can rent a canoe or a rowboat near Como Park or at Studley Park in Kew for A$10 to A$12 an hour.

The best place to jog is the 2 1/2-mile running track around King's Domain Park. The Tan Track, as it is known, is where Melbourne's fitness freaks race at dawn and dusk.

The world's strangest football game

Australian football—a game all its own that is based on Gaelic football—is a strange combination of soccer and rugby. You can see this one-of-a-kind game at the Melbourne Cricket Ground in Yarra Park, one of Australia's biggest sports stadiums. The best football game, if you can get tickets, is the Grand Final in September, Australia's biggest sporting event.

Melbourne's best restaurants

Without question, Melbourne beats Sydney when it comes to restaurants. **Fanny's,** *Lonsdale Street; tel. (61-3)663-3017,* is one of the best restaurants in Australia, a cozy little place with international fare. If you want an elegant night out, eat upstairs. If you'd rather save your Australian dollars, eat in the little bistro downstairs. It is less chic but serves the same food at much lower prices.

The city's best seafood restaurant is **Jean Jacques,** *502 Queensberry St., Melbourne; tel. (61-3)328-4214.*

Two Faces, *149 Toorak Road, South Yarra; tel. (61-3)266-1547,* serves French-Swiss cuisine made from only the freshest ingredients. The wines are good, too.

Mietta's Melbourne, *Alfred Place; tel. (61-3)654-2366,* is a lovely restaurant in an old Victorian building. A piano bar is located downstairs. **Stephanie's,** *405 Tooronga Road; tel. (61-3)208-8944,* is another romantic place, in an elegant historic mansion.

Melbourne is famous for its ethnic cuisine. Chinatown (Little Bourke Street), for example, is a thriving neighborhood with pagoda-style buildings. The aroma of hanging ducks and ginseng fills the air. The best restaurant here is **Flower Drum,** *103 Little Bourke St.; tel. (61-3)663-2531.*

Turkish and Mideastern restaurants are sprinkled along Sydney Road. The Richmond district, just east of downtown Melbourne, off Swan Street, is also heavily ethnic, with Greek, Turkish, Argentine, Indian, Vietnamese, and Mexican restaurants. Lygon Street, near the university, is a busy row of Lebanese and Italian restaurants.

The best hotels

One of the great landmarks of Melbourne is the **Windsor Hotel,** *Spring Street; tel. (61-3)630361.* Recently restored, the Victorian hotel has a domed Grand Dining Room, decorated with silk wallpaper and crystal chandeliers. Visiting statesmen stay here.

The **Regent,** *25 Collins St.; tel. (61-3)630-321,* is a work of modern art, with a sky-lit atrium filled with little white bulbs. Occupying the top 15 floors of a 50-story building, the hotel has panoramic views of the city. Jackie Collins stayed in the Kensington Suite on the top floor, which has windows from floor to ceiling.

Rockman's Regency, *Lonsdale and Exhibition streets; tel. (61-3)662-3900,* has suites with private jacuzzis that hold five people at a time. The bar is nice, but it's open only to guests. John McEnroe stays here.

The dullest night life

In Melbourne, lights generally go out well before midnight. However, you can enjoy the arts at the city's new theater complex and concert hall. Luciano Pavarotti praised the Melbourne concert hall as the finest in the world.

Melbourne does have one New York-style dance spot. **Inflation,** *60 King St.; tel. (61-3)623674,* has a gigantic video screen and a huge dance floor. The crowd is lively.

Palace, *Lower Esplanade, St. Kilda; tel. (61-3)534-0655,* is also a fun place.

The best of Perth

Perth, the largest city on Australia's west coast, is the most isolated city in the world. Adelaide, the closest town, is more than 1,000 miles away. It takes three days to get to Perth by train from Sydney. Because of their isolation, the 900,000 residents of Perth are close-knit and friendly.

Perth has many parks and wide-open spaces, miles of great beaches, good hotels, and a wide variety of ethnic restaurants. But best of all, it has the most ideal weather in Australia, more like the Mediterranean than Down Under. Although it's not as hot as Sydney, it offers more continuous hours of sunshine.

Perth's pride

King's Park, a 1,000-acre wilderness area, tops Mt. Eliza and offers panoramic views of Perth. At its heart is a fountain dedicated to pioneer women. If you lose track of the time, look for the floral clock.

King's Park is a place to stroll at your leisure, enjoying some of Australia's exotic flora and fauna. When you tire, stop for a snack at the park's restaurant.

Other top sights

The **Art Gallery,** *47 James St.,* is one of the best art museums in Australia. It is a dramatic modern building that cost US$10 million to build. Masterpieces by Van Gogh, Cézanne, Picasso, and Monet are displayed, as well as works by contemporary Australian artists. Look for the "Art of the Western Desert," created by the Panunya, a tribe of aborigines.

The **Old Mill,** at the end of Narrows Bridge, ground flour during the gold rush in the 1800s. Today it houses colonial tools and artifacts.

Perth's best bets

Burswood Restaurant and Casino, *Great Eastern Highway; tel. (61-9)362-7777,* is the largest resort complex in the Southern Hemisphere and the second-largest gaming floor anywhere in the world.

Perth's best restaurants

The most romantic restaurant in town is the **Ord Street Café,** *27 Ord St., West Perth; tel. (61-9)321-6021.* A cozy place, the café serves light fare on the veranda or in the drawing room.

Perth's best seafood restaurant is **Jessica's Fine Seafood,** *Shop 1, Merlin Centre, 99 Adelaide Terrace; tel. (61-9)325-2511,* which has a view of the Swan River. Try the grilled dhufish, a firm, sweet fish found only in Western Australia.

Other good bets are the **River Room** at the Sheraton Perth; the **Oyster Bar,** *88 James St., Northbridge;* and **Lombardo's,** *Fishing Boat Harbor, Fremantle.*

Perth's most pleasant hotels

The **Merlin,** *99 Plain St.; tel. (61-9)323-0121* or *(800)223-9868* in the United States, is the flashiest hotel in Perth. This 5-star affair has a lobby with a pink Italian granite floor and a 13-story atrium topped by a domed glass roof. Rooms are spacious.

Celebrities stay at the **Parmelia Hilton,** *Mill St.; tel. (61-9)322-3622.* Excellent service is the main attraction.

Other good hotels are the Orchard, the Parkroyal, the Langley, and the Sheraton Perth.

The best of Queensland

Queensland, Australia's northeastern province, is a diverse land containing many different worlds: the fluorescent Great Barrier Reef in the Coral Sea; the aboriginal reservation in the Daintree Rain Forest; the gold and opal mines at the jungle's edge; and sacred natural art galleries in the pitiless Outback.

The best of Brisbane

Complete with a surfing subculture (at nearby Surfer's Paradise on the Gold Coast), **Brisbane** is often compared to Los Angeles. Homes in Queensland's sprawling capital city sport red-tile roofs and blue swimming pools. The hot sun fosters a casual dress code—men often wear shorts, knee socks, and ties to work. In the fields they wear kepis, military hats with wide brims that snap to the crowns on one side.

Founded as a penal colony for convicts supposedly too tough to be sent to Sydney, Brisbane originally was home to Australia's mining and agricultural industries. Today, tourism is making a bid for first place in the local economy.

While in Brisbane, stop by **Queensland Aboriginal Creations,** *135 George St.,* run by the Department of Aboriginal and Islanders Advancement. You can buy tribal masks, musical instruments, weapons, and bark paintings.

For a boost to your patriotic ego, stop by the memorial called **They Passed This Way,** *Lyndon B. Johnson Place, Newstead Park,* erected as a tribute to the United States after General MacArthur made his headquarters here during World War II.

The **Forest Park** is an oasis of eucalyptus trees and tropical birds just outside Brisbane.

Carefully designed walking paths lead through the park and its Botanical Gardens. Stop by the **Sir Thomas Brisbane Planetarium,** the largest in Australia.

The best place to see cuddly koalas is the **Lone Pine Sanctuary,** *Fig Tree Pocket,* west of Brisbane. About 100 of the little bears live here, along with kangaroos, emus, and other Australian animals. You can hold the koalas and feed the kangaroos by hand.

The place to stay in Brisbane is the **Sheraton Brisbane Hotel,** *249 Turbot St.; tel. (61-7)835-3535.* Rooms are beautifully furnished and offer views of the Brisbane River.

Another good bet is the **Hilton International Brisbane,** *190 Elizabeth St.; tel. (61-7)231-3131.*

Surfer's Paradise: the best of the Gold Coast

Just south of Brisbane is **Surfer's Paradise,** the largest and liveliest resort on Australia's 20-mile Gold Coast. The sandy beaches are perfect, the water warm, the surf, as you would expect, terrific—and behind it all are the MacPherson Mountains. Believe it or not, the beach here is even better than in Hawaii. However, the crowds can be unbearable, especially around Christmas and Easter.

A good place to stay is **The Hub,** *21 Cavill Ave.; tel. (61-75)31-5559,* a motel near the beach. Each unit has its own balcony, bathroom, refrigerator, and television. Double rooms are A$30 per person; single rooms are A$40.

Cairns: a tropical best

Cairns (pronounced "Cans") is a tropical town filled with the aromas of coffee, sugarcane, and orchids. You can walk from one end of Cairns to the other. The jungle encroaches wherever someone hasn't mowed his lawn or raked pesky mangoes from his yard.

A languid town, Cairns sprawls along the northern fringes of the Great Barrier Reef, overlooking blue Trinity Bay. The ramshackle houses, surrounding jungle, and fields of sugarcane lend the town its colonial mystique. Palm trees sway in the wind, and tropical fruits are mainstays of the local diet. Trading ships line the oceanfront.

Cairns can be a best or a worst for women, because it is home to many more men than women. A common assumption is that a woman on her own is a working girl. Pubs are often partitioned into separate rooms for men and women, and signals can get crossed if the boundaries are violated.

For decades, Cairns has been a fishing capital of the world, abounding in barramundi, shark, and marlin. It's also the stepping-off point for the world's best black marlin fishing grounds. Although they aren't particularly good eating, black marlin put up one heck of a fight, making for a good battle.

Cairns' real attraction is the nearby **Great Barrier Reef,** which is described below.

Cairns' best hotels

Cairns does have a celebrated hotel or two, including **Harbourside Village,** *209 The Esplanade; tel. (61-70)51-8999,* with rooms for A$80; the **Pacific International,** *43 The Esplanade; tel. (61-70)51-7888,* with rooms for A$90; and the good old **Hilton International,** *Wharf Street; tel. (61-70)52-1599,* with rooms for A$140.

Palm Cove, not far from Cairns, has a jet-set resort called the **Reef House,** where bougainvillea scents the air and palm trees rustle in the wind. The resort's restaurant is good.

The Great Barrier Reef

Extending 1,260 miles, from New Guinea to the Tropic of Capricorn, the **Great Barrier Reef** passes along the coast of Queensland. Containing more than 2,000 coral reefs, coral islands, and cays, the reef is home to the world's greatest variety of marine life, nearly 1,400 kinds of sea creatures. It is a must see if you are in Australia. The coral forms stunning natural patterns, and clear and brightly colored fish swim in unison.

Scuba divers from around the world come here to swim among the exotic fish. If you'd rather, you can walk across much of the reef at low tide, when the water recedes. (Wear tennis shoes, the coral is sharp.) Or you can go beyond the danger zones around this coral paradise and swim to your lungs' content.

The Great Barrier Reef is a beautiful but dying world. The underwater castles created by coral were once multicolored. Slowly, they are turning white—the sign of a dying reef. The killer is the crown of thorns, a starfish that grows to two feet across. These seemingly harmless creatures eat the living coral and leave behind skeletons. Shell collectors who take giant triton mollusks from the water are also to blame—these shellfish prey upon the crown of thorns.

Some scientists forecast the end of the reef; others say this is merely a natural cycle that began in 1979, will run its course, and then end. Coral eventually regenerates itself.

Australia's best island

Green Island is the best place to stay while exploring the reef. You can see the submarine world through windows at the island's **Underwater Coral Observatory** or from a glass-bottomed boat, which departs the island regularly.

The beaches that edge the mile-square island are empty except for driftwood trees. Cool coconut palm groves offer refuge from the hot sun. Blue and white herons prance along the sand paths. Even the pigeons here are beautiful—they're green and yellow, not the soot color of North American pigeons. Between the chirping crickets and slapping palms, Green Island is a lively spot.

The cheapest way to get to the island is to book a trip with Great Adventure Tours in Cairns. For about A$19, you get a boat ride to and from the reef. If the six-hour stay is too short, you can rent a bungalow from **Hayles Resort,** *tel. (61-70)51-4644,* for A$60 per night. Other reef resorts cost triple that.

Another beautiful reef resort is **Dunk Island,** owned by **Australian Airlines,** *tel. (212)986-3772,* where you can sleep in a beachfront cottage for A$130. You can spend your days snorkeling, swimming, walking in the rain forest, and playing golf and tennis.

Queensland's best market

Take the train from Cairns to **Kuranda,** which has an outdoor market selling Indonesian batiks, native opals, and sapphires. The town is a short walk from the market, past a reconstructed settlers' village and an aboriginal art gallery that sells bark paintings (these barks cost less and look better than those in Sydney or Melbourne).

Tarzan's favorite: Queensland's rain forests

Not far from Brisbane are misty rain forests where orchids scent the air and parrots sing from thick canopies of leaves hundreds of feet in the air. More than 800 kinds of trees grow in these forests, many with buttressed trunks that form church-size caves. Giant ferns, orchids, ginger plants, and organ-pipe funguses grow together in a thick web that blocks out the sun. You can swing like Tarzan from thick vines. Butterflies, tree frogs, snakes, and bugs make their homes here. (The best time to visit is during the less-buggy dry season, from May to November.)

The rain forest closest to Brisbane is at **Mt. Glorious,** a 45-minute drive away. Slightly farther on, at **Mt. Tamborine,** are six rain forest parks. While hiking here, stop at the Maiala Rain Forest Café to enjoy English tea served with fresh scones, jam, and thick cream, while savoring the fragrance of jasmine and watching colorful parrots. Two-and-a-half hours south of Brisbane is the **Lamington Plateau,** where you can stay at Binna Burra or O'Reilly's lodges.

The densest and least spoiled rain forests are 1,000 miles north of Brisbane (closer to Cairns): Kurando, Lake Eachem, Lake Barrine, Daintree River, and Cape Tribulation.

Hayles Tours runs a private bus service from Cairns to Cape Tribulation. The one-store town is near a good youth hostel with compound huts that surround a free-form swimming pool and a patio of logs sliced in cross sections. The restaurant serves fresh fish on ginger rice topped with coconut milk and flanked by mango strips—all for A$5.

Peacocks and parrots roam Cape Tribulation, which begins the **Daintree Rain Forest,** said to be the oldest on earth. The controversial new road that cuts through the forest is threatened by roots reaching down from branches to reclaim the red mud.

Wear long pants, long sleeves, and a hat to protect yourself from bugs and thorny plants. (Look out for ticks, which are unusually tenacious here; the wait-a-while plant, which has savage thorns; snakes; and leaches.)

Tropical Walkabouts, *tel. (61-70)98-5304,* offers guided day bushwalks to Daintree River and Cape Tribulation National Park for A$59.

For information on transportation to the rain forests, contact the **Queensland Government Travel Centre,** *196 Adelaide St., Brisbane, Queensland 4000.*

Australia's oldest residents

The aborigines lived in Australia for at least 39,000 years before Britain sent its prisoners to colonize the country. On the shores of Lake Mungo in western New South Wales, evidence remains of a cremation that took place 30,000 years ago. And caves on the Nullabor Plain and a Bass Strait island were occupied 20,000 years ago. Anthropologists estimate that 300,000 aborigines lived in Australia before 1770. They spoke 500 different languages.

The aborigines believe in Dreamtime, an age that existed at the dawn of creation and is still present, a timeless otherworld linking the past, present, and future. Mythological characters from Dreamtime, painted by the aborigines on rocks, can be seen at the **Nourlangie Rock Northern Territory** and other places throughout the country.

North of Cairns, in Laura, is the **Quinkon Reserve**, which boasts three rock galleries. Some of the paintings date from 13,200 B.C. The cracked and overhanging rocks were chosen because they face east and the rising sun.

The best of the three galleries is the **Split Rock Gallery,** a natural gallery displaying ancient aboriginal cave paintings. Two routes lead from Cairns to the gallery. The easier of the two is through the Outback; the more interesting but riskier route is via the well-named Cape Tribulation through the jungle. You will need an odometer to find the rock walls that are decorated with the murals, because all traces are invisible from the road.

Aborigines continue the artistic ways of their forefathers, decorating weapons, tools, and totems with colorful religious patterns and figures. Tribal dancers hold onto the steps and music symbolizing events in Dreamtime. The best-known dance is the Corroboree, performed by dancers covered with white paint and wearing leafy pompoms around their knees. Australia's 160,000 aborigines maintain their tribal traditions mainly in northern and Central Australia (Queensland is populated with more aborigines than any other state). About two-thirds of the aborigines are living a relatively modern lifestyle in the big cities. They are the poorest group in Australia, plagued by health problems, alcoholism, and culture shock.

Wujal Wujal, an aboriginal reserve, is in the Daintree Rain Forest, 30 miles from the nearest town of Helensvale. This village of impoverished shacks is littered with crashed cars, mysteriously parked on end, nose down, against trees. This position represents the ritual return to Dreamtime in aboriginal paintings.

The world's most mysterious rock

An island-size red monolith called **Ayer's Rock** lies in the heart of Australia. The largest rock on earth, it draws thousands of curious visitors and is part of a national park run by tribal elders and white officials. Situated in the Northern Territory, 200 miles southwest of Alice Springs, it could be considered the navel of the Australian Outback.

The Pitjantjatjara tribespeople call the rock Uluru and attach religious significance to it. On the north surface of the rock is a series of caves and grooves known as the Skull. Tribespeople believe this area of the rock served as the camp of their ancestors in Dreamtime before the world began. They perform initiation ceremonies here.

Resorts have been built near the rock. The best is the **Sheraton Ayers Rock,** *Yulara Drive, Yulara; tel. (61-89)562200.* Painted in the red hues of Ayer's Rock, it is kept cool by a huge white awning that stretches over the entire complex.

Yulara, 15 miles from the rock, has the **Four Seasons Hotel,** *(800)445-5505,* and campgrounds.

Between Alice Springs and Ayer's Rock are the **Desert Oaks Resort Centre,** *tel. (61-56)0984;* the **Wallara Ranch Motel and Camping Ground,** *tel. (61-56)2901;* and the **Curtin Springs Roadside Inn,** *tel. (61-56)2934.*

The best time to visit Ayer's Rock is during the Australian winter, from May to September, when rain makes the desert flower. Temperatures are in the 70s, rather than 140 degrees Fahrenheit, as they can be in the summer. For more information on visiting the rock, contact the **Northern Territory Tourist Commission,** *3550 Wilshire Blvd., Suite 1610, Los Angeles, CA 90010, (800)468-8222.*

A taste of the Outback

Australia's great **Outback,** a vast, hot, wilderness land in the heart of the continent, is inhabited by leathery stockmen and ancient aborigines. A little-known land, it stretches from the heart of Australia to the northwest. It was once known as the Back of Beyond. Cattle graze on million-acre ranches, or stations as they are known, on dusty turf that conceals diamonds, iron, aluminum, and uranium.

To really get to know the Outback, arrange a farm stay—a few days living with a family on a working farm or ranch. For more information, contact **Bed and Breakfast International,** *18-20 Oxford St., P.O. Box 442, Woollhara, Sydney, NSW 2025, Australia.*

Or live like a ranch hand at Escott Station, a rambling cattle ranch in the wilds of northern Queensland. You'll stay in a rustic guest cottage on the homestead, eat with the ranch hands, and get acquainted with the cattle.

Don't expect a luxurious, California-style dude ranch. The place has a bar, a swimming pool, and electricity, but you are not pampered with resort-type service. You won't spend your days enjoying planned recreational activities—life on a ranch involves hard work. If you're up to it, tag along with the stockmen and watch the bulls being castrated. Or you can help out with more palatable jobs, such as breaking horses, catching crocodiles, and fishing. You also can canoe on the Nicholson River and go on a wild pig shoot.

Bed and board is A$30 a day. Or you can stay in a tent out in the bush for A$38 a day, including a trained guide. For more information, contact Lyn Stolk, **Escott Barramundi Lodge,** *Escott Station, c/o Post Office, Burketown, Queensland 4830, Australia.*

A gem-studded land

The Outback, in places, is paved with gems. Towns in the region have names such as Sapphire, Rubyvale, and Emerald and are connected by dirt roads made from piles of earth heaped up by old-time miners. From time to time, valuable gems overlooked by miners are found in the dirt.

Finding a sapphire, emerald, or ruby could turn a vacation into a jackpot. A book on Australian gems advises that "although it's not recommended that gem hunters should begin to dig up roads in search of stones, many fine gemstones have been found on the sides of roads." The odds against finding a gem on the road are like those against winning big in Las Vegas. But in the road, you don't have to pay to play.

It's not as easy as stepping from your vehicle and picking up a rock or two along the road; however, you could get lucky. Roy Spencer, a 12-year-old boy, did. He picked up the Black Star of Queensland, a 1,156-carat sapphire, in a field. It was cut to a 733-carat star sapphire valued at US$450,000.

It's hard to see stones in the road. That sparkle you spy is most likely quartz or shards of glass from countless windshields that have been shattered along the way. Giant road trains— tractor trailers that tow huge dollies packed with freight or cattle—roar along the dirt tracks, shooting up rocks that demolish windshields. Because of this, most Australian vehicles that travel through the bush are outfitted with wire windshield guards or curved plastic shields.

The best way to set off on an Outback mining journey is to rent a camper in Sydney, then head north for the gem fields. Vans rent for about A$32 a day, plus 9 cents a mile. They are well-equipped, but you will need a few extra items, such as a shovel, a block and tackle, a spare gas can, a thermos, and some plastic bowls. Small refrigerators that run on 220 volts, generators, or porta gas are provided. Finding water can be a problem. The bore water brought up by windmills is drinkable, but it acts as a laxative. Carry your own supply.

Mining licenses cost US$15, but you don't need one for just a few days. Just don't try your luck on any claims you see pegged out.

Emerald is the first of the gem-field townships. Beyond this town are the fields near the mining village of **Sapphire,** a dingy, huddle of slapped-together shacks and tents. The main post office is a tiny one-room shanty. The Rough and Ready Pub is just down the dirt road.

If you don't manage to find a gem on your own, you can buy some in this region and sell them in the United States for a fine profit. One Yankee miner recently gave up on the quest for gems and bought one instead—a star sapphire (in Sapphire, of course) for A$30 (about US$20). Back in the United States, the stone was appraised at US$50.

If you'd rather search for the world-famous Australian opal, head for Coober Pedy or Lightning Ridge, in the center of the country, where 90% of the world's opals are mined.

Coober Pedy is an underground town on the edge of the formidable Simpson's Desert. Miners in this 120-degree desert live in underground caves, where the temperature is an even 65 degrees Fahrenheit. Water is trucked in and sold at 15 cents a gallon.

Opal buyers throng to this settlement to buy wholesale opal rock clusters or polished opals. Dutch buyers predominate.

Top train trips

Australian trains are the best way to see the Outback. Two routes are especially scenic.

The transcontinental **Indian-Pacific** runs from Sydney on the Pacific Ocean to Perth on the Indian Ocean. This route cuts through the Great Dividing Range and the pasture country to the west, the mining country around Broken Hill, along the shores of the Great Australian Bight, and across the vast expanse of the dry Nullabor Plains. The trip takes three days and costs A$543 first class (it's worth the extra money—economy class tends to be uncomfortable, noisy, and unpleasant). Book a few months in advance—berths are in demand, particularly in September and October, when the wildflowers are blooming.

The **Ghan** runs from Adelaide on the south coast to Alice Springs in the center of Australia, skirting the beautiful Simpson Desert and its dry salt lakes. This overnight journey is about A$220 first class, one way, including meals. The train has an entertainment car with slot machines, a hairdresser, a gift shop, VCR rentals, and video games for children.

Western Australia—the faraway land

Western Australia, the westernmost province, is about as far from Sydney and the east coast as you can get. This gigantic region's beauty is natural. Only 300,000 people live outside Perth, in an area four times the size of Texas.

The hottest town in Australia is in this province. **Marble Bar** has an average temperature of 96 degrees Fahrenheit.

The most beautiful sights in Westralia, as this region is known, are the fields of wildflowers. No ordinary fields these. They roll to the horizon, a patchwork quilt of blue, purple, red, and orange. Between August and October, more than 7,000 native species (some not found anywhere else on earth) blossom here. The most famous fields are near Albany on the southern coast and Geraldton, north of Perth.

Westralia also houses Australia's best ghost town. **Coolgardie,** once home to 15,000 rowdy, brawling gold miners, is now deserted except for tourists. Old covered wagons remain on the main street, where 29 hotels and bars once thrived. **Goldfields Exhibition,** *Bayley Street,* displays memorabilia from the gold rush of the 1890s, which brought nearly 200,000 miners to Westralia.

Kalgoorlie was the area's largest mining town, with two stock exchanges, seven newspapers, and some of the most expensive real estate in the country. Kalgoorlie still mines gold, but the pace has slowed.

The **Kimberley Plateau** raises its flat head in the northern corner of Westralia, covering a region larger than California but home to only 6,000 brave souls. The green Fitzroy River carves a gorge through the limestone plateau, its water filled with sharks, crocodiles, and stingrays. Caves once used by the aborigines as burial grounds can be seen at Windjana.

The world's cheapest ranches

Property has always been cheap in Australia, primarily for two reasons: low population and long distances. If you were to buy a cattle ranch on the ocean, with 10 miles of area, paddocks, houses, and a few thousand head of cattle, you could expect to pay about US$500,000, or less than US$1 an acre, with the improvements and livestock thrown in free. This is difficult to understand until you realize you're a day's drive from the nearest small town and if the car breaks you can forget about calling a mechanic.

For more information, contact the **Australian Land Development Company,** *1096 Doncaster Road, Doncaster East, Melbourne, Victoria, Australia; tel. (61-3)842-2288;* or **Budget Farmlets,** *Country Property Sales, Melbourne, Victoria, Australia; tel. (61-3)329-2244.*

Australia's best foods

Australia's culinary delights often have strange names—but don't let that stop you from trying them. Look for Moreton Bay bugs and Victorian yabbies (both are crustaceans, not insects), Sydney rock oysters, Queensland snapper, barramundi, John Dory fish, Tasmanian scallops, and shrimp from anywhere along Australia's 35,000-mile-long coastline. If you can find it, try some kangaroo-tail soup. For dessert, order pavlova, a delicious fruit, whipped cream, and meringue concoction.

Australian wines can be good. They have been compared favorably to those produced in France. The Baroosa Valley near Adelaide and Hunter Valley near Sydney are the prime wine-producing regions. The whites are superior to the reds.

Dinki-di: how to speak Strine

Australians don't speak English the way Americans do—they fracture it in their own way. They speak very fast and raise their voices at the ends of sentences, making every one sound like a question. They also invert subjects and objects, as in "nice buy, this" or "good ale, that."

Most Australian slang is based on rhyming Cockney slang. Septic and sepo are derogatory terms for Americans. (Yanks rhymes with tanks, as in septic tanks.) It's not easy to pick up.

Australians also shorten everything. A milkman is called a milko, a garbage man is a garbo. A postal worker is a postie. And they have a habit of answering questions with questions. If you ask, "What time does the movie start?" the ticket seller probably will answer, "You want to see the feature, do you?"

A few words of strine to keep in mind: a bathing suit is a cozzie; the real thing is dinki-di; an appetizer is an entrée; a sidewalk is a footpath; a popsicle is an ice block or icy pole; napkins are serviettes; thank you is ta; and a can of beer is a tinny or a tube.

Top travel tips

Qantas, Air New Zealand, United, Continental, and UTA French Airlines provide service between the United States and Australia, and Canadian Pacific Air connects Australia with Canada. Most carriers offer advance-purchase fares that include layovers in the Pacific Islands, and Qantas usually has fares that include stops in the Far East. The around-the-world fares range from US$1,345 to US$1,745. APEX fares through Qantas range from US$1,195 to US$1,545. Continental is cheapest, with Los Angeles to Sydney prices ranging from US$995 to US$1,545 round trip. In general, fares are highest from December to March.

Qantas' Circle 8 fare is the best bargain at US$1,580 from September to November and US$1,730 from December to March round trip from Los Angeles or San Francisco. **Qantas, (800)227-4500,** also has a special around-the-world offer in conjunction with **TWA, (800)221-2000,** for US$2,599.

You can save on the cost of rail travel within Australia by purchasing an Austrailpass, similar to the Eurailpass, before you leave home. First-class and economy versions are available, and the cost depends on class and the length of your stay rather than distance traveled. For more information, contact **Australian Travel Service/Tour Pacific,** *P.O. Box 2078, 116 South Louise, Glendale, CA 91205, (818)247-4564.*

Chapter 23

THE BEST OF NEW ZEALAND

New Zealand is a land of spectacular scenery: shooting geysers, cloud-shrouded mountain peaks, bubbling hot springs, deep-blue fjords, and secluded coves. It is also a land of extremes, with both tropical beaches and icebergs.

The Kiwis, as the people of New Zealand are affectionately known, love their land and are among the most ardent conservationists in the world. They are as varied and interesting as the landscape they seek to preserve. The Maoris, a Polynesian people who lived here long before the Europeans arrived, maintain their ancient traditions. The Europeans, too, preserve their old ways. Scottish dances seldom seen even in Scotland are danced by kilted sheep farmers.

This is the best place in the world for nature lovers, thrill seekers, and sports buffs. You can raft down a wild mountain river, battle a fighting rainbow trout, explore magnificent fjords, climb or ski the Southern Alps, or hike the awe-inspiring Milford Track.

New Zealand, which is made up of three main islands (North, South, and Stewart) and a number of smaller ones, stretches 1,000 miles along the southern tip of Polynesia. Its nearest neighbor is Australia, 1,300 miles to the northwest.

New Zealand's largest city

Auckland, huddled on an isthmus separating Waitemata and Manukau harbors, has 14 volcanoes, each with tremendous views. The best panorama is from **Mt. Eden,** the highest point in the city. Hike up the cowpath or road and picnic in the volcano's grassy bowl while enjoying the view.

Known as the Queen City among its inhabitants, Auckland has restaurants, cinemas, shops, theaters, concerts, and art galleries. It also has 102 mainland beaches and 23 secluded islands. The Hauraki Gulf is a favorite among boaters (and Auckland has a lot of boaters—one in every four homeowners also owns a boat).

The world's best Polynesian museum

The **War Memorial Museum,** built in memory of the New Zealanders who died fighting in World War I, houses the world's best collection of Maori and Polynesian artifacts, some dating back to A.D. 1200. The pièce de résistance is a 98-foot war canoe carved from a giant totara tree. It carried 80 Maori warriors at a time.

The best Kiwi art

The world's biggest collection of paintings by New Zealand artists is at the **Auckland City Art Gallery,** *Kitchener and Wellsley streets.* Especially worth seeing are works by John Webber and William Hodges, both of whom accompanied Captain Cook on his voyages in the South Pacific in the 18th century.

Animal bests

Animal lovers should make time to visit one of Auckland's three race courses (**Epsom, Ellerslie,** and **Avondale**); the **Auckland Zoo,** where the nocturnal, flightless kiwi bird can be seen; and the **Lion Safari Park** in Massey.

The best bargains in town

Good, inexpensive shops are located downtown, near Quay and Queen streets. Just east of the intersection is the **Old Customhouse,** which has been converted into a mall with a movie theater, arts and crafts shops, a tavern, and a bookstore. Built in 1889, the Customhouse is one of the few examples of Victorian architecture in Auckland.

A 10-minute walk west from the corner of Queen and Quay is the **Victoria Park Market,** located in the city's former trash dump (it's quite picturesque, believe it or not). You can buy kiwi fruit for a few cents apiece, fresh fish, and inexpensive clothing.

Polynesian bests

Karangahape Road (known as K Road) is where Auckland's Polynesian population shops. You can buy brilliantly colored cloth and tropical foods here alongside matrons from Samoa, Fiji, Tonga, and Cook islands. (Auckland has the largest Polynesian population of any city in the world. More than 70,000 residents have Maori ancestry, and 58,000 Pacific islanders have immigrated here.)

Auckland's best dining

Most of the better restaurants in Auckland don't have liquor licenses. But you usually can bring your own wine (which brings down the price of dinner considerably).

Auckland's best is **Antoine's,** *333 Parnell Road; tel. (64-9)798-756,* a French restaurant in a sun-drenched colonial house with linen-covered tables. Wine *is* served here. Ring the doorbell to enter.

Another good bet is **Le Gourmet,** *1 Williamson Ave., Grey Lynn 2; tel. (64-9)769-499.* Chef Warwick Brown creates dishes using only fresh ingredients.

August Moon is Auckland's best Chinese restaurant, with hand-carved teak decor and dancing.

The best hotels

Auckland's only five-star hotel is the newly built **Regent,** *Albert Street; tel. (64-9)398-882.* Rooms are about NZ$200 per night.

Other good hotels are the impersonal but efficient **Hyatt Kingsgate Auckland,** *Waterloo Quadrant and Princes Street; tel. (64-9)797-220;* and the **Sheraton Auckland,** *83 Symonds St.; tel. (64-9)795-132.* Both are centrally located and have double rooms for about NZ$180.

The most interesting night life

The bar at the **Abbey Hotel,** *Wellesley and Albert streets,* is known as the watering hole for Auckland's literati. A British-style lounge, it is frequented by sociable intellectuals, always looking for a lively battle over ideology. If you plan to get involved in the nightly squabble (it's all in good fun) be sure to read up first. The Kiwis have a good grasp of current events.

K Road, Auckland's red-light and theater district, intersects Ponsonby Road, which is lined with restaurants.

The Quay, a key travel hub

The **Quay,** in addition to offering a view of Harbor Bridge, is a transportation center. You can get a Bus-About pass here that allows you to ride public buses for less. You also can catch a ferry here to take you to the islands and beaches in Hauraki Gulf.

Capital Wellington

The growing city of **Wellington,** the capital of New Zealand, sprawls along the southern tip of North Island. For a view of Wellington's harbor and skyline, ascend **Mt. Victoria.** (A Maori burial ground was bulldozed to make room for the viewing platform.) White wooden houses cover the green hills surrounding the city. The beaches of the Inner Harbor are popular, and on summer weekends the harbor is filled with yachts.

Wellington is a cultural center, with two professional theater companies, numerous amateur dramatic and musical societies, the New Zealand Symphony Orchestra, and the Royal New Zealand Ballet Company. The recently completed Michael Fowler Center and St. Paul's Cathedral (built in 1866) both sponsor plays and concerts.

From **Lambton Quay,** bright red cable cars carry pedestrians 397 feet over the suburbs to the beautiful **Botanical Gardens.**

The **National Museum and Art Gallery** in the suburb of Newtown has superb Maori artifacts, items used by Captain Cook, geological collections, colonial history displays, and works of art by national and international masters.

Wellington's best restaurant is the **Plimmer House,** *Boulcott Street; tel. (64-4)721-872,* in a lovely restored building. Order the duckling or venison.

Pierre's, *342 Tinakori Road, Thorndon; tel. (64-4)726238,* is a good French-style bistro.

The highlights of North Island

North Island is the cradle of New Zealand. It was here that the Europeans first landed and faced off with the native Maori. The island's beauty belies its violent past—it is fringed with beautiful, palm-shaded beaches and blessed with hospitable weather year-round. Explore it from north to south.

New Zealand's northernmost point

Cape Reinga, the country's northernmost point, affords a magnificent view of the Pacific Ocean and the Tasman Sea. Its graceful white lighthouse seems frail and vulnerable, facing the rage of two great bodies of water from the ridge of a narrow point of land.

The Maoris believe this is where spirits of the dead depart for their journey back to the ancestral land, which they call Hawaiki.

The cape is a pleasant 3 1/2-hour drive on Highway 1 or 1-hour flight from Auckland. It is a great place to camp, but it lacks hotels. Try camping at Houhora or Taputupoto bays.

The best beaches

Doubtless Bay is a crescent of perfect sandy beaches that draws throngs on holidays. **Houhora** is a beach favored by fishermen, smugglers, picnickers, and campers.

Ninety Mile Beach (which is only 57 miles long) is a seemingly endless stretch of golden sandy beaches lined with dunes and embroidered with seashells. This is the scene of a fishing contest each summer and the prime spot to find toheroa, a much sought-after shellfish.

The largest private museum

The **Wagner Museum** at Houhora Heads is the country's largest private museum, containing rare pre-European Maori artifacts, an excellent natural history display, and extensive exhibits from the Victorian era.

The Bay of Islands

The **Bay of Islands** is where Captain Cook landed, Charles Darwin researched, and the mighty Hongi Hika (the Maori chief who ruled over New Zealand until his death in 1828) lived. The bay is a boaters' paradise, offering every imaginable craft for charter. Numerous world-record catches of marlins, tuna, yellowtails, threshers, mako sharks, and hammerhead sharks have been made on local deep-sea fishing launches.

The **Waitangi Treaty House,** on the Bay of Islands, is where Maori chiefs and English gentlemen signed a treaty in 1840 ending conflict, giving the Maoris land rights, and admitting New Zealand to the British Empire. Next to the little white house, now a museum, is a splendidly carved wooden Maori meeting house. On the grounds is a 13-foot-long Maori canoe. And nearby, close to the Waitangi Bridge, is the **Museum of Shipwrecks.**

Russell was the first European settlement and the first capital of New Zealand. The town's 19th-century buildings give it a Victorian flavor, but Russell has been known as the sin center of the Pacific. Today the yacht crowd frequents the town.

Paihia is the best place to stay along the bay, because of its many restaurants, bars, and places to rent boats. But its red sand beaches are less seductive than the golden ones farther north. From **Fuller's Launch** you can hop aboard a cream trip, once made to collect milk from dairy farmers, now made to deliver mail and provisions.

The hottest beach

The **Coromandel Peninsula,** on the east coast of North Island, has New Zealand's hottest (and strangest) swimming spot: **Hot Water Beach.** Named for the hot springs that seep through its sand, the beach literally steams. You can create your own thermal pool by digging into the sand.

The peninsula is also the mecca of alternative lifestyles and naturalists. The back-to-nature movement is as healthy here in the 1980s as it was in the United States in the 1960s.

Best view, best spring

Kaikohe has spectacular views of both the Tasman and the Pacific coasts, as well as a museum called Pioneer Village. Nearby are **Ngawha Springs,** which have the highest mineral content in the world and are known for their curative qualities.

The most magnificent trees

Magnificent native kauri trees stand along the road that runs through the 6,100-acre **Waipoua Kauri Sanctuary.** The largest is the mighty Tane Mahuta (Lord of the Forest), which is estimated to be 1,200 years old. The oldest is 2,000-year-old the Te Matua Ngahere (Father of the Forest).

Waikato: the best of the Maoris

North of **Hamilton,** which is the capital of New Zealand's rural Waikato region and the largest inland city, is the center of Maori culture. **Turangawaewae Marae** is the focal point of a Maori revival movement organized in the 1920s by Princess Te Puea Herangi, who established a complex of buildings on the river. The complex includes traditionally carved meeting houses and a concert hall. It is not generally open to the public, but you can see it from across the river at the bridge downstream. The sacred burial ground of the Waikato Maoris is 2.5 miles downstream at **Mt. Taupiri.**

The scene of the last battle of the Wakato Land Wars in 1864 is southwest in **Orakau.** Maori leader Rewi Maniapoto and 300 men, women, and children fought off 1,400 colonial soldiers for three days before they lost their fortified village.

The finest Maori carved meeting house is in Te Kuiti in southern **Waitomo.** Maori leader Te Kooti Rikirangi built the wooden structure to thank the local Maniapoto people, who gave him refuge when he was in danger.

The rose of New Zealand

The magnificent rose gardens of **Te Awamutu,** southwest of Hamilton, have earned this town the title, Rose Town of New Zealand. The roses are best seen in November during the annual Rose Festival. New Zealand's oldest and loveliest church is here; **St. John's Anglican Church** was built in 1854.

New Zealand's largest lake

Lake Taupo, at the heart of North Island, is the largest New Zealand lake, extending over 232 square miles and filling an old volcanic crater. The trout fishing is terrific in the lake and the rivers and streams that feed it. You can fish here year-round.

One of New Zealand's most attractive lodge-hotels is on the banks of Lake Taupo: **Huka Lodge,** *P.O. Box 95, Huka Falls Road, Taupo; tel. (64-74)85791.*

The best adventures

At the southern end of Lake Taupo are the renowned trout-fishing and river-rafting waters of the Tongariro and Wanganui rivers, Kaimanawa State Forest Park, and Tongariro National Park, all accessible from Turangi.

Tongariro National Park, with its snow-capped mountain peaks, is a superb ski resort in winter and a scenic place to hike in summer. An extensive network of paths and huts makes it easy to explore the park and its historic Maori sights. The volcanic peaks of Tongariro, Ruapehu, and Ngauruhoe are the focal points. **Château Tongariro,** *Mt. Ruapehu; tel. (64-812)23-809,* is a luxurious hotel at the heart of the park's spectacular mountains.

On Wanganui River you can take boat trips, guided canoe treks, and white-water rafting expeditions.

Rotorua: a heavenly Hades

"I was pleased to get so close to Hades and be able to return," said playwright George Bernard Shaw after visiting the area around **Rotorua City**—the boiling, bubbling, steaming center of North Island.

Located on this volcanic rift that once inspired great fear, Rotorua is New Zealand's number-one tourist spot, surrounded by thermal springs, Maori villages, and 10 trout-filled lakes. Boiling mud, erupting geysers, steaming terraces of sulphur, and colorful silica deposits combine to create an other-worldly landscape.

Rotorua has the greatest concentration of Maori residents of any New Zealand city. The historic Maori village of **Ohinemutu,** on the lake, has a 19th-century traditional meeting house that took 12 years to carve. The Christian church, **St. Faith's,** built in 1910, has a window with a Maori Christ, elaborate carvings, and a bust of Queen Victoria presented to the Maoris by Britain for their loyalty to the crown.

The Maoris live their traditional lifestyle at **Whakarewarewa,** where they use the boiling pools for cooking and washing. The **Maori Arts and Crafts Center** displays traditional works of wood carving, weaving, and greenstone carving. A replica of a pre-European Maori fortified village is featured, and traditional Maori concerts are presented.

On Geyser Flat in Whakarewarewa is New Zealand's greatest geyser, **Pohutu** (Splashing), which shoots 100 feet into the air several times a day. The smaller geyser next to it usually erupts just before Pohutu does.

Rotorua City was established as a sanatorium in 1880, when the New Zealand government leased the land from the Maoris. **Tudor Towers,** which houses a museum and an art gallery, was the original bathhouse. To its right are the **Polynesian Pools,** whose sulphurous waters are still used at the Queen Elizabeth Hospital to treat rheumatism and arthritis. Another good hot pool is **Hinemoa,** on Mokoia Island, in the middle of Lake Rotorua.

New Zealand's most beautiful drive

The road around the **East Cape** is one of the most rugged yet beautiful coastal drives in New Zealand, passing small historic settlements, pleasant coves and beaches, and wild countryside that remains rich in Maori tradition and culture. Some of the finest Maori carvings can be seen in the traditional meeting houses of this district, which is the first in the world to greet the morning sun.

The world's only mainland gannet reserve

The world's only mainland gannet (a large yellow-headed seabird) sanctuary is to the south of Cape Kidnappers, where large flocks can be seen between April and October. The reserve can be reached by four-wheel-drive vehicles or on foot.

The world's best sheep shearing

Masterton, on the southern tip of North Island, hosts the annual Golden Shears competition—a sheep-shearing contest that attracts shearers from all over the world. The town, located in the rich Wairarapa farming country, is filled with craftspeople.

South Island: the most beautiful

New Zealand's most spectacular scenery is on **South Island.** At **Punakaiki,** for example, nature has carved limestone rocks into what look like giant stacks of pancakes. The Tasman Sea rushes into bore holes in these oddly shaped rocks, making great shuddering booms. The island's most memorable sights are described below, starting at the north end, following along the Pacific Coast, crossing the Southern Alps, and then following the Tasman Coast.

The best boat charters

Ferries from North Island land in **Picton,** a busy little port in South Island's incredibly beautiful Marlborough Sounds, 597 miles of waterways sheltered by bays and coves. Picton is the base for charter boat companies that take you cruising, fishing, and diving.

The **Picton Hotel,** *Waikawa Road; tel. (64-57)37-202,* is pleasant, with a pool, private bathrooms, and a restaurant. **Bellevue,** *34 Auckland St.; tel. (64-57)36-598,* is a cozy little guesthouse.

The least-traveled trail

New Zealand is crisscrossed by well-marked trails leading through spectacular scenery. One of the least known, and therefore least crowded, is the **Nydia Trail,** along the Marlborough Sounds. Passing through genuine wilderness, the trail has no access road. A mailboat that serves farms and vacation homes also delivers hikers to any starting point along the 80-mile trail. If prearranged, the mailboat will pick you up again farther north. Check with the ranger station or public information office in the harbor town of Havelock for maps and to arrange transportation.

One good route along the trail begins at Shag Poing in Kauma Bay. Heading north, you will cross two fast-running jade-green rivers near a deer farm. (The Japanese buy the velvet of the deer antlers and use it as an aphrodisiac.) The trail then climbs the first of several 1,000-foot saddles with a view of the valley below. You can quench your thirst at a waterfall before continuing across a stretch of private property. Keep an eye out for wild goats and boars—and take cover if you spot any.

You'll definitely need an accurate map and a compass if you're going to hike the Nydia Trail—it is barely marked and rarely tramped.

The wildest coastline

South of Picton, at **Kaikoura,** the Pacific Coast is at its wildest. The town is on a narrow peninsula buffeted by the ocean and protected by rocky cliffs and a narrow beach. Nearby are limestone caves and seal colonies. The Kaikoura Mountains are a dramatic backdrop. The peninsula is popular among fishermen and known for its large crayfish.

The most English town

Nestled at the base of Banks Peninsula on the edge of the Canterbury Plains is the garden city of **Christchurch,** a very English town. The river that meanders through its center, past old stone buildings and terraced houses, is called the Avon.

The city museum houses an excellent exhibit on the history of Antarctic exploration that includes equipment used by the English and Norwegian teams that competed to reach the South Pole. The museum also has an exhibit demonstrating the movement of continents.

Noah's Hotel, *corner of Oxford Terrace and Worcester Street; tel. (64-3)794-700,* is a first-class, centrally located hotel with an elegant restaurant called the Waitangi Room.

The **Cotswold Inn,** *88-90 Papanui Road; tel. (64-3)553-535,* is pleasant, with authentic period furnishings.

The best fishing

The **Canterbury** region, especially the town of Methven, is a mecca for salmon and trout fishermen. During the summer, quinnat salmon run in the Rangitata and Ashburton rivers near Geraldine. Three major salmon-fishing contests are held each year on the Rangitata, Rakaia, and Waitaki rivers.

New Zealand's only castle

The Edwardian and Victorian houses of **Dunedin,** on the southernmost Pacific Coast, embrace Otago Harbor, a 12-mile fjord. On one of the hills overlooking the city is New Zealand's only castle, **Larnach,** a century-old manor built in 1871 by J.M. Larnach, minister of the crown. The castle took 14 years to build, its ceilings 12 years to carve. The strangely European edifice was built to impress Larnach's French wife. Perhaps it didn't work; she committed suicide in Wellington's parliament building years later. The castle has been restored, and its 43 rooms are open to the public.

The world's largest flying bird

The world's largest bird of flight, the rare royal albatross, can be seen in all its glory at **Taiaroa Head,** at the tip of Otago Peninsula near Dunedin. The graceful bird has a 10-foot wingspan and hovers above the sea like a kite. The oldest-known wild bird in the world is an albatross. Since 1937, when she was banded, this albatross has returned here each year.

About 20 pairs of royal albatrosses circle the globe each year, at speeds of up to 66 miles per hour, to roost at Taiaroa. They mate for life and produce one chick every two years. You can observe the birds up close from a newly opened lookout.

The Devil's Marbles

North of Dunedin, on a beach near the fishing village of **Moeraki,** are the intriguing Moeraki boulders known as **The Devil's Marbles,** strange spherical rocks weighing several tons. The huge stones were formed 60-million years ago by the accumulation of lime salts.

The shortest route across the Alps

The shortest route across the Southern Alps passes through the Alpine playground that is **Arthur's Pass National Park.** The picturesque mountain village of Arthur's Pass is a great base for mountain climbing, hiking, hunting, skiing, and breathing fresh mountain air. If you'd like to savor the area, stay a few nights at the **Chalet,** *P.O. Box 5; tel. (64-516)34-506,* a Swiss Alpine-style chalet with five rooms.

The Tasman Coast—a nature-lover's best

The **Tasman Coast,** on the other side of the island, is a good place to go if you like hiking, mountain climbing, rafting, or watching animals. It has three major national parks and is flanked by rugged mountains and washed by turbulent rivers.

New Zealand's best glaciers

The 217,000-acre **Westland National Park** has New Zealand's two most beautiful glaciers: Fox and Franz Josef. Arrange a (strenuous) guided hike across the icy masses at the park headquarters in the town of Franz Josef (the native forest is crisscrossed with 68 miles of trails). Or take a helicopter or ski plane over the shining glaciers.

New Zealand's highest peak: Mt. Cook

Mt. Cook, at 12,349 feet, is New Zealand's highest mountain. Sir Edmund Hillary, the first man to climb Mt. Everest, trained here. The mountain is at the heart of **Mt. Cook National Park,** which also features the beautiful 18-mile Tasman Glacier (and four other very high, very large glaciers). Ski planes operate regular flights to the head of Tasman—an exhilarating experience.

One of the best hotels in the area, the **Hermitage,** *Glentanner; tel. (64-562-1)809,* is a chalet at the foot of Mt. Cook.

The most spectacular park

Fjordland National Park, at the southern tip of South Island, is one of the largest national parks in the world, much of it unexplored. Lonely fjords lap at the mountains, while waterfalls tumble thousands of feet into the densely forested valleys. The fourth-largest waterfall in the world, **Sutherland Falls,** drops 1,873 feet through the forest. The gateway to the park is the town of **Te Anau,** which is the place to go for hotels and restaurants.

Fjordland Travel Limited, *P.O. Box 1, Te Anau, New Zealand; telex Fjord NZ 4183,* offers boat and bus tours of Doubtful Sound that take you to see Lake Manapouri, the Wilmot Pass, and many beaches.

The eighth wonder of the world

According to Rudyard Kipling, the **Milford Sound,** which leads from Fjordland National Park to the sea, is the eighth wonder of the world. And who are we to argue with Kipling? The scenery is indeed spectacular: misty peaks, waterfalls tumbling down green cliffs, and cottony clouds reflected in the mirror-like water. The sound is dominated by 6,247-foot **Mitre Peak,** a pyramid-like mountaintop. And it is fed by the spectacular **Bowen Falls,** which drop 531 feet.

The most beautiful walk in the world

The 33-mile **Milford Track,** which makes its way through Fjordland National Park to the Milford Sound, is the most beautiful walk in the world. To get here, take a boat across Te Anau Lake to Glade House. Leading through rain forests, meadows, and mountain passes, the trail passes wild rivers, deep fjords, and crashing waterfalls. The clearly marked track takes five days to hike; it is suitable even for the novice.

You can hike independently or join a group (which costs about NZ$726). You stay in shelters along the way. Only a limited number of hikers (64) are permitted on the trail each day, so write to the **Milford Track Office,** *Tourist Hotel Corporation of New Zealand, Private Bag, Wellington, New Zealand,* as far in advance as possible (up to one year) to make arrangements. Reservations also can be made by travel agents in the United States through the New Zealand Central Reservations Office in California.

The most southerly Alpine pass

Haast Pass is the most southerly, and the most historic, of the trans-Alpine passages, following an ancient Maori route through a rugged, breathtaking landscape. The contrast between the east and west sides of the pass is dramatic—**Westland** is lush; **Otago,** on the other side of the pass, is a dry region, relieved by lakes.

The pass runs through **Mt. Aspiring National Park,** a 100-mile reserve that covers most of the southern Alps. Looming above the park is 9,961-foot Mt. Aspiring. Much of the park's activities (hiking and fishing) are centered in its headquarters at Lake Wanaka.

The most beautiful lakes

Mackenzie Country (named for a Scottish shepherd who tried to hide stolen sheep in this isolated area at the heart of South Island) is a rural area known for its six glacial lakes, the largest of which are Tekapo, Pukaki, and Ohau. Lake Tekapo is an unbelievable turquoise color (the result of powdered rock ground by the glaciers feeding the lake). All the lakes offer great fishing. A nice place to stay is **Parkhead Holiday Motel,** *Pioneer Drive, Lake Tekapo; tel. (64-5056)868,* on the lake shore.

Queenstown: the most sophisticated resort

Nestled on the shores of clear blue Lake Wakatipu is Tyrolean-style **Queenstown.** Once a sleepy lakeside town, Queenstown has become the country's most sophisticated resort, with restaurants, hotels, an airport, and ski slopes. Any adventure is possible here: jet boating, white-water rafting, canoeing, sailing, jet skiing, water skiing, horseback riding, snow skiing, back-country safaris, and helicopter flights. You can cruise Lake Wakatipu on the *TSS Earnshlaw* steamer or follow its southern border aboard the Kingston Flyer steam train.

The **A Line Motor Inn,** *27 Stanley St.; tel. (64-294)27-700,* is a nice hotel with a restaurant overlooking Queenstown Bay. Rooms are about NZ$170.

The **Lakeland Regency,** *Lake Esplanade; tel. (64-294)27-600,* has scenic views, its own restaurant, and private bathrooms. It also has a pool. Rooms are about $NZ150.

The **Nugget Point Club,** *Arthurs Point Road; tel. (64-294)27-630,* is a luxury sporting resort.

Stewart Island, the unspoiled

Across Foveaux Strait from South Island is **Stewart Island,** an untouched haven of dense forest with birds, animals, and flowers. The tiny fishing village of **Oban** is the main town on the island. Bush walks and paths spread out from it to strategically placed huts throughout the northern part of the island. You can hike one of the many trails that circle the island.

Stewart Island is a bird-watcher's paradise. You can see tuis, bellbirds, wekas, tomtits, and wood pigeons. And you can hear their songs year-round from the woods and meadows.

Buffeted by both the Arctic and the Pacific oceans, Stewart Island's early settlers had a hard life. Many abandoned the island, fed up with the harsh storms and the cold winters, and left behind their homes, sawmills, tin mines, and whaling stations.

The place to stay is **South Seas Hotel,** in the middle of Oban. This is where the island's inhabitants meet for a beer. If you're not interested in a beer, just enjoy the view of the harbor.

The world's best summer skiing

When it's summer in the United States, it's winter in New Zealand, and the mountains are cloaked in heavy snow. Summer skiing in New Zealand is much cheaper than winter skiing in the United States (not counting the air fare, of course). Lift tickets are NZ$18, about half the price of those at U.S. ski resorts. And hotels and restaurants are much less expensive.

The largest ski area

The largest and most popular ski area in New Zealand is the **Whakapapa Skifield** in Tongariro National Park on North Island. The slopes descend from Mt. Ruapehu, a dormant volcano. Skiers are warned that part of the ski area is in a mudflow danger zone.

The park is a comfortable one-day drive from Auckland. Head south on State Highway 4, then turn on to Provincial Highway 48, which takes you into the park and eventually up to the slopes. If you arrive early in the morning, the road to the top of Ruapehu is usually clear of snow and ice, allowing you to drive all the way to the parking area. Midday, however, usually brings fresh snowfall, and you may be forced to leave your car below and ride up the hill on a goat (a comfortable, four-wheel-drive bus).

An adult full-day lift ticket is about NZ$30; a half-day ticket is about NZ$20; and a season pass is about NZ$495. These fees allow you to use the platter lift, four chair lifts, four T-bars, two pomas, and seven rope tows. With a capacity of 10,000 skiers per hour, these lifts provide access up to 7,200 feet. Whakapapa has slopes for every level of skier, including a superb national downhill course for experts.

Skiing across the top of the last face of the High Traverse, you can look up into the chimney at the end of the run. The chimney isn't very long, but when you drop in from the top you can't see the slope below—and you have no retreat. It's a bit like stepping into an empty elevator shaft. A thrill for even the most jaded.

On the flanks of **Mt. Ruapehu,** accommodations range from the luxurious Château Tongariro to the rustic cabins at Skotel, from high-class motels and club chalets to a trailer park. If you want to stay at the Château Tongariro, make your reservations well in advance. An elegant restaurant in the basement serves delicious steak and seafood.

The longest ski season

Mt. Hutt, on South Island, has New Zealand's longest ski season, extending from May through November. It boasts the earliest operating date of any skifield in the Southern Hemisphere. The field itself is set in a huge bowl that collects snow. Early in the season is the best time to ski powder snow; little patches of powder hide in the shadows of ridges.

Mt. Hutt has several great routes that offer 700 vertical meters of skiing and a range of slopes and snow types. Facilities include one chair lift and four T-bars. You can heliski here, too, with the help of Methven Heliski, which flies to the upper Rakai Ranges. Ski lessons at Mt. Hutt are NZ$16; ski rental is NZ$21; and ski lifts are NZ$32.

New Zealand's wooliest bargain

New Zealand supports a flock of 70-million sheep. So it shouldn't be a surprise that fleece is a way of life for many and the backbone of the New Zealand economy. An army of home knitters stands by to turn the raw material into sweaters, gloves, hats, and scarves. The handiwork of New Zealanders pays off in apparel that is sturdy and well-designed.

The wool varies from breed to breed, but most is incredibly dense and full of lanolin, which makes it water-resistant (and gives knitters baby-soft hands). Undyed yarn, enough to make three to four sweaters, can be bought for NZ$100.

For those who like their wool still on the hide, New Zealand is also one of the world's greatest marketplaces for sheepskin. A sheepskin throw rug is less than NZ$75.

The best travel bargain

A New Zealand **Railways Travelpass** makes traveling through the country easier and less expensive. Unlimited travel, including the boat between North and South islands, is $NZ540 for 15 days; $NZ625 for 22 days. For information, write **Travelpass,** *c/o Passenger Business Group, New Zealand Railways Corporation, Private Bag, Wellington, New Zealand.*

THE BEST OF LATIN AMERICA AND THE CARIBBEAN

North Americans tend to laud the charm and culture of Europe and Asia, while ignoring the wonders to the south. What a mistake! Latin America and the Caribbean have some of the world's most gorgeous beaches, tallest waterfalls, ancient cultures, mystifying ruins, exotic foods, and friendly people. What's more, Latin America and parts of the Caribbean have yet to be overwhelmed by hordes of tourists, and hotels and restaurants are often cheap.

Chapter 24

THE BEST OF MEXICO

Mexico is the best choice for an inexpensive vacation in a warm and exotic foreign country. It is perfect for sun worshippers, hardy adventurers, high rollers, and those on a tight budget. South of the border you'll find beautiful beaches, unexplored wilderness, cosmopolitan cities, historic monuments, and good food—all for next to nothing.

The telephone situation in Mexico is complicated. To call Mexico City, dial 1-905, then the local telephone number. For the rest of Mexico, dial 011 (the international operator), then 52 (the country code for Mexico), then the city code and local number.

In general, Mexico's telephone system functions poorly. It is not uncommon, for example, to get a busy signal time after time, even though the number you are calling is not in use.

Most Mexican hotels and some of the larger restaurants accept dollars as well as pesos. However, we recommend exchanging dollars for pesos at a bank and paying in pesos; banks give a much better exchange rate than hotels and restaurants.

Keep in mind that prices in this chapter may have changed by the time you read it, because the inflation rate in Mexico is high. In 1987, the inflation rate was 132%.

Mexico City: the world's largest landlocked city

Mexico City is the largest city in Mexico, with the largest population of any city in the world. It is the cultural, political, and commercial hub of the country. Located on a plateau, it is surrounded by mountains. Colonial architecture gives it a Spanish air.

The best place to put the city in perspective is the rooftop bar of the 44-floor **Latin American Tower,** *Eje Central Lazaro Cardenas.*

The best museums

The best place to begin your tour of the city is the **Museo de la Ciuded** (City Museum), *Pino Suarez 30.* Formerly the Palace of the Counts of Santiago (early Spanish conquistadors who came to the New World seeking their fortunes), it documents Mexico City's history in chronological order from the Aztecs through the 20th century. The museum is open Tuesdays through Sundays from 9:30 a.m. to 7:30 p.m., and a small admission fee is charged. Tours in English are conducted at least once a week.

The **National Museum of Anthropology,** *Paseo de la Reforma,* in Chapultepec Park, houses most of Mexico's excavated pre-Columbian treasures, including artifacts from the Palenque tombs, Mexico's most spectacular Mayan site. The architecture and figurines at Palenque strangely resemble those at ancient Oriental sites in Cambodia, which is possible evidence of a direct ancestral link.

The museum also houses an Aztec calendar stone that divides the year accurately into a 52-week cycle, providing evidence of early Indian civilizations' ability to use astronomy to divide time. On the second floor a display depicts present-day Indian lifestyles in Mexico. Bilingual guides are available for tours. The museum is open from 9 a.m. to 7 p.m. daily except Mondays.

Bellas Artes Museum, *Lazaro Cardenás,* has a permanent collection of Mexico's world-famous muralists, including a duplicate of the Diego Rivera mural commissioned for the Rockefeller Center in New York City. (Because Rivera depicted John D. Rockefeller as a greedy capitalist, the copy in New York is now covered by another less provocative mural.)

If you visit the Bellas Artes Museum on a Sunday or a Wednesday, you can see a performance by **Ballet Folklorico,** a lively folk ballet company. The glass curtain hung across the stage was commissioned from Tiffany's. The museum is open from 10:30 a.m. to 6:30 p.m. daily except Mondays.

A bit of Austria-Hungary

In Chapultepec Park, once the royal hunting grounds of the Aztecs, is **Chapultepec Castle,** once the imperial residence of the Hapsburgs, whose quarters are now on display. This unlikely bit of Austria-Hungary in the heart of Mexico was engineered by Napoleon III of France, who in 1864 installed the Hapsburg prince Maximillian as the governor of Mexico. Needless to say, this ill-thought-out bit of colonialism didn't work. In 1867, this outpost of Napoleon's empire collapsed, Maximillian was killed, and his widow went mad.

The castle, which is a museum today, also displays a collection of 19th-century art and costumes. It is open to the public from 9 a.m. to 5 p.m. daily except Mondays. A small admission fee is charged.

The best crafts

Mexico is known for its regional crafts, including leatherwork, furniture, blown glass, ceramics, pottery, textiles, tinwork, and woodcarving. At the **Museum of Popular Art,** in Chapultepec Park, you can inspect the country's handicrafts, then purchase your favorites at the adjacent stores. Prices are relatively cheap, and the quality is usually good. The museum is closed Mondays.

The zocalo: the heart of the city

Many of Mexico City's attractions are on the zocalo, the main city square. The grandest is the **National Palace,** which houses most of Mexico's government offices. It is a beautiful example of colonial architecture, especially dramatic when illuminated during Mexico's many holidays. Inside are Diego Rivera murals depicting this country's history through the Revolution of 1910. The National Palace is open from 9 a.m. to 6 p.m. daily except Mondays.

Mexico's grandest cathedral

The **Cathedral of Mexico,** the largest in the country, is also on the zocalo. Built over a 200-year period beginning in the 16th century, the cathedral incorporates many architectual styles. Its massive sanctuary houses 16 chapels, 27 altars, and a valuable collection of religious artwork from the Spanish colonial period.

The **Altar of the Kings** is a highly ornamental creation built in the wild baroque style known as churrigueresque, which was introduced by Spanish architect and artisan José Churriguera. Popular in the late 17th century, this style ignored the restraint employed by Renaissance artists and used elaborate designs and rich materials, such as gold and silver.

The greatest archeological find

Located just off the zocalo is the greatest accidental archeological find of the century: the **Great Temple of Tenochitlan.** Unearthed in 1978 by the Mexican Power and Light Company, it was once the holiest temple of the Aztecs. It depicts the legend of the god Huitzilopochtli, who avenged the murder of his mother Coatlicue by his sister Coyolzauhqui on the Hill of the Serpents. Although many of the artifacts found here are displayed in museums around the country, the site is still impressive, with intricate, artistic wall sculptures. Admission is free. The site is closed Mondays.

The city's best house

The 17th-century **Casa de los Azulejos** (House of Tiles), *Av. Madero 4,* which is completely covered in tiles, was built by the son of one of the counts of Orizaba. The young man became wealthy despite his father's prediction that he would never have a house of tiles (a Spanish saying that meant he would never be successful). To spite his father, he bought a house and had it completely covered in tiles.

The House of Tiles is now a drugstore called Sanborns.

Mexico City's best shopping

The best shopping in Mexico City is at the huge open-air markets. **Lagunilla,** *Avenida Allende,* is a massive, sprawling market that sells everything from false teeth to expensive jewelry. The best day to shop is Sunday, when Lagunilla combines with the **Thieves' Market** to become the largest market in Mexico City.

The **San Juan Crafts Market** (also called the Curiosities Market), *Ayuntamiento,* a modern three-story complex of artisans' shops, sells kitschy artwork. A better place to shop is the **Bazaar Sabbado,** *San Jacinto 11,* a more fashionable Saturday bazaar in the suburb of San Angel. This is where some of the best craftsmen sell their wares, everything from jewelry to paintings. The bazaar is set up in the refurbished remains of a 17th-century convent.

Look for fine leatherwork at **Aries,** *Florencia 14,* which sells everything from boots to knifeholders.

Good (but expensive) silver products are available at **Tane,** *Amberes 70,* and **Flato,** *Amberes 21.* Wherever you buy silver, always check the back for the Mexican double eagle mark or the number 0.925, which guarantees that the product contains the proper amount of silver.

Although it is better to buy textiles in the regions where they are made (the quality and prices are better), Mexico City has shops selling excellent government-approved items. At **Girasol,** *Calle Genova 39,* for example, you can buy sarapes, wool blankets, wall hangings, and shawls. The best are made of lightweight white wool. You also can buy *huipils,* white cotton dresses embroidered with tiny flowers; *rebozos,* long multicolored scarves made of silk or wool; and *guayabera* shirts, light, gaily decorated shirts popular with Latin American men.

Mexico City's best restaurants

Hosteria Santo Domingo, *Belisario Dominguez 72; tel. (905)510-1434,* is the best restaurant in town. Located in a perfectly preserved 19th-century building, it serves traditional Mexican dishes. The *chillis in nogada* (a Poblano pepper stuffed with walnuts, cream, pomegranate seeds, and mince) is especially good.

San Angel Inn, *Palmas 50; tel. (905)548-6746,* is the most beautiful restaurant in Mexico, situated in a 250-year-old building that has been completely restored. It has hosted Pancho Villa, Pavlova, Caruso, and Gershwin. Chef Manual Lozano cooks up a good *pompano en papillote.*

The **Hacienda de los Morales,** *Vasquez de Polanco Mella 525; tel. (905)540-3225,* is an elegant, reasonably priced restaurant specializing in both Continental and Mexican cuisine. Reservations are a must at this beautifully restored 16th-century hacienda.

La Fonda el Refugio, *Liverpool 166; tel. (905)525-0805,* is decorated with primitive art and locally blown glass. Order the *mole poblano* (thin tortillas fried and stuffed with shredded chicken and covered with *mole,* a rich sauce made with 25 ingredients, including hot peppers, tomatoes, raisins, and chocolate). Finish your meal with *café de olla* (black coffee served with brown sugar, cinnamon, and cloves). Dinner for two is less than 34,000 pesos ($15). Reservations are recommended.

Meson del Cid, *Humboldt 61; tel. (52-5)521-1940,* is a three-level dining room that serves open-hearth cooking. Baby suckling pig *à la segovia* is the house specialty. Pheasant *à la meson del cio* is good, too.

Del Lago Restaurant, *Nuevo Bosque de Chapultepec; tel. (905)515-9585,* has a clear view of Chapultepec Lagoon through its grand windows. Trees and hanging plants give the interior an outdoor look. The seafood is good. Save room for dessert, and order the *mango flambé au tequilla.*

San Angel Inn, *Palmas and Altavista; tel. (905)5-548-6746,* set in an old hacienda with beautiful gardens, serves good Mexican food. Men must wear ties. Make reservations. Dinner for two is about 68,000 pesos ($30).

The capital's best hotels

Camino Real, *Mariano Escobedo 700, 11590 Mexico City; tel. (52-90)5-203-2121* or *(800)228-3000,* is the only deluxe hotel in Mexico City. Located at the edge of Chapultepec Park, its seven-acre spread includes pools, tennis courts, three entertainment bars, a disco, a coffeeshop, and two restaurants. Double rooms range from 190,000 pesos to 214,000 pesos ($85 to $95) a night.

El Gran Hotel de la Ciudad de Mexico, *Merchant's Arcade, 16 Septiembre 82, Zocala; (800)334-7234,* is centrally located, comfortable, and has excellent service. It has cage elevators and a Tiffany glass ceiling in the lobby. A double room is 130,000 pesos ($50) a night.

Hotel Majestic, *Francisco Madero 73; tel. (5)521-8600,* is another good hotel. From its rooftop terrace, the view of the city is panoramic. The Mexican color guard marches by the hotel every day at 6:30 p.m.

Hotel Cortes, *Av. Hidalgo 85; tel. (5)585-0322* or *(800)528-1234,* a restored 18th-century hacienda, is a moderately priced hotel—rooms are about 101,000 pesos ($45) a night. The hotel is clean, comfortable, and efficient. It is also popular, so make reservations well in advance.

The **Maria Cristina,** *Lerma 31; tel. (5)546-9880,* is a small hotel with a pretty garden and a piano bar. A double room is less than 130,000 pesos ($40) a night.

The hottest night life

The **Bellas Artes,** *Plaza Central Alameda,* presents the Ballet Folklorico on Wednesdays and Sundays at 9 p.m. You also can attend a concert, symphony, ballet, or opera. Check the *Mexico City News* for the schedule.

Popular nightclubs include **Can Can,** which has a lively floorshow; **Magic Circus,** *Rodolfo Gaona 3;* the **Disco Club** at El Presidente, *Campos Eliseos 218;* and **Hotel Aristos,** *Paseo de la Reforma 276* (this is the place to go to hear rock bands). The leading gay bar in the city is **9,** *Londres 156.*

Single women aren't usually allowed in clubs or bars in Mexico City by themselves. The only bars lone women may attend are hotel lounges.

The best day trips

Midway between Mexico City and Tula, the capital of the ancient Toltec Indians, is the **Tepotzotlan Monastery,** a beautiful example of Spanish architecture, encrusted with intricate gold carvings made by local Indians. You can visit Wednesdays through Sundays from 11 a.m. to 6 p.m.

Cholula was the site of thousands of human sacrifices. In fact, although it was built long before the Aztec civilization flourished, this gory monument was still in use when the Spanish came. Hearing that they were to be killed here, Hernan Cortes and his entourage killed thousands of Aztecs. The site is open daily.

The pyramids of **Teotihuacan,** built sometime between A.D. 400 and A.D. 800, make up the largest, most complete archeological site in this hemisphere, covering more than 35 square miles. The Indians who built the pyramids, probably Mayans or their predecessors, marked time in 52-year cycles, building a new pyramid on top of the old one every cycle. The site includes hundreds of small temples, two large ones (the Pyramid of the Sun and the Pyramid of the Moon), and a large enclosed arena that was probably used for religious spectacles or ceremonial ball games. From mid-October to mid-May, a narrated sound-and-light show begins at 7 p.m. in English and at 8:15 p.m in Spanish. The site is open daily. A small admission fee is charged.

San Miguel de Allende: a town for artists

Situated in a small valley surrounded by hills, **San Miguel de Allende** has retained its colonial charm while blossoming into a center for the arts. Burros line the streets, and flowers fill every corner. Homes are hidden behind tall, bougainvillea-draped stucco walls. And art galleries, cafés, and restaurants serve the thriving expatriate community.

Located on the high central plateau about 250 miles northwest of Mexico City, San Miguel is in the agriculturally rich Bajio region on the colonial route. The entire town is a historic national monument; all architecture conforms to the colonial style.

La Parroquia, the imposing pink cathedral on the main zocalo, is a 19th-century Indian mason's interpretation of a French Gothic cathedral. The bells chime every 15 minutes.

San Miguel earned its reputation as an international arts center in 1938, with the opening of the first English-speaking school, the **Instituto Allende,** *Bellas Artes, Centro Cultural El Nigromante.* The institute is now the largest Latin American fine arts school for English-speaking students.

The city is also the home of the **San Miguel Writing Center,** *Ancho de San Antonio 20, C.P. 37700 San Miguel de Allende, Mexico; tel. (52-2)01-90.* The teachers here are all published writers.

A favorite among expatriates, San Miguel is home to an eccentric blend of Yankee artists, writers, gays, and retired folks.

Buying handicrafts and antiques

This is one of the best places in Mexico to buy handicrafts. Most shops are within three blocks of the main square. Its a good idea to visit several before buying—quality varies. Although you can do some bargaining, most of the prices are set.

Casa Maxwell, *Canal 14,* and **Llamas Brothers,** *Zacateros 11,* are two of the best handicraft shops in San Miguel. They're both quite expensive. Two cheaper shops are **La Ventana,** *Canal Street,* and **La Balaiza Mercantil,** *Mesones 42.*

By Appointment Only, *Salida de Queretaro 45; tel. (2)0205,* in a private home, sells high-quality clothes, jewelry, and leather goods. (As the name implies, you must make an appointment.)

San Miguel is also a good place to buy antiques. Although no pre-Columbian antiques may be sold legally in Mexico, you can buy Spanish antiques from the colonial period. Try the antique shops that line the main square. Be careful—many items offered for sale are merely convincing reproductions.

The best restaurants

The best restaurant in San Miguel de Allende is the **Villa Jacaranda,** *Aldama 53; tel. (52-2)1015.* The food is superb, but the atmosphere alone makes the place worth a visit. Set in a vast stone hacienda, the quiet and relaxing restaurant is surrounded by gardens filled with flowers and trailing vines. Try the house specialty, drunken chicken, which is breast of chicken sautéed in onions and peppers. Or try the *chilis nogadas,* a tangy blend of peppers covered in a sweet cream sauce. Order the crisp, dry local white wine called Calafia. Dinner for two costs about 57,000 pesos.

The restaurant at the **Casa de Sierra Nevada,** *Hospicio 35; tel. (2)0415,* is the most elegant in town. A jacket and tie are required, as are reservations.

La Posada Carmina, *Cuña de Allende 7; tel. (2)0548,* set in a cool, inviting courtyard filled with flowers, is also good. Try the cheese and vegetable salad or the *paella Valenciana.* You don't need to make reservations or to wear a suit. A meal for two costs about 33,800 pesos.

El Patio, *Correo 10,* is less expensive. It's a good place for a quick lunch. Although the food is ordinary, the setting is pleasant. You can enjoy music at the piano bar. Dinner for two is about 2,300 pesos.

The sweetest dreams

La Posada San Francisco, right on the main square, *tel. (52-1)8960,* is within walking distance of just about everything in San Miguel. A spacious suite, suitable for a family of four, costs 90,000 pesos to 113,000 pesos per night. The hotel serves delicious breakfasts for about 11,250 pesos ($5) for two.

Casa de Sierra Nevada, *Hospicio 35; tel. (2)0415,* is an old Spanish villa. Rooms, which are luxurious, cost about 180,000 pesos a night. The hotel has an excellent restaurant.

The spiciest nights

Cantinas, nightclubs, and cocktail lounges in San Miguel stay open until 1 a.m., and many will stay open later at the request of guests. The **Ring,** *Avenida Hidalgo,* is a disco popular with the over-35 crowd. **Laberintos Discoteque,** *San Antonio,* is popular with a younger set and has loud music. You must pay a cover charge.

Mama Mia, *Umaron 5,* has live music, from Andean folk to jazz, Wednesdays through Mondays on its patio. **La Princesa,** *Recreo 5,* is a quiet place, where you can listen to music while enjoying an early evening drink.

The steamiest side trip

Just a few miles from San Miguel, in **Taboada,** you can soak in steaming hot springs while a waiter brings you drinks. And at **La Gruta** (in El Cortijo) you can swim in an Olympic-sized heated pool or take a steam bath in a cave of hot mineral water.

Taxco: the silver capital

Taxco is a mining town in the mountains. About a day's ride outside of Mexico City and off the main tourist route, it is less crowded than Guanajuanto or Cuernavaca. It is also the place to buy silver jewelry.

William Spratling introduced silversmithing to Taxco in 1929. Now the town has more than 300 fine jewelry shops. And the mines show no signs of cutting off the supply of metal.

Original Spratling pieces are difficult to come by, but most of the jewelry sold throughout Taxco is styled upon his original models. All silver products, from jewelry to candelabra, cost about 25% less than American counterparts and about 50% less than European pieces.

The best jewelry shops are **Los Castillos,** *Plazuela Bernal 10,* **A. Pineda y Virgilios,** *Av. J.F. Kennedy 28,* and **Real de Plateros,** *Calle Celso Munoz 4.*

Taxco's early wealth led to ornate local architecture. Most of the old Spanish buildings on the zocalo have been restored. Several reflect Taxco's wealth, their interiors liberally decorated with gold and jewels.

Santa Prisca Church, built in the 18th century by Juan de la Borda, is a gorgeous example of Spanish colonial architecture both inside and out. It has twin 130-foot baroque towers, a massive blue-tile dome, and pink walls. Inside are 12 altars, gold altarpieces, and original paintings by Miguel Cabrera.

Casa Borda mansion, also on the zocalo, is another impressive example of colonial architecture, towering five stories above the square. The house is so large that Juan de la Borda lived in only half of it.

The two most colorful times to visit Taxco are during Holy Week and the National Silver Fair, at the beginning of December. Make reservations far in advance.

Taxco's best tables

La Ventana de Taxco, *Hotel Hacienda del Solar; tel. (732)20587,* in a pink stone house on a hill just south of town, serves delicious Italian food for reasonable prices. Tables look out at the red-roofed houses of Taxco and the mountains beyond. The view is loveliest at sunset. Hollywood publicist Ted Wick, who lives in town, once owned this building—he still plays the grand piano in the lounge.

La Pagaduria del Rey, *Cerro de Bermeja; tel. (465)2-3467),* serves steaks, seafood, and Mexican food. The menu is limited, and the restaurant opens whenever the staff feels like it, but the food is good. A meal for two is about 56,000 pesos ($25), not including tip or wine.

The best hotels

The most beautiful hotel in Taxco is **Rancho Taxco-Victoria,** *Carlos J. Nibbi 14; tel. (73-2)2-0004,* with large rooms, a pleasant restaurant, a bar, a swimming pool, and beautiful gardens. Double rooms are about 13,000 pesos ($50) a night.

Hotel de la Borda, *Cerro del Pedregal 2; tel. (732)2-0226,* is cozy, with a restaurant overlooking the city, a pool, and large bathrooms. Double rooms are about 108,000 pesos (or $56) per night.

Montetaxco, *off Route 95; tel. (465)2-1300,* a mountainside hotel on the north side of town, has 160 rooms and 50 villas and suites. It offers color televisions, air conditioning, a pool, spa facilities, a golf course, a tennis court, horseback riding, and a restaurant with nightly entertainment. A double is about 147,000 pesos ($65) a night.

Cuernavaca, where spring springs eternal

Cuernavaca is the city of eternal spring, with temperatures that hover around 75 degrees Fahrenheit year-round and lush vegetation. The Mexicans were not the first to recognize this city as an ideal resort. The Aztecs used Cuernavaca (or Cuauhnahuac, as the city was originally called) as a retreat.

Cortes also recognized its appeal. He built **El Palacio de Cortes** as his personal residence here. This massive fortress is now home to the **Cuauhnahuac Historical Museum,** which houses murals by Rivera, Siquieros, and Orozco.

Cuernavaca has become expensive by Mexican standards, in part because of the year-round expatriate community. Prices are substantially higher than in Taxco or San Miguel de Allende, and the area is more touristy than other cities.

See the cathedral that Cortes founded in 1529, the summer palace of the Hapsburgs, and the beautiful Borda Gardens, where a botanical festival is held each year in April.

The speediest way to learn Spanish

The fastest way to learn Spanish is to enroll in a course at the **Center for Bilingual Multicultural Studies,** *San Jeronimo 304, Cuernavaca, Guerrero, Mexico* (or contact **Ruth Ann Rayel,** *7316 S. Ridge Trail, Fort Worth, TX 76133, (817)294-1189 or (817)731-0851).* Students may speak only Spanish, even if they are novices, and are fined 1 peso each time they break the rule. They live with Mexican families, who include them in their everyday lives, and spend three hours a day in grammar classes, two hours in history and culture classes.

The program is reasonably priced. Registration is $100, and classes are $125 per week. Expenses for room and board (including three meals a day) vary from $10 to $15 per day.

Cuernavaca's best restaurants

Las Mananitas, *Ricardo Linares 107; tel. (73)14-14-66,* is set in an exotic tropical garden where peacocks, cranes, macaws, and myna birds roam among diners. Try the shrimp Patricia or the Patzcuaro whitefish with Lorenzo sauce.

The **Château René,** *Atzingo 11; tel. (73)17-23-00,* serves excellent French and Italian food. Dinner for two is about 50,000 pesos.

Harry's Bar, *Gutenberg 3; tel. (12)7679,* attracts a lively crowd. House specialties are barbecued ribs and chicken. A meal for two is about $15.

Yucateco, *Francisco Villa 112; tel. (73)13-3758,* serves Mayan food. House specialties include *panuchos* and chicken *pibil.* Dinner for two is less than 22,500 pesos.

The best hotels

The most luxurious place to stay in Cuernavaca—and the most expensive—is the **Rancho** (or Hacienda) *Cortes, Plaza Kennedy 90, Atlacomulco; tel. (73)15-8844.* This resort hotel has tennis courts, spa facilities, pools, lounges, two restaurants, lovely gardens, and weekend concerts. A double room is about 105,000 pesos ($50) a night.

Posada las Mañanitas, *Ricardo Linares 107; tel. (73)12-4646,* a long-time favorite of the rich and famous, is another luxurious hotel with an excellent restaurant. Peacocks strut proudly through the gardens surrounding the hotel. A double room is about 180,000 pesos ($50) a night. Credit cards are not accepted.

Posada Jacarandas, *Cuauhtemoc 805; tel. (73)15-7777,* is a large estate with a lovely outdoor restaurant, two sunken grotto pools, tennis courts, a small golf course, beautiful gardens, and spacious suites with fireplaces, terraces, and televisions. A double room is only 79,000 pesos ($35) a night.

Oaxaca: the best Indian territory

Oaxaca, the most Indian region, is the best place to explore present-day Indian culture as well as ancient Indian ruins. The colonial city of Oaxaca is a good base. Plan to stay at least a few days—there is a lot to see.

The age-old tradition of weaving lives on in the village of **Teotitlan del Valle.** You can watch weavers at work then buy decorated carpets and sarapes for 45,000 pesos to 450,000 pesos ($20 to $200).

About eight miles outside Teotitlan del Valle is the **Yagul** site, dating from about A.D. 700. Earlier this century, precious Zapotec artifacts were taken from this series of multiple tombs. The site includes a hill fortress, a group of palaces and temples, and a ball court.

Mitla, the City of the Dead, is 26 miles outside Oaxaca. Built by the Zapotecs, Mitla was later enlarged by the Mixtecs. Although this is a touristy spot (Indian women mill around trying to sell souvenirs), it is also impressive, with intricate mosaics and strange stone carvings on the walls.

In the opposite direction from Oaxaca is another impressive archeological site: **Monte Alban.** This massive group of Zapotec ruins covers 15 square miles. The Temple of Danzantes and the ceremonial ball court are the two most impressive sites. However, you can spend hours wandering among literally hundreds of ceremonial altars, winding staircases, and stone carvings. The site is open daily from 8 a.m. to 6 p.m.

To see what was found in the tombs of Mitla and the ruins of Monte Alban, visit the **Regional Museum** in Oaxaca, *Calle M. Alcala,* where most of the treasures are kept.

Keep in mind that when exploring the region of Oaxaca, you should use your camera guardedly; the natives don't like to have their pictures taken.

Oaxaca's best buys

The region of Oaxaca is a good place to shop. Prices for textiles, jewelry, and handicrafts tend to be much lower than those in Cuernavaca and Mexico City. Visit the village of **Tlacolula** on a Sunday, when a huge market is set up by Indian vendors and artisans selling clothing, pottery, rugs, wall hangings, and gold jewelry styled upon the original Zapotec and Mixtec patterns. Visit the village of **Atzompa** on a Tuesday for superb green-glazed ceramics. The village of **Ejutla** is famous for its intricately carved knives, **San Bartolo Coyotepec** for its black pottery, and **Octolan** for its straw baskets.

If you prefer to shop in stores, visit **Casa Brena**, *Pino Suarez 58,* or **Aripo**, *Garcia Vigil 809.*

Oaxaca's best food and lodging

El Asador Vasco, *Portal de Flores 11; tel. (951)6-2092,* overlooking the zocalo, is the best restaurant in town. Chef Juan Hernandez takes cuisine seriously, and his restaurant is worth a special trip. Both Spanish and Mexican dishes are served. Try the house specialty, *cazuelas,* small casseroles of baked cheese, mushrooms, and garlic. Dinner for two is about 34,000 pesos ($15), not including drinks.

El Sol y La Luna, *Murguia 105; tel. (951)6-2933,* is a combination coffeehouse, restaurant, and gallery. Although the restaurant is small, and you may have to wait for a table, it's worth the wait. Dinner for two is about 34,000 pesos ($15).

No matter where you eat, you probably will smell chocolate. Oaxaca is known for it. Try the famous *mole* sauce (a mixture of chocolate, cinnamon, chile peppers, and bananas), which is served on meat and poultry.

Although hotels here don't have the amenities of those in the resort cities, they are clean, comfortable, and cheap. The **Victoria**, *Km 545, Route 190; tel. (5)2633,* atop a hill overlooking town, is one of the best, with a heated pool, tennis courts, a disco, and large breakfasts. Double rooms start at 116,250 pesos ($55).

El Presidente, housed in the former Santa Catalina Convent, *Cinco de Mayo 300; tel. (6)0611* or *(800)472-2427,* is comfortable and serves an excellent luncheon buffet that is open to both guests and visitors. A double room is about 124,000 pesos ($55) per night.

Oaxaca travel tips

You can reach Oaxaca from Mexico City on one of Mexicana's daily flights. Round-trip air fare is about $75. Once in Oaxaca, rent a car to get to the archeological sites.

Guadalajara: Mexico at its best

Guadalajara is the home of the Mexican hat dance, mariachi bands, tequilla, Mexican horsemen, and rodeos. It is also a bustling, sophisticated city with a large American community, attracted by the easy lifestyle and the pleasant climate.

This is a good place to admire Spanish colonial architecture. Many of the buildings in the **Plaza Tapatia** have been restored to their former glory. Hospicio Cabañas, built in 1801 as an orphanage, has been renovated and converted into the Cabanas Institute, a center for the arts.

Its chapel contains Orozco's famous mural, *Four Horsemen of the Apocalypse*. Other colonial buildings of interest include the cathedral at the center of the city, the Jalisco Supreme Court, the Government Palace, and the Legislative Hall.

Gaudalajara is a city of parks. The largest, **Parque Agua Azul,** *Gonzales Gallo and Avenida Independencia,* has an open-air theater, a bird sanctuary, and special sections designed for children and the blind. The park also houses the House of Handicrafts, which contains superb examples of colonial furniture, ceramics, blown glass, tinwork, and textiles produced in the State of Jalisco. Most of the products are for sale at reasonable, fixed prices.

Mexico's largest open-air market

The huge **Libertad Market,** *Avenida Independencia,* is the largest open-air market in Mexico. After shopping, retire to the **Plaza de los Mariachis,** across the street, and listen to the strolling musicians while sipping a cool drink.

Delicious dining

For a late lunch, try the **Guadalajara Grill,** *Lopez Mateos Sur 3771,* where the band strikes up at 3 p.m. and then again at 10 p.m. Another favorite is **Cazadores,** *Av. Union 405.* Both serve Mexican food.

Luxurious hotels

Most hotels in Guadalajara are more like resorts than hotels, with extensive recreational facilities and restaurants and bars on the premises.

El Camino Real, *Av. Vallarta 5005; tel. (36)21-7217,* is a luxurious hotel with lovely gardens, a putting green, a tennis court, a bar, and a restaurant. A double room is about 158,000 pesos ($60) a night.

The new **Hyatt Regency,** *Avenida Lopez Mateos; tel. 36-22-7778,* boasts the only indoor skating rink in Mexico. A double room is about 192,000 pesos ($80) a night.

The best day trips

Tlaquepaque, a suburb of Guadalajara, has a wide selection of artisans' shops selling textiles, blown glass, and brass. Lunch at the **Restaurant Sin Nombre.** You'll have to ask for directions—because the restaurant doesn't have a sign. It serves a creative mixture of Provençal and Mexican food. Dress is casual, and dinner for two is less than 56,250 pesos ($25).

Jalapa: the flower garden of Mexico

Jalapa, the capital of Veracruz, is known as the flower garden of Mexico, because of its many parks. This small and friendly colonial city is seldom visited by tourists, even Mexican.

The city is 4,700 feet above sea level, and all the streets run at steep angles. Walking is thoroughly exhausting, so hire a taxi to take you sight-seeing. Taxis are plentiful, and the rates are regulated—you can go anywhere in the city for less than $1.

Begin your tour in the main square. Visit the **Palacio de Gobierno** (Government House), which houses the famous *Liberation* mural by Diego Rivera, depicting man's struggle through life, and the massive colonial cathedral, built in 1773.

El Mercado Jauregui, one of the four local markets, has booths selling food, furniture, clothes, and flowers.

After the crush of the market, visit the small **Barrio Xalitic,** said to predate Christopher Columbus. Women scrub their clothes in the public water trough, and children play in a small park among tapped springs and small Christian shrines. The little park is especially delightful at Christmastime, when a Nativity village is constructed.

At centrally located **Parque Juarez,** vendors sell balloons, flowers, and food, and boys offer to shine your shoes. Steer clear of the food sold by vendors; it looks good but carries Montezuma's Revenge.

Try some of Jalapa's famous coffee at the café in the park, shaded by red-and-white striped umbrellas. The café serves an excellent *lechero*—hot milk poured into rich coffee extract and sweetened.

Walk along the artificial lakes of Paseo de Los Lagos to the **La Casa de los Artesanos** (House of the Artisans), a colonial building where local craftsmen sell their wares. Then stop by the **Museum of Anthropology,** *Avenida Jalapa,* to view its large collection of pre-Columbian artifacts.

Mexico's best symphony

Jalapa boasts the best symphony orchestra in Mexico. For 6,800 pesos ($3), you can listen to two hours of classical music and new creations in the modern **State Theater.** During intermission, members of the audience are allowed backstage to meet the orchestra.

Jalapa's best food

Jalapa's best restaurants are **La Casona del Beatro, El Diamante, La Barranquilla,** and **La Casa de Mama.** For seafood, go to **La Palma.**

Jalapa's best hotel

The **Maria Victoria,** *Zaragosa 6,* is the best hotel in Jalapa. It has a good restaurant and a bar. A double room is about 68,000 pesos ($30) a night.

Chihuahua: land of the best bandito

Chihuahua was home to Pancho Villa (Emiliano Zapata), the Mexican Robin Hood. The house where the beloved bandito lived is a museum of the revolutionary era as well as Villa's life. (In 1910 Villa joined rebels and fought for President Madero and against General Huerta and President Carranza. He and his men killed American citizens in Columbus, New Mexico in 1916 and were pursued unsuccessfully by the U.S. Army for 11 months.) Villa's house was inhabited until just four years ago by his aging widow. The featured artifact on display is the bullet-riddled Dodge in which Villa was assassinated in 1923.

Also in Chihuahua is the **Museo de Arte Popular,** which has an exhibit featuring the Tarahuamara culture, with woven blankets, full-sleeved blouses, whirling skirts, carved wooden masks decorated with goat hair, and palm baskets. Attached to the museum is a gift shop, where you can buy copies of these items as well as books on the indigenous cultures of Mexico and Mexican history.

El Palacio del Gobierno (Government Palace) is noteworthy for its gorgeous murals depicting the history of Mexico, including the arrival of the first priests, the Spanish Conquest, and the Mexican Civil War and its heroes.

The **Museo Regional** is housed in a beautiful art-deco mansion with well-preserved stained-glass windows and elaborately carved mantels. Parts of the mansion have exhibits of Mormon and Mennonite settlements in Chihuahua. The toy display includes Tarahuamara miniatures, Mennonite playthings, and antique dolls.

You can see a replica of an adobe house from the ancient Paquime Indian culture in the northern part of Chihuahua, at **Casa Grandes.**

Chihuahua has a **Holiday Inn,** supposedly the finest hotel in the area, as well as a **Hotel Presidente,** Mexico's answer to the Hilton chain. However, the town's best deal is the Hotel Turista, where you can get a room with a shower and a comfortable bed for about 9,000 pesos ($4) a night for two.

After dinner, stop by the **Bar Jardin** at the Hotel El Presidente and enjoy a few beers while listening to local crooners. Two popular styles of Mexican music are *staples,* the traditional romantic Mexican sound, and the *bohemio,* roughly equivalent to French nightclub music.

The world's grandest canyon

Mexico's **Barranca del Cobre** (Copper Canyon) has the U.S. Grand Canyon beat. It is four times larger and 300 feet deeper, with mountain peaks that rise 10,000 feet and valleys that drop 1,500 feet.

Until 1961, when the Chihuahua al Pacifico train line opened, the canyon was inaccessible and known only to isolated Tarahumara Indians living in caves. The train line climbs from sea level at Los Mochis on the Pacific to 8,000 feet, then descends to Chihuahua. It passes the most spectacular scenery in Mexico—sheer cliffs that change color as the sun sets, giant rock formations, deep gorges, and mountain peaks. You can catch the train every day in Chihuahua at 7 a.m. or in Los Mochis at 6 a.m.

The best place to stay in the canyon is **Hotel Cabañas Divisadero-Barrancas,** in Divisadero, midway along the route. This rustic log-cabin hotel is perched on the rim of the canyon and has dizzying views. Several Indian families live in caves nearby. These timid people sell handwoven baskets for less than 11,000 pesos ($5), wood carvings, and necklaces. Surrounding the hotel are trails that the Indians follow to the bottom of the canyon, 5,000 feet below.

Acapulco: Mexico's most sophisticated resort

Since the 1920s, the rich and famous have retreated to **Acapulco** for the winter. The tropical Pacific Coast resort is famous for its fine beaches, luxury hotels, and deep-sea fishing facilities. Slim, tanned bodies line the beach, and colorful parasails float above it.

Acapulco isn't quite as nice as it used to be. It has become a smoggy, crowded city of 14 million with bumper-to-bumper traffic. And on the hills above the city, crowded, dirty barrios have developed that house the cheap labor serving the many hotels and restaurants.

But you can forget all that, if you choose, by not driving and by frequenting places such as **Hoy,** a chic restaurant on La Condesa Beach, where the langostas and margaritas are as perfect as the view.

Blackbeard's, also on La Condesa Beach, is another popular restaurant. Have the fish kabobs and the house rum with pineapple juice. **Villa Demos,** *Av. Del Prado 6,* serves good Italian food in a tropical garden.

The place to stay, if you can afford it, is **Las Brisas,** *Carretera Escenica Clemente Mejia 5255; tel. (748)41650.* Guests stay in individual casitas on a hill overlooking Acapulco Bay, surrounded by bougainvillea and hibiscus. Each little cottage has its own pool. The cost per night is 563,000 pesos ($250).

Puerto Vallarta: the most charming resort

Puerto Vallarta, that sleepy little fishing village discovered by Hollywood in 1964, is one of Mexico's foremost resort towns. And unlike Acapulco, Puerto Vallarta hasn't lost its traditional charm. Native vendors push their wares in barrows up cobblestoned streets. Local fishermen roast pompano and red snapper on the beach. And Indian women pound their laundry on rocks by the stream.

The town doesn't have fine examples of Spanish architecture or a preponderance of pre-Columbian ruins, but it does have 25 miles of beaches, superb restaurants, and luxurious hotels, and most of the beachfront hotels have parasailing facilities.

The fishing is good here, too. Marlin season is from November to January. And every year in November an international fishing competition is held off the coast of Manzanillo. You can charter a deep-sea fishing boat in town at the bay.

Puerto Vallarta was carved out of the jungle, which still encroaches on the town. You can join a jungle tour for about $6. Most involve a three-hour van ride through back country. Douse yourself with insect repellent—the mosquitoes eat gringos.

Los Arcos, just south of town, is an underwater national park that you can tour by glass-bottomed boat.

Eating well

La Perla, *Camon Real Hotel, Playa Las Estacas; tel. (52322)2555,* is the best restaurant in town, with a Continental menu and a fine wine list. You can try gourmet treats, such as poached quail eggs with red caviar or crayfish salad with broccoli and morels.

Carlos O'Brian's, *Paseo Diaz Orcaz 786; tel. (2)1444,* is a popular restaurant—long lines form hours before the 7 p.m. opening. The food is delicious, and the margaritas are strong. Dinner for two is about 45,000 pesos ($20).

Las Palomas, along the Malecon, is open for breakfast, lunch, and dinner. Steak and lobster are served, and 1950s dance music is played late into the evening. A meal for two, including wine, is about 68,000 pesos ($30).

La Margarita, *Calle Juarez 592; tel. (2)1215,* is a quiet garden restaurant with excellent service. A superb full-course meal is about 79,000 pesos ($35)for two.

Chico's Paradise, 30 minutes south of Puerto Vallarta off Mismaloya Road, is perched high above a waterfall in the midst of the jungle. House specialties include drunken shrimp, which is baby shrimp marinated in beer, wine, orange juice, and herbs; barbecued ribs; a steak and lobster combination; and Chico's black-bean soup. Dinner for two is about 68,000 pesos ($30).

The best hotels

The best hotel in Puerto Vallarta is **Garza Blanca,** *Playa Palo Maria; tel. (322)21023.* You can stay in suites right on the beach or in a villa with its own garden and pool.

El Camino Real, *Playa las Estacas; tel. (322)2-0002,* two miles south of Puerto Vallarta, is particularly fine. Double rooms are about 506,000 pesos to 754,000 pesos ($225 to $335) a night, but rooms are spacious, with two double beds, a large bathroom, a fully stocked refrigerator, and a small lounging area. Buffet lunches are served.

Hotel Plaza Careyes, north of town, is quiet and elegant, with eight miles of beach, a disco overlooking the ocean, and facilities for water sports. A double room is about 338,000 pesos ($150) a night.

Plaza las Glorias, *Avenida de las Garzes; tel. (322)2-2224,* is another five-star hotel. Each room has a full-service bar and cable television. Guests can use the John Newcombe Tennis Center next door. Double rooms are about 225,000 pesos ($100) a night.

El Oceano, *Galeana 103; tel. (322)2-1050,* is smaller, with comfortable rooms overlooking the bay, a nice restaurant and bar, and a rooftop pool. Rooms are as little as 34,000 pesos ($15).

Molino de Agua, *Ignacio Vallarta; tel. (322)2-1907,* has comfortable bungalows around a jungle garden. Double rooms are about 101,000 pesos ($45) per night.

The Pacific at its best

Acapulco and Puerto Vallarta are busy resort towns, much changed from the sleepy little fishing villages they once were. However, you still can experience the peaceful ways of the Pacific in **San Blas,** 40 minutes south of Mazatlan, off Highway 15.

This is a land of endless summer, with rain forests, orchids, and warm waves. Life is lazy, and no one worries about the time. Giant shrimp and fresh fish roasted over coals are served in the cafés. For a few cents, you can take a bus from San Blas to **Matanchin Bay,** the most beautiful beach on the Pacific, where the waves are giant and clear and carry surfers miles before breaking.

The Huicholes Indians, who live in the mountains above San Blas, consider the Pacific holy. Shamans wearing feathered sombreros lead awe-struck Indians into the waves.

When you tire of the beach, take a jungle boat for a few dollars into the marshy forest. You will see iguanas, blue herons, and parrots. The boat stops at a little cantina overlooking a deep pool. Have a beer, then take a swim.

The best whale watching

In October, hundreds of gray whales migrate from the Bering Straits to the warm lagoons of the **Baja Peninsula** to mate and have babies. The best place to see them is **San Ignacio Lagoon,** halfway down the peninsula on the Pacific Coast. The whales are so friendly that they'll probably come close to you as you watch them.

The bright green lagoon is mirror-like, ringed with sandy hills and rocks. The hazy Santa Clara Mountains stand in the background. Because whale watching has become so popular here, it is carefully regulated by the Mexican government. San Ignacio, Ojo de Liebre, and Guerrero Negro are official sanctuaries. Boats must have permits to enter, and only two are permitted in at a time.

Baja's Frontier Tours, *2223 C St., San Diego, CA 92102; (619)232-1600,* arranges camping and whale-watching expeditions in San Ignacio. Seven-day trips are $885, including camping equipment, transportation, two nights in the La Pinta hotel in San Ignacio, and meals. Air fare is not included.

The best of the Mexican Caribbean

Until the early 1970s, Mexico's idyllic Caribbean coast was undeveloped, inhabited only by Mayan Indians. Then the Mexican government realized the area's potential as a resort and began developing the Yucatan Peninsula. The empty island of Kankune became **Cancun**—the trendiest resort town in Mexico. Its neighbors, Cozumel and Isla Mujérès, also have benefited from the exposure, sprouting luxury hotels and restaurants and attracting tourists in larger numbers each year.

Considering their temperate climate, white-sand beaches, and clear waters, it's amazing that these islands took so long to attract notice. The weather is mostly sunny from October through April, and even during the rainy season (July through September), showers are often only brief afternoon events. If you tire of the sand and surf, you can visit the nearby Mayan ruins at Tulum, Coba, and Chichen Itza.

While Cancun and Cozumel are primary resort towns, with superb restaurants, luxurious hotels, excellent beaches, and facilities for water sports, Isla Mujérès is less sophisticated, still a place for Mexican families on holiday. One recent visitor reported that some of the islanders were less than friendly. However, Isla Mujérès does have a Mayan temple and excellent scuba diving.

The most seductive beaches

The Caribbean side of Cancun has the best beaches, with sand as soft as talcum powder, aquamarine water, and exhilarating waves. The beach in front of the **Hyatt Caribe** is especially pretty, shaded by coconut palms and studded with lounge chairs that can be used by anyone, not just guests at the hotel. If you tire of the beach, splash in the Hyatt's series of pools connected by a canal that is crossed by a little bridge.

Cancun's best beach playground is at the **Camino Real,** a hotel on a point of land. On one side, the Caribbean crashes against an inviting beach; on the other is the calm Bahia de Mujérès, where you can snorkel among fluorescent fish. The hotel has a saltwater pool fed by the bay and inhabited by giant tortoises and tropical fish. You can snorkel here or sun on the raft in the middle. Then wash the salt off your body in the ice-cold futuristic freshwater pool. (You don't have to be a guest to use the pools.)

On Cozumel, the beaches north and south of San Miguel are superb. Most of the island's hotels hug these beach coves, so guests walk directly from their rooms onto the beach each morning. Because the currents off Cozumel are tricky, you should never swim alone.

Isla Mujeres' most beautiful beach is **El Garrafon.** The beaches at Tortugas and Marias are less crowded.

Super snorkel, super scuba

Outside Cancun, on the road to Tulum, is an idyllic lagoon called **Xel-Ha,** where you can enjoy the best snorkeling in the Mexican Caribbean. Netting keeps the sharks out, while letting all the colorful fish in. You can glide among the rocks, circle around the edge, or explore coves on the far side. You will see electric-blue fish, yellow fish with black stripes, and schools of tiny darters moving in unison. Although the lagoon is deep, the water is so crystal clear that you can see to the bottom. You can rent equipment here, but the flipper sizes are limited.

The best scuba diving is off the coast of Isla Mujeres, which is surrounded by reefs. You can rent equipment at Mexico Divers on the waterfront for 68,000 pesos ($30) a day.

About 500 yards off Cozumel, along **El Cantil,** is a series of reefs where you can dive to see tropical fish and underwater wrecks. Water visibility averages about 100 feet, perfect for photographs. You can rent diving equipment in San Miguel from **Aqua Safaris,** *tel. (988)2-*

0101, or **Dive Cozumel,** *tel. (988)2-0002.* Tank and weights rent for about 22,500 pesos ($10) an hour, regulators 22,500 pesos ($10), and fins, masks, and snorkels about 11,250 pesos ($5).

Most hotels charge higher prices for their diving facilities, but the on-site convenience is sometimes worth it. And some hotels offer scuba lessons. A two-hour lesson is 56,250 pesos ($25), and a three-day progressive scuba seminar with a certified instructor costs about 180,000 pesos ($80). A one-day guided diving tour from Cozumel to Palancar Reef costs about 79,000 pesos ($35), including lunch and equipment.

Cancun's best scuba diving is in the waters off its southern point. You can arrange guided diving expeditions and equipment rental through your hotel for 68,000 pesos ($30).

The best of the mysterious Mayas

Remnants of the great civilization of the Mayas, which mysteriously disappeared long before Europeans appeared in Mexico, can be explored near Cancun. Descendants of the Mayan workers can be seen on its streets of the city and in surrounding villages—friendly, small, dark-eyed people with round faces. Many live as they have for centuries in one-room, palm-thatched huts furnished with hammocks and a table.

However, no traces remain of the ancient Mayan priests and mathematicians, who designed and built the great monuments and developed a calendar more accurate than the Gregorian.

Chichen Itza is worth the three-hour drive from Cancun. The most famous and complete of the ancient ceremonial sites, it was built by the Toltecs (an invading Indian group) on top of a smaller Mayan site. The 1,000-year-old temple complex includes burial grounds, sacrificial altars, and royal ball courts. Plan to get here early in the day, and wear low-heeled shoes and sunscreen.

The most impressive monument at Chichen Itza is the **Temple of Kukulcan,** which is a perfect calendar as well as an engineering feat. The 91 steps to the top of each of the pyramid's four faces, plus the one step to the temple at the top, add up to 365, the number of days in a year. Fifty-two panels decorate the sides of the pyramid, one for each year of the Mayan century. The 18 terraces equal the 18 months of a Mayan year. During the spring and fall equinoxes, the sun creates a shadow on one face of the wall that resembles a serpent, the sign of the god Kukulcan.

Although the climb is steep, the view from the top of the pyramid makes it worthwhile. Ascending is actually easier than descending the tall, narrow steps. The easiest way to get back down to the ground is to walk sideways, holding onto the chain provided for that purpose. Experts say this is the correct way to descend anyway, as it is considered impolite to turn your back on the gods.

Another impressive sight at Chichen Itza is the ceremonial **ball court,** used by the Mayans to play a game that was a cross between soccer and basketball. The goal was to get the ball through 1 of 2 hoops placed 25 feet high on opposing walls. The winning captain was beheaded as a sacrifice to the gods. However, before he was dropped down the 390-foot sacrificial well (which you still can see), the sacrificee was given hallucinogenic drugs and wine. And he was consoled with the fact that he was guaranteed a place in heaven.

To get to Chichen Itza from Cancun, you can rent a car and drive yourself (be careful of villagers and their animals, who cross the country roads with abandon). Or you can hire a taxi and a guide to take you there for about $30 a day. Another alternative is to join a bus tour at your hotel. These cost about $35 a person, including a guide and lunch. Beer and Coke (only) are sold on the buses for a pittance.

The walled city of **Tulum** is on a cliff overlooking the sea. The piles of ancient rock are brightened by flowering trees. Parts date back to A.D. 500. Climb the steep, narrow steps to the top of the main pyramid, the **Temple of the Descending God.** Below, white-sand beaches stretch in either direction. Human sacrifices were once pushed over this cliff. Note the carving of the upside-down god. Some say it is the god of rain; others claim that it is a being from outer space descending to earth.

You can arrange a bus tour from Cancun to Tulum and Xel-Ha for about 45,000 pesos ($20). Tours to Tulum and Chichen Itza can be arranged from Cozumel for about 56,250 pesos ($25).

The largely uncharted city of **Coba,** about 30 miles west of Tulum, has the tallest pyramid in the Yucatan—at 1,150 feet, it is twice the height of El Castillo at Chichen Itza. Once it has been completely studied, Coba may prove the most important Mayan city of all. It once had as many as 40,000 inhabitants, and more than 7,000 stone structures have survived. Carvings of the Descending God can be seen on the temple that tops the pyramid. From the summit you can see Coba's five lakes, surrounded by jungle.

Uxmal is the best-preserved of the Mayan cities on the Yucatan Peninsula. It's also one of the prettiest, with reservoirs rather than wells. Built and abandoned three times between A.D. 325 and A.D. 900, it boasts richly carved temples. One of the most intriguing buildings here was named the **Nunnery** by conquistadores, who knew little about the Mayas. Some scholars believe the name is almost correct, because the building housed priestesses, who would be sacrificed to the god Chac. Others say it was just an administrative center. The **Palace of the Governor** is enormous—occupying a platform that is longer than a football field. The **Pyramid of the Magician** contains five temples, built one above the other.

A fisherman's paradise

Fishing is fabulous in the Mexican Caribbean. From March to mid-July, the sailfish run. From May to early June, the bonito and dolphin run. From May to September, it's the wahoo and kingfish. And barracuda, bluefin, mackerel, white marlin, and grouper can be fished year-round.

The best place to arrange a charter is in **Puerto Juarez,** where rates are $125 to $250 a day for two. Isla Mujérès also has good rates—you can arrange an all-inclusive deep-sea fishing expedition for four people for about $200 a day through Mexico Divers. Rates are much higher in Cancun and Cozumel—from $250 to $350 a day.

The best shopping

Shopping in the Caribbean takes patience, persistence, and a poker face. The basic rules of haggling apply. Ask the price of something, then offer half as much. The shopkeeper inevitably will reply that what you're offering won't even cover the costs of the materials. Your best response is to shrug your shoulders and walk away. The shopkeeper probably will follow you.

Cancun

Cancun's major market area is downtown along **Avenida Tulum.** As you walk by this open-stall market, which stretches for about two blocks, the shopkeepers call to you—some even reach out to grab you by the arm as you pass. Blankets, sweaters, silver bracelets, and straw hats are thrown across boxes and tables in these stalls, and nothing is marked with a price. Feel free to rummage, but wait to ask for help until you're sure of what you want to buy. Once you have the attention of a salesperson, you won't get rid of him easily.

One of our editors found a handmade cardigan sweater in this market. The salesperson (a 16-year-old boy) asked for 225,000 pesos ($100). She offered 90,000 pesos ($40). The boy laughed. But when she walked away, he grabbed her arm. She eventually bought the sweater for $40.

The sweaters and blankets at this market are good quality, but the gold and silver may be less so. Buy a piece of jewelry (if you can get a good price) because you like it, not because you think you're investing in gold. Real silver is marked with a government symbol that shows an eagle with a snake in its mouth leaning against a cactus.

If you'd rather avoid the market, good shops are located along Avenida Tulum. **La Casita,** for example, stocks traditional Mexican clothes and silver and coral jewelry.

El Parian, Cancun's main square, also is a good place to shop. **Anakena** sells Mayan art. **Ronay** specializes in black coral and gold jewelry. And **Victor** has an excellent collection of Mexican ceramics, Christmas ornaments, jewelry, and textiles.

Little boys on the streets sell marionettes dressed in Mexican costume that make good gifts for children and cost next to nothing.

Isla Mujeres

The place to go for handmade, brightly embroidered cotton dresses is **Isla Mujeres.** As you step from the boat onto the dock, you'll be bombarded by people selling blankets, lace tablecloths, necklaces, and conch shells. However, the better merchandise is in the shops in town. These shops keep their doors open to the sun, and the maracas and hats seem to pour from the shops onto the streets and sidewalks. The pastel blue and green dresses, which hang in the doorways and wave in the wind, go for 68,000 pesos ($30). One of our editors found a pair of silver earrings shaped like roses, with fine individual petals, for 11,250 pesos ($5). You can bargain in some of these shops, but not all.

Cozumel

On Cozumel, **Bazaar Cozumel,** *Rafael E. Melgar Boulevard,* sells high-quality Mexican art, including silverwork, tapestries, and pottery, at good prices. And **Plaza del Sol** has about a dozen craft and jewelry shops.

Cancun's best restaurants

El Pescador, *Tulipanes,* off Avenida Tulum, is immensely popular, with long lines for dinner. The food is good, and the ambience colorful. Vendors selling everything from roses to Mexican hats stop by the tables. It's all in good fun. And the prices are great.

Cancun 1900, *El Parian; tel. (988)3-0038,* is decorated as a turn-of-the-century dance hall. House specialties include seafood and prime rib. Dinner for two is about 79,000 pesos ($35), not including drinks, tip, or tax.

Hacienda el Mortero, *tel. (988)3-1133,* set in a quiet, elegant hacienda, serves excellent Mexican cuisine. You can't go wrong, no matter what you order. Dinner for two, not including drinks, tip, or tax, is about 79,000 pesos ($35).

Although you may have to wait a half-hour to be seated, **Maxime,** *tel. (988)3-0438,* is worth it, especially if you tire of Mexican food. The fare is French, and house specialties include *terrine de canard au poivre vert, feuilleté d'escargot,* and *soufflé orange.* Dinner for two is about 79,000 pesos ($35).

Papagayo, *Claveles 31,* is a charming and inexpensive restaurant made up of little Tiki huts. Try the Papagayo omelet, seafood tacos, lime soup, and margaritas. A meal for two is only 34,000 pesos ($15).

Los Alemandros, *Avenida Bonampaht and Sayil; tel. (4)0807,* serves good local Yucatec food.

Cancun's best hotels

The **Camino Real,** *tel. (988)3-0100,* is the best hotel in town. It has 300 rooms, 2 good restaurants, a saltwater swimming pool, a freshwater pool with a swim-up bar, and one of the hottest discos on the island. Double rooms are more than 450,000 pesos ($200) a night during high season (December to May).

The **Exelaris Hyatt Regency,** *tel. (988)3-0966,* offers villas as well as hotel rooms, four restaurants, tennis courts, facilities for water sports, and a pool with a waterfall. A double room costs about 450,000 pesos ($200) a night.

The **Casa Maya,** *tel. (988)3-0555,* is a huge hotel popular with families. Its rooms are spacious, with walk-in closets and large bathrooms. The hotel offers moped rentals, a pool, and tennis courts. A double room is about 405,000 pesos ($180) a night.

The **Club Lagoon,** *tel. (988)3-1111,* is a quiet group of adobe dwellings on Laguna Nichupte. The hotel has two good restaurants and two bars. A double room is about 325,000 pesos ($140) a night.

Cozumel's best fare

Fernando's, *Rafael Melgar 35-B,* has good steaks. Dinner for two is about 79,000 pesos ($35).

Pepe's, *Avenida Rafael Melgar,* serves superb seafood in a romantic setting. Dinner for two is 56,000 pesos ($25).

El Portal, *Malecon,* is an inexpensive place for a good breakfast.

Cozumel's best hotels

Although other luxury hotels have arrived in the last few years, **El Presidente,** *tel. (987)2-0322,* remains the best, with large rooms, a pretty beach, a pool, tennis courts, and an excellent dining room. A double room is about 225,000 pesos ($100) a night.

Sheraton Sol-Caribe, *North Zone; tel. (987)2-0700,* has good diving facilities, an excellent dining room, and three tennis courts. A double room is about 360,000 pesos ($160).

The **Galapago Inn,** *South Zone; tel. (987)2-0663,* is a small, quiet hotel with access to good diving areas. A double room is about 124,000 pesos ($55) a night.

Isla Mujeres' best restaurants

Maria's, *El Garrafon,* five miles outside town, serves excellent food in elegant, peaceful surroundings. Dinner for two is about 68,000 pesos ($30).

Ciro's Lobster House, *Matamoros 1,* serves lobster, red snapper, and a wide selection of Mexican wines. A meal for two is about 56,000 pesos ($25).

Restaurant Gomar, *Hidalgo 5,* is romantic, with both indoor and terrace dining. The lobster and fresh fish are the best bets. Dinner for two is about 56,000 pesos ($25).

Isla Mujeres' best hotels

El Presidente Caribe, *tel. (988)2-0002,* is the island's best hotel. A double room is about 180,000 pesos ($80) a night.

Posada del Mar is a comfortable, small hotel across from the beach. It has tennis courts, a pool, a restaurant, a bar, a laundromat, and air conditioning. A double room is about 124,000 pesos ($55) a night.

Hottest night life

The night life in Cancun and Cozumel is growing. **Cristine's** at the Krystal, **Aquarius** at the Camino Real, and **Tabano's** at the Sheraton are the current hot spots in Cancun. On Cozumel, go to **Scaramouche, Grips,** and **Morgan's.**

Tips on getting around

Although both Cancun and Cozumel have efficient, inexpensive bus service, you might as well take taxis, which are incredibly cheap. Cancun's green and white taxis are equipped with meters. Fares seldom exceed 7,800 pesos ($3.50). The cabs in Cozumel do not have meters, so make an arrangement with the driver before you get in. The fare should be less than 2,250 pesos ($1).

Minibuses transport tourists and their luggage from the airport to hotels for less than 6,800 pesos ($3) per person.

Cancun, Cozumel, and Isla Mujeres all offer moped and auto rentals. The Casa Maya and Krystal hotels on Cancun charge about 34,000 pesos ($15) for an eight-hour rental. On Cozumel, you can rent a moped from Reuben's for about 34,000 pesos ($15) a day. On Isla Mujeres, you can rent a motorbike near the ferry dock for about 27,000 pesos ($12) a day.

In Cancun, you can rent a car from **Avis,** *tel. (988)4-2147;* **Budget,** *tel. (988)4-1709;* **Econorent,** *tel. (988)4-1435;* and **Holiday,** *tel. (988)4-1061.* Each charges about 79,000 pesos ($35) a day with a 125-mile limit. Hertz and Avis are represented on Cozumel, where they charge about 110,000 pesos ($49) a day.

The cheapest ways to get there

Inexpensive package trips to Cancun are available from the Baltimore/Washington area. American Express can arrange a trip, including round-trip air fare and seven nights hotel accommodations, for $675. Apple Vacations and Wainwright offer less expensive packages, but they are often booked up. Wainwright has a "Cancun Fling" package that ranges from $299 for three nights, including air fare and hotel accommodations, to $889 for seven nights. Apple Vacations offers three- to seven-night deals for about the same prices.

Destinations   456

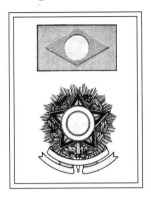

Chapter 25

THE
BEST
OF
BRAZIL

Brazil—the largest South American country—is watered by the Amazon rain forest, the largest in the world, and drained by the Amazon River, which carries more water than any other river in the world. The country's spectacular shoreline—which is lined with broad beaches and high mountains that circle the harbors—is among the most beautiful in the world. But Brazil has more to offer than spectacular scenery. It boasts the continent's most exciting city, Rio de Janeiro, and South America's largest industrial city, São Paulo.

Brazilians are beautiful, an exotic blend of Indian, African, and European ancestry. Half the population is under 25, adding to the beauty quotient, but creating social problems.

A fun-loving nation, Brazil has the world's best Carnival, with glittering costumes, immense processions, mesmerizing music, and gala balls. Year-round, scantily clad Brazilians line the country's beaches.

Restaurants in Brazil are excellent and cheap. Food supplies are abundant and varied, and the chefs are talented. Once you have tried the national dish, *feijoada* (a spicy black-bean stew), take advantage of the international cuisine.

Brazil has the highest inflation rate in the world—229% in 1987. So prices rise rapidly. As of press time (spring 1988), five-star hotels charged about 19,500 cruzados ($130) for a double, and good hotels charged about 9,000 cruzados ($60). However, you should take these prices as rough guides only, considering the incredible inflation rate and the constantly changing values of the dollar and the cruzado.

Rio: Brazil's cultural center

Rio de Janeiro is Brazil's most cosmopolitan city. It is most famous for its pre-Lenten Carnival, but it has much more to offer than simply a festival. A beautiful city surrounded by low mountains, Rio hugs Guanabara Bay, which is rimmed with palm-lined beaches and dotted with 84 islands. Jet-setters from around the world soak in the sun all day, then dance the samba all night.

The world's best Carnival

People from around the world flock to Rio for its **Carnival,** a four-day extravaganza that concludes Ash Wednesday. Poor Cariocas (residents of Rio) often put a year's savings into their costumes for the round of wild parties and balls.

Carnival officially begins when the mayor hands the key to the city to King Momo, the mock king of the festivities, who appears at all major Carnival events (parades, balls, costume contests) and orders everyone to have fun. King Momo is elected by the residents of Rio; the primary requirement is that he be very fat.

Samba schools are the focus of glittering processions beginning at 6 p.m. Sunday and Monday and continuing until noon on Shrove Tuesday. These enormous groups compete for prizes and go to great lengths to come up with the most fantastic and outrageous costumes and themes. The competition is always passionate, and at times it gets violent.

Traditionally, each of the city's samba schools (which number up to 5,000 members each) paraded through the streets of downtown Rio displaying their floats and gaudy costumes. A few years ago, the rowdy parades were taken off the streets and put into the **Sambo'dromo,** a stadium about a half-mile long and about as wide as a street. Brazilians and visitors of all backgrounds pay from a few cents to up to more than $200 to crowd into this structure and watch the samba schools perform. It is the equivalent in spectacle of a halftime show at the Super Bowl, but the majorettes are topless. And the show lasts 17 hours.

Rio's elite, disguised in fantastic costumes, attend elaborate balls. The best are at Canecão Nightclub, the Yacht Club, the Flamenco Football Club, La Scala, and Sugarloaf Mountain. Local nightclubs also arrange elaborate parties, with samba bands and costumes.

Tickets for Carnival balls and parades go on sale in November and sell out early.

The most exotic New Year's celebration

As colorful as Carnival—but less known—is Rio's New Year's celebration. Just before midnight, thousands of white-robed worshippers carrying candles gather on the city's beaches to make offerings to the goddess of the sea, Lemanja. At midnight, fireworks go off, and crying, singing worshippers rush into the ocean carrying flowers and gifts for their deity.

The view from Christ's feet

Rio's best-known landmark is the huge statue of **Christ the Redeemer,** overlooking the harbor from the top of Corcovado Mountain, 2,250 feet above sea level. A little train takes you to the statue.

From this vantage point on the top of the mountain, the view of the harbor is spectacular, particularly as the day turns to dusk, then dark, and the city below begins to glitter against the aquamarine blue of the sea. Have a drink in the café at the top of the mountain.

Another beautiful view of Rio is from the top of **Pau de Açucar** (Sugarloaf Mountain), a rock rising 390 feet above the bay. A cable car makes the trip from 8 a.m. to 10 p.m.

Rio's best museum

The **Quinta da Boa Vista** (National Museum), *São Cristóvão,* in the former Imperial Palace, displays objects that once belonged to the royal family. The Bendego meteorite is one of the largest ever found on earth. The Amazon Indian display is also worth seeing. Surrounding Quinta da Boa Vista is a quilt of lawns, flower beds, and hothouses that can be explored by horse-drawn carriage.

Brazil's best books

The **National Library,** founded in 1810, has a collection of one-million volumes in various languages, including a parchment copy of the Guttenberg Bible (one of four existing) and an astonishing collection of Hebraica.

South America's best beaches

Rio has spectacularly beautiful beaches—Botafogo, Copacabana, Ipanema, Leblon, São Conrado—where women wearing the world's skimpiest bikinis bask in the sun. Called *tangos,* the bikinis here consist of three tiny triangles of fabric held in place by string.

The prettiest beach is the one most distant from the center of the city, **São Conrado,** where the Hotel Intercontinental has taken root. This beach is not as crowded as Copacabana and Ipanema, and the water is cleaner.

São Conrado is also the best place to go hang-gliding—or just to watch the colorful gliders hover in the air for hours, held aloft by updrafts coming off the ocean and up the mountainside. They look like huge butterflies leisurely enjoying the afternoon sun.

Copacabana, lined with luxury hotels, restaurants, and nightclubs, is the chicest beach in South America. It is the longest and widest in Rio. Stroll along **Avenida Atlântica,** which is tiled with mosaic and lined with first-class hotels and expensive shops.

Close rivals of Copacabana are Ipanema (which is less congested and draws a younger crowd), Leblon, and Barra da Tijuca. Southern Ipanema is a fashionable residential area.

Two hours north of Rio are the beaches of **Bujios,** the playgrounds of the elite. Called the jewel of the Brazilian Riviera, Bujios is filled with expensive boutiques. The pace is languid. People sleep until noon and dine in the wee hours of the morning. You can walk to the beach from anywhere in this little fishing village. Houses have no doors, and drums can be heard.

About 90 miles north of Rio is **Cabo Frio,** whose forts and 17th-century convent are a dramatic backdrop to a wide, almost deserted beach.

The world's largest stadium

Maracana Stadium, the world's largest sports arena, which holds more than 200,000 people, is the locale of Rio's wild soccer matches. The games are second in importance only to Carnival here. Buy a Cadiera Especial ticket for 1,500 cruzados—this allows you to enjoy the matches in an area fenced off from the mobs of raucous fans. Most hotels offer packages that provide transportation to and from the stadium as well as seats for the games.

The best bets

The **Jockey Club** holds horse races Thursday nights and weekends. The most important is the Grande Premio Brasil, held the first Sunday in August. Everyone who is anyone shows up in fancy dress to watch South America's best horses run.

The best way to see the bay

The best way to see **Guanabara Bay** is to take a day or half-day cruise among its islands. Boats dock along Avenida Nestor Moreira, next to the Sol e Mar restaurant. Paqueta, where Rio's lovers meet, is the loveliest island. Cars aren't allowed here, only bikes and carriages. A ferry to Paqueta takes about an hour-and-a-half; hydrofoils take 30 minutes.

Rio's best drive

The road that winds through Rio's mountain backdrop, passing through Itatiaia National Park toward Visconde de Maua, is breathtaking. En route is **Petropolis,** once the emperor's summer palace, which has been preserved complete with royal belongings, including the Brazilian imperial crown. You must remove your shoes to visit the interior of the palace, which is open to the public daily except Mondays. About an hour farther along is **Teresopolis,** a national park that attracts mountain climbers.

The world's best colored gems

Brazil is the world's major purveyor of colored gems. Aquamarines, topazes, amethysts, and turmalines are abundant and cost 20% to 25% less in Brazil than in New York. Emeralds are also in great supply—large deposits have been discovered recently. Settings and mountings are tremendous bargains, because of the low cost of labor.

Two good places to shop for colored gems are **H. Stern** and **Amsterdam Sauer**—the largest dealers in Brazil. H. Stern offers free round-trip transportation from all major hotels in Rio to its headquarters in Ipanema. It also conducts tours of its lapidary and goldsmith workshops, as well as of its gem museum, which features outstanding pieces from Brazil, including a 42-pound aquamarine.

The best shopping

In addition to gemstones, Rio also has great deals on leather goods. You'll find good deals at all the city's department stores, including **Rio Sul,** on the west side of the tunnel leading from Avenida Princesa Isabel. Or stroll along Avenida Atlantica in the evening, where you'll find a wide assortment of leather products.

Feirarte (formerly known as the Hippie Market) is a good place to buy arts and crafts. It is held Sundays at Praça General Osorio in Ipanema.

Rio's best restaurants

Rio's best gourmet restaurants include **Le St. Honoré,** *Meridien Hotel; tel. (55-21)275-2922,* inspired by Paul Bocuse; **Le Pré Catalán,** *Rio Palace Hotel; tel. (55-21)521-3232,* created by Gaston Lenôtre; and **Le Bec Fin,** *Av. Copacabana 178A; tel. (55-21)542-4097.*

For authentic Brazilian food, the best restaurant in town is **Moenda,** *Trocadero Hotel, Second Floor, Av. Atlantica 2064, Copacabana; tel. (55-21)257-1834.* The decor is not deluxe, but the food is scrumptious. Try the *feijoada completa.* Prices are moderate.

Ouro Verde, attached to the hotel of the same name, is one of the best restaurants in Copacabana. The most romantic is **Copacabana,** in the Copacabana Hotel. **Enotria,** *Rua Constante Ramos,* serves delicious northern Italian food.

In old Rio, try **Chale,** *Rua da Matriz 54,* or **Maria Thereza Weiss,** *Rua Visconde Silva 152.* Both are in old colonial houses full of Brazilian antiques.

In new Rio, try **La Tour,** *Rua Santa Luzia,* a revolving restaurant at the top of the Aeronautical Club building near the American Consulate.

Brazil has good barbecue restaurants, called *churrascaria.* These all-you-can-eat places serve grilled meats—pork, beef, marinated chicken livers—with salad and rice. The food is inexpensive and usually superb.

The best *churrascaria* is **Gaucha,** *Rua Laranjeiras 114.* **Mariu's,** *Avenida Atlantica,* just up from Copacabana, is one of the few *churrascarias* on the beach. **Porcao,** *Barra,* past São Conrado, is also good.

Rio's best seafood is served at the **Sol e Mar**, *Av. Nestor Moreira 11*, in Botafogo, which has a view of the bay. A string quartet entertains as you enjoy your South Atlantic fish. Another good place for seafood is Alba Mar, also overlooking the water downtown.

Rio's best hotels

Rio's most inviting hotel, in a glitzy modern way, is the **Meridien**, *Copacabana Beach; tel. (55-21)275-9922.*

Other first-class hotels are **Rio Palace**, *Copacabana Beach; tel. (55-21)521-3232;* **Caesar Park**, *Ipanema; tel. (55-21)287-3122;* and **Marina Palace**, *Leblon; tel. (55-21)259-5212.*

Copacabana Palace, *Av. Atlantica 1702; tel. (55-21)255-7070*, is the grand old dame of Rio's hotels, the first major hotel built on Copacabana Beach. Until recent years, jet-setters from around the world returned here year after year. However, despite cosmetic surgery, the old girl can't match the attractions of the newer hotels on Copacabana and Ipanema beaches.

The hottest night life

Rio's residents don't sit down to dinner until 9 p.m. or so. By the time dinner is finished, it's nearly 11 p.m. This is when the city's night spots wake up.

The most popular *discotecas* (discos) are Hippopotamus, Caligula, and Help. They are like discos everywhere, with loud music, light shows, and lively crowds. Many are organized as private clubs. Ask the concierge at your hotel to make a reservation for you.

Rio's *gafieiras* are a better bet if you want to see authentic Brazilian night life. These large dance halls draw people of all ages. The places have little or no decor, the bands vary, and the crowds are noisy. But the noise is distinctly Brazilian, and the crowds are charmingly unsophisticated. One of the more sophisticated *gafieiras* is **Asa Branca**, *Av. Meme de Sa 17; tel. (55-21)252-0966*, a fairly new dance hall owned by one of Rio's most energetic entertainment moguls, Chico Recarey.

Two of the best clubs for live entertainment are **Karaoke de Limelight**, *Rua Min-Viveiros de Castro 93, Copacabana; tel. (55-21)542-3596;* and **Karoake de Canja**, *Av. Ataulfo de Paiza 375; tel. (55-21)511-0484.*

You'll find a more sophisticated piano bar and a live band at **Café Un, Deux, Trois**, *Rua Bartolomeu Mitre 123; tel. (55-21)239-0198*. **Biblos**, *Av. Epitacio Pessoa 1484; tel. (55-21)521-2645*, is a good place to dance.

If you're in the mood for a quieter evening, try the **Bâteau Mouche Bar**, next to the Sol e Mar restaurant. The tunes date back to the 1940s, and there's dancing, of course.

For a Las Vegas-type show, go to **Plataforma**, *Rua Adalberto Ferreira 32; tel. (55-21)274-4022*, or **Scala Rio**, *Av. Afranio de Melos Franco 296; tel. (55-21)239-4448.*

South America's most modern city: Brasilia

Brasilia is a futuristic fantasy situated in the middle of the great central plain of Brazil. The white structures of this capital city are striking, set against the rich red soil. The capital is laid out in the shape of an airplane, with government buildings down the middle and residential and commercial areas along the two wings.

Brasilia came into existence in 1960. President Juscelino Kubitschek decided the nation's capital should be in the center of the country, rather than on the coast, and began construction of the city, which took three years to complete. He drew on the talents of urban planner Lucio Costa, who designed the city, and architect Oscar Niemeyer.

However, the seeds of Brasilia were sown in the 1800s by St. João Bosco, who wrote in his memoirs, "Repeatedly a voice spoke out, saying: When they come to excavate the mines hidden in the breasts of these mountains (between the 15th and 20th parallels), here the promised land will arise, giving forth milk and honey. It will be of unimaginable riches, and this will happen before the second generation passes...before 120 years go by."

Bosco's vision inspired Brazilian leaders to stipulate in the constitution of 1891 that the new capital should be established in the area between the 15th and 20th parallels, the location of modern-day Brasilia. The saint is commemorated at **Dom Bosco Church,** which has tall and brilliant blue stained-glass windows.

Brazil's tallest tower

Brasilia has one of the tallest telecommunications towers in the world, the 600-foot **Torre de Televisão.** Take an elevator to a platform at 225 feet or another elevator to a restaurant and bar that offer an extensive view of the city.

The best place to begin

Catetinho, the temporary residence of President Juscelino Kubitschek in 1956 and Brasilia's first building, is the best place to begin a tour of the city. The white-clapboard house on stilts was built in 10 days for the former president, when he and city planners were plotting the city's future. It is modestly furnished, with a bed and a plain wooden table, around which city planners gathered.

Brazil's ultramodern cathedral

The architecturally noteworthy **National Cathedral** is an ultramodern structure designed in the shape of the crown of thorns. A statue of St. Peter is suspended from the roof in the Passage of Reflection, which leads to the underground nave. A pool, which surrounds the concrete building, is reflected in the nave's glass roof panels, giving the interior an airy brightness.

The prettiest palace

Brasilia's most famous building is the **Itamarati Palace,** which rises out of the beautiful water gardens that hold the city's well-known sculpture the **Meteor.** The pool is filled with yard-wide lily pads called Victoria Regia, native to the Amazon. Inside is a splendid collection of Brazilian art, including works by Portinari, the country's premier painter.

Brazil's boldest architecture

The **National Congress Complex** looks more like an outer-space colony than a political center. The long, narrow building is reached by ramp-like staircases and topped by two eggshell domes, one inverted and known as the cup and saucer. The building glows at sunset.

The **Planalto Palacio** is the city's most graceful building, its roof supported by marble arches, its facade mirrored in a reflecting pool. Next door, a man-made waterfall washes the face of the Justice Ministry.

The president's house

The **Palacio da Alvorada,** the home of the president of Brazil, is outside town on Lake Paranoa. The sumptuous building has glass walls, rosewood floors, and panels of gilded tile.

To visit the palace, which is open to the public most weekends, obtain a pass from the Palacio do Planalto in Brasilia.

Brasilia's best dining

The *churrascarias* along the lake are good places to eat. The best is **Churrascaria do Lago,** *tel. (55-61)223-9266.* Good international cuisine is served at the **Piantella,** *tel. (55-61)224-9408,* which has live music.

First-class hotels

Brasilia's best hotel is the first-class **Nacional,** *Setor Hoteleiro, Sul Lote 1; tel. (55-61)226-8180,* which has a lovely central view of the government buildings.

Hotel Das Americas, *Setor Hoteleiro, Sol 4, Bl. D.; tel. (55-61)223-4490,* in the southern hotel area, is air-conditioned. Rooms have refrigerators. Double rooms are $35 to $45.

Eron Brasilia, *Setor Hoteleiro Norte, A5, Lote A; tel. (55-61)226-2125,* has air-conditioned rooms with refrigerators. Rooms are $50.

Brazil's best theater

The **Teatro Nacional** (National Theater) has one of the most flexible modern stages in South America, as well as two auditoriums. The building was designed to look like an elongated Aztec pyramid.

São Paulo: South America's richest city

São Paulo, a city of nearly 13 million, is the industrial center of Brazil and the largest city in South America. It employs the largest labor force in Latin America, with more than 400,000 workers, and has the highest standard of living in Brazil. It also has the largest number of Japanese in the world outside Japan.

South America's biggest cathedral

The **Catedralo Metropolitano of São Paulo** is the largest—and one of the most beautiful—in South America. The vaulted neo-Gothic structure holds 8,000 worshippers and dominates the **Praça da Sé** (Cathedral Plaza), where fountains gurgle and Paulistas gather. The cathedral's underground crypt contains the remains of ecclesiastical figures.

The world's biggest zoo

São Paulo's **zoo,** *Av. Miguel Estefano 4241, Auga Funda; tel. (55-11)276-0811,* is the largest in South America, with more than 400 animals and 600 birds. It is open daily from 9 a.m. to 6 p.m.

After visiting the zoo, stop by the **Jardim Botanico,** *Av. Miguel Estefano 3031,* an orchid farm that displays more than 35,000 species. Open Tuesdays to Sundays 9 a.m. to 5 p.m.

South America's best art gallery

The **Museu de Arte de São Paulo,** *Av. Paulista 1578; tel. (55-11)251-5644,* has a collection of Western art from the Gothic Age to the present, the only such collection in South America. The museum has Raphael's *Resurrection,* painted when the 16th-century artist was just 17, a Rembrandt self-portrait, and 13 works by Renoir.

The closest thing to Japan

São Paulo's **Liberdade** (Japantown)—south of Praça da Sé along Praça da Liberdade and Rua Galvão Bueno—is the closest thing to Japan in the Americas. Entered through red lacquer gates, it has tranquil rock gardens, Japanese grocers, and herbal-remedy stores. To realize the importance of São Paulo's Japanese population (nearly 800,000 strong), visit the **Museu da Imigração Japonesa** (Japanese Immigration in Brazil Museum), where exhibits explain the 75-year history of Japanese immigration.

The world's second-best religious art museum

São Paulo's **Museu de Arte Sacra** (Sacred Art Museum), *Av. Tiradentes 676,* is second only to the Vatican when it comes to collections of Western religious art. Room after room of the museum is filled with carved altars, gold altarpieces, statues, and paintings.

The top sights

Ibirapuera Park was built for São Paulo's fourth centennial celebrations. Inside the grounds is an exact reproduction of Japan's Katura Palace. Willows border the lakes, and eucalyptus groves scent the air.

Casa do Bandeirante, *Praça Monteiro Lobato,* is an 18th-century pioneer house preserved for tourists. You can see firsthand the Spartan lifestyles of early settlers, who slept in hammocks and used trunks as tables. On the grounds are ox carts and three mills for sugarcane and corn.

You can see how Brazil's wealthier colonists lived at the **Museu da Casa Brasileira** (Brazilian Home Museum), *Av. Brigada Faria Lima 774.* Built in 1945, the mansion contains photos and sketches of early homes, as well as antique furniture and religious pieces.

In the old center of town, several churches and a Byzantine Franciscan convent still stand, as well as São Paulo's oldest building, a Jesuit chapel built in 1554.

Another attraction (so to speak) is the largest snake farm on the continent, the **Instituto Butantã,** *Av. Vital Brasil 1500,* where venom is collected for medicinal uses. It is open from 9 a.m. to 5 p.m Tuesdays through Sundays; from 1 p.m. to 5 p.m. Mondays.

Shopping bests

São Paulo is known for its shopping. The best buys include clothing, antiques, and Brazilian jewels. The steep Rua Augusta, lined with little boutiques selling native art and unusual clothing, is a good place to begin your shopping spree. In addition, the city has many large shopping malls. The jeweler Henry Stern has an office in São Paulo as well as in Rio.

A huge Sunday fair is held along the **Praça da Republica.** A colorful street fair is held Tuesdays and Thursdays through Saturdays in **Pacaembú Stadium,** *Praça Charles Miller.*

The best restaurants

O Profeta, *Alameda Dos Aicas 40; tel. (55-11)549-5311,* serves food from all over Brazil. The specialties are fish and *feijoada.*

The best place in São Paulo for *feijoada* is **Bolinha,** *Av. Cidade Jardim 53; tel. (55-11)852-9526,* a popular place that usually has long lines (reservations are not accepted). Have a drink at the bar and watch the people while you wait.

If you tire of Brazilian food, you can have a good French meal at **Marcel's,** *Rua Epitácio Pessôa 98; tel. (55-11)257-6968.* Chef Jean Durand is good friends with Paul Bocuse, with whom he shares a love of delicate dishes. The restaurant is closed Sundays. Credit cards are not accepted.

São Paulo also has good *churrascarias* (**Rodeio,** *Rua Haddock Lobo 1498; tel. (55-11)993-2322,* which has great cowboy atmosphere, is the best) and a great many restaurants.

The best hotels

Maksoud Palace, *Alameda Campinas 150; tel. (55-11)251-2233,* is the most luxurious hotel in São Paulo, with a swimming pool, a sauna, squash courts, eight restaurants, and a Scandinavian smorgasbord. Top-floor rooms have maid, butler, and valet service. Built in 1979, it is a modern 22-story structure surrounding an atrium, where a 1-ton sculpture by the Brazilian artist Toyota hangs.

The chicest hotel in São Paulo is **Caesar Park,** *Rua Augusta 1508; tel. (55-11)285-6622,* surrounded by lush vegetation. The lobby is an elegant place for a rendezvous. Breakfast is served in the garden, and at night a band plays in the rooftop bar.

The **Mofarrej Sheraton,** *Alameda Santos 1437; tel. (55-11)284-5544,* is a five-star European-style luxury hotel.

The **São Paulo Hilton,** *Av. Ipiranga 165; tel. (55-11)256-0033,* has a pool, a sauna, four restaurants, five bars, and jewelry and gift stores. But it is near the red-light district.

The best night life

São Paulo's most popular nightclub, **Club 150,** *Alameda Campinas 150, Maksoud Hotel; tel. (55-11)251-2233,* is a good place to listen to jazz.

St. Paul, *Alameda Lorena 1717; tel. (55-11)282-7697,* is the best place for singles. Couples are admitted only on weekends.

Plataforme 1, *Av. 412; tel. (55-11)287-1234,* has a samba show with beautiful dancers. Patrons also can dance. Dinner is served. Because it's located on the 42nd floor (the penthouse), it offers a spectacular view. The club opens Mondays through Saturdays at 8:30 p.m.

Barracao de Zinco, *Av. Ibirapuera 2441; tel. (55-11)531-6740,* is a good samba house.

Salvador—center of voodooism

Salvador de Bahia is the center of the **candomble** cult, created by African slaves who were forced to practice Catholicism but who wanted to preserve their own religion. The slaves merged their gods with Christian saints and Biblical characters and worshipped both. The deity of lightning, Chongo, for example, was combined with St. Barbara, also associated with lightning. And Iemanja is another name for the Virgin Mary. Candomble has become an accepted part of Roman Catholicism. Salvador has 166 churches and 4,000 candomble *terreiros* (temples).

You can attend a candomble ceremony (as long as you don't bring a camera or cross your hands or feet, which is considered unlucky). The god to be honored at the ceremony has its own special costume, and its colors are donned by candomble followers. Men and women are seated opposite each other. As the ritual progresses, worshippers fall to the ground in convulsions, their bodies apparently possessed by the spirits being conjured. They speak in voices completely unlike their own.

Most ceremonies begin at 8:30 p.m. and continue until 11 p.m. or midnight. Call **Bahiatursa,** *tel. (55-71)245-8433,* for a schedule of ceremonies. Or ask your hotel operator to arrange a visit to a candomble ceremony for you.

Another ritual dating back to the days of slavery is the *capoeira,* a dance-fight. This strange and beautiful performance was begun by slaves, who, forbidden to fight, learned to disguise their aggressions in the graceful forms of a dance.

Carnival is even more colorful here than in Rio, although it is less-known. And it is longer, beginning one month before Lent. Participants pay homage to Iemanja, the goddess of the sea, and don the *mortalha,* a costume made of bedsheets. Groups, called *afoxes,* dance to drums and throw a powder called *efu,* which is made from the horns of sheep and supposedly possesses mystical powers.

The most beautiful churches

Igreja da São Francisco, *Praça Pae. Anchieta 1; tel. (55-71)243-2367,* is one of the most beautiful baroque churches in the world. Built in the 18th century by Franciscans, the interior walls are covered with gold leaf and hand-carved rosewood. Portuguese stone was imported to construct the church; Portuguese tiles to illustrate the life of St. Francis. Men can visit the monastery next door, but women can only peer through the door.

Salvador's cathedral, **Terreiro de Jesus,** *tel. (55-71)243-4573,* is massive, also covered in gold leaf. The Jesuits built the cathedral from 1657 to 1672, before they were ousted from Brazil. It is closed to the public during Carnival.

The most popular church in the city is the **Igreja de Nosso Senhor do Bonfim** (Church of Our Lord of the Good Ending), *Adro do Bonfim.* It is dedicated to Oxalá, the father of candomble gods and goddesses, who is also known as Jesus. Worshippers often wear silver and white, the colors of Oxalá. A tiny room in the back of the church contains creepy testimonials to the power of faith—wax castings of injured or sick human body parts that have been miraculously cured.

A beautiful little **Carmelite church,** *Largo do Carmo; tel. (55-71)243-1935,* founded in 1585, has been made into a museum that displays religious objects in precious metals and stones and an exhibit explaining candomble.

Igreja da Boa Viagen (Church of the Good Voyage), *Boa Viagen Beach; tel. (55-71)226-1800,* is known for its 18th-century Portuguese mosaics.

The oldest church in Salvador is **Igreja e Mosteiro de Nossa Senhora da Graça,** *Largo da Graça; tel. (55-71)247-4670.* The 18th-century church includes part of a monastery built in 1557.

Igreja e Convento de Santa Tereza, *Rua do Sodré 25; tel. (55-71)243-6310,* was built in the 17th century for the Shoeless Carmelite's Order of St. Teresa. It has been restored and made into the Museu de Arte Sacre. The museum is open Tuesdays through Saturdays from 10 a.m. to 11:30 a.m. and from 2 p.m. to 5:30 p.m.

Salvadore's best food

In addition to religion, African culture also has influenced local cuisine, most of which you'll find fantastic, some of which you'll find strange. It is characterized by creoles and jambalayas, spicy and served with rice. The primary ingredients are pork, seafood, and coconut.

Solar do Unhão, *Avenida do Contorno; tel. (55-71)245-5551,* is in an old stone sugarcane factory washed by the Bahía de Todo los Santos (Bay of All Saints), which gives Bahia its name. Brazilian politicos and jet-setters come here.

Casa da Gamboa, *Rua Gamboa de Cima 51; tel. (55-71)245-9777,* is located in a colonial house with antique furniture and lace curtains. Bahian specialties are served. The restaurant is closed Sundays.

The best hotels

Luxor Convento do Carmo, *Largo de Carmo 1; tel. (55-71)242-3111,* is the most charming hotel in town, occupying the former convent of a 16th-century Carmelite Church. Guests sleep in nuns' cells, which have been outfitted with decadent modern additions, such as air conditioning, color televisions, and refrigerator-bars. The central courtyard has a large pool. Although the hotel is not near the beaches, it is convenient base for exploring town. The hotel restaurant, **Forno o Fogão,** serves good local fare.

Quatro Rodas Salvador, *Farol de Itapuã; tel. (55-71)249-9611,* is a spanking-new hotel located on the beach 40 minutes from town. It has an ocean-view rooftop nightclub, two excellent restaurants, a bar, tennis courts, a concert hall, and satellite television.

Niagara's superior

Iguaçu Falls, at the border with Argentina, is even bigger than Niagara Falls, a spectacular sight. One of the world's greatest waterfalls, it is is on the Igauçu River, near its confluence with the Paraná River. Iguaçu Falls is actually made up of 200 separate falls, some very tiny. The biggest is Devil's Throat, 330 feet high. (Iguaçu means *great waters* in the language of the local Guaraní tribes, who were once cannibal and the subject of the movie *Missionary.)*

To best see the falls, take the elevator down to the river's edge and walk out onto the platform that reaches into the middle. From this angle you will see rainbows glimmering through the water.

Nearby is the great **Itaipú Dam** and the world's largest hydroelectric power complex.

The best place to stay is the **Hotel das Cataratas,** *Radovia das Cataratas, Km. 28; tel. (55-455)74-2666,* which overlooks the falls. It has a pool, a restaurant, and a bar.

The world's largest rain forest: the Amazon

The world's largest rain forest and the world's wildest river share the same name: the **Amazon.** The river flows 3,550 miles, is fed by 1,000 smaller rivers and tributaries, and is home to 2,000 species of fish (including the life-threatening piranha, with its razor-sharp teeth, and the candiru, which swims up human orifices and lodges itself in the body).

The forest is home to exotic animals, such as the tapir and anaconda. You'll see colorful parrots deep in the jungle. About 158 Indian tribes live in the Amazon. When they first visited the New World, Christopher Columbus and Sir Walter Raleigh both reported hearing of Amazon warrior women, who, like the characters in Greek legend, lived independently of men.

Encompassing an area of 2.3-million square miles, the Amazon is overwhelming. The only practical way to see it is by boat—few roads make their way through the dense jungle. Don't expect to see all the Amazon's mysteries when traveling down the river—at points the river is so wide that the shore cannot be seen on both sides.

The Brazilian government hosts one-way Amazon cruises twice a month on the **ENASA Line,** *Av. Presidente Vargas 41, Belem; tel. (55-91)223-3011.* These ships, modern catamarans, have staterooms, dining areas, and air conditioning. The trip takes six days from Belem to Manaus, five days from Manaus to Belem.

If you're interested in a jungle excursion, take a trip on a smaller boat. Riverboats (with room for 4 to 20 passengers) depart weekly from Manaus for 3-day adventures that return to Manaus. Some riverboats are equipped with what is called jungle air conditioning (cooling provided by old generators) and individual cabins. Others simply supply hammocks, and you sleep on deck in the open air. (The hammocks are not as uncomfortable as you might expect, because mosquitoes and other bugs do not, in fact, ravage the river.) The boats stop at various jungle sites, where English-speaking guides lead the way through the terrain.

Another way to explore the jungle is to stay at jungle lodges, which range from Spartan to deluxe. You can arrange for a van to pick you up at Manaus and drop you off for two or three days at a lodge.

Another alternative is a private boat, which can be found by asking around the docks of Belem near the Ver-O-Peso Market. Bring your own hammock.

It is best to plan these adventures from the United States. For more information, contact one of the following tour operators: **LADATCO,** *2220 Coral Way, Miami, FL 33145; (800)327-6162 or (305)854-8422 in Florida;* **LATOUR,** *114 E. 28th St., New York, NY 10016; (800)348-3401 or (212)532-3020 in New York;* or **Brazil Nuts,** *81 Remsen St., Brooklyn Heights, NY 11201; (800)553-9959 or (718)834-0701 in New York.*

Take proper medical precautions against malaria before and during a trip to the Amazon. Anti-malaria pills, such as Aralen (chloroquinephosphate, 500 milligrams), are available with a prescription. Yellow fever shots are also required for travel in the Amazon.

Belem, the gateway to the Amazon

Belem—the gateway to the Amazon—is a modern city with vestiges of its colonial past. Nearby, at the mouth of the Amazon, is **Marajo Island,** which is bigger than all of Denmark. Archeologists are studying burial grounds on Marajo, where remnants of a long-lost people can be seen. The island also has huge buffalo farms and herds of wild buffalo, whose ancestors escaped the captivity of earlier farms. Buffalo hunts are organized out of Belem.

The newest and most expensive hotel in town is the **Hilton,** *Av. Presidente Vargas 882; tel. (55-91)223-6500,* across from the Praça da Republica. You can make reservations from the United States, *(800)445-8667.* **Vanja,** *Rua Benjamin Constant 1164; tel. (55-97)222-6688,* is a downtown hotel with air-conditioned rooms, a restaurant, a bar, and a beauty salon (if the jungle takes its toll on your appearance).

A block away, on Avenida Presidente Vargas, is the **Excelsior Grão Para,** *tel. (55-91)222-3255,* with small, rather drab, but inexpensive rooms. The recently renovated **Hotel Regente,** *Av. Governador José Malcher 485; tel. (55-91)224-0755,* is an inexpensive three-star place.

Manaus: at the heart of the rain forest

If you want to really experience the Amazon, go to **Manaus.** The architecture in this town is a mix of European styles and modern wooden structures that blend into the jungle surroundings. The waterfront market sells live animals and birds and voodoo and Indian artifacts, as well as the usual assortment of merchandise. Because Manaus is a free port, you can buy imported merchandise for at least two-thirds less than elsewhere in Brazil.

Manaus is the best base for taking day excursions upriver into narrow tributary channels. **Capitania do Porto** (Office of the Port Captain), *Rua Marques de Santa Cruz,* has information on boat trips, including several one- and two-day trips up the River Negro. A one-day trip costs about 4,550 cruzados, including guides, lunch, and drinks. Four or more people can hire a smaller boat for about 1,300 cruzados a head for trips on the river or into the small, jungle-roofed canals. Hunting and fishing safaris also can be arranged.

The best hotel in Manaus is the five-star **Tropical,** *tel. (55-92)238-5757,* on the beach of Ponta Negra outside town. It is well worth its price. Owned by Varig Airlines, the Tropical is situated on a 10-acre site, cleared from virgin jungle, running along the River Negro from Manaus. It has a private zoo. Architect Adolpho Linden designed the hotel to look like a Portuguese colonial country house. The hotel's restaurant is first-class, known for its superb regional fish dishes. For reservations contact **Varig Airlines,** *tel. (55-92)234-0251,* or the hotel.

South America's most spectacular wildlife

Travelers are just beginning to discover **Pantanal,** a region similar to the Florida Everglades, located south of the Amazon in western Brazil. Pantanal has the most spectacular concentrations of wildlife in South America, if not the world. Pantanal can be reached from either Campo Grande or Cuiaba via a jeep safari or a riverboat trip. The same groups that arrange trips to the Amazon (listed above) organize trips to Pantanal.

Chapter 26

THE BEST OF THE CARIBBEAN

The Caribbean is speckled with beautiful little worlds—islands rimmed with white sand, coral reefs, and palm trees. Each is unique. Some have volcanoes, others are flat as pancakes. On some, the residents speak French; on others, the people speak Spanish, Dutch, or English. A few of the islands have luxurious resorts with gambling casinos and fine restaurants that draw the jet set. Others are remote, with thick jungles and few inhabitants.

(Because most Caribbean islands accept U.S. dollars as well as their own local currencies, prices for hotels, restaurants, and travel are quoted in dollars throughout the chapter.)

St. Barthélemy (the best beaches)

St. Barthélemy has the most gorgeous beaches in the Caribbean. This millionaire's island is dotted with the vacation homes of such illustrious families as the Rockefellers and the Rothschilds. Mick Jagger, Peter Jennings, Beverly Sills, Mikhail Baryshnikov, and Billy Joel frequent the island. They are drawn to St. Barts (as the island is affectionately known) by the seductive langor of its lifestyle and its sophisticated French atmosphere.

The island's most beautiful beach is **Anse du Gouverneur,** on the south coast. The sand is as soft as talcum powder, and jagged cliffs protect the beach on two sides, giving it a secluded air. It is never crowded.

Despite the jet-setters who frequent the island, life on St. Barts is homey and small-scale. However, it has become pricey. One of the island's most exclusive resorts is Les Castelets, founded by a financier on the board of the American Ballet.

St. Barthélemy is one of only two completely free trading ports in the Caribbean (the other is St. Martin), and it sells French perfume and champagne at lower prices than in Paris.

The Cayman Islands—a mecca for scuba divers

The most varied scuba diving in the Caribbean is off the **Caymans,** three islands (Grand Cayman, Cayman Brac, and Little Cayman) surrounded by almost continuous rings of reefs. This spectacular underwater frontier contains 325 coral-encrusted shipwrecks, some rumored to contain treasure. The water is crystal clear, with a visibility of 200 feet. Craggy coral formations extend to the North Canyon Wall, where the ocean floor drops off a mile deep.

More than 20 diving companies offer scuba-diving lessons and gear rental in the Caymans. The oldest and largest on Grand Cayman is **Bob Soto's Diving,** *tel. (809)949-2022,* run by owner Ron Kipp out of four locations, including the Holiday Inn on Seven Mile Beach.

The inhabitants of the Caymans are among the best seamen in the world and are heavily recruited by international freighting companies. Until tourism became their bread and butter, every able-bodied man went to sea at age 18.

Aside from scuba diving, the national pastimes are barhopping and churchgoing. Barefoot Man and other island bands play nightly, except Sundays, at the **Grand Cayman Holiday Inn.** Another popular night spot is **Silver's Nightclub** at the Treasure Island Hotel.

Blue laws close bars at midnight on Saturdays. Bars can open again at noon on Sundays; however, on Sundays, live music can't be performed.

Pedro's Castle, *Savannah; tel. (809)947-3388,* on Grand Cayman, is the oldest building on the islands. Once a pirates' hangout frequented by Blackbeard, Pedro's Castle is now a restaurant that serves light refreshments.

The **Tortuga Club,** *P.O. Box 496; tel. (809)947-7551,* on the east end of Grand Cayman, is the most romantic place to stay. It offers reasonably priced package tours.

Jamaica: the sensuous island

Jamaica is a sensuous place, a land of sunshine, ganja, reggae, colonial houses with verandas, and thick tropical jungle. The pace is slow and languid. The sexiest place on the island is the **Blue Lagoon,** where Brooke Shields starred in a romantic movie by the same name.

Jamaica's longest, most beautiful white sand beach is **Negril,** discovered by hippies almost two decades ago. The hippies have gone, but Negril is still a place for the younger set. The beach is lined with hotels, including the Hedonism II (whose name reflects its philosophy of life). Nude sunbathing is allowed on a section of the beach.

At the westernmost point on the island is **Rick's Café,** propped 10 feet from the edge of a cliff. The water below is deep and clear, prompting thrill seekers to dive from the top of the cliff into the water 30 or 40 feet below. Try to get here in time for the sunset, the most fantastic in the Western Hemisphere.

The most beautiful of Jamaica's great houses (mansions left from the colonial days) is **Rose Hall,** once inhabited by the infamous white witch Anne Palmer. It was bought by John Rollins, the former lieutenant governor of Delaware, in the 1960s and restored with meticulous attention to the original detail.

Avoid **Kingston,** unless you go with a friend who knows the city well. Some sections of the city can be downright dangerous. If you decide to spend time in Kingston, the best place to make contacts is the **Pegasus Hotel,** the meeting place for Kingston's expats.

The best way to hear reggae

Jamaica's reggae is an urban outgrowth of the Rastafarian religion, which grew up on this island among a group of escaped African slaves, called Maroons. To hear reggae visit **Montego Bay** and **Negril.** Appearances by top reggae artists, including Third World, The Mighty Diamonds, and Dennis Brown, are advertised in local newspapers. Outdoor concerts are held every Friday at Cornwall Beach in Montego Bay.

If you have Jamaican friends, ask them to take you to clubs outside the tourist areas. These are cheaper and feature smaller reggae bands. Don't go to these clubs unless you are accompanied by a Jamaican. And don't object to the ever-present ganja.

Jamaica inns

The best place to stay in Jamaica is the **Sans Souci,** *Ocho Rios; tel. (809)974-2353,* about two hours down the coast from the Montego Bay Airport. It has multilevel pools and terraces connected by leafy walks. The entrance is imposing, with a guardhouse. The outer walls are beige and pink. Inside, the decor is casual—white rattan and wicker furniture on a tile floor in the foyer, overhead fans, and a mahogany bar fancifully done up as the Ballroom Bar. Rooms are $150 during the winter (high season).

The Sans Souci features a local band that performs Bob Marley tunes with the same ease and grace it handles Elvis hits. When the band takes a break, the pianist in the bar, who is a dead-ringer for Sam in the movie *Casablanca,* takes over. You'll hear *As Time Goes By* at least once during the course of the evening.

The **Half Moon Club,** *tel. (809)953-2211,* is near the airport at Montego Bay. Dining rooms, hallways, and verandas are done in the open plantation style. The service and food are good. Guests can use a Robert Trent Jones-designed golf course, pools, tennis and squash courts, and watersports equipment. The private beach is one-mile long. Rooms range from $100 to $240, depending on the season.

The best of the Bahamas

Just a few hours from New York or Miami are the 700 islands of the **Bahamas,** an idyllic chain of islands stretching from Bimini, just 50 miles off the coast of Florida, toward Haiti. The islands are mostly flat and bordered by white-sand beaches. Only 20 of them are inhabited. **Nassau,** the biggest tourist center, acts as the seat of government. It is not particularly attractive, plagued by crime, unemployment, and resentment.

However, Nassau does have a splendid health club, the **Royal Bahamian Hotel,** *West Bay Street, Cable Beach; tel. (809)327-6400.* A first-class hideaway, this $7-million complex offers guests use of a gym, a whirlpool, a sauna, steam baths, a massage room, tennis courts, swimming pools, and a private white-sand beach. What's $100 to $215 per night, when good health is at stake?

A planned paradise in the Bahamas

The best thing to do when you get to Nassau is leave. Cross the bridge from Nassau to **Paradise Island**, leaving the shabby, graffiti-stained city behind. You will be engulfed in growth as green and thick and dark as a jungle.

This is a planned playland for vacationers. All the trappings are here: quick and easy access from the United States; a benevolent June-like climate year-round; accommodations of every degree of luxury; sandy beaches and calm, clear water; a championship golf course; tennis courts; restaurants and nightclubs; and a large casino.

One of the most beautiful places on the island is **Versailles Gardens,** located behind the Ocean Club Hotel. This landscaped series of terraced gardens stretches across the island from the hotel grounds to the water's edge. The gardens were begun years ago by Dr. Axel Wenner-Gren, who owned the island (then named Hog Island) and wanted to recreate the gardens at the Château de Versailles in France. When Wenner-Gren sold the island in 1960, the new owner, Huntington Hartford, continued to develop the gardens, adding statues, fountains, and—the crowning touch—a 14th-century Augustinian cloister brought from France.

Night life on Paradise Island is Las Vegas revisited. Most of the action is at the **Paradise Island Resort and Casino,** a loud and gaudy place with a casino and nightclubs. Your best bet is the variety show at the **Tradewinds Lounge,** located within the Paradise Island Resort and Casino. The show is corny but worth seeing for Bill Bonaparte, a steel drummer.

The finest (and oldest) hotel on Paradise Island is the **Ocean Club,** *P.O. Box N4777, Nassau.* It's a small, tasteful 71-room place. A doorman, in top hat and tails, stands by to greet you. The hotel's restaurant, the Courtyard Terrace, is beautiful and romantic. Double rooms range from $105 to $750.

The **Paradise Paradise Resort,** *tel. (809)326-3000,* attracts a young, lively crowd with free water sports. Doubles range from $95 to $185 per night.

To make reservations at the above hotels, call *(800)321-3000* or *(305)895-2922*

The purest of the U.S. Virgins

St. John, the smallest of the U.S. Virgin Islands, seems to be escaping the fate of its overdeveloped sisters. Two-thirds of its mere 20 square miles are set aside as national parkland. Campsites dot the park, just a few yards from the surf.

The favorite pastime on St. John is snorkeling. One of the best places to watch the fish is **Watermelon Bay,** past the ruins of the Annaberg sugarcane factory near Leinster Bay.

At the tip of Frances Bay is **Mary's Point,** a haunted promontory. Legend has it that during the revolt against the Danes in 1733, slaves leapt to their deaths from the cliff above to avoid being captured. They believed their souls would return to Africa.

Maho Bay—a 14-acre private campground—is our favorite place to stay on the island. When Maho Bay was first built, materials were carried to the site by hand to keep the natural beauty intact. Innovative water and sewage systems help to conserve precious supplies (St. John must import one-million gallons of water a day). Hot water is not available.

The 102 cottages at Maho Bay are actually canvas tents on 16-foot platforms connected by a labyrinth of walkways. Each includes a sleeping area with two beds, a living room with one bed, a cooking area, and a porch with a table and chairs. Electric lamps, bed linens, blankets, and towels are provided.

If you aren't up to camping, try **Caneel Bay Plantation,** *St. John, U.S. Virgin Islands 00830; tel. (809)776-6111,* the most luxurious place to stay on St. John. The 170-acre 18th-century sugar plantation is dotted with tennis courts and exotic plants. Cottages are clustered around seven beaches. The posh cottages don't have air conditioning or telephones. To make reservations, contact **Rockresorts Reservations,** *30 Rockefeller Plaza, Room 5400, New York, NY 10112; (800)223-7637.*

Anguilla—a peaceable kingdom

On **Anguilla,** one of the Caribbean's least-discovered islands, you apologize shyly if you pass someone on the beach. Anguilla has no discos, no casinos, no high-rises—just lots of beach and solitude.

The Anguillans are a peaceful people with a peaceful history. Slavery didn't pay here. Cotton and bananas wouldn't grow, and the workers were a strain on water supplies. So plantation owners left the islanders to lead their own lives.

In 1969, when the English Parachute Regiment landed in Anguilla to put down what they thought was a revolt, they were met by Anguillans waving Union Jacks. The islanders wanted to remain a Crown Colony.

Serene beaches border the island. The best is at **Shoal Bay Villes,** a two-mile stretch that is popular but still uncrowded. The ocean bottom is evenly sloped to a distant string of rocks that attracts sea creatures and snorkelers. Underwater, you can look around for coral gardens, reefs of elkhorn, and star and flower coral, as well as squirrelfish, sergeant fish, and damselfish. Snorkeling and rafting equipment can be rented at **Happy Jack's,** *tel. (809)497-2051,* a restaurant in the Shoal Bay Villes complex.

Malliouhana Hotel, *Meads Bay, Anguilla, BWI; tel. (809)497-2111* or *(800)372-1323 in the United States,* is the most exclusive and expensive hotel in the Caribbean. (Guests have included Kissinger and Onassis.) The hotel has Mediterranean and Far Eastern furnishings, hardwood and tile floors, brass fixtures, and balconies off every room. The 30 acres surrounding the hotel are dotted with swimming pools perched high on the cliffs. Rooms are $2,430 per week.

A more rustic, less expensive place to stay is the **Mariners,** *Sandy Ground; tel. (809)497-2671* or *(800)223-0079 in the United States.* The hotel complex is made up of nine gingerbread cottages on the beach, each with trellised doorways and tiled floors.

St. Kitts and Nevis: the first British colony

St. Kitts and **Nevis,** an independent two-island nation since 1983, were the first British colonies in the Caribbean. They retain a British-colonial flavor, with English inns, sugar plantation houses, and a lovely 19th-century port. St. Kitts has forested volcanic hills and sheltered beaches. Nevis is quiet and civilized.

St. Kitts' best hotel is the **Golden Lemon,** *Dieppe Bay; tel. (809)465-7260,* an elegant place with ceiling fans, canopied beds, and a walled garden. The Kennedys have stayed here. Rooms range from $250 to $400, including meals.

The best place to stay on Nevis is the **Montpelier Plantation Inn,** *tel. (809)469-5462,* which is popular among writers and artists. Fruit and vegetables grown on the grounds are served at mealtimes. Rooms are $150 to $280, including meals.

The most varied island (St. Martin/Sint Maarten)

The French and Dutch **St. Martin/Sint Maarten** is the most varied of the Caribbean islands. It has tropical scenery and cultures of two European countries.

Sint Maarten, the Dutch half of the island, has luxurious Dutch inns frequented by the royal family of the Netherlands. Cruise ships dock in the Philipsburg Harbor to allow passengers to take advantage of duty-free prices on jewelry, linens, crystal, and cameras.

The French half of the island is more affordable (although several of the large new hotels tend to be expensive) and has better restaurants. Artists come to **Marigot,** St. Martin's waterfront square, to set up their easels. Small fishing boats pull into port with the day's catches, vendors sell their wares under brightly colored umbrellas, and travelers meet at La Vie en Rose to chat over fresh, exquisitely prepared seafood. Accommodations range from luxury resorts in the French-Mediterranean style to downright cheap guesthouses.

Away from the main towns you'll find secluded bays and long sandy beaches protected by coral reefs. In the center of the island, mountain peaks rise sharply. Palm trees grow along with orange bougainvillea and magenta hibiscus. The sun shines year-round. Temperatures hover around 80 degrees Fahrenheit.

Thanks to the island's French legacy, dining is a pleasure worth taking time to enjoy. More than 150 restaurants are spread over both sides of the island. Our favorite is **La Caravelle** in Philipsburg. The entrance is on Front Street opposite the Caribbean Hotel. The romantic covered terrace is candlelit and looks out over the ocean.

The best hotels in St. Martin/Sint Maarten are La Samanna, Mullet Bay, Caravanserai,

Oyster Pond, and L'Habitation. La Belle Creole is one of the island's most charming hotels, built in the form of an old Mediterranean village.

Martinique: the most sophisticated

Martinique is the most sophisticated and developed island in the Caribbean, with gourmet restaurants and nude beaches. It is lush, covered with flowers. Fort-de-France is known as the Paris of the western Atlantic, with the same wrought-iron grillwork and narrow-street charm as the European city. And Martinique (along with Guadeloupe) has the best Creole food in the region. French luxury goods are sold at bargain prices, and luxury to rock-bottom accommodations are available.

The Caribbean's second-liveliest Carnival (after Trinidad's) is held in Martinique. The week before Lent bubbles with color, music, and parties. Each day has a special significance. On Devil Day, for example, children dress in red to ward off the devil. Near the end of the week a Carnival queen is crowned, people line the streets to watch the grand parade, and parties continue through the night.

Fort-de-France—the Paris of the western Atlantic

Fort-de-France, Martinique's capital, is a cosmopolitan city, where the people speak and act French. However, only a short drive outside the city are places where you'll have to wait for cows to cross the streets, you'll have to compete with the jungle for the land, and you'll hear people speaking Creole.

In Fort-de-France, seek out the tiny bakeries, where French pastries and breads are sold at reasonable prices. Don't miss the **Pre-Columbian Art Museum,** *rue de la Liberté,* and the nearby **Schoelcher Library,** with a statue of the local abolitionist (who was from Alsace). Along **rue Victor Hugo** are shops selling island crafts and paintings and French imports.

The island's best beaches

Martinique has both silvery beaches and rocky cliffs. Inland are rain forests and a volcano. The island's most appealing beaches, as well as several petrified wood savanna forests, are in **Ste. Anne.** The church in the center of town is planted with beautiful tamarind trees. Ste. Anne has two good restaurants: Chez Jack and l'Etoile de Mer.

Off Martinique's coasts are the wrecks of 13 ships, which can be explored by scuba divers. For equipment, visit the Carib Scuba Club in Carbet.

Martinique's most powerful mountain

Climb Martinique's extinct volcano, **Mt. Pelée**. Ask for a guide at the town hall. Needless to say, the view from the mountain is spectacular. For a glimpse of the fierce power of Mt. Pelée, visit the ruins of the town of St. Pierre, destroyed by the volcano in 1902.

The island's most famous resident

La Pagerie, on the Southwest Peninsula, is the birthplace of Empress Josephine. A museum here contains mementos and love letters to her from Napoleon. It is open Tuesdays to Sundays from 9 a.m. to 5:30 p.m. The entrance fee is 15 francs.

Martinique's best digs

The best place to stay in Martinique is **Hôtel Plantation de Leyritz,** *Basse-Pointe,*

Martinique; tel. (596)78-53-92 or *(596)78-53-32,* an isolated 18th-century French-colonial plantation that has been made into a hotel with a first-class health spa that offers beauty and health therapy, horseback riding, and French food. Double rooms are $60 to $150.

Trinidad—the Caribbean's best Carnival

Trinidad—a cosmopolitan island, oil-rich and industrialized—rivals Rio as host of the world's best Carnival. Its Carnival parades have developed into an art form, as carefully choreographed and costumed as any Broadway musical. They have casts of thousands.

Participants in Trinidad's spectacular parades are grouped into theme bands. As many as 3,000 people can be part of one costume band, while steel bands have 80 to 100 musicians, playing up to 500 steel pans.

The steel band competition begins about three weeks before Carnival and culminates on the Saturday before, when the champions are chosen from the island's 100-odd bands. The drums are so well-tuned and the musicians so talented that they have been known to play classical symphonies with expertise.

The Carnival activities climax in the big parade on Shrove Tuesday. Revelers work themselves into a frenzy and join the bands in their dances.

For information on specific Carnival events, contact the **Trinidad and Tobago Tourist Board,** *118-35 Queens Blvd., Forest Hills, NY 11375; (718)575-3909.*

The Grenadines—the Tahiti of the Caribbean

St. Vincent and the **Grenadine Islands** are billed as the Tahiti of the Caribbean, because of their tropical beauty. Here, Captain Bligh brought the breadfruit that survived the mutiny on *The Bounty.* The 100 Grenadine Islands are connected by local mailboats and offer inexpensive accommodations.

Mustique is the Grenadine hideout of celebrities, including Princess Margaret. Try the **Cotton House,** *tel. (809)456-4777,* a hotel in an 18th-century cotton warehouse built of stone and coral. The hotel restaurant, Roft, and Basil's Bar are good.

The easiest—and cheapest—destination

Puerto Rico has the most extensive air service in the Caribbean, with daily flights from all major North American cities. And because it is a U.S. territory, American visitors don't have to worry about passports or changing money.

The island's beaches are lined with modern, self-contained resorts, as well as budget hotels and charming guesthouses. But the island also has a huge modern city with a historic core—**San Juan.** Old San Juan, a cluster of cobblestoned Spanish streets with old houses and churches, is built in and around a fort. The city offers posh boutiques, horse races, cockfights, casinos, flamenco dancing, Las Vegas-style shows, discos, and brothels.

Puerto Rico's best town

One of Puerto Rico's most charming towns is **Rincon,** on the unspoiled southwest coast. A friendly fishing town, it draws American retirees with its easygoing pace and low prices. Panoramic roads curve down from the green hilltop farms to the Caribbean beaches. Trade winds from the east dump moisture on the 4,500-foot-high rain forest. In the morning, you can help fishermen pull their nets onto the beach. While the main plaza has a supermarket, a bakery, a tropical bar, and restaurants, the town does not have high-rise hotels, casinos, gourmet food, fancy boutiques, or tourists.

Rincon's beach is shaded by palm trees and backed by squatters' shacks surrounded by mango, banana, citrus, papaya, and breadfruit trees.

Last year, Rincon was blessed with a *parador*—a government-owned country inn. For information, call *(800)443-0266*.

Another good hotel in town is **Villa Antonio,** *P.O. Box 68, Route 115, Rincon, PR 00743; tel. (809)823-2645,* which has rooms for $45 to $65 a night.

Puerto Rico's best-kept secret

Puerto Rico's best-kept secret is **Vieques,** a little-known 21-mile-long island due east of the big island. A U.S. naval base is located here, and from time to time bomb tests are held.

Despite this, Vieques is a nice vacation cove. Wild horses and cattle roam the roads, hills, and empty beaches. Small boats cruise **Phosphorescent Bay** on moonless nights, allowing you to see the brilliant streaks emitted by phosphorescent organisms. Mahogany and rubber trees reach through the ceiling of the small rain forest. And white sand beaches, some near colorful coral reefs, slip into clear calm waters.

Home to 8,000 Spanish-speaking natives and 100 U.S. sailors and Marines, Vieques is an informal, low-key, and low-cost hideaway. You can hire a ketch for scuba diving through **Vieques Divers** in Esperanza for $40 per person, including food and drinks.

To get to Vieques, take a plane from San Juan or drive from San Juan to Fajardo, then take the ferry to Vieques. For information, call *(809)722-1551*.

The most central place to stay is **Parador Villa Esperanza,** *tel. (809)741-8675,* in the little fishing village of Esperanza. Double rooms are about $65. The marina has mooring facilities and tennis courts. To the right of the front door is restaurant row.

Landlubbers might prefer **Casa del Frances,** *P.O. Box 458, Vieques, PR 00765; tel. (809)741-3751,* a guesthouse that features horseback riding. This former plantation has French doors, pillars, balconies, an atrium, a large pool, and an outdoor bar with tropical plantings. It is a mile or so from the beach and Esperanza. Winter rates are about $100 per night for a double room.

Haiti: the most exotic island

It's a shame **Haiti** is politically unstable and dreadfully poor, because it is the most unique island in the Caribbean. The Haitians' exotic culture is a blend of French, African, and voodoo traditions. You can see African dances, attend one of the most colorful Mardi Gras, and indulge in Creole feasts. Accommodations range from luxury villas and antique mansions to quaint hostelries, including **Habitation Leclerc,** the West Indian palace of Napoleon's sister Pauline. Jackie Onassis and Catherine Deneuve have stayed here. **Cap Haitien** is one of the most beautiful cities in the West Indies, with artists' studios and a port.

The voodoo capital

Haiti's dramatic mountains and flawless black and white beaches set the stage for the true drama of the island: voodoo. Superstition and ritual abound, even among the most educated inhabitants. Haitians believe the island gods are all around you, moving through the air and living in the mountains, rivers, seas, rocks, caves, and sacred trees.

Spirit-worship rituals are performed by priests or priestesses, known by their followers as *hungans*. Accompanied by the hypnotizing rhythm of sacred drums, bells, and rattles, the *hungans* dance and chant, beckoning the spirits to possess them and their followers.

The climax of these ceremonies is always the blood sacrifice, when an animal's sacred powers are believed to be released. The adorned and painted animal, typically a chicken, is mutilated, dismembered, and placed on the altar as an offering to the gods. Sometimes the blood is collected and drunk by the worshipers to sate the thirst of the spirit.

As the frenzy of the drumbeats and the singing increases, the believers become possessed, and their bodies begin to convulse and contort. Once the believers are in the trance state, the spirits speak through them, giving advice and threatening evildoers in the assembly.

To display the miraculous powers of the spirits, called *loas,* the possessed may repeatedly stab themselves, handle red-hot coals or bars of iron, or eat broken glass, apparently causing themselves no harm.

If you would like to see a voodoo ceremony, ask for information at your hotel or contact the **National Office of Tourism** in Port-au-Prince, *tel. (509-1)21720.*

Magical nights

Haiti's best hotel is the **Grand Hotel Oloffson,** *Port-au-Prince; tel. (509-1)20139,* whose rooms are named after celebrities who have stayed in them—Mick Jagger, Marlon Brando, Graham Greene, and Anne Bancroft.

The Dominican Republic—the New World's first settlement

Columbus called the **Dominican Republic** the most beautiful island in the world when he landed here in 1492. One year later, his brother Bartholomeo established here the first permanent European settlement in the Americas, New Isabella (known today as Santo Domingo). Historic monuments, monasteries, and fortresses remain from the colonial days, giving the island a Spanish air.

The Dominican Republic covers 1,900 square miles, approximately two-thirds of the island of **Hispaniola,** which it shares with Haiti. It has lovely beaches, lively night life, excellent restaurants, and many hotels. The tallest mountains in the Caribbean (more than 10,000 feet) are here.

Santo Domingo, the oldest city

Santo Domingo, the capital of the Dominican Republic, is the New World's oldest European-style city. It has one of the largest botanical parks in the world and an enormous zoo. Visit the **Casas Reales Museum,** downtown, to see treasures recovered from the *Concepcion,* a 16th-century Spanish galleon. The cathedral, **Santa Maria la Menor,** is also worth seeing. The **National Pantheon,** *Calle Las Damas,* houses the bodies of the country's heroes and martyrs.

The **Alcazar,** often called the Columbus Fortress Palace, was home to Don Diego Columbus (Christopher's son) from 1509 to 1516. It was restored in 1957.

The city's most unusual restaurant is the **Meson de la Cava,** *Paseo de los Indios; tel. (809)533-2818,* located in a cave with stalactites and stalagmites.

Another unusual restaurant is **La Roca,** *tel. (809)586-2898,* in the town of Sosua, originally settled by Marranos (hidden Jews who pretended to be Catholics). The cuisine is similar to the dishes of Ladino Jews (who speak a form of Spanish) in Greece and Turkey.

One of the best and least expensive places to stay in Santo Domingo is 16th-century **Hostal Nicolas de Ovando,** *53 Calle las Damas, Santo Domingo; tel. (809)687-3101.*

The Caribbean at its most posh

The poshest resort in all the Caribbean is the **Casa de Campo** at La Romana in the Dominican Republic. Frank Lloyd Wright designed the main building, and the interior was designed by Oscar de la Renta. Celebrities, including de la Renta, have private mansions on the grounds.

Accommodations at the resort include private villas along the golf course and sea. Waitresses wear long white gowns with pink bows, and you can hire a horse and buggy to take you dining. The nephew of the maharaja of Jodhpur introduced polo to the Dominican Republic, and you'll find the best riding horses in the Caribbean at the Casa de Campo resort.

Curaçao—Holland in the Caribbean

Curaçao, the largest of the Netherlands Antilles, is a bit of old Holland in the New World. **Willemstad,** the capital, resembles Amsterdam, complete with canals and 17th-century canal houses; the tallest pontoon bridge in the Caribbean (named after Queen Juliana); Indonesian restaurants; and a museum featuring wooden shoes and Delft tiles.

History buffs should visit the Willemstad forts. **Fort Nassau** is situated in the ramparts above town. **Fort Amsterdam,** on the sea, is the site of the Governor's Palace and the 18th-century Dutch Reformed Church, which still has an English cannonball embedded in its walls.

Try to see **Ronde Klip** in northeast Curaçao, a privately owned *landuis,* or plantation, and **Jan Kok Landhuis,** built in 1650 and used as a restaurant.

The prettiest natural sight in Curaçao is in **St. Christoffelberg,** where wild orchids grow. (You have to climb 1,213 feet to the highest spot on the island to see the flowers.)

The oldest Jewish settlement in the New World

The Dutch tradition of religious tolerance spread early to the New World, and in 1651 a group of Jews established the oldest Jewish settlement in the Americas on this island. Services are held on Friday nights and Saturday mornings at the synagogue, **Congregation Mikve Israel-Emanuel,** which is right by Schottegat Harbor. Also visit the Jewish graveyard, **Beth Haim,** also the oldest in the Americas.

Curaçao's exotic food

Curaçao features a mélange of Dutch, Latin American, and Indonesian cuisines.

Outside Willemstad, on the western tip of the island, is **Westpunt,** a fishing port, where you'll find excellent seafood restaurants, including **Jaanchie's** and **Playa Forti.** Dutch-French food is served at **De Taveerne,** not far from Willemstad in an 18th-century manor house complete with antiques of the period.

Saba: the most scenic

Although **Saba,** a five-square-mile volcanic island, has no beaches, it is incredibly scenic. Twenty-eight miles from St. Martin in the Netherlands Antilles, this rugged, mountainous island is a wall of jagged black and gray rock that shoots up 3,000 feet from the white caps of the surf. Its summit is lost in the clouds. Roads snake through picturesque villages with names such as Hell's Gate, Windwardside, and The Bottom. Small white houses with red-tile roofs peek through the thick tropical vegetation produced by the rich volcanic soil. Because most of the houses are built on slopes, each one has a magnificent view. Cultivated crops cut into the sides of steep hills like steps.

Saba has no casinos and no high-rises, and you won't find air conditioning. But lush rain forests hug the mountainsides, mist shrouds the summits, and gabled Dutch architecture distinguishes the small towns. If you stay overnight, the local radio station probably will announce your visit.

Saba is world-famous for its scuba diving, with more than 25 different diving areas. Diving instruction and certification are offered at **Saba Deep,** a diving shop at the LAI Chance Harbor, which is owned and operated by two Americans.

After all that exercise, you'll want a good meal. Try **Scout's Place** or **Lime Time.** Local specialties are curried barbecued goat and lobster.

Saba's most popular hotel is **Captain's Quarters,** *tel. (599-4)2201,* formerly the residence of a famous Saban sea captain. This comfortable hotel has one of the few swimming pools on the island. The food at the restaurant is delicious and moderately priced.

Montserrat—the best refuge

Montserrat is a lush green island that was colonized primarily by Irish Catholics from nearby St. Kitts in the early 17th century. (Because of its Irish heritage, Montserrat is known as the Emerald Isle. It is now a British colony, but Irish influences remain.)

In the 17th century, Montserrat became known as a safe place to avoid Protestant persecution, and it drew Catholic refugees from neighboring islands and Virginia. The most important heritage left by religious dissent on Montserrat is privacy and freedom.

Plymouth, the island's largest town, is remarkably quiet. Chickens cross the road here as often as people. Shops along **Parliament Street** sell handmade cotton goods and local fruits. Stop by **Anthony's Church** to see its exquisite interior, as well as the 200-year-old tamarind tree outside. Try Montserrat's rum liqueur punch at **Perk's Factory.**

Montserrat's black sand beaches (which set it apart from other Caribbean islands) were formed from volcanic ash. The only white sand beach is also one of the best (and least accessible): **Rendezvous Beach.** (The other beaches are gray.) To get to the beach, board a local charter from the **Vue Point Hotel,** *tel. (809)491-5210.*

Montserrat has miles of hiking trails across its mountains. The most spectacular is to the **Great Alps waterfall,** a 70-foot cascade. A slightly more difficult walk takes you along **Galway's Soufrère,** where water bubbles out of the ground.

The world's best recording studio

Rock stars Elton John, Phil Collins, Sting, Stevie Wonder, Duran Duran, Paul McCartney, Wham, and James Taylor have been drawn to Montserrat by George Martin's recording studio, **Air Studios,** recognized as one of the best in the world.

The best way to sample the islands

What better way to explore the Caribbean islands than by sail? And you don't have to sell the family jewels to afford a trip like this. Prices for bareboats (you bring your own provisions and sail the boat yourself) range from $175 to $360 per day during the summer and from $340 to $575 during the winter, depending on the size and type of boat.

Unlike Greece and its islands, the Caribbean knows no winter. And unlike their counterparts in the South Pacific, the Caribbean islands are close enough to each other to make knowledge of a sextant unnecessary.

Charter companies will check your sailing skills to make sure you can operate its expensive vessel safely. The company may decide to appoint a professional skipper to accompany you (at extra cost) or refuse to rent you a vessel altogether if you don't have enough experience handling sailboats.

If you want relatively calm waters and a few hours of sailing each day, consider the British Virgin Islands. The entire chain is only about 50 miles long, and large charter fleets are based on St. Thomas and Tortola. The islands are small, with scores of quiet bays off sandy beaches. One of the nicest places to anchor is **Cane Garden Bay** on Tortola's north shore, a narrow fjord cut into tall, steep hills. You can row a dinghy ashore for a dinner of fresh lobster and a steel drum concert at **Stanley's Welcome Bar,** right on the beach.

If you are in for more adventurous sailing and more diverse islands, consider the Leeward or Windward islands. Beginning with St. Martin, about 80 miles east of the Virgin Islands, the Lesser Antilles island chain turns south. Distances between the islands are greater here than in the Virgins, and the ocean swells that roll in from Africa can make the inter-island passes wet and rough. You might spend entire days beating from one island to the next.

The months from July through November are hurricane season. High season is from mid-December to mid-April, when the weather tends to be settled, the trade winds reliable, and the prices highest.

The Moorings, *P.O. Box 139, Road Town, Tortola, British Virgin Islands; (800)535-7289,* is the oldest and most reliable bareboat charter fleet. Marinas are located in the British Virgin Islands and Hurricane Hole, St. Lucia.

Tortola Yacht Charters, *P.O. Box 432160 Miami, FL 33243* (or **Nanny Cay,** *Tortola, BVI; tel. (809)494-2221*) operates from a full-service marina at a new 26-acre resort complex on Nanny Cay in Tortola. This company has the largest bareboats in the Caribbean.

North South Charters, *(800)387-4964,* is a good company located in the British Virgin Islands. It rents bareboats and bareboats with skippers.

THE BEST OF NORTH AMERICA

Nature is at its best—and most varied—in North America. From the arid and desolate beauty of the Grand Canyon to the moose-filled forests of northern Canada, North America is a nature-lover's dream. People come here from around the world to see the Rocky Mountains, the California shoreline, and the serene beauty of Nova Scotia—yet North America's own residents take her for granted. This is a shame, because many of the world's greatest sights are here, within driving distance.

Chapter 27

THE
BEST
OF
CANADA

Canada, one of the most fascinating countries in the world, is just to our north. Covering 3.8-million square miles, it is the second-largest country on earth. Within its wide boundaries are a rainbow of cultures and a kaleidoscope of natural sights. To the west are cloud-piercing mountain peaks, the rugged Pacific coastline, and cities with large Chinese communities. In the east are quaint British towns, French-speaking Quebec, and secluded islands. The interior is home to cowboys, rodeos, and ranches.

Canada is a nature-lover's dream, offering some of the world's best skiing, fishing, boating, hiking, bird watching, and hunting. But it's a great place for those who love big-city life as well. Montreal, Toronto, Edmonton, and Vancouver are metropolises with fine restaurants, high-fashion boutiques, cosmopolitan populations, artistic communities, and good theater and dance companies. However, the best thing about Canada is its easy access. You just drive north.

The best of Montreal

Montreal, Canada's largest city, is the world's second-largest French-speaking city (after Paris). Parisian sophistication and Canadian friendliness blend here. The air smells of good coffee and French cooking.

Located on Montreal Island in the St. Lawrence River, the city faces the entrance to the St. Lawrence Seaway. Dominating the city is Mt. Réal (Mt. Royal), for which the city is named.

The city is informally split in two: the English section in the west and the French section in the east. Street names reinforce this division.

The oldest section

The oldest section, which hugs the waterfront, is called, appropriately, **Vieux Montreal** (Old Montreal). The seed of the city was an Indian village called Hochelaga. French settlers took it over in 1642 and called their town Ville Marie de Montreal. The French town was surrendered to the British 118 years later, in 1760. For one year (1775 to 1776), the British ceded the town to the Americans. The quarter has been patiently restored and is filled with antique shops, cafés, and boutiques.

A futuristic contrast

At the other end of the time scale is **Man and His World,** a permanent mini-version of the international exposition EXPO '67. Situated on an island in the St. Lawrence River, it is a fascinating, ultramodern collection of spheres and towers, some of which are slowly rusting and falling apart.

Montreal's prettiest churches

The **Basilica of Notre Dame,** *Place d'Armes,* is an elaborate neo-Gothic affair with two tall spires. Built in 1829, the church houses an immense organ with 5,772 pipes. The altar, too, is monumental. And the wood carvings are carefully detailed. The basilica was designed by New York architect James O'Donnell, whose grave is in the church. The **Sacred Heart Chapel,** adjacent to the basilica, has stained-glass windows illustrating the history of Montreal. The church is open daily.

Notre-Dame-de-Bonsecours, *400 St. Paul St. E.,* in Vieux Montreal, is the city's oldest church, built in 1657, destroyed by fire, then rebuilt in 1771. The facade is from 1895. Located near the water, it also is known as the Sailor's Chapel. It is closed Mondays.

Underground Montreal: the warmest shopping

Because Montreal can be buried in as much as 100 inches of snow during the winter, many of the city's shops have taken refuge in a seven-mile mall beneath the city. Designed by architect I.M. Pei and developer William Zeckendorf in the 1950s, the underground complex has shops, sports facilities, theaters, exhibits, restaurants, apartments, hotels, and banks.

The nucleus of the complex is **Place Ville Marie,** where shops surround a sculptured fountain. Corridors link Ville Marie with similar complexes at Place Bonaventure and Place du Canada. The three areas together contain 280 shops, 20 restaurants and bars, and entrances to three hotels.

Place des Arts is a lavish performing-arts center, home of the Montreal Symphony Orchestra and the Montreal Opera. To get there, take the metro to the Place des Arts stop.

Montreal at night

Montreal doesn't close until 3:30 a.m., a liberty that spoils other cities for many Montrealers. The center of the city's nighttime activity is charming and sophisticated **Crescent Street,** Montreal's version of the Latin Quarter. Prince Arthur, Duluth, and St. Denis streets are also lined with bars, cafés, and restaurants.

On summer nights in early July, you can take in the jazz festival at the Théâtre St. Denis, and in late August you can enjoy the film festival at cinemas throughout the city.

For something unique, go to a *boîte à chanson,* a Quebec-style café with French folk music.

Finest French cooking

The best restaurant in Montreal is **Les Mignardises,** *2307 rue St. Denis; tel. (514)842-1151.* Chef Jean Pierre Monnet creates masterpieces, and the service is superb. Dinner is C$60 to C$100 per person, with wine. The restaurant is closed Sundays and Mondays.

Chez la Mère Michel, *1209 Guy St.; tel. (514)934-0473,* is cozy, with an outstanding French provincial menu and a pretty garden patio. Try the *homard soufflé Nantua* (fresh lobster added to mousseline potatoes and served on a bed of spinach). Closed Sundays.

Les Chênets, *2075 Bishop St.; tel. (514)844-1842,* is decorated with original works of art. The dishes, too, are masterpieces, smothered in delicious sauces. The selection of Cognac and Armagnac brandies is the best in the Americas. Dinner is served daily; lunch is served Mondays through Fridays.

Le St. Honoré, *Faubourg Ste. Catherine, 1616 Ste. Catherine St. W.; tel. (514)932-5550,* has a good fixed-price French menu for only $19.95. Located in a 200-year-old stone house, this restaurant is divided into two sections. The first floor, which is open every day, is informal and has good steaks. The second floor is fancier and serves exquisite French specialties. The second-floor restaurant is closed Saturdays after lunch and all day Sundays.

The best hotels

Montreal's best hotel is the **Ritz Carlton,** *Sherbrooke West; tel. (514)842-4212.* A luxurious, Continental-style hotel, it is near fashionable boutiques, restaurants, and galleries.

Less expensive hotels include **L'Hôtel de la Montagne,** *tel. (514)288-5656,* and the **Hotel Château Versailles,** *tel. (514)933-3611.*

Montreal's bed and breakfasts are small, cozy places to stay. For a list, contact **Gîte Montreal,** *331 Clarke St., Suite 29, Westmount, Montreal PQ H3Z 2E7; tel. (514)932-9690.*

Quebec: the French heart

Quebec City, the capital of the French-speaking province of Quebec, is the focal point of French Canadian nationalism. It is also the first French settlement in North America (95% of the population is French) and the oldest city in the New World (the walled fortress was founded by Champlain in 1608). Quebec is the only walled city in North America. It is set high on Cape Diamond, 350 feet above the St. Lawrence River.

Vieux Quebec

In **Vieux Quebec** (Old Quebec), you'll see 17th- and 18th-century stone houses similar to those in the villages of Normandy and Brittany in France.

The heart of Vieux Quebec is the beautiful **Place d'Armes**. A good introduction to the history of Quebec is the sound-and-light show at the **Musée du Fort.** The **Seminary,** dating from 1663, houses a museum containing a rare collection of Canadian money, including Indian wampum and playing cards used as legal tender in colonial times. In the museum at the **Hotel Dieu,** you can see the stone vaults where Augustinian nuns took refuge during the 1759 siege. The skull of French general Montcalm is on view at the **Ursulin Convent Museum.**

Looming over the Place d'Armes is the **Château Frontenac,** a magnificent Victorian hotel with turrets and towers. Built in 1892, it perches at the top of Cape Diamond, a 300-foot bluff.

Next door is the **Jardin des Gouverneurs,** originally the private garden of the Château St. Louis. It is best known for its statue of General James Wolfe and Marquis de Montcalm, erected in 1828. On it is written, "Their courage gave them the same lot; history, the same fame; posterity, the same monument."

Canada's most important battle

The **Plains of Abraham** in Quebec were the site of a battle that determined the fate of Canada. On Sept. 13, 1759, the British army under Wolfe defeated the French under Montcalm, and Canada was turned over the British. (However, the French inhabitants held on to their language and culture.) Both Wolfe and Montcalm were killed during the battle. According to legend, at the end of the battle, a voice was heard across the plains crying, "*Je me souviens*" (I remember), which became the motto of the province of Quebec.

Today the battlefield is part of the 230-acre **Parc des Champs de Bataille.** From the observation post, you'll have a wide view of the field and the river.

The **Quebec Museum** is also on the park grounds. It contains displays illustrating Québec's history, paintings by Quebecois artists, and a section devoted to 17th-century decorative arts. The museum is open from 9:15 a.m. to 9 p.m. daily.

Remnants of war

The **Citadel,** a massive star-shaped fortress above the city, was built in 1820 by the British to protect against American invasion following the War of 1812. It was never used in battle. The changing of the guard takes place here daily during the summer at 10 a.m.

The oldest section

The oldest section of the city is around Place Royale in a district known as **Lower Town.** When Champlain started his colony here, it was a trading post, with a store, a few houses, and fortifications. In later years, Place Royale became the center of the fur-trading industry. As colonists and missionaries arrived, the settlement gradually moved uphill, to Vieux Quebec.

Today, Lower Town is a busy port. Designated a historic area by the Canadian government, the section surrounding Place Royale is being restored. It has the greatest concentration of 17th- and 18th-century buildings in North America.

The oldest church in Quebec, **Notre Dame des Victoires,** is located on Place Royale. This small stone church built in 1688 is decorated inside with elaborate woodwork. The altar is carved in the shape of an old fort. The church is open daily.

A funicular will take you from Place d'Armes down to Place Royale, where you can walk along cobblestoned streets past 17th-century buildings and sunny squares. **Rue de Trésor** is the best place to stroll; painters sell their masterpieces along here.

The best French architecture

Quebec's **Assemblée Nationale** (parliament buildings)—bounded by rue Dufferin, boulevards St. Cyrille and St. Augustin, and Le Grande Allée—are imposing French structures built in 1877 and 1886. Twelve bronze statues commemorating famous Canadians rest in niches in the facade. They are the works of the Quebec sculptor Hébert. Guided tours are conducted daily during the summer and on weekdays during the winter. The assembly is not in session from June 24 to Oct. 1.

The best time to visit

The **Carnival de Quebec,** a 10-day celebration beginning on the first Thursday in February, is the most festive time to visit the city. A huge party to commemorate the end of winter, it includes two parades, fireworks, and winter sports. The official mascot is a seven-foot snowman called Le Bonhomme Carnival.

If you plan to visit during Carnival, you will be competing for hotel rooms with more than a half-million people from all over North America. Make reservations. If you can't find a room, contact the **Carnival lodging committee,** *tel. (418)524-8441.*

Quebec's best restaurants

The best restaurant in town is **À le Table de Serge Bruyère,** *Livernois Comples (upstairs), 1200 rue St. Jean; tel. (418)694-0618,* where a special prix-fixe menu of seven courses is served (C$40.25). Try the filet of Quebec lamb with green shallots and fresh tomatoes. Reservations are required. The restaurant is closed Sundays from Sept. 5 to May 1 and Mondays year-round.

Restaurant Louis Hebert, *668 Grande Allée Ouest; tel. (418)525-7812,* is also good, serving light French fare. Set in a 17th-century fieldstone building, it has a French provincial atmosphere, with calico lampshades and an outdoor terrace. It is open daily.

The best place for local French-Canadian fare is **Aux Anciens Canadiens,** *34 rue St. Louis; tel. (418)692-1627.* Located in the former home of the 19th-century historical novelist Philippe Aubert de Gaspé (which was built in 1675), the restaurant serves Canadian yellow pea soup, *tourtière* (meat pie), and maple syrup pie with heavy cream. Reservations are suggested. The restaurant is open daily.

The best hotels

The most elegant place to stay is **Le Château Frontenac,** *1 ave. des Carrières; tel. (418)692-3861.* It is grand, historic, and expensive (rooms are C$110 to C$400). The cocktail lounge and many of the rooms have views of the St. Lawrence. However, because this is a tourist hotel, expect to be one of many Americans.

Auberge du Trésor, *20 rue Ste. Anne; tel. (418)694-1876,* is a 300-year-old inn on the Place d'Armes. Its 20 guest rooms have private bathrooms, televisions, and air conditioning. Prices are moderate (C$50 to C$80).

Le Château de Pierre, *17 ave. Ste. Geneviève; tel. (418)694-0429,* is a 15-room mansion built in 1853. Its large rooms all have color televisions and air conditioning. Prices are moderate (C$60 to C$90).

The best of Provincial French Canada

Most American visitors, smitten by Quebec City's charms, overlook the nearby countryside (unless they snow ski in the Laurentides, Quebec's Little Switzerland). This is a big oversight. Farmstays are available in fascinating villages, where people wake up with the roosters.

An island lost in time

Nearby **Ile d'Orléans** is a lovely island with historic Quebecois homes, old farming villages, and French restaurants. Until 1935, the island could be reached only by boat. Because of this, it retained its old French ways longer than its neighbors. Many of the houses here are from the 17th and 18th centuries. Most residents are farmers and descendants of French immigrants from Normandy and Brittany.

Miraculous cures

Farther on is the village of **Ste. Anne de Beaupré,** whose massive cathedral is a famous Catholic shrine. Invalids from all over the world come here to be cured—the fountain in front of the church is said to cure diseases. And some of them have been, to judge from the plethora of crutches, canes, and walkers left behind by cured believers—some of the paraphernalia is hung from the church's ceiling. Built in 1922, the cathedral holds 10,000 people.

A best for *les artistes*

Just an hour north of Quebec City, on the north shore of the St. Lawrence River, is a bustling resort for artists and patrons called **Baie St. Paul.** Dozens of galleries display works of the Group of Seven—painters who portray the Charlevoix region.

The Gaspé Peninsula

An hour northeast of Baie St. Paul, the port of Rivière du Loup marks the beginning of the **Gaspé Peninsula,** a French fishing and farming region. The Gaspé begins dramatically. Mountains plunge into the sea. Little fishing towns brave the pounding surf. Although rugged, the peninsula is accommodating—many manor houses have been converted to inns.

Gaspé is an old French fishing village, three hours north of Rivière du Loup on the northern tip of the peninsula. The French spoken here, *joual*, sounds to the French of France as Middle English would sound to us. Gaspé is where Cartier first stepped ashore in North America in 1534. A large granite cross marks the spot. The **Gaspé Museum** has exhibits on the history and folklore of the area.

Around the point from Gaspé is **Bonaventure,** founded by French-speaking Acadians fleeing British troops in 1755. Nearby are limestone rock formations that reach out of the sea—popular among small-boat sailors and sea birds. You can walk to **Percé Rock** at low tide. **Ile Bonaventure** is a boat ride away. This bird sanctuary was once a pirate hideout.

One of Quebec province's best restaurants perches 1,000 feet above Percé Rock. **L'Auberge du Gargantua,** *tel. (418)782-2852,* serves excellent French provincial cooking. Specialties include periwinkles in court bouillon, fresh fish, and giant crab. But the best dish is the bouillabaisse Gargantua. Reservations are required. The restaurant is open daily.

Ottawa, a capital city

Canada's capital, **Ottawa,** is a small beautiful city with only 301,567 inhabitants. Set high on a bluff overlooking the confluence of the Ottawa, Gatineau, and Rideau rivers, it has lovely views in all directions. Man has added to the scenery: the Gothic Parliament Buildings create a romantic skyline. The Rideau Canal is pretty, cutting through the city.

Ottawa has a British flavor. The language is predominantly English, and you're more likely to be served scones than croissants. Established by Queen Victoria in 1858 as the capital of the United Provinces of Canada, the city is filled with elaborate Victorian architecture. It became the capital of modern Canada in 1867.

Ottawa's top sights

Parliament Hill, on a bluff over the Ottawa River, is the pedestal for the spectacular Parliament Buildings, with their tall copper roofs. The 302-foot **Peace Tower** dedicated to Canadians who lost their lives in World War I forms part of the main entrance to the buildings. Its walls and floors are made of stones from the battlefields. Its tower contains a 53-bell carillon. You can go to the Visitor's Galleries in the House of Commons and the Senate. Or take a tour of the Center Block, which passes through the Memorial Chamber, the Library, and the Peace Tower lookout. During the summer, you can watch the changing of the guard on the lawns of Parliament Hill daily at 10 a.m.

The **National Gallery of Canada** is located in the **Lorne Building,** *Elgin Street,* between Albert and Slater Streets. It contains six floors of galleries devoted to European and

Canadian art, displaying works by Canada's Group of Seven, including Paul Kane's paintings of Indians and Cornelius Kreigoff's paintings of pioneers. European masters Rembrandt, Chardin, El Greco, Cézanne, Van Gogh, Monet, and Picasso are also represented.

Bytown Museum, near the junction of the Rideau Canal and the Ottawa River, is filled with artifacts of the Ottawa Indians: furniture, clothes, guns, tools, and toys.

Ottawa's best hotels

The best hotel in town is **Château Laurier,** *Confederation Square; tel. (613)232-6411.* An institution in Canada since 1912, it is a favorite among politicians and big-time businessmen. The hotel's restaurant, the Canadian Grill, is dignified. Rooms are C$120 to C$135.

The **Four Seasons,** *150 Albert St.; tel. (613)238-1500,* has all the modern luxuries: whirlpool baths, tanning rooms, and saunas. The dining room and wine bar are popular. This is Ottawa's most expensive hotel—rooms are C$145 to C$165.

The **Park Lane,** *111 Cooper St.; tel. (613)238-1331,* is a moderately priced hotel.

The best of Shakespeare

Try to make it to Stratford's annual summer **Shakespearean Festival.** The town, which is modeled on Stratford, England, has swans, green lawns that sweep down to the river, and pretty cottages. You can picnic in **Queen's Park** beneath tall shade trees. Past the Orr Dam and the 90-year-old stone bridge is the **Shakespearean Garden,** a formal English garden with a sundial that was presented to the town by a former mayor of England's Stratford-upon-Avon. For more information, contact the **Stratford Shakespearean Festival,** *P.O. Box 520, Stratford, Ontario, N5A 6V2; tel. (519)273-3424.*

The most curious place to dine in Stratford is **The Church,** *Brunswick and Waterloo streets; tel. (519)273-3424,* which has delicious food and church-like decor—organ pipes, an altar, a vaulted roof, and stained-glass windows. Reservations are required.

Shrewsbury Manor, *30 Shrewsbury St.; tel. (519)271-8520,* a charming old Victorian house, has been turned into a bed and breakfast. Rooms are only C$30 per couple.

Niagara from the other side

Just 20 minutes from Niagara-on-the-Lake, down Niagara Parkway, is the Canadian side of **Niagara Falls,** which is both prettier than the U.S. side and less crowded. You can take an elevator below the falls at Table Rock House. And the ship *Maid of the Mist* takes you practically under the falls. Boats leave from the dock on the parkway just down from the Rainbow Bridge. The cost is about C$5 for adults, C$3 for children.

The best place to stay is the **Foxhead Hotel,** *5685 Falls Ave.; tel. (416)374-4444,* which has a perfect view of the falls. Rooms are C$50 to C$150, depending on the season.

The best of Toronto

Toronto, situated on the Great Lakes, is the second-largest city in Canada. Towering buildings, such as the CN (Canadian National) Tower, the world's tallest free-standing structure, punctuate the city's dramatic skyline. Canada's most modern city, Toronto boasts avant-garde architecture, especially on Eaton Square and at the O'Keefe Center.

Despite its modern appearance, Toronto is old, occupying the site of a French fort (1749-1759) in an area purchased by the British from the Indians in 1787. It was settled largely by

Loyalists who left the Thirteen Colonies during and just after the Revolutionary War. Americans raided the city twice, destroying parts of it during the War of 1812. Then known as York, it was renamed Toronto in 1834.

Toronto is an Indian word meaning "place of meeting," which is appropriate, considering the huge and varied ethnic groups that populate the city. Because of the diversified population, the choice of restaurants is astounding.

Toronto is second only to New York in number and variety of stage productions. It has a progressive urban spirit and a sophisticated cosmopolitan outlook, without the big-city problems of Chicago and New York.

The world's tallest building

Toronto's most visible landmark, the **CN Tower,** has an observation deck at 1,136 feet that affords a panoramic view of the city. At the top is the revolving Top of the Tower restaurant (the highest and largest revolving dining room in the world) and a communications tower. On a clear day you can see for about 75 miles.

Toronto's top sights

The best place to begin exploring the city is at its heart: **City Hall,** a modern superstructure that looks something like the landing pad for a spaceship. Topped with a white dome and flanked by 20- and 27-story curved towers, the building's twin clamshell design won an international competition for Finnish architect Viljo Revell, one of 530 contestants.

The nine-acre plaza in front of City Hall, called **Nathan Phillips Square,** was named after the Toronto mayor responsible for the project. It provides a community meeting place for concerts and self-appointed orators. In the winter, the reflecting pool doubles as a skating rink. The focal point of the square is a Henry Moore sculpture called *The Archer.* When city fathers balked at buying it, the people of Toronto raised the money to buy it themselves. Moore was so touched by their enthusiasm that he donated many of his works to the Art Gallery of Toronto.

Across the street is **Old City Hall,** an imposing Romanesque fortress that houses the Provincial Courts. Built in 1899, it has marble columns, stained glass, and grained flooring from Georgia. The building is embellished with carved gargoyles, said to be furtive caricatures of city councillors with whom the architect battled in the 1890s.

In Queen's Park, the **Provincial Parliament Building** stands on the site of a former lunatic asylum. Wander through the pink sandstone complex and listen to the lawmakers debating in the legislative chambers.

Casa Loma is a 98-room medieval-looking castle created by financier Sir Henry Pellant. Built between 1911 and 1914, the extravagance boasts gold-plated bath fixtures, a gigantic pipe organ, and one of the largest wine cellars in North America. An 800-foot underground tunnel leads to stables furnished in marble, mahogany, and Spanish tile.

Old Fort York, *Garrison Road,* was built in 1793 and destroyed during the War of 1812, then rebuilt. The officers' quarters, center blockhouse, and battlements have been refurbished. Members of the Fort York Guard are dressed in uniforms of British troops of the era.

Finest art

The **Art Gallery of Ontario** is renowned for its collection of works by Canadian artists and for its important collection of Henry Moore sculptures.

The **Royal Ontario Museum,** *Avenue Road and Bloor Street West,* displays Chinese art and artifacts, extensive ethnological collections, dinosaurs, fossils, and minerals.

The **McMichael Canadian Collection of Art,** in Kleinburg, about 25 miles north of Toronto, has 30 gallery rooms constructed from timbers that once enclosed pioneer homes and barns. More than 1,000 paintings by the Group of Seven and their contemporaries are on display, along with West Coast and Woodland Indian and Inuit works.

The most inviting parks

Toronto has 15,000 acres of parkland that display signs reading, "Please walk on the grass." **Toronto Islands Park** can be reached by ferry from across the harbor. **Exhibition Place,** *Lakeshore Boulevard West,* is the site of the Canadian National Exhibition, held from the third week in August to the first Monday in September. **High Park,** near the west end of the Queen streetcar route, is a lovely place for sailing, picnicking, and strolling.

The best shopping

The hub of downtown shopping is **Eaton Center,** an 860-foot-long shopping center docked on Yonge Street. The mall is shaped like a large ocean freighter, with a series of railings, big exposed ducts, greenhouse glazing, and three-dozen sculptured geese swooping from the glass-domed ceiling. The Eaton Center does more gross sales than any other shopping mall in North America.

The retail giants Simpsons and Eaton's are anchored at each end of the mall, with 300 shops, banks, boutiques, and fast-food outlets on three levels in between.

The best entertainment

Ontario Place, along the lakefront, is an overwhelming futuristic entertainment complex built over the water on three man-made islands. It includes a disco, a roller rink, a marina, numerous restaurants, and snack bars. The main attraction is the **Cinesphere,** a ball-shaped theater where films are projected on a six-story curved screen, the world's tallest.

Harborfront, another recreational development, stretches 1 1/2 miles from York Street to just past Bathurst. Divided into four sections, the attractions include antique shops, art galleries, cafés, studios, theaters, picnic facilities, and a multicultural media center.

Toronto has its own symphony and is home to both the Canadian Opera Company and the National Ballet. The **O'Keefe Center,** *Front and Yonge streets,* is a modern hall with seating for 3,200. The **St. Lawrence Center,** *Front and Scott streets,* contains an 830-seat theater that accommodates a resident repertory company, visiting theater groups, and opera and dance companies.

Incomparable cooking

Toronto's best restaurant, and the granddaddy of haute cuisine in Canada, is **Winston's,** *104 Adelaide St. W.; tel. (416)363-1627.* You'll feel like royalty here, surrounded by magnificent decor. Try the lamb or the *escalope de veau*, and save room for crepes suzette. The wine list is extensive. Dinner is about C$60, with wine. Reservations are required. Winston's is closed Sundays and holidays.

Canada's best Thai restaurant is **Bangkok Garden,** *18 Elm St.; tel. (416)977-6748,* a beautifully decorated place. Try the steamed gingerfish or the mussels in spicy coconut sauce. The restaurant is closed Sundays.

The most charming restaurant in town is **Le Bistingo,** *349 Queen St. W.; tel. (416)598-3490,* a fashionable French restaurant with scrumptious desserts. It is closed Sundays and major holidays.

The best place for nouvelle cuisine is **Chiaro's,** *37 King St. E.; tel. (416)863-9700,* in the newly renovated King Edward Hotel. Dishes are not only light and delicious, but they are also beautifully presented. Try the duck, *aiguillette de caneton,* and fruit ices. Chiaro's is closed Sundays and holidays.

Il Posto, *York Square, 148 Yorkville Ave.; tel. (416)968-0469,* is Toronto's best Italian restaurant, with imaginatively prepared pasta dishes.

The best hotels

The **Royal York Hotel,** *100 Front St. W.; tel. (416)368-2511,* is the biggest hotel in the British Commonwealth. A landmark since 1929, it is a favorite among royalty, movie stars, and visiting prime ministers. Service is superb.

Toronto's most charming hotel is the **King Edward,** *37 King St. E.; tel. (416)863-9700.* This Edwardian-style classic was recently renovated. Rooms are C$210 to C$250.

The **Sheraton Center,** *123 Queen St. W.; tel. (416)361-1000,* outdoes itself with imaginative decor. A three-story waterfall cascades in the lobby, and the hotel complex houses 40 stores, 2 theaters, 10 restaurants, and 6 bars. Outside are lovely gardens. And, of course, modern luxuries, such as saunas and indoor and outdoor pools, have not been forgotten. Rooms are C$126 to C$189.

A pleasant moderately priced hotel is the **Delta Chelsea Inn,** *33 Gerrard St. W.; tel. (416)595-1975,* between Yonge and Bay streets.

The best of New Brunswick

Along **New Brunswick's** 1,400-mile shoreline are some of the oldest cities and towns in Canada, founded by Loyalist refugees from the American Revolution. The coast is also home to small Acadian French towns. Forests cover 88% of the province. Life is serene. Along the **Fundy Coast,** residents pass the time predicting the weather and discussing the price of seafood.

Campobello Island, a president's favorite

Campobello Island is where President Franklin Roosevelt retreated from the tensions of his job. His house is open to the public. The **Roosevelt Campobello International Park,** a joint Canadian-American preservation effort, is open May to October from 9 a.m. to 5 p.m. Benedict Arnold also lived on Campobello Island for a time, at Snug Cove.

St. Andrews, a moving town

St. Andrews is a Loyalist settlement with a unique history. The first settlers built their town at Fort George (later Castine, Maine). When that area became part of the United States, the townspeople actually lifted their homes and moved them to the Canadian side of the border. Today St. Andrews is a peaceful summer haven with swimming, golfing, and tours of Passamaquoddy Bay.

St. Andrews Blockhouse National Historic Site, at the northwest end of Water Street, is the only surviving wood fortress of several built for the town's defense during the War of 1812. Also see **Greenock Church,** a pretty church built in 1824.

Visit the aquarium at Huntsman Marine Laboratories, northwest of town on Brandy Cover Road, and the **Ross Memorial Museum,** *188 Montague St.,* in an old house filled with antiques, paintings, and curios.

The best place to stay in town is the quirky **Rossmount Inn,** *tel. (506)529-3351.* The Victorian house is decorated with a mishmash of Persian rugs, English wallpaper, and French art. Smoking is not permitted on the grounds. Credit cards are accepted.

The best bird watching

New Brunswick is an excellent place for bird watching. More than 350 species of birds can be seen; all you need are a pair of binoculars and a North American field guide. During the winter, New Brunswick attracts such rare birds as the Bohemian waxwing, pine grosbeak, common redpoll, and purple finch.

For bird watchers, the event of the year is the **Christmas Bird Count,** sponsored by the National Audubon Society. As many observers as possible are needed on the count day, which usually falls during the last two weeks of December. Write to the **New Brunswick Museum,** *Natural Science Department, 277 Douglas Ave., St. John, New Brunswick E2K 1E5,* for the names and addresses of count compilers.

The New Brunswick Federation of Naturalists sponsors field trips several times a year. For more information, write to the **New Brunswick Museum,** *277 Douglas Ave., St. John, New Brunswick E2K 1E5.*

St. John: the oldest town

St. John is the oldest incorporated town in Canada, inaugurated in 1785. Actually, it was founded by Samuel de Champlain on St. John the Baptist Day (June 24) in 1604. The Loyalists turned this city into one of the world's greatest shipbuilding ports. Vessels from every country call here.

The St. John River's **Reversing Falls** will leave you wondering. The falls, which appear to flow backward, are actually rapids beneath the bridge on Highway 100. A Tourist Information Center here shows a film explaining the phenomenon. Usually the river empties into the Bay of Fundy. But as the tide rises, the estuary water reverses the river current, creating climbing rapids.

New Brunswick's best seafood

Shediac, which holds a six-day Lobster Festival every July, is known for its incredibly fresh and inexpensive lobster. The city is also known for having New Brunswick's warmest water, thanks to sand bars and shallow depths.

Paturel Shore House, *tel. (506)532-4774,* on the ocean next to a seafood-packing plant, is the best place in the area to get seafood. Take Highway 15 east from Shediac and watch for signs to Cape Bimet and Paturel. Lobster is caught locally and prepared to your specifications. The lobster stew (C$7) can be a meal in itself.

The best places to stay are **Chez Françoise,** *93 Main St., Shediac, NB E0A 3G0; tel. (506)532-4233;* and **Vacation Motel,** *L.A. Crossman, Box 1893, Shediac, NB E0A 3G0; tel. (506)532-2199,* where rooms are C$28 to C$50.

Nova Scotia: more Gaelic than Scotland

Nova Scotia, a 375-mile peninsula separated from New Brunswick by the Bay of Fundy, is more Gaelic than its grandfather, Scotland. The province, which is made up of two main sections, Nova Scotia proper and **Cape Breton Island,** drew boatloads of Scotsmen during the wave of immigration from the Highlands in the 18th century. The Cape Breton immigrants left before they felt the full impact of King James VI's law of 1616, which prohibited the use of Gaelic and the wearing of kilts. Today, even in such remote regions of Scotland as the Isle of Skye, the use of Gaelic is rare. However, on western Cape Breton Island, most adult residents have Gaelic-speaking parents. (Nova Scotia is actually a better place to learn Scottish Gaelic than Scotland. You can take summer classes at St. Anne's in Cape Breton. For more information, contact the **Canadian Association for Scottish Studies** in Ontario, *tel. (519)824-4120.)*

Fiddlers in this province retain a Scottish style abandoned by most Scottish musicians long ago. "This, not Scotland, is the real McCoy," says Celtic record distributor Dan Collins of Shanachie Records. The stretch along the coast of Cape Breton from the causeway at Port Hastings to Margaree Forks known as the **Ceilidh Trail** is the place to go to enjoy traditional music and dance. Check with the proprietors of pubs in the area for details.

Hale and hearty contestants in the **Highland Games,** held annually in Antigonish in mid-July, are likely to roll into the local pubs for a pint of ale and a boast about their bravado in the caber (log) toss. For more information on the Highland Games, contact the **Nova Scotia Department of Tourism,** *(800)341-6096.*

The Micmac Indians also have annual summer games. These have evolved from a reunion, lasting three months, that has been held since the 18th century. Originally, a continental Indian congress met and planned survival tactics against the encroaching Europeans. They succeeded at least to a degree—to this day, the Micmacs on rural reservations retain their native language.

The Micmacs' summer games include tributes to St. Ann, such as dances to the beat of the sacred drum, and field games, including archery, canoeing, and *waltes,* a dice game.

To arrange a visit to the Micmacs' summer games, call the Micmac **public information office,** *tel. (902)535-3311.*

The best treasure hunting

Oak Island, Nova Scotia has frustrated treasure hunters for nearly 200 years. Convinced that Captain Kidd and his fellow pirates hid their loot here, many fortune seekers have tried the hunt and failed. Millions of dollars have been spent and six lives have been lost trying to find the treasure. So far, nothing has been found.

The first treasure hunt was in 1796, when some men spotted a depression in the land and figured something might have been buried. They began digging and uncovered a layer of planks every 10 feet. When they got down 96 feet, water from the ocean flooded the pit, which had been ingeniously designed to thwart digging. A shaft stretches from the pit to the ocean, permitting water to enter the main well if it is tampered with.

The oldest colony: Newfoundland

Newfoundland is at once the newest of the Canadian provinces and the oldest of the British colonies. Sir Humphrey Gilbert landed on this North Atlantic island in 1583 and claimed it for Queen Elizabeth. But it didn't become part of Canada until 1949.

Legions of hunters, hikers, fishermen, campers, boaters, and photographers take advantage of the natural bounties of this northern province's 47 provincial park wilderness areas and 2 national parks: Terra Nova in the east and Gros Morne in the west.

Marine Atlantic Reservations Bureau, *P.O. Box 250, North Sydney, NS, B2A 3M3 Canada; (800)341-7981* or *(800)794-8109 in Maine,* operates a year-round vehicle and passenger ferry service between North Sydney, Nova Scotia, and Port-aux-Basques, Newfoundland. During the summer, an additional service operates between North Sydney and Argentia, 78 miles from St. John's.

Gros Morne: the most beautiful scenery

Gros Morne National Park is a jaw-dropping wilderness area on the west coast of Newfoundland. The 750-square-mile park has the most spectacular fjords in North America. Gros Morne (which translates as Big Knoll in French) is a flat-topped extinct volcano rising 2,000 feet from the Gulf of St. Lawrence. Climb the 2 1/2-mile **Names Callaghan Trail** to the top of Gros Morne for the best view of the tundra and the roaring sea below. Look for moose, caribou, bald eagles, black bears, and beaver.

Hike along the elevated boardwalk through the marshes to **Western Brook Pond.** At the end of the path is a dock, where you can catch a tour boat and cruise the pond. (You can register for a boat tour at the park's visitor center.) Boats sail beneath towering rocky cliffs to a misty 2,000-foot waterfall. Three boat trips depart daily, weather permitting, from mid-June to mid-September. Boat capacity is 25 to 30 people. The fare is C$16 for adults, C$5 for children. To get to the pond, drive north of the visitor center on Highway 430, about 18 miles, past Sally's Cove.

Canada's loveliest drive

Canada's most beautiful drive is **Highway 430,** north of Gros Morne, on the coast of the **Great Northern Peninsula.** The waters of jagged fjords lap at the steep Long Range Mountains. At the northern tip of the peninsula, hundreds of icebergs rise as much as 300 feet out of the water. You can get more information from the Information Center in Wiltondale, which is open from 9 a.m. to 9 p.m. in the summer.

Canada's best archeological sites

The Great Northern Peninsula is the site of some of Canada's most interesting archeological sites. **Porte-aux-Choix** has a 5,000-year-old Red Paint Indian burial mound and the remains of later Inuit cultures. Three Red Paint burial mounds have been excavated here, uncovering the remains of 100 people, weapons, and artifacts. The relics can be seen in the visitor center, which is open from June through Labor Day. (The Red Paint lived here about 2340 B.C. Later, Dorset Eskimos, known for their fine stone tools, lived here for 2,000 years. About A.D. 1100, the Beothuck Indians took over the region.)

At the tip of the Great Northern Peninsula is **L'Anse aux Meadows National Historic Park,** the site of a Viking settlement dating from A.D. 1000 (492 years before Columbus). These early Norse settlers built six thatched houses, three of which have been reconstructed. Historians believe the first European child born in America was Snorri Thorfinnson, born here to Icelandic trader Thorfinn Karlsefni in A.D. 1005. The child is mentioned in Viking sagas.

While visiting the park, stay at the **St. Anthony Motel,** *P.O. Box 187, St. Anthony, NF, A0K 4S0; tel. (709)454-3200.* Single rooms are C$45; double rooms are C$52.

The best of the Beothucks

For a glimpse of the life of the Beothuck Indians, head east on the **Trans-Canada Highway** (Highway 1) to Grand Falls. The **Mary March Museum,** *Cromer Avenue,* is dedicated to the study of the Beothuck Indians, who inhabited the region when the first European settlers of the 1600s came ashore. Mary March was the last of the unassimilated Beothucks, and her knowledge was the foundation of the museum.

While in Grand Falls, stay at the **Mt. Peyton Hotel-Motel,** *214 Lincoln Road, Grand Falls, NF A2A 1P8; (800)563-4894* (for reservations only).

A Red Barron best: Gander

Gander, 60 miles east of Grand Falls on Highway 1, played an important role during World War II. Thousands of aircrafts flew here from all parts of Canada and the United States to refuel before heading to Europe.

A visit to Gander, which is also famous for its hunting and fishing, is a great adventure. You can take a floatplane from here to the interior of the island to fish for salmon or to set up a hunting camp.

Most of Gander's hotels and motels line the Trans-Canada Highway. Try the **Albatross Motel,** *tel. (709)256-3956.*

Terra Nova: the best wildlife

Terra Nova National Park, southeast of Gander, is famous for its Atlantic beaches and its wildlife (including moose, black bear, red fox, Canada geese, beaver, and lynx). Keep an eye out for the park's unusual pitcher plant, which is carnivorous. You can rent cabins, canoes, and bikes at the park headquarters, *tel. (709)533-2296.*

France in the New World

Off the southern coast of Newfoundland are two French islands: **St. Pierre** and **Miquelon.** You must clear customs to travel to these islands, but a passport is unnecessary if you have identification.

Both islands truly feel like forgotten French towns, with French architecture, fashion, and culture. French wines are a good buy here, even though the islands lost their tax-free status recently.

The best place to stay on St. Pierre is **Hôtel Robert,** *tel. (41)2419* (it is not possible to call here from the United States), a small old-fashioned hotel. For reservations at any of the hotels in St. Pierre, call **SPM Tours,** *tel. (709)722-3892.*

The most romantic town

St. John's, a natural rock-bound harbor on the Avalon Peninsula, is Newfoundland's most romantic town. Quaint houses with brightly colored facades recall the town's wild past, when pirates raided and great feasts were held. While St. John's is one of the oldest towns in North America, inhabited by fishermen since the 15th century, its buildings are Victorian. Earlier dwellings all were destroyed by fire.

Signal Hill, which looms above the harbor, was the site of the first trans-Atlantic reception of a radio signal, sent by Guglielmo Marconi on Dec. 12, 1901. About two-thirds of the way up Signal Hill is **Queen's Battery,** built in the late 18th century. Across the narrows from Queen's Battery is **Fort Amherst.** The Battery and the Fort, together with a chain that stretched across the narrows, were effective in closing the port to enemies.

St. John's has two beautiful churches: the twin-spired **Roman Catholic Basilica** and the **Anglican Cathedral,** one of the best examples of Gothic architecture in North America.

If you're looking for restaurants, shops, and people, stroll downtown along Duckworth and Water streets. (**Water Street** is known as the "oldest main street on the continent," because it served as a pathway for the early explorers.)

To dine in an old-time colonial atmosphere, visit the **Woodstock Colonial Inn,** *tel. (709)753-9510.*

Most hotels in St. John's are expensive. The best are the **Hotel Newfoundland,** *tel. (709)726-4980* or *(800)268-8136 in Canada,* located on Cavendish Square, and the **Stel Battery Hotel,** *tel. (709)726-0040* or *(800)267-STEL,* which has panoramic views.

The best of Alberta

The peaceful and vast prairies of **Alberta** retain much of the open space and freedom that drew settlers into the Canadian wilderness a century ago. Alberta's prairies stretch for miles, a flat quilt at the foot of the Canadian Rockies.

While Alberta does have thriving, colorful cities, most of this vast 255,285-square-mile province is unpopulated—it has fewer inhabitants than the city of Philadelphia. And most of the population (more than half) lives in Edmonton and Calgary.

Calgary: the best cow town

Calgary is both a colorful remnant of the Wild West and a huge, modern city. Known as Cowtown, because of its cattle industry, Calgary is a thriving business center located less than an hour from the Rockies. This lively, crazy town is best known as the home of the **Calgary Stampede,** a wild rodeo of horse racing and high jinks.

Calgary got its start as a Royal Canadian Mounted Police post in 1875, back in the days when buffalo hunters, whiskey traders, pioneers, and Indians required the likes of Sergeant Preston of the Yukon to keep them in line. The post was founded at the junction of two rivers, the Bow and the Elbow. Colonel J.F. Macloud, the commander of the Mounties who founded the post, named it Calgary after his favorite fishing spot on the Bay of Mull in Scotland. The log fort attracted 600 settlers.

Four years later, the Canadian Pacific Railway reached Calgary in its rush to "save the West from the Yankees." The population of the post promptly doubled, as Chinese were brought in from the Pacific to lay railway tracks and European settlers—mostly English—poured in from the Atlantic Coast.

Tremendous beef herds were built up around Calgary, and it soon became a cattle metropolis. With the discovery of oil at nearby Turner Valley in 1914, Calgary boomed. The province of Alberta (the nation's richest) provides 85% of Canada's oil. (The province is so rich, in fact, that residents don't have to pay any Provincial taxes.)

Outside the downtown area, Calgary is beautiful. The Rocky Mountain foothills begin to the west. The prairie stretches forever to the east. Northeast of Calgary are the **Drumheller Badlands,** where dinosaur skeletons have been found. Southwest is the **Glenmore Reservoir,** surrounded by parks and trails. Farm towns and huge cattle ranches begin south of the city.

The best rodeo

If you want to brave the **Calgary Stampede,** make sure you have reservations—the city swells with participants and spectators. (To make reservations, contact **Calgary Exhibition & Stampede,** *P.O. Box 1860, Calgary, AB T2P 2M7.*)

The stampede is big and rough, drawing an immense and enthusiastic crowd. Cowboys from all over the continent ride bucking broncos and bulls, rope calves, and wrestle steers for prizes. The **Stampede Stage Show** features chorus girls, clowns, bands, and glamour. The funniest event is the **Chuckwagon Race,** in which old-time cowboy chuck wagons race around the track. The total prize money for the 10-day meet is C$274,490. Sudden Death, the last heat, takes place the final night and is worth $50,000.

The best view of the city

The revolving restaurant at the top of the 626-foot **Calgary Tower,** *Ninth Avenue and Center Street; tel. (403)266-7171,* has the best view in town. You can see the Rockies when it's clear. If you don't want to pay for dinner, enjoy the view from the observation deck.

Calgary's top sights

Fort Calgary, *750 Ninth Ave. S.E.; tel. (403)290-1875,* is a 40-acre natural history park on the site of the original Mounted Police fort. Exhibits explain the history of Calgary. The fort is open daily year-round. Free tours can be arranged.

The **Glenbow Museum,** *130 Ninth Ave. S.E.; tel. (403)264-8300,* has extensive displays of Indian and Inuit art and artifacts. The art gallery has carvings and ceramics from all over the world. The museum is closed Mondays.

Explore **Heritage Park,** west of *14th Street and Heritage Drive S.W.; tel. (403)255-1182,* an authentic pre-1915 Alberta town. Original pioneer buildings from all over Alberta have been transported here, including a log church, a blacksmith's shop, a newspaper office, and a bakery. The park is open May through mid-October.

The best shopping

If you have a secret urge to look like Roy Rogers, head to **Western Outfitters,** *128 Eighth Ave. S.E.; tel. (403)266-3656.* (If you go to the Calgary Stampede, you'll need your spurs!)

The best food

The most elegant restaurant is the **Owl's Nest,** *320 Fourth Ave. S.W.; tel. (403)266-1611.* Before dinner, women are given roses. After dinner, men are presented with cigars. Have the British Columbia salmon, Beluga caviar, turtle soup, or quail. Reservations are suggested. Major credit cards are accepted.

The finest of Alberta's beef is served at the **Rimrock Room,** *Palliser Hotel, Ninth Avenue and First Street S.W.; tel. (403)262-1234.*

Calgary's best hotel

The **Palliser,** *133 Ninth Ave. S.W.; tel. (403)266-8621,* is an institution in Calgary, built in 1914 by the Canadian Pacific Railroad. The gracious old hotel has brass doors, marble pillars, and chandeliers.

Canada's most beautiful national parks

Banff and Jasper national parks, on the border between British Columbia and Alberta, are among the most beautiful nature reserves in the world. Together, they comprise 6,764 square miles in the Rocky Mountains. Imagine snow-topped peaks rising out of deep-green forests, cascading rivers, mountain sheep, bears, and silent blue lakes.

Banff is the older of the parks, Jasper the larger. They run together and stretch from Mt. Sir Douglas in the south to Resthaven Mountains in the far north. Many nature trails climb into their remote valleys and peaks. Banff lies 81 miles from Calgary via Highway 1; Japser is 225 miles from Edmonton on Route 16.

Highway 93, from Banff to Jasper, which passes the Athabasca Glacier, is spectacular. You'll see bighorn sheep, mountain goats, and bears from the road.

The 160-square-mile **Columbia ice fields** spread across Jasper. Rent a snowmobile in the park, then take off to explore them. Jasper also boasts Alberta's highest peak, **Mt. Columbia** (12,294 feet), and the spectacular **Athabasca Falls,** which rush through a narrow gap.

The **Banff Springs Hotel,** *Spray Avenue; tel. (403)762-2211,* which has views of the mountains and two rivers, is the best place to stay while exploring the parks. Established in 1928 to bring visitors to the nearby hot springs, the castle-like hotel has four dining rooms, an espresso bar, cocktail lounges, and a post office. Its golf course is considered one of the most scenic in the world. Single rooms cost from C$150 to C$175; double rooms from C$160 to C$195.

Edmonton: the best boomtown

Edmonton has been a boomtown three times in its life: the fur trade brought hundreds of trappers and trackers in the 18th century; the gold rush attracted thousands in the 1890s; and the discovery of oil and natural gas brought industrial development in the 1960s. Despite its spurts of sudden growth, Edmonton is well-designed, with 10,000 acres of parks. And city leaders have made a tremendous effort to preserve historic buildings.

Edmonton's best festival

The **Klondike Days,** which celebrate the days of gold prospecting, take place in late July. Everyone must dress in period costumes (those who don't may find themselves temporarily incarcerated in the Klondike clink!), the streets are filled with performers, and parades make their way through the streets. The new coliseum hosts rock'n'roll and Western entertainment.

Edmonton's best sights

Fort Edmonton, a replica of the fur-trading post established in 1795, stands in a 158-acre park off Whitemud Freeway in the suburbs. It is complete with a stockade, a fur-processing plant, a clay oven, McDougall's General Store, the Northwest Mounted Police Jail, and a Masonic Temple. The original trading post has been replaced with **Alberta's Legislative Building,** *109th Street and 97th Avenue,* which was built in 1912.

The **Muttart Conservatory and Horticulture Center,** *98th Avenue and 96th Street,* is a complex of four ultramodern pyramid-shaped greenhouses that act as a botanical incubator. Each pyramid has a specific climate and is filled with flora of appropriate regions. The complex is open daily.

Edmonton Civic Center, *100th Street and 102nd Avenue,* is a gigantic structure containing the Edmonton Art Gallery, City Hall, a convention center, the law courts building, and the Centennial Library.

Edmonton's best restaurants

Hy's Steak Loft, *10013 101st St.; tel. (403)424-4444,* serves superb steaks (Alberta is famous for its beef). The restaurant is closed Sundays. Reservations are required.

Vi's, *9712 111th St.; tel. (403)482-6402,* has good, hearty food for a reasonable price. Try the thick homemade soup; finish your meal with the chocolate-glazed pecan pie. The restaurant is open daily.

The best hotel

The **Westin Hotel,** *100th Street at 101st Avenue; tel. (403)426-3636,* is where Princess Di and Prince Charles stayed when they visited in 1983. The swimming pool and sauna are inviting, and the restaurant is one of the best in the city.

Play cowboy for a while

Rafter Six, *Seebe, AB T0L 1X0; tel. (403)673-3622,* is a typical guest ranch 50 miles west of Calgary. The package cost is C$85 to C$96 per person, per day.

The best of British Columbia

British Columbia, Canada's westernmost province, has snow-capped mountains that rise out of the Pacific, providing backdrops for Vancouver and Victoria. In the north of this region are tiny settlements lost in a stark wilderness; in the center are wide-open ranchlands that cowboys call home. Throughout the area, glacier ice fields jut into birch and maple forests.

More than one-million acres of British Columbia have been set aside for five national parks. The area also contains 11-million acres of provincial parks.

Throughout this coastal province are **petroglyphs,** rock drawings made by unknown tribes long ago, which are carefully preserved by the government. Mementos of the early fur traders, explorers, and pioneers can be seen at **Fort Langley,** a restored fur trading post in Fort Defiance on Vancouver Island, and at **Fort James,** near Prince George. Artifacts of the Cariboo gold rush of the 1860s are preserved at **Barkerville.** And the Royal Mounted Police left its mark at **Fort Steel.**

Vancouver: a best city

Vancouver is surrounded on all sides by snow-capped mountains, and glass-sided skyscrapers are reflected in the glittering blue harbor. The air is pure, and the climate is mild. At the western edge of the city, cliffs drop to the sea. Totem poles stand near the Strait of Georgia, a reminder of the Northwest Indians, who were the first inhabitants in this region. Canada's third-largest city, Vancouver has 1.3 million residents.

The city's main thoroughfare is **Georgia Street,** where you'll find the old Hotel Vancouver, the Vancouver Art Gallery inside an old granite courthouse, and entrances to underground shopping malls.

Near Georgia Street, between Howe and Hornby, is **Robson Square,** a three-block complex designed by Arthur Erickson. Inside the square are international kiosks, a skating rink, and terraced gardens with pools and waterfalls. At the edge of the square is a seven-story glass pyramid—the **Law Courts Building.** During the week, you can wander into an open courtroom, sink into an upholstered chair, and watch a hearing.

Stanley Park, just north of downtown, is a wilderness playground with performing whales and a zoo. The best way to see this immense, 1,000-acre preserve is by bike (a six-mile scenic drive circles the park). **Stanley Park Rentals,** *676 Chilco St.,* just outside the park, rents 10-speed and tandem bicycles.

Gastown, east of the Sea Bus terminal, is the birthplace of Vancouver. This renovated 19th-century area is filled with pubs, restaurants, galleries, and boutiques. Stop by **Hill's Indian Crafts,** *Water Street,* for baskets, moccasins, carvings, jewelry, prints, and sweaters.

South of Gastown, along Pender Street, is **Chinatown.** Sidewalk stalls sell Chinese food and knicknacks, and herbalists offer deer horns, dried sea horses, and exotic teas. The **Chinese Cultural Center,** *Pender Street,* has maps of the area. Stroll through the **Dr. Sun Yat-Sen Classical Garden,** 2 1/2 acres of miniature fountains, pavilions, ponds, and bridges.

Granville Island has galleries, theaters, cafés, and an open market. Have dinner at **Bridges.** Afterward, stop by Granville Island Hotel's **Pelican Bay Lounge** to enjoy some jazz. Return downtown from Granville aboard the False Creek Ferry, which departs from a dock near Bridges.

The stern-faced totem poles in the **Museum of Anthropology** at the University of British Columbia are a sharp contrast to the modern lines of the museum itself, which was designed by Erickson.

The best restaurants

La Cachette, *2036 W. 41st Ave.; tel. (604)266-0824,* as its name suggests, is hidden away. While it is difficult to find, it's more than worth the search, a cozy but elegant restaurant with an ever-changing menu. Everything is homemade. The prix-fixe menu includes six courses. The restaurant is closed Sundays and Mondays. Reservations are a good idea.

Le Pavillon, *Georgia and Howe streets; tel. (604)689-9333,* in the Four Seasons Hotel has a superb menu that features game and seafood. The wine list is extensive. The restaurant is closed Sundays. Reservations are required.

Umberto's is an institution in Vancouver, with three restaurants serving three different cuisines. The original, *1380 Hornby St.; tel. (604)687-6316,* specializes in northern Italian cuisine. **La Cantina di Umberto,** *1376 Hornby St.; tel. (604)687-6621,* has fresh local seafood. And **Il Giardino,** *tel. (604)669-2422,* serves fowl and wild game. All three are excellent.

The **Only,** *20 E. Hastings St.; tel. (604)681-6546,* serves the freshest seafood in town. A cheap, informal place in a down-at-the-heels neighborhood, it has booths and counter seats, all with views of the gas burners and frying pans where the fish is cooked. No liquor is served, and credit cards are not accepted. The restaurant is closed Sundays.

Vancouver's best beds

Vancouver's best hotel is **The Mandarin,** *645 Howe St.; tel. (604)687-1122,* which offers every luxury and convenience imaginable, from a gourmet restaurant to a health club. Double rooms are C$190 to C$205.

The **Bayshore Inn,** *1601 W. Georgia St.; tel. (604)682-2377,* once hosted Howard Hughes, who took over the top two floors. Yachtsmen stay here, mooring their boats at the hotel dock. Doormen in red jackets and tall fur hats guard the doors. Rooms have floor-to-ceiling windows with lovely views of the water and the city. Shops, lounges, restaurants, and a pool are available to guests.

If you're watching your budget, stay at the **Sylvia Hotel,** *1154 Gilford St.; tel. (604)681-9321.* This nine-story hotel, which has a good dining room, is popular, so make reservations in advance.

Vancouver Island: the most beautiful

Vancouver Island, which stretches 170 miles along the western coastline of British Columbia, is sheltered along its southern border by Washington State's Olympic Peninsula. You can take a ferry from Vancouver City to Nanaimo.

Most of the half-million people on Vancouver Island live along its east coast, which is rich in timber, farmland, and fishing streams, or at the southern tip in the city of Victoria. The wild and rugged west coast is sparsely inhabited, with few villages. It is deeply cut by fjords and piled high with mountains. The south end of the island is mountainous, reaching a height of 7,200 feet; the north end is flat.

Victoria, the provincial capital, was first settled by Europeans in 1843. It has been the site of coal mining, logging, fur trading, and fishing.

One of the most beautiful sights on the island is **Butchart Gardens,** near Victoria, across the Saanich Peninsula from Sydney. Originally (in 1905) this area was a limestone quarry; today it offers entertainment on summer evenings.

Victoria, the most British city

"A tweedy, daffodilish, green-fingered sort of place, a golfish, fly-fishing, 5 o'clock teapot place." That's how Canadian author Bruce Hutchinson described **Victoria,** which feels more British than any other city in the Americas. While it is the largest city on Vancouver Island, the atmosphere is relaxed. The air smells of flowers and the sea. The climate is mild, less rainy than on the island's west coast.

Go behind the **Tweed Curtain,** as it is known, along Oak Bay. Enjoy the thick British accents and stop for tea at the Oak Bay Beach Hotel, the Blethering Place Tearoom in Oak Bay Village, or the dining room in the Butchart Gardens Mansion.

Activity in Victoria centers around the harbor, which is surrounded by Victorian buildings, including the Empress Hotel, the Provincial legislative buildings, the old steamship terminal (now a wax museum), and the Belmont Building. The Visitors and Convention Bureau, an art-deco building, offers maps and information.

Victoria's **Provincial Museum** traces life before and after glaciers covered Vancouver Island with a sheet of ice 3 1/2 miles thick. Walk through the rain forest, which includes a reconstructed 19th-century town and an Indian longhouse.

Outside the Provincial Museum complex is **Thunderbird Park,** which has a collection of coastal Indian totem poles. You can watch Indian craftsmen carving reproductions of traditional designs. Just beyond the park is the **Helmcken House,** the oldest house still standing in British Columbia.

The **Tong-Ji Men** (Gate of Harmonious Interest), at the corner of Fisgard and Government in Chinatown, is a 30-foot arch with 4,500 ceramic tiles and 1,008 decorative panels that was made in Taiwan.

Craigdarroch Castle, *Joan Crescent,* was built in 1885 by the multimillionaire coal baron Robert Dunsmuir for his wife Joan. A nonprofit society is refurbishing the castle, which was auctioned off for a dollar after Joan's death.

Along Rockland Avenue is the **Government House,** where the lieutenant governor of British Columbia resides. Its gardens are more than 100 years old.

Most restaurants in Victoria serve mostly bland English fare—fish and chips and the lot. Two exceptions are **Periklis,** *531 Yates St.,* where you can enjoy Greek food, and **Foo Hong,** in Chinatown, a popular and inexpensive lunch spot.

Stay at the Gothic **Empress Hotel,** *721 Government St.; tel. (604)384-8111,* which is great fun but rather touristy and expensive. Built in 1906 on the harbor, it has lovely views as well as a bar, a restaurant, and a disco. Have high tea in the afternoon.

A good, moderately priced hotel is **Helm's Inn,** off Government Street, near the Provincial Museum, *tel. (604)385-5767.* Comfortable, nicely decorated double rooms are only C$52

The most shopping space

Nanaimo, the second-largest city on Vancouver Island, has the largest amount of retail shopping space per capita of any city in Canada. The city is also filled with preserved pioneer buildings and sites, which you can see on the historic walking tour.

Stroll around Nanaimo's waterfront, where you'll see the **Bastion,** the former Hudson's Bay Company Fort, erected in 1852 by settlers as protection against raiding Indians. **Fishermen's Wharf** has an abundance of fresh seafood. The **Georgia Park Promenade** leads to the modern seaplane base and on to Swy-A-Lana Lagoon and Maffeo Sutton Park.

Georgia Park is dedicated to the Indian tribes who first inhabited this area and features a display of authentic Indian canoes and totem poles. **Swy-A-Lana Lagoon** features a man-made tidal pool. Next to the lagoon, native Indians operate a traditional carving shed, where you can watch craftsmen carving masks and other artifacts.

The best bathtub race

Nanaimo's annual **Bathtub Race** in mid-July is a zany spectacle. Hundreds of daring tubbers challenge the wild waters of Georgia Strait in a 30-mile race to the beaches of Vancouver. It's hilarious.

The most romantic town

One of the loveliest places on the island is **Parksville,** a little town off Route 19 on the east coast. From the highway the town doesn't look like much—a few trailers and gift shops. But behind the ever-present towering pines are wide beaches with calm, clear waters. On the horizon are purple, snow-topped mountain ranges. The beach extends out for nearly a mile at low tide, and sea lions cavort not far from land. The water is surprisingly warm as early as May.

Tigh Na Mara, *R.R. 1, Site 114, C16 Parksville, V0R 2S0; tel. (604)248-2072,* has the most romantic accommodations on Vancouver Island. You stay in log cabins (with fireplaces) next to the beach and have use of a jacuzzi, canoes, paddle boats, and rowboats.

The best whale watching

You can track the great gray whale each spring as it migrates northward along the west coast of Vancouver Island. The first migrants appear in late February; by mid-April the waters are filled with hundreds of them. As many as 40 or 50 gray whales like the area so much that they spend the summer here.

The best time for whale watching is from late February through June. The whales can be spotted from the headlands of Pacific Rim National Park, from the restaurant at Wickaninnish Bay, or from the rocky shores of Little Beach, Big Beach, or Amphitrite Point in Ucluelet. However, the best way to watch is from the deck of a charter boat that specializes in whale-watching trips.

You'll usually see only a small portion of the whale. When spouting, whales roll forward and seem to lift partly out of the water, revealing their scarred gray backs and the bumps of their vertebrae, which are known as knuckles. While diving in deep water, whales occasionally show their graceful, barnacle-encrusted tails, displays called fluking. When whales poke their heads out of the water for a look around, they are spy-hopping. The most breathtaking sight is when whales breach, jumping almost completely out of the water to land on their backs with a huge splash.

Canadian Princess Resort offers whale-watching cruises that depart from Vancouver and Victoria. A two-day, one-night cruise costs C$89 per person; a three-day, two-night cruise is C$139. For more information, contact the resort at **Oak Bay Marina Ltd.,** *1327 Beach Drive, Victoria, BC V8S 2N4; tel. (604)598-3366, or Ucluelet, BC; tel. (604)726-7771.*

Subtidal Adventures, *P.O. Box 253, Ucluelet, BC V0R 3A0; tel. (604)726-7123* or *(604)726-7336,* also offers a whale-watching cruise. The three-hour trip runs from 9 a.m. to 1 p.m. in March and April. The cost is C$24 for adults, C$19 for children.

The highest city

British Columbia boasts the highest city in Canada: **Kimberley,** in the Rocky Mountains just north of the U.S. border. This mining town-turned-ski resort resembles a Bavarian Alpine village. The townspeople sponsor a **Julyfest** modeled after the German Oktoberfest (but held earlier in the year) that includes parades, folk dances, beer tents, and international entertainment.

Kimberley's real claim to fame is its excellent downhill skiing. The city's mountain rises 2,300 feet and has 32 runs served by chair lifts and T-bars. The mountain also has one of North America's longest lighted ski runs (1,600 feet). For information on ski packages, contact **Kimberley Ski Resort,** *P.O. Box 40, Kimberley, BC V1A 2Y5; tel. (604)427-4881.*

Canada's only desert town

Osoyoos is a Spanish-influenced desert town in a 252-mile desert pocket east of Vancouver. It is watered by deep Lake Osoyoos, where you can fish for trout and bass. You can swim here, too, if you don't mind sharing the water with painted turtles. Try your luck panning for gold in the Okanagan Valley above Osoyoos.

An authentic Indian village

Hazelton (known as Kiran-maksh among the Indians), in the heart of British Columbia, is a modern Indian town next to a reconstructed Gitskan Indian village built to look as it did before the arrival of the white man. The village, called **Ksan,** has six longhouses, totem poles, and birchbark canoes. The House of Treasures contains the tribal regalia of Gitksan chiefs. A campground and trailer park adjoin the village.

Canada's best skiing

Skiing in Canada is as exhilarating as skiing in the Alps. British Columbia and Alberta have some of the most spectacular peaks in the world, beginning at the Pacific Coast. The Canadian Rockies are rugged, wild, and challenging. And Quebec's Laurentians offer après-ski activities with a French flavor.

The best heli-skiing

Heli-skiing, a relatively new sport, uses helicopters instead of chair lifts to allow you to

Kootenay Heli-skiing, *P.O. Box 717, Nakusp, BC V0G 1R0; tel. (604)265-3121* or *(800)663-0100,* offers trips into the open bowls and steep tree-lined runs of the unspoiled Selkirk and Monashee mountains. (Because the terrain is difficult, you must be an accomplished skier to participate.) Seven-day packages, available from Jan. 3 to April 17, cost from C$1,595 to C$2,670, depending on the season and accommodations.

Whistler Heli-skiing, *P.O. Box 386, Whistler, BC V0N 1B0; tel. (604)932-4105,* offers packages out of Whistler and Bralorne that take you into the Spearhead and Chilcotin ranges.

Mike Wiegele Helicopter Skiing, *P.O. Box 249, Banff, Alberta, Canada T0L 0C0; tel. (403)762-5548* or *(800)661-9170,* takes you to the Cariboos and Monashees in the Canadian Rockies.

The best powder skiing: British Columbia

British Columbia's ski slopes are a sparkling, powder-covered paradise. And they are varied, including the Rockies, Bugaboos, Purcells, Selkirks, Chilcotin, Cariboo, and Monasheesr. The longest fall-line runs in North America are here, as well as the highest serviced vertical drop.

Whistler, a trendy, fast-growing resort with gorgeous powder-bowl skiing above the tree line, has the longest vertical drop in the Americas (4,278 feet). Nearby **Blackcomb Mountain** opened recently. For more information, contact **Whistler Resort Association,** *P.O. Box 1400, Whistler, BC V0N 1B0; tel. (604)932-4222.*

Alberta's best slopes

Calgary, Alberta, the jumping-off point for some of the world's finest downhill and cross-country skiing, hosted the 1988 Winter Olympic Games. About an hour from Calgary are the magnificent Rocky Mountains and **Mt. Allan,** the site of many Olympic events. Thirty minutes farther into the mountains is **Banff National Park,** whose beautiful terrain is reminiscent of Lake Tahoe and Yosemite National Park.

Banff, the best resort

Banff is the area's best ski resort, with both the easiest and most difficult trails and superb facilities. **Mt. Norquay** has some of the best beginner trails in the park, as well as three of the most difficult runs in North America: the North American, the Bowl, and the Lone Pine. The **Lone Pine** is a favorite among residents of Calgary, but it often intimidates tourists. The **North American** and the **Bowl** have acted as training grounds for many of Canada's world-class downhill racers. The mountain rises from 2,680 feet to 7,005 feet; the longest run measures 1.6 miles.

The best time to visit Banff (unless you dislike crowds) is during the **winter festival,** which as been held every January since 1917. Teams from around the country meet for the Mountain Madness Relay Race—a pentathalon of downhill skiing, running, skating, snow-shoeing, and cross-country skiing.

The **Banff** Springs Hotel is the best ski lodge in Canada. Built in 1888, it was once the world's largest hotel. Not only does it look like a castle, but it operates like one, too. A medieval banquet—complete with period costumes and mead—is staged once a week in the imposing two-story Mt. Stephen Dining Hall.

The longest season

Another ski area popular among Calgarians is **Sunshine Village,** about 20 minutes from

Another ski area popular among Calgarians is **Sunshine Village,** about 20 minutes from Mt. Norquay. Located at the tree line in an Alpine bowl, it is known for its powder snow. It has the longest ski season in the region, lasting through mid-June—an average snowfall of 30 feet enables the resort to stay open so long. Trails range from tight tree-lined runs to open bowls at the top. Sunshine's runs cover 1,200 acres, with a vertical drop of 3,420 feet to an on-the-mountain village. Stay at the **Sunshine Inn.**

Sunshine Village's **Nordic Center,** which opened in 1982, offers excellent high-country touring and programs for the novice and the telemark cross-country skier. Tracks to look for include the Spray River Loop, the Cascade Fire Road, the Red Earth Creek, the Pipestone Loop, and a telemark trail on Moraine Lake Road.

The world's biggest ski jump

The world's biggest ski jump is in **Thunder Bay, Ontario,** the newest hot spot for ski-jump fans. Four major Alpine areas have scores of slopes, including dozens of cross-country trails, for both beginners and experts. Canada's famous ski-jump champions practice here. Daily air service is available from Toronto, Winnipeg, Sault Ste. Marie, and Minneapolis.

North America's oldest ski slopes

The **Laurentians** (Laurentides in French), 40 minutes north of Montreal, are the oldest ski areas in North America. The world's first rope tow was installed here in 1932 in the Quebec village of Shawbridge. Since then, these mountains have catered to skiers from around the world.

Mt. Tremblant, the highest peak in the Laurentians, has a spectacular view of lakes, valleys, and forests. Its 3,000-foot vertical drop makes all kinds of skiing possible. **Gray Rocks** also offers tremendous skiing. **St. Sauveur** is the place to ski and be seen.

If you're looking for accommodations in the Laurentians, try **Station Mt. Tremblant,** which can handle up to 800 guests. **Manoir Pinoteau** has the best view of Tremblant and serves excellent food.

The world's best fishing

Some say Canada, which is bordered by three oceans and the Hudson Bay and dotted with thousands of lakes, rivers, and streams, has the best fishing in the world. Inland waters are filled with major freshwater fish, while the Atlantic and Pacific coasts run with striped bass, bluefin tuna, shark, and other deep-sea fish. Generally, the farther north you go, the better the fishing. In the Yukon and Northwest Territories, the open-water fishing season runs from June to late September. Water in these Arctic regions is ice cold, and the fish fight harder, making the sport more challenging and exciting.

British Columbia: the best fishing

In British Columbia, which many claim has the best fishing in Canada, you can fish year-round. With so many miles of streams and rivers and thousands of lakes spread across a sparsely populated land, it is a fisherman's paradise. Despite all this, the region isn't crowded.

Five species of salmon can be caught in the coastal waters off British Columbia. Pacific-Gulf Charters offers three-day packages in British Columbia for about C$439, including accommodations, fishing equipment, and meals. Contact **Whittomes Ltd.,** *58 Station St., Duncan, BC, Canada V9L 1M5; tel. (604)748-8128.*

Fred Kuzyk is one of the best fishing guides in the business. His company, **Coho Fishing and Guiding Services,** *104 E. 49th Ave., Vancouver, BC Canada V5W 2G2; tel. (604)324-8214* or *(604)872-2856,* can organize every detail of your trip, including all the necessary fishing licenses. All packages include transportation, accommodations, meals, equipment, tackle, and guide.

The wildest fishing

The Atlantic coast of **Labrador** is a wild and woolly place to pit yourself against trout and salmon. **Powell's Outfitters Limited,** *Charlottetown, Labrador, Canada A0K 5Y0; tel. (709)949-4640,* can arrange a wilderness trip for you, providing accommodations in a lodge.

The northwestern woods of Ontario is another remote and beautiful place to fish. **Reserve-A-Resort,** *P.O. Box 647 (T), Kenora, Ontario, Canada P9N 3X6; tel. (807)468-6064* (call collect), can arrange fishing trips here.

The happiest hunting grounds

Canada has a profusion of wildlife: brown bears and grizzly bears in British Columbia and the Laurentian Mountains of Quebec; buffalo in Alberta; and elk and moose in Saskatchewan. The Northwest Territories and the Yukon have polar bears, musk oxen, caribou, seals, walruses, and penguins. Most of the animals are protected. Hunting laws are detailed and involve specific seasons and registrations. For more information, contact the Ministry of Natural Resources of the area where you want to hunt.

The most adventurous hunt

Adventurous and experienced hunters can track polar bears in the Northwest Territories with the help of Eskimo guides. However, the total quota of polar bears that can be hunted is 400 a year, and the local Eskimos decide how many of these are to be shot by tourists. You must use an Eskimo guide, and you can't use mechanical vehicles. Such a hunt means two weeks of travel over huge ice ridges via dogsled.

If the polar bear quota is filled, plenty of other game can be hunted in the Northwest Territories: musk ox, caribou, reindeer, wolf, wolverine, mink, lynx, otter, beaver, seal, walrus, and whale.

The best hunting camps and lodges

For a real wilderness adventure, stay at an Indian camp in Ontario, where a sure-footed Indian guide can show you the trails. **Big Trout Lake Indian Band** operates a lodge, where you can hunt moose, bear, and grouse. Access is by aircraft. For more information, contact **Tom Morris,** *Bugg River Camp, Big Trout Lake, Ontario P0V 1G0.*

Sylvester Jack, *P.O. Box 210, Atlin, BC V0W 1A0,* operates a big-game hunting camp in northwestern British Columbia. He can guide you on sheep, bear, and moose hunts.

Canada's best sailing

Nova Scotia is a Shangri-La for boaters. Its calm harbors and rolling hills are a perfect refuge for Atlantic sailors. Boaters can dock at: **Armdale Yacht Club,** *Halifax, North West Arm;* **Bedford Basin Yacht Club,** *Halifax;* **Bras d'Or Yacht Club,** *Baddeck;* **Canadian Forces Sailing Association,** *P.O. Box 280, Shearwater;* **Chester Yacht Club;** **Dartmouth Yacht Club,** *Bedford Basin;* **Lennox Passage Yacht Club,** *D'Escousse;* **Lunenburg Yacht**

Club, *Herman's Island;* **Royal Western Nova Scotia Yacht Club,** *Montague Row, Digby.*

The rugged island is filled with boat charter and rental companies. **Cheticamp Boat Tours** (Capt. Bill Crawford), *P.O. Box 10, Grand Etang, Nova Scotia B0E 1L0; tel. (902)224-3376,* offers whale-watching cruises and scenic boat tours and charters that depart Government Wharf at Cheticamp Harbor 9 a.m., 1 p.m., and 6 p.m. during July and August. Special group rates and charters can be arranged.

The most exciting rafting

Adventures en Eau Vive, *Quebec, RR 2, Chemin Rivière Rouge, Calumet J0V 1B0; tel. (819)242-6084,* arranges rafting groups on the Rouge River from April through October for C$64 per day on weekends, C$54 per day during the week, and C$141 for a two-day camping and rafting trip.

The best on horseback

What better way to see the wilds of Canada than on horseback? The best way to go is with **Trail Riders of the Canadian Rockies,** *P.O. Box 6742, Station D, Calgary, Alberta, Canada T2P 2E6; tel. (403)263-6963,* a nonprofit group that leads riders through the uninhabited valleys of Banff National Park. A six-day trip is C$615, including accommodations in Indian tepees, horses, saddles, meals, and guides.

The best ways to get around

VIA Rail Canada is an efficient, comfortable, and scenic way to travel across Canada. Tickets are relatively inexpensive: Vancouver to Halifax is about C$341; Montreal to Edmonton is C$223; Ottawa to Montreal is about C$20; and Edmonton to Toronto is about C$207.

The **Canrailpass** offers unlimited transportation on VIA trains in a designated region at a fixed cost. A 30-day pass costs C$560 during peak season.

Chapter 28

THE BEST OF THE UNITED STATES

Americans go to great lengths and expense to travel to the far corners of the earth in search of the world's bests. The irony is that we can find many of them right in our own back yards. People from around the world flock to the United States to see New York, Washington, San Francisco, New Orleans, the Rocky Mountains, the Grand Canyon, and Niagara Falls. Yet we often take for granted the beauty of our homeland.

New York is the most exciting city in the world. California is the world's trendsetter. The Grand Canyon is one of the world's major wonders. Texas is a world unto itself. Hawaii has the world's best surfing. Alaska is one of the world's last frontiers. And decisions affecting the entire world are made in Washington, D.C.

Where do you begin? If you like big cities, go to New York or Chicago. If you prefer nature, go to Yellowstone or Yosemite national parks. Beach lovers should head for California.

We will begin on the East Coast with New York City, continue on to New England, then head south along the East Coast. Next we will head west through Texas and the Southwest. Then we will explore the Rockies and California, before heading north on the Pacific Coast. We won't overlook the Midwest and Chicago, an often misunderstood area of the country. And last, but not least, we will describe the bests of Alaska and Hawaii. (This order is not meant as a rating.)

New York City: America's number-one sight

Ask any foreign visitor where he would most like to go in the United States and his reply most likely will be New York City. People around the globe dream of visiting New York, America's great melting pot, a stew of colorful traditions and peoples. New York is also the creative center of the United States. Ambitious young Americans hoping to make it big make their way to the Big Apple—the country's best dancers, artists, writers, musicians, and fashion-designers. This mixture of exotic, ambitious, and energetic people makes New York electric.

Manhattan: the heart of the City

Manhattan Island, the liveliest of New York's five boroughs, is the heart of the City, as New Yorkers call their town. The famous **Midtown** area, stretching from 34th to 59th streets, contains the most important sights, including the Museum of Modern Art (MOMA), Rockefeller Center, St. Patrick's and St. Bartholomew's cathedrals, Times Square, Grand Central Station, the United Nations, Macy's and Bloomingdales, and the Empire State Building.

The southern tip of the island houses most of the city's historic sights, as well as the financial district. Farther north are ethnic neighborhoods: Little Italy, Chinatown, and the Lower East Side. SoHo, an artists' haven, is west of Little Italy. North of SoHo is Greenwich Village, the famous student and artist district, which has become more polished and expensive in recent years. Andy Warhol and Arthur Miller frequented Chelsea, just north of the Village. East of Chelsea is Gramercy Park, with its 19th-century mansions and brownstones.

The **Lower East Side,** between Houston and Canal streets and Allen and Essex streets, is a Jewish and Latino community with great bargain clothing stores. The best are on **Orchard Street.** For Jewish treats, visit **Yonah Schimmel's Knishery,** *137 E. Houston St.; (212)477-2858,* or **Moishe's Bakery,** *181 E. Houston St.; (212)475-9624.*

Chinatown, surrounding Mott Street, is the largest Chinese community east of San Francisco, with hundreds of Chinese restaurants and stores. The **Chinese Museum,** *8 Mott St.,* explains the history and culture of New York's Chinese community and leads tours through the neighborhood.

SoHo's best galleries are the **Museum of Holography,** *11 Mercer St.,* and **O.K. Harris,** *383 W. Broadway.* The shops along Canal Street, especially **Canal Jean,** have the best and most interesting buys.

Greenwich Village is filled with homes and haunts of American writers and artists. Louisa May Alcott once lived at 132 MacDougal St. Anarchists from the 1920s met at 137 MacDougal St. in the Liberal Club. Eugene O'Neill saw his first plays produced at the Provincetown Playhouse. Edgar Allen Poe lived at 85 W. Third St. Look for Picasso's colossal sculpture *Sylvette* on Bleecker Street.

Washington Square Park is the place to go to see first-class street performances. For a bit of spare change, you can watch comedians, musicians, and other performers do their stuff here. (You'll also see sunbathers, drug pushers, office workers, and lovers.)

If money interests you, visit the **Financial District.** Tour the **Federal Reserve Bank** (The Fed), located between Nassau and William streets, and the **New York Stock Exchange** (for free), where you can see the trading floor from the visitors' gallery. **Federal Hall,** facing the Stock Exchange, is where George Washington took his oath of office.

The symbol of freedom

The recently restored **Statue of Liberty,** on an island off the tip of Manhattan Island, has become a symbol of America at its best—welcoming with open arms immigrants from poor and oppressive nations. The best view of the statue, a gift from France, is from the the **Staten Island Ferry,** which leaves from the ferry dock on South Street. For a trip to the statue itself, take a ferry from **Battery Park.**

The best city park: Central Park

New York's **Central Park** is the best city park in the world—and one of the biggest. Here, New Yorkers escape the pace of their frenetic city. This playground for all ages has a zoo, a carousel, an ice-skating rink, a boating lake, gardens, soccer fields, horseshoe courts, baseball diamonds, tennis courts, jogging paths, basketball courts, wading pools, bird watching, bike rentals, marionette shows, concerts, lawn bowling, horse-and-buggy rides, and refreshment stands. Free Shakespearean plays are performed during the summer. Be careful in the park at night.

The top sights

The **Empire State Building,** *Fifth Avenue, between 33rd and 34th streets,* was for years the tallest building in the world. Designed by Shreve, Lamb, and Harmon, it was built in 1930-1931. From the top of this 102-story building you have a breathtaking view of New York.

Radio City Music Hall, *50th Street and Sixth Avenue,* next to Rockefeller Center, is New York's most extravagant theater. The long-legged, feathered Rockettes and their cancan are the main attractions. The interior is art-deco.

St. Patrick's Cathedral, *51st Street and Fifth Avenue,* is the largest Roman Catholic cathedral in the United States. Built between 1858 and 1879, it was designed by James Renwick. This Gothic Revival church has 12 side chapels and contains the shrine of St. John Neumann (1811-1860), the first American male to be canonized.

The **United Nations,** *between 42nd and 48th streets,* on the East River, is a large complex with a garden and an esplanade. Free tickets to General Assembly meetings are available in the lobby 30 minutes before each 10:30 a.m. and 3 p.m. meeting (weekdays).

Former Beatle John Lennon lived in the **Dakota Apartments,** *Central Park West,* between 72nd and 73rd streets, until his murder there Dec. 8, 1980. This elegant apartment building, home to many celebrities, was built in 1884.

New York's best museums

The **Metropolitan Museum of Art,** *Fifth Avenue and 82nd Street,* houses more than three-million works of art, including the Rockefeller Collection of Primitive Art, European paintings, and Egyptian art. The Met, as it is known, is New York's number-one museum and a must-see.

The **Museum of Modern Art,** *11 W. 53rd St.,* has the best collections of modern art in the world. Permanent shows range from Impressionist to Contemporary. Innovative special exhibits are arranged by MOMA's renowned curator.

The **Cloisters,** in a rebuilt medieval monastery in Ft. Tryon Park in upper west Manhattan, displays Romanesque and Gothic art. Highlights are the Unicorn Tapestries, the Cuxa Cloister, and the Treasury.

The **Guggenheim Museum,** *Fifth Avenue and 89th Street,* a modern spiral building designed by Frank Lloyd Wright, displays the best of contemporary art, including works by Kandinsky, Miro, Calder, and Klee.

The **American Museum of Natural History,** *Central Park West and 79th Street,* houses the fossilized remains of prehistoric animals, as well as reconstructed homes of present and past civilizations. See the show of stars at the planetarium.

The **International Center of Photography,** *1130 Fifth Ave. and 94th Street,* is America's only major museum of photography. The **Jewish Museum,** *Fifth Avenue and 92nd Street,* has a comprehensive collection of Jewish ceremonial art.

The **Museum of the American Indian,** *Broadway and 155th Street,* is the largest Indian museum in the world.

El Museo del Barrio, *1230 Fifth Ave. and 104th Street,* is devoted to Latin American art and culture.

The **Museum of the City of New York,** *103rd Street and Fifth Avenue,* illustrates the city's past.

The **Museum of Broadcasting,** *1 E. 53rd St.,* is one of the least known and most interesting museums in the city, showing old television shows and playing old radio recordings.

The **Whitney Museum,** *945 Madison Ave. and 75th Street,* is a futuristic structure housing modern American art by Hopper, Soyer, de Kooning, Motherwell, and Warhol.

The City's best shopping

Fifth Avenue is lined with some of the world's chicest and most expensive stores. Look at the gigantic gems in Tiffany's windows. Take stock of the latest fashions on show at Bergdorf Goodman and Saks. Or stop in at F.A.O. Schwartz, where you can spend from $20 to $20,000 for a toy. Also look for Cartier, Gucci, Steuben Glass, Godiva Chocolates, and the famous Trump Tower.

Other elegant shopping streets include Madison, Park, and Seventh avenues and 39th, 56th, and 57th streets.

If you prefer bargains over elegance, go to Orchard and Delaney streets. **Annemarie Gardin Inc.,** *498 Seventh Ave.,* where prices are very low, is open Mondays through Fridays only from 9 a.m. to 5 p.m. The **Better Made Coat and Suit Company,** *270 W. 38th St.,* has designer labels for less than designer prices.

The world's best diamond market

The **Diamond Exchange,** *47th Street and Sixth Avenue,* is responsible for more than 80% of the world's wholesale diamond trade. The exchange is dominated by the Orthodox Jewish community.

New York's best food markets

Zabar's, *2245 Broadway; (212)787-2000,* has the greatest variety of delicacies and the biggest crowds, attracting 30,000 customers per week. The coffee is roasted by Saul Zabar himself. Twenty-six kinds of salami, 42 kinds of mustard, and 30 varieties of honey are sold.

Balducci's, *424 Avenue of the Americas; (212)673-2600,* has fresh produce and herbs, pasta, homemade dishes, and candy. Prices are high.

Dean & Deluca, *121 Prince St.; (212)431-1691,* is another deli with an incredible variety, including edible ferns in season. The Italian foods are good.

New York's best beaches

While New York isn't known as a beach town, it does have 20 miles of beaches. The best are **Rockaway Park** (not Far Rockaway, which is seedy) and **Jones Beach;** the worst is **Coney Island,** which has become a slum. Take the A or CC subway train to Rockaway; the Long Island Railroad to Jones. **Brighton Beach** is a Russian enclave called Odessa by the Sea.

How to see a television show live

Free tickets to television shows are offered occasionally at the **New York City Visitors Bureau,** *2 Columbus Circle; (212)397-8200.*

The best entertainment

Midtown, on the west side, is New York at its most entertaining. You'll see everything from Broadway shows to X-rated movies. The **Theater District** stretches from 44th to 54th streets on Broadway. The most beautiful theaters are the **St. James** and the **Shubert,** *44th Street,* the **Booth,** *45th Street,* and the **Majestic,** *44th Street.*

Lincoln Center is the hub of New York's haute couture. More than 13,000 spectators can be accommodated in the center's six buildings: Avery Fisher Hall, the New York State Theater, the Metropolitan Opera House, the Library and Museum of Performing Arts, the Vivian Beaumont Theater, and the Julliard School of Music. The **Metropolitan Opera House** is spectacular, with gigantic Chagall murals, a beautiful central fountain, and glittering chandeliers.

The best on and off Broadway

If you're looking for lights, luster, and glitter, see a show on Broadway. For a more intimate or avant-garde evening, see an off-Broadway show. In either case, you'll be seeing some of the world's best theater.

At **TKTS,** *Duffy Square, 47th Street and Broadway; (212)354-5800,* you can get tickets to shows for half-price—but you have to buy tickets for shows that same day. **Hit Shows,** *630 Ninth Ave; (212)581-4211,* sells "two-fers" for a discount. **QUIKTIX** at **Joseph Papp's Public Theater,** *425 Lafayette St.; (212)598-7100,* sells tickets at half-price at 6 p.m. on the night of a performance (as do many other theaters, on and off Broadway).

Joseph Papp's **New York Shakespeare Festival** performs at the Delacorte Theater in Central Park from June through September. Tickets are given out free at 6:15 p.m. for the 8 p.m. performance. Arrive at 5 p.m. and bring a picnic to ensure a good place in line.

The world's best opera company

The **Metropolitan Opera Company,** *(212)362-6000,* is the largest in the world, with a cast that sometimes includes Joan Sutherland and Luciano Pavarotti. The sets are incomparable. From September through April, the company performs at the Metropolitan Opera House in Lincoln Center. During the summer, free performances are given in city parks.

The best dance and music

The **New York City Ballet,** *(212)870-5570,* is the oldest ballet company in the United States. It presents classics, including the *Nutcracker Suite* at Christmas.

The **American Ballet Theater,** *(212)477-3030,* directed by Mikhail Baryshnikov, engages such stars as Baryshnikov himself.

The **Joffrey Ballet** and the **Alvin Ailey Dance Company** are innovative troupes that perform in the City Center. Joffrey does classic revivals. Ailey concentrates on modern dance. For more information, call *(212)265-7300.*

The **New York City Opera,** *(212)870-5570,* managed by Beverly Sills, presents bold productions, often in English. Foreign-language operas have supertitles.

The **New York Philharmonic,** *(212)580-8700,* is well-respected, performing works from Bach to Bernstein from September through May.

The best jazz joints

New York's best places to hear jazz include: the **Blue Note,** *131 W. Third St.; (212)475-*

8592; **Sweet Basil,** *88 Seventh Ave. S.; (212)242-1785;* **The Village Vanguard,** *178 Seventh Ave. S.; (212)255-4037;* **The Bottom Line,** *15 W. Fourth St. and Mercer Street; (212)228-6300* (all in Greenwich Village); and **West End Café,** *2904 Broadway; (212)666-8750,* near Columbia University.

The best rock'n'roll and folk music

The **Ritz,** *119 E. 11th St.; (212)228-8888,* rocks with the tunes of musicians such as Chuck Berry.

The **Lone Star Café,** *Fifth Avenue and 13th Street; (212)242-1664,* has good country-western music, a surprise in the middle of such a cosmopolitan city.

The **Back Porch,** *488 Third Ave.; (212)685-3828,* has a terrific pianist.

Brazilian music is played at **Sounds of Brazil,** *204 Varick St.; (212)924-5221.*

New York's best restaurant

The **21 Club,** *21 W. 52nd St.; (212)582-7200,* in the heart of Midtown Manhattan, has an elegant dining room for those who wish to keep a low profile. Dr. Armand Hammer and Aristotle Onassis have been patrons.

This establishment began as a speakeasy during Prohibition; Jack Kriendler and Charlie Berns opened the club on New Year's Day in 1930. Away from the scrutiny of federal agents, it became a haven for politicos, actors, and journalists. Tallulah Bankhead once said there wasn't much point in getting up on Sundays, because 21 is closed that day. Dinner for two at 21 is about $100, not including drinks.

Other superb restaurants

The **Quilted Giraffe,** *550 Madison Ave.; (212)593-1221,* serves the innovative creations of Barry and Susan Wine. The beggar's purses are especially good, little crepes filled with *crème fraîche* and caviar. The prix-fixe menu is $75. The restaurant is closed Sundays.

Johnathon Waxman, *154 E. 79th St.; (212)772-6800,* serves American food with flair—the french fries may be the best in the United States. Try the venison in season. The place is expensive.

Four Seasons, *99 E. 52nd St.; (212)754-9494,* is a popular place for lunch. The menu varies with the season, a combination of classic and contemporary cuisines. The wine list is long. Save room for the chocolate-chocolate mahogany cake.

Lutèce, *249 E. 50th St.; (212)752-2225,* is the best French restaurant in New York. Only the finest ingredients are used, and the preparation is imaginative.

Café des Artistes, *1 W. 67th St.; (212)877-3500,* has been a New York institution since the 1930s. Try the potted and roasted duck *confit.* The restaurant is open daily for dinner and Sundays for brunch.

Le Cirque, *58 E. 65th St.; (212)794-9292,* is one of the best French restaurants in Manhattan, an elegant, spacious place with impeccable cuisine. Its *crème brulée* is the best in the United States. Reservations are required. The restaurant is closed Sundays.

Enoteca Iperbole, *137 E. 55th St.; (212)759-9720,* has the largest wine cellar in the United States. Try the pheasant with your wine. The restaurant is closed Sundays.

The best ethnic restaurants

The best Mexican restaurant in New York (and perhaps the United States) is **Rosa Mexicana,** *1063 First Ave.; (212)753-7407.* Try the red snapper in cilantro sauce.

The best restaurant in Chinatown is **Auntie Yuan,** *1191A First Ave.; (212)744-4040,* which has nouvelle Chinese cuisine. The four Taiwanese chefs return to China every year to hone their skills.

Benito's II, *163 Mulberry St.; (212)226-9012,* in Little Italy, is one of the city's best Italian (Sicilian) restaurants. **Elaine's,** *1703 Second Ave.; (212)534-8103,* is also good, especially popular among publishers and writers. Nancy Reagan and friends lunch at **Primavera,** *1578 First Ave.; (212)861-8608.* And **Sandro's,** *420 E. 59th St.; (212)355-5150,* should not be overlooked. Chef Sandro Fioriti goes all out with spices and imagination when preparing his pasta. The fried ricotta with tomato sauce is tasty.

The **Russian Tea Room,** *150 W. 57th St.; (212)265-0947,* near Carnegie Hall, has Russian specialties and a glamorous clientele. Try the blini with caviar, the borscht, and the icy vodka drinks. The restaurant is open daily.

The **Ukrainian Restaurant,** *132 Second Ave.; (212)533-6765,* is humble and cheap—but the food is excellent.

Darbar, *44 W. 56th St.; (212)432-7227,* is the best Indian restaurant in town, an elegant place with white-linen tablecloths and correct service.

New York's best hotels

The best place to stay is the **Carlyle,** *35 E. 76th St.; (212)744-1600,* an old-fashioned, Old World hotel with perfect service. The attention to detail is remarkable.

Morgans, *237 Madison Ave.; (212)686-0300,* is an exclusive hideaway for celebrities, including Margaux Hemingway and Rod Stewart. An enthusiastic young staff (owner Steve Rubell says he hired no New Yorkers) takes care of guests' needs. Andy Warhol paintings adorn some of the rooms. Guests are guaranteed admission to the Palladium.

The **Algonquin,** *59 W. 44th St.; (212)840-6800,* is a first-class, old-fashioned hotel.

The **Helmsley Palace,** *455 Madison Ave.; (212)888-7000,* is a modern skyscraper rising out of a 19th-century mansion. The lobby and dining rooms are elegant old rooms with antiques. Bedrooms are spacious and modern, with fantastic views of New York.

The **Ritz Carlton,** *112 Central Park S.; tel. (212)757-1900,* is a very English, very luxurious modern establishment with views of Central Park and a central location near the main shopping areas. The popular Jockey Club dining room is here.

The **Pierre,** *Fifth Avenue at 61st St.; (212)838-8000,* is a peaceful place, where celebrities stay when they want privacy. The view is of Central Park.

The new **Grand Bay Hotel,** *152 W. 51st St.; (212)765-1900* or *(800)237-0990,* is a bit of old Europe in the middle of Manhattan. Each of the 180 rooms is decorated differently, but all have bathrooms of Italian marble. Hotel services include courtesy limousine service to Wall Street and use of nearby health-club facilities. The concierge is especially helpful.

The best of New York State

Don't spend all your time in the City; **New York State** also is worth seeing. Unspoiled forest and rolling farmland still exist in this fertile state, which is watered by lakes Champlain, George, Erie, and Ontario, as well as the Hudson River. The Adirondack and Catskill mountains offer retreat from the noise and pollution of New York City.

Niagara Falls: the best honeymoon spot

You'll hear **Niagara Falls** long before you see them. This 180-foot waterfall, which pours 40-million gallons of water a minute, is actually made of three great torrents: Canada's **Horseshoe Falls,** the **American Falls,** and **Bridal Veil Falls.** Horseshoe is the most spectacular.

The best way to see Niagara is aboard the *Maid of the Mist*, which departs Prospect Park and the landing on the American side. The half-hour cruise costs about $4. Another good way to see the falls is from the Observation Tower in Prospect Park.

You also can view the cascade from below. Take an elevator 125 feet down to the **Scenic Tunnels,** which lead to a two-level observation deck near Horseshoe Falls. Wear a slicker; it's wet.

Bridges and wooden walkways lead across the base of Bridal Veil Falls, within 25 feet of the river, to the **Cave of the Winds** below Goat Island. The roar of the water and the heavy spray are overwhelming.

Look for accommodations on the Canadian side, 20 minutes north on Niagara Parkway, in the 164-year-old town **Niagara-on-the-Lake.** This lovely retreat is the home of the Shaw Festival. The **Oban,** *tel. (416)468-7811,* is one of the oldest inns; the **Moffat Inn,** *tel. (416)468-4116,* and the **Prince of Wales,** *tel. (416)468-3246,* are pleasant.

The best of the Adirondacks

You can hike in the **Adirondacks** for days without leaving the wilderness. The most beautiful area is between lakes Placid and Saranac, where the forest is untouched and the streams are pure.

Adirondack National Park is the largest wilderness area east of the Mississippi, bordered by lakes George and Champlain. One of the most beautiful sights in the park is the **Ausable Chasm,** on Route 9 near Interstate 87, a mile-long gorge near Lake Champlain.

Ft. Ticonderoga, used during the French and Indian War and the Revolutionary War, guards the junction of lakes Champlain and George. A museum today, it is open from May through October.

Lakes Placid and Saranac, at the heart of the Adirondacks, offer canoeing, boating, and fishing. Lake Placid has tremendous skiing—good enough for the Olympics, in fact, which were held here in 1980.

The best place to stay on Saranac Lake is **The Point,** *Star Route, Saranac Lake; (518)891-5674,* an 11-room inn with a private beach. Originally a camp, The Point is elegant now, decorated with fine paintings. The bedrooms are enormous. You can sail or canoe on the lake, hike or cross-country ski through the woods, or play tennis, golf, badminton, billiards, ping pong, or croquet.

High Peaks Base Camp, 13 miles from Lake Placid, *tel. (518)946-2133,* is situated on 200 acres ringed by the Sentinel Wilderness Range and the Hurricane Mountain Primitive area. It has miles of cross-country ski trails and is just five miles from the downhill ski slopes at Whiteface Mountain. Enjoy a home-cooked meal in the Wood Parlor. The price is unbelievable—$15 for a bunk, $45 for a double room. Weekly rates are $65 to $90.

The Baseball Hall of Fame

Cooperstown, in central New York State, is a small town with a big drawing card—the **Baseball Hall of Fame.** Three floors of baseball memorabilia fill this museum, a mecca for baseball fans. You can see enlarged photographs of the world's best baseball players, sculptures of Babe Ruth and Ted Williams carved from single pieces of laminated basswood, and

1,000 artifacts and photos from the early Negro baseball leagues. Also on display are baseball cards from 1900, Lou Gehrig's uniform, and Joe DiMaggio's locker.

Cooperstown has several good restaurants. The best is the **Dining Room,** *Main Street; (607)547-2211,* where you can indulge in homemade fare and rich desserts.

Our favorite place to stay is **Angelholm,** *14 Elm St.; (607)547-2483,* a restored home built nearly 175 years ago. This bed and breakfast has only four bedrooms, and baths are shared. But full breakfast is included in the price of a room ($55 to $80).

Lake Champlain's bests (and beasts)

Between New York, Vermont, and Quebec lies **Lake Champlain,** where more than 200 sightings of a controversial monster called Champ have been reported. Champ's existence is debatable, but the beauty of the lake and its islands is not.

Lake Champlain's major islands—North Hero, South Hero, and Isle La Motte—are dotted with sugar maple and oak trees, red barns, and silos. Although they look serene, they have had a tumultuous history. The French, British, and Americans have warred over the lake, because of its importance as a natural highway from New York to Canada.

Samuel de Champlain discovered the islands in 1609, claiming them for the French. Later, the British claimed them, and finally the Americans. The turning-point battle of the War of 1812 was fought at Plattsburgh, where nearly 30,000 British troops were defeated by 2,000 Americans.

Isle La Motte is the site of the first settlement in Vermont, **Ft. St. Anne,** which was built by the French in 1666 for defense against the Indians. Today open-air Masses are held here. **Ft. Blunder,** built by the Americans in 1777, was so named because its builders didn't realize it was on Canadian soil.

The best place to stay on the lake is **North Hero House,** *(802)372-8237,* an inn built in 1800. Double rooms are $50 to $90.

The best of New England

One of the oldest and most historic areas of the United States is **New England,** whose quaint, shingled homes and simple churches have a unique charm. Boston harbors intellect, art, ethnic variety, and beauty. Cape Cod has the most beautiful coastline on the Atlantic. And the mountains of northern New England are green and rolling.

The best of Boston

Boston, one of the most livable cities in America, is a collection of interconnected small towns. Despite its folksy atmosphere, it is sophisticated, with a large intellectual community and many universities and colleges. It is also the best place to trace American colonial history. Historic figures, such as Samuel Adams, Paul Revere, and Ben Franklin, lived here. Walk by the **Old North Church,** where lanterns were hung to signal an attack by the British during the Revolutionary War. Or climb **Bunker Hill,** the site of one of the war's major battles. And visit the place where Boston Tea Party participants dumped tea into the harbor.

American writers Ralph Waldo Emerson, Henry David Thoreau, Louisa May Alcott, and Daniel Webster found inspiration in Boston. In more recent years, Boston has spawned the Kennedys. And many of America's best minds have graduated from Harvard University near Boston.

The best way to see Boston

The easiest way to see Boston is to follow the **Freedom Trail**—a red brick or painted line that leads past the city's greatest landmarks. The trail takes you past the **Old State House,** where the Boston Massacre occurred, the **Old North Church,** where the light was hung to signal Paul Revere, the **Old South Meeting House,** where the Boston Tea Party was planned, the **Boston Tea Party Ship and Museum,** and the **Granary Burial Ground,** where the victims of the Boston Massacre are buried.

Boston's must sees

The best view of the city is from **Bunker Hill,** but you'll have to climb 294 steps to enjoy it.

Beacon Hill is an elegant neighborhood with trees, cobblestoned streets, and beautiful old brownstones. Louisa May Alcott once lived at 10 Louisburg Square. Bluebloods now live where Puritans once settled.

The **Black Heritage Trail** passes 16 important landmarks of black history over the past 300 years.

The **State House,** a gold-domed building in Beacon Hill, is open to visitors.

The world's oldest public library

Boston's **Public Library** is the oldest in the world, founded by Benjamin Franklin and decorated with paintings by Sargent.

Boston's best museums

The **Museum of Fine Arts,** near Northeastern University, has Egyptian, Impressionist, and Americana collections.

The **Isabella Stuart Gardner Museum,** *280 Fenway,* is a small Venetian-style palace filled with great works of art, including Titian's *The Rape of Europa,* Raphael's *Pieta,* and paintings by Rembrandt, Sargent, Whistler, and Matisse.

Boston's **Institute of Contemporary Art,** *955 Boylston St.,* in a former fire station, displays works by contemporary artists.

The museum at the **John F. Kennedy Library,** *Morrisey Boulevard,* contains photos and documents about John and Robert Kennedy.

The world's largest fish tank

The **New England Aquarium** on Central Wharf is the world's largest fish tank, containing the world's greatest collection of sharks.

Boston's best parks

Boston is a city of parks. The best is the **Boston Common,** where you'll see inviting green lawns, sunbathers, frisbee players, musicians, and picnicking families. Swans swim in the little ponds.

Boston's **Public Gardens,** between Arlington, Boylston, Beacon, and Charles streets, are just across from the Boston Common.

The **Arnold Arboretum,** a 265-acre park on the Arborway in Jamaica Plain, is one of America's oldest parks, containing 6,000 varieties of trees.

Boston's best laughs

The **Comedy Connection,** backstage at the Charles Playhouse, has uproarious comedians every night. **Catch a Rising Star,** *Harvard Square, Cambridge,* and **Stitches,** *Commonwealth and Boston avenues,* are also good.

The most festive times to visit

Patriot's Day (April 19) is celebrated with the re-enactment of Paul Revere's ride. The hero sets out from the North End and gallops past the Old North Church yelling, "The British are coming. The British are coming." In Concord, Minutemen re-enact the battle of the Old North Bridge. This is also the day of the Boston Marathon.

Boston's best ice cream

Every Boston-area neighborhood has its favorite ice-cream parlor. The best is **Toscanini's,** *899 Main St.,* in Cambridge, a small shop serving 16 homemade flavors, including ginger, grape-nut raisin, Vienna finger cookie, and Belgian chocolate.

A roster of great restaurants

The best seafood restaurant in Boston is **Anthony's Pier 4,** *140 Northern Ave.; (617)423-6363,* which is decorated with pieces of scrimshaw and old navigational equipment. Order the lobster.

The most elegant restaurant in town is **Aujourd'hui,** in the Four Seasons Hotel, *200 Boylston St.; (617)338-4400,* where New England fare is spiced up with European and Asian accents. White linen and Royal Doulton china dress the tables.

The most romantic restaurant is **Café Budapest,** *90 Exeter St.; (617)266-1979,* where exotic flowers decorate the Old World dining rooms and spicy Central European dishes scent the air.

One of the oldest restaurants in Boston is the **Locke-Ober Café,** *3 Winter Place; (617)542-1340,* which opened in 1875. Try the filet of lemon sole *bonne femme.*

Boston's finest hotels

The oldest hotel in America and Boston's best is the **Parker House,** *60 School St.* Dickens, Emerson, and Longfellow all stayed here. The famous Parker House roll was first baked here a century ago. Ho Chi Minh once worked at the Parker House as a busboy.

The **Ritz Carlton,** *15 Arlington St.; (617)536-5700,* is an elegant place with a dignified staff and luxurious rooms. The hotel restaurant offers lovely views of Boston's Public Gardens and exquisite meals.

The **Copley Plaza,** *138 St. James Ave.; (617)267-5300,* is an elegant 460-room hotel opened in 1912. While it is grand, it has an intimate air, with a library where you can take tea. The bedrooms are spacious and richly furnished. The Copley has three restaurants, three bars, and shops.

The best of Cambridge

Across the Charles River from Boston is **Cambridge,** a charming area encompassing Harvard University (the oldest in the nation), the Massachusetts Institute of Technology (MIT), and lots of bookstores and movie houses.

The trendiest shops and restaurants are on **Harvard Square,** where you'll also find street performers, five ice-cream parlors, and seven bars. **Harvard Yard,** part of the campus, is quieter and more dignified.

The **Harvard University Museum,** *24 Oxford St.,* is actually four museums: the Peabody Museum of Archeology and Ethnology, the Museum of Comparative Zoology, the Mineralogical and Geological Museum, and the Botanical Museum. The museum's Ware Collection of glass flowers is the finest array of decorative glasswork in the world.

The **Fogg Art Museum,** *32 Quincy St.,* is the best university art collection, a formidable assortment of Oriental and late 18th-century European art.

One of the largest comic book stores in the United States is the **Million Year Picnic,** *99 Mt. Auburn St.*

The **Grolier Bookstore,** *6 Plympton St.,* is the oldest poetry bookstore in the country.

Two historic towns

Just outside Boston are two towns that played essential roles in American history: Lexington and Concord.

Paul Revere rode through **Lexington** the night of April 18, 1775 warning that British troops were approaching. On Lexington Green, the first shots of the Revolutionary War were fired and the first blood was drawn.

Founding fathers Samuel Adams and John Hancock slept at the **Hancock-Clarke House,** *36 Hancock St.,* today a museum.

Concord is the town next door, where Minutemen gathered to head off the British. The Old North Bridge over the Concord River is the site of the Revolutionary War's first battle. It was made famous by these words: "Here once the embattled farmers stood and fired the shot heard round the world."

Concord produced some of America's most famous writers. Louisa May Alcott lived with her family at the Wayside and wrote *Little Women* at the Orchard House. You can visit the **Ralph Waldo Emerson House,** *28 Cambridge Turnpike.* Nathaniel Hawthorne rented the **Old Manse,** *Monument Street,* but bought Wayside.

The **Concord Museum,** *Lexington Road and Cambridge Turnpike,* displays possessions of Emerson and Thoreau.

Cape Cod: the most beautiful coastline

Cape Cod, a hook-shaped sandy peninsula in southeast Massachusetts, has the most beautiful coastline on the Atlantic: sand dunes covered with sea oats, silvery driftwood, seagulls basking in the sun, huge rocks, and the crashing ocean. The Cape Cod National Seashore protects 44,600 acres of the cape from development.

The liveliest town

Provincetown, at the northern tip, is the cape's hot spot, a maze of clapboard houses, some dating back to the 18th century, galleries, guesthouses, and shops. Popular and busy, it draws artists, gays, and families. The town lies within the Cape Cod National Seashore and is surrounded by dunes, ocean beaches, marshes, and woods.

Commercial Street, the main thoroughfare, is lined with art galleries, shops, and crowds of pedestrians, bikers, cars, horse-drawn buggies, hawkers, and skate boarders. Here, also, is the **Provincetown Playhouse,** where playwright Eugene O'Neill spent a lot of time.

Provincetown has a long history. Although Plymouth claims to be the oldest colony, the pilgrims actually landed at Provincetown first, before heading on to Plymouth, where they settled. A monument to these hardy souls sits atop a 100-foot hill at the heart of town. The 252-foot granite column can be climbed via 116 steps. From the top you can see for 50 miles on clear days.

Provincetown boasts one of the few British-style links (sand) golf courses in the United States, the **Highland Golf Club,** *Highland Road, Truro; (617)487-9201.* You can play for $8 to $12.

For dancing, go to **Captain John's,** *Shankpainter Road.* More novel entertainment can be found at the **Surf Club,** *MacMillan Wharf,* where you can marvel at the Provincetown Jug and Marching Band—four musicians who play 20 instruments, including washboards, jugs, and kazoos.

The **Moors,** *Bradford Street; (617)487-0840,* has good Portuguese dishes and fresh seafood.

Our favorite inn is **Bradford Gardens,** *178 Bradford St.; (617)487-1616,* built in 1820, one block from the beach. The two-story main house and the four additional cottages are decorated with fireplaces and old-fashioned furnishings. Double rooms are $89 to $150 in high season, including breakfast.

New England's oldest settlement

Plymouth, where the *Mayflower* landed in December 1620, is the oldest European settlement in New England. Half the colony died the first terrible winter here. **Plymouth Rock,** the landmark boulder marking the spot where the pilgrims disembarked, is kept behind bars at **Pilgrim Hall,** *Water Street.* The Plymouth of 1627 and the Wampanoag Indian summer campsite have been recreated here in a Williamsburg-style complex called **Plymouth Plantation,** where actors play the parts of the pilgrims and Indians. Explore the *Mayflower II,* a reproduction of the original.

The **Sleepy Pilgrim,** *182 Court St.; (617)746-1962,* is a pleasant 12-unit motel with double rooms for $57.

The best whale watching

Whale-watching cruises depart Plymouth and Provincetown for the Stellwagen Bank north of Cape Cod, one of the few areas in the United States where great whales can be seen on a regular basis. Each year thousands of these beautiful giants take up residence on the 20-mile-long shoal. Fifteen kinds of whales have been seen in these waters, as well as dolphins, porpoises, and rare birds. Marine biologists accompany the cruises to identify and describe the fish and birds and explain their behavior. The price is about $16 for adults, $12 for children.

Groups offering cruises from Plymouth include **Captain John Boats,** *(617)746-2643;* **Web of Life Science Center,** a nonprofit marine research and education center (whale-watching money goes to support whale research), *(617)866-5353;* and **Captain Tim Brady & Sons,** *(617)746-4809.* Whale-watching cruises from Provincetown include **Portuguese Princess,** *(617)487-2651;* and **Provincetown Whale Watch,** *(617)487-3322.*

Provincetown Inn, at the tip of Provincetown, *(800)343-4444,* offers a whale-watching package that includes a cruise, two dinners, two breakfasts, and two nights lodging for $155 per person, double occupancy in high season, $85 in low season.

The most beautiful island

Martha's Vineyard Island, off the coast of Cape Cod, is the most beautiful on the

Atlantic Coast, protected by bluffs and dunes. Rocky and sandy beaches edge the island. Inland are pine forests and peaceful lakes and ponds, where you can canoe among rare seabirds. At the far end of the island are the brightly colored cliffs of Gay Head and a small Indian reservation. Shingled Cape Cod houses nestle among the island's rolling hills, and bayberry scents the air.

You can catch a ferry to Martha's Vineyard from the Cape Cod town of **Woods Hole.** If you plan to bring a car, make reservations well in advance; you'll have to wait in line for hours if you don't.

Edgartown is the most elegant town on the island, its narrow streets lined with expensive shops and guesthouses.

Oak Bluffs is a honky-tonk town, less stuffy than most of the towns on the island. Gingerbread houses make this slightly seedy town look quaint. The largest carousel in the world, the Flying Horses, is here.

Gay Head is the most beautiful spot on Martha's Vineyard. It is also home to the remaining Indians on the island, who live on a reservation nearby. An Indian-operated lunch counter at the top of the cliffs serves the best milkshakes anywhere. The view from the patio is the best on the island.

Seafood is fresh and plentiful on Martha's Vineyard. For lobster, go to the **Homeport** restaurant, *Menemsha; (617)645-2679,* where dinner is about $23, including appetizer and dessert. Bring your own wine. Reservations are advised.

If you're feeling more adventurous, buy your own fresh lobster and a steamer in Menemsha, a small fishing village, and prepare your own feast.

Edgartown is home to the island's two most elegant restaurants: L'Etoile and Warriners. The seafood at **Warriners,** *Post Office Square; (617) 627-4488,* is good, and the wine list is extensive. But it's a bit stuffy. **L'Etoile,** *Charlotte Inn, 27 S. Summer St.; (617)627-5187,* is pretty, and the service is superb.

Our favorite inn is the **Kelly House,** *South Water Street,* in Edgartown. A cozy place decorated in the style of the 1890s, it is open year-round. The dining room is good and inexpensive; dinner for two is about $20.

The **Captain Dexter House,** *100 Main St., Vineyard Haven; (617)693-6564,* is a good inn with reasonable prices (double rooms are $95 to $140 during the summer, including Continental breakfast). This old sea captain's home was built in 1843 and is filled with antiques.

Nantucket—the most exclusive

Nantucket is a lovely island east of Martha's Vineyard. This wealthy resort has long, sandy beaches and quaint, cobblestoned streets. If you love to shop, you'll love Nantucket. Look for Nantucket woven baskets and scrimshaw jewelry (carved from whale teeth). **Seven Seas Gifts** is a good gift shop with an enormous variety.

The best way to see Nantucket is by bike. Pedal out to **Seaskonset Beach** (pronounced Skonset) and check out the island's many old lighthouses.

Nantucket was the greatest whaling town in the United States during the 18th and 19th centuries. Visit the **Nantucket Whaling Museum** and **Hadwen House** and **Peter Foulger House,** old whaling homes that are open to the public.

The island's best restaurant is the **Jared Coffin House,** *Broad Street, (617)228-2400,* which is internationally acclaimed.

Two pleasant old inns are the **Carriage House,** *5 Ray's Court; (617)228-0326,* in a converted 1865 carriage house; and the **Ships Inn,** *13 Fair St.; (617)228-0040,* in a sea captain's house built in 1812. Both have antique furnishings. Double rooms at the Ships Inn are from $95 to $100 in high season, including Continental breakfast; rooms at the Carriage House are slightly more expensive.

New Hampshire's bests

The highest peak on the East Cost is **Mt. Washington** in the White Mountains of New Hampshire. Located in the **White Mountain National Forest,** this 6,288-foot mountain is a popular ski resort. Take the train to the top. **Crawford Notch State Park,** nearby, has sparkling waterfalls. Take Route 3 to the flume at the southern end of Franconia Notch. This glacier-covered chasm has 70-foot walls. A rock formation called The Old Man of the Mountains looks over Profile Lake.

Mt. Washington Hotel and Resort, *Bretton Woods; (603)278-1000,* is the most peaceful of the Shite Mountain resorts. Excellent stables, a championship golf course, fishing, skiing, and tennis are offered. Rooms are $85 to $150 per person, depending on the season.

Maine's main sights

The best thing about **Portland** is the area surrounding it. Casco Bay, the Casco Bay Islands, and Sebago Lake are typical New England areas, with quaint houses and good boating and swimming. Portland also has great lobster, good night life, and the poet Longfellow's house. **Cap'n Newick's Lobster,** *740 Broadway St., South Portland; (207)799-3090,* is the best place in town for lobster (although the decor isn't much).

Bar Harbor

Bar Harbor, once a mecca for the wealthy, welcomes a broader spectrum of visitors today. The quaint harbor town shares **Mt. Desert Island** (so named by Champlain in 1604 because of its rocky summit) with **Acadia National Park,** an expanse of mountains, spruce forests, rugged coastline, and deep lakes. Along the shore is Somes Sound, the deepest fjord on the East Coast. The air is pure and the drinking water is the best we have ever tasted. The local restaurants serve fresh lobster for next to nothing.

Acadia National Park is surrounded by a 10-mile park road loop. Along the road is **Thunder Hole,** where waves rush into a rocky canyon producing a thundering boom and sending up towers of foam; **Jordan Pond,** an idyllic, mirror-like pond reflecting the Bubbles, two rounded mountains; **Jackson Memorial Library,** the world's largest center for mammalian genetic research; and **Sand Beach,** the island's only sandy swimming area.

It's worth rolling out of bed early to see the sun rise from the summit of **Cadillac Mountain,** a windswept bald spot, the highest on the island, with views of forests, ocean, and neighboring islands. If you do get here at dawn, you are the first person in the United States to see the sun rise.

The best place to dine on the island is the **Jordan Pond House,** *Park Loop Road, Acadia National Park; (207)276-3316,* a rambling old house. You can dine on the lawn when it's warm or by the fireplace when it's not.

A good place to stay is the **Bluenose,** *90 Eden St., Bar Harbor; (800)531-5523* or *(800)445-4077,* set on a cliff just outside town. Rooms have French doors that open onto private balconies overlooking Frenchman's Bay. The pool is heated, a real asset in chilly Maine.

Rhode Island's bests

Newport, Rhode Island has New England's finest mansions (which belong to families such as the Astors and the Vanderbilts), as well as the region's top music festival and sailing events (before the America's Cup was won by Australia, the regatta began here, at the mouth of the Narragansett Bay).

For two weeks every July, Newport hosts a music festival with concerts featuring premier and recently discovered works and thematic programs, such as "Emperor's Court," works composed in Austria-Hungary during the reign of Franz Josef. The spectacular mansions of Newport are converted to concert halls for this 19-year-old event. The long list of debuts by major talents at this festival is indicative of its quality. You can get tickets through the **Music Box,** *(401)849-6666.*

The best restaurant in town is the **White Horse Tavern,** *Marlborough and Farewell streets; (401)849-3600,* America's oldest tavern. Built in 1673, it later became a tavern run by a notorious Red Sea pirate. It is open daily.

A good place to stay the night is **Mill Street Inn,** *75 Mill St.; (401)849-9500,* where double rooms are $135 to $165 during the summer, including Continental breakfast.

Classic New England in Vermont

Rural **Vermont** offers the rolling Green Mountains, lovely Lake Champlain, covered bridges, bridle trails, farmland, and little villages.

Stowe, in northern Vermont, is the state's biggest vacation center. It is best visited during its Winter Carnival in mid-January, which includes ice sculpture and winter sport competitions. **Mt. Mansfield** provides downhill and cross-country skiing and hiking on its Long Trail.

The quintessential New England town is **Newfane,** Vermont. North of Brattleboro, this town is gorgeous in the fall, when autumn leaves splatter it with color and the air smells of apples. The white clapboard houses have dark shutters. During the winter, neighbors gather around the potbelly in Union Hall.

The **Old Newfane Inn** (1787) dates back to when Vermont was a republic. **Union Hall,** built in 1832, was once a house of worship. The **Newfane Store** sells homemade cider and fudge. The famous **Marlboro Music Festival** is held nearby each summer, on the campus of Marlboro College.

Double rooms at the **Old Newfane Inn,** *Court Street; (802)365-4427,* on the green, cost $75 to $115.

One of Vermont's best resorts is **Stratton Mountain Resort,** *(802)297-2200,* in the Green Mountains. Lessons are given in downhill and cross-country skiing, golf, tennis, and fishing. Two nights here cost $130 per person (there's a two-night minimum).

New Jersey: the most maligned state

New Jersey is the most maligned state in the Union, probably because most people know only the long and ugly turnpike. Despite odorous industrial cities, such as Newark and Elizabeth, New Jersey does deserve to be called The Garden State. A patchwork quilt of farm communities and historical parks, New Jersey offers the top per-acre value for agricultural production.

The state's beaches are natural, white, and extend the entire length of the coast. At the heart of New Jersey are the **Pine Barrens,** an unspoiled wooded area. Northern New Jersey has pretty lakes, and in the northwest are mountains leading into the Poconos. Along the Delaware border are historic towns with legends that date back to the Revolutionary War.

More than 100 clashes occurred on New Jersey soil during the Revolutionary War, including pivotal battles in Trenton, Princeton, and Monmouth.

Princeton: New Jersey's prettiest town

Princeton, a beautiful, historic town founded in the 17th century, is the site of an Ivy League university, stately private mansions, and an intimate downtown area. In addition to **Princeton University,** Princeton is the home of the Institute of Advanced Study founded by Einstein, the Princeton Theological Seminary, and Westminster Choir College, famous for its choir.

Built around Princeton University, a center of thought since 1756, the town has been embellished by such wealthy benefactors as Andrew Carnegie (who funded the building of a lake used as a training area for the Princeton Crew and as an ice-skating rink in winter). Another benefactor refurbished the central downtown square (called **Palmer Square**) in Tudor motif, complete with an old-fashioned inn. Palmer Square is especially lovely at Christmas, when the giant pine at its center is decorated. Princetonians gather around the tree to sing carols.

Nassau Hall at the university was the seat of the Continental Congress from June to November 1783.

Buy a gourmet picnic lunch from **Squire's Choice,** *Palmer Square,* and enjoy it on **Princeton Battlefield,** where George Washington's army won a victory against the British on Jan. 3, 1777, or in **Marquand Park,** which has more variety than most botanical gardens. Late in the summer, community theater groups stage plays on the battlefield beside the four marble columns left standing from a home burned down during the Revolutionary War. The cool pines protect the audience from the summer sun.

The **Annex Restaurant,** *Nassau Street,* is an Italian restaurant,where you can get a relatively inexpensive but delicious meal. After 10 p.m., you can mingle with professors and students at the bar.

The **Nassau Inn,** at the center of town, has several dining rooms, including the **Yankee Doodle Tap Room,** which has live music. Initials carved in the inn's tabletops date back to 1919.

The best of the Jersey shore

One-hundred miles of boardwalk and beaches trim the New Jersey coast, offering both honky-tonk towns and quiet enclaves.

Atlantic City: a gambler's best

Almost every American knows the streets of **Atlantic City,** a honky-tonk town famous for its gambling, by heart—they are on the *Monopoly* game board. Before the Civil War, Atlantic City was the seaside getaway for the high society of New York and Philadelphia. The town fell on hard times during the mid-20th century. However, in 1978, Resorts International opened the first casino here, and since then the town has revived. A dozen casinos have opened along the Boardwalk and on the bay.

The former Million Dollar Pier has been reborn as **Ocean One,** a shopping and dining arcade. Like visitors of 100 years ago, you can ride a canopied wicker chair on wheels from one end of the Boardwalk to the other, stopping to see saltwater taffy being pulled.

The best restaurant in town is the **Knife and Fork,** near Bally's Grand. Service is fabulous; customers are treated like royalty. The seafood dishes are excellent, especially the bouillabaisse, which is chock-full of fish and large pieces of lobster.

Cape May: a Victorian surprise

At the southern tip of the Jersey shore is a Victorian surprise: **Cape May.** Victorian mansions with wide porches, gables, and elaborate woodwork line the streets. Many are guesthouses. The wide sandy beach is inviting.

The **Barnard-Good House,** *238 Perry St.; (609)884-5381,* is a Victorian house with a wraparound porch decorated with lacy wood trim. The parlor has an antique pump organ and a hand-carved and tiled false fireplace. An iron, pewter, and brass gasolier hangs above the dining room table. The breakfast served here is delicious—fresh juice, omelets, croissants, homemade breads, and crepes. Each of the six bedrooms is decorated differently; some have four-poster beds, others have bathrooms with antique tubs.

The **Summer Cottage Inn,** *613 Columbia Ave.; (609)884-4948,* was built in 1867 as a summer home. Verandas and tall ceilings keep the house cool. This Victorian bed and breakfast is decorated with walnut- and oak-inlaid floors and period wallpaper. Afternoon tea is served in the sitting room, where wicker furnishings are placed around the fireplace. Three of the bedrooms have private baths.

A best for Bruce fans

Bruce Springsteen fans should visit the **Stone Pony,** in Asbury Park, where he and Southside Johnny got their start. Rock'n'roll stars still come through here now and then. The Stone Pony's marquis includes up-and-coming regional bands that you might see on the charts some day.

New Jersey's best inn

The **Woolverton Inn,** *Woolverton Road, Stockton; (609)397-0802,* is on the New Jersey/ Pennsylvania line at the Delaware River. Shaded by two spacious front porches and big old trees, this stone manor house was built in 1793 by John Prall, who ran a quarry in what is now the garden. In 1957, Sir John Terrell, the owner of the popular Music Circus, bought the property, and many of the celebrities performing in the Music Circus have stayed here. Every room is filled with antiques. Some bedrooms have canopied beds, others have four-poster beds.

Philadelphia: a historian's best

Philadelphia is the most historically important city in the United States. Founded in 1681 by William Penn as a Quaker colony, Philadelphia is where Thomas Jefferson wrote the Declaration of Independence, signed at Independence Hall, and where the Bill of Rights was adopted at Congress Hall. The Continental Congress met in Philadelphia, which was the national capital from 1777 to 1800.

All the city's major historic sights are in **Independence National Historic Park:** Independence Hall; the Liberty Bell; Carpenter's Hall, where the First Continental Congress met in 1774; City Tavern, a reconstruction of the tavern where delegates of the Continental Congress gathered; Congress Hall; Graff House, where Thomas Jefferson lived; Old City Hall; and the Betsy Ross House.

Bordering the one-mile-square park is **Society Hill,** Philadelphia's oldest neighborhood, which has been completely restored. Society Hill was named for the Free Society of Stock Traders, a company created by William Penn. However, most people presume it was named for the somewhat snooty residents.

The most important sights

The Declaration of Independence and the Constitution were signed at **Independence Hall,** *Chestnut Street.* Half-hour tours are offered. Across the street is the **Liberty Bell Pavillion,** where you can touch the cracked bell that rang out in July 1776 to proclaim the Declaration of Independence (the bell cracked in 1835 and again in 1846).

The **Betsy Ross House,** *Arch Street between Second and Third streets,* is where musket balls were made for the Continental Army and flags were made for the Pennsylvania Navy. In the house are Betsy Ross' spectacles, snuffbox, and Bible.

The **National Portrait Gallery,** *420 Chestnut St.,* houses paintings of great American figures, many painted by artist Charles William Peale.

Penn's Landing is the largest freshwater port in the world. You can visit several ships here, including the *Gazela Primeiro,* a Portuguese square-rigger built in 1883; the *Moshulu,* the largest all-steel sailing ship afloat; and the *SS Olympia,* Admiral Dewey's flagship for the battle of Manila Bay during the Spanish American War.

The **Edgar Allan Poe House,** *532 N. Seventh St.,* is where Poe wrote *The Raven, The Tell-Tale Heart,* and *The Murders in the Rue Morgue.*

Germantown: the most historic neighborhood

Philadelphia's most historic neighborhood is **Germantown.** In 1688 its residents made the first formal protest against slavery in this country. The British quartered their troops here during the Revolutionary War. In the 18th century, Philadelphian society built mansions in the area. The most elegant is **Cliveden,** *6401 Germantown Ave.,* built in 1763 for Benjamin Chew, a friend of the Penns. The **Wyck Mansion,** *6026 Germantown Ave.,* and the **Stenton Mansion,** *Windrim Avenue and 18th Street* (which served as Washington headquarters for a time), are also beautiful.

The city's best museums

The **Philadelphia Museum of Art,** *26th Street and Benjamin Franklin Parkway,* houses one of the best art collections in the United States. Especially good are the John G. Johnson Collection of European old masters and the paintings by Eakins. The building is a 1928 reproduction of the Parthenon. See Ruben's *Prometheus Bound,* Van Eyck's *St. Francis Receiving the Stigmata,* and Brueghel's *Village Wedding.*

The **Barnes Foundation Museum,** *300 N. Latches Lane, Merion; (215)667-0290,* displays a superb collection of Impressionist paintings, including works by Renoir, Cézanne, and Matisse. You must have a reservation to visit this museum, which is open Fridays and Saturdays from 9:30 a.m. to 4:30 p.m. and Sundays from 1 p.m. to 4:30 p.m. It is closed in July and August. Children under 12 are not admitted.

The Rare Book Department of the **Philadelphia Library,** *Logan Square,* is a treasure trove of letters, manuscripts, and original prints, including letters by Dickens, folios by Shakespeare, and Edgar Allan Poe manuscripts.

The **Franklin Institute,** *20th Street and Benjamin Franklin Parkway,* is a hands-on science museum founded in 1824, where you can walk through a giant human heart, check out a steam engine, or watch a giant clock that works by gravity. This is the best museum for children in the entire country.

The **Norman Rockwell Museum,** *601 Walnut St.,* in the Curtis Building, houses more than 600 reproductions of the painter's works and 324 of his *Saturday Evening Post* covers.

The **Pennsylvania Academy of Fine Arts,** *Broad and Cherry streets,* contains famous American paintings, including Benjamin West's *Penn's Treaty with the Indians* and Winslow Homer's *Fox Hunt.*

The **Rodin Museum,** *22nd Street and Benjamin Franklin Parkway,* has the most complete Rodin collection outside Paris.

The **Rosenbach Museum,** *2010 Delancey Place,* has the Rosenbach family collection of rare books, antiques, paintings, and drawings. The original manuscript of James Joyce's *Ulysses,* first editions of *Don Quixote,* a rough draft of *Lord Jim,* and Keats' famous love letters to Fanny Brawne are kept here.

Three tip-top restaurants

Le Bec-Fin, *1523 Walnut St.; (215)567-1000,* is an elegant restaurant with only 14 tables. The prix-fixe menu includes six courses and changes with the season. Seatings are at 6 p.m. and 9 p.m. The restaurant is closed Sundays.

The **Garden,** *1617 Spruce St.; (215)546-4455,* as its name implies, has a lovely garden for dining outdoors. It also has five inviting dining rooms. Try the roast chicken flambé. The restaurant is closed Saturdays and Sundays in July and August.

Old Original Bookbinders, *125 Walnut St.; (215)925-7027,* is the place for seafood. This Philadelphia fixture was founded at the end of the Civil War by Samuel Bookbinder and has always been popular. Nearly every president since Lincoln has eaten here.

Philadelphia's best hotels

The crème de la crème of Philadelphia hotels is the **Four Seasons,** *One Logan Square; (215)963-1500,* an elegant institution with 24-hour room service, a health spa, an indoor pool, complimentary shoeshines, valet parking, a restaurant, and a lounge. Double rooms are $120 to $235; suites are $450 to $1,200.

The **Sheraton Society Hill,** *One Dock St.; (215)238-6000,* is centrally located in Society Hill, near the historic sights. Facilities include an indoor pool, a health spa, a restaurant, an entertainment lounge, and 24-hour room service. Double rooms are $165 to $195.

The best of Washington, D.C.

Washington, D.C. has more open space than any capital city in the world. At its heart is the **Mall,** a two-mile expanse of lawn stretching from the Capitol to the Lincoln Memorial and from the George Washington Monument to the Jefferson Memorial. The city's main roads are wide as well, giving a sense of that valued American commodity—elbow room.

Capital sights

The **Capitol,** a domed white building topped by a statue of an Indian symbolizing freedom, is Washington's bulls-eye. The main avenues begin here and head out toward the suburbs like spokes on a bicycle wheel. The building is open to the public; you can sit in on congressional hearings. Free tours are offered every 10 minutes to the congressional visitors' galleries of the Senate and the House of Representatives.

From the visitors' gallery of the **Supreme Court Building,** behind the Capitol, you can watch as the laws of the United States are shaped. Sixteen marble columns line the front of this classic Greek-style structure. Six-ton bronze doors guard the main entrance, which is flanked by two huge statues: *The Contemplation of Justice* and *The Guardian, or Authority, of Law.* The court is in session from October through April.

The **White House** is the nation's number-one residence. The best way to see the president's house is to have your congressman arrange a tour. If that's not possible, regular tours are conducted in the morning. Be prepared for a long wait. You'll see the public rooms, not the rooms where the first family actually lives. For more information, call *(202)456-2200.*

The **Library of Congress,** *First and East Capitol streets,* is one of the world's most comprehensive libraries, with 83-million books, magazines, maps, photos, and films. It is made up of one main building and two annexes and grows at a rate of 7,000 items per day. The original Library of Congress building opened in 1897, a grand Italian Renaissance structure with a dome, columns, murals, and carved balustrades. Three Gutenberg Bibles, a collection of Stradivarius violins, and rare books and prints are kept here. All adults can use the facilities for research, but you cannot take books out. A librarian can explain how to find materials.

The **Folger Shakespeare Library and Theater,** *201 E. Capitol St.,* has one of the world's best collections of Shakespearean books and manuscripts. Its theater is a replica of the Globe Theater in London.

Ford's Theater, *511 10th St. N.W.,* where Lincoln was assassinated, is still in use. Plays are presented from October through May.

The Smithsonian: America's treasure-house

The stated purpose of the **Smithsonian Institution,** founded by Congress in 1846, is "the increase and diffusion of knowledge among men." In its quest to fulfill this goal, the institution has expanded many times and now comprises 15 museums, galleries, a theater, and a zoo.

The most fascinating of the Smithsonian museums is the **National Air and Space Museum,** *Independence Avenue between Fourth and Seventh streets.* It houses the Wright brothers' *Kitty Hawk,* Lindbergh's *Spirit of St. Louis,* and spacecraft. Don't miss the three-dimensional movies on flight.

The **Hirschorn Museum,** *Seventh Street and Independence Avenue N.W.,* contains the most comprehensive collection of modern sculptures in the world. The circular building has ramps that lead upward in a spiral past works of art. Outside the Hirschorn, on the Mall, is the museum's sculpture garden, which contains works by Rodin.

The **Freer Gallery of Art,** *12th Street and Jefferson Drive S.W.,* displays Far Eastern art and artifacts and a splendid collection of works by James Whistler. The president's inaugural reception is held in the garden.

The **National Gallery of Art,** *Sixth Street and Constitution Avenue N.W.,* hosts first-rate art shows. The East Wing, opened in 1978, is an architectural feat, a triangular shape that comes to a perfect point. The West Wing houses one of the world's greatest collections of 19th-century European paintings.

The **National Museum of Natural History,** *10th Street and Constitution Avenue,* has dinosaur skeletons and the Hope Diamond.

The **National Museum of African Art,** *950 Independence Ave.,* has one of the best collections of African art in the world, as well as an extensive collection of photos and films about Africa.

The **National Museum of American History,** *10th Street and Constitution Avenue,* displays the earliest American bicycles, the ruby slippers worn by Dorothy in *The Wizard of Oz,* a 240-pound brass pendulum, tapes of the Watergate hearings, tapes of old *Superman* television shows, recordings of radio shows from the 1940s, and reproductions of log cabins.

The nation's greatest monuments

The **Washington Monument** is the tallest and can be seen from most places in the capital. To enjoy the view from the top, you'll have to wait in a seemingly endless line.

The **Lincoln Memorial** is the most impressive of the monuments. This imposing statue of Honest Abe looks over the reflecting pool. The words of the Gettysburg Address are engraved in the marble walls around him. It is most beautiful at night, when spotlights bring out Lincoln's craggy features.

The **Jefferson Memorial** is the most beautiful, a white marble structure softened by a dome and reflected in the Tidal Basin. It is loveliest in the spring when the cherry trees surrounding it are in bloom.

The **Kennedy Center for the Performing Arts** commemorates President Kennedy. Tour the building and its many theaters even if you don't see a show.

The most moving monument is the **Vietnam War Memorial,** a long black marble wall sunk into the earth, on which the names of every American soldier killed in Vietnam are inscribed. War veterans from around the country make pilgrimages to the site.

The grandest cemetery

Arlington National Cemetery is the final resting place of thousands of soldiers and famous Americans. The tomb of the Unknown Soldier and the graves of John and Robert Kennedy, Pierre L'Enfant (the architect who designed the city), and Chief Justice Oliver Wendell Holmes are also here. The cemetery is located across Memorial Bridge.

Mt. Vernon: the most beautiful home

George Washington's home, **Mt. Vernon,** is located in a beautiful spot along the Potomac, in Virginia. The pillared colonial mansion house of the tobacco plantation has a gorgeous view of the river. See the slave cemetery, a sad reminder of the days when some Americans were not free. To get to the house, drive south from Alexandria.

The most beautiful parks and gardens

Dumbarton Oaks Museum and Garden, *1703 32nd St. N.W.,* has the district's most beautiful gardens. The museum has a choice collection of Roman and Byzantine art and a display of Columbian jewelry. The French and Italian gardens become more informal as they descend the hill toward woods.

The **National Zoological Park,** *the 3000 block of Connecticut Avenue N.W.,* is one of the largest zoos in the country. And it's free. The giant pandas were a gift from China. In warm weather, the monkeys play outside on jungle gyms.

Joggers, bikers, hikers, and horseback riders get away from the city in **Rock Creek Park.** If you follow the wooded trails, you will find yourself alone in the forest. It's hard to believe you're in the middle of the city.

The **Chesapeake and Ohio Canal National Historic Park** provides 185 miles of biking and hiking trails along the Potomac River.

The capital's finest fare

Jean-Louis, at the Watergate Hotel, *2650 Virginia Ave.; (202)298-4488,* is the most elegant restaurant in Washington, a favorite of President Reagan. Chef Jean-Louis Palladin prepares prix-fixe meals with an endless array of courses. As you might expect, it's expensive.

The **Palm,** *1225 19th St. N.W.; tel. (202)293-9091,* is an elegant restaurant, the best in town for steak.

Dominique's, *1900 Pennsylvania Ave. N.W.; tel. (202)452-1126,* serves exotic and tasty game dishes.

Washington's best ethnic food

Au Pied du Cochon, *1335 Wisconsin Ave. N.W.,* is a good, inexpensive French bistro.

Le Gaulois, *Pennsylvania Avenue,* near George Washington University, is a popular French restaurant. Make reservations, or you'll wait in line forever.

Thai Taste, *Connecticut Avenue and Calvert Street,* is a good Thai restaurant with reasonable prices. Expect to wait in line if you come here on a weekend.

Café de Artistas, *3063 M St. N.W.,* is a great Cuban restaurant with jazz and flamenco music.

Iron Gate Inn, *1734 N St. N.W.,* has terrific Mideastern food. The outdoor courtyard is charming.

Nanking, *901 New York Ave. N.W.,* is the city's best and least expensive Chinese restaurant.

Washington's most elegant hotels

The **Sheraton Grand,** *525 New Jersey Ave. N.W.; (800)325-3535,* on Capitol Hill, has a breathtaking lobby (decorated with a four-story atrium and a three-story waterfall) and a 100-foot-long hall with marble floors and walls. The Signature Room restaurant has protected alcoves where diners' privacy is preserved.

The **Four Seasons,** *2800 Pennsylvania Ave. N.W.,* in Georgetown, is the oldest and, until recently, the most elegant hotel in Washington.

The **Vista International Hotel,** *1400 M St. N.W.; (202)429-1700,* is built around a 14-story atrium. This hotel's facade is a 130-foot high window. The six floors of suites were decorated by Givenchy himself.

The **Washington Plaza Hotel,** *Massachusetts and Vermont avenues; (800)424-1140,* is five blocks from the White House and five blocks from the Convention Center. Oriental art decorates the lobby of this nine-story building, which has one of the nicest swimming pools in Washington.

The **Mayflower Hotel,** *1127 Connecticut Ave. N.W.; (800)468-3571,* was one of the greatest hotels in the world when it opened in 1925. John F. Kennedy, Lyndon B. Johnson, and Harry S. Truman stayed here.

The **Capitol Hilton,** *16th and K streets N.W.; (202)393-1000,* was renovated recently but still has its old marble walls. **Trader Vic's,** a well-known restaurant in the building, serves seafood and fancy alcoholic drinks.

Hay-Adams, *H and 16th streets; (800)424-5054,* facing the White House, is the best situated hotel in Washington. The lobby has rich walnut paneling and two 17th-century tapestries.

The **Omni Shoreham,** *Calvert Street and Connecticut Avenue N.W.; tel. (800)228-2121,* is surrounded by 11 acres of parks and woods. Built in 1930, the hotel's 770 rooms have been renovated.

The **Watergate Hotel,** *2650 Virginia Ave. N.W.; tel. (800)424-2736,* was the scene of the famous Watergate burglaries during the Nixon years. Museum-quality Oriental art and top-class restaurants draw visitors.

The best night life

Blues Alley, *1069 Wisconsin Ave. N.W.; (202)337-4141,* in Georgetown, is a great place to see big-name acts. Because the room is so small, you can get close to the stage.

One Step Down, *2517 Pennsylvania Ave. N.W.; (202)331-8863,* has good jazz musicians on weekends.

The **Bayou,** *K Street; (202)333-2897,* in Georgetown, has live local and national bands.

Cities, *18th Street,* in Adams Morgan, is a restaurant with a really hot disco upstairs, where everyone is dressed to the hilt. The restaurant is fun. The decor, which always has a city theme, changes monthly; one month it will look like Nairobi, the next month like Paris.

If you prefer a quieter evening, see a Shakespeare play at the **Folger,** *201 E. Capitol St. S.E.; (202)546-4000.* Or take in a show at the **Kennedy Center,** *2700 F St. N.W.;* the **National Theater,** *1321 E St. N.W.; (202)628-3398;* or **Arena Stage,** *Sixth Street and Maine Avenue S.W.; (202)448-3300.*

The best of Dixie

The **South** offers a traditional yet laid-back lifestyle all its own. Southern hospitality is alive and well below the Mason Dixon Line.

Williamsburg: America's best colonial town

Williamsburg, Virginia is a completely reconstructed colonial town. Originally, Williamsburg was an outpost of Jamestown, the first permanent English settlement. By the late 1600s, it was the capital of Virginia. However, when the capital was moved to Richmond during the Revolutionary War, Williamsburg was forgotten. In 1926, John D. Rockefeller had the town restored. Today, costumed actors act out the roles of Williamsburg's early settlers.

William and Mary, the second oldest college in the country, is located in Williamsburg. The Sir Christopher Wren Building is the oldest classroom building in the United States.

Old plantations line the banks of James River near Williamsburg, remnants of the colonial days. **Carter's Grove** is the most beautiful. A dirt road leads from Williamsburg through plantation fields to this Georgian mansion, located on US 60.

Berkeley Plantation—not Plymouth—between Williamsburg and Richmond on Route 5, was the site of the first Thanksgiving in 1619. Both Benjamin Harrison and William Henry Harrison were born here.

Atlanta: the South's most important city

Atlanta, the city that suffered the most during the Civil War, has become the South's most prominent city. The federal headquarters of Reconstruction following the war is bustling and modern.

Reverend Martin Luther King Jr. began his crusade against racism in Atlanta, which became one of the first southern cities to erase the vestiges of the old slave system. King and his father were pastors at **Ebeneezer Baptist Church,** *407 Auburn Ave. N.E.* King's tomb is in the churchyard here.

Paces Ferry Road is one of the prettiest residential areas in the area. Magnificent estates line the road. The finest is the **governor's mansion,** *391 W. Paces Ferry Road,* with its antiques, gardens, and fountains. The **Atlanta Historical Society,** *3101 Andrews Drive,* includes the Swan House, an elegant mansion, the Tullie Smith House, a restored antebellum farmhouse, and McElreath Hall, which has historic exhibits.

The Margaret Mitchell Room in the **Public Library,** *Carnegie Way and Forsythe Street,* houses autographed copies of *Gone With the Wind.*

Uncle Remus fans should see the **Wren's Nest,** *1050 Gordon St.,* where Joel Chandler Harris lived.

Atlanta's best restaurants and hotels

The **Abbey,** *163 Ponce de Leon Ave.; (404)876-8831,* is meant to look like an abbey, with stained-glass windows and waiters wearing monks' robes. The food is sinfully good and rich. Try the *feuilleté d'agneau* (lamb in a pastry crust).

The **Dining Room,** *3434 Peachtree Road N.E.; (404)237-2700,* just outside Atlanta in Buckhead, has uncompromising service and scrumptious food and wine. Afternoon tea is served. A two-course dinner is $37; a three-course dinner $47; a four-course meal with dessert is $69.

Two of the finest hotels in the South are the **Westin Peachtree Plaza,** *Peachtree Street and International Boulevard; (404)659-1400,* and the **Hyatt Regency,** *265 Peachtree St.; (404)577-1234.* The Plaza has a lake, birds, and floating cocktail lounges. The Hyatt has a 27-story atrium and revolving bars. Double rooms in both begin at $150.

Savannah and Charleston: the best of the Old South

Savannah and Charleston retain the charm of the Old South, with pastel houses and near-tropical greenery. **Charleston** is a museum, with old homes, historic monuments, and gardens. Mansions line Church, Meeting, and Battery streets. The two most splendid are the **Nathaniel Russell House,** *51 Meeting St.,* and the **Edmonston-Allston House,** *21 E. Battery St.*

The **Charleston Museum,** *360 Meeting St.,* is the oldest in America. The **Gibbes Gallery,** *135 Meeting St.,* has a collection of works by American artists. Also visit the **Old Slave Market,** *6 Chalmers St.,* and **Ft. Sumter,** where the Civil War began when South Carolina attacked the Union stronghold.

Savannah, Charleston's sister city, has a pirate past but an aristocratic southern ambiance. For two centuries, piracy and shipping flourished here. Today, mansions and gardens dot the town, and the renovated waterfront is filled with shops and restaurants.

Visit the **Ships of the Sea Museum,** *503 E. River St.,* which displays ship models and figureheads. Also see the **Owens-Thomas House,** *124 Abercorn St.,* and the **Davenport House,** *Columbia Square.* The Owens-Thomas House was built in 1816 and has formal gardens and a restored kitchen. The Davenport House is older and has a beautiful china collection. The grave of Tomochichi, the Indian who allowed settlement in the area, is at Wright Square.

The **First African Baptist Church,** *Franklin Square,* built in 1788, is one of the oldest black churches in the country.

Savannah's best restaurant is **Wilkes Dining Room,** *107 W. Jones St.* Mrs. Wilkes says grace at each table. Long lines wait to enjoy the food at this inexpensive place.

Johnny Harris Restaurant, *1651 E. Victory Drive,* serves the best barbecue in the South.

The best swamp: Okefenokee

This huge wild-life sanctuary is home to rare birds and alligators. Immense cypress trees spread their roots in the black water. Known as Land of the Trembling Earth by Indians, Okefenokee is surrounded with legend. The northern entrance is south of Waycross, Georgia. For information on swamp excursions, call *(912)283-0583.*

The country-western capital: Nashville

Nashville, the town from which most of America's greatest country musicians hail, is a Mecca for country music fans.

The **Grand Ole Opry** is where country music achieved its fame. The Opry opened in 1943 at the Ryman Auditorium, drawing country music fans from far and wide. In 1974, the Grand Ole Opry moved to the newer, bigger **Grand Ole Opry House,** *just off I-40; (615)889-6700.* The best seats in the house cost $12.39—and they are in high demand, so call early for reservations.

Nashville's top sights

Centennial Park is the place to laze as you listen to local jazz musicians do their thing. The 140-acre park, located on the fringe of downtown Nashville, has a lake, rose gardens, and people throwing frisbees and playing soccer.

Centennial Park's reproduction of the Greek Parthenon gave Nashville its nickname, the Athens of the South. This impressive structure was built in 1897 to celebrate Nashville's centennial. Housed inside the Parthenon are a collection of oil paintings by American artists from the late 1800s and a statue of Athena—a Nashville sculptor's rendering of a demolished statue described in a fifth-century B.C. critique. For more information on the park, call *(615)259-6358.*

The **Hermitage,** *off Old Hickory Boulevard near I-40; (615)889-2941,* was the home of Andrew Jackson, the seventh president of the United States, built in 1819. Here, Jackson made the decision to move the Cherokee from their homeland to Oklahoma. Some 18,000 Indians passed not far from his house as they marched the Trail of Tears in 1838. The house escaped harm during the Civil War; it was guarded by Federal troops. The house is open daily from 9 a.m. to 5 p.m.; admission is $3.75.

The **Country Music Hall of Fame,** *4 Music Square E.,* houses Elvis' solid gold Cadillac and other memorabilia. Across the street is a pool shaped like a guitar.

Ft. Nashborough, *First Avenue below Church Street,* is a re-creation of the original settlement of Nashville.

The best country-western clothing

The **Alamo of Nashville,** *324 Broadway; (615)244-3803,* sells the epitome of Western clothing. Celebrities, including Elvis, Rudolph Nureyev, James Brown, and Ronald Reagan, have been fitted here. You can choose from ready-made Western wear or have a suit made to order.

Top entertainment

Although Nashville is home to country music, that's not the only kind of entertainment you'll find here.

The **Tennessee Performing Arts Center (TPAC),** *505 Deaderick St.,* offers Broadway road shows and performances by the Nashville Ballet and the Tennessee Repertory Theater. For ticket and scheduling information for the Tennessee Repertory Theater, call **Centratik,** *(615)320-7171.* For other TPAC events, call **TicketMaster,** *(615)714-2787.*

For live music (including blues, jazz, rock, and country), go to the **Bluebird Café,** *4104 Hillsboro Road; (615)383-1461.* Get here early or reserve a table.

The best restaurants

Julian's, *2412 W. End Ave.; (615)327-2412,* offers the best a la carte classic French cuisine in Nashville. Because the rooms are small, with only one table per room, privacy is ensured. Dinner for two is $70, not including wine.

Arthur's, *off Hillsboro Road; (615)383-8841,* in the mall at Green Hills, is an elegant four-star restaurant with a prix-fixe seven-course meal for $38 per person, not including wine. Princess Anne, President Ford, and country music stars have dined here. Arthur's won the 1988 *Travel-Holiday* magazine award.

The best hotel

The most luxurious accommodations in town are at the **Hermitage,** *231 Sixth Ave. N.; (800)251-1908,* built in 1910. This hotel, voted the most romantic in Nashville, offers only suites: choose from contemporary, traditional, and Oriental. Hotel limousines will meet you at the airport. Suites are $99 to $150.

Memphis—home of the king of rock'n'roll

Memphis, located on the banks of the mighty Mississippi, was home to Elvis Presley (known affectionately as The King) and the cradle of blues music. The music lives on on Beale Street and at Graceland, Elvis' home.

Take a guided tour of **Graceland.** You'll see the King's vast car collection, his trophy room, and the Meditation Gardens, where he and his family are buried. Elvis paid $100,000 for the house in 1957, when he was 22 years old. Die-hard Elvis fans come here to mourn at the singer's grave, often wearing Elvis costumes (white pantsuits, dark glasses, and slicked-back hair). The cost of the tour is $7.50 for adults, $4.75 for children under 12. For more information, call *(901)332-3322* or *(800)238-2000.*

New Orleans: the best party town

New Orleans is famous for its outrageous Mardi Gras, when residents don splendid costumes and hold all-night parties and balls. But it also has some of the nation's best food. And it is one of the prettiest cities in the country.

The **French Quarter** is the oldest, loveliest, and zaniest section of town. Wrought-iron balconies and railings decorate French- and Spanish-style buildings. Female impersonators dance in the bars. Artists, musicians, and partiers roam the streets. **Jackson Square,** the heart of the French Quarter, is marked by St. Louis Cathedral and a statue of Andrew Jackson. The **Moonwalk** provides a view of the river.

Most of the city's bars, which stay open 24 hours a day, are located along **Bourbon Street.** College students, transvestites, bums, tourists, and locals stroll up and down the street in a never-ending, colorful parade.

Lafitte's Blacksmith Shop is New Orleans' most historic saloon. It originally belonged to the pirate John Lafitte, who sold his booty here and plotted to rescue the exiled Napoleon.

The **Pontalba Apartments,** *525 St. Ann St.,* where William Faulkner lived, are the oldest apartments in the country.

The best museums in New Orleans

The **Jazz Museum,** *833 Conti St.,* has old Louis Armstrong records.

The **Cabildo,** near Jackson Square, houses a death mask of Napoleon. This building was at various times the seat of French, Spanish, English, and American rule of the Louisiana Territory.

The **Chalmette National Historic Museum,** *St. Bernard Highway,* is the site of the Battle of New Orleans (1815), where Andrew Jackson defeated the British.

The **Conti Wax Museum,** *917 Conti St.,* is one of the world's finest. The voodoo display and the haunted dungeon are the best.

The **Voodoo Museum,** *739 Bourbon St.,* has a voodoo altar and educational displays.

Mardi Gras: the biggest party

Mardi Gras—a famous celebration that includes balls, parades, and a costume contest—begins shortly after Christmas and lasts until Lent. Most of the activity is in the French Quarter and along Canal Street. The most popular event is a transvestite **He Sheba Contest.** Make reservations well in advance.

The best jazz festival

The New Orleans **Jazz and Heritage Festival** lasts for 10 days in late April and early May, featuring jazz, blues, gospel, and Cajun music. Big-name artists, such as Fats Domino, the Fabulous Thunderbirds, and Wynton Marsalis, have played. Tickets are $6 in advance, $8 at the gate. For information, contact the **New Orleans Jazz and Heritage Foundation Inc.,** *P.O. Box 2530, New Orleans, LA 70176; (504)522-4786, (504)888-8181,* or *(800)535-5151.*

The best way to dine

The **Grill Room,** at the Windsor Court Hotel, *300 Gravier St.; (504)523-6000,* is the most elegant place in town. It has hosted Nancy Reagan and Princess Anne. The menu and wines are superb. The restaurant is open daily for lunch and dinner.

Arnaud's, *813 Bienville St.; (504)523-5433,* in the French Quarter, is the best Creole restaurant. The decor glitters: crystal chandeliers, antique ceiling fans, beveled windows, and delicate china. Try the oysters Bienville, and save room for the crepes suzette.

The best bars

In the **Napoleon House,** *500 Chartres St.,* pictures of the emperor hang on the wall beneath ceiling fans.

The **Old Absinthe House**, *240 Bourbon St.*, once served absinthe, an extract of worm-wood that is now outlawed because it causes insanity. Here pirates, artists, and gentlemen drank absinthe from a fountain. Today, the bar offers a tasty Absinthe Frappe made with anisette or Pernod.

Pat O'Brien's, *718 St. Peter St.*, has a pianist, lots of singles, and an unusual fountain. **Antoine's**, *713 St. Louis St.*, has New Orleans' best wine cellar. **K-Paul's Louisiana Kitchen**, *416 Chartres St.*, serves gin marinated with jalapeno peppers. **Crazy Shirley's** is the home of Dixieland music. And **Maple Leaf**, *8316 Oak St.*, specializes in ragtime.

The best hotels

Pontchartrain, *2031 St. Charles Ave.; (504)524-0581*, is the most romantic hotel in town. Double rooms are $115 to $320.

A pleasant, more affordable place to stay, is the **Frenchmen Inn**, *417 Frenchmen St.; (504)948-2166*, in two townhouses built in 1860. Rooms are decorated with antiques and have balconies overlooking the courtyard, the pool, and the patio. Double rooms are $64 to $99.

Florida: the most tropical state

Florida is the closest North Americans get to the tropics. Thousands of Yankees and Canadians descend on the Sunshine State during the winter and spring to escape the snow and cold of their home states. It's the most popular winter escape, complete with sandy beaches, palm trees, tropical drinks, resort hotels, seafood restaurants, and lively crowds.

The most peaceful beaches

Most people think of the Atlantic Coast when they think of Florida. But some of the prettiest and least crowded beaches are along the Gulf of Mexico. **Pensacola Beach,** on the panhandle, has fine, white sand and temperate, clear water. **Ft. Walton Beach** is attractive and has a 1,200-foot observation pier. Farther south are the white sand beaches of **Belleair** and **Clearwater.** The finest sand is at **Madeira** and **Redington** beaches. **Long Boat Key** is posh and not too crowded. **Point O'Rocks,** an isolated beach near Siesta Key, is famous for its colorful rocks. **Venice Beach** is known for the sharks' teeth that wash up on shore. **Ft. Myers Beach** has the most beautiful sunsets. And **Sanibel** and **Captiva** islands are the best places in the state to look for seashells.

Our favorite hotel on the Gulf of Mexico is the **Don CeSar,** on St. Petersburg Beach, *(813)360-1881,* an amazing pink Spanish-style castle surrounded by palm trees overlooking the ocean. Once the hideaway of F. Scott Fitzgerald, it is the playground of celebrities. Rooms are $135 to $150 during the winter.

The **Belleview Biltmore**, *25 Belleview Blvd., Belleair-Clearwater; (800)237-8947* or *(800)282-8072*, is a spa. Here you can soak in whirlpools and Swedish showers and work up a sweat in the exercise room. Double rooms are from $110 to $250.

The **Buccaneer Inn**, *595 Dream Island Road; (813)383-1101*, is the best restaurant on Longboat Key, situated on a marina. The house specialty is prime rib cooked very rare and then roasted over live charcoal.

Where the action is: the Atlantic Coast

The Gulf of Mexico is nice, but the surf and the crowds are more exciting on the Atlantic.

Daytona Beach has 23 miles of sandy beach and a boardwalk. High-rise hotels and condominiums line the ocean. Alas, cars can drive on the beach (a real nuisance).

The most beautiful dunes and beaches along the Atlantic Coast are at **Ponte Vedra** and **South Ponte Vedra** beaches, the site of two exclusive resorts: the Sawgrass and the Ponte Vedra Inn.

The quietest East Coast beach is **New Smyrna,** between Daytona Beach and Titusville. One of the state's last unspoiled beaches is **Playalinda,** part of the Canaveral National Seashore.

Southern Florida's Atlantic Coast has some of the world's most famous resort towns: **Palm Beach, Ft. Lauderdale,** and **Miami Beach.** College students flock here for spring vacation, and Americans in general migrate here during the winter.

Our favorite place to stay on Florida's Atlantic Coast is the **Breakers,** *South County Road, Palm Beach; (305)655-6611.* The lobby of this grand Italianate resort has frescoed vaulted ceilings and 15th-century Flemish tapestries. The original Breakers, built in 1903, burned, as did the second. The present building was built in 1926. The National Register of Historic Places lists the Breakers as "culturally significant in its reflection of 20th-century grandeur." It has 2 18-hole golf courses, a private beach with cabanas, 14 tennis courts, an outdoor saltwater pool, a sauna, lawn bowling, croquet, and programs for children. The hotel dining room is large, and its 100,000-bottle wine cellar is one of the world's biggest.

Ft. Lauderdale has some of the finest beaches south of Daytona—and the best night life. The **Candy Store Disco,** *1 N. Atlantic Blvd.,* is a lively spot.

The **Bonaventure Resort Spa,** *250 Racquet Club Road; (305)389-3300,* is surrounded by palm trees and waters. You can put your body through a Swiss needle shower, a shiatsu massage, or an herbal wrap. Double rooms are $125 to $175.

Miami Beach is the most famous resort, drawing 13-million visitors each year to its luxurious beachfront hotels. South Beach's **Lummus Park** is the best beach area. Eighth Street in **Little Havana** is lined with great Cuban restaurants. The affluent **Coral Gables** neighborhood has more elegant restaurants.

The Keys: Florida at its best

The **Florida Keys,** a 100-mile chain of gorgeous islands, stretch into the Gulf of Mexico from Florida's southern coast. They are less commercial, less spoiled, and more relaxed than most of Florida's other beaches.

Four towns dot the islands: Key Largo, Islamorada, Marathon, and Key West. **Key West,** at the tip of the Keys, is known as a place for all-out parties. **Key Largo** is peppered with beaches in small coves: **Smathers** is the longest; **Memorial** has a 100-yard pier over the water; **South** is the most peaceful. Tavernier and Plantation islands have pretty Atlantic beaches. Big Pine Key has white sand coves on the Gulf side.

The best place to stay in the Keys is the **Marriott Casa Marina,** *1500 Reynolds Ave.; (305)296-3535* or *(800)228-9290,* literally the last resort in the United States, situated at the south end of the southernmost city in Florida. Originally, it was a stopover for travelers heading to Havana, Cuba. This posh four-story resort hotel has vaulted ceilings, polished mahogany, arched windows, sea views, and landscaped gardens. Hemingway liked this hotel, as did Harry Truman. During the Cuban Missile Crisis in 1962, the hotel housed American troops. In 1978, it was renovated and returned to its original splendor.

St. Augustine: America's oldest settlement

Decades before Plymouth or Jamestown, the Spanish established **St. Augustine,** America's oldest permanent settlement, in 1565. In 1740, the fortified town fought off the English. Its fortress, **Castillo de San Marcos,** built in 1672 of coquina rock, has been preserved and can be visited. The courtyard is surrounded by guardrooms, storerooms, a jail, and a chapel.

The **Oldest Store Museum,** *4 Artillery Lane,* has tools and machines from the 1800s, including high-wheeled bicycles, a steam-powered tractor, a Gibson Girl corset, and animal-powered treadmills.

The **Kenwood Inn,** *38 Marine St.; (904)824-2116,* is a charming old inn in the historic section of St. Augustine. Built in 1865, it has been restored and is furnished with antiques and reproductions. Guests can use the inn's pool. Double rooms are $40 to $65, including Continental breakfast.

Wakulla Springs—America's deepest

Johnny Weissmuller grappled with alligators at **Wakulla Springs** in his famous Tarzan role. Located 10 miles south of Tallahassee, this deep spring has no bottom, or so divers claim, which is why the water is so incredibly cold. If you want to get away from the Florida heat, this is the place. Mastadon bones have been found in this spring.

A beautiful old hotel, the **Wakulla Springs Lodge,** *(904)224-5950,* overlooks the spring, surrounded by giant oaks draped with Spanish moss. The lodge is decorated with wood-beamed ceilings, marble floors, massive doors, and antiques. And the food in the dining room is good. Double rooms are $45 to $65 year-round.

Texas: the Lone Star State

Texas, the second-biggest state (after Alaska), is a land of extremes. Here, the J.R. Ewings of the world gamble great fortunes, while the women dress in furs, despite the scorching heat, and keep the makeup manufacturers of the world in business. At the same time, cowboys roam the stark, wide-open ranges. And Mexicans risk their lives to cross the border illegally. Going to Texas can be as much a cultural experience as visiting a foreign country.

Houston: the fastest-growing city

Houston has grown faster than any other American city, sprawling across 532 miles. Twenty-five oil companies have their headquarters in the city's skyscrapers.

The coolest way to tour hot, humid Houston is through the **Houston Tunnel System,** a series of air-conditioned passageways that connect all the major buildings downtown. For a map of the tunnels, which are lined with shops and restaurants, stop by the Houston Library, Penzoil Place, or the Texas Commerce Bank.

Penzoil Place is Houston's cultural showpiece. Designed by the prominent architect Philip Johnson, this glass complex includes the Jesse H. Jones Hall for the Performing Arts and the Alley Theater. The Jesse H. Jones Hall is home of the Houston Symphony Orchestra, the Grand Opera, and the Houston Ballet Company. Its lobby features Richard Lippold's *Gemini II* sculpture.

Hermann Park contains the Museum of Natural Science and Burke Baker Planetarium, the Houston Zoological Gardens (where you can see a colony of vampire bats), and the Miller Outdoor Theater. Nearby are the **Museum of Contemporary Arts,** *5216 Montrose Blvd.,* and the **Museum of Fine Arts,** *1001 Bissonet.*

Also worth seeing are the **Bayou Bend,** *1 Wescott St.,* off Memorial Drive, the former home of Ima Hogg, daughter of the first native-born Texas governor, and the **San Jacinto Museum of History,** *3800 Park Road,* located at the base of the San Jacinto Monument (which is taller than the Washington Monument) on the San Jacinto Battlegrounds.

One of the world's greatest sports complexes is Houston's immense **Astrodomain,** which includes the Astrodome.

The **Menil Collection,** *1515 Sul Ross St.,* is a wide-ranging gallery with prehistoric to modern art and special exhibits on tribal cultures.

Houston's best bar

Gilley's, *4500 Spencer Hwy.,* in Pasadena, is Houston's most well-known bar. Owned by country-western music star Mickey Gilley, it was filmed in the movie *Urban Cowboy.* For 25 cents you can ride the mechanical bull.

Houston's best rodeo

Every February, the **Houston Livestock Show and Rodeo** is held in the Astrodome. The largest show of its kind in the world, it draws cowboys from all over North America.

Houston's best restaurants

Brennan's, *3300 Smith; (713)522-9711,* is a well-loved Houston institution with fine food and bargain prices. Try the eggs Creole or the catfish with roasted pecans; save room for praline parfait.

Charley's 517, *517 Louisiana; (713)224-4438,* has imaginative fare, including fresh venison and buffalo. The wine list is extensive.

La Reserve, *Inn on the Park, Four Riverway; (713)871-8181,* is an elegant restaurant surrounded by reflecting pools where black swans glide. Inside are beveled ceiling mirrors, antiques, and crystal chandeliers. The menu changes daily but always includes fresh fish, beef, game, and produce.

Houston's best hotel

The best hotel in town is **Remington,** *Post Oak Park, 1919 Briar Oaks Lane; (713)840-7600* or *(800)231-9802,* a beautifully decorated place with a homey feel. Little extras make it special: handmade soaps, fresh fruit and chocolates in the bedrooms, and brass razors. Double rooms are $100 to $225.

Dallas: fact is better than fiction

Dallas is famous for J.R. Ewing of the television series *Dallas,* the Dallas Cowboys and their cheerleaders, and the assassination of John F. Kennedy. What many people don't know is that it is the most sophisticated city in the South.

Be prepared for the **Dallas-Ft. Worth Airport,** the world's largest—larger than Manhattan Island.

The saddest sight

The most sobering sight in Dallas is the spot where John F. Kennedy was shot, a grassy knoll at Market and Main streets marked by a large black granite marker. The **John F. Kennedy Museum** is scheduled to open Nov. 22, 1988 to mark the 25th anniversary of his assassination. It will be located on the sixth floor of the School Book Depository, where Lee Harvey Oswald hid and took aim at the president.

Dallas' best sights

Dallas City Hall, *1500 Marilla,* rises 560 feet and surrounds a pleasant plaza.

The **Dallas Zoo,** *621 E. Clarendon Drive,* has the finest collection of rare birds in the nation.

Thanksgiving Square has a bell tower, the Chapel of Thanksgiving, and the Hall of Thanksgiving, which exhibits costumes and artifacts from seven continents.

The **Museum of Fine Arts,** *1717 N. Harwood St.,* displays classic, pre-Columbian, European, and American paintings and sculpture.

The best collection of museums

State Fair Park, *off I-30 East,* has five museums within walking distance of each other. **Science Place** is one of the best science museums in the United States, housing exhibits on astronomical phenomena, human anatomy, shells, and the workings of radios. The **Dallas Hall of State** covers 400 years of state history. The **Age of Steam Railroad Museum** exhibits an old Dallas depot, a streetcar, an old passenger train, and the world's largest steam locomotive. The **Museum of Natural History** features the wildlife of the Southwest. The **Dallas Aquarium** and the **Dallas Planetarium** are favorites with children.

Dining bests in Dallas

Lawry's The Prime Rib, *3008 Maple Ave.; (214)521-7777,* serves the best roast beef in Texas, carefully dry aged 14 to 21 days, then roasted on a bed of rock salt. It is carved and served warm at your table. When it was founded 50 years ago, Lawrence Frank and Walter Van de Kamp agreed that their restaurant should be elegant but friendly—no snooty waiters and no foreign languages on the menu.

The **Routh Street Café,** *3005 Routh St.; (214)871-7161,* has a five-course prix-fixe menu for $42 that includes American, Mexican, and Continental cuisines. This renovated prairie-style house has art-deco decor. Reservations are required.

San Simeon, *2515 McKinney Ave.; (214)871-7373,* is an elegant restaurant with great food. Save room for the white chocolate crème de menthe ice cream on a chocolate pecan shell.

Dallas' best digs

Mansion on Turtle Creek, *2821 Turtle Creek Blvd.; (214)559-2100* or *(800)527-5432,* a 1920s mansion-turned-hotel, is cozy, with wood fires, leaded windows, and a good dining room. The lobby has polished floorboards, a domed ceiling, and tall arched windows. Double rooms are $205 to $2,800.

The best place for rabid anti-smokers is the **Non-Smokers Inn,** *9229 Carpenter Freeway; (214)631-6633* or *(800)253-7377.* It has a hot tub, a sauna, a pool, cable television, and an exercise room. Double rooms are $38 to $50, including Continental breakfast.

Austin: the most laid-back city in Texas

A large student population and a rebellious history make Austin the most laid-back and free-thinking city in Texas. It is also one of the prettiest.

Austin's top sights

The **Texas State Capitol,** *Congress Avenue,* built in 1888, is colossal. It is open 24 hours a day when the legislature is in session, and free tours are conducted from 8:30 a.m. to 4:30 p.m. The **Texas Archives and Library Building** is located on the capitol grounds.

The **Laguna Gloria Art Museum,** *3809 W. 35th St.,* has the city's best art collection. Concerts, plays, and festivals are held on the grounds, which are lovely.

The **Lyndon Baines Johnson Library,** *2313 Red River St.,* contains the former president's speeches.

Austin's Area Garden Center, *2200 Barton Springs Road,* in Zilker Park, has gardens, a 19th-century pioneer cabin, a log-cabin school, and an old blacksmith shop.

A country-western Hollywood

Young country-western musicians flock to Austin to try to make it big. Willie Nelson and Jerry Jeff Walker are among those who have succeeded. The **Austin Opry House,** *200 Academy Drive,* is owned by Willie Nelson, who brings in top-name entertainment. The **Broken Spoke,** *3201 S. Lamar,* is the best place for foot stompin'.

A bed for the night

The best place to stay in Austin is the **Drishill Hotel,** *604 Brazos St.; (512)474-5911* or *(800)228-0808,* a renovated 19th-century building. Double rooms are $45 to $75.

San Antonio: the best of Tex-Mex

San Antonio is the site of the battle of the **Alamo** between 200 Texans (including Davey Crocket) and 4,000 Mexicans led by Commander Santa Anna. The Texans turned a mission building into a fort and fought to free Texas from Mexico. When the siege ended, all but six Texans were dead. Crocket survived, but he was later killed at the orders of Santa Anna. "Remember the Alamo" became a battle cry. The people of San Antonio still commemorate March 6, the day the siege ended.

Founded in 1718 as a Spanish military mission, the city is now more than half Mexican-American. The Tex-Mex atmosphere is thick and spicy.

The best Mexican food north of the border is prepared in San Antonio. Try **El Mirador,** *722 S. St. Mary's St.* (order the *huevos rancheros*); **Los Patios,** *2015 N.E. Loop 410* (which has the best location); or **Casa Rio,** *430 E. Commerce St.* (which is the oldest and most popular).

The best of the missions

Spanish Franciscan missionaries built five missions in San Antonio to convert local Indians to Christianity. Two of them, the Alamo and Mission San Jose, are downtown.

The **Alamo,** *Alamo Plaza,* is actually the Mission San Antonio de Valero, with a chapel and barracks. The **Mission San Jose,** *6539 San Jose Blvd.,* is the largest. It has its own irrigation system, built by the Spaniards, and a beautiful rose window. Mass is still held here, and a mariachi band plays on Sundays.

The **Mission San Francisco de la Espada,** *10040 Espada Road,* has a beautiful chapel. A mile-long aqueduct, built between 1731 and 1745, supplies it with water. The **Mission San Juan Capistrano,** *9102 Grof Road,* built in 1731, differs from other, more architecturally elaborate missions in its simplicity.

The best museums

The **San Antonio Museum of Art,** *200 W. Jones Ave.,* is housed in the restored Lone Star Brewery building, which has towers, turrets, ornate columns, and huge rooms. The collection includes pre-Columbian, American Indian, Spanish Colonial, Mexican, and European art and Texas furniture.

The new **Lone Star Brewing Company,** *600 Lone Star Blvd.,* displays animal heads, horns, antlers, birds, and fish. You can sample free beer at the Buckhorn Bar.

Best restaurants and hotel

San Antonio's two best restaurants are **La Louisiane,** *2632 Broadway; (512)225-7984,* which is beautifully decorated and has good French cuisine, and **San Angel Restaurant,** *La Mansion del Norte, 37 N.E. Loop 410; (512)341-3535,* which has a Continental menu and a Spanish look.

Amerisuites, *11221 San Pedro Ave.; (512)342-4800* or *(800)882-2266,* is a good, inexpensive hotel with double rooms for $53, including Continental breakfast. The hotel has a heated pool and a whirlpool.

The Southwest: nature at its most powerful

The **Southwest** is a region of awe-inspiring natural beauty, much of which is preserved in the area's national parks. The most famous is the **Grand Canyon** in Arizona. If you think the reality can't possibly match the Grand Canyon's reputation, you're wrong. This is a sublime place, carved over the course of eons by the Colorado River. The descent to the bottom is rugged. From the base, the canyon looks like some otherworldly Shangri-La, a rainbow of colors and powerful bastions.

The best place to stay while you explore is **El Tovar Hotel,** *(602)638-2401,* on the South Rim, an elegant but rustic lodge perched on the edge. All other hotels are outside the park limits and do not have views of the canyon. For more information, contact the **Grand Canyon South Rim Visitors Center,** *(602)638-7770.*

Zion National Park, in Springdale, Utah, is less famous. It is so named because its beauty reminded Mormon pioneers of paradise. The best view in all the Southwest is from **Angel's Landing,** a 2 1/2-mile trail from the Grotto picnic area in Zion. For information, contact the park's **Visitors Information Center,** *(801)772-3256.*

Bryce Canyon National Park, five hours south of Salt Lake City, has a delicacy that differentiates it from other canyons. Some consider it the most beautiful, with its lacy rock formations. For information, contact **Visitors Center,** *(801)834-5322.*

Phoenix—the best oasis

The power of nature in the Southwest—the giant rocks and the lack of water—is unrelenting. **Phoenix** is a welcome oasis in the middle of this desert. The capital of Arizona is actually a chain of resort towns. The Valley of the Sun, ringed by mountains, is inhabited by 1 1/2-million people, many of them wealthy retirees. Outside Phoenix are 23 reservations, home to 50,000 Indians.

Both the best view and the best meal can be found at **Etienne's Different Point of View,** *Pointe Tapatio Resort, 11111 N. Seventh St.; (602)863-0912.* This restaurant at the top of a mountain has a 360-degree view of the city and the surrounding desert. The best view is at sunset.

Frank Lloyd Wright designed the valley's greatest hotel, the **Arizona Biltmore,** *24th Street, Missouri, Phoenix; (800)228-3000* or *(602)955-6600.* Gold leaf lines the ceilings. The color scheme and decor are Southwestern, with stained glass, murals, paintings, and Indian tapestries. The Biltmore has 2 18-hole golf courses, 18 tennis courts, 3 swimming pools, a health club, and a sauna.

The best of Tucson

Tucson, surrounded by the Sonora Desert, has both the easygoing atmosphere of a small town and the cultural offerings of a big city, including opera, symphony, theater, and art. With an influx of newcomers from the East Coast, Tucson is losing some of its Hispanic and Southwestern flavor. But old Spanish festivals are still held, and good Mexican restaurants can be found throughout the town.

Most of Tucson's sights are within walking distance of the University of Arizona campus. The **Arizona State Museum,** for example, has a collection of Southwest Indian artifacts and exhibits on area plants and animals. The **Arizona Historical Society,** *949 E. Second St.,* illustrates the state's history, with colorful exhibits about early settlers and outlaws.

El Presidio is a walled fortress built by Spanish settlers. Nearby are the **Spanish Colonial Pima County Courthouse,** built in 1928, and the **Tucson Museum of Art.**

Old Town Artisans, *186 N. Meyer Ave.,* next to El Presidio, displays Western handicrafts, including Navajo rugs, in a 19th-century adobe building.

Fourteen miles west of Tucson is the **Arizona-Sonora Desert Museum,** where you can see jaguars, mountain lions, beavers, and bighorn sheep, as well as a cave and a garden with 300 kinds of plants.

The **Mission of San Xavier del Bac,** nine miles south of Tucson on Mission Road on the Tohano O'Adham Indian Reservation, was founded in 1692 by the Jesuits. It is one of the most beautiful churches in the Southwest, a white Mexican Renaissance structure surrounded by brown desert. Visit during the Mariachi Mass, held at 12:30 on Sundays during the winter. This adobe structure has frescoes, carved figurines of saints, and two lions that wear satin bow ties.

Tuscon's best restaurant is the **Tack Room,** *Rancho Del Rio Resort, 2800 N. Sabino Canyon Road; (602)722-2800,* in an old adobe hacienda in the desert. Try the veal or the rack of lamb Sonora. Breads and desserts are homemade.

The best place for closet cowboys

If you've always dreamt of riding horses across the desert, the **Tanque Verde Guest Ranch,** *14301 E. Speedway Blvd.; (602)296-6275,* is your best bet. Located 12 miles from Tucson, this hostelry, a working ranch until the 1920s, welcomes you into ranch life. You can eat well, swim in the indoor pool, and ride horses.

The Southwest's mysterious cliff dwellings

North Americans take long and expensive voyages to Machu Picchu and Chichen Itza to see ancient Indian ruins. However, the most extraordinary pre-Columbian ruins are right in our own back yard. The mysterious Anasazi Indians built beautiful, complex cliff dwellings in the **Four Corners** region of the American Southwest long before Europeans arrived. Great cities were carved out of reddish-gold sandstone cliffs by these unknown people, whom the

Navajo named the Anasazi, or Ancient Ones. Their civilization flourished from the time of Christ until 1300, then disappeared without a trace.

No one knows exactly what became of the Anasazis, but you can explore their ancient dwellings, perched in gigantic cliffside caves on plateaus in the open plain, at times five stories high with as many as 800 rooms (the caves are tiny compared with the sheer cliffs that loom above them). The caves went unseen by the white man until December 1888, when they were discovered by two cowboys searching for stray cows.

The most extensive cliff dwellings (4,000 in all) are in the 52,000-acre **Mesa Verde National Park** in Colorado. The largest and most famous cliff dwelling is **Cliff Palace,** where about 250 people lived in the 13th century. Its towered ruins look like a fantasy castle protected by a gigantic cave 100 yards wide and 30 yards deep, almost perfectly preserved because it is shielded from the elements by the cliff overhang. It is one of the five dwellings in the park that you can visit.

Hiking is limited in the park, but you are permitted to walk along five marked trails. The best is the loop called **Petroglyph Trail.**

Most cliff dwellings are closed on snowy days, usually between September and May. During this winter season, ranger-guided tours of **Spruce Tree House,** one of the cliff dwellings, are conducted daily. And the **Archeological Museum** is open from 8 a.m. to 5 p.m. For more information, contact the **Park Superintendent,** *Box 8, Mesa Verde National Park, CO 81330; (303)529-4475 or (303)529-4461.*

Mesa Verde National Park is a two-hour drive from the airport at Durango, Colorado, where rental cars are available.

The best place to stay is the **Far View Lodge,** *Box 277, Mancos, CO; (303)529-4421,* near the cliff dwellings. Each room has a private balcony with a view. Double rooms are $62 during the summer; in May and October, you can get a double room for two nights for $50.

You also can see Anasazi dwellings in Navaho National Monument in **Monument Valley Tribal Park,** near Kayenta, Arizona. Unfortunately, overuse is wearing down the three dwellings here—Inscription House, Betatakin, and Keet Steel. Inscription House has been closed, and entrance to Betatakin and Keet Steel houses is limited.

The best of Indian country

Modern-day Indians maintain their traditions throughout the Southwest. Their pueblos are living communities, not museums.

The **Navajo reservation** in Monument Valley covers 16-million acres, mostly in northeastern Arizona. About 160,000 people make up the Navajo Nation. They are shepherds, silversmiths, weavers, and tour guides. The largest and most famous (active) Navajo trading post is **Hubbell's,** a national historic site. For more information on the Navajos, contact **Recreational Resources Department,** *Navajo Tribe, Box 308, Window Rock, AZ 86515; (602)871-4941.*

The **Hopi reservation** is enclosed by Navajo country. The 6,000 Hopis (whose name means Peaceful Ones) occupy 1.4-million acres of land. Believed to be the descendants of the Anasazi, the Hopis are farmers and craftspeople. They believe spirits live in the nearby San Francisco Peaks.

The Hopis live on three main mesas. The Indians on **First Mesa** produce the best pottery. Those on **Second Mesa** create beautiful baskets, kachina doll carvings, and silver jewelry. The Hopis on **Third Mesa** are known for decorative wicker plaques.

Old Orabi on Third Mesa vies with Acoma Pueblo as the oldest inhabited town in the United States. The centuries-old village of **Walpi,** high on the edge of First Mesa, has tiny winding streets and houses crowded into the cliffs. For more information, contact the **Hopi Cultural Center,** *Box 67, Second Mesa, AZ 86043; (602)734-2401.*

Santa Fe: the nation's oldest capital

Set atop a 7,000-foot plateau at the base of the Sangre de Cristo Mountains in northern New Mexico is **Santa Fe.** The air is pure, the adobe homes are ancient, and the people are a mixture of Spanish, Indian, and Anglo.

The oldest capital in the nation is inhabited by families who have been here for 14 generations. Outside the city are weathered mountains and old Indian pueblos. The desert is dotted with cacti and piñon pines.

Spanish conquistadores arrived here 400 years ago and named the town La Villa Real de la Santa Fe de San Francisco. The Spanish town was built on the site of abandoned Pueblo Indian villages that had been built 300 years before the arrival of the conquistadores.

The central plaza of Santa Fe was laid out by the Spanish in 1610. The **Palace of the Governors,** built of adobe in 1610, is the oldest public building in North America. It houses the **Museum of New Mexico** and occupies the entire north side of the plaza. Along its porch, Indians spread blankets and sell handmade jewelry and pottery.

An inn has existed at the site of the **Hotel La Fonda,** off the plaza, since before the opening of the Santa Fe Trail. A faded sign on the hotel wall marks the end of the trail.

Around the corner is **St. Francis Cathedral,** completed in 1886. The two gold towers of this stone structure glow in the sun. Inside is a 16th-century wooden statue called *La Conquistadora,* said to be the oldest madonna in North America. A block away is the Loretto Chapel, which houses the circular Miraculous Staircase built without nails or other visible means of support by an unknown carpenter. Legend says the carpenter was St. Joseph. The chapel itself was modeled after the Ste. Chapelle in Paris.

The best fiesta

The **Fiesta de Santa Fe,** held in September, has music, dancing, and candlelight processions that begin at the cathedral. Zozobra, a 40-foot puppet representing Old Man Gloom, is burned to the delight of the crowds.

The biggest bomb

The scientists responsible for the atomic bomb met at 109 E. Palace St. beginning in 1943. Members of the **Manhattan Project** entered here and then went out a back way to Los Alamos. A plaque on the wall says, "All the men and women who made the first atomic bomb passed through this portal to their secret mission at Los Alamos. Their creation in 27 months of the weapons that ended World War II was one of the greatest achievements of all time."

The best restaurants

The **Pink Adobe,** *406 Old Santa Fe Trail; (505)983-7712,* in a 300-year-old adobe building, serves native specialties with creative variations. It is closed on major holidays.

Arturo Jaramillo and his family serve some of the region's best traditional food at **Rancho de Chimayo,** *(505)351-4444* or *(505)351-4375,* in the village of Chimayo. Reservations are advised.

The best accommodations

The **Bishop's Lodge,** *Bishop's Lodge Road; (505)983-6377,* is set on 1,000 acres in the foothills of the Sangre de Cristo Mountains and offers horseback riding, tennis, swimming, and a fine dining room. Archbishop Latour in Willa Cather's *Death Comes for the Archbishop* retreated here. In reality, the archbishop's name was Lamy, and he left his little chapel with painted glass windows. At the turn of the century, the archbishop's retreat was purchased by newspaper tycoon Joseph Pulitzer, who added two houses to the estate before selling it to James R. Thorpe. Thorpe turned it into a dude ranch.

Taos: a town of artists

Artists and writers flock to **Taos,** the most picturesque town in the Southwest. About 3,000 people live here at the foot of Mt. Wheeler, the highest peak in the state. **Taos Plaza,** built in 1617, became an artists' colony in the 1890s and is still inhabited by artists today. Museums around the plaza include the 200-year-old **Blumenschein House,** *LeDoux Street,* where pioneer artist Ernest Blumenschein lived from 1919 to 1962. The **Harwood Foundation Museum and Library** contains the paintings of the first Taos artists. The **Kit Carson Museum** was bought by the scout in 1843. Also on the plaza are the **Millicent Rogers Museum of Southwestern Arts and Crafts** and the **D.H. Lawrence Shrine and Ranch,** where the writer lived in the 1920s.

Just north of Taos on Route 68 is the most striking and best-preserved adobe pueblo in New Mexico. This town, which dates from 1100, is home to about 2,000 Taos Indians. Wooden ladders lead to the five-story tiered homes. For more information, contact **Taos Pueblo Tourism Director,** *P.O. Box 1846, Taos, NM 87571; (505)758-8626.* For a chuck-wagon tour of the reservation, organized by the **Taos Indian Horse Ranch,** call *(505)758-3212.* The tour lasts from 3 p.m. to 4:30 p.m. and costs $15.50. Make reservations two weeks in advance.

The best place to stay in the area is the **Sagebrush Inn,** *(505)758-2254,* where Georgia O'Keeffe painted some of her best canvases. The adobe walls are 24 inches thick, and the interior ceilings are supported by log beams. Spanish-tile floors and fireplaces give the inn a rustic look. Navajo Indian rugs and works by Taos artists decorate the lounge. The inn has a swimming pool and tennis courts.

The best of the Rockies

Glacier Park, *(406)888-5441,* in northwest Montana contains some of the most spectacular and least-touched scenery in the **Rocky Mountains,** including glaciers, high peaks, lakes and streams, and a great variety of wildlife (including grizzly bears, so be careful). The park straddles the Continental Divide. **Going to the Sun Road** is a 50-mile stretch leading to hiking trails.

Glacier Park Lodge, *(406)226-5551,* in the park, draws nature lovers, fishermen, hikers, and backpackers. This scenic resort also offers naturalist programs, golf, horseback riding, swimming, cruises, and nightly entertainment. Rooms are $17 to $105 per night.

Rocky Mountain National Park, *(303)586-2371,* is the best place in Colorado for hiking and horseback riding. Two hours from Denver, the park has 20 peaks rising more than 12,000 feet. You'll see bighorn sheep, deer, and elk on the park grounds.

Yellowstone National Park, *(307)344-7381,* is the world's greatest geyser area, with more than 200 geysers and 10,000 hot springs. The most famous geyser is **Old Faithful,**

which erupts at regular intervals. **Steamboat** is the largest geyser in the world, lasting 20 minutes and shooting higher than 300 feet.

The **Yellowstone River** has carved a canyon through the rock at Yellowstone National Park. Waterfalls and lakes reflect the blue sky. More than 1,000 miles of trails crisscross the park. Be careful if you hike the backcountry; grizzly bears have become a problem. You'll also see moose and bison. Park employees say swimming in the warm waters of Firehole River can be exhilarating; however, this isn't encouraged, because you can be scalded. Yellowstone is the oldest national park in the United States, established in 1872.

The best skiing in the United States

Taos, New Mexico and **Jackson Hole, Wyoming** are challenging ski areas that are remote enough not to attract big crowds. Both have serious ski schools, but neither has much après-ski activity. Taos does have French-run inns and an Indian culture. Jackson Hole has views of the magnificent Tetons, and from time to time you'll see a graceful elk leaping through the snowfields. **Grand Targhee,** the backside of the Tetons, offers world-class powder and empty slopes. The resort at **Sun Valley, Idaho** has all the amenities but little charm. **Snowbird, Utah** has the best powder skiing in the country.

The best of California

During the past century, Americans have flocked to **California** with visions of fame, fortune, and freedom. They have been drawn by dreams of striking it rich or of making it big in Hollywood. The energy created by these imaginative and ambitious people has made this state one of the most productive in the Union—and one of the most unusual.

The best of San Francisco

San Francisco is the most inviting city in the United States—even if it also is one of the most expensive. It's beautiful, surrounded on two sides by water—the Pacific Ocean and the San Francisco Bay. When the fog rolls in, the city becomes mysterious and soft. When the sun shines, the city glitters. Situated atop steep hills, San Francisco has been the setting for many a chase scene in the movies. Nearly every neighborhood has a hill with a spectacular view. This city is remarkably clean—and very cosmopolitan.

The **Golden Gate Bridge,** which crosses the Golden Gate Strait between the Pacific Ocean and San Francisco Bay, is the city's most famous landmark. Actually a reddish color, the bridge is especially beautiful when partially shrouded in fog. The bridge connects the city to exclusive Marin County, home of Sausalito's artists' colony. It is also one route to the Napa Valley wineries.

The **Golden Gate Promenade** in Aquatic Park is a 3 1/2-mile hike to the bridge that passes beaches, a yacht harbor, the Palace of Fine Arts, the Presidio Army Museum, and Ft. Point.

Golden Gate Park offers 1,017 acres of hiking trails and bridle paths. Free concerts are held in the **Music Concourse** on Sundays at 2 p.m. One of the city's major art museums, the **MH de Young Memorial Museum,** which has a splendid Rodin collection, is in the park. Next door is the **Asian Art Museum.** The **California Academy of Sciences,** which features the Wattis Hall of Man, the Steinhart Aquarium, and the Morrison Planetarium, is also located here.

The most interesting neighborhoods

San Francisco's **Chinatown** is the largest Chinese community in the United States. Walking these streets, you can actually imagine you are in China. Most of your fellow pedestrians are Oriental. The signs are in Chinese. Little shops sell silk Chinese jackets and little black slippers. Food stores have unidentifiable items in their windows. And the architecture of the buildings is Chinese; many were built long ago by the first Chinese immigrants, brought to America to help build the railroad. The best time to visit is during the Chinese New Year celebration in January or February. The highlight is the Dragon Parade, but there also are marching bands, fireworks, and a beauty pageant. For more information on the festival, call *(415)982-3000.*

Nob Hill, an area with plush hotels and a lovely park, is San Francisco's most elegant neighborhood. The **Stanford Court Hotel,** *905 California St.,* serves high tea and delicious dinners. Leland Stanford, a railroad mogul, once owned this mansion. **Huntington Park,** between Taylor and Mason streets, with a lovely view of Grace Cathedral, is the most romantic place for a picnic.

North Beach, between Chinatown and Fisherman's Wharf, is home to hippies, the Italian community, and many of the city's best restaurants and bars. The Cathedral of Saints Peter and Paul looms above the neighborhood, making sure its residents keep their faith. You are likely to see elderly men playing boccie in the parks. The most colorful time to visit is during the Blessing of the Fishing Boats the first weekend in October, when the community parades from the cathedral to Fisherman's Wharf.

San Francisco's best time

Holy City Zoo Comedy Club, *408 Clement St.; (415)386-4242,* features good country, rock'n'roll, and folk musicians, as well as uproarious comedians. All the fun takes place in an 80-year-old high-ceilinged barnhouse.

Superb restaurants

Nob Hill Restaurant, *The Mark Hopkins, Number One Nob Hill; (415)392-3434,* is the best in San Francisco. It has a gentlemen's club atmosphere, with wood paneling and a quiet dining room. Chef Peter Morency creates dishes such as lobster and avocado wonton with ginger and orange sauce. Dinner is expensive.

Le Castel, *3235 Sacramento; (415)921-7115,* in an old San Francisco home, has delicious poached salmon. Make reservations at this popular restaurant, which is closed Sundays and Mondays.

The **Mandarin,** *900 N. Point St.; (415)673-8812,* is the city's best Chinese restaurant. And it has a spectacular view of San Francisco Bay. This is the place to get Peking duck. Save room for the mandarin glazed bananas for dessert.

Maxwell's Plum, *Ghiradelli Square; (415)441-4140,* is decorated with crystal chandeliers, Tiffany glass, and art-nouveau and art-deco statues. The food glitters as well as the decor.

Favorite inns

Our favorite inn in San Francisco is the **White Swan,** *845 Bush St.; (415)775-1755,* in the heart of town. Each room is individually decorated, with four-poster beds, fireplaces, antique chairs and desks, and shelves and shelves of books. Guests are provided with thick terry-cloth bathrobes, and at night the sheets are turned down and chocolates are left on the pillows. Soft teddy bears lounge on the beds, and the air smells of the homemade cookies being baked in the kitchen. Breakfasts are enough to keep you going until dinner. Afternoon cocktails and hors d'oeuvres are served in the cozy sitting room. The young staff is extremely helpful and friendly. Double rooms are $145 to $160, including breakfast and tea and cocktails.

La Petite Auberge, *863 Bush St.; (415)928-6000,* has a French motif. Fresh flowers scent the rooms, and floral wallpaper, French country antiques, quilts, handmade pillows, and working fireplaces make them cozy. Continental breakfast and afternoon tea are served in the dining room.

The **Archbishop's Mansion Inn,** *1000 Fulton St.; (415)563-7872,* is the lavishly restored home of the archbishop of San Francisco. In 1934, the pope spent the night here. Rooms, which are named after operas, are decorated with carved beds, fireplaces, and antiques. Breakfast, cocktails, and meals are included in the cost of the room. Smoking is permitted only in the drawing room.

The **Mansion Hotel,** *2220 Sacramento St.; (415)929-9444,* is the most amusing place to stay, owned and operated by zany Bob Pritikin, who entertains visitors with his musical saw on weekend evenings. The hotel is decorated with oddball antiques and is set in a grand old home that was built in 1877 by Senator Chambers. His daughter Claudia haunts the house, or so they say. The art collection is museum-worthy, the furniture Victorian, and the service first-class.

The best side trip

Sausalito, across Golden Gate Strait by bridge or ferry, is a pretty port and beach resort. The population of this former Bohemian haven doubles on summer weekends. Situated between San Francisco and Mt. Tamalpais, Sausalito has lovely views, unusual crowds, great bars and restaurants, and a profusion of shops.

Sausalito's two best hotels are the **Alta Mira,** *(415)332-1350,* and the **Casa Madrona,** *(415)332-0502.*

Los Angeles: the most eclectic city

Although **Los Angeles** is often obscured by smog and deafened by the din of traffic, it has the stuff of which dreams are made: Hollywood, Beverly Hills, Malibu, and Marina del Rey. This is the stage for the jet-set world of the Beautiful People.

Hollywood: the best of the limelight

Northwest of downtown Los Angeles is the center of the entertainment world: **Hollywood.** Major film and television studios are here, as well as great cinemas and theaters. **Hollywood Boulevard** is a fascinating mishmash of shops and people. **Mann's Chinese Theater** is a garish building. Outside the theater, in the cement, are the foot- and handprints of famous Hollywood movie stars. **Sunset Boulevard,** or The Strip, is lined with nightclubs, bars, and performance halls, and **Melrose Avenue** is lined with pleasant restaurants, where you can stargaze. Hollywood is seedy at night, frequented mainly by prostitutes.

The best studios

Universal Studios, *Universal City; (818)508-9600,* the birthplace of box-office hits and prime-time television shows, offers the most elaborate tour, lasting seven hours. It costs $17.95 for adults; $12.95 for children under 12; free for children under 3.

NBC Television Studios, *3000 W. Alameda Ave., Burbank; (818)840-3537,* is smaller, but the one-hour tour is better. You are more likely to see a show being taped or a star. The tour is $5.50 for adults; $3.50 for children.

Free tickets to some show tapings are offered by all the television studios on a first-come, first-served basis. You can get them at the Visitors Information Center in the Greater Los Angeles Visitor and Convention Bureau. Or send a self-addressed, stamped envelope to **ABC-TV,** *4151 Prospect, Hollywood 90027; (818)557-7777;* **CBS-TV,** *7800 Beverly Blvd., Hollywood 90036; (818)852-4002;* or **NBC-TV,** *3000 W. Alameda Ave., Burbank 91523; (818)840-3537.*

LA sights

The oldest buildings in the city are in the **Pueblo de Los Angeles State Historical Park,** a 19th-century area in the northwest section of downtown. The **Old Plaza,** with 100-year-old trees, stands at the center. You can tour the Avila Adobe, the Pico and Sepulveda houses, and ancient Chinese gambling and opium dens.

Visit the **Huntington Library, Art Gallery, and Botanical Gardens,** *1151 Oxford Road, San Marino.* The library houses one of the world's most important collections of rare books, including a Gutenberg Bible and original editions of *The Canterbury Tales,* Thoreau's *Walden,* and Benjamin Franklin's autobiography. The art gallery contains 18th- and 19th-century British paintings, including Thomas Gainsborough's *Blue Boy* and Sir Thomas Lawrence's *Pinkie.* The botanical gardens are immense, with desert, Japanese, and Elizabethan sections.

The **J. Paul Getty Museum,** *17985 Pacific Coast Hwy.,* in Malibu, is located in the mansion of the late billionaire, a replica of a first-century Roman villa situated on a cliff overlooking the coast. Inside are pieces of Greek and Roman sculpture, 18th-century French decorative art, and European paintings.

The **Watts Towers,** *1765 E. 107th St.,* are three concentric towers built single-handedly by Simon Rodia out of pieces of trash. The old man took 33 years to build these works.

Venice: the craziest beach

Venice, a crowded, crazy, somewhat seedy beach area on the edge of Los Angeles, is the best place in the city to people watch. **Ocean Front Boulevard,** a coastal walkway, is lined with vendors, street musicians, roller skaters, drug addicts, lovers, beachboys, new-wave fans, gays, senior citizens, artists, and tourists from all over the world. Venice was so named because of its many canals and Italian-style buildings. Abbot Kinney attempted to build an American Riviera here at the turn of the century, with canals and gondoliers.

Disneyland: the world's best theme park

Disneyland, outside Los Angeles, is the original theme park (Walt Disney World outside Orlando, Florida was built later). The oldest and still the best, it brings Mickey Mouse to life, offers trips through the stars, and creates a disconcertingly convincing haunted house. In August 1985, Disneyland recorded its 250-millionth visitor.

The best song and dance

The **Los Angeles Philharmonic** plays at the **Hollywood Bowl,** *2301 N. Highland Ave.,*

Hollywood, during the summer. The rest of the year it plays at the Dorothy Chandler Pavilion in the **Music Center,** *First Street and Grand Avenue.*

Troubadour, *9081 Santa Monica Blvd., West Hollywood; (213)276-6168,* saw Linda Rondstadt, Miles Davis, Joni Mitchell, and Blood, Sweat, and Tears before they hit the big time.

The **Roxy,** *9009 Sunset Blvd., West Hollywood; (213)276-2222,* is a fashionable night-spot and a testing and recruiting ground for the music industry.

The **Comedy Store,** *8433 Sunset Blvd., Hollywood; (213)656-6225,* hosts well-known comedians, including Richard Pryor, Steve Martin, Redd Foxx, and Robin Williams.

The best restaurants

The **Polo Lounge,** in the **Beverly Hills Hotel,** *9641 Sunset Blvd.; (213)276-2251,* is where celebrities are made—and then fade. The many windows of this fishbowl offer views of a swimming pool and tropical plants. The Polo Lounge attracts the likes of Barbra Streisand, Gore Vidal, and Joan Collins. If the celebrities don't interest you, concentrate on the food, which is scrumptious.

Le Dome, *8720 Sunset Blvd; (213)659-6919,* serves better down-home French country cooking than you'll find in France. The *choucroute garnie* is delicious, and the wine list is good. The restaurant is closed Sundays.

The **Dynasty Room,** *Westwood Marquis, 930 Hilgard Ave.; (213)208-8765,* is a gourmet restaurant, with classic Continental cuisine. The decor is lovely, with crystal chandeliers and T'ang Dynasty pottery.

Scandia, *9040 Sunset Blvd., West Hollywood; (213)278-3555,* is the best Scandinavian restaurant in the United States. Have brunch or a late supper after the theater at this popular place.

Los Angeles' heavenly hotels

Celebrities who don't live in Beverly Hills stay at the Beverly Wilshire or the Beverly Hills hotels. The **Beverly Wilshire Hotel,** *9500 Wilshire Blvd; (213)275-4282,* has cobblestoned pavements and Louis XIV gates. The older wing, called the Wilshire, is a lavish neo-Renaissance building. The newer Beverly Wing is decorated with French tapestries, Spanish furniture, and Italian marble. Prince Charles stayed in the most opulent suite, the Christian Dior.

The **Beverly Hills Hotel,** *9641 W. Sunset Blvd.; (213)276-2251,* a pink-stucco Spanish villa, is surrounded by palm-shaded lawns where movie stars lounge. Less-famous folks have a hard time getting a room here.

The **Bel Air,** *701 Stone Canyon Road, Bel Air; (213)472-1211,* is a pink mission building with red-tiled roofs and a courtyard fountain. Despite its old-fashioned appearance, it has modern luxuries, including outdoor whirlpool baths. Dolly Parton likes the Bel Air.

The **Terrace Manor,** *1353 Alvarado Terrace; (213)381-1478,* is a Tudor-style house built in 1903 by the owner of a glass factory, who fitted the windows with art-nouveau leaded stained glass. Victorian antiques look stately against the mahogany and oak wall panels. Caruso recordings are played while cocktails are served in the parlor in the late afternoon. Owner Sandy Spillman performs magic tricks.

Bacchus' favorite: Napa Valley

The beautiful **Napa Valley,** 40 miles north of San Francisco on Highway 101, produces

America's best wines. From September through November, the area's wineries are busy harvesting grapes. More than 60 wineries in Napa and Sonoma counties invite visitors to tour their facilities and sample their wines. The best is the three-hour tour of the **Robert Mondavi Winery,** designed for people who already know something about wine.

A lovely place to stay in the valley is **Beazley House,** *1910 First St., Napa; (707)257-1649,* a two-story shingled residence built in 1902. The Beazley House is noted for its woodwork and stained-glass windows. Sherry, coffee, and tea are served to guests in the living room, next to a large fireplace.

America's most beautiful drive

The drive along the Pacific Coast from San Francisco south to Big Sur is the most spectacular in the United States. **Highway 1** is a dizzying twisting ribbon edging high cliffs above the pounding surf. Many movie chase scenes have been filmed on these precipitous roads. Stop from time to time to look over the edge at the deep-blue water and empty beaches below. Because the undertow along the coast is so fierce, swimming is usually forbidden. In places you'll hear colonies of sea lions barking on the rocks. The most spectacular scenery is at **Big Sur.** Waves crash through holes worn in giant rocks, and fierce winds whip along the sand. When you get here, ask how to get down to the beach. The roads often aren't marked.

The **Ventana Inn,** *Highway 1, Big Sur; (408)667-2331* or *(408)624-4812,* is a modern cedar structure. Rooms have carved arched headboards and handmade Nova Scotian quilts. Some have fireplaces, saunas, and hot tubs. The hotel has a heated swimming pool. Continental breakfast is served in the lobby, and a complimentary cheese and wine buffet is offered in the afternoon. The inn's restaurant has good food and a view of the ocean and mountains.

America's most exclusive golf resort

Pebble Beach, 120 miles south of San Francisco and 337 miles north of Los Angeles, has America's best golf course. **Pebble Beach Golf Links** has hosted two U.S. Open golf tournaments (1972 and 1982), two U.S. Amateur tournaments, and the annual Bing Crosby National Pro-Am. It is 6,357 yards long, very narrow, and draped across a magnificent landscape.

The **Cypress Point Club,** also in Pebble Beach, is the most exclusive golf course in the world and one of the prettiest. You must be invited to play here.

This area is worth a visit even if you aren't a golfer. **Carmel,** a quaint beach town with chic shops and inviting inns, is nearby. The best view of the sun setting over the Pacific Ocean is from the beach in Carmel. Residents flock here each evening to watch the red orb sink behind the sea. And the **Del Monte Forest,** stretching along the coast, offers some of the most scenic—and expensive—real estate in the world. The forest is surrounded by **17-Mile Drive,** a loop that passes beaches, sea lions, blowholes, grand estates, and scenic overlooks.

The **Lodge at Pebble Beach,** *17 Mile Drive, Pebble Beach; (408)624-3811,* is a gorgeous resort with tennis, swimming, horseback riding, saunas, hiking, fishing, and hunting. Rooms start at $200 per night in the summer.

The premier auto show in the world is the **Pebble Beach Concours d'Elegance,** held on the lawn of the Lodge at Pebble Beach.

The tallest trees in the world

Redwood National Park in northwest California contains the world's tallest tree, 367 feet high. Magnificent stretches of virgin redwood forest, many of the trees 2,000 years old, are the main attraction. The park borders the Pacific coastline, where sea lions, seals, and birds live unthreatened.

The highest falls in North America

Yosemite Falls, which drop 2,425 feet, are the highest in North America. Located in Yosemite National Park, in east central California, they are one of the many natural spectacles in the **Sierra Nevada,** whose cliffs and pinnacles were formed by glaciers. The famous photographer Ansel Adams took many of his best-known photographs in this park.

The **Ahwahnee Resort** in Yosemite, *(209)252-4848,* built in 1927, has views of Yosemite Falls and Glacier Point. The six-story pseudo-castle is decorated with Western and Indian motifs. Movie stars and heads of state have stayed here. The 77-foot Great Lounge has two fireplaces. Facilities include a pool, tennis courts, horseback riding, hiking trails, and winter sports.

The Northwest: nature at its best

The **Pacific Northwest** has managed to keep its natural beauty from being commercialized and overdeveloped. The rugged, untouched coasts of Washington and Oregon are breathtaking. The mountains are protected by national parks. The cities are lively without polluting the countryside.

The Northwest gets a lot of rain. If you can put up with the drizzle, you'll love its result. This is the greenest place in North America. Grass is an emerald color. Pine trees grow straight and tall, to heights unheard-of on the East Coast.

Seattle: where the grass is greenest

Seattle is one of the nation's most gorgeous cities. Surrounded by mountains on nearly all sides, it sits on Puget Sound and Lake Washington. The Cascade and Olympic mountains are only two hours away, and the lone white peak of Mt. Rainier can be seen from anywhere in the city. In addition to all its natural wonders, the city also offer restaurants, bars, and cultural activities.

The best view of the city is from the **Space Needle** in Seattle Center, a remnant of the 1962 World's Fair.

The most bizarre place in Seattle is **Ye Olde Curiosity Shop,** *Pier 54; (206)862-5844,* where shrunken heads and mummified humans are displayed

The best place for restaurants and night life is **Pioneer Square,** the renovated section of Old Seattle. **Grand Central Arcade,** *First Avenue and Occidental Street,* has the best shops.

The best tour of the city is the **Underground Seattle Tour,** which leaves from 610 First Ave. and shows you the remains of the original city, which burned in 1889.

Seattle's finest food

Pike Place Farmer's Market, *First Avenue and Pike Street,* has stalls filled with colorful fresh vegetables and fruits. It also has good restaurants. One of Seattle's best is **Chez Shea,** *(206)467-9990,* a cozy room on the top floor of the Corner Market Building. You can enjoy gourmet food while looking out over Puget Sound and the Olympic Mountains. **Café Sport,** *(206)443-6000,* at the north end of the Pike Place Market, is a casual restaurant with good seafood.

Le Gourmand, *425 N.W. Market St.; (206)784-3463,* is an intimate restaurant with three-course prix-fixe meals. It is open Wednesdays through Saturdays.

The **Georgian Room,** *Four Seasons Olympic Hotel, 411 University; (206)621-7889,* is a stately dining room serving nature's best. Try the red Alaska king salmon with black currant sauce.

Seattle's two best inns

Galer Place, *318 W. Galer St.; (206)282-5339,* is a quaint turn-of-the-century shingled home with a lush garden. This bed and breakfast has only three rooms, each furnished with antiques. A hot tub bubbles among the flowers in the back yard. Continental breakfast and afternoon tea are served.

Chambered Nautilus Bed and Breakfast Inn, *5005 22nd Ave. N.E.; (206)522-2536,* is a rambling old house on a steep hill with views of the Cascade Mountains. Country antiques are sprinkled throughout the house, and most rooms have their own porches. Wine and tea are served by the fireplace in the parlor. Breakfast is served in the dining room and usually includes fresh-baked bread or muffins.

The best of the wilderness

Mt. Rainier, a 14,410-foot mountain in **Mt. Rainier National Park,** has more glaciers than any other mountain on the U.S. mainland. The 4 1/2-mile **Skyline Trail** is the longest loop trail on the mountain. From Panorama Point you can see glaciers and the summit. Mt. Rainier was sacred to the Yakima and Klickatt Indians, who believed evil spirits inhabited a crater lake at the summit and caused storms and avalanches.

You can stay in Mt. Rainier National Park at the **Paradise Inn,** *off Route 123; (206)569-2275,* which looks out over Mt. Rainier and the valley below. This rustic inn was built in 1916 of notched cedar logs, with no nails. The open-beamed lobby has 50-foot cathedral ceilings and 2 stone fireplaces.

The **Olympic National Forest** has wildly beautiful beaches along the Pacific Ocean. Inland, the Hoh, Queets, and Quinault river valleys have non-tropical rain forests. Up to 140 inches of rain fall here each year, and moss covers everything. **Mt. Olympus** rises 7915 feet, challenging mountain climbers.

Stay at **Quinault Lodge,** *(206)288-2571,* an old-fashioned log building on Lake Quinault in Olympic National Park. Facilities include a pool, a health club with a sauna, boats, hiking trails, fishing areas, and horseback riding.

To truly understand the power of nature, visit **Mt. St. Helens,** a volcano that erupted in 1980 causing mass destruction. You can tour the barren, burned-out area around the mountain. This peak is 50 miles northwest of Portland.

America's deepest lake

Crater Lake in Oregon, which fills a 1,932-foot crater, never freezes because of its depth. Located 6,000 feet above sea level, it is surrounded by snow-capped mountains. This beautiful, deep-blue lake is five hours south of Portland. While the park is open year-round, only the south and west entrance roads are open during the winter. And the Rim Drive is open only from July 1 through late October. For more information, call *(503)594-2211.*

You can spend the night by the lake in cottages operated by **Crater Lake Lodge,** *(503)594-2511.* The cottages are equipped with cold running water, blankets, and electricity.

The best of the Great Lakes

In the middle of America's northern prairies are the five **Great Lakes.** Surrounding these mammoth, freshwater lakes are some of the nation's best farmland and most prosperous cities. **Lake Superior** is the deepest, the most treacherous, and the most beautiful. **Lake Michigan** is the best for fishing, swimming, and sailing. And its high western dunes are excellent for hang gliding.

Chicago: the biggest city

The greatest thing about this rough-and-tumble town is its beautiful, clean beaches. Its architecture is memorable also, showing off the genius of Frank Lloyd Wright and his ilk. The second-largest city in the United States, **Chicago** has three of the world's tallest buildings. And its neighborhoods are varied, filled with ethnic groups.

The best architecture

Chicago was the birthplace of modern architecture as developed by Louis Sullivan, his disciple Frank Lloyd Wright, and other members of the unofficial Chicago School of Architecture. Many of this group's first skyscrapers are still standing, next to taller, more modern buildings designed by the likes of Mies van der Rohe and Helmut Jahn. The **Archicenter,** *330 S. Dearborn; (312)922-3432,* is the place to learn about Chicago's diverse architecture (for tour information, call *(312)782-1776*).

The tallest building

Standing proudly over Chicago is the **Sears Tower,** *233 S. Wacker Drive,* the world's tallest building. Its 110 stories are reached by 103 elevators and lit by 16,000 windows. It covers an entire block. You can visit the skydeck on the top floor, from which, on a clear day, you can see as far as Wisconsin to the north, Indiana to the south, and Michigan to the east.

The most magnificent mile

The 16-block stretch of Michigan Avenue between the Chicago River and Oak Street is called the **Magnificent Mile**—with good reason. Here are Chicago's best and most exclusive department stores, as well as hundreds of small specialty shops and many of the best restaurants in Chicago.

Along the Magnificent Mile is **Water Tower Place,** *835 N. Michigan Ave.; (312)751-3681,* by far Chicago's best—and most beautiful—indoor shopping mall, six stories of shops and restaurants.

The **Chicago Water Tower** and the **Pumping Station,** *Michigan and Chicago avenues,* were the only buildings that survived the great Chicago Fire of 1871.

The best museums

The **Art Institute of Chicago,** *Michigan Avenue and Adams; (312)443-3600,* is a world-class art museum with the finest collection of Impressioinist paintings in this country and an outstanding collection of Renaissance, Oriental, and post-Impressionist art. Admission is $5 (free on Tuesdays).

The **Field Museum of Natural History,** *Roosevelt Road and South Lake Shore Drive; (312)922-9410,* is a huge museum with a collection of jewels, Egyptian mummies, and free-standing dinosaur skeletons. Admission is $2 (free on Thursdays).

The **Museum of Broadcast Communications,** *800 S. Wells; (312)987-1500,* pays tribute to Chicago's glory days, when many national radio and television broadcasts originated here. You can watch or listen to more than 400 classic radio shows and 900 television shows.

The **Museum of Contemporary Art,** *237 E. Ontario; (312)280-2660,* features art being created today. Admission is $3 (free on Tuesdays).

With more than 2,000 displays—including a coal mine, a World War II German submarine, and the Apollo 8 command module—the **Museum of Science and Industry,** *57th Street and South Lake Shore Drive; (312)684-1414,* is the most popular in the city. The **Omnimax Theater** features a five-story domed screen that puts the viewer in the middle of the action. Admission to the museum is free; the Omnimax Theater is $4.50 for adults, $3 for children.

The **Oriental Institute,** at the University of Chicago, *1155 E. 58th St.; (312)702-9520,* is a first-rate museum of the ancient Near East (Egypt, Mesopotamia, Iran, and the holy land). Highlights are Egyptian mummies, fragments of the Dead Sea scrolls, and a huge winged bull from the throne room of King Sargon II of Assysia. Admission is free.

Chicago's newest museum, the **Terra Museum of American Art,** *666 N. Michigan Ave.; (312)664-3939,* which opened in 1987, has a strong collection of works by American Impressionists.

The most colorful neighborhoods

Hyde Park, the home of the University of Chicago, is an intellectual's dream, with six bookstores (four new, two used) and hundreds of people itching for good conversation. Hyde Park is also home to the Museum of Science and Industry, the Oriental Institute, and Frank Lloyd Wright's famous Robie House. Every June, Hyde Park hosts its annual **57th Street Art Fair.**

The wealthiest part of town, known as the **Gold Coast,** is an area of old mansions and luxury apartment buildings, conveniently close to Lake Michigan, Oak Street Beach, and the Magnificent Mile.

Chicago's old Bohemia was Old Town, where many of the city's artists and hippies lived. But as Old Town gentrified, rising rents drove the artists, actors, and writers out. The new Bohemia is **Lake View,** the neighborhood around Belmont and Clark, which is filled with restaurants, bookstores, small theaters, new-wave bars, coffee shops, and used-clothing stores.

Chicago's newest neighborhood is **River North,** an old warehouse district that in the past 10 years has become a chic loft area. Bounded by the Chicago River on the south and Chicago Avenue on the north, River North is an area of fashionable shops, trendy nightclubs, and popular new restaurants.

An art gallery district—not unlike SoHo in New York City—thrives along West Erie, Huron, and Superior streets, between Wells and Sedgwick.

The best parks and zoos

Chicago has 29 miles of lakefront parks. Lake Michigan offers clean water and pleasant swimming. The most popular beaches are **Lincoln Park** and **Oak Street.** Smaller, rockier, and less crowded are the beaches in **Hyde Park,** *between 49th and 57th streets.*

Grant Park, on the waterfront between Roosevelt Road and Randolph Street, east of Michigan Avenue, is attractive. The Grant Park Orchestra gives free outdoor concerts here on Wednesday, Friday, and Saturday evenings. At night, a light display dances across the **Buckingham Fountain,** which sprays 90 feet into the air.

On the grounds of the **Lincoln Park Zoo,** *2200 N. Cannon Park,* are beaches, yacht harbors, and the Lincoln Park Conservatory, which is the city's music capital. Good music can be heard in the bars and theaters along Clark Street and Lincoln Avenue. Look out for muggers.

The **Brookfield Zoo,** *First Avenue and 31st Street,* in Brookfield, recreates the Sahara Desert and the Australian Outback, as well as the habitat of the Siberian tiger.

The best town for theater

Twenty years ago, Chicago had no live theater to speak of. However, today more than 100 groups perform in the city. In fact, Chicago's theater scene rivals even those of New York and London. Although many are shoestring operations performing in storefronts and church basements, Chicago also has a respectable number of strong, well-established theaters.

No other Chicago theater group comes close to the **Steppenwolf Theater,** *2851 N. Halsted; (312)472-4141.* Many of its best shows have gone on to perform off Broadway in New York City.

Chicago's best laughs

For almost 30 years, **Second City,** *1616 N. Wells; (312)337-3992,* the best comedy theater in the city, has provided Chicago with consistently popular comedy revues. John Belushi, Shelly Long, Gilda Radner, and Alan Arkin all began their careers here. If you want to go, make reservations at least a week in advance.

Second City recently opened a second stage, **Second City ETC,** *1608 N. Wells,* which is just as funny.

The most outrageous entertainment

Believe it or not, one of Chicago's most popular nightspots is the **Baton Lounge,** *436 N. Clark; (312)644-5269,* an outrageous club, where funny, ravishing female impersonators attract an eclectic crowd. Straight and gay, young and old all come to see such local legends as Chili Pepper and Leslie. Reservations are essential.

The best jazz and blues

For music lovers, Chicago is synonymous with jazz and blues. And **Joe Segal's Jazz Showcase,** in the Blackstone Hotel, *636 S. Michigan Ave.; (312)427-4300,* has been the place to hear great jazz in Chicago for decades.

No blues bar comes close to the **New Checkerboard Lounge,** *423 E. 43rd St.; (312)624-3240,* where blues greats such as Buddy Guy and Junior Wells perform regularly and rock stars such as Mick Jagger and Keith Richard drop by (sometimes they even jam with the old bluesmen). The club itself is friendly and safe, but it is located in a dangerous neighbor-hood—so park near the club or take a cab. Don't take a bus or the subway—Chicago's southside is rough.

If you love the blues but prefer to stay in a safer neighborhood, visit the **Kingston Mines,** *2548 N. Halsted; (312)477-4646,* in the heart of Lincoln Park. The Kingston Mines attracts many of the acts that play at the New Checkerboard Lounge as well as newer bands during the week.

The best classical music and opera

Under the leadership of Sir George Solti, the **Chicago Symphony Orchestra** (CSO) has become a world-class orchestra, popular not only in its home city, but also in Europe and the Orient. The CSO performs in **Orchestra Hall,** *220 S. Michigan Ave.,* across the street from the Art Institute of Chicago. For a schedule, call *(312)435-8122;* for ticket information, call *(312)435-6666.*

The **Lyric Opera,** *20 N. Wacker Drive; (312)332-2244,* is world-famous for its grandly staged operas.

The best deep-dish pizza

A quick way to start an argument in Chicago is to ask who has the best pizza in town. Everyone has his favorite place for pizza. The world-famous Chicago-style pizza was first served in the late 1940s at **Pizzeria Uno,** *29 E. Ohio Ave.; (312)321-1000.* And everyone agrees (even in Chicago) that Pizzeria Uno and sister restaurant **Due,** *619 N. Wabash Ave.; (312)943-2400,* still serve great pizza.

The best barbecued ribs

Chicago, not the South, has the best barbecued ribs. At **Ribs 'n Bibs,** *East 53rd Street,* you can get a bucket of mouthwatering ribs for $21.

The best ethnic restaurants

A city of ethnic groups—Poles, Irish, Lithuanians, Serbs, Croatians, Italians, and Hispanics—Chicago has hundreds of great ethnic restaurants. The best is a Serbo-Croatian restaurant called the **Golden Shell,** *100063 South Ave. N.; (312)221-9876,* on Chicago's far southeast side. The food is great, and on weekends authentic folk bands and belly dancers perform.

The best gourmet restaurant

In a city of excellent restaurants, **Le Français,** *269 S. Milwaukee Ave.; (312)541-7470,* in the nearby suburb of Wheeling, is la crème de la crème. Close to O'Hare International Airport and a 45-minute drive from the Chicago Loop, Le Français serves a classically French menu that will please the most finicky gourmet palate. The restaurant is closed Mondays.

The best grand hotel

The **Mayfair Regent,** *181 E. Lake Shore Drive; (312)787-8500,* is Chicago's first-class hotel, the place where important businessmen want to be seen. The penthouse restaurant has a wide view of the lake, as do most of the rooms.

The best little hotel

The **Whitehall Hotel,** *105 E. Delaware Place; (312)944-6300,* just off the Magnificent Mile, is one of Chicago's most elegant little hotels. A short walk from Michigan Avenue and the Oak Street Beach, the Whitehall couldn't be more conveniently located. For $20, Whitehall's chauffeured limousine, stocked with your favorite beverages, will take you wherever you want to go in Chicago.

The Great Lakes' best resort

Mackinac Island, Michigan, where Lake Huron meets Lake Michigan, is a beautiful, peaceful place with no automobiles, just horse-drawn carriages and bicycles. Indians once lived here in lodges that are preserved in an open-air museum. During the Revolution, British forces built a fort here, now restored and open to the public. The island became a fashionable resort in the late 19th century, and it was the second area (after Yellowstone) to become a national park.

Today, the island is a refuge for city dwellers, a place for sailing, golfing, horseback riding, and tennis. Victorian homes and white church steeples dot the town. Sailboats bob in the lakes, and the waterfront is filled with shops and restaurants.

The **Grand Hotel,** *(906)847-3331* (call collect for reservations), on Mackinac Island, was built in 1887 by railroad and steamship companies. Constructed in Greek Revival style, with a long veranda supported by columns, it has a lovely pool (where Esther Williams swam in *This Time for Keeps*), as well as a golf course and tennis courts. The food is good, but the main dining room is stuffy. Tea is served in the parlor.

The **Island House,** *(906)847-3347,* is an old Victorian resort on Mackinac Island. The enormous white building is fringed with shaded porches and topped with corner turrets and dormer windows. Built in 1848, it is the island's oldest hotel. Breakfast and dinner are served in the hotel dining room. You can sleep late, then have cocktails on the front porch while savoring the view of the Straits.

The newest hotel on the island is **Mission Point Resort,** *(800)833-7711,* set on 18 acres of Lake Huron shoreline. It has a heated outdoor swimming pool, two hot tubs, three tennis courts, a fully equipped health and fitness center, a pool hall, and an arcade. The main lobby is a spacious circular room with five huge stone fireplaces and a soaring, vaulted ceiling of 40-foot hand-hewn timbers. Rooms overlook Lake Huron. Double rooms begin at $83, including breakfast and dinner (special weekday rates begin at $75).

Alaska: the wildest (and coldest) state

Alaska is the last frontier in the United States. Having more unexplored territory than the rest of the 49 states combined, Alaska's virtues lie not in its few major cities but in the beauty of its frozen landscape, home to only 300,000 fishermen, prospectors, and Eskimos. Our largest state has excellent fishing, unlimited trails, and an endless reserve of wildlife.

Alaska is a land of superlatives. **Mt. McKinley,** at 20,320 feet, is the tallest mountain in North America. Astounding amounts of gold and oil have been discovered in this state. And Alaska is the last area in the country where native populations keep their traditional ways undisturbed by the white man. Alaska has the longest winter in the United States, lasting from October to April. June and July have days of continuous light. This is the best time to visit— unless you really like the snow.

Alaska's most spectacular sight

The most spectacular sight in Alaska is **Glacier Bay National Monument,** where myriads of ice boulders float in fjords bordered by thick forests. The park was covered by ice thousands of feet deep until just 200 years ago. Nowhere else can you get so close to glaciers. In this ever-changing area, humpback and killer whales spout, porpoises and seals play, and bears, mountain goats, and more than 200 species of birds, including the bald eagle, live. The waters are filled with trout, salmon, and halibut. During the summer, Glacier Bay is a rainbow of flowers.

The top of the world

Across the **Arctic Circle** is the land of the Eskimo, where the sun never sets during summer. All you can see for miles is vast, gently rolling tundra.

Barrow is the northernmost point of the continent, located 330 miles north of the Arctic Circle. North America's largest Eskimo settlement is here—Barrow covers 88,000 square miles. This is also the whaling capital of the Arctic.

Kotzebue is the trading center of the Arctic. Part of the ancient land bridge that once joined Siberia and North America, it has been a major settlement and trade center for 6,000 years. **Front Street,** the city's main street, is also the beach, where fishing boats pull up and fish and meat are hung on racks to dry. You can shop here for jade, ivory carvings, furs, native handicrafts, and artifacts.

The Pribilof Islands

The **Pribilof Islands,** in the Bering Sea, are home to North America's largest seal herd and the biggest seabird colony in the world (more than 190 bird species have been sighted). Each summer, 1.7-million northern fur seals migrate here to bear their young.

The best of the Alaskan panhandle

The history of Alaska began in its panhandle, a scenic fishing, timber, and mining area filled with thousands of wooded islands, mountains covered by glaciers, and waterfalls. The entire southeast of the state is the huge, wild **Tongass National Forest.** One of its glaciers, the Malaspina, is as big as Rhode Island. Lonely, isolated towns are blocked from the mainland by the Coastal Mountains.

Juneau, the capital

Juneau, the capital of Alaska, was founded 100 years ago as a fishing and gold-mining town. It has 18,000 residents, who are watched over by Mt. Roberts and Mt. Juneau. Behind the state capitol is **Gold Creek,** where a mining museum shows what it was like to tunnel through the mountains. North of town is the splendid **Mendenhall Glacier.**

Juneau's best hotel is the **Westmark Juneau,** *51 W. Egan Drive; (907)586-6900,* across from the waterfront. Beautifully carved wood decorates this hotel, which has modern furnishings, cable television, and a good restaurant and lounge. Double rooms are $138 during the summer; $88 during the winter.

The best drive

The most spectacular drive from Juneau is north to **Haines.** Forty miles of road wind through the mountains to the border. **Klukwan,** near Haines, has the largest concentration of bald eagles in North America. The **Chilkoot Trail,** which begins in the gold-rush town of Skagway, is littered with wagon wheels, horse skeletons, and commemorative plaques that trace the steps of gold-crazed miners.

Luxury in Alaska

The most luxurious place on the panhandle is a hot-springs resort on Chichagof Island called **Tenakee Springs.** The springs (about 107 degrees Fahrenheit) are therapeutic. The town is made up of wooden houses on stilts connected by plank walkways. Stay at the **Tenakee Inn and Tavern,** *(907)736-9238* or *(907)586-1000,* a Victorian hotel where double rooms are $45.

Sitka: where Russia meets America

Alaska's tourist center is **Sitka,** at the base of Mt. Edgecumbe. When Alaska was part of

Russia, this was its capital. You can still see the Slavic influence, especially in the Russian Orthodox cathedral. Visit the **Sitka National Historical Park,** at Lincoln Street and the Indian River. Here, Russians captured a Tlingit Indian stronghold in 1804. You can see totem poles, the battlefield, and a museum with displays of Tlingit and Russian culture.

The **Westmark Shee Atika,** *330 Seward St., Sitka; (907)747-6241,* is decorated with native art, including a wall mural illustrating Tlingit history. A sunken living room surrounds the fireplace. The best views are from the rooms on the third floor. Double rooms are $98.

Where the people are: Anchorage

Half of Alaska's population (about 180,000 people) lives in **Anchorage.** This big city boasts two daily newspapers, performances by celebrities and internationally recognized orchestras, theater, fast-food joints, glass and steel buildings, supermarkets, and department stores.

The best thing about Anchorage is its night life. This is where those with cabin fever go to let off steam. Bars, massage parlors, restaurants, nightclubs, and strip joints keep the money changing along Fourth Avenue and Spenard Road.

Visit the **Anchorage Museum of History and Art,** *121 W. Seventh Ave.; (907)343-4326.*

Shop for native crafts at the **Alaska Native Arts and Crafts Association Showroom,** *333 W. Fourth Ave.; (907)274-2932.* Look for the soft, warm clothing of Alaska at the **Oomingmak Musk Ox Cooperative,** *604 H St.; (907)272-9225.*

The best time to visit Anchorage is during the **Winter Carnival,** held each year in mid-February.

Alaska's best restaurants and hotel

Even hotel restaurants in Alaska, which is known for its seafood, are surprisingly good. The best restaurant is the **Crow's Nest,** at the Captain Cook Hotel in Anchorage. Other good restaurants include **Elevation 92,** *Third Avenue and K Street,* and **Simon and Seaforths,** *410 L St.*

The state's best hotel is the **Anchorage Westward Hilton,** *(907)272-7411,* which will seem like paradise after the rough cold of the Alaska wilderness.

The largest island: Kodiak

Kodiak, the largest island in the United States, is also the largest fishing port and the home of the king crab. This island, where you will see Russian architecture, has the oldest European settlement in Alaska. The Kodiak bear is the world's largest species of bear.

A heavenly sight

One of the most beautiful sights in Alaska can be seen from anywhere in the state. Electromagnetic fluctuations in the atmosphere and the magnetic pull of the North Pole create the magnificent spectacle of the **Aurora Borealis,** a rainbow of colors that glimmers on the horizon.

Hawaii: America's paradise

The most beautiful place in the United States is halfway around the world—**Hawaii.** Long, sandy beaches, palm trees, jungles, exotic people, luxurious resorts, and some of the world's best surfing combine to make this state a true paradise.

Maui, the second-largest of the Hawaiian Islands, has both luxury resorts and large undeveloped areas. The **Kaanapali Beach Resort** has restaurants, shops, and hotels. The **Hyatt Regency Maui** is splendid. Its open-air lobby is decorated with antique Asian vases. The **Kapalua Bay Hotel** is more subtle.

On the east coast of Maui is **Hana,** a ranch town (the drive here is breathtaking). Maui's best adventure is a helicopter ride over the **Haleakala volcano.** You will see waterfalls and sacred pools, as well as the grave of Charles Lindbergh. You also can join a bicycle tour down Mt. Haleakala. A van carries you to the rim of the volcano, where you enjoy breakfast and the sunrise. Then you coast downhill for 38 miles.

The most civilized island is **Oahu,** where Honolulu is located. The **Kahala Hilton** is superb, as is the **Halekulani.** Visit the Iolani Palace, the Bishop Museum, and Pearl Harbor.

Hawaii, the biggest island

Waterfalls, black sand beaches, cliffs, surf, soft trade winds, and beautiful views make **Hawaii** gorgeous. The Big Island, as it is known, is also the most historic, settled by Polynesians more than 1,000 years ago. The island has plantation towns, royal homes, missionary churches, and burial grounds. Its extraordinary resort hotels, which draw people from around the world, lie on the **Kohala Coast.**

Hawaii is a 93-mile-long diamond-shaped island with four active volcanos. A trip around the island leads past fields of sugarcane, rain forests with wild orchids, steam vents, volcanoes, black sand beaches, petroglyphs, ancient temples, coffee trees, shacks, grasslands, and cacti.

While exploring Hawaii, you may also see the Night Marchers, ghost warriors who chant along the ancient **King's Trail,** which winds through several resorts. The **Puuhonua O Honaunau National Historical Park** was a place of refuge, where Hawaiians could escape the king's wrath in ancient times. Near the town of **Hawi** is the birthplace of Kamehameha, the first king to rule all the islands. Nearby is the **Mo'okini Heiau,** a temple dating back to A.D. 480, still cared for by the Mo'okini family, which has watched over it since it was built.

The beach town of **Kailua** has reasonably priced hotels, fishing charters, shops, and stone churches built in the 1800s. **Hulihee Palace,** now a museum, provides a view of the harbor. Built as a summer palace for Hawaiian royalty, its architecture is a curious blend of elements from New England, France, England, and Hawaii.

Hawaii Volcanoes National Park encompasses the island's two active volcanoes: **Kilauea** and **Mauna Loa.** An 11-mile drive circles Kilauea's huge collapsed summit, or caldera, which passes near man-size lava tubes and the **Halemaumau,** a fire pit where the goddess Pele is said to live. The most beautiful drive is along the **Chain of Craters Road,** which winds 25 miles down Kilauea and takes you as close as you are permitted (and as close as you would want to get) to **Puu Oo Vent,** which erupts regularly.

Mauna Kea is the best place on earth to conduct infrared studies. This peak is 13,796 feet above a huge, dark ocean, protected from the lights of civilization; it is also above 40% of the earth's atmosphere. The **Manua Kea Observatory** has six astronomical telescopes.

If you can afford it, stay at the **Kona Village Resort,** *P.O. Box 1299, Kaupulehu-Kona; (808)325-5555* or *(800)421-0000.* Rooms are from $310 to $510.

Kauai: the lushest isle

Kauai, the fourth-largest Hawaiian island, is the most beautiful. *Fantasy Island, The*

Thorn Birds, Raiders of the Lost Ark, and *South Pacific* were filmed here. The **Na Pali Coast,** which can be reached by helicopter, is the island's most spectacular area.

The air seems green on this lush island. Waterfalls cascade down sharp peaks into the **Hanalai River.** Orchids and ginger line the river, which meanders through taro fields toward the sea. Three beautiful parks line Hanalei Bay: Hanalei Beach Park, Hanalei Pavilion, and Waioli Beach Park. Two large peaks, Hihimanu and Namolokama, watch over the valley.

Waimea Canyon is often called the Grand Canyon of the Pacific. It is 3,600 feet deep and 10 miles long. Its valleys are green, and its ridges are blanketed with flowers. The **Kukui Trail** leads down 2,000 feet to the fertile canyon floor, where you can explore ancient Hawaiian ruins.

The wettest place on earth is **Mt. Waialeale,** where 450 inches of rain fall each year. On the western slope of this 5,080-foot peak lies the **Alakai Swamp,** a 10-mile area where birds and plants (but no mosquitoes) flourish. The **Pihea Trail** (which translates as Din of Voices) leads to the swamp, where giant ferns and tree-size violets grow.

Hawaii's most luxurious resorts

Honolulu has two grand hotels: the **Moana,** *2365 Kalakaua Ave.; (808)922-3111* or *(800)325-3535,* and the **Royal Hawaiian,** *2259 Kalakaua Ave.; (808)923-7311* or *(800)325-3535.*

The Moana, one of Hawaii's first hotels, opened in 1901. Robert Louis Stevenson came here to write. The 75-room white clapboard hotel is a classic South Seas design, with overhead ceiling fans, a veranda with wicker furniture, and rooms furnished with antiques. It is on the beach.

The Royal Hawaiian is a pink Moorish-style palace built in the 1920s. The hotel's first guest was Princess Kawanakoa, who would have been queen of Hawaii if the islands had been left alone. The hotel is on the beach and has a pool.

The **Kahala Hilton,** *5000 Kahala Ave., Honolulu, Oahu; (808)734-2211,* is a first-class hotel with a beach and a swimming pool. It also has a pool filled with dolphins. The hotel's beachfront restaurant is good.

The **Mauna Kea Hotel,** *P.O. Box 218, Kamuela; (800)228-3000,* was built 20 years ago by Laurence Rockefeller on the white sands at Kaunaoa Point.

Kona Village, *P.O. Box 1299 Kaupuleha-Kona; (800)367-5290,* is on a kipuka, an area of land left untouched by surrounding lava flows. This recreation of a South Seas island community was built by Johnno Johnson. Johnson sailed to this protected cove for years before opening the resort, where coats and ties are banned. You stay in individual thatched huts in a tropical setting.

CURRENCY EXCHANGE TABLE*

Country	Currency	Foreign Currency in Dollars	Dollars in Foreign Currency
Australia	Dollar	0.82	1.23
Austria	Schilling	0.08	12.55
Brazil	Cruzado	0.006	181.85
Britain	Pound	1.77	0.57
Cameroon	CFA Franc	0.003	295.30
Canada	Dollar	0.83	1.21
China	Yuan	0.27	3.72
Czechoslovakia	Koruna	0.19	5.21
East Germany	Ostmark	0.56	1.78
Egypt	Pound	0.43	2.30
Finland	Markka	0.24	4.20
France	Franc	0.17	6.00
Greece	Drachma	0.007	141.95
Hong Kong	Dollar	0.13	7.80
Hungary	Forint	0.02	48.99
Iceland	Krona	0.02	44.38
India	Rupee	0.07	13.90
Ireland	Punt	1.51	0.66
Israel	Shekel	0.63	1.60
Italy	Lire	0.0007	1320.00
Ivory Coast	CFA Franc	0.003	295.30
Japan	Yen	0.008	128.85
Kenya	Shilling	0.06	16.78
Macao	Pataca	0.12	8.03
Mexico	Peso	0.0004	2290.00
New Zealand	Dollar	0.71	1.40
Nigeria	Naira	0.24	4.17
Norway	Krone	0.16	6.42
Poland	Zioty	0.002	429.80
Portugal	Escudo	0.007	145.00
Romania	Leu	0.12	8.55
Rwanda	Franc	0.013	76.08
Senegal	CFA Franc	0.003	295.30
Seychelles	Rupee	0.19	5.30
Spain	Pesata	0.008	118.05
Sweden	Krona	0.16	6.16
Switzerland	Franc	0.68	1.48

Tanzania	Shilling	0.01	96.45
Togo	CFA Franc	0.003	295.30
Venezuela	Bolivar	0.03	32.60
West Germany	Mark	0.56	1.78
Yugoslavia	Dinar	0.0005	2031.69
Zimbabwe	Dollar	0.56	1.79

* Currency exchange rates as of June 1988.

INDEX

AGORA BOOKS

Undiscovered Europe

More than 600 pages of little-known, undiscovered places as well as major monuments and museums. This book is designed as a practical guide to help you discover Europe for the first time, or the fiftieth time. It tells you about what is well-known and worth discovering...and what is completely undiscovered and worth getting to know. Handy when planning a trip, and a great book to take with you when you travel. **Soft cover—$14.95**

The World's Top Retirement Havens

The 12 best overseas Edens covered in detail. Complete information on immigration restrictions, crime, cost of living, real estate, household help, travel and much more. 172 pages. **Soft cover—$12.95**

Paris Confidential

Paris Confidential, written by Warren and Jean Trabant, will introduce you to Paris in a way that you could never get from a standard tourist guidebook. This book is for those who really want to get to know the heart and soul of this special city, as true connoisseurs know it. 134 pages. **Soft cover—$12.95**

The 1988 Passport Companion

All the inside travel information you need to make the most of every travel dollar you spend. This pocket-sized reference clues you in to how the travel industry really works. It's a guide to less expensive and less troublesome travel—with specific names, addresses, telephone numbers, and useful information on tourist offices, embassies, major airlines, discount travel agencies, cruise lines, national railroads, rent-a-car agencies, and much more. **Soft cover—$6.95**